SAP PRESS e-books

Print or e-book, Kindle or iPad, workplace or airplane: Choose where and how to read your SAP PRESS books! You can now get all our titles as e-books, too:

▶ By download and online access
▶ For all popular devices
▶ And, of course, DRM-free

Convinced? Then go to **www.sap-press.com** and get your e-book today.

SAP PRESS

SAP PRESS is a joint initiative of SAP and Rheinwerk Publishing. The know-how offered by SAP specialists combined with the expertise of Rheinwerk Publishing offers the reader expert books in the field. SAP PRESS features first-hand information and expert advice, and provides useful skills for professional decision-making.

SAP PRESS offers a variety of books on technical and business-related topics for the SAP user. For further information, please visit our website: *www.sap-press.com*.

Joe Darlak, Jesper Christensen
SAP BW: Administration and Performance Optimization
2014, 652 pp., hardcover
ISBN 978-1-59229-853-2

James Wood
Getting Started with SAP HANA Cloud Platform
2015, approx. 575 pp., hardcover
ISBN 978-1-4932-1021-3

Schneider, Westenberger, Gahm
ABAP Development for SAP HANA
2014, 609 pp., hardcover
ISBN 978-1-59229-859-4

Jeffrey Garbus
SAP ASE 16 / Sybase ASE Administration
2015, approx. 725 pp., hardcover
ISBN 978-1-4932-1182-1

Richard Bremer and Lars Breddemann

SAP HANA® Administration

Rheinwerk®
Publishing

Bonn • Boston

Editor Kelly Grace Weaver
Copyeditor Melinda Rankin
Cover Design Graham Geary
Photo Credit Shutterstock.com/112252583/© Anteromite
Layout Design Vera Brauner
Production Kelly O'Callaghan
Typesetting III-satz, Husby (Germany)
Printed and bound in the United States of America, on paper from sustainable sources

ISBN 978-1-59229-952-2
© 2015 by Rheinwerk Publishing Inc., Boston (MA)
1st edition 2014, 1st reprint 2015 with corrections

Library of Congress Cataloging-in-Publication Data
Bremer, Richard.
SAP HANA administration / Richard Bremer and Lars Breddemann. -- 1st edition.
pages cm
ISBN 978-1-59229-952-2 (print) -- ISBN 1-59229-952-0 (print) -- ISBN 978-1-59229-953-9 (ebook) --
ISBN 978-1-59229-954-6 (print and ebook) 1. Database management. 2. Business enterprises--Data processing.
3. SAP HANA (Electronic resource) I. Breddemann, Lars. II. Title.
QA76.9.D3B7135 2014
005.74--dc23
2014022965

Contents at a Glance

Dear Reader,

In my experience, book writing is one of those things that picks up momentum at the end. It takes almost a year to get through the entire process, and then—just when you think you can see the light at the end of the tunnel—the last two months really do you in. After weekly phone calls, endless reviews of edited (and re-edited, and re-re-edited) chapters, and back-and-forth debates about how to capitalize things like BACKINT/BackInt/Backint (read on to find out, curious reader!), the process of writing a book can feel like it takes a lifetime.

The end product, though, reflects the effort that went into it. Your authors, Richard Bremer and Lars Breddemann, have persevered—in the midst of a new baby, an international move, and more—to write the very first book on SAP HANA administration. Though you weren't there for all the phone calls, dear reader, I trust you'll see the time that went into it, and take an equal measure of value from it.

Of course, even a book requires a little tuning every now and then, so we at SAP PRESS would be interested to hear your opinion. What did you think about *SAP HANA Administration*? How could it be improved? As your comments and suggestions are the most useful tools to help us make our books the best they can be, we encourage you to visit our website at *www.sap-press.com* and share your feedback.

Thank you for purchasing a book from SAP PRESS!

Kelly Grace Weaver
Editor, SAP PRESS

Rheinwerk Publishing
Boston, MA

kellyw@rheinwerk-publishing.com
www.sap-press.com

Contents

3   Installation and Updates 75

Preface

In the years since its release in 2011, SAP HANA has grown and matured in an impressive way. It started as a redundant data store in BI solutions or as an accelerator add-on, and now, several years later, the database can power all business applications of large corporations. With constantly growing adoption in increasingly serious use cases, there comes a need for skills in all matters related to the database system. Although there is no shortage of books related to implementing or marketing SAP HANA, the topic of database administration has been somewhat neglected in the past. In the more than 700 pages that follow, we will address this gap.

Who Should Read This Book?

Database administration does not suddenly become important with the go-live of a project. On the contrary, system design and the requirements of system operation must be taken into account when planning the implementation. They will play an important role during system setup and in the implementation phase—and if everything has been done well, the administration of the running system will be a walk in the park.

With this in mind, we developed the contents of this book so that they will aid project members responsible for the SAP HANA system setup and the definition of an operational concept for the system.

We did, of course, not ignore the most obvious target group—that is, the administrators of SAP HANA systems—who will find a wealth of information from system architecture through table management and from session handling, backup mechanisms, and high-availability features to aspects of user management and security.

In addition, database developers will find valuable information on how to analyze query performance and efficiently work with traces and log files. They will also gain insight into how SAP HANA processes information models, procedures, and SQL statements.

Last but not least, project managers must also understand how proper setup of the system itself and the operational procedures will be crucial to the success of the project. Chapter 2 and Chapter 14 in particular have been written for those who are responsible for SAP HANA projects.

Structure of This Book

When we sat down and planned the table of contents of this book, we felt that the book should have two major and inseparable themes that would guide the content creation of each chapter: concepts and skills. Even though there is already a wide range of publications available on SAP HANA, database administrators will need an understanding of the database system on a more fundamental level than is usually provided. At the same time, administrators need the ability to derive from such conceptual understanding the appropriate actions in a given situation. Experience is a catalyst for this process, and we used our own experience in working with SAP HANA systems to include detailed examples or best-practice recommendations throughout the book.

The first two chapters are entirely dedicated to an introduction to the SAP HANA system and its most typical application in IT landscapes. In all of the following chapters, you will find a balanced mix of teaching concepts and conveying hands-on skills. Chapters 3 to 6 are related to the database system, with topics such as installation and update, persistence and business continuity, and scaling SAP HANA. Chapters 7, 8, and 9 deal with objects in the database in general and database tables in particular. In Chapters 10 to 13, we cover transaction handling, the repository as a backend for managing development artifacts, and the topics of user management, system security, authentication, and authorization. We put everything learned so far together in Chapter 14 with an end-to-end view of planning and setting up an SAP HANA system before rounding out the book with an in-depth discussion of performance and root-cause analysis. A more detailed preview of the chapters follows:

▶ **Chapter 1: Architecture of the SAP HANA Database**
We lay the foundation for all the following chapters by zooming into an SAP HANA system and explaining the core components of the database along with the boundary conditions of system setups, such as hardware choices, deployment options, and more.

▶ **Chapter 2: SAP HANA Scenarios: Administration Considerations**
SAP HANA systems have a variety of aspects that may be important for the DBA—depending on how the system is being used. We introduce the most common usage scenarios, such as BI solutions, SAP BW on HANA, or SAP Business Suite on HANA, and highlight the most important skill sets for each scenario.

▶ **Chapter 3: Installation and Updates**
The act of installing or updating the database software is in itself fairly simple. It is the related tasks, such as the preparation of the operating system, that lead to considerable complexity. In addition to describing these preparatory steps in detail, we help you to choose the best option from the range of available installation and update tools, and we guide you through the process of installation and update, both interactively and in batch mode.

▶ **Chapter 4: Administration Tools**
With SAP HANA Studio, SAP delivers a feature-rich tool for the database administrator. We introduce the basic usage aspects of this tool, as well as an overview of the SAP HANA flavor of DBA Cockpit—the well-known SAP NetWeaver standard tool for database administration.

▶ **Chapter 5: The Persistence Layer**
In this chapter, we start with a look at data and log writing in SAP HANA. We then progress to backup mechanisms, including log backup, data backup, and storage snapshots. Finally, we cover disaster-recovery setups based on SAP HANA's system replication technology.

▶ **Chapter 6: Scale-Out Systems and High Availability**
SAP HANA systems can be scaled horizontally by combining multiple physical hosts into one single database cluster. We first describe the working principle of such scale-out systems and then dive into administration tasks, such as adding or removing hosts. Finally, we describe the high-availability features of SAP HANA scale-out systems.

▶ **Chapter 7: Objects**
In a database system, you find not only tables but also other objects. We use this chapter to tell you about all the types of objects you can find in SAP HANA, including tables (briefly), views, indexes, stored procedures, sequences, triggers, and more.

▶ **Chapter 8: Table Types**

Tables are the most important kind of object in a database, and we dedicate two entire chapters to them. In this first one, we explain the different types of tables that SAP HANA offers, with—of course—a focus on columnar tables.

▶ **Chapter 9: Working with Tables**

The second table-centered chapter explains the most important tasks related to table management in SAP HANA. We cover SAP HANA-specific processes— such as the loading of tables into main memory or the delta merge procedure— and we discuss the partitioning and distribution of tables in scale-out systems.

▶ **Chapter 10: Sessions and Transactions**

Sessions and transactions are the basic elements that enable applications to communicate with the database system. Database developers will appreciate our introduction to session management in SAP HANA, and administrators need to know how to monitor and manage sessions and transactions.

▶ **Chapter 11: Working with the Repository**

The repository is SAP HANA's store for development artifacts, such as information models, stored procedures, or applications. Although this book is not about developing in SAP HANA, administrators should know about the mechanisms of managing development content in the repository.

▶ **Chapter 12: User Management and Security**

Database systems often contain sensitive information that must be protected. We have two chapters related to security topics, starting with coverage of user management and aspects of system security, such as authentication options, network encryption, and audit logging.

▶ **Chapter 13: Roles and Privileges**

SAP HANA offers two different role concepts and a variety of privilege types for implementing user authorizations. In this second security-related chapter, we tell you everything you need to know about roles and privileges.

▶ **Chapter 14: Planning and Setting Up an SAP HANA System Landscape**

This chapter starts with a discussion of the most important aspects of planning SAP HANA systems: sizing, deployment choices, system landscape considerations, and so on. We then guide you step-by-step through the necessary and recommended postinstallation steps that will lead to a well-prepared SAP HANA system that is ready for productive usage.

► **Chapter 15: Tools for Performance Analysis**
A typical task for a database administrator or a database developer is to assess the performance of a single statement. Like other systems, SAP HANA offers multiple tools that may help in this process, and as is the case in other systems, some of these tools are more useful than others. We briefly introduce all of these tools, help you choose the most useful ones, and guide you through the use of the immensely valuable Plan Visualizer tool.

► **Chapter 16: Monitoring and Root-Cause Analysis**
Our final chapter guides you through the built-in and external offerings for system monitoring and then gives an overview of tools and functionalities for root-cause analysis. These include error messages and diagnostic files generated by the system as well as traces of the database server and the client interfaces.

Whether you read the book cover-to-cover or use it as a reference to look up details on the task at hand, we are confident that you will learn a great deal about today's most exciting SAP product.

Acknowledgments

We would like to thank our families and loved ones for their support and understanding over countless long nights and many weekends that we needed to invest in the completion of this book. To Barbara, Ronja, Luise, and Henrike Bremer: Without your love and patience, we could not have completed this book.

To Karen: Thank you so much for your support, for your love, and for enduring "half-day" vacations during the writing phase.

We also thank our colleagues Werner Steyn, Lucas Kiesow, and Marc Hartz for reading parts of this book and providing valuable feedback. Throughout the past years, we also had many a good discussion with our colleagues in SAP HANA development, SAP HANA product management, and the former RIG. Whether directly related to the book or not, these discussions provided fuel for the text at hand. In no particular order, we thank Martin Kittel, Torsten Strahl, Henning Zahn, Elke Zietlow, Rocco Himmer, Werner Thesing, Sascha Schwedes, Martin Frauendorfer, Nora Roch, Peter Stockinger, Christiane Hienger, Andrea Kristen, Melanie Handreck, Florian Müller, Ralf Czekalla, Serge Muts, Matt Kangas, and Mark Heffernan.

We'd also like to thank Kelly Grace Weaver, our editor at SAP PRESS, for her patience, for competently guiding us through the process of creating our first ever book, and for helping us to eventually get everything ready. In the final stage of review, she probably slept even less than we did. Thank you in particular for the passionate discussions of semantics, the use of language, and details of typesetting—a beautiful change from the daily business of IT.

Although the variety of components and setup options for SAP HANA
may seem confusing, the system is not so complex if you understand the
building blocks. The purpose of our first chapter is to help you understand
how simple and beautiful SAP HANA systems really are.

1 Architecture of the SAP HANA Database

Since its first release three years ago, SAP HANA has evolved beyond being just another relational database management system. In this chapter, we will help you understand what this means for you, the administrator. In the first few sections, we will approach SAP HANA from the outside and slowly zoom in, shedding light on the hardware composition of the system, showing you what the operating system will see, and finally looking into the database processes to understand the internal architecture of the system. In addition to this, we will shed some light on distributed SAP HANA instances that allow scaling out the database, thereby increasing data storage and computing capacity. Following this journey into the database, we will again take a step back and talk about the appliance concept of SAP HANA before finishing up with some insight into the software release cycle.

1.1 The Basics

Before we really dive into the details, let's try to make good on our promise in the chapter's introduction and spend a page explaining what SAP HANA actually is. Today, SAP HANA is a technology platform for the new generation of SAP. (Notice that we say new, not next! SAP HANA is already a reality at SAP.)

The SAP HANA system contains many components that administrators need to understand (which you'll learn all about in this book). However, for the interactions of end users and developers in an SAP HANA system, only two are visible: a relational database system fulfilling the famous *ACID* requirements (atomicity, consistency, isolation, and durability) and a development platform and application server within the same environment. By bringing application development and data storage more closely together than in previous SAP systems, SAP HANA extends the toolset available to SAP developers to cater to all requirements in the modern world of business software.

Consider the highly simplified architectural overview of systems with SAP HANA in Figure 1.1; the two main components described in the previous paragraph are represented by two "server" components of the SAP HANA system. The database management system is the *index server component*, and most components of the development platform reside in the *XS server*.

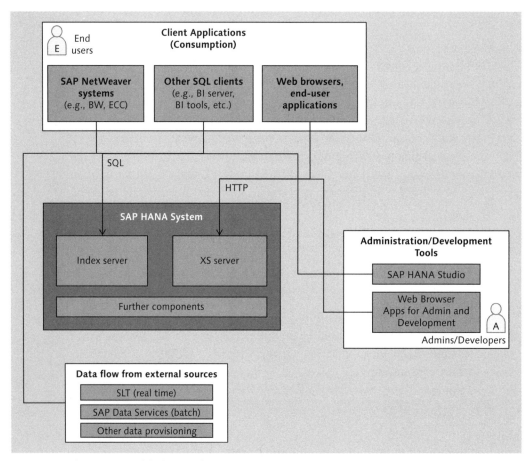

Figure 1.1 Simplified View of an SAP HANA System

In Figure 1.1, the world outside of SAP HANA is divided into three parts (we hope the French do not mind); the client applications inhabit one of these, the administrators and developers another, and the external data sources the third. As opposed to the people of Gaul 2,000 years back, these parts communicate via the same language—or rather, the same two languages (by and large)—depending on which component of SAP HANA they converse with. SQL is the most prominent native language of the index server, and applications of the XS server are mostly exposed via HTML5 user interfaces.

Because we promised to keep it simple, we will stop here, and feed you the rest of the details step-by-step in the rest of the chapter. Before we go any further, though, we want to establish a few definitions that we'll use consistently throughout the book:

► **Instance**

We will use the term *SAP HANA instance* (or simply *instance*) to refer to the collection of those processes that make up one SAP HANA environment on a single-node database server. For all practical purposes, these are the processes and programs that are created when you run the install program for the server components of the SAP HANA database. The instance consists mainly of the start processes, the core database processes, and some of the SAP HANA auxiliary processes (all of which we'll describe in more detail in this chapter).

As with other SAP systems, an instance has two identifiers: the system ID (SID)—which is a three-letter alphanumeric identifier starting with a letter—and the two-digit instance number. The SID uniquely identifies the database instance. Except for special setups, there is a 1:1 mapping of SID to instance number, that is, the instance number is often a unique identifier as well. The instance number is used in defining the internal and external network ports of the SAP HANA system.

It is possible to install more than one SAP HANA instance on a single physical database server, and you can even operate SAP NetWeaver and SAP HANA instances on the same server.

Note

In the context of distributed systems that we will cover in Section 1.5 and in Chapter 6, we will not use the term "instance." The reason is that "instance" is a widely used term in SAP NetWeaver systems, and the concept of instances in distributed SAP NetWeaver systems can't be applied perfectly to the individual hosts of a distributed SAP HANA system.

▶ **System**

We will mostly use the term *system* to refer to the physical database server, the operating system, and the SAP HANA instance (or instances) installed on that server, as well as any required auxiliary components.

▶ **Host and scale-out system**

We use the term *host* to refer to a physical machine. A host is a device you can touch. We continue the definition of system as the entire database system, including its hardware and software components. A *scale-out system* therefore is a collection of multiple hosts, with SAP HANA software running on all of them.

▶ **Node and distributed system**

Especially in the context of scale-out systems, we use the term *node* to refer to the SAP HANA software that runs on one host. There is, however, no fixed relationship between a node and a host; that is to say, one can move a node from one host to another (for example, in a failover situation). There is to our knowledge no good term referring to only the software processes on all hosts of the database system. We therefore use the term *distributed system* also to refer to a collection of multiple nodes.

Within this choice of terminology, we mainly use the term *node* to define a semantic relationship. There can be different types of nodes, and the node type defines the role of this node within the SAP HANA system.

1.2   The Physical View: SAP HANA Servers

Let's begin the architectural overview with a glimpse at the hardware of an SAP HANA server. Assume that your server is a typical computer server, consisting of a mainboard with CPU and RAM, network interfaces, disks, and other devices you would expect to find in a computer system.

In Figure 1.2, we have cut down the database into its three most prominent internal and one very important external building blocks: the data and processing layer, the persistence layer, and the network layer. We will now discuss each of these building blocks in more detail.

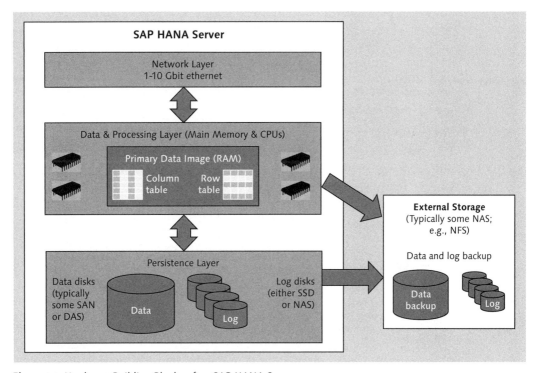

Figure 1.2 Hardware Building Blocks of an SAP HANA Server

1.2.1 Data and Processing Layer

The heart of SAP HANA is what we call here the *data and processing layer*, represented in the hardware world by the main memory and the CPUs (and auxiliary components). You may have heard that SAP HANA is an in-memory database, which means that the *primary* image of all data is in RAM and that all internal algorithms are optimized to work on data that is present in memory. Put simply, the database attempts to keep all database tables fully in main memory during regular operations. This leads to extreme demands for the amount of main memory installed in the database, and SAP HANA systems come with copious amounts of this once-rare resource.

The maximally possible amount of main memory in a single database server is determined by two choices made by SAP:

- **The type of CPUs supported**
  Presently, SAP HANA will only run on the Intel X86 architecture; more specif-

ically, the database code is optimized for the newer generations of the Intel XEON architecture (Westmere-EX and Ivy Bridge-EX), making use of its advanced SIMD instruction sets like SSE3 and SSE4.

At the time of writing, SAP HANA servers can contain a maximum of 8 CPUs with 10 CPU cores each (15 cores for Ivy Bridge), that is, 80 (120) CPU cores in total.

▸ **The maximum ratio of main memory to number of installed CPUs**
Based on use-case studies, SAP has set a maximum ratio of main memory to number of installed CPUs of about 16 GB per CPU core for analytic use cases. In response to these two restrictions, the current generation of SAP HANA servers comes with at most one or two terabytes (TB) of main memory installed for the Westmere- and Ivy Bridge-based models, respectively.

For operating SAP Business Suite systems—which have mostly an OLTP workload—SAP allows larger amounts of main memory in a single server, bringing the currently available maximum to 6 TB of RAM.

Intel's Processor Architecture

Readers interested in more details about how SAP makes use of Intel's processor architecture can consult a joint white paper by Intel and SAP on the topic, which is referenced in "Intel & SAP HANA Solution Brief: Scaling Real-Time Analytics across the Enterprise—and into the Cloud":

www.saphana.com/docs/DOC-2592

1.2.2 Persistence Layer

SAP HANA could not be a database if it did not store data on a nonvolatile medium. Of course, the system also comes with enough disk storage to keep all data and other required information. Similar to most other database systems, SAP HANA writes transaction logs synchronously and keeps a full data image in asynchronously updated data volumes.

In general, these two systems come with two dedicated sets of disks. The data volumes always reside on classical discs whose total capacity must equal three times the installed RAM of the server according to the *SAP HANA Server Installation Guide* (downloadable from the SAP Community Network: *https://scn.sap.com*). For the log volumes, SAP initially required SSD storage with a capacity equaling the amount of installed RAM.

In certain systems, classical hard drive technology is also supported. Both sets of disks need to fulfill SAP's specifications for data throughput, I/O operations per second, and so on, which are available to SAP HANA hardware partners. Additional disks are needed for the software installation of SAP HANA and all related SAP components.

Internal or External Disks

As for the interesting question of whether the disks are internal to the database server or whether you may make use of your existing enterprise storage—we'll get to that in Section 1.6.

Although the data and log disks are intrinsic components of the database, SAP does not define the required nature of the devices to keep data and log backups. There are two backup methods available: file-based backup and network-pipe-based backups. For file-based backup, a dedicated storage device must be available in the file system of the SAP HANA server, and customers are free to choose the storage technology.

1.2.3 Network Layer

The number of network interfaces required in an SAP HANA system depends on several aspects of the system setup, such as clustering, implemented high-availability concepts, and more. These options will be covered later. For now, we will make some simplifications and only state that an outbound network interface must be available for SAP HANA to communicate with other IT systems. This interface must have a nominal throughput of at least 1 gigabit (Gbit), and 10 Gbit Ethernet is recommended.

Network topologies around SAP HANA systems can vary widely, but generally speaking SAP HANA can be treated like other databases in terms of network considerations for SAP NetWeaver systems or SAP BusinessObjects BI systems.

1.3 The Operating System View: Database Processes

If you log on to the operating system of an SAP HANA database, the first thing you will notice is that it is a Linux OS. Up to and including SPS 7, the only supported operating system was SUSE Linux Enterprise Server (SLES) 11 or SUSE Linux

Enterprise Server for SAP Applications 11, most probably on service pack level 2 or 3. With SPS 8, SAP introduced support also for Red Hat Enterprise Linux 6.5; see SAP Note 2009879.

We have divided the processes that belong to an SAP HANA database server into four factions, as displayed in Figure 1.3. We will now walk you through this quartet of process groups.

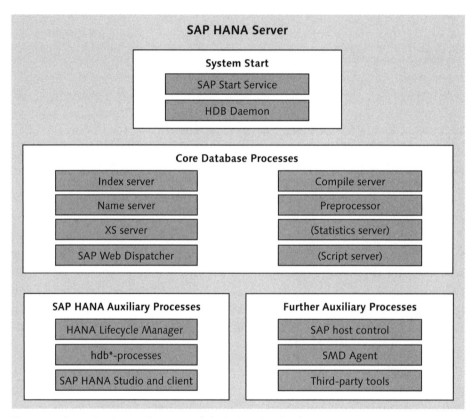

Figure 1.3 Operating System Processes of the SAP HANA Database

1.3.1 System Start

All SAP systems are started by a process named *SAP Start Service* (see Figure 1.4), which in Linux operating systems is represented by the `sapstartsrv` OS process. SAP HANA is no exception to this rule. You will find `sapstartsrv` running for each instance of the SAP HANA database on your server.

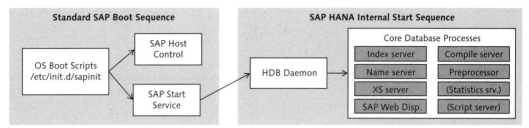

Figure 1.4 Boot Sequence of an SAP HANA System

SAP Start Service

Documentation for SAP Start Service is available as part of the public documentation of SAP NetWeaver available via the SAP Help Portal.

We will not go into much detail here, because SAP Start Service is well known to SAP administrators. For those not familiar with the service, it provides functionality to start and stop the SAP system along with rudimentary monitoring capabilities, such as access to trace files, logs, and configuration of the system, through a common API regardless of what SAP system is being monitored.

The generic SAP Start Service only kicks off one single process of the SAP HANA system, which is called the *HDB daemon*. Even though the daemon is in fact a core process of the database, we moved it into the group of processes for system start to accentuate its purpose. The daemon process has two tasks: start all required core processes of the SAP HANA database system, and keep them running, that is, restart them if a process should fail.

The list of required processes is mostly predefined by SAP, but there are a few choices an administrator can make, because there are a few nonmandatory core processes in SAP HANA. All processes to be started by the HDB daemon have entries in the daemon configuration file *hdbdaemon.ini*.

1.3.2 Core Database Processes

The most interesting processes for us are of course the core database processes. Purists might argue that our definition is not quite correct, because we include here the SAP Web Dispatcher, which is not an SAP HANA process but rather a standard SAP component. However, for our purposes a "core process" is an OS process that is started by the HDB daemon, and the SAP Web Dispatcher is one of them. It is also the only process whose activity is not monitored in the list of running services in SAP HANA Studio (Figure 1.5).

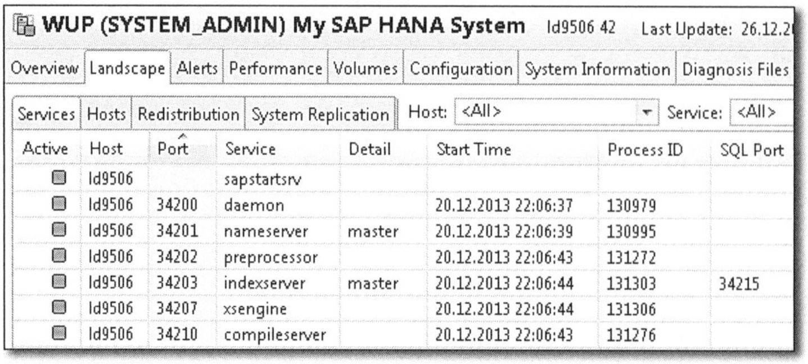

Active	Host	Port	Service	Detail	Start Time	Process ID	SQL Port
☐	ld9506		sapstartsrv				
☐	ld9506	34200	daemon		20.12.2013 22:06:37	130979	
☐	ld9506	34201	nameserver	master	20.12.2013 22:06:39	130995	
☐	ld9506	34202	preprocessor		20.12.2013 22:06:43	131272	
☐	ld9506	34203	indexserver	master	20.12.2013 22:06:44	131303	34215
☐	ld9506	34207	xsengine		20.12.2013 22:06:44	131306	
☐	ld9506	34210	compileserver		20.12.2013 22:06:43	131276	

Above the table: 🗃 **WUP (SYSTEM_ADMIN) My SAP HANA System** Id9506 42   Last Update: 26.12.2

Overview | Landscape | Alerts | Performance | Volumes | Configuration | System Information | Diagnosis Files

Services | Hosts | Redistribution | System Replication || Host: ‹All›   ▾ Service: ‹All›

Figure 1.5 Active Processes of a Typical SAP HANA Database System

Next, we will give you an idea of the purpose of all of these processes that, combined, represent a fully functioning SAP HANA database. We will choose a somewhat arbitrary ordering, based on what we perceive are the most important processes. (Here again, we will keep it simple and provide further details for some processes in Section 1.4.)

The Index Server

For most practical purposes, the *index server* is *the* database process in SAP HANA. It has the following jobs:

▸ It provides the SQL interface on SAP HANA's SQL port.

▸ It manages all database tables and other objects of the database catalog.

▸ It processes all SQL queries in the database.

As such, the index server will under normal circumstances have the largest resource footprint among all the processes on the SAP HANA server—for memory as well as for CPU usage.

The Name Server

SAP HANA needs a logical view of itself—for example, its components and locations of data—which is called the *topology*. The topology is managed by the *name server* component. The name server becomes particularly important in distributed database systems (which we have not mentioned yet; they will be covered in Section 1.5). The name server also hosts the backup manager, responsible for coordinating synchronized backups of all system components.

The XS Server and the SAP Web Dispatcher

Since the beginning, but especially since the SPS 5 release, SAP HANA has been a development platform built around the integrated database kernel. Of course, the database itself (index server) offers development capabilities, such as designing database schemas, views, and SAP HANA data models or stored procedures. The *XS server*—which was introduced with SPS 5—targets the development layer on top of these rather technical tools.

Among the features provided by the XS server, you can find:

▶ Server-side JavaScript

▶ OData services and XMLA

▶ Development of user interfaces (HTML5) with SAPUI5

▶ Application definitions to expose sets of development artifacts as applications

Applications created in SAP HANA XS server are exposed through HTTP. As a web-server component, SAP HANA uses the *SAP Web Dispatcher*, which will be well-known to all SAP NetWeaver administrators.

SAP Web Dispatcher

Documentation of the SAP Web Dispatcher is available as part of the documentation of the SAP NetWeaver Application Server on the SAP Help Portal.

The Compile Server

With the release of SAP HANA SPS 6 (revision 60), the compiling of L-script procedures has been moved from the index server process into the newly established compile server process. This is a mandatory, automatically installed component of SAP HANA that, in our experience, you do not need to know much about.

The Preprocessor

For processing unstructured data, SAP HANA's *preprocessor* component creates searchable, full-text indexes and offers capabilities such as tokenization, normalization, stemming, and extraction processing. It might be regarded as a supporting component to the index server for text search and text analysis.

The Statistics Server

The *statistics server* is a database process which provides the *statistics service*. Starting with SPS 7 (revision 70), it is possible to have the statistics service integrated into the index server and name server processes, thus eliminating the need for a dedicated further database process. The statistics server is thus an optional process that is enabled in the default configuration of SPS 7.

Statistics Service

The statistics service, on the other hand, is not optional; it has to be available for the database to be functional. It is SAP HANA's offering for information collection, checking, and alerting on all system components.

The Script Server

The *script server* is an optional component that is at present only required for certain functionalities associated with the Application Function Library (AFL). It is not enabled by default.

1.3.3   SAP HANA Auxiliary Processes

All processes mentioned so far are required for the regular operations of an SAP HANA system. The auxiliary components we discuss next are native parts of SAP HANA but are only used for specific tasks, such as updating the software.

SAP HANA Lifecycle Manager

Software updates are the main topic of the SAP HANA Lifecycle Manager (HLM), which is a graphical application that supports updating just the database or all components of a so-called SAP HANA Support Package Stack (see Section 1.7.1) by using corresponding components installed on the database server. The frontend application is available from within the administration tool SAP HANA Studio and also accessible through a web interface. HLM's functionality extends beyond updating, with support for system landscape modification (renaming the system, provisioning additional database instances, etc.) and more.

In the SPS 8 release of SAP HANA, the functionalities for system lifecycle management have mostly been switched off, and hdblcm (discussed ahead) is now the preferred tool for all related tasks.

The hdb* Tools

SAP HANA comes with a range of command-line tools, which we here summarize as *hdb*-tools*, because their names begin with the acronym hdb. These tools are installed into the directory */usr/sap/<SID>/HDB<instance>/exe*. Among these tools, you can find:

▸ **hdblcm and hdblcmgui**
These are new applications for installing and updating the database introduced with SPS 7. It is planned that hdblcm will become the backend tool used by HLM in higher support packages.

▸ **hdbsql**
This is a command-line SQL console that comes with the client package (it is thus available on any computer that has the SAP HANA client installed).

▸ **hdbuserstore**
This is a secure store for database credentials that can be used for password-free authentication, for example, in hdbsql. It is also used by SAP NetWeaver Application Servers on SAP HANA to store their database credentials. hdbuserstore is also part of the client package.

SAP HANA Studio and Client

With a fully installed instance of the SAP HANA database, you will always also get SAP HANA Studio and the client locally installed on the database server. However, in most cases, database administrators (DBAs) will use a local installation of SAP HANA Studio to connect to the server. The local installation of these tools is meant for emergency and bootstrapping DBA tasks when a remote connection is not available.

1.3.4   Further Auxiliary Processes

As an SAP system, SAP HANA comes with several standard SAP components used for basic operation and monitoring. There may also be additional components installed by vendors other than SAP.

SAP Host Agent

The SAP Host Agent is a tool for monitoring and controlling SAP instances. Part of this tool is the already mentioned SAP Start Service. There are further components, for example, `saposcol`, which collect information on an operating system level, and `saphostctrl`, which is used by HLM for providing user access to the HLM backend (for more information, see Section 12.4.1 in Chapter 12).

> **Further Resources**
>
> Database administrators who may not be familiar with traditional SAP landscapes can find information about the SAP Host Agent in the SAP NetWeaver documentation on the SAP Help Portal.

SMD Agent

The SAP Solution Manager Diagnostics Agent (SMD Agent) is another tool for collecting status and other monitoring information. In this case, it collects information to feed SAP Solution Manager. For information on integrating SAP Solution Manager with SAP HANA, see *https://service.sap.com/solman-hana/*.

Third-Party Tools

Depending on preferences and requirements, customers may operate certain non-SAP software components on their SAP HANA servers, such as antivirus software, monitoring agents, or backup management tools.

1.4 The Logical View: Internal Architecture of the Database

Let's now take a look at the architecture within the database core processes. Figure 1.6 shows how these processes interact with each other. In the figure, we only highlight a few internal components of each of the core processes to keep it simple.

We also show optional services in the figure, such as the script server and the statistics server. You may remember that the statistics service can be moved from the dedicated statistics server process into the other database processes. In that setup, the statistics scheduler will run in the name server, and all other parts of the statistics service will be integrated into the index server (see Chapter 5 for details).

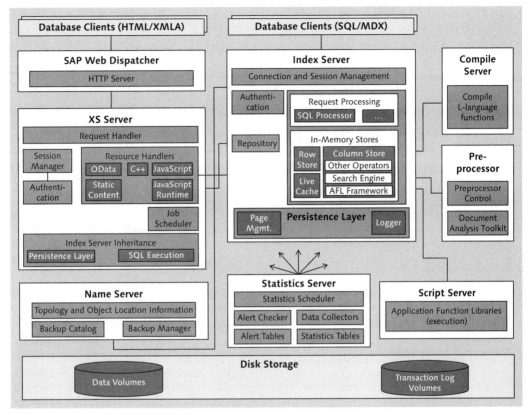

Figure 1.6 Internal Architecture of SAP HANA Database

Note that there are two entry points for the interactions of database clients with the SAP HANA system: the index server for SQL-based requests (including MDX) and the XS server for HTTP-based requests. Because it is the server relevant for administrators, this section focuses on the index server. For the sake of completeness, we briefly mention the XS server, but a detailed discussion would be outside the scope of this book.

1.4.1   Index Server Architecture

Any SQL-based or MDX-based interaction with SAP HANA will enter the index server component and (assuming successful authentication and authorization tests) be executed by the SQL processor. Depending on the nature of the query and the database objects accessed, different internal engines of the database will be involved in the query execution, such as the processing engines of the row and column store. Also—and especially in distributed SAP HANA systems—the name server component will be involved to find the location of database objects required for query processing.

For certain functionalities, the index server will delegate a part of the workload to other processes: to the compile server for compiling functions in the SAP-internal L-language; to the script server for executing L-functions of the Application Function Libraries (AFL); or to the preprocessor for creating full text indexes and for other parts of processing unstructured data. The database clients will not notice these delegations; they simply converse with the index server.

L-Language

L-language is an internal, C-like language that is dynamically compiled with an optimizing compiler. It is not available for application development to SAP HANA users.

Both the index server and the XS server make use of SAP HANA's repository for storing development artifacts. Although the XS server—which is technically an extended index server—comes with its own repository, all processes use the repository in the index server.

Underlying all of these database components is the disk storage, in which those processes that control data on their own create data and log volumes; see Chapter 5.

Note

Multiple core processes of SAP HANA own data and thus create data and log volumes. Processes creating data and log volumes are the index server, the name server, the XS server, the statistics server, and the script server.

A simplified schematic of the index server is shown in Figure 1.7.

When communicating with the database, clients first need to open a connection and acquire a session through the connection and session management component, which will also involve the authentication manager to validate the credentials provided with the connect attempt.

Upon successful authentication, the clients can send commands to the database, typically in the form of SQL statements. All statements are executed in the context of a transaction—coordinated by the *Transaction Manager*, which is responsible for transactional isolation and keeping track of open and closed transactions. Upon events such as committing or rolling back transactions, the Transaction Manager informs the involved relational stores so that they can take appropriate action. In combination with the persistence layer, the Transaction Manager is also responsible for achieving atomic and durable transactions.

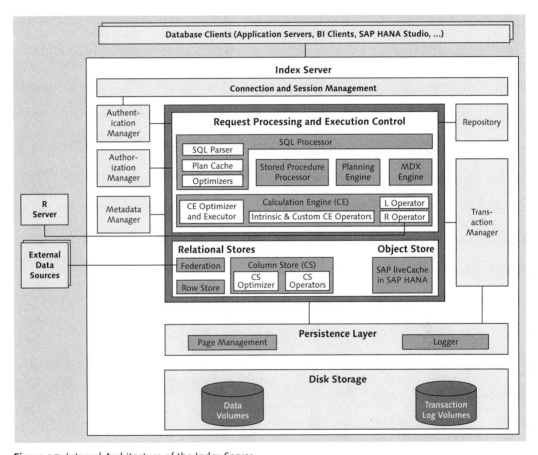

Figure 1.7 Internal Architecture of the Index Server

Note

For an in-depth discussion of session and transaction management, including concurrency control, see Chapter 10.

Actual statement execution involves the components listed under Request Processing and Execution Control in Figure 1.7. Statements first have to be parsed, checked, and optimized to generate an execution plan. Depending on the nature and content of the statement, different execution engines might be involved, such as the stored procedure processor (for SQLScript procedures) or the planning engine.

Several functionalities of the database have been implemented in a common infrastructure called the *calculation engine*. To many people, the calculation engine will be best known for its set of intrinsic calculation engine operators that can be used within SQLScript procedures. There is, however, more to this engine, such as operators for L and R, or planning operators.

All of these processing engines operate on top of the in-memory stores of the database. SAP HANA presently offers four such stores. The most important one is the *column store*, which manages column store tables that are typically used to store application data; it also contains, for example, the text-search capabilities of the database. The *row store* is a row-oriented in-memory store, typically used for system/basis tables (e.g., for basis tables of SAP NetWeaver systems) but not for application data. *Data federation* allows transparent access to objects in remote databases (a concept typically termed Smart Data Access in SAP HANA) and is in fact a virtual store, as its data has no local persistence within SAP HANA. Finally, the *liveCache* is an in-memory object store, well-known from the SAP Business Suite, where it is used in applications such as the SAP SCM component SAP Advanced Planning and Optimization (APO).

The *Metadata Manager* is a component for maintaining metadata of the database catalog, such as table and view definitions. It is a single metadata catalog for all in-memory stores, technically implemented as a collection of row store tables.

The interface between the in-memory store and the data volumes on disk is implemented in the *persistence layer*. This component manages the data pages for the in-memory stores and their persistence in the data volume; it also controls the writing of transaction log entries to the log volumes.

1.4.2   XS Server Architecture

As we mentioned earlier, a detailed discussion of the XS server is outside the scope of this book; however, Figure 1.8 shows a diagram of its basic architecture.

HTML access enters the system through the SAP Web Dispatcher, which delegates the access request to the XS server. Depending on the request, different processors in the XS server will be involved in the request processing, for example, the JavaScript runtime or the OData handler.

In most cases, the request will involve application data, which in SAP HANA is always stored in one of the relational stores of the index server process. Hence, the XS server will involve the appropriate index server component for such data access through a database-internal network protocol (even if both components are on the same physical server).

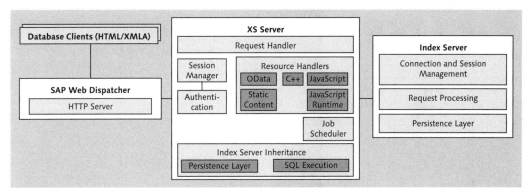

Figure 1.8 XS Server Architecture

1.5   Distributed SAP HANA Systems

Now that you know the fundamental concepts behind SAP HANA systems, we will go one step further and introduce distributed SAP HANA systems.

As we mentioned earlier, the database size of SAP HANA servers is restricted to 2 TB of main memory (6 TB for SAP Business Suite systems). If that was the end of the story, we would not need to talk about SAP HANA as a serious player in today's database market. The way to implement larger database systems is through scaling out, that is, building database systems that span multiple physical servers. To avoid confusion with the server processes, from now on we will use the term *host* to denote a single physical server machine in an SAP HANA system. Hence, there can be single-host database systems (which we have covered so far) and multihost systems, also called *distributed systems* or *scale-out systems*.

In a distributed SAP HANA system, most core components of the system exist on each of the individual hosts, as depicted in Figure 1.9. In some cases, a component can play different roles, depending on which host it is running on, such as the name server, which runs as an active master name server on one host (host 1 in our figure) and as a read-only slave on the other hosts. In Figure 1.9, we have marked in **bold** those components that can play different roles on the different hosts of the scale-out instance.

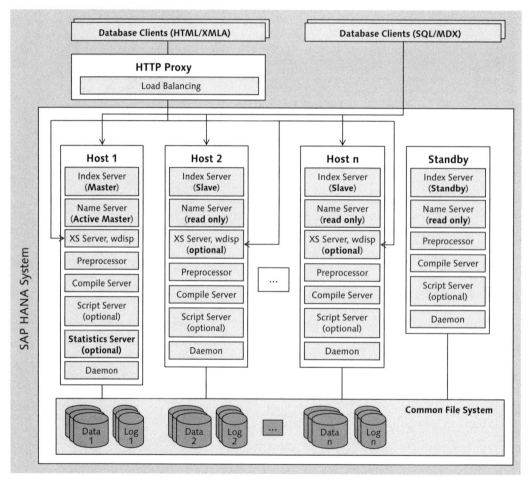

Figure 1.9 SAP HANA Core Components in a Distributed System

In this figure, hosts 1 through n are active, that is, they control data and take part in database operations, such as query executions. The last host is called standby.

This host is a high-availability component, technically identical to the others, but on standby and ready to take the workload of an active host that might fail for whatever reason. For more details on high-availability features in SAP HANA scale-out systems, see Chapter 6.

More on Nodes

Recall our definition of nodes from Section 1.1. In Figure 1.9, the first host houses the master node of our SAP HANA system, whereas hosts 2 through n house the slave nodes, and the master and slave nodes combined are the worker nodes. The standby hosts house standby nodes. In the case of a host failure, the node of the failing host will be moved to a standby host.

In this section, we discuss the three major components that allow SAP HANA to operate as a single database over several nodes. Conceptually, it boils down to one index server process per node, which all access a shared storage system. These multiple index server processes are coordinated by the name server process. Let's look into this one by one.

1.5.1 The Name Server in Distributed Systems

In distributed SAP HANA systems, the name server process plays a particularly important role. It maintains the system topology, which describes the system in two aspects: the logical description of the database (which hosts exists, what is the role of the hosts, etc.) and the map of data locations (the mapping of database objects to hosts and processes on the hosts).

This topology information will be required for query execution in the distributed database system. In order to avoid excessive network communication, a copy of the topology is held available on each host.

To avoid the complexities involved in keeping a resource consistent even though it is changed by multiple processes, there is at any point in time only one name server process that is allowed to modify topology information. This process is named the *active master name server*. All other name servers only hold a read-only copy of the topology.

Because the topology is a highly critical resource, there is built-in redundancy in the topology management: The system can have up to three configured *name server masters*. One of these—initially the first one that becomes active upon system start, typically the one on the master node—is the active master name server. The other two masters constantly monitor the availability of the active master name server. If the active master name server fails, one of the other master name servers will be appointed the new active master name server and thus gain write access to the topology. This redundancy process for the name server functionality is independent from the host failover we mentioned earlier.

1.5.2 Distributed Index Servers: Data and Query Distribution

Many data objects in the SAP HANA database can be distributed across multiple database nodes, either by moving entire objects from one host to another, or—in the case of database tables—by partitioning the table into multiple physical partitions and distributing these partitions across the nodes (see Chapter 9).

In a scale-out scenario, one of the index server processes plays a special role. It is called the *master index server* and typically resides on the first host of the database system (the order of hosts is determined at installation time). The extended responsibilities of the master index server include (but are not limited to) the following items:

- **Metadata management**
  Similar to topology management, the metadata catalog of the database is centrally managed and replicated to all other index servers. If metadata changes are required on an arbitrary host, this host will signal the metadata change to the Master Metadata Manager on the master index server.

- **Transaction management**
  Transaction handling in distributed architectures requires particular efforts to ensure consistency throughout the transactions. In SAP HANA, this is implemented via *distributed transactions* and a *two-phase commit* mechanism. If a transaction is started that involves data owned by different index server processes, a primary transaction will be started on the Master Transaction Manager, and all other involved index servers will start local transactions that are linked to this primary transaction.

  During the commit phase, the Master Transaction Manager will send requests to all of these local transactions to prepare the commit and will, upon successful acknowledgement, finally commit the transaction—or upon an error message, it will initiate a rollback.

▶ **Row store**

The row store in SAP HANA can be distributed as well, albeit with a smaller feature set than the column store. It is, for example, not possible to partition row store tables. In a typical system configuration, all row store tables of applications are located on the master index server.

▶ **liveCache**

The SAP liveCache cannot be distributed. If implemented in a distributed landscape, it will reside on an additional dedicated host (not on the master index server).

1.5.3 Distributed Persistence

All processes that own data create data and log volumes. Hence, if a system consists of four worker nodes, the four index server processes (and other data-owning processes) will each create a data volume and log volumes. In Table 1.1, we give an overview of all database processes and whether or not they have their own data and log volumes on the master or slave nodes of an SAP HANA system.

Process	Persistence on Master	Persistence on Slave
Index server	Yes	Yes
Name server	Yes	No
XS server	Yes	Yes (if enabled on slave)
Statistics server	Yes (if dedicated process)	N/A
Script server	Yes (if running)	Yes (if enabled)
Compile server	No	No
Preprocessor	No	No

Table 1.1 Data Persistence in SAP HANA Scale-Out Systems

In the terminology of nodes and hosts we introduced earlier, data volumes in a distributed SAP HANA system belong to a node, not to a host. This becomes evident if you consider a failover of a node from one host to another; in this case, the previous failover-host must assign all data volumes of the worker node on the failing host.

In order to facilitate host-independent data volumes, they must reside on a common file system that can be accessed from all hosts of the database system. Such a common file system may be established by using traditional filer concepts or by other means, such as file systems that stretch across local disks of multiple hosts. In SAP HANA setups, this is a choice made by the hardware vendor. We will not cover vendor-specific details in this book.

1.6 The Appliance Concept of SAP HANA

Initially, SAP HANA was only available as a so-called appliance, that is, a bundle of SAP software preinstalled on a certified piece of hardware from one of the SAP HANA certified hardware vendors. By 2014, SAP partially lifted some of the restrictions related to SAP HANA by introducing a concept called *Tailored Data Center Integration* that adds the ability to reuse certain data center components for an on-premise installation of SAP HANA. Meanwhile, SAP HANA is also available as a hosting or cloud offering from different service providers, including SAP itself.

In this section, we will briefly discuss these three installation options. We will conclude the section by diving into some details of how SAP HANA may and may not be used.

1.6.1 SAP HANA Appliance Offerings

When planning an on-premise installation of SAP HANA, the easiest way to make sure the system hardware is tailored for optimal system performance and matches SAP's requirements is to choose a system from the wide range of SAP HANA appliance offerings from certified hardware partners.

The list of all certified appliance systems based on the Intel Westmere architecture is maintained in the Product Availability Matrix (PAM) for SAP HANA, available on SAP Service Marketplace at *https://service.sap.com/sap/support/pam*. The certified systems based on the more recent Intel Ivy Bridge architecture are listed on SCN at *https://scn.sap.com/docs/DOC-52522*.

Appliance systems are usually classified by the system size in terms of installed main memory or other characteristics, such as disk space or number of CPUs, that follow directly from that choice. For the system sizes of single-host systems, there is a schema similar to T-shirt sizes in the fashion industry, as listed in Table 1.2. In this table, we denote Ivy Bridge configurations with the addendum "Ivy" in the first column. There is also now more liberty regarding the file system sizes for log and data volumes, which we indicate by listing typical minimum configurations.

Size	RAM	CPUs * Cores	Data file system	Log file system
XS	128 GB	2 * 10	1 TB	160 GB
S	256 GB	2 * 10	1 TB	320 GB
M	512 GB	4 * 10	2 TB	640 GB
L	1024 GB	8 * 10	4 TB	1280 GB
XS Ivy	128 GB	2 * 15	> 1 TB	> 128 GB
S Ivy	256 GB	2 * 15	> 1 TB	> 320 GB
M Ivy	512 GB	2 * 15	>= 1.5 TB	>= 512 GB
L Ivy	1 TB	4 * 15	>= 3 TB	>= 512 GB
XL Ivy	2 TB	8 * 15	>= 6 TB	>= 512 GB

Table 1.2 General-Purpose Configurations of SAP HANA Appliance

Amount of Disk Storage Built into SAP HANA Systems

In Table 1.2, we explicitly list file system sizes, not storage sizes, because all hardware vendors build some sort of redundancy into their storage components. The amount of installed disk space will typically be much larger than the required file system sizes, at least for the data and log areas.

When deciding on a SAP HANA system setup, several aspects have to be considered. The most important ones—scaling the right size, whether or not the system should be used for a SAP Business Suite system, and how the actual deployment will be handled—are discussed next.

Scaling SAP HANA System Sizes

As the amount of data in a database system grows, the system's hardware needs to be scaled to accommodate the added data volume (or the increased workload). In the world of SAP HANA, there are two options available: *scale up* and *scale out*.

For database sizes up to 1 TB of RAM, several hardware vendors have setups that are ready for scale up. You might start with a database size of, say, 256 GB of RAM and if needed increase the database size to 512 GB or 1 TB of RAM by adding more CPUs, disk space, and RAM to the existing hardware server.

Scale-out systems are typically configurations of multiple M- or L-sized hosts, but some vendors also offer configurations based on S-sized hosts. Be warned, though, that with most hardware vendors a scale-out system does not use the same hardware components as a single-host system, especially when it comes to "external" factors, such as the chassis and so on. As an example, for a given vendor a single-host system might be delivered as a rack-mounted server, whereas the same vendor's scale-out systems are based on blade server technology.

In most cases, the transition from a single-host system (database sizes of up to 1 TB of RAM) to a scale-out system requires an exchange of hardware in the system being scaled. In most likely all cases, hardware components such as additional network devices, additional disks, or other storage system components will need to be added.

Specific details on the scalability options are available from the individual hardware vendors.

SAP HANA for SAP Business Suite Systems

The system configurations from Table 1.2 are available for all types of SAP HANA installations. For SAP Business Suite systems only, with their typical OLTP workload and comparatively large amounts of data that is not accessed frequently, special configurations are available with a higher ratio of RAM to CPU power, as listed in Table 1.3. These configurations are not supported for installations other than SAP Business Suite.

RAM	CPUs * Cores	Data file system	Log file system
1 TB	4 * 10	4 TB	1 TB
2 TB	8 * 10	8 TB	2 TB
4 TB	8 * 10	16 TB	4 TB

Table 1.3 SAP HANA Appliance Configurations for Business Suite Systems

Deployment Process of SAP HANA Appliance Systems

Next to the preselection and certification of hardware components, the appliance concept comes with further simplifications related to the deployment of an SAP HANA system. The initial installation of the operating system, file system layout, and SAP HANA software will be performed by the hardware vendor so that customer teams do not need to have dedicated installation knowledge for SAP HANA systems.

There is also an integrated support concept, in which SAP customer incidents serve as a single point of entry for all issues related to the SAP HANA system. SAP Support will distribute these incidents to the support teams of the hardware or OS vendor if necessary.

1.6.2   Tailored Data Center Integration

Especially for larger customers with standardized hardware landscapes and tiered IT operations, the appliance concept for SAP HANA servers will often not fit well into the existing structure of the data center. To address this situation, SAP started opening up the appliance concept in 2013 with Tailored Data Center Integration.

In this concept, the supported hardware systems are still restricted to those certified systems listed in the Product Availability Matrix for SAP HANA. Customers can, however, buy these servers without disks (this refers to storage for data and logs) and use their existing enterprise storage systems instead. For this purpose, the integration of custom storage adapter technologies, such as fiber channel adapters for SAN boot, is permitted.

> **Note**
>
> Not all storage systems are supported in SAP HANA Tailored Data Center Integration. Supported storage systems will be made available online in SAP's Partner Information Center at *https://global.sap.com/partners/directories/SearchSolution.epx*.
>
> Currently (July 2014), the list of certified storage solutions is available on SCN. "SAP Certified Enterprise Storage Hardware for SAP HANA" can be found at *https://scn.sap.com/docs/DOC-48516*.

Further steps are already planned for Tailored Data Center Integration, such as opening of the network layer to use the existing enterprise network.

With Tailored Data Center Integration, responsibility is shifted from the hardware vendor to the project team in multiple areas. One area is the hardware setup—in particular, the integration of the existing enterprise components into the SAP HANA server. SAP provides a tool for measuring throughput and latency between the SAP

HANA server and enterprise storage system as part of the SAP HANA software, starting with SPS 7. Documentation of this tool is available in SAP Note 1943937.

The second area of shifted responsibility is software installation. With Tailored Data Center Integration, hardware vendors are no longer responsible for installing the SAP HANA software. Instead, this is (generally speaking) the responsibility of the project team. SAP only supports SAP HANA installations that have been performed by persons who have successfully achieved the "SAP Certified Technology Specialist [Edition 2013] – SAP HANA Installation" (E_HANAINS131) certification.

1.6.3 Hosting and Cloud Offerings

In addition to on-premise installations, SAP HANA is also available through hosting and cloud offerings. For classical hosting, many service providers offer SAP HANA as part of their hosting portfolio; contact your favorite service providers for details.

For cloud offerings, there are presently three categories available:

▸ **Cloud on SAP HANA**
  Cloud on SAP HANA refers to applications hosted by SAP on SAP HANA hardware, such as SAP Sales and Operations Planning (S&OP).

▸ **Cloud platform services**
  Developers or partners who want to develop applications on SAP HANA that can be hosted on cloud infrastructure should look into the *SAP HANA Cloud Platform*. This offering allows development and operation of applications on SAP HANA hosted in SAP's data centers. The development toolset includes SAP HANA's native development capabilities as well as a full, Java-based development environment.

  For simpler use cases, there is also the *SAP HANA One* offering, which is a SAP HANA system hosted on Amazon Web Services. It is mostly intended for test cases and prototypes but also supported for production usage.

▸ **Cloud infrastructure services**
  Similar to hosting, SAP HANA cloud infrastructure services allow running SAP HANA systems (and other components of the SAP landscape) in a "foreign" data center. One such offering is *SAP HANA Enterprise Cloud* (HEC); an alternative offering is the *SAP HANA Infrastructure Subscription*, presently offered by SAP and by Amazon Web Services.

1.6.4 Generic Deployment Considerations

Regardless of how SAP HANA is installed—on premise or hosted, appliance or tailored—there are certain generic restrictions and guidelines regarding the usage of the SAP HANA system, especially on production instances. We will now touch on several of these properties.

Multiple SAP HANA Instances on One Hardware System

If an SAP HANA instance is used in the production tier of a system landscape, there is only one SAP HANA instance allowed on the physical SAP HANA system. That is, you must not install multiple SAP HANA instances on the same single-host or scale-out server in production usage.

In nonproduction tiers of the system landscape, such as development, test, quality assurance, or sandbox systems, multiple SAP HANA instances may be installed on the same physical server. See Chapter 3 for details, and refer to SAP's statement in SAP Note 1681092.

Multiple Applications on One SAP HANA Instance

If you want to run multiple applications which use (i.e., store data and perform queries in) the same instance of SAP HANA, the situation is less restrictive but more complicated. SAP supports concurrent applications on the same SAP HANA instance in many cases, but there is a body of rules surrounding this topic.

The rule set is maintained in several SAP Notes, starting with SAP Note 1661202. This note lists all applications that may be set up with the same SAP HANA instance as the primary database. Because the content of this white list is changing with time, we will not reproduce it here. The range of applications includes SAP BW on SAP HANA, custom data marts, accelerators, and many more.

For the particular case of planning an SAP BW on SAP HANA system, more detailed considerations are listed in SAP Note 1666670. The most important of these may be that SAP does not support running multiple instances of SAP BW on the same *production* instance of SAP HANA. For the nonproduction tiers of the system landscapes, multiple SAP BW systems may be using the same physical SAP HANA system, but each SAP BW instance will need its dedicated SAP HANA instance.

Finally, for the SAP Business Suite, there is a dedicated white list maintained in SAP Note 1826100, which lists those applications that may be installed on the same database instance and server (in production) as an SAP Business Suite component, with specific considerations for individual components of SAP Business Suite.

In the scope of this book, more important than the application white lists themselves are the administration considerations that should in many cases discourage you from running multiple applications on the same database—at least if one of these applications is critical in some sense (security, business processes, etc.). We briefly mention the most prominent of these considerations here without going into detail yet; that's what the rest of the book is for:

▶ **Lifecycle management**
You can only patch the entire database software at once, not "the portion of the database used by application <x>." The same is true for database backup and recovery.

▶ **Resource and workload management**
The resource and workload management features of SAP HANA currently (as of SPS 8) are limited in scope but constantly improving. Today, depending on the criticality of the applications it may not be recommended to operate multiple applications on the same database system.

▶ **Security**
Although you can restrict developers to work only in a certain area of the database system, this is not entirely possible for database administrators and, in many scenarios, also not for application support staff.

SAP HANA and SAP NetWeaver Application Servers

Starting with SAP NetWeaver 7.40 and SAP HANA SPS 7, operating instances of SAP NetWeaver Application Server on the same hardware as instances of the SAP HANA database is supported. See SAP Note 1953429 and *www.saphana.com/docs/ DOC-4391* ("Overview—SAP HANA and SAP NetWeaver AS ABAP on One Server") for details.

Support of Scale Out for Specific Scenarios

Although scale out is a generic, publically available feature of SAP HANA, managing data appropriately in a distributed landscape and for performance-critical application is far from a trivial operation.

Although SAP BW on SAP HANA actively manages data distribution in distributed SAP HANA instances, such application support is not possible in all circumstances, especially not in custom data marts. SAP recommends that customers planning to use SAP HANA scale out for scenarios other than SAP BW contact SAP HANA product management for best practices and expert advice.

> **Note**
>
> Scale-out support for SAP Business Suite systems is in a pilot phase as of July 2014.

Virtualization

On-premise operation of SAP HANA on virtualized servers is for production (since SPS 8) as well as nonproduction (since SPS 6) use, as described in SAP Note 1995460 and *www.saphana.com/docs/DOC-3334* ("SAP HANA Virtualized—Overview"). Several restrictions apply for the deployment of SAP HANA on virtualized hardware. We list the most relevant ones here:

- The only hypervisor supported for production usage is VMware vSphere 5.5. vSphere 5.1 is supported only for nonproduction use.
- Virtual machines must be hosted on certified SAP HANA hardware, and only single-host systems are supported as hardware platforms.
- The initial VM installation (including SAP HANA instance in the VM) must be performed by the hardware vendor team or a certified person.
- Memory overcommittment is not supported.

1.7   Release Cycles of SAP HANA Database Software

SAP HANA software is released in two categories of software bundles: Support Package Stacks and revisions. Support Package Stacks are major releases of SAP HANA in which new functionality and significant changes can be introduced, including, in rare cases, even incompatible changes. Revisions are patches to the software for the purpose of minor improvements and bug fixes.

1.7.1   Support Package Stacks

An *SAP HANA Support Package Stack* (SPS) is a bundle of the core database software (SAP HANA database, client [driver] package, SAP HANA Studio, etc.) with additional components that are part of (at least certain) SAP HANA license bundles, such as the real-time data replication technology SAP Landscape Transformation Replication Server (SLT).

Support package stacks presently have a loosely defined release cycle: SAP intends to release (and has released since the beginning of SAP HANA) a new support package stack every six months, in May and in November of each year. We write "loosely defined," because there are no fixed and committed release dates for future support package stacks, and it may happen that the release of a support package stack is delayed by a few weeks.

SAP intends to end the lifecycle of a support package stack a few months after the release of the successive SPS; customers operating an older SPS level will have to upgrade to the latest SPS after the end of the lifecycle for their SPS.

1.7.2   Revisions

An SAP HANA *revision* (also called an *SAP HANA Support Package* or SP) contains the core database software, including the database clients and SAP HANA Studio, as well as certain add-on components, such as the Application Function Libraries (AFL). Revisions do not follow a fixed release cycle; instead, they are released when needed. If there are very important bug fixes, there might be two revisions within two weeks, and there may be a month or more without a new revision.

In order to support better planning of SAP HANA patching, SAP introduced two special types of revisions, as described in SAP Note 2021789.

SAP HANA Datacenter Service Points

SAP HANA Datacenter Service Point revisions are only released after testing in SAP's own production systems. Next to the regular scenario and regression testing performed for all revisions, they have undergone real-life testing in production systems with significant workloads, including SAP BW and SAP Business Suite components. SAP plans to release one such revision for each Support Package Stack of SAP HANA approximately three months after the release of the SPS.

SAP HANA Maintenance Revisions

SAP HANA Maintenance Revisions contain major bug fixes and—as opposed to reg-ular revisions—may be made available on the code base of an older SPS (e.g., for the code base of SPS 7 after the release of SPS 8). Sometimes, there are restrictions for updating from a maintenance revision to certain higher revisions; these restrictions are maintained in SAP Note 1948334.

SAP intends to end provisioning of new maintenance revisions for a given SPS with the release of the SAP HANA Datacenter Service Point revision of the succes-sor SPS.

1.8 Summary

You should leave this chapter with a good understanding of the major building blocks of SAP HANA systems in the hardware world as well as in terms of pro-cesses running on the operating system of your SAP HANA server.

If you remember that the database server is a typical server and that the three main processes in the database are the index server (the database itself) and the XS server (development platform/application server) as the system's work horses and the name server (owner of the system topology) as the bookkeeper of the system's overall structure, then you have understood the big picture.

You should now also have a basic understanding of the properties of distributed SAP HANA instances and of the different options of deploying SAP HANA, includ-ing the concepts of SAP HANA appliances and Tailored Data Center Integration.

We hope that we have accomplished the goal of this chapter: to make you feel that SAP HANA systems are not that complicated to understand after all. Continue reading, and we will thoroughly destroy this impression by showing you thou-sands of fascinating details that administrators can and should know about our favorite SAP technology platform.

There are multiple fundamentally different ways of making use of SAP HANA systems. In this chapter, we give some hints about where you will have to invest time and skills for your planned or running SAP HANA implementations.

2   SAP HANA Scenarios: Administration Considerations

The nature of SAP HANA projects today can vary wildly. There are typical SAP BW installations that use SAP HANA as a database instead of other relational database management systems (RDBMS); there are installations that use SAP HANA as a data mart platform, with BI tools from SAP or other vendors as a reporting layer; there are installations that offer a custom-built web application in the XS server on top of a data mart in SAP HANA's database; there are installations that use SAP HANA as an accelerator for existing classical SAP Business Suite systems; and by now there are also customers who operate their SAP Business Suite systems with SAP HANA as the primary database.

These different usage scenarios have different levels of complexity with regard to the processes happening in the database, and thus they also have different requirements for aspects of system administration.

In this chapter, we sort these use cases into two major groups: one in which an application server (more specifically, an SAP NetWeaver Application Server) is involved and SAP HANA merely plays the role of a relational database system; and a second group, in which SAP HANA is used as a development platform and potentially even as an application server. We will discuss on a high level what areas of administration are very relevant in these groups and what ones play a minor role.

Finally, we will do our best to convince you that reality is in fact more complicated, because you will very likely not have such a nicely defined scenario. The real world does not bother with our rules of categorization.

2.1   SAP HANA as a Database in Application Servers

When we talk about application servers in this book, we have mostly SAP NetWeaver Application Servers in mind. Its application server capabilities notwithstanding, we will not consider the SAP BusinessObjects BI server as a contender for the application server category for the simple reason that in scenarios with an SAP BusinessObjects BI server on top of SAP HANA there is significantly more direct development and administration required in the database than in a pure, SAP NetWeaver-based system.

Before considering individual setups, including SAP NetWeaver Application Servers operating in conjunction with SAP HANA, let's talk a little bit about SAP NetWeaver itself.

> **Further Resources**
>
> For a more detailed discussion of the SAP NetWeaver Application Server, we recommend reading the SAP Help documentation, which can be found at *https://help.sap.com/nw_platform* • APPLICATION HELP • FUNCTION-ORIENTED VIEW • APPLICATION SERVER.

SAP NetWeaver is a technology platform that includes the SAP NetWeaver Application Server and further core components, such as SAP Enterprise Portal, SAP Business Warehouse, and more. The SAP NetWeaver Application Server is the runtime for SAP applications that exists in an ABAP and a Java variant. SAP NetWeaver systems operate on top of databases and thus provide a three-tier architecture (client, application, and database server). Although this architecture might introduce performance challenges compared to direct connectivity between clients and the database, the application server offers a wide range of features that assist with the operation of business applications.

An important aspect of the interaction between SAP NetWeaver Application Servers and databases is that the application server has its own end-user accounts, but any communication with the database happens via one central technical connection user in the database. This allows for a strict separation between application users and database users; at the same time, user management in the database does not play a big role.

There are three ways in which SAP HANA can be used as a database for an SAP NetWeaver Application Server: as an accelerator, as a database for SAP BW, and as a database for SAP Business Suite. We'll discuss each of these scenarios in this section.

2.1.1 SAP HANA Accelerators for SAP Applications

The first and simplest systems with SAP NetWeaver-based applications directly involving SAP HANA were the so-called accelerators for SAP Business Suite applications. These accelerators all have in common that an application adds SAP HANA as a redundant persistent store for its data and uses this persistence to speed up selected operations (typically read access for reporting purposes but also for other processes), as depicted in Figure 2.1.

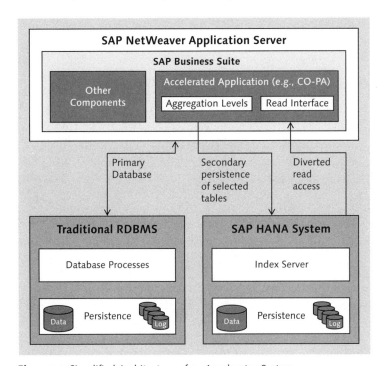

Figure 2.1 Simplified Architecture of an Accelerator System

All accelerated applications have in common that the application itself has been modified only minimally and that for the end user there are no differences between the accelerated and nonaccelerated versions, except for greatly improved performance of the accelerated aspects.

On SAP HANA, an accelerator requires only minimal administration efforts and skills. Topics such as user management do not play a role, because all application access uses the SAP NetWeaver connection user. SAP HANA-side development also does not play a role in these applications.

Backup and recovery can usually be ignored, because the data in SAP HANA is just a redundant copy that can simply be reloaded if required. If backup and restore are used, one faces the usual complications of point-in-time recovery of a secondary system, the data content of which needs to be synchronized with the primary system at all times.

SAP HANA administrators for accelerator systems will thus mostly need a generic understanding of the database and knowledge of the update process and of transaction and session management and similar topics that may play a role for monitoring and troubleshooting.

2.1.2   SAP HANA as the Primary Database for SAP BW Systems

In an SAP BW System, SAP HANA can simply be used as the primary database. You can have more complex scenarios, but the vanilla SAP BW on SAP HANA uses SAP HANA as a replacement for traditional RDBMS, supported by modifications under the surface of the SAP BW system to optimize the interaction between SAP BW and the database for SAP HANA.

The simplified architecture shown in Figure 2.2 will not surprise any reader; it is an SAP NetWeaver stack running SAP BW and using SAP HANA as the primary database. Certain functionalities are partially pushed down from the application server layer into the database layer, for example, in query processing (selected features of the SAP BW OLAP processor).

For database administrators, this setup does not bring significant new responsibilities compared to operating an SAP BW system on traditional database systems; they only need to transfer their skills to the new database system.

Of the special aspects of SAP HANA, some play a particularly big role in SAP BW systems. One such aspect is table management—including table partitioning and behavior during data loading. Administrators will benefit from a solid understanding of this topic; we encourage reading Chapter 9 with particular dedication.

Figure 2.2 includes hints of several technologies that have been newly introduced with and that are only available in SAP BW 7.4 on top of SAP HANA (SPS 5 or higher).

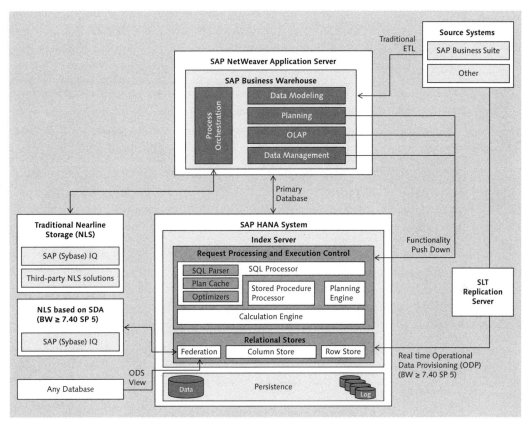

Figure 2.2 Architecture of SAP BW on SAP HANA

The first one is a new functionality for nearline storage. In SAP BW, nearline storage (NLS) is a data storage method orchestrated by the NLS interface of the SAP BW system that transfers data into the dedicated nearline storage system through the application server layer. As opposed to classical archiving, data in the NLS system remains available for reporting if explicitly demanded, typically with a performance penalty compared to online storage in the primary database. With SAP HANA's data federation mechanism *Smart Data Access* (SDA), an NLS integration based on direct transfer between the primary database (SAP HANA) and the NLS system (SAP [Sybase] IQ) has become possible, starting with SAP NetWeaver 7.40 SP 5.

There are two more recent developments in SAP BW that make use of the Smart Data Access feature; a composite provider and the new ODS view allow modeling of data in SAP BW (with or without local persistence in the SAP HANA database) based on remote data sources exposed through Smart Data Access. Both features are available with SAP NetWeaver 7.40 SP 5.

Although we will not dive into the details of these SAP BW capabilities, we want to make administrators aware that the data federation topic can play a role in SAP BW implementations based on SAP HANA.

Another new and SAP HANA-specific functionality of SAP BW on SAP HANA (NetWeaver 7.40 SP 5 or higher) is the ability to create data sources based on the real-time replication technology of SAP Landscape Transformation Replication Server (SLT). This approach enables simplified data flows by bypassing the usual data-acquisition layer (PSA) of the SAP BW system and extends the real-time data-acquisition capabilities of SAP BW.

The previously mentioned extensions in the SAP BW system can have a huge impact on the SAP BW architecture in a given implementation, both in terms of interfaces as well as data warehouse architecture. They do not, however, influence the database administration in a fundamental way.

This will change when you start using the native development capabilities of the SAP HANA system through the SAP BW layer. We will discuss the impact of such setups in Section 2.3.

2.1.3 SAP HANA as the Primary Database for SAP Business Suite

SAP Business Suite is the most complex SAP standard application you can operate on SAP HANA, both in terms of the intrinsic complexity of the application and the way it makes use of SAP HANA. Although SAP Business Suite on traditional RDBMS uses the database purely as a data store and handles all application logic in the application server layer, SAP Business Suite on SAP HANA (Figure 2.3) includes native SAP HANA content, such as stored procedures or virtual data models that are used in data-intensive processes of the SAP Business Suite applications. This also means that in order to operate an SAP Business Suite system you need skills not only in database administration and SAP NetWeaver administration but also in managing the SAP HANA repository (see Chapter 11).

Because this mixing of classical SAP NetWeaver techniques and native SAP HANA development techniques increases the overall system complexity, the SAP Business Suite development team intends to decrease the dependency of the SAP Business Suite on native SAP HANA content.

End users do not access these content objects directly but only through the SAP Business Suite applications; there are therefore no end-user accounts needed directly in the database.

> **Note**
>
> SAP Business Suite applications do not make use of SAP HANA Live—the native SAP HANA content offered by SAP for a wide range of SAP Business Suite applications. SAP HANA Live is, from an administrator's perspective, another type of data mart (see Section 2.2.1).

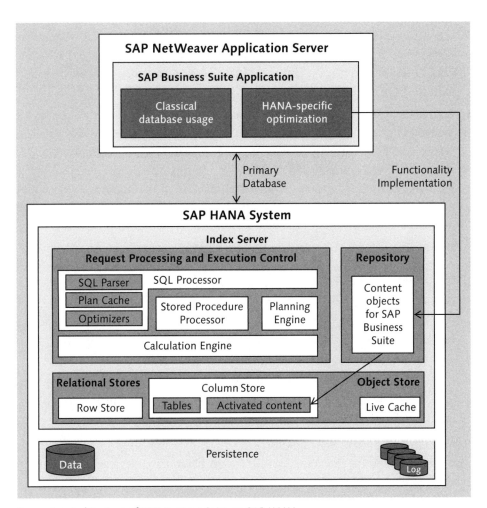

Figure 2.3 Architecture of SAP Business Suite on SAP HANA

2.2   SAP HANA as a Development Platform

The SAP HANA system can of course also be used outside of SAP NetWeaver-based landscapes. You may implement new applications simply by using SAP HANA as a database through its JDBC/ODBC interface; you might make use of the built-in data mart features; or you might employ the integrated development platform and lightweight application server functionalities of SAP HANA XS.

All of these use cases have generic properties in common that influence the requirements for system administration and security:

▶ **Development in the database layer**
The most obvious consequence of developing in the database (as opposed to developing in the application server layer) is that there will be database users with developer privileges. This means that user management will play a role at least in those landscape tiers that have active developers.

At the same time, application support and administration knowledge of the development system will become more important. This involves topics such as application lifecycle management, transports, or change management, and it also touches on topics such as repository administration or debugging in the new development environment of SAP HANA. (Note that these topics also play a role in the SAP NetWeaver Application Server; SAP HANA simply introduces new tools, different functionalities, and other terminology.)

▶ **Direct access from the end-user network to the database layer**
When the application server tier is removed from the system landscape, end users will need direct access to the database layer. In some cases, for example, when the access uses the HTTP protocol, it will be possible to install network proxies, but in many cases, there will be direct communication between the end-user device and the database server.

▶ **Named end users in the database**
In many cases, such a scenario will also require named end users in the database, which will create the need for user management, control of privileges, and so on, especially in the production tier of the system landscape.

The two most typical scenarios involving SAP HANA-side development and direct end-user access to the database are SAP HANA-based data marts and applications developed using SAP HANA's XS server.

2.2.1   Data Marts with SAP HANA (Standalone Implementation)

Data marts are arguably the most typical development scenario in SAP HANA. For the purpose of this book, a data mart is a redundant store of data in a system that is dedicated to reporting off of this data set. In many cases, you would build data marts to remove OLAP-like workload from transactional systems. In this sense, an SAP BW system also has data mart aspects—but because SAP BW is mainly a data warehouse and not primarily dedicated to the purpose of reporting, we do not consider SAP BW systems data marts.

An SAP HANA data mart typically has a number of features, which are depicted in Figure 2.4 and which we discuss next.

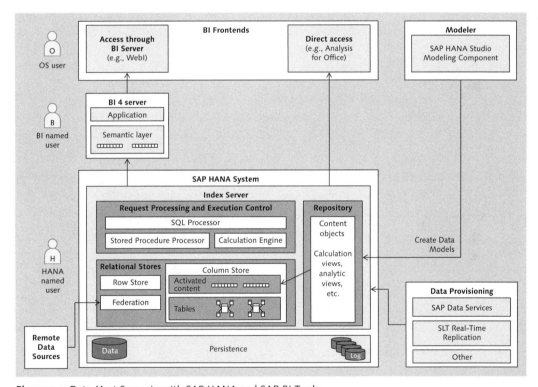

Figure 2.4 Data Mart Scenario with SAP HANA and SAP BI Tools

Data Provisioning

Somehow, you need to get your data into the SAP HANA system. The two most common tools for this task are SAP Data Services for batch-mode ETL and SAP

Landscape Transformation Replication Server (SLT). There are other technologies available, such as data federation, which is called Smart Data Access in SAP HANA and supports most of the popular database platforms as remote data sources, including Oracle Database, Teradata Database, Microsoft SQL Server, and Hadoop clusters. There are also third-party ETL tools certified to work with SAP HANA.

Data provisioning is treated at great length in multiple publications about SAP HANA, so we will not discuss it here.

Virtual Data Models

Data modeling may refer to the act of creating the physical data model in the database, sometimes also termed "database schema," that is, the designing of database tables. It may also refer to the creation of virtual data models on top of the physical table layout. We will use the term "data modeling" in this second sense.

The primary purpose of such data modeling is to ease the task of report development by implementing the semantic relationship between database tables in a central location. That is, the virtual data model represents a semantically guided abstraction from the technical database table layout. With a well-defined data model, this relationship does not need to be recreated individually in each report.

In SAP HANA, virtual data models are created with a data modeling component embedded into SAP HANA Studio. The modeling objects are three types of views (called attribute views, analytic views, and calculation views), stored procedures, and privilege objects to control row-level access to modelled views (called analytic privileges). Data modeling is covered extensively in a multitude of publications, and we will only mention this topic when it is directly related to administration jobs. Analytic privileges are an exception to this rule; we cover them in detail in Chapter 13.

Data Consumption

The data models in SAP HANA are represented to the outside world as database views. These views are in most cases consumed by business intelligence (BI) applications through the SQL interface of the database by using the SQL or MDX query languages, but they may also be accessed through SAP HANA XS with OData or XMLA. In the simplified architecture shown in Figure 2.4, we have ignored the XS-based data consumption.

Depending on the BI application used, there might be direct interaction between the client and the database server, or there might be an intermediate BI server such as the SAP BusinessObjects BI server. The existence of such an intermediate server component offers advantages such as network separation and making use of the user-management capabilities (including identity-management integration) that might be more advanced than SAP HANA's present offering. At the same time, some of these applications—for example, SAP BusinessObjects Web Intelligence or SAP BusinessObjects Dashboards—will increase the system complexity by introducing another semantic layer on top of SAP HANA.

If reporting applications directly establish a point-to-point connection to the database server, this not only opens up the database layer towards the end-user network, it also means that in virtually all cases each end-user will need a named user in the database system. As a consequence, questions of user management, authentication, and authorization in the database will play a significant role, and one should not forget that such a scenario will even introduce the need for end-user-oriented application support with skills in SAP HANA technologies.

The choice of BI tools to be placed on top of SAP HANA will thus be influenced by functional considerations, aspects of administration and security, and performance requirements. One could probably write an entire book about this particular topic, but we won't cover more details here.

User Management and Other Security Aspects

User management plays a two-fold role in data mart scenarios; in the development system, development accounts must be managed, which might require complex authorizations but typically only affects a small number of accounts so that mass maintenance of users may not be necessary.

In the production tier, we will in most cases find named database users for all end users who retrieve information from the data mart. Hence, user provisioning and management of users will play an important role, as well as the design and administration of proper authorizations. Depending on the requirements, you might also need to implement security audit processes in the database layer.

Content Lifecycle Management

One of the great advantages of virtual data models is that they allow immense flexibility in the process of building and managing data models. Changes to a virtual data model can take effect in mere seconds, because no physical data changes are required.

If you want to manage this flexibility appropriately, you will need to implement some lifecycle management; fortunately, SAP HANA offers tooling for this purpose. See Chapter 11 for more details.

If you consider these aspects, you will probably notice that with a data mart, unsurprisingly, you find yourself in a world that combines basis administration and application administration within the same system. This is no different in SAP HANA than it is on other databases offering integrated development environments.

2.2.2 Applications in SAP HANA

For our purposes, applications in SAP HANA are applications developed with tools offered by SAP HANA, such as the XS server and the modeling environment but also classical database development with stored procedures and so on. This is opposed to applications developed on top of the SAP HANA system, that is, applications that make use of SAP HANA's external SQL or HTTP interfaces to communicate with the SAP HANA system.

In terms of administration, these systems have mostly the same requirements as the data marts we discussed in the previous section; they require a combination of application administration (repository administration, content lifecycle management, end-user integration, etc.) and classical database administration.

In addition to data marts, however, there are even more security aspects to be considered, most of which are related to authentication options that can be configured on an application level. Because this book is mostly focused on database administration and not on aspects of the SAP HANA development platform, we will relegate you to the product documentation of SAP HANA, especially the database administration guide and the developer guide: *https://help.sap.com/hana/SAP_HANA_Administration_Guide_en.pdf* and *https://help.sap.com/hana/SAP_HANA_Developer_Guide_en.pdf*.

2.3 Mixed Scenarios

Until now, we have described nicely separated scenarios with one particular application using SAP HANA in a particular way. These deployments are only extremes in the multidimensional space of thinkable system architectures; reality will in most cases fall into a spot somewhere away from these fringe areas.

When talking to active or prospective customers of SAP NetWeaver-based systems on SAP HANA, most of them expect that they will start with a plain vanilla implementation of their application (i.e., with systems like those we introduced in Section 2.1) and that there will be pressure to introduce some sort of database-side development in the future. We will use SAP BW on SAP HANA as the most common example for such mixed scenarios.

The term *SAP BW mixed scenario* is often used to refer to an SAP BW implementation on SAP HANA, in which data modeling using the SAP HANA modeling component is also employed. There are two fundamentally different ways in which such data modeling can be used in the context of a SAP BW system:

▶ SAP HANA data models may be created on top of application data tables of the SAP BW system (i.e., on top of master data tables and fact tables of InfoCubes and DataStore objects [DSOs]). These models can then be consumed in the typical fashion of SAP HANA-based data marts by BI tools, bypassing the SAP BW BEx and OLAP layers for reporting.

▶ SAP HANA data models may be created on non-SAP BW tables, for example, tables provisioned with SAP Data Services or SLT. These data models can then be exposed within the SAP BW system by means of composite providers, virtual providers, transient providers, and whatever other beautiful tooling the SAP BW system offers for this purpose.

For both of these cases, one can think of a multitude of good reasons to implement them or not to implement them; they clearly can provide great value in extending an SAP BW system with more ad-hoc data modeling techniques.

We will not enter into a battle over the merits and downsides of such solutions here. It may suffice to say that we certainly do not oppose them. It is, however, our intention to make you aware that such mixed scenarios do add to the intrinsic complexity of the SAP BW–SAP HANA compound and thus will create a more interesting job for the administrators of the SAP HANA database powering the SAP BW system.

One important aspect of practically running two applications (SAP BW and the data mart) on the same database system is that in many aspects you cannot separate these applications in the database. There is, for example, no application-aware workload management, and processes such as backup/recovery or database software updates will always affect the entire system.

In Figure 2.5, we display many (though not all) of the ways in which data and objects can be used within a landscape consisting of an SAP HANA database, SAP BW on SAP HANA, and BI tools, such as the family of SAP BusinessObjects BI products.

We have already mentioned the different options for data provisioning for SAP BW in Section 2.1.2 and for data marts in Section 2.2.1 — so there is not much new in this area except for the fact that in such mixed scenarios the primary database of the SAP BW system may contain significant amounts of data not managed through the SAP BW layer.

The more interesting part is the way in which native content of the SAP HANA system and content of the SAP BW stack may function together. We can distinguish two major cases: (a) SAP HANA representations of SAP BW models and (b) consumption of SAP HANA models through the SAP BW layer. We discuss these in a bit more detail next.

2.3.1 SAP HANA Representations of SAP BW Models

Starting with SAP NetWeaver 7.40 SP 5, the SAP BW system can create representations of SAP BW data models (e.g., InfoCubes or DSOs) in the SAP HANA repository, that is, as analytic views or calculation views. Changes made to the SAP BW object will automatically be transferred also to the SAP HANA information models.

If there is an association between named users in the SAP HANA system and application users in the SAP BW system, this functionality can even include authorization management. The SAP BW system can then also generate analytic privileges and roles in SAP HANA that reproduce as far as possible the authorizations of the SAP BW application users.

The data models that have been pushed into SAP HANA can be reused and extended in information models created with the modeling component of SAP HANA Studio; they can also be directly consumed from BI tools. This is an option for customers who want to bypass the SAP BW reporting layer (SAP BW's OLAP processor and the BEx layer) but require a well-managed data warehouse.

Even though analytics is not the subject of this book, we encourage customers who consider this option to evaluate how much of the extensive OLAP functionalities of the SAP BW system they are presently using and how much of this can be easily reproduced using the tools of SAP HANA and the chosen reporting solution.

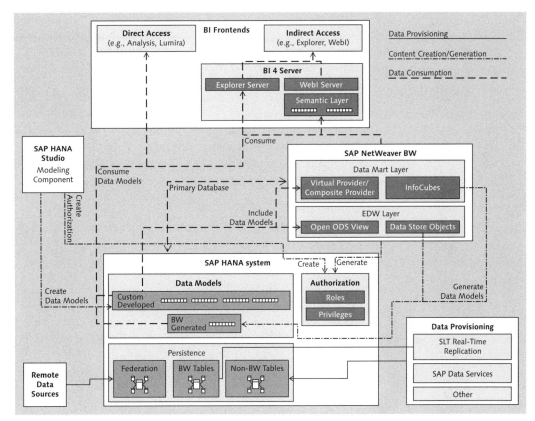

Figure 2.5 Options for Data Flow and Content Usage in SAP BW Mixed Scenarios

It must be noted also that in SAP NetWeaver 7.30 on SAP HANA it is possible to generate SAP HANA models representing InfoCubes and DSOs of the SAP BW system. In this first release of SAP BW on SAP HANA, however, this mechanism is not yet integrated in a fashion that would make it generally recommendable. Instead of having the originating SAP BW system manage the content generated in SAP HANA—including integration of lifecycle management—the 7.30 implementation relies on a pull mechanism controlled through a wizard in SAP HANA Studio. Also, generation and management of data access privileges are far more mature in the implementation created with SAP BW 7.40.

These two aspects—synchronized lifecycle management between SAP BW and SAP HANA objects and consistent reporting authorizations in both worlds—are particularly important in a system that exposes the same content for consumption with largely different reporting mechanisms.

2.3.2 Consumption of SAP HANA Models through the SAP BW Layer

The second major use case for mixing SAP HANA's native capabilities with those of the SAP BW stack is the consumption of SAP HANA information models in Info-Providers of the SAP BW system. In general, this approach is driven by the desire to provide more ad hoc capabilities, such as faster provisioning of new functionalities in reports. Because it doesn't require changes to the physical table layout, the impact of creating new SAP HANA information models or modifying existing ones is far smaller than the comparable action in classical SAP BW modeling.

In the SAP BW layer, the SAP HANA information models can be consumed in multiple types of providers, such as the virtual provider, the composite provider, or the new open ODS view of SAP BW 7.40 (SP 5 or higher).

In this scenario, the lifecycle of SAP HANA information models and the related SAP BW objects must be controlled across the interface between the two systems, and here the integration is not as good as it is in the case described previously.

If SAP HANA information models are only consumed through the SAP BW layer, tasks such as user management or the creation of reporting authorizations can be delegated to the SAP BW layer. If the same models can also be consumed directly through BI tools, one again faces the challenge of synchronizing end-user accounts and privileges in both sides of the setup.

An SAP BW mixed scenario introduces one major new aspect that did not play a role in classical SAP BW implementations: Application administration now extends from the SAP BW layer into the database layer.

This has consequences for database administration, for example, due to the fact that the database administrators are no longer the only persons with named users in the database. Also, resources are now consumed by two entirely different mechanisms, and appropriate monitoring must be set up to account for the needs of both worlds.

It also makes it necessary to determine the limits of influence of database support personnel and application support personnel. A good collaboration between the teams of database administrators and application administrators will make life much easier for everyone.

2.4   Summary

The intention of this chapter was to give the reader a feeling for the skill sets that database administrators will need in their SAP HANA scenario. We have explained that there is one most important deciding factor: Is the database operated as persistence for SAP NetWeaver-based applications or not?

In SAP NetWeaver systems, the SAP HANA administrators will need to master the SAP HANA flavor of classical database administration while user management, other security aspects, or the operation of SAP HANA's development platform will only play a minor role.

In scenarios in which SAP HANA is used as a development system and which allow direct end-user aspects into the database, these concepts will often play a dominant role in the administration parts of system setup.

In reality, very often a mixture of those two use cases will be implemented. An SAP HANA administrator should therefore be prepared to dive also into those areas of the database system that might be considered less important in the original project plan.

Although installing and updating an SAP HANA database is a task that you will not normally do every day, there are still multiple tools and mechanisms for this purpose.

3 Installation and Updates

Even though for most customers the SAP HANA software will come preinstalled with the hardware, we recommend that all administrators understand how to install SAP HANA instances. Once an instance is installed, updates are inevitable—so we discuss both topics in this chapter.

We will first tell you about necessary preparations for installing SAP HANA, outline the tools that SAP offers for installing and updating the SAP HANA database, and tell you why it is easy to choose the most appropriate of these tools. We will then guide you through the standard processes of installing and updating the database, including step-by-step instructions and including installing and patching from the command line or in batch mode. We will also offer some advice about installing and updating scale-out systems and troubleshooting an install.

We will not cover any post-installation steps in this chapter—even if they are mandatory, such as installing a license key. These actions will be mentioned individually in the following chapters of this book, and an overview of all necessary and recommended postinstallation steps is given in Chapter 14.

3.1 Preparing for Installation and Updates

Installing SAP HANA systems has prerequisites on multiple levels, including the expected skill set, server hardware, operating system setup, and file system setup.

3.1.1 Skill Set

In the first years of SAP HANA, only trained personnel of SAP HANA hardware partners were permitted to install the initial instance of the database software on an SAP HANA server. SAP now has partially lifted this restriction and supports SAP HANA installations if the system has been installed by a certified person. The installation certification exam *SAP Certified Technology Specialist (Edition 2013) — SAP HANA Installation*, booking code E_HANAINS131, is required for database installations through customer and partner teams.

> **Note**
>
> When performing the initial installation of the SAP HANA database software, the installing party also assumes responsibility for the correct installation and configuration of the operating system and related components (e.g., the file system layout).

3.1.2 Server Hardware

The SAP HANA database may only be installed on validated or certified hardware systems. The list of available server systems is maintained in the Product Availability Matrix (PAM) for SAP HANA (search for "HANA" on *https://service.sap.com/sap/support/pam*) and for the most recently available server system on SAP Community Network (SCN) (*https://scn.sap.com/docs/DOC-52522*).

As stated in Chapter 1, an SAP HANA system based on the Tailored Data Center Integration concept also requires use of certified or validated appliance hardware, with exceptions for storage or network components.

3.1.3 Operating System

Prior to SPS 8 of SAP HANA, the only supported OS for SAP HANA systems was SUSE Linux Enterprise Server 11 (SLES 11) or SUSE Linux Enterprise Server for SAP Applications 11 (SLES for SAP 11); SLES is thus the focus of this section. We will not deal with the actual installation and configuration of the operating system in this book, but we do intend to point you toward all important resources that will help you. SAP summarizes many OS-related recommendations in SAP Note 1944799. We provide a more extensive view here.

> **Red Hat Enterprise Linux 6.5**
>
> With SPS 8, support was added for Red Hat Enterprise Linux 6.5. You can find all information regarded to the installation on Red Hat Enterprise Linux 6.5 in SAP Note 2009879.

Note

Please refer to the PAM or contact your chosen hardware partner to find out whether your particular SAP HANA server system has been validated for SLES 11, SLES for SAP 11, Red Hat Enterprise Linux 6.5, or all of them. Most server systems are validated for Service Pack (SP) 2 and SP 3 of their respective SLES flavor, but maintenance for SLES 11 SP 1 ended in late 2013.

Software Packages to Install

SUSE Linux Enterprise Server comes with multiple preselections of installable software packages, named *patterns*. For SAP HANA servers, the minimal pattern is sufficient. In regular SLES 11, this pattern is named "Server Base System," and in SLES for SAP 11 it is named "SAP Application Server Base." In addition to the package selection from these base packages, SAP HANA requires a small list of additional packages. As of July 2014, you need the packages listed in Table 3.1 (for the most recent list, refer to the SAP HANA server installation guide at *https://help.sap.com/hana_platform/*).

Package	Comment
gtk2	Use version that comes with the operating system. Required for some OS-level tools shipped with SAP HANA.
java-1_6_0-ibm	Use version that comes with the operating system. Required for SAP HANA Studio installed on the server.
libicu	Use version provided with the operating system. Provides Unicode libraries.
mozilla-xulrunner192-1.9.2.xx-x.x.x	Use version provided with the operating system, but at least the given minimum version. Required by the XS engine.
ntp	Recommended for automatic synchronization of server clock.
sudo	Run programs with the privileges of another user: part of typical Unix administration concepts.
syslog-ng	Use version provided with the operating system. Used for security audit logging.
tcsh	Some SAP HANA-related scripts assume the existence of the tcsh OS shell.

Table 3.1 Required Additional Software Packages on the Server OS

Package	Comment
libssh2-1	For encrypting network connections.
autoyast2-installation	Makes it possible to install SLES automatically in parallel on multiple servers of identical hardware configuration.
yast2-ncurses	Text-mode version of the SUSE OS setup tool yast2.
unrar	Tool required to extract the SAP HANA installation medium download.

Table 3.1 Required Additional Software Packages on the Server OS (Cont.)

In the course of SAP HANA-related support incidents, SAP Support may need additional software packages. The most commonly required packages are maintained by SAP in SAP Note 1855805. We provide the current (July 2014) package list in Table 3.2 for your convenience.

Package	Comment
bing	Point-to-point bandwidth measurement tool
bonnie	File system benchmark
cairo	Vector graphics library
findutils-locate	Tool for locating files
graphviz	Graph visualization tools
iptraf	TCP/IP network monitor
krb5-32bit	MIT Kerberos5 Implementation: libraries
krb5-client	MIT Kerberos5 Implementation: client programs
sensors	Hardware health monitoring for Linux
sapcrypto	Required for SSL encryption of network connections
SAPCAR	Tool for extracting SAP archives: also included with the database installation media

Table 3.2 Additional OS Packages Recommended for Supportability

Operating System Configuration

SAP recommends several changes to the operating system configuration, of which we summarize the most important ones here. Note that these changes typically require root access and that in scale-out systems they must be applied on all hosts. Some changes even require a reboot of the operating system.

- **General OS configuration guidelines**

  SAP publishes optimal configuration settings for the different Service Pack levels of SLES. These settings are listed in SAP Note 1944799—SAP HANA Guidelines for Operating System Installation. In particular, see SAP Note 1824819 and SAP Note 1954788 for SLES 11 SP2 and SP3, respectively.

  In addition, SAP advises against certain changes to the OS configuration and keeps a blacklist of known potentially harmful modifications in SAP Note 1731000.

  For assisting the support staff with analysis of an SAP HANA system, SAP recommends keeping track of all changes made to the default OS configuration; see also SAP Note 1730999.

- **Swap space**

  As opposed to the generic SAP recommendation regarding swap space (SAP Note 1597355), it is not useful, let alone necessary, to set up swap space in the amount of twice the installed main memory. Instead, the configured swap space should at most be 50 GB (in scale-out systems this is the maximum per host). In fact, we see no reason to configure more than 20 GB of swap space on an SAP HANA host (which is consistent with SAP's recommendation in SAP Note 1310037, which contains installation notes for SLES 11 in the general context of SAP applications).

- **Disable CPU power save mode**

  The CPUs in SAP HANA servers should always be configured for maximum performance. If the CPUs are configured in a power save mode (such as "on demand"), then the CPU governor might not handle CPU frequency adaptions efficiently, leading to high system CPU times. See SAP Note 1890444 for more details.

- **Additional non-SAP and non-SUSE software**

  The SAP HANA database software is designed to make use of all hardware resources of the database server as efficiently as possible. It is therefore not recommended to operate other software on the database server unless required for data center operation. In SAP Note 1730928 and further notes therein, SAP explains what third-party software may be used on the database server. If a particular version of such third-party software is known to cause issues with the SAP HANA database, the software components or versions will be listed in SAP Note 1730996.

- **Recommended file system for storage components**

  Unless your hardware partner explicitly makes a different choice, SAP recommends the XFS file system for all storage components of the database (data, log, and software installation); see SAP Note 1944799.

► **Scale-out systems: connectivity choices**
When setting up scale-out systems, the handling of host names as well as the separation of the external network from the network for internal (inter-node) communication may be challenging. Refer to SAP Note 1743225 for advice.

► **Support connections**
It is advisable to prepare system access for SAP Support by means of SAP support connections as early as possible. Before the actual SAP HANA software is installed, the most useful connections will be those that enable remote access to the operating system of the SAP HANA server. Multiple such connections are available, as listed in SAP Note 1635304, such as the WTS connection (provided it is possible to connect from the WTS server to the SAP HANA server) or an SSH connection. These connections require setup on the SAP HANA server and on the SAProuter.

► **Time zone settings**
The time zone setting of the operating system also determines the time zone setting of the SAP HANA database. This affects, for example, time-related entries in database system tables or the time stamps of entries in the database's log files.

3.1.4   File System Setup

Once the server hardware is in place and the operating system is set up correctly, there is only one important step to do before you can start the actual system installation, and this is setting up the necessary file systems and the recommended directory structure.

Please always refer to SAP's documentation for the latest recommendation regarding the file system layout. You can find this in the *SAP HANA Server Installation and Update Guide*, which is available at *https://help.sap.com/hana_platform/*. The file system layout proposed by SAP has been stable through the last several support package stacks. We give you here SAP's recommendations and a few annotations.

The SAP HANA software itself needs file system space by and large for four categories of file system objects (and each of these categories should have its own dedicated file system):

► **Installation path /hana/shared**
This is the target directory for the software installation. The binaries of the database and typically other components, such as SAP HANA Studio and client,

will be placed here. In a scale-out cluster, this directory must be accessible to all hosts in the cluster.

When installing an SAP HANA database system with a given SID, a new directory, */hana/shared/<SID>*, will be installed, and all installed software components of that instance will reside there. This enables multiple database instances with different software versions to be installed on the same host.

Note also that trace files written by the database system will end up in this directory.

SAP's requirement is that the size of this file system matches the amount of physical RAM installed in the database host; in a scale-out system, this must be identical to the sum of the RAM of all worker hosts.

▶ **System instance directory /usr/sap**
This is the standard path to the local instance of any SAP system. It contains the `saphostcontrol` installation and a directory, */usr/sap/<SID>*, for each installed SAP system instance. In the case of SAP HANA, most of the content of */usr/sap/<SID>* is linked symbolically from */hana/shared/<SID>*.

This file system should be at least 50 GB in size. If multiple SAP HANA instances are installed on one host, you should increase the file system size accordingly.

This file system is specific to the physical host, including in scale-out clusters (i.e., it is not a shared file system in a cluster installation).

▶ **Database data volumes /hana/data**
There must be a dedicated file system used to store the data volumes of the SAP HANA database. This file system must have a size equal to three times the installed main memory of the database host (in scale-out clusters, the total data storage must equal three times the sum of the amount of main memory installed on all worker nodes of the system).

In scale-out systems, the data volumes must be available to all hosts in the scale-out cluster. The most common option is to use some type of shared storage or shared file system. Another option is block storage with the SAP HANA storage connector API (SAP Note 1900823). The actual technology will depend on the choice of hardware vendor.

SAP HANA also offers a process to capture a consistent image of the database in a file system–based snapshot. If the storage system supports efficient means of creating snapshots, this mechanism can be the fastest way of creating or restoring a full data backup. If you plan to make use of snapshots, you should include the necessary requirements when choosing the storage system hardware.

▶ **Database log volumes /hana/log**
For the log volumes of the SAP HANA database, a dedicated file system is required as well. In single-node instances, this file system will in most cases reside on a solid state disk, whereas it is usually (but not always) located on regular storage technology in scale-out clusters.

The size of the log area must equal the amount of main memory installed in the database host (in scale-out clusters, the sum of the amount of main memory installed on all worker nodes). For the new Ivy Bridge generation of SAP HANA servers, different log file system sizes have been introduced; see "SAP Certified Appliance Hardware for SAP HANA" at *https://scn.sap.com/docs/DOC-52522*.

In scale-out clusters, the log area must be available to all hosts in the cluster. The available options are the same as for the data volumes.

In addition to these mandatory file systems for the database software itself, the following file systems should not be overlooked. Some of them will be installed in a standard installation; others are optional but should be included in your system planning:

▶ **Operating system installation (root file system)**
The root file system, containing the installation of the Linux operating system itself, should be at least 10 GB in size and must use a file system type supported by the hardware partner and SAP, such as ext3. If you plan to install additional software components—for example, monitoring software—then make sure that either the root file system or dedicated additional file systems have sufficient disk space. SAP has no further strict requirements regarding the OS file system, allowing customers to set up the Linux environment for SAP HANA systems to match the guidelines of their data centers. This includes, for example, the choice to set up swap space on a dedicated storage partition or in a swap file (setting up a dedicated partition on a fast storage device is clearly recommended) or to define a dedicated storage partition for temporary files (the */tmp* file system).

▶ **Space for data and log backups**
The SAP HANA database offers two distinct targets for data and log backups (see Chapter 5 for details). The *BackInt* mechanism enables control of the

backup system through a third-party backup tool and writing the backups to network pipes. When using this mechanism, there is no need for a backup file system on the SAP HANA server. With traditional file-based backups, on the other hand, the database needs a locally available file system of sufficient size to maintain data and log backups.

The appropriate sizing of such a backup file system is not a trivial matter, and we address this challenge in the context of Chapter 5. It is a file system that should, however, be included in the system planning from the start, and it is the only one of the mentioned file systems that is not included in the appliance definition and will not be taken care of automatically by your server hardware vendor.

Any backup—whether file-based or not—should be located on storage devices external to the originating server hardware, and SAP allows the usual technologies, such as NFS, for mounting the backup file system into the SAP HANA server, with the exceptions listed in SAP Note 1820529. Data and log backups may reside on the same storage device.

In scale-out installations, the file system path for data and log backup must be the same and valid for all hosts of the cluster. Although it is technically possible to have individual storage devices for each host all mounted at the same file system path on their respective hosts, SAP strongly recommends using shared storage for the backup location.

Note

It should be noted that if you do not explicitly set up locations for data and log backup, these files will be written to a location underneath the installation path /hana/shared.

▶ **Space for provisioning software updates**

It can be very useful to prepare a network storage location to provision software downloads (e.g., updates of the database software) to your SAP HANA system. Such a shared location for software images can be very useful if you maintain multiple SAP HANA systems and want to automate software updates.

Because SAP does not mention a preferred location to place software images for installation or update of the SAP HANA system, we have taken the liberty of suggesting the following idea:

Place software updates into the file system path /hana/shared/media. If you are using a network file system for software provisioning, mount this file system into the proposed path. If not, this location is a safe place, because it typically has copious free space (as opposed to the root file system) and does not interfere with the data or log file storage. On small SAP HANA servers, there is a chance that disk space in */hana/shared* can be scarce (remember that the file system size of */hana/shared* must equal the amount of installed main memory). To give you an estimate of the required disk space, consider that the installation files of SAP HANA have a size of approximately 10 GB, and you will need twice that amount temporarily in order to unpack the files. Also, a simple update of the server software alone amounts to about 3 GB.

A typical file system layout (excluding file systems for database backups and software provisioning) for an SAP HANA system is depicted in Figure 3.1. That figure contains all necessary information to deduce the file system layout of a scale-out cluster. In single-node systems, the counter <m> always has the value 1, and storage devices marked as "shared" may also be local devices of the database server.

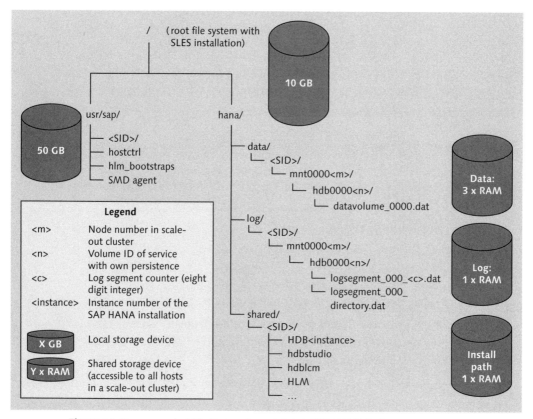

Figure 3.1 Recommended File System Layout for an SAP HANA System

3.2   Tools for Installing and Updating SAP HANA Systems

The SAP HANA database software comes with four different installation tools, some of which can also be used for updates. In addition, there are also tools that are *only* for updates. All of these tools are listed in Table 3.3.

Out of these tools, only the first three listed can be recommended for use in production landscapes. The other tools are either deprecated (Unified Installer) or are not aware of the database system as a whole, focusing just on single components (hdbinst, hdbupd).

Tool name	Purpose	GUI	Batch mode	Comment
hdblcm	Installation and update	No	Yes	Standard tool for nongraphical installation and update (starting with SPS 7).
hdblcmgui	Installation and update	Yes	No	Standard tool for GUI-based installation or update with local logon to database server (starting with SPS 7), using hdblcm as backend.
HLM	Update, installation of additional instances	Yes	No	Tool for updating the database or adding further instances to an existing database, with remote access from SAP HANA Studio or a web browser. *Note:* In SPS 8, most of this functionality has been removed from HLM. The recommended tool for all these actions is now hdblcm(gui).
hdbinst	Installation	No	No	Built-in installer of individual components. Should not be used for customer installations, because it does not install supporting components (HLM or similar).
hdbupd	Update	No	No	Built-in update program of individual components. Should not be used in customer installations.
Unified Installer	Installation	Yes	No	Deprecated installation tool, replaced by hdblcm(gui).

Table 3.3 List of Tools for Installing and Updating SAP HANA

It took us just one sentence to cut the offering of installation/update tools in half, but it will take slightly longer to help you choose the right one from the set of remaining tools. We will guide you first through the installation and then add a brief word on the update tools.

3.2.1 Installation Tools

The tool for installing the database (or adding components to the database installation) is the `hdblcm` tool, which comes in two flavors: a text-mode installer that can be used interactively as well as in batch mode via a prepared configuration file and a graphical variety that guides you through the installation process with an easy-to-follow wizard. These flavors (or, to make things easier: tools) are named `hdblcm` and `hdblcmgui`, respectively. We will frequently use the notation `hdblcm(gui)` if an explanation applies to both flavors. Both tools have a lot in common:

▸ They require OS access with the root user (or an equivalently privileged user) of the database server.

▸ They enable the installation of single-node systems and scale-out systems.

▸ They let you install additional SAP HANA instances on the database server.

▸ They both use the same installation libraries and thus produce the same log files for the install process.

▸ They are available via the "installation and upgrade image" option of the database software as well as the "update and patch" download of updates to the database server software.

There is a third tool, SAP HANA Lifecycle Manager (HLM), that can only be used to add an additional instance to an already installed database server; it cannot be used for performing the initial installation.

> **Note**
>
> In SPS 8 of SAP HANA, most functionalities for system lifecycle management have been removed from HLM so that in SPS 8 the only tool for installation and update is the `hdblcm(gui)` tool.

Choosing hdblcmgui

In our eyes, `hdblcmgui` is the perfect tool for someone who does not frequently install SAP HANA database systems and thus will appreciate a little more guidance and comfort than a text-based tool offers. For example, the tool checks the validity of entries (file system paths, etc.) and displays comprehensible messages if something seems to be not in order.

The drawbacks of using the hdblcmgui tool compared to the command-line version include the obvious necessity of X-server forwarding when accessing the SAP HANA server (which may or may not be easy to accomplish in your data center) and the perceived speed of the application, which sometimes feels a bit unresponsive (but has been improved greatly in SPS 8).

On the other hand, especially when installing a scale-out system, you will be grateful for the assistance offered by the hdblcmgui application.

Choosing hdblcm

For the regular database installation master who knows what he or she is doing, the hdblcm command-line tool will typically be the tool of choice, especially when installing single-node instances. In interactive mode, this is the fastest way to install a new complete SAP HANA instance, be it the first one on the database server or an additional system on a nonproduction server. For automated system provisioning—for example, for server hosting or for setting up training instances—the batch mode is invaluable.

Choosing HLM

As HLM cannot be used at all for system installation in SPS 8, we do not recommend it.

3.2.2   Update Tools

For updating the SAP HANA system, you can use the hdblcm(gui) tools. The strengths of these two tools have already been discussed in the context of installation, and they can be transferred to the update process.

Before SPS 8, the third tool available for updating the database (or adding a new instance to an existing database installation) is the IILM tool. In our experience, however, the overall update process is much simpler with hdblcmgui, and this tool is also more fault tolerant than HLM. Because virtually all functionality has been removed from HLM in SPS 8, we decided not to cover the tool in this book.

3.3 Installing an SAP HANA Database

Now that we have laid the groundwork, we can start our first SAP HANA installation. First, we will tell you what to download, where to get the files from, and
where to place them. After this, we will guide you step-by-step through the installation of a single-node system with the graphical `hdblcmgui` tool.

Unless stated otherwise, all installation steps have to be carried out by the root
user of the Linux operating system.

> **Note**
>
> Batch-mode installation and upgrade are covered in Section 3.6.

3.3.1 Downloading and Preparing the Software

In order to install the SAP HANA database, you need to download the installation
image of the software from SAP Service Marketplace. You can find the software at
the following location: *https://service.sap.com/swdc/* • INSTALLATIONS AND UPGRADES •
A-Z INDEX • H • SAP HANA PLATFORM EDITION • SAP HANA PLATFORM EDITION 1.0 •
INSTALLATION.

From that location, download all files belonging to the support package you want
to install. SAP HANA installation files are offered as self-extracting RAR archives.
The first file therefore has the file type (extension) EXE, and all subsequent files
have the extension RAR. For SPS 7 of SAP HANA, you need to download 10 files
with a total size of almost 10 GB.

> **Note**
>
> Once you have downloaded all files, do not extract them on a Windows machine using
> the self-extract functionality (i.e., do not run the <first_file >.exe file). If you extract the
> files on a Windows OS, all file access permissions will be erased, and this will lead to vir-
> tually irreparable issues when you try installing the software.
>
> Only extract the download either locally on the SAP HANA server or on a Linux server
> from which you can directly provision the extracted archive to the target SAP HANA
> server in a way that preserves file access information.

Now, let's assume that you have placed the download into a directory accessible
on your SAP HANA server, for example, the location */hana/shared/media/* that we

proposed in Section 3.1.3. We will refer to this location as "<media_path>" throughout this chapter.

After placing the RAR archive into <media_path>, change into that directory and unpack the download using the unrar program. Most likely the unrar package will not have been installed on your SAP HANA system, because it is not part of the SLES 11 Server Base System. It is, however, part of the SLES 11 distribution and can thus be added using your preferred method of installing additional packages from the distribution.

> **Note**
>
> On Linux operating systems, you must extract the installation archives of SAP software (including SAP HANA) as the root user. The installation process will verify file ownership during the installation process. See also SAP Note 886535 for extracting multivolume archives of SAP installation media.

In order to unpack the files, log on with the root operating system user and change into the <media_path> directory. The extraction will create a directory labelled with an eight-digit number (we will call this number <dvd_label>). That number is SAP's identifier for the installation medium, and it does not have an obvious translation into SAP HANA version numbers. We therefore recommend setting up a target directory for the extraction with an appropriate directory name. For the remainder of this chapter, we will use the placeholder <installation_base_path> to refer to the location into which you extract the archive.

Then, unpack the multivolume self-extracting RAR archive using, for example, a command following the pattern given in Listing 3.1.

```
# Change directories to your software download (if you follow
# our suggestion, <media_path> = /hana/shared/media/)
cd <media_path>
# Create the target directory for extracting the files
# (in our example for SPS 7). With reference to the text
# above, the <installation_base_bath> in our example is
# <installation_base_path> - <media_path>/SPS7_install/
mkdir SPS7_install
# Extract the archive into that target directory
unrar x <dvd_label>_part01.exe SPS7_install/
```

Listing 3.1 Linux Commands to Extract the SAP HANA Installation Archive

After extracting the archive, you will find the following directory and file structure inside of the target directory of the installation:

▸ **Directory <installation_base_path>/<dvd_label>**
Contains multiple files with version information and so on, which will typically not concern you, except for the file MD5FILE.DAT, which contains the MD5 check sums of every single file of the extracted archive.

▸ **Directory <installation_base_path>/<dvd_label>/DATA_UNITS**
This directory contains all components of the SAP HANA database that are part of the installation medium. For each component, there is one subdirectory within DATA_UNITS. We list those components that can be deployed in the course of the database installation in Table 3.4, ordered subjectively by the importance they play for the installation process of a typical SAP HANA installation.

Component	Directory Name(s)	Comment
hdblcm	HDB_LCM_LINUX_X86_64	New installation programs hdblcm and hdblcmgui (recommended as of SPS 7)
SAP HANA database	HDB_SERVER_LINUX_X86_64	The software of the SAP HANA database itself
SAP HANA Studio	HDB_STUDIO_LINUX_X86_64 HDB_STUDIO_WINDOWS_X86 HDB_STUDIO_WINDOWS_X86_64	Versions of SAP HANA Studio for Linux (64 bit), Windows 32 bit and Windows 64 bit
SAP HANA client	HDB_CLIENT_LINUX_X86_64 (and versions for all other supported architectures)	The client package, including JDBC driver, ODBC driver and multiple useful tools
HLM	SAPHANALM_LINUX_X86_64	SAP HANA Lifecycle Manager (HLM)
AFL	HDB_AFL_LINUX_X86	Functional extension "Application Function Library"
Unified Installer	HANA_IM_LINUX__X86_64	Deprecated (as of SPS 7) installation tool
Hardware Check Tool	SAP_HANA_HWCCT	Tool to verify hardware properties (for Tailored Data Center Integration)

Table 3.4 SAP HANA Components for the Install Process

There are more components contained in the installation medium, but they do not play a role in the installation of the database itself. Depending on your intended usage scenario, you may need to deploy some of these later, using the installation procedure of the individual component (installation functionality for these components is not contained in `hdblcm`):

▶ Server components to set up the data federation technology Smart Data Access (SAP_HANA_SDA_10)

▶ The SAP liveCache add-on for running SAP liveCache integrated in SAP HANA (HANA_LCAPPS_10_LINUX_X86_64)

▶ SAP-provided optional content (name starts with HCO_), for example, the demo content of SAP HANA Interactive Education (SHINE)

▶ SAP NetWeaver components such as the SAP NetWeaver Kernel, SAP Host Agent, and SAP Software Provisioning Manager (SWPM), a part of the Software Logistics (SL) toolset

▶ SAP HANA Information Composer—a Java-based application that aims to add agile modeling capabilities on top of SAP HANA's modeling component

▶ The RSA-plugin for SAP HANA Studio, which adds functionality that was used in a deprecated workflow for integrating with SAP Data Services (usually not needed anymore)

3.3.2 Running the Installation Tool

Now, we are ready to start the actual system installation with the graphical `hdblcmgui` tool.

1. As the root user on the Linux operating system of your SAP HANA server, navigate to the location of the `hdblcm` tools on your installation medium: *<installation_base_path>/<dvd_label>/DATA_UNITS/ HDB_LCM_LINUX_X86_64*. In that directory, start the installation program by executing the command `./hdblcmgui`.

This will open the installation tool, which on its first screen shows you the installable components it detected (Figure 3.2). On this screen, you can also point the tool to other installation medium locations if necessary. If you prepared the installation software as we advised earlier, you can simply continue to the next step.

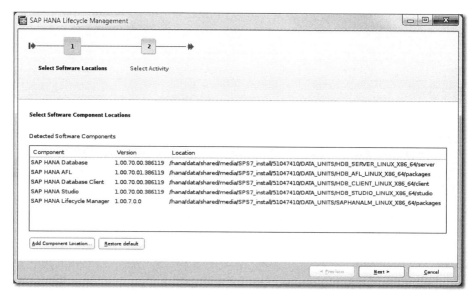

Figure 3.2 Detected Installable Components on the First Screen of hdblcmgui

2. The `hdblcmgui` tool supports the installation of new SAP HANA instances (and updating existing ones). The second step of the workflow lets you choose between these two activities; if you are installing the first SAP HANA instance on a given server, you will not be able to select UPDATE EXISTING SYSTEM. It will be grayed out, as shown in Figure 3.3.

Figure 3.3 Choosing the Activity to Perform

3. Once you have selected INSTALL NEW SYSTEM, the next screen of the wizard offers the installation of additional optional components with the new database instance (note that the SAP HANA database itself is not optional).

We recommend always installing SAP HANA Studio, SAP HANA client, and SAP HANA Lifecycle Manager (HLM) with every instance of the database. These three are useful tools (or contain useful tools) and therefore should be installed at least with the first instance of SAP HANA on a given server. Even if you install multiple instances on the same server, it is useful to have local Studio, client, and HLM installations for each instance, as this is the best way to guarantee that you always have the perfectly matching version of the additional tools.

As can be seen in Figure 3.4, we will continue with this minimum recommended setup, installing everything except the Application Function Libraries (AFL).

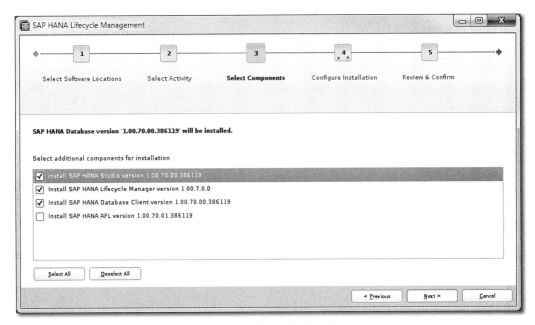

Figure 3.4 Selecting Software Components to Install with the SAP HANA Instance

4. The next step (CONFIGURE INSTALLATION) breaks down into seven substeps, in which we define all necessary properties of the database system to be installed. First, we have to tell the installer about the most significant hardware

characteristic: Is our database system on a single host, or is it distributed in a scale-out cluster? In our example, we are installing a single-host database (Figure 3.5).

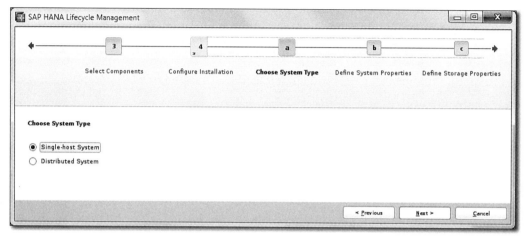

Figure 3.5 Choosing the System Type

5. The next piece of information to provide is the basic characteristics of the new database, as shown in Figure 3.6:

  ▸ For INSTALLATION PATH, we recommend using the default value "/hana/ shared"; this is where the database software will be installed and also where certain runtime data, such as trace files or configuration files, will be located.

  ▸ The SAP HANA SYSTEM ID (SID) is the unique identifier of your SAP system to be installed. In our example, we use the SID "WUP".

> **Note**
>
> SAP recommends that no two SAP systems within a customer environment should have the same SID.
>
> The SID must consist of three alphanumeric characters. Only uppercase letters are allowed, and the first character must be a letter (not a digit). Several possible SIDs are reserved and cannot be used; see the *SAP HANA Server Installation Guide* for details.

  ▸ Finally, choose the INSTANCE NUMBER from the dropdown box. Our database system "WUP" will be equipped with instance number "42".

Note

The INSTANCE NUMBER is a second identifier for the SAP system to be installed, but it does not need to be unique throughout your system landscape (it must be unique among the SAP systems installed on a given host or host cluster). In an SAP HANA system, the instance number determines the external and internal communication ports of the software.

The instance number is a two-digit number in the range of 00 to 99.

If you plan to set up a disaster-tolerant SAP HANA system by using the system replication technology, be aware that such a system will internally need two consecutive instance numbers: the one you choose here and the next-highest number. Hence, if you plan to make use of system replication you must not choose instance number 99, and if you might install multiple SAP HANA instances on the same server and make use of system replication, you might want to implement a schema such as "only use even instance numbers."

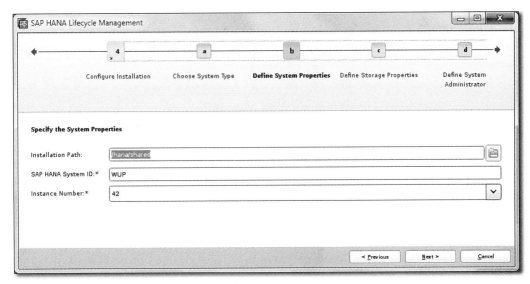

Figure 3.6 Entering Properties of the Database System

6. Next on the agenda is the definition of the storage system properties. In this dialog, we need to enter the locations of the data and log volumes. Note that you have to enter the SID-specific path names, that is, *<data_path>/<SID>* and *<log_path>/<SID>*. The system will already make appropriate proposals, as you can see from the automatically inserted suggestions in Figure 3.7.

The suggested <data_path> directory is */hana/data*, and the suggested <log_path> directory is */hana/log*, which leads to the selection of:

▶ LOCATION OF DATA VOLUMES: "*/hana/data/WUP*"

▶ LOCATION OF LOG VOLUMES: "*/hana/log/WUP*"

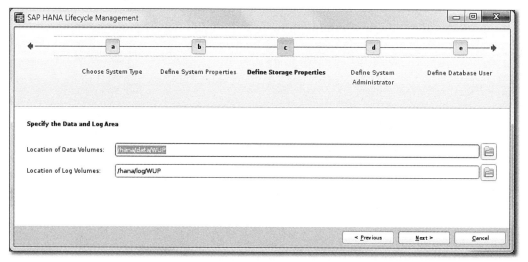

Figure 3.7 Defining Locations for Data and Log Storage

7. On the next screen, we have to define the system administrator for the SAP HANA system on the OS level (Figure 3.8).

For each SAP HANA system with a given <SID>, there is a dedicated administration user on the operating system. The name of this user is <sid>adm (all in lower case), and it will be automatically created by the installation program. In our case, the user will be named "wupadm".

All administration users of SAP systems on the Linux operating systems are added to the group SAPSYS.

Although you cannot change the user and group names, you are free to choose the user and group IDs. The installation program automatically determines the first free user and group IDs, and typically there will be no reason to deviate from this choice.

The following information can be entered or modified from the proposed input values:

▶ PASSWORD and PASSWORD CONFIRMATION: The password of the <sid>adm OS user. Choose a password that complies with your IT department's security guidance.

▶ SYSTEM ADMINISTRATOR LOGIN SHELL: The executable program of the OS shell to use when logging on with the <sid>adm user. Administrators will typically choose either bash (in modern Linux distributions, the default executable /bin/sh is a symbolic link to /bin/bash) or C-shell (/bin/tcsh). We leave the choice to your personal preference.

▶ SYSTEM ADMINISTRATOR HOME DIRECTORY: We recommend not changing this path from its default value.

▶ SYSTEM ADMINISTRATOR TIMEZONE: This choice only affects the time zone setting of the operating system administrator; it does not affect the time zone settings of the database itself. The database time zone is determined from the global time zone setting of your Linux operating system. In order to avoid confusion, we recommend setting the user's time zone to the server's time zone.

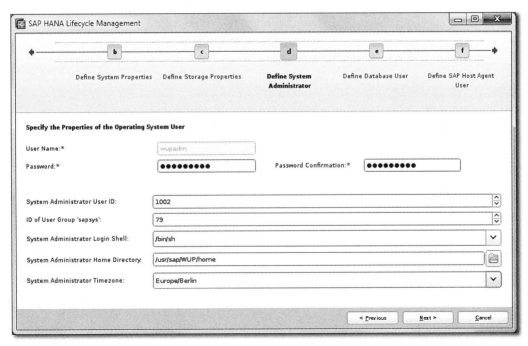

Figure 3.8 Defining the Administration User on the Operating System

8. Your SAP HANA database comes with one preinstalled, logon-enabled database user, which is always named "SYSTEM". This user is highly powerful, and it is intended for use during the system setup (bootstrapping) and in emergencies. During times of regular database usage, the SYSTEM user should be retired (deactivated).

   You need to specify and confirm the password for the SYSTEM user (Figure 3.9). If you plan to set up a high level of system security, we do not recommend using the same password for the database user SYSTEM and the OS user <sid>adm.

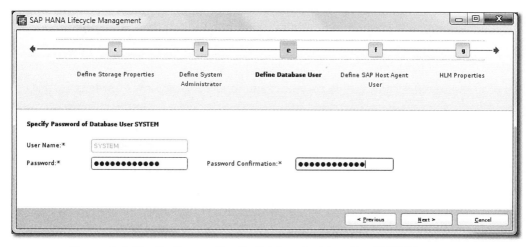

Figure 3.9 Setting the Password for the Database Bootstrap User (SYSTEM)

9. HLM uses self-signed SSL certificates in its communication with the database server. Because internal and external host names may be different, we need to set up a mapping accordingly.

   For example, a given SAP HANA host might have the internal hostname "hanahost1," and you might use "hserver01.mycompany.com" externally. In this case, you would have to fill in "hanahost1" for HOSTNAME and "hserver01.mycompany.com" for CERTIFICATE HOSTNAME.

   In our example, internal and external host name are identical (Figure 3.10).

10. At this point, all preparations are finished. The installation wizard displays a summary of all defined properties for the installation (Figure 3.11). If you agree, you can start the actual installation by clicking INSTALL.

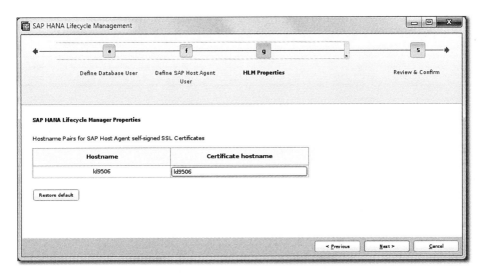

Figure 3.10 Defining the Hostnames for SAP Host Agent SSL Certificates

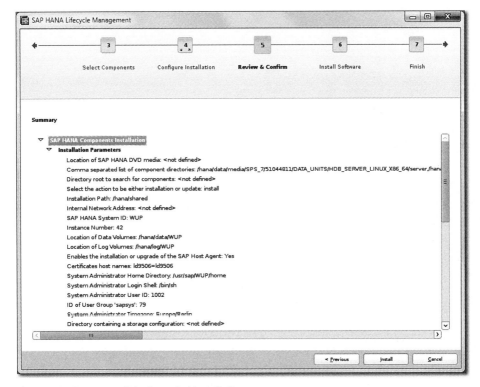

Figure 3.11 Summary of the Intended Installation

11. While the installation is running, progress bars indicate the progress (Figure 3.12).

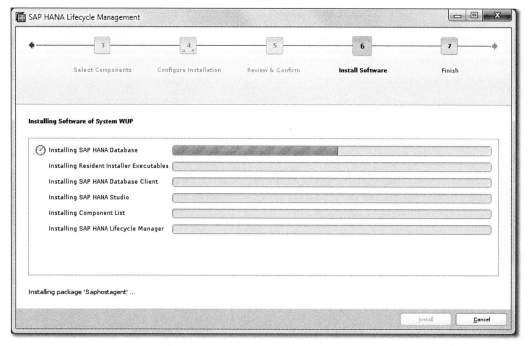

Figure 3.12 Progress Indication during the Install Process

12. The installation of a new database on a single-host system typically takes around 10 minutes. At the end of this process, if all goes well, the database will be started and ready for your first logon.

    Whether or not the installation was successful can easily be seen on the final screen of the installation wizard (Figure 3.13). This screen also gives access to the log files of the installation process for the individual components that have been installed.

If there are errors in the course of the installation, the log files will contain information as to what went wrong. In our experience, the installation process is pretty robust, as long as your system meets the requirements for hardware and operating system setup.

You can now start using the database system, which means that you should prepare the system for its actual purpose. There is a long list of steps that you should follow in order to make sure you have an easily manageable system. We walk you through typically recommended steps in Chapter 14. (The reason we place that chapter so far back in the book is that those steps touch virtually every aspect of database administration.)

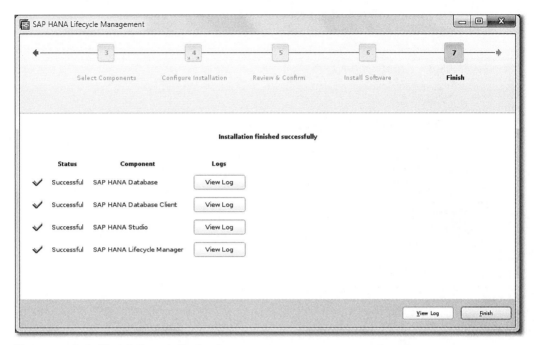

Figure 3.13 End of Installation—Indicating Success

We recommend not removing the extracted installation archive of a given support package stack from the SAP HANA server if you are operating database instances of that support package level. You will need the installation packages for the support package stack if you want to add further instances of the database at a later point in time.

3.4   Updating an SAP HANA Database

For updating the database and related components on the database server, there are in principle three options. You might install all components individually with their respective installation program, or you might use one of the two tools that can update all system components at once. These tools are the HLM tool and the hdblcm(gui) tool.

We cannot see a good reason to update each component individually, and out of the other tools, hdblcm(gui) has proven more robust in our experience compared to the HLM tool, which appears less tolerant with regards to deviations from a hypothetical perfect system setup. We will therefore demonstrate a database update via the hdblcmgui tool. As with installation, the preparations for the update are more complex than the actual update process. We will therefore give you as much detail as possible about these prearrangements. The prerequisites for the graphical tool are the same as those for updating the database using the hdblcm tool on the command line or in batch mode.

3.4.1 Prerequisites

The most important prerequisite for updating the database is of course the downloading of the new software packages and the appropriate placing of those packages on your SAP HANA server. There are a few more steps that help you perform the update without glitches.

Choosing the Target Revision for an Update

In most cases, you can directly upgrade the SAP HANA database server software to any target revision from your current revision. A few restrictions apply if you are coming from a maintenance revision (see Chapter 1), because these revisions may have specific requirements regarding the target revisions of updates. These update paths are listed by SAP in SAP Note 1948334. Even if you upgrade from one SPS to another, you do not have to first upgrade to the SPS release version itself; you can usually directly upgrade to the intended target revision. In fact, the update paths for maintenance revisions in most cases exclude an upgrade to the initial revision of the successor SPS.

More difficult is—as always—the question of whether you will want to upgrade to the latest revision or an older one. Generally speaking, you can either upgrade to revisions of the highest current support package stack, or to the maintenance revision of the previous support package stack (as long as your system is currently on the previous SPS level).

In light of SAP's release strategy, our general advice is not to move to the latest support package stack (SPS) before the SAP HANA Datacenter Service Point revision of that SPS has been released, unless you have specific requirements for new functionality that may only be available in the latest SPS.

You should keep in mind that SAP intends to stop providing maintenance revisions shortly after the SAP HANA Datacenter Service Point revision of the successor SPS has been released, so you will need to schedule an SPS upgrade sooner or later.

Download Archives

Before you can update the database, you will need to download the software packages to update. The required download files will depend on the set of components installed on your database server and on the target version of the upgrade.

In theory, you can upgrade either to individual revisions (sometimes also referred to as individual support packages) or to a higher support package stack. Assuming that most customers will be operating maintenance revisions before upgrading to the successor SPS, the upgrade to the SPS release itself will usually be prohibited by incompatible upgrade paths. We will therefore only cover the case of updating to a specific revision, for which you will have to download a number of individual software packages. If you have installed our minimum recommended components, you will have to download the following packages:

▶ SAP HANA Server (Linux X86 64 bit)

▶ SAP HANA Studio (Linux X86 64 bit)

▶ SAP HANA Client (Linux X86 64 bit)

▶ SAP HANA Lifecycle Manager (HLM) (Linux X86 64 bit)

If you have installed add-on components, such as the AFL, you will have to download those packages too.

In addition to the packages for the database server, you will typically also need the SAP HANA Studio and client for all other platforms on which you are running these components in your landscapes. In most cases, you should at least download the 32- and 64-bit Windows versions of SAP HANA Studio and client. You may operate servers that need the SAP HANA client software on other operating systems, and you should download the client package for these operating systems as well.

Next we will only cover updating the software on the SAP HANA database server.

All downloads are available from the software download center on SAP Service Marketplace at *https://service.sap.com/swdc* • Support Packages and Patches • A-Z Index • H • SAP HANA Platform Edition • SAP HANA Platform Edition 1.0 • Entry by Component. At that location, choose the component to download—for example, HANA database for the database server software—and then the version for the selected component.

For any given update process, you should always download all required packages with the same revision level. The HLM tool is an exception, because HLM does not use the revision labeling of SAP HANA. You should always download the highest patch level of HLM for the given support package stack.

Unpack Archives

The software updates you downloaded are in the format of SAP Archives (SAR files). If you update the database using the hdblcm(gui) tool, you will first need to extract these archives.

In our example, we will assume that you downloaded the archives into a location that we will call <download_path> on the SAP HANA database server and that you extracted them into a directory we will refer to as <update_base_path>.

Continuing the suggestions we made in Section 3.3.1, you might choose:

▸ <download_path> = */hana/shared/media/REV_<x>_download*

▸ <update_base_path> = */hana/shared/media/REV_<x>*

Having these two separate locations allows you to easily remove the extracted versions after a successful update process but still keep the SAR files themselves in case you need them again at a later point in time.

In order to extract the archives, you will need the SAPCAR program. On any correctly installed SAP HANA system, this program will already have been installed. You can find it with the HLM installation for your given instance (SID) in the location */usr/sap/hlm_bootstraps/<SID>/HLM/exe/*.

With these points in mind, you can unpack the archives by using the syntax given in Listing 3.2.

```
# Change directories to your software download for the given
# revision <x> (if you follow our suggestion,
# <download_path> = /hana/shared/media/REV_<x>_download/)
```

```
cd <download_path>
# Create the target directory for extracting the files (in
# our example, for revision <x>). With reference to the previous
# text, the <update_base_bath> in our example is
# <update_base_path> = /hana/shared/media/REV_<x>/
mkdir ../REV_<x>
# Extract all archive files into that target directory.
# Generally, the SAPCAR syntax is
# SAPCAR -xvf <.SAR_file> -R <extraction_target_directory>
# We will use the SAPCAR installed with our database SID. For
# each archive file <file_i>.SAR, run the following statement:
/usr/sap/hlm_bootstraps/<SID>/HLM/exe/SAPCAR
-xvf <download_path>/<file_i>.SAR -R <update_base_path>/
```

Listing 3.2 Unpacking the Update Archives

Special Treatment for the HLM Package Download

Most SAP HANA archives will extract into a dedicated subdirectory of <update_base_path>. One exception is the HLM package (file name SAPHANALM*.SAR), which will extract its content files directly into the target directory of the SAPCAR command. In a deviation from the guidance given in Listing 3.2, you should create a dedicated subdirectory for the HLM tool (e.g., *<update_base_path>/HLM*) and extract the HLM archive into that subdirectory.

Also, the update process of the HLM tool itself requires not only the extracted HLM tool but also the SAR file of the HLM tool in the same directory. You should therefore copy the SAPHANALM*.SAR file into the target directory for extracting that file (e.g., *<update_base_path>/HLM*).

Other Prerequisites

If you update the HLM component of your database system (and if you are not using HLM itself for the update), you should now stop HLM for the <SID> to be updated, as shown in Listing 3.3.

```
/hana/data/shared/<SID>/HLM/stop-hlm.sh -f
```

Listing 3.3 Stopping the HLM Process for a Given SID

If, as recommended by SAP, you have deactivated the SYSTEM user of your SAP HANA database, you will have to activate it again for the update process.

3.4.2   Steps in an Update

Regardless of which tool you use to update the database, the main steps of updating the software will always be the same:

1. The update program installs the new software version in a shadow location.

2. The database processes are shut down.

3. The new software version is switched for the old one; because the new software version has already been installed on the same file system, this process takes mere seconds.

4. The database processes are restarted immediately (unless you explicitly prohibit the restart).

During the update of the database software, the `hdblcmgui` tool will not only replace the program files of the database software but also update the SAP Host Agent installed on the database server to the version that is contained in the database software archive (unless the installed version of SAP Host Agent is already higher than the packaged version, and unless you explicitly disable the SAP Host Agent update); it will also update the resident `hdblcm` and `hdblcmgui` programs in */hana/shared/<SID>/hdblcm*.

Database Downtime during Update

The required restart of the database software naturally has the effect that the database will be unavailable for a period of time. The duration of this downtime depends on the data content of the database server, as will be explained in Chapter 5. The main contribution to long downtimes comes from the row store. It may be as short as about one minute if the database has negligible data volume in the row store—or it may take the better part of half an hour, if the row store is several hundred GB in size. After loading the row store tables, the database is available to applications.

Following the restart, it will also take some time until all typically required column store tables are loaded into main memory. The database will automatically preload with low priority those tables that were in main memory before the last shutdown. In addition, any query requiring table columns that are not yet in main memory will trigger the loading of those columns. It is also possible to mark entire tables or individual table columns for preload.

The duration of this warm-up phase depends on the data content of the database and also on the usage of the data. Especially if the update is performed within a scheduled downtime window, it is a good idea to define appropriate prewarm queries to trigger the loading of essential data into main memory and to include the execution of those queries in the overall update process.

You may need to plan downtimes of all connected components in the course of the upgrade. This is particularly important for any data-provisioning processes that target the SAP HANA database. Make sure that no data-loading jobs are active when you start the upgrade (depending on your scenario, these might include SAP Data Services jobs, SAP BW process chains, or other jobs); if you are using SLT for real-time replication, pause all replication jobs.

Near-Zero-Downtime Upgrades

SAP offers a method for near-zero-downtime upgrades for customers who are running a disaster-tolerant SAP HANA system using the system replication technology. We cover these in Chapter 5 in the context of system replication.

These near-zero-downtime upgrades will make the downtime during upgrade practically independent from the data volumes in row store and column store. That is, there is no significant downtime for loading row store data, and there will be no significant warm-up phase for loading column store data into main memory.

3.4.3   Running the Update Tool

In order to run the update process in `hdblcmgui`, it is easiest if you simply run it as the root user. If that is not possible, you can run the program with other users, but you will need to enter the root user's password in the course of the update.

1. As the root user on the Linux operating system of your SAP HANA server, navigate to the location of the `hdblcm` tools on your installation medium. You have two options for running the tool:

   Either use the version that comes with the SPS installation medium, located in the file system path *<installation_base_path>/<dvd_label>/DATA_UNITS/ HDB_LCM_LINUX_X86_64* (if you followed our guidance in Section 3.3.1, <installation_base_path> will be */hana/shared/media/SPS<y>_install*).

Or use the tool version that comes with the SAP HANA database server package that you want to update to. You will find the `hdblcm` tools in the file system path *<update_base_path>/SAP_HANA_DATABASE*. In our case, this is */hana/shared/media/REV_<x>/SAP_HANA_DATABASE*.

Whichever tool location you choose, start the update program by executing the command `./hdblcmgui`.

2. If you start the update program from the SPS installation medium, the automatically detected component versions are those of the support package stack (Figure 3.14). You have to make the program aware of the directory into which we extracted the downloaded archives. Click on ADD COMPONENT LOCATION... and enter the <update_base_path> you prepared in Listing 3.2.

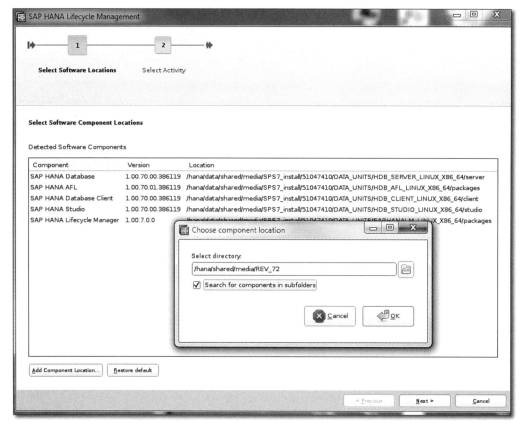

Figure 3.14 Entering Installation Source Location

Make sure to enable searching in subfolders before confirming the pop-up window. The tool will now scan for SAP HANA software components in the given path and refresh the list of detected components.

Note

If you started hdblcmgui from the extracted archive of the SAP HANA database server package in *<update_base_path>/SAP_HANA_DATABASE*, then the program will automatically detect all components extracted into *<update_base_path>*.

3. In the next step of the wizard, you have to choose to update, and you have to select the database system to update from the dropdown menu. You can only update one system at a time.

4. For the selected system, you have to choose the components that you want to update. Typically, this will be all components that you have downloaded. You can also use this step to add new components, such as the AFL, if you have downloaded and extracted the correct version of those (Figure 3.15).

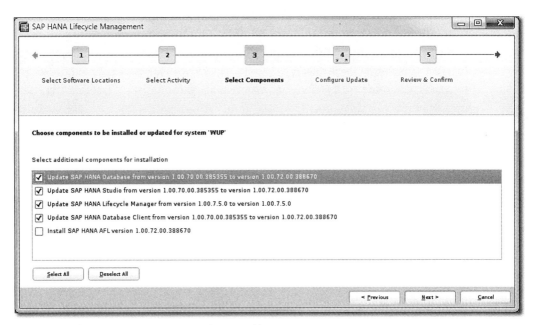

Figure 3.15 Choosing Components to Update or Add

5. In the final interactive step, you have to enter the passwords for the operating system administrator user <sid>adm and the database administrator user SYS-TEM. If you used this update process to also add HLM to the system, there would be an additional step for HLM properties.

6. The next screens of the update wizard will present you with a summary of the intended update and then a progress indicator during the update process. At the end of the update process, you will see success or failure messages, and you will be able to check the update logs of all components.

3.5   Installing Multiple Instances of an SAP HANA Database on the Same Physical Server (Nonproduction)

SAP supports installing multiple instances of SAP HANA database on the same physical host but only on systems that are not used in production. If a database instance is used as production system, it must be the only instance on the host. One reason for this restriction is that the database software assumes that it has all hardware resources at its command, and multiple instances may therefore attempt to overallocate resources, especially CPU time.

In order to make optimal use of their nonproduction hardware, customers may install multiple database instances, such as development, test, or sandbox systems, on the same host. When installing such multi-instance systems (typically referred to in SAP's documentation as "multi-SID systems"), one must be aware of several limiting factors, especially in the main memory management.

The database size of an SAP HANA system is limited by the amount of main memory available to the database. With its primary data image in RAM, the database can only work efficiently if it has sufficient amounts of memory available. If multiple databases are installed on the same host, the main memory must be allocated fairly to prevent memory overcommits.

The SAP HANA database has a database parameter named global_allocation_limit that limits the amount of extended memory that all processes of one SAP HANA instance combined may allocate. If the database instances approach this limit, the parameter will attempt to free memory resources, and in the worst case it will terminate ongoing transactions.

The first database instance installed on a given host has a default global allocation limit that is calculated as follows: 90% of the first 64 GB of RAM plus 97% of the

RAM above 64 GB. On a 1 TB system (1024 GB), this would amount to 90% of 64 GB + 97% of 960 GB = (57.6 + 931.2) GB = 988.8 GB available to the database. This typically leaves sufficient memory for the operating system itself and auxiliary processes, such as monitoring agents. If you add more instances, you will need to adjust the limit of the existing and the newly installed instances such that the sum of all allocation limits does not exceed the default setting for a single-instance installation.

If you install additional instances using HLM, you can modify the allocation limits of all installed instances and the new instance in the course of the installation process. If you use the `hdblcm(gui)` tool, you will need to verify and potentially adjust the allocation limits of all instances on the host manually. See Chapter 4 for information on how to modify the database configuration. The parameter to modify is `global.ini` • `[memorymanager]` • `global_allocation_limit`. The unit of measurement for the parameter is megabytes.

Adding a New Instance Using hdblcm(gui)

The process of installing an additional database instance via the `hdblm` or `hdblcmgui` tool is exactly the same as the process for installing the first instance.

3.6   Installation and Update in Batch Mode

If you have to install or update SAP HANA systems frequently, the `hdblcm` tool will most probably become your friend. It has been built for interactive as well as non-interactive installation and update from the command line.

An installation or update process can be described via a set of parameters of the `hdblcm` tool. For any required parameter, there are up to three ways of entering the parameter: You may specify it as a command-line parameter; you may specify it in a configuration file; or, if the parameter has not been supplied in either of these two ways, the `hdblcm` tool will request it interactively.

You can thus run a fully interactive installation or update by not specifying any parameters on the command line or in the configuration file. You can also run a fully automated installation or update by specifying all parameters on the command line or in the configuration file. And you can also mix those options, specifying some parameters on the command line and some in the configuration file and have the tool ask you interactively for all others.

In addition to checking the *SAP HANA Server Installation and Update Guide* (*https:/ /help.sap.com/hana_platform*) for a reference of all parameters and command-line options, you can also get very useful help from the hdblcm tool itself. The tool can generate template configuration files for updating or installing the database, and it can print all supported parameters in a help screen.

```
# Print help screen for installation or update, with
# documentation of all possible arguments (native to the
# hdblcm tool, as well as passed through to underlying
# components such as hdbinst:
./hdblcm --action=install|update --help --pass_through_help
# Generate template configuration file for update or
# installation:
./hdblcm --action=install|update --dump_configfile_template
```

Listing 3.4 Assistance Available on the Command Line for Using hdblcm

For many parameters, the install or update program provides well-chosen default values. In a database system set up following SAP's recommendations, these default values will usually be sufficient.

The default values play an important role for batch-mode installation or update. If you specify the option --batch (or -b), the hdblcm program will insert the default values for any value not specified on the command line or in the configuration file.

In this section, we provide simple examples of installing and updating an SAP HANA system, using a configuration file for typically needed parameters. We will build the configuration file in such a way that we can use it for installation, update, or both. We will also demonstrate the proposed way to handle passwords securely.

3.6.1 Password Treatment

For installation or update of SAP HANA systems, you will need to specify up to four passwords:

▶ You will always need to give the password of the <sid>adm database administrator on the OS and of the SYSTEM database user. At install time, the SYSTEM user's password must adhere to the default password policy: eight characters, at least one lowercase, uppercase, and numeric.

▶ If you start the installation or update with a user other than the root user, or if you install a scale-out system, you will need to give the root user's password.

▶ If you install the first SAP HANA instance on a given server (and if no SAP Host Agent is installed yet), you will also need to enter a password for the sapadm user, the administration user of the SAP Host Agent.

Because of security considerations, we cannot recommend specifying these passwords on the command line. After all, the passwords will be visible in the operating system's process list.

You can enter passwords interactively, but this will not be possible in batch mode. For a batch-mode installation, you may enter passwords into the configuration file, but then you'll have to modify the configuration file if the passwords are changed. The final and recommended option is to put the parameters into an XML file, which can be used in the installation or update process. This way, you can have one generic configuration file that is independent of password changes and a dedicated password file for each system.

We show an example XML file for all four passwords in Listing 3.5; in this listing, anything not in **bold** is a comment.

```
<?xml version="1.0" encoding= "UTF-8"?>
<Passwords>
   <!-- Password for <sid>adm user: -->
   <password>DontBother!</password>
   <!-- The other entries are self-explanatory: -->
   <system_user_password>WeAlreadyKnow99</system_user_password>
   <!-- Root password not needed if you install a
        single-node system as root -->
   <root_password>AllYourPasswords</root_password>
   <sapadm_password>OfCourse</sapadm_password>
</Passwords>
```

Listing 3.5 Example XML File for Password Specification

SAP's recommended way of using this password XML file is to pipe the XML file content into the invocation of the hdblcm program. This requires using the command-line option --read_password_from_stdin=xml, which is only available in batch mode, so we also have to use the option --batch. The password XML file should be located in a directory that is only accessible to the root user—for example, the root user's home directory. A typical invocation of hdblcm will thus look like Listing 3.6.

```
cat ~/passwords.xml | ./hdblcm --read_password_from_stdin=xml --batch
--action=<action> [... other parameters]
```
Listing 3.6 Example Invocation of hdblcm with Password File

3.6.2 Preparing the Configuration File

We recommend specifying all generic but required options in a configuration file instead of passing them as command-line parameters. In a typical SAP HANA installation, you will have to change only a very few parameters from their default values. If a parameter (e.g., a SID) is specified in the configuration file and also given on the command line, the command-line parameter supersedes the setting from the configuration file.

Generate the configuration file template as shown in Listing 3.4. You can remove any unnecessary parameters. A minimal configuration file is shown in Listing 3.7.

```
[General]
# Index (Default: studio,hlm,client)
components=server,hlm,afl,client,studio
[Server]
# Root User Name (Default: root)
root_user=lroot
# System Administrator Timezone (Default: UTC)
timezone=CET
[LifecycleManager]
# Certificate Host Names
certificates_hostmap=ld9506=ld9506
```
Listing 3.7 Example Configuration File

3.6.3 Performing the Installation

If you install an SAP HANA system in batch mode, adhere to the following instructions for specifying parameters:

▶ Parameter --batch must be given on the command line to enable batch-mode.

▶ action=install must be specified.

▶ sid=<SID> must be specified.

▶ number=<instance> should be specified. If not given, the system will automatically choose the lowest available instance number—which might not be intended, for example, if you are using system replication.

▶ If your root operating system user is not named root, you must specify the correct name in parameter root_user=<name>.

▶ When also installing the HLM component, you must specify the parameter certificates_hostmap=<hostname>=<certificate_hostname>.

In the example configuration file in Listing 3.7, we did not specify action and sid in the configuration file, so these parameters need to be given on the command line.

It is useful to redirect the console output of the installation program to a text file so that you can easily analyze this log at a later point in time if required. Also, and especially if your network connection to the SAP HANA server may be unreliable, you might want to use standard Linux functionality, such as nohup or screen, to protect the installation process from being interrupted by network disconnects.

With our configuration and password files prepared, we can now install a new SAP HANA instance. In Listing 3.8, we install a new system named NSA with instance number 52 in batch mode.

```
# Install SAP HANA System NSA with instance number 52, using
# a configuration file, with passwords from an XML file.
# The output of the installation file is redirected to a log
# file, and the process is protected from network disconnects.
nohup cat /root/hana_passwords.xml | ./hdblcm --action=install
  --configfile=/root/install_update_template.cfg
  --sid=NSA --number=52 --read_password_from_stdin=xml
  --batch &> /root/install_log_nsa.txt
# Monitor the output during installation.
tail -f /root/install_log_nsa.txt
```

Listing 3.8 Installing an SAP HANA Instance in Batch Mode

3.6.4 Performing the Update

Performing a DB update in batch mode is very similar to the installation. There are, however, a few differences:

▶ You must not enter the instance number; the SID is sufficient.

▶ When running the installer from the extracted archive of the SAP HANA server, it does not—at least in our setup—automatically detect the HLM installation files. We therefore have to use parameter --component_root to point the program to our <update_base_path> (/hana/shared/media/REV_72 in our example).

In Listing 3.9, we show the command line for updating our newly installed instance NSA to the release level of the archives extracted into directory */hana/shared/media/REV_72*, using the same configuration and password file as for the installation.

```
# Update SAP HANA instance NSA in batch mode.
nohup cat /root/hana_passwords.xml | ./hdblcm --action=update
  --configfile=/root/install_update_template.cfg
  --sid=NSA --read_password_from_stdin=xml
  --batch --component_root=/hana/shared/media/REV_72
  &> /root/update_log_nsa.txt
# Monitor the update process using tail.
tail -f /root/update_log_nsa.txt
```
Listing 3.9 Updating Instance NSA in Batch Mode

3.7   Installing and Updating Scale-Out Systems

In the previous sections, we only installed single-node instances of the SAP HANA database and you might—rightfully—ask yourself whether or not setting up a scale-out system might be more troublesome. We have some good news: There is hardly any difference compared to installing and updating single-node systems, with the obvious difference that you have to manage multiple hosts. In this section, we'll call out the major differences between installing and updating single-node vs. scale-out systems.

3.7.1   Preparation

When installing a scale-out system, all preparation steps mentioned in Section 3.1 have to be fulfilled on all hosts of the distributed system. In addition, there are a number of requirements specific to scale-out systems:

▶ **File system layout**
  The file systems for the installation path (*/hana/shared*), the data volumes of the database system (data path */hana/data/<SID>*), and the log volumes (log path */hana/log/<SID>*) must exist as a shared file system that is available on all hosts; see Section 3.1.4. Data and log paths must exist before you start the installation; the installer will not create them for you.

  Especially if you plan to install multiple instances of SAP HANA on the scale-out hardware, we recommend setting up */hana/data* and */hana/log* as shared file systems (as opposed to having */hana/data* as a local directory on the server and only */hana/data/<SID>* as a shared file system).

▶ **Root operating system user**
The root operating system user must be the same on all hosts of the scale-out cluster, that is, the user must have the same name and password on all hosts.

▶ **DB administrator on operating system (<sid>adm)**
The database administrator <sid>adm must have the same user ID and password on all hosts of the scale-out cluster. If the user does not exist yet, the installer will create it for you. If, however, the user already exists on at least one of the hosts (e.g., left over from a previous installation of a system with the same SID), you will have to manually make sure that the requirements are met.

3.7.2 Installing a Scale-Out System with hdblcmgui

The only difference between installing a scale-out instance and a single-node instance is that you need to define multiple hosts and their logical roles (worker or standby) in the course of the installation process. You can therefore follow the instructions given in Section 3.3.2.

The main difference is the screen for choosing the system type. Here, you must now select DISTRIBUTED SYSTEM, which will present you with further input fields (Figure 3.16):

▶ For ROOT USER NAME and ROOT USER PASSWORD, enter the credentials of the root OS user that are valid on all hosts.

▶ For INSTALLATION PATH, we recommend using the default value */hana/shared*.

▶ You can leave the field NON-STANDARD SHARED FILE SYSTEM empty in a typical installation.

▶ You can add additional hosts one by one via the ADD HOST... button. This will open a pop-up window in which you can enter the hostname of the host to add as well as the host type (worker or standby) and a high-availability group. See Chapter 6 for more details on these scale-out topics.

Note that the host on which you are running the installation program will always be added as the first host into your database cluster, and it will be a worker. This host will not show up in the table of ADDITIONAL HOSTS. You only need to specify details for the additional hosts. In our example, we are installing a five-host cluster, with four worker hosts and one standby host.

The subsequent steps of the installation are again the same as for single-node instances.

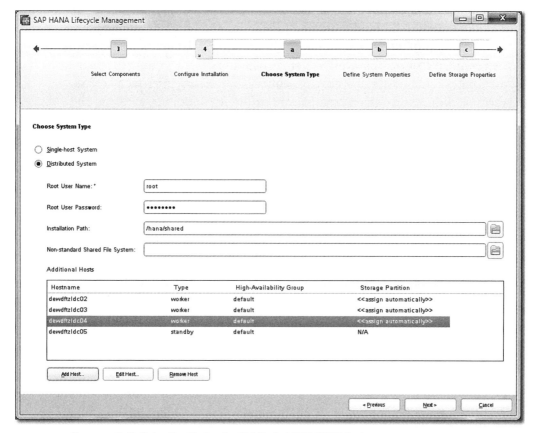

Figure 3.16 Defining the Hosts of a Distributed SAP HANA Instance

Note

You can of course also use the command line version, hdblcm, for the installation of scale-out systems. However, the tool's main advantage of batch-mode installation is less prominent with scale-out systems. The reason is that batch-mode installation is not independent from the host names, so you cannot use the same configuration file for installing multiple systems.

If you need to treat systems individually anyway for the singular process of installation, you may unashamedly enjoy the assistance offered by a graphical tool.

3.7.3   Updating a Scale-Out System

There is no difference to the update procedure when updating a scale-out system. You should only make sure to update a scale-out system while all hosts of the cluster are functioning. Unless it can absolutely not be avoided, you should not perform an update in a failover situation.

The update procedure will restart the database software automatically on all hosts of the scale-out system.

3.8   Troubleshooting

The installation and update process—especially using hdblcm(gui)—is very robust if the operating system has been set up correctly. If you run into issues during the installation or update process, you will need to study the log files for details. We will first show you how to find these log files. After this, we introduce a small set of command-line tools that will help you to prepare and verify a database installation.

3.8.1   Log Files of hdblcm

The hdblcm tool writes its log files into dedicated directories for each invocation of hdblcm or hdblcmgui. These directories are named */var/tmp/hdb_<SID>_hdblcm_install_<timestamp>*, where <SID> is the SID of the SAP HANA system being installed or updated (the directory name always contains the substring "install", regardless of the selected action). In these directories, you will find two files: hdblcm.log and hdblcm.msg. The log file is easily human readable and in case of issues typically contains understandable error messages. The message file hdblcm.msg is more technical and will in most cases only be useful for SAP Support staff.

During installation or update, hdblcm will invoke install or update programs of the individual components being installed or updated (database server, SAP HANA Studio, client ...). The log files of these subprocesses are also placed into */var/tmp*. You can most easily find them by listing the directory contents in temporal order (ls -ltr /var/tmp) and looking for files and directories whose names start with "hdb" and that have been created while hdblcm was active.

If you are using hdblcmgui, the tool gives direct access to the log files of all subprocesses and of the overall installation on the final screen of the install process.

3.8.2 Useful Tests on the Command Line

Finally, we offer you a few useful checks on the command line that can help you during or after the installation process.

Listing All Installed SAP Systems on the Server

Especially if you are installing multiple database instances on the same server, you will appreciate a quick way to list all SAP systems with their SID and instance number. This can most easily be achieved using the `saphostctrl` program, as shown in Listing 3.10. For each SAP system, the output contains the SID, the instance number, the hostname, and the version of the SAP Host Agent installed with the SAP system. Information on the database version can be obtained from the `saphostctrl` program with the function `ListDatabases`.

```
/usr/sap/hostctrl/exe/saphostctrl -function ListInstances
Inst Info : NSA - 52 - ld9506 - 740, patch 36, changelist 1[...]
Inst Info : WUP - 42 - ld9506 - 740, patch 36, changelist 1[...]
Inst Info : OMG - 01 - ld9506 - 740, patch 36, changelist 1[...]
```

Listing 3.10 Command Line and Output for Listing All Installed SAP Systems

Checking the Active Processes of a Given Database Instance

You might want to see all running processes on the operating system that belong to a given instance of the SAP HANA database, for example, after installing or updating the database instance. If you are logged on to the database server as the <sid>adm administrator user of the database instance, you can use the `HDB info` command, as shown in Figure 3.17.

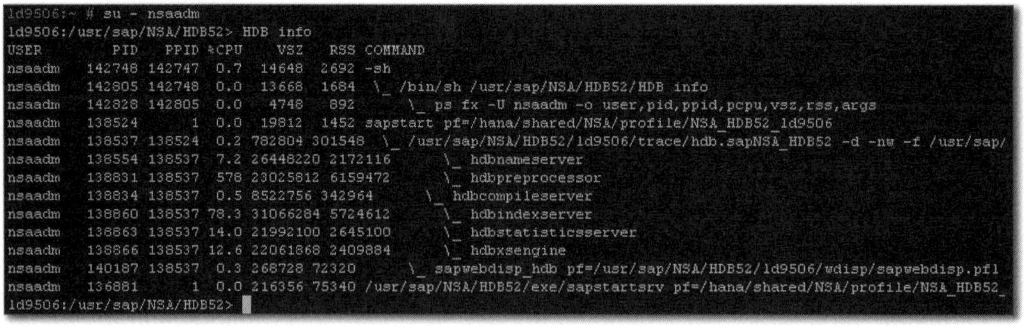
```
ld9506:~ # su - nsaadm
ld9506:/usr/sap/NSA/HDB52> HDB info
USER        PID   PPID %CPU    VSZ   RSS COMMAND
nsaadm   142748 142747  0.7  14648  2692 -sh
nsaadm   142805 142748  0.0  13668  1684  \_ /bin/sh /usr/sap/NSA/HDB52/HDB info
nsaadm   142828 142805  0.0   4748   892      \_ ps fx -U nsaadm -o user,pid,ppid,pcpu,vsz,rss,args
nsaadm   138524      1  0.0  19812  1452 sapstart pf=/hana/shared/NSA/profile/NSA_HDB52_ld9506
nsaadm   138537 138524  0.2 782804 301548  \_ /usr/sap/NSA/HDB52/ld9506/trace/hdb.sapNSA_HDB52 -d -nw -f /usr/sap/
nsaadm   138554 138537  7.2 26448220 2172116      \_ hdbnameserver
nsaadm   138831 138537  578 23025812 6159472      \_ hdbpreprocessor
nsaadm   138834 138537  0.5 8522756 342964      \_ hdbcompileserver
nsaadm   138860 138537 78.3 31066284 5724612      \_ hdbindexserver
nsaadm   138863 138537 14.0 21992100 2645100      \_ hdbstatisticsserver
nsaadm   138866 138537 12.6 22061868 2409884      \_ hdbxsengine
nsaadm   140187 138537  0.3 268728 72320      \_ sapwebdisp_hdb pf=/usr/sap/NSA/HDB52/ld9506/wdisp/sapwebdisp.pfl
nsaadm   136881      1  0.0 216356 75340 /usr/sap/NSA/HDB52/exe/sapstartsrv pf=/hana/shared/NSA/profile/NSA_HDB52_
ld9506:/usr/sap/NSA/HDB52>
```

Figure 3.17 Listing All OS Processes of a Given SAP HANA Instance

3.9   Summary

The most difficult steps of installing or updating an SAP HANA database system are the preparatory ones, that is, setting up the file system correctly, downloading the proper components, and extracting them (or not) appropriately. We spent a great amount of time on these steps, hopefully clarifying all the important preparation steps of OS configuration, software downloads, and so on.

Another obstacle can be choosing the right installation or update tool from the range of SAP's offerings. We discussed the advantages of the individual tools for different purposes so that you can make a well-informed choice. In our experience, the best tool for all circumstances is the `hdblcm` tool, which supports installation and update in batch mode, interactively on the command line, and even with an easy-to-follow wizard in a graphical user interface. Our detailed step-by-step instructions clarify all questions you might have regarding the installation or update process using this tool.

We also gave the most important advice on troubleshooting the installation or update process, pointing out the locations of install logs and introducing useful checks to verify the success of your install or update activities.

Now that you have learned how to install and update SAP HANA database systems, you can start using them—and of course, as database administrator, your first contact will be with the tools for database administration. These are the topic of the following chapter.

SAP offers multiple tools for administrators to use with an SAP HANA database system. The main tool is SAP HANA Studio, which you will get to know in this chapter. We also provide an overview of other administration tools available for SAP HANA.

4   Administration Tools

When asked about their idea of a perfect database administration tool, many administrators tell us that the best tool is one that they never have to use. This, in fact, is a statement about the database system itself, rather than a statement about the administration tools. Quite understandably, administrators do not want to manually administer their database systems regularly—and they may not even be able to do that, depending on the number of database systems they are responsible for. Instead, they need a system that can monitor itself, offers proactive alerting, and can be automated or remotely controlled for any standard administration tasks.

So why do database vendors create and document administration tools at all? The answer, naturally, is "because they are needed." They are needed by small IT departments for whom the cost of automation is higher than the cost of manual administration; they are needed for the treatment of exceptional events, that is, events that occur outside of those repetitive scenarios that are documented in the operating manual for a given system landscape; they are needed for the first few steps on a new database system, before any intended automatisms have been set up; and, last but not least, they are useful for getting to know the database system, because they provide a sort of guided tour of the more important aspects of the software.

SAP provides two main tools to SAP HANA administrators: the standalone tool SAP HANA Studio, which can be installed centrally on the database server and locally on any Windows or Linux PC, and the SAP HANA flavor of SAP NetWeaver's DBA Cockpit program for database administration.

Because it's the most important, we will spend the greater part of this chapter with SAP HANA Studio. In the last section of the chapter, we'll give an overview of the SAP HANA-specific functionality in DBA Cockpit.

4.1   Introduction to SAP HANA Studio

There is often confusion about what *SAP HANA Studio* really is. It is in fact not easy to give a simple answer, because there is a lot of diverse functionality built into the software. We will give you our view.

Primarily, SAP HANA Studio is the standard tool for operating and monitoring an SAP HANA database system. It is a standalone program that is available for Linux and Windows operating systems. In addition to a number of predefined UI elements for various typical administration purposes, SAP HANA Studio also offers an SQL Editor for running arbitrary SQL statements against the database.

Along with administration functionality, the tool also features a data modeling environment. With this modeler, you can create multidimensional data models that contain specific optimizations for the purpose of analytical reporting. SAP HANA Studio also contains an integrated development environment for creating applications based on SAP HANA XS and SAPUI5.

SAP HANA Studio is based on the Eclipse IDE, and thus its look and feel will be familiar to many users. It offers multiple predefined *perspectives* (user-interface layouts) for different user personas, such as a database administrator, developer, or modeler.

Throughout this book, we will almost exclusively deal with the administration aspects of SAP HANA Studio, naturally using the ADMINISTRATION perspective. In this section, we'll introduce you to SAP HANA Studio by walking you through its UI, the process of connecting to an SAP HANA database system, and the basic principles of working with SAP HANA Studio.

4.1.1   Your First Contact with SAP HANA Studio

In order to start SAP HANA Studio on Windows, execute the hdbstudio.exe program; in a standard installation, it resides in *C:\Program Files\SAP\hdbstudio\hdbstudio.exe* (64-bit installation of SAP HANA studio) or *C:\Program Files (x86)\SAP*

hdbstudio\hdbstudio.exe (32-bit version). The Studio installer will also create entries in the Windows start menu in the SAP HANA folder. When you start SAP HANA Studio for the first time, you will be greeted with a WELCOME screen from which you can choose the initial operating mode for your Studio installation, as shown in Figure 4.1. From the earlier discussion, you will probably have guessed that this screen in fact lets you choose the perspective to work with.

As a database administrator, you will probably choose OPEN ADMINISTRATION CONSOLE here. When using SAP HANA Studio, you can change the perspective at any point in time without even having to restart the program. You can therefore easily change between different types of system usage if needed.

Before we proceed to more details of SAP HANA Studio, let's mention that SAP has invested significantly in enriching the integrated help system of SAP HANA Studio. You can, for example, access integrated copies of parts of the SAP HANA product documentation by selecting SAP HANA HELP CONTENT (which will open a new window). Among other items, you can find there the *SAP HANA Administration Guide*.

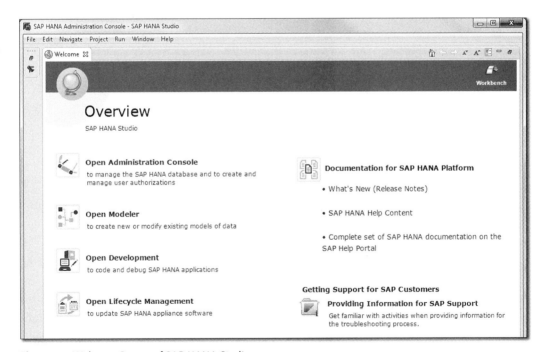

Figure 4.1 Welcome Screen of SAP HANA Studio

Assuming you have chosen to enter the ADMINISTRATION CONSOLE, SAP HANA Studio will present itself with an initial view of the ADMINISTRATION perspective, as shown in Figure 4.2.

It is not connected to a database system yet, but SAP HANA Studio nicely shows the overall UI elements in the default layout of the ADMINISTRATION perspective: On the left-hand side there is the SYSTEMS view, as shown in ❶. Once you connect your Studio to a database system, this view will display a navigator through which you can access objects of your database system.

The largest screen area, shown in ❷, is reserved for "editors." Most of your work with SAP HANA Studio will happen in such editors, for example, a Table Editor or the Administration Editor—a complex user interface summarizing most aspects of the database system for administrators. We will touch on those editors later.

Figure 4.2 Initial View of the Administration Perspective

Underneath the editor area, there is space for other views (see ❸), such as the PROPERTIES view, which displays detailed properties of objects selected in the SYSTEMS view or the active editor in a context-sensitive way. Every time you change the selected object in the SYSTEMS view, and every time you switch to another editor, the content of the PROPERTIES view will be adjusted. In the top-right corner, there is the perspective switcher, as shown in ❹, the fastest way to change between the different perspectives of SAP HANA Studio.

The major screen areas of SAP HANA Studio can be tabbed, similar to the tabbed user interfaces of modern web browsers. You can, for example, have multiple editors open at the same point in time, or there may be multiple additional views opened in the area for other views (see ❸), such as the ERROR LOG in addition to the PROPERTIES view. This error log contains error messages of the Eclipse framework, which, in our experience, are of no relevance to the end user. We therefore always close the ERROR LOG and never look at it again.

> **Usage Hint**
>
> We will share many useful details with you about working with SAP HANA Studio in the course of this chapter. The first and most important of these is that in SAP HANA Studio the context menu is highly important; you will frequently make use of the right mouse button.

4.1.2 Connecting to SAP HANA Database Systems

The most beautiful administration tool is worth nothing without a backend system to administer, so the first thing to do is to connect our SAP HANA Studio instance to our new database system. We'll explain the process for this next.

Creating a New Connection

The first step is shown in Figure 4.3. Right-click in the background area, shown in ❶, of the SYSTEMS view and choose ADD SYSTEM... from the context menu.

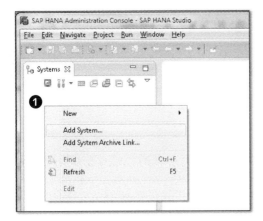

Figure 4.3 Connecting to a Database System in SAP HANA Studio

On the first screen of the wizard that now opens (Figure 4.4), we have to enter the essential details of the system we want to connect to. Any SAP HANA instance is uniquely identified by the hostname of the SAP HANA server and the SAP System ID or the instance number. Because the instance number determines the port of the SQL interface, connection details are always based on HOST NAME and INSTANCE NUMBER.

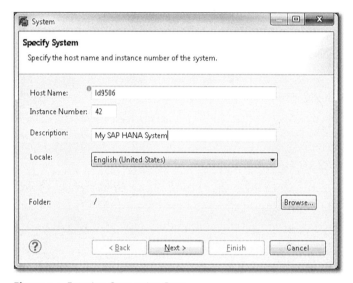

Figure 4.4 Entering Connection Data

The HOST NAME usually does not need to be entered in its fully qualified form— as long as it can be resolved correctly. In a scale-out system, it is sufficient to enter one of the host names. A good choice is the first host of the cluster, which usually runs the active master name server and the master index server. SAP HANA Studio will automatically collect information about all other hosts in the cluster and will distribute queries. For the DESCRIPTION, you may choose any short term that suits you.

> **Locale**
>
> The LOCALE is only relevant for data modeling. Formatting of numbers or dates in the administration screens of SAP HANA Studio is based on the locale of the operating system user who started the program. This is why—because we the authors are German— our screenshots show German-style formatting of numbers, dates, and so on. Most importantly, the decimal separator in German formatting is a comma, and the dot is used for separating orders of magnitudes.

On the second screen of the wizard (Figure 4.5), you must enter the credentials for the database user you want to use in the connection. This user must already exist in the database.

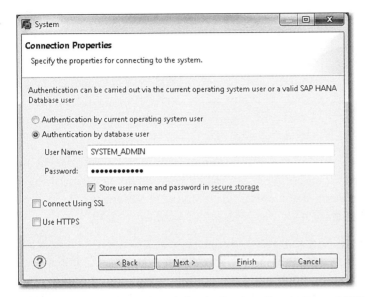

Figure 4.5 Entering the Credentials for the Database User to Connect With

If this is the first connection to a freshly installed SAP HANA database system, the only available user will be SYSTEM. Because we try to convince customers not to work with the SYSTEM user, we have already prepared our system with a number of dedicated user accounts. For regular administration purposes, we defined a database user named "SYSTEM_ADMIN" with appropriate privileges, and we use that one in the following parts.

SAP HANA Studio supports authentication by database user name/password or by the current operating system user (Kerberos authentication). Depending on your setup, choose the appropriate option.

If you are using name/password authentication, we recommend selecting the checkbox STORE USER NAME AND PASSWORD IN SECURE STORAGE—at least if you are the only person that has access to the operating system account you use for running SAP HANA Studio. This option will place your credentials into the secure credential store of the Eclipse framework so that SAP HANA Studio can authenticate you automatically in the future.

SAP HANA Studio usually communicates with the database through its SQL interface. If SSL encryption of SQL connections is enabled, you should make use of encryption also in your connections with SAP HANA Studio by selecting the checkbox CONNECT USING SSL. (For necessary preparations on the server and client sides, refer to the *SAP HANA Administration Guide*; you can find this by searching at *https://help.sap.com/hana_platform*.)

In some situations, such as during restore of a database backup, the communication will happen through the interface of the SAP Start Service and uses the HTTP (port 5<xx>13) or HTTPS (port 5<xx>14) interface (<xx> is the instance number of your SAP HANA database). To encrypt communication with the SAP Start Service, select the checkbox USE HTTPS.

Because the third screen of the wizard does not contain content that is needed in typical use, we can skip it and immediately click FINISH. If valid credentials have been entered, the system connection will be added to the SYSTEMS view (Figure 4.6), and you can start working with the SAP HANA database.

If your database user account still uses its initial password, you will now be asked for a new password. In a pop-up window, you will be asked for the initial password as well as a new one. Should your chosen new password not comply with the password policy of the database system, you will be informed about the rules that you have violated.

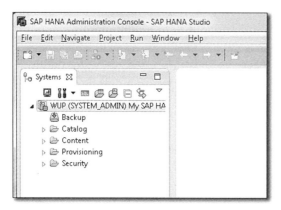

Figure 4.6 System Connection Added to SAP HANA Studio

Adding Connections to Further SAP HANA Systems

If you have multiple SAP HANA database systems to manage, you can add connections to all of these systems within the same instance of SAP HANA Studio. Simply repeat the procedure for adding the first connection, and enter the connection details of the additional database.

Adding Connections for Multiple Database Users of One SAP HANA System

If you have multiple database users on the SAP HANA system and want to be able to work with those users, you do not need to re-enter all connection details. Instead, as shown in Figure 4.7, you can right-click the top node, shown in ❶, of the system entry of an existing database connection in the SYSTEMS view and choose ADD ADDITIONAL USER... from the context menu. This will open a wizard in which you only need to enter the credentials of the additional database user you want to connect with.

> **Note**
>
> In SPS 8, the context menu entry has been changed to ADD SYSTEM WITH DIFFERENT USER...; see the right-hand side, shown in ❷, of Figure 4.7. The functionality remains unchanged.

Context Menu in SPS 7   Context Menu in SPS 8

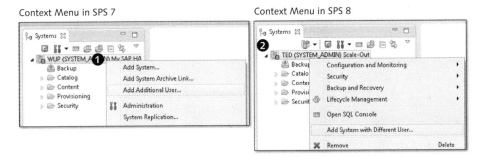

Figure 4.7 Adding Additional Users for an Existing Database Connection

4.1.3 Principles of Working with SAP HANA Studio

SAP HANA Studio allows you to perform actions on entities of the database system. These entities might be database tables or schemas, development objects in the SAP HANA repository, database users or roles, or even the database itself. You can navigate to these entities in the navigator tree of the SYSTEMS view, and then execute an action for the selected entity.

Many of these actions will open an editor. An editor is always specific to an entity (object, user, or the system itself), the database system to which this entity belongs, and the database user who executed the action.

Even though SAP HANA Studio offers a graphical user interface that is easy to learn and use in general, we will next point out several useful working principles that will help you make the most efficient use of the software.

Handling Multiple Database Connections

We have already hinted at one important aspect of working with this software: You can have multiple database connections (combinations of database instance and database user) registered in your Studio, as was shown in Section 4.1.2. You must therefore pay attention, choose the entity from the correct system, and perform the action with the correct user. It is advisable to only expand the navigator tree of one system/user combination at a time and to close editors that are no longer needed.

To provide additional assistance when working with production systems, SAP HANA offers the option to define the system usage type as of SPS 8. For systems with usage type production, SAP HANA Studio will display a visual indication and additional confirmation requests. The system usage type is defined by the database parameter global.ini • [system_information] • usage. Set this to production for production-like systems.

Actions in the Systems View

At the top of the SYSTEMS view you can find a toolbar with several buttons that allow you to immediately start selected important actions. These actions will either be effected on all SAP HANA systems registered in your Studio or on the currently selected system. In Figure 4.8, we have selected the entry for system TED with user SYSTEM_ADMIN; this means that system-specific actions would be executed on system TED, as long as user SYSTEM_ADMIN has the required privileges.

The SYSTEM MONITOR button, shown in ❶, will open an editor containing a condensed view of the most important KPIs for all registered SAP HANA systems. The ADMINISTRATION button, shown in ❷, opens the ADMINISTRATION EDITOR for the currently selected database system. To open an SQL EDITOR for the currently selected system, use the SQL CONSOLE button, shown in ❸, and search for database tables on the selected systems with the FIND TABLE button, shown in ❹. Finally, there are three buttons that can assist you with handling the navigator trees if you have a very large number of systems registered in your Studio: The FIND SYSTEM button, shown in ❺, allows you to search for systems by SID, user name, or folder name (not by description, though); you can COLLAPSE ALL navigator trees in the SYSTEMS view with the corresponding button, shown in ❻; and if you are currently working with an editor for a given entity (e.g., a database table) on a given system, with a given database user, you can immediately find that entity in the corresponding navigator tree by clicking the LINK WITH EDITOR button, shown in ❼.

In SPS 8, the FIND TABLE button has been removed from the toolbar, and the new ADD SYSTEM button, shown in ❽, has been introduced.

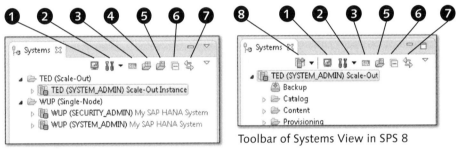

Toolbar of Systems View in SPS 7

Toolbar of Systems View in SPS 8

Figure 4.8 Actions Directly Available in the Systems View

Usage Hint

The system-specific actions, such as opening the SQL EDITOR or finding tables, are also available from the context menu when clicking on the top node of the navigator tree for a given connection entry.

Elements of the System Navigator Tree

The system navigator tree is the most important element for your work in SAP HANA Studio. It has up to five main subtrees, depending on the privileges of the active database user. In Figure 4.9, we show the navigator tree for two different users on two different systems: The SYSTEM_ADMIN on system TED, shown in

❶, has permissions related to database backups, whereas the SECURITY_ADMIN on system WUP, shown in ❷, does not.

On the TED system, shown in ❶, we have expanded all main subtrees. These subtrees have the following purpose:

❸ BACKUP

The BACKUP node provides access to the user interface for manually executing, restoring, and managing database backups.

❹ CATALOG

The CATALOG is a representation of all database objects, such as tables, views, procedures, or sequences (users or roles are not database objects in the catalog). All such objects always belong to a database schema, and the CATALOG folder provides access to schemas and catalog objects.

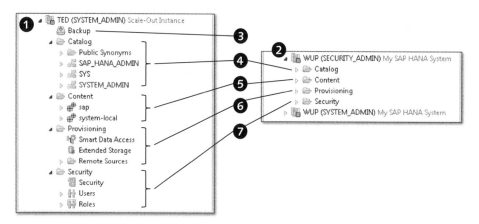

Figure 4.9 Elements of the System Navigator Tree

❺ CONTENT

SAP HANA contains a development environment. If you use this environment, the design-time versions of development objects will be stored in the so-called repository. The repository is structured using a package hierarchy. In SAP HANA Studio, the CONTENT folder gives access to the package hierarchy and the design-time objects therein.

Through activation of repository objects, a runtime version can be created. Depending on the object type, these runtime versions are accessible via the CATALOG or SECURITY folders.

❻ PROVISIONING

Several data provisioning technologies have been developed for or integrated into SAP HANA, such as Smart Data Access for direct access to tables on remote systems or SLT for real-time data replication. Such scenarios can be customized and controlled from the PROVISIONING folder.

❼ SECURITY

Database users and catalog roles can be managed from within the SECURITY folder. Within that folder, you can also find an additional item named SECURITY that provides access to security-related functionality, such as audit logging, password policy, or disk encryption.

Roles

SAP HANA offers two different concepts for creating and managing roles, referred to as *catalog roles* and *repository roles*. Only catalog roles can be created and edited from within the SECURITY folder of the navigator tree. See Chapter 13 for more details.

Usage Hint

Sometimes, folders in the navigator tree contain a larger number of objects. In this case, it can be very useful to filter the objects in that folder. Simply right-click on the folder and select FILTER from the context menu in order to enter a filter pattern.

4.2   Database Administration with SAP HANA Studio

In this section, we will summarize general administration tasks that you can accomplish using SAP HANA Studio. These tasks include changing the database configuration and starting or stopping the entire database system or individual server processes. Certain specialized administration tasks related to backup, user, or security administration are covered in dedicated chapters.

4.2.1 Managing the Database Configuration

The database configuration of the SAP HANA database is maintained in multiple configuration files—similar to other database systems. Each component of the database—the index server, name server, and so on—has its own configuration file. These configuration files are text files with a pleasantly simple syntax.

Within each configuration file, parameters are grouped into sections. The section names are enclosed in brackets—for example, [memorymanagement]—and parameters are always specified in the format <name>=<value>.

For each parameter, there can at any point in time be up to two or three different settings. On the file system of the database server, these three layers of parameter settings are located in three different sets of configuration files:

- **Default value**
  The default value as defined by SAP. It is valid unless a customer-chosen value is defined.

  The default values are maintained in configuration files that in a standard installation are located in the file system path */hana/shared/<SID>/exe/linuxx86_64/HDB_<version>/config/*.

- **System-wide customizing**
  A customer-defined value that is valid on all hosts of the database system. If for a given parameter a system-wide customer-chosen value is defined, this overrides the default value.

  System-wide deviations from the default values can be found in the file system path */hana/shared/<SID>/global/hdb/custom/config*.

- **Host-specific customizing**
  A customer-defined value that is only valid for a given host. Host-specific values usually exist for the list of database processes on the different hosts, because some processes will only be running on a subset of hosts. Host-specific values can also make sense if you are operating an inhomogeneous scale-out system in which not all hosts have exactly the same hardware setup. A host-specific customizing overrides system-wide or default values.

  Host-specific customizing is not possible for all parameters. In fact, for most configuration files, host-specific customizing is not available.

  On the file system, you can find host-specific parameter settings in the directory */hana/shared/<SID>/HDB<instance>/<hostname>*.

> **Warning**
>
> Under no circumstances should you edit the configuration files containing default values. There is never any reason for such modifications.
>
> In regular operation, there is never any reason to modify the other configuration files directly on the file system. Instead, you should always use the comfortable Configuration Editor in SAP HANA Studio or the provided SQL syntax, or—if available—the Configuration Editor in DBA Cockpit for SAP HANA (see Section 4.4).
>
> Modifying the configuration files on the file system can be necessary if the database software is not running and can no longer be started for reasons that may be related to a misconfiguration. This is the only exception to the previously mentioned rule.
>
> The database provides audit logging functionality, which can also log changes to the database configuration. If you modify the settings directly on the file systems, the database system's audit-logging mechanism will not capture these changes.

SAP HANA Studio offers an easy-to-use interface for displaying and changing the database configuration. We will now show you how to optimally work with this interface.

Displaying the Database Configuration in SAP HANA Studio

In order to manage the database configuration with SAP HANA Studio, log on with an administrator user and open the Administration Editor of the database system. In that editor, navigate to the CONFIGURATION tab.

> **Privilege Information**
>
> In order to change database parameters using the Configuration Editor, your database user must have the system privileges CATALOG READ and INIFILE ADMIN.

This tab displays the database configuration in a hierarchy on configuration file, section, and parameter. Initially, all of the configuration files are collapsed. For the example shown in Figure 4.10, we have expanded the global.ini configuration file, shown in ❶, and, within that file, the sections MEMORYMANAGER, shown in ❷, and PERSISTENCE, shown in ❸.

Gray diamonds, shown in ❹, indicate in which configuration files there are parameters that deviate from the default values on the system or host level. If customizing exists for a given parameter, a green circle, shown in ❺, indicates what value is active system wide or on a given host. In Figure 4.10, we show that the system-wide customizing setting is active for parameter `global.ini` • `[persistence]` • `basepath_datavolumes`.

If host-specific values are not available for a given file, section, or parameter, this is indicated by the DISABLED icon, shown in ❻.

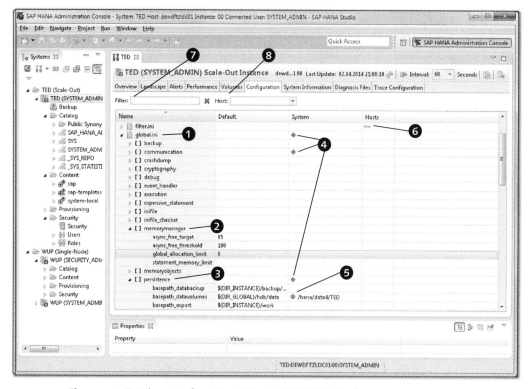

Figure 4.10 Database Configuration Editor in SAP HANA Studio

When you need to view or change the value of a specific parameter, the fastest way to find the parameter is often to simply search for the parameter name in the FILTER box, shown in ❼. The system starts searching as you type, and the search finds pattern matches in the names of configuration files, sections, and parameters.

In scale-out systems, the default setup of the Configuration Editor does not show individual hosts—which administrators of large scale-out systems will appreciate. If you need to show host-specific values, you can select the hosts to show from the HOSTS dropdown box, shown in ❽.

Changing Database Settings in the Configuration Editor

In order to change a parameter value, double-click on the parameter (you can click anywhere within the row of the parameter) to open an input box in which you can specify new system-wide and host-specific values (Figure 4.11).

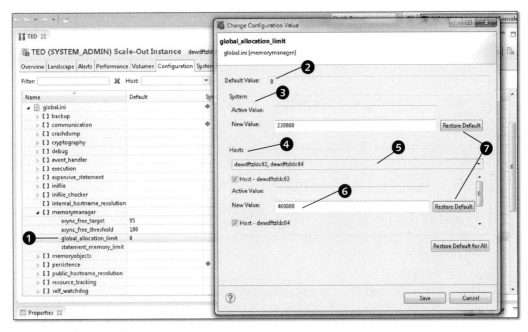

Figure 4.11 Changing a Parameter

In our example, we are changing the parameter global.ini • [memorymanager] • global_allocation_limit, shown in ❶. The input box displays the DEFAULT VALUE, shown in ❷, on top of a box for the SYSTEM-wide settings, shown in ❸, where you can enter a NEW VALUE that will be valid for all hosts of the database system.

In the HOSTS box, shown in ❹, a dropdown box, shown in ❺, allows you to select the hosts for which you want to define host-specific settings. These hosts will be displayed in the area below, giving you the opportunity to enter a NEW VALUE, shown in ❻, for each selected host. The input window does not provide any parameter documentation, be it a definition of the parameter, unit, or measurement, or other interesting properties.

You can always switch back to the default value by clicking the RESTORE DEFAULT button, shown in ❼.

> **When Do Parameter Changes Take Effect?**
>
> Most parameter changes take effect immediately without requiring a restart of the entire database or the affected database process. The `global_allocation_limit` parameter from Figure 4.11 is one of the exceptions.
>
> Unfortunately, there is no consistent documentation of database parameters yet. Some parameters are documented in different parts of the SAP HANA product documentation, and others are mentioned in SAP Notes. In most cases, the necessity of a full or partial system restart is mentioned.

4.2.2 Starting and Stopping the Database

Under normal circumstances, you will not need to start, stop, or restart the database processes explicitly. Parameter changes that require a system restart or certain updates or configuration changes to the operating system are among the rare reasons to shut down the database system.

> **Privilege Information**
>
> You can only stop, start, or restart the entire database system if you have the credentials of the operating system administrator <sid>adm. There are no specific *database* privileges required.
>
> For those actions, the communication between SAP HANA Studio and the database server does not use the SQL interface of the database but the HTTP(s) interface of the SAP Start Service.

If you do need to stop or restart the system, though, there are a few things you should know. This section describes them.

Stopping or Restarting the Database System

There is one golden procedure for stopping or restarting the entire database system; this procedure uses SAP HANA Studio to restart the database processes and monitor the activity in the course of the restart.

To stop or restart the database system, right-click on the system entry in the SYSTEMS view of SAP HANA Studio, and choose the intended action from the context menu.

The system will now ask you for the credentials of the <sid>adm user on the operating system of the database server (unless these credentials are stored in the Eclipse Secure Store).

For stop and restart, a wizard appears (Figure 4.12), which allows you to choose the mechanism of shutting down the system (SHUTDOWN TYPE):

❶ SOFT

Soft shutdown allows the database to wait for open transactions to finish. The system will shut down as soon as all ongoing transactions are closed, but it will wait at most until the shutdown DATE and TIME, shown in ❷, are reached. The proposed value for this maximum wait time is 10 minutes.

The soft shutdown also allows the database system to perform a savepoint operation before stopping the database processes. This will lead to a faster restart of the system (see Chapter 5).

This is the preferred and recommended method of shutdown.

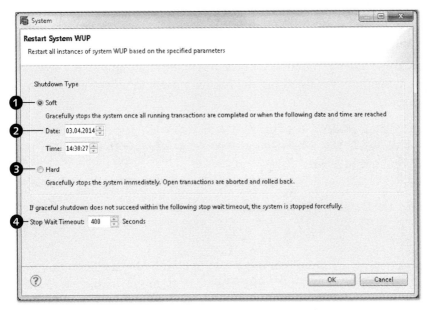

Figure 4.12 Options for Restarting or Stopping the Entire Database

❸ HARD

A hard shutdown instructs the database processes to start the shutdown sequence immediately. It does not kill the database processes, but it still represents a graceful shutdown in which the system processes can terminate in a controlled fashion.

Compared to the soft shutdown, the database does not wait for open transactions to finish, cancelling them instead. The system also does not trigger a savepoint. The shutdown process itself is therefore faster than with a soft shutdown. The next database start, on the other hand, will in general take longer because of the necessary transaction rollback and the greater volume of redo logs that must be applied.

It may happen in exceptional situations that the graceful shutdown of some database process has no effect, because the process will not react to any reasonable means of interacting with it. In these cases, you will need to apply more force, and the database system will—if needed—also kill unresponsive processes. This forceful stop will happen if a process has not terminated within a given time interval after the attempt to gracefully stop it. You can configure this STOP WAIT TIMEOUT, shown in ❹, on the stop/restart dialog.

Starting the Database System

If a database is presently shut down, you can also start it up from SAP HANA Studio: Choose the START... action from the context menu of the system entry in the SYSTEMS view.

After entering the credentials of the <sid>adm Linux user, you can enter a START WAIT TIMEOUT value. This value determines the time after which the SAP Start Service will consider the system start to have failed.

Monitoring the Database during Start, Stop, or Restart

Once you have selected the START..., STOP..., or RESTART... action, SAP HANA Studio will open an Administration Editor for the database system in diagnosis mode. You can manually open this editor (Figure 4.13) by selecting the OPEN DIAGNOSIS MODE action from the dropdown menu, shown in ❶, of the ADMINISTRATION button on the toolbar of the SYSTEMS view.

The diagnosis mode offers two functionalities: status monitoring of the database processes on a high level (see Figure 4.14) and access to the diagnosis files of the database.

The process monitoring in diagnosis mode is limited to the process status. There is one entry in the table for each process of each node of the database instance. The colored icons as well as the entries in column STATUS indicate the status of the given process, such as RUNNING, STOPPING, STOPPED, SCHEDULED, or INITIALIZING.

Figure 4.13 Manually Opening the Diagnosis Mode

Active	Host	Process	Description	Process ID	Status	Start Time	Elapsed Time
⬚	ld9506	hdbcompileserver	HDB Compileserver	152332	Running	26.03.2014 22:24:01	183:05:18
△	ld9506	hdbdaemon	HDB Daemon	152158	Stopping	26.03.2014 22:23:55	183:05:24
△	ld9506	hdbindexserver	HDB Indexserver	152357	Stopping	26.03.2014 22:24:02	183:05:17
⬚	ld9506	hdbnameserver	HDB Nameserver	152174	Running	26.03.2014 22:23:56	183:05:23
⬚	ld9506	hdbpreprocessor	HDB Preprocessor	152328	Running	26.03.2014 22:24:01	183:05:18
△	ld9506	hdbxsengine	HDB XSEngine		Scheduled		
△	ld9506	sapwebdisp_hdb	SAP WebDispatcher		Scheduled		

System: WUP
Host: ld9506 STEM_ADMIN) My SAP HANA System   ld9506 42   Last Update:
Instance: 42
Version: 1.00.72.00.388670 (NewDB100_REL)

Processes | Diagnosis Files

Host: <All>

Figure 4.14 System Editor in Diagnosis Mode

If you need more information regarding what happened during the start or stop process—for example, for troubleshooting if the system does not start up—then the following diagnosis files are most important (for a problem with processes of the SAP HANA system with instance number <instance> on host <hostname>):

▸ **The daemon trace file**
The daemon process orchestrates the startup of all further database processes. You can see log entries regarding these actions in the file *daemon_<hostname>.3<instance>00.<max>.trc* (we use <max> to denote the maximum value of the three-digit trace file rotation indicator for the given file).

▸ **The nameserver trace file**
During system startup, the name server process performs several consistency checks of the system topology and other plausibility tests. This is why you can often find information regarding start-up problems in the name server trace file *nameserver_<hostname>.3<instance>01.<max>.trc*.

▶ **The indexserver trace file**
Because the index server is basically "the database," the highest probability for issues lies with this process. In case of trouble, check its trace file, *indexserver_ <hostname>.3<instance>03.<max>.trc.*

4.2.3 Starting and Stopping Individual Database Processes

There may be situations in which you have to restart individual database processes (usually referred to as services in the SAP HANA documentation and in SAP HANA Studio), for example, in order for a parameter change to take effect. In order to restart a single process, you have to stop or kill it. The daemon process will immediately realize that the process is not running anymore and restart it. Under normal circumstances, you should never kill processes. This should only be necessary if the process is not responding to any interaction.

You can restart processes in the Administration Editor of SAP HANA Studio. In the editor, go to the tab LANDSCAPE, and stay on the first tab, SERVICES. Right-click on the process you want to restart, and choose the STOP... or KILL... action from the context menu.

Privilege Information

You need system privilege SERVICE ADMIN to stop, kill, or restart a service. In addition, you need system privilege CATALOG READ in order to open the Administration Editor.

In the same context menu, you can also choose to start all missing services of the database instance—which may be needed if some services did not start up properly during a start of the database.

Finally, you can reconfigure the service, which will apply all current parameter settings that do not require a restart. If you follow our recommendations from Section 4.2.1 about managing the database configuration, you will not need this action.

4.3 Monitoring the Database with SAP HANA Studio

SAP HANA offers a wealth of monitoring information in dedicated system views. Most of these system views are exposed as public synonyms and available through the SQL interface to all users of the database.

The most important monitoring aspects are summarized in user-friendly elements of the Administration Editor in SAP HANA Studio. The database system also contains a component for proactive alerting in the form of the statistics service.

In this section, we will show you how to gain a first-glance overview of the SAP HANA database systems that the SAP HANA Studio is connected to. We will cover monitoring views as windows to the runtime internals of the system and the statistics service as the bookkeeper of important SAP HANA system operations figures as well as the alerting functionality based on it. Finally, a brief overlook of recent additions to the monitoring tool set is provided.

4.3.1 Getting an Overview of the Database System

SAP delivers two system overview screens with SAP HANA Studio. The System Monitor can be opened using the first button in the toolbar of the Systems view (see Figure 4.8). It provides a brief overview of the most important aspects of all SAP HANA databases connected from your SAP HANA Studio.

Privilege Information

If you have multiple connections configured for one SAP HANA system, the system monitor will simply pick the first of these connections alphabetically by user name to retrieve the relevant system data. That user will need at least system privilege CATALOG READ and object privilege SELECT on the _SYS_STATISTICS schema in order to display all information correctly.

The System Monitor is presented in a tabular view (Figure 4.15), with one line per SAP HANA system. The entry for a scale-out instance, shown in ❶, can be expanded to yield one line per host; entries for single-node instances, shown in ❷, cannot be expanded.

In the monitor, you can easily determine the overall state of multiple SAP HANA systems at once. The indicator in the Operational State column will only be green if all processes of the corresponding instance are alive. You also find disk and memory usage information here as well as current CPU usage.

By double-clicking on the entry of a given database system, you can navigate forward to the more detailed overview screen of the Administration Editor of the system. An exception is the Alerts column; double-clicking a cell of that column will open the alerting information of the corresponding system.

The SYSTEM MONITOR refreshes its display automatically. You can configure this mechanism through the PROPERTIES button, shown in ❸.

Many tabular monitoring views have more information to offer than in their initial configuration. In these cases, there is a CONFIGURE VIEWER button, shown in ❹, which gives access to a configuration screen from which you can add or remove fields.

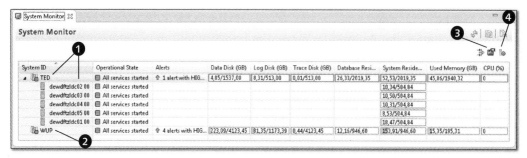

Figure 4.15 System Monitor for All Connected SAP HANA Systems

A more detailed system summary (Figure 4.16) can be obtained from the OVERVIEW tab, shown in ❶, of the Administration Editor. This is the initial tab that opens when you start the Administration Editor for a given SAP HANA database system.

Privilege Information

In order to open the Administration Editor, you need system privilege CATALOG READ.

This overview screen—like many other monitoring screens—can be refreshed either manually via the REFRESH CURRENT PAGE button, shown in ❷, or you can define an automatic refresh by using the START AUTOMATIC REFRESH button and UPDATE INTERVAL input field, shown in ❸.

The OVERVIEW screen offers forward navigation to many different detail views by clicking on any of the underlined texts, as shown in ❹. It is divided into several sections, as follows:

❺ GENERAL INFORMATION
   Here you can find important overview information, such as the software version of database and operating system, the system size (Single-node or scale-out?

Number of nodes?), and more. The forward navigation for the VERSIONS entry gives an overview of the database version history (date and version for each software update).

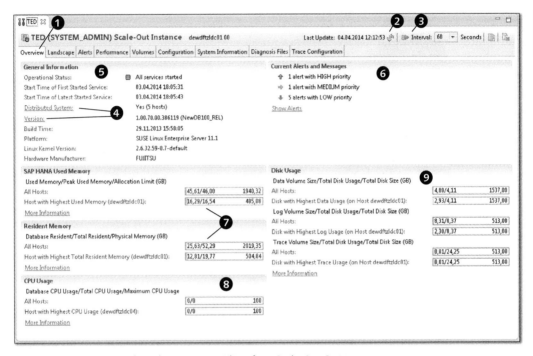

Figure 4.16 Overview in the Administration Editor for a Scale-Out System

6 CURRENT ALERTS AND MESSAGES
This area simply gives the number of active alerts of the three categories—high, medium, and low—with forward navigation to the alert details.

7 SAP HANA USED MEMORY and RESIDENT MEMORY
In SAP HANA USED MEMORY, the system displays the amount of RAM used by the database processes at the moment and the peak usage since the last database restart in relation to the maximum available memory for all processes of the instance combined, represented by the ALLOCATION LIMIT (parameter global_allocation_limit).

In RESIDENT MEMORY, on the other hand, the system displays the amount of resident memory on the OS for the database processes and for all processes that are active on the OS.

> **Further Resources**
>
> For a complete explanation of memory usage in SAP HANA, please refer to *www.saphana.com/docs/DOC-2299* ("SAP HANA Memory Usage Explained").

❽ CPU USAGE

The CPU usage is given for the database processes and for all processes on the OS as a percentage of the total available CPUs. You can find out the number of physical CPU cores of the database from the tooltip that appears when you hover with the mouse over the CPU USAGE indicator.

❾ DISK USAGE

DISK USAGE is also split into usage by the database processes and by all processes on the OS for the data, log, and trace file systems separately. In most cases, the trace file system will be the same as that for the system installation (*/hana/shared/<SID>*). These are the three file systems into which the database adds data, so the file system usage must be monitored the most closely.

For a scale-out system (like the one displayed in Figure 4.16), the usage indicators display the consumption of the given resource for the entire database system as well as for the host that has the highest usage of the resource.

4.3.2 Monitoring Views in the Administration Editor

The Administration Editor offers a multitude of further monitoring views. At this point, we will not explain any of these views in particular, as the different monitoring views are covered at length in the following chapters.

A typical monitoring view looks like the one in Figure 4.17. In this case, we display the THREADS view, shown in ❷, of the PERFORMANCE tab, shown in ❶, of the Administration Editor for our system TED. You will find elements that we mentioned before, such as the CONFIGURE VIEWER button or the refresh buttons, shown in ❸. On top of the view, there is often an expandable SUMMARY pane, shown in ❹, followed by a tabular view of the monitoring information.

Most monitoring views offer filtering capabilities and other customizing options that differ from view to view depending on what is most appropriate for the information being displayed. In most cases, you can export the current content of the view to a CSV, HTML, or XML file.

Figure 4.17 Typical Monitoring View in SAP HANA Studio

Dedicated user interfaces exist for the most important monitoring views offered by the database system but not for all of them. A further group of important views is exposed with a simple table viewer in the SYSTEM INFORMATION tab, shown in ❻, of the Administration Editor. The set of views on this tab can be extended by uploading further SQL queries, as shown, for example, in SAP Note 1969700.

4.3.3 The Statistics Service

The statistics service is SAP HANA's offering for automated checks and proactive alerting. It manages a set of monitoring tables and the data collection into these tables, and it keeps the definition of a number of checks that it invokes using its built-in scheduler. These checks cover a wide range of database aspects, from monitoring the fill level of the disks through critical CPU and RAM usage to license expiration or missing backup configuration. SAP is also open to introducing new checks and has done so on several occasions in the past—for example, based on incident reports from customers.

Next, we cover the most important actions in the ALERTS tab.

Displaying Alert Information

You can manage and monitor the statistics service from within SAP HANA Studio by opening the Administration Editor for a given SAP HANA instance and changing to the ALERTS tab (Figure 4.18). On that tab, you will find an alert SUMMARY, as shown in ❶, which shows the current alerts by priority and check (multiple alerts of the same check will lead to just one entry here).

Privilege Information

In order to view the alerts of the statistics service, you need the SELECT privilege on schema _SYS_STATISTICS. To also customize the service, you need system privilege INIFILE ADMIN as well.

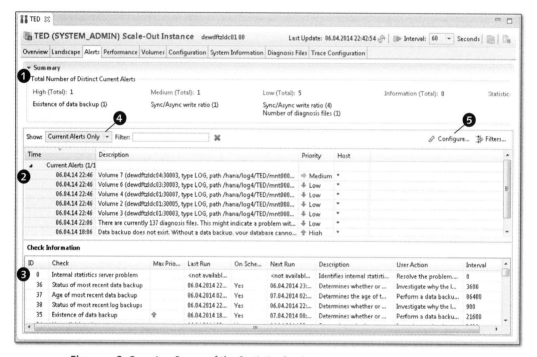

Figure 4.18 Overview Screen of the Statistics Service

Below that summary, there is a detailed table, shown in ❷, that displays all current alerts individually. If you want to also see historic alerts, you can enable this from the SHOW dropdown box, shown in ❹. At the bottom, the system displays CHECK INFORMATION, as shown in ❸, on all alert checks that are defined in the database software. This display includes a description of the check and recommended user actions (which, owing to the required brevity, may not always be helpful). You can also find out whether a given check is scheduled and what the scheduled check interval is. In the column MAX PRIORITY, you can see whether there has ever been an alert for the given check and what the maximum priority of that alert was.

Finally, you can open a wizard to configure the statistics service by clicking the CONFIGURE... button, shown in ❺.

Customizing the Statistics Service

This configuration wizard has three tabs (Figure 4.19). On the first tab, shown in ❶, you can customize e-mail alerting by providing information such as an SMTP server and so on.

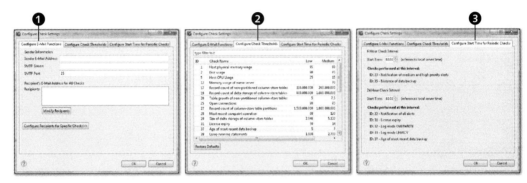

Figure 4.19 Customizing the Statistics Service

On the tab CONFIGURE CHECK THRESHOLDS, shown in ❷, you can customize threshold values for individual checks if the check is based on threshold values.

> **Usage Hint**
>
> In the list of checks, you can hover over the CHECK NAME fields to see a more detailed check description, and you can hover over the fields in columns LOW, MEDIUM, and HIGH to see information on the unit of measurement and default values for the given check threshold.

Some of the checks monitor slowly changing variables (such as the age of the last data backup, which is measured in days). These checks are scheduled in intervals of 6 or 24 hours. On the tab CONFIGURE START TIME FOR PERIODIC CHECKS, shown in ❸, you can customize the start time of these checks in order to move them into appropriate time windows if necessary. In the default configuration, the checks are executed at 2 a.m. system time (and repeated every 6 or 24 hours).

4.3.4 Other System Monitors

Starting with SPS 7, SAP HANA Studio comes with a number of new system-monitoring dashboards that are based on small SAPUI5 components delivered as part of the database's preinstalled content. As of July 2014, there are three distinct dashboards available:

▶ MEMORY OVERVIEW
You can open this dashboard by right-clicking on a connection entry in the SYSTEMS view and choosing MEMORY OVERVIEW from the context menu.

The dashboard offers a highly useful summary of the memory consumption of the database system (see Figure 4.20), including the number of tables, total size of all tables, and so on. In a scale-out system, the overview is shown per host, and you can switch between the hosts within the dashboard.

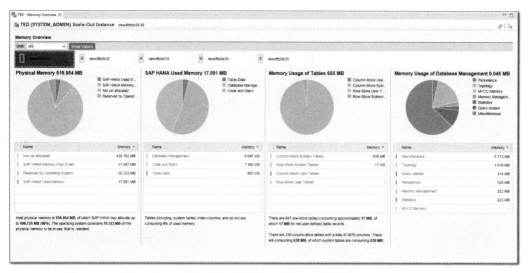

Figure 4.20 The Memory Overview Dashboard for a Scale-Out System

▶ RESOURCE UTILIZATION
You can open this dashboard by right-clicking on a connection entry in the SYSTEMS view and choosing RESOURCE UTILIZATION from the context menu. You can

choose the host (in scale-out systems) and one or several KPIs to display from the KPI groups CPU, MEMORY, and DISK. To select multiple KPIs from one group, hold down the $\boxed{\text{Ctrl}}$ key while selecting.

▶ MEMORY ALLOCATION STATISTICS
The MEMORY ALLOCATION STATISTICS dashboard can only be opened for specific database processes, such as the index server process on a given host. To access the dashboard, open the Administration Editor, go to the LANDSCAPE tab and the subtab SERVICES, and right-click on the service you want to display. Then, choose MEMORY ALLOCATION STATISTICS from the context menu.

The dashboard breaks down the memory usage of the selected database process into components such as row tables, column tables, code segment, and so on.

The information displayed in these dashboards is based on data collected by the statistics service, that is, on tables and views in schema _SYS_STATISTICS.

Privilege Information

The usage of all mentioned dashboards requires the privileges granted by role `sap.hana.admin.roles::Monitoring`, which comes predelivered with any SAP HANA system starting with revision 70.

4.4 DBA Cockpit for SAP HANA

Administrators of SAP NetWeaver-based systems will be familiar with Transaction DBACOCKPIT for administration of the SAP system's database. This transaction has special flavors for all database systems supported by SAP NetWeaver, and naturally there is also an SAP HANA variant.

Note

In terms of functional completeness, SAP HANA Studio is the leading system and may offer some features that are not yet implemented in DBA Cockpit.

DBA Cockpit for SAP HANA is part of any SAP NetWeaver installation that uses SAP HANA as the primary database and in any SAP NetWeaver system starting with SAP NetWeaver 7.30 SP 5 as well as in SAP Solution Manager version 7.01

SP 4 or higher. The Performance Warehouse component of DBA Cockpit is only available in SAP Solution Manager systems.

Because DBA Cockpit generally will be known to most SAP NetWeaver administrators and the content is very similar to that of SAP HANA Studio, we will keep this section short. You can find the official documentation for DBA Cockpit for SAP HANA with the SAP NetWeaver documentation at *https://help.sap.com/nw74* under APPLICATION HELP • FUNCTION-ORIENTED VIEW • DATABASE ADMINISTRATION • DATABASE ADMINISTRATION FOR SAP HANA • DBA COCKPIT FOR SAP HANA.

To run DBA Cockpit, you need certain permissions in the SAP NetWeaver system, and full functionality is only available if the database user has sufficient privileges. All of these privileges are summarized on the "Authorizations" page in the documentation of DBA Cockpit. Because this list may change with time, please refer to the documentation when setting up DBA Cockpit.

After starting DBA Cockpit in an SAP HANA system, a summary screen is displayed that is similar to the overview screen of the ADMINISTRATION CONSOLE in SAP HANA Studio (Figure 4.21). It displays generic information, such as the database version, as well as alerts and resource consumption.

In the left-hand panel, you can select further functionalities from the following groups:

▶ CURRENT STATUS
This category offers monitoring information on resource usage and alerts.

▶ PERFORMANCE
This section gives access to monitoring views that are relevant to performance analyses, for example, the threads overview, expensive statements trace, and more. In SAP Solution Manager systems, you also find the Performance Warehouse in this section.

▶ CONFIGURATION
The CONFIGURATION section displays the overall database configuration (e.g., details of a scale-out configuration), and it allows you to read and modify the database configuration files.

▶ JOBS
One part of DBA Cockpit for any database system is a scheduling functionality for database jobs, such as the creation of data backups. This functionality is available from the JOBS section, including for the SAP HANA database system.

▶ DIAGNOSTICS

The DIAGNOSTICS section gives access to a wide range of diagnosis functionalities, starting with an audit log (which is an SAP NetWeaver functionality, not to be confused with SAP HANA's intrinsic audit-logging functionality), to an SQL EXPLAIN PLAN, an SQL Editor, functionality to configure and view the database traces, and more.

The section also contains database-related functionality that is special to SAP NetWeaver systems, such as the SQLDBC trace or the ability to compare the state of tables and indexes in the database to the information maintained in the ABAP dictionary.

▶ SYSTEM INFORMATION

Finally, as in SAP HANA Studio, for some monitoring views of the database there is no dedicated UI in the Administration Editor tool. The most important of these monitoring views are exposed in the section SYSTEM INFORMATION.

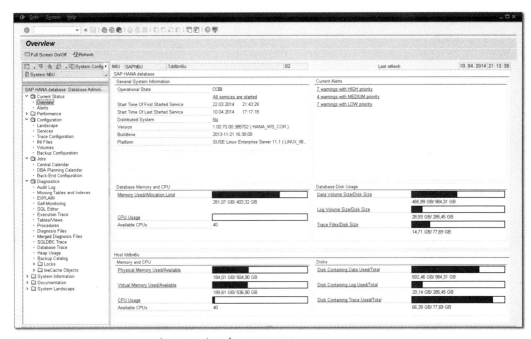

Figure 4.21 Overview Screen of DBA Cockpit for SAP HANA

4.5 Summary

SAP HANA Studio is the tool of choice for active administration and monitoring of the database system. The main intention of this chapter was to give you guidance on usage aspects of the tool so that you will have no trouble making use of it in the context of the following chapters. And don't forget: Help will always be given to those who remember the F1 key!

In order to achieve the "D" in ACID, in-memory databases also need to write all committed data to disk—and SAP HANA is no exception. This is where the persistence layer comes into play.

5 The Persistence Layer

In the early days of SAP HANA, one of the most frequent technical questions we had to answer was "What happens if you pull the plug?"—alluding to one of the most prominent features of SAP HANA, namely that it's an in-memory database. You may take the fact that one does not hear this question very often anymore—if at all—as an indication that with SAP HANA, SAP has indeed made an impression in the database world.

The answer to the now-forgotten question is of course that either the UPS (uninterruptable power supply) takes over or the database is switched off abruptly. This then turns into an opener to an exciting topic: How does the nonvolatile data store in SAP HANA work? How can I recover if a situation like a sudden power outage leads to inconsistencies in the data image (because the database processes, the operating system, and the storage layer may not have time to finish data-modifying transactions)? How can I continue database operations with as little disruption as possible? These questions will be answered in the course of this chapter.

Not all databases processes of a running SAP HANA system actively manage data that needs to be stored persistently. The processes that do—the *data-persistent processes*—write data and log files of their own. A consistent state of the database can only be described by the data persistence of all these processes combined. In Table 5.1 we list all database processes, pointing out whether or not they are data-persistent on a master or slave host. In the table we also list the port by which the processes are identified internally in the database system. You need to know this port number, because it is used to identify the database process in most monitoring views of the persistence layer. As usual, xx in the port number denotes the instance number of the database system.

Process	Internal Port	Data-Persistent on Master	Data-Persistent on Slave
Name server	3xx01	Yes	No
Preprocessor	3xx02	No	No
Index server	3xx03	Yes	Yes
Script server	3xx04	Yes (if enabled)	Yes (if enabled)
Statistics server	3xx05	Yes (if dedicated process)	N/A
XS server	3xx07	Yes	Yes (if enabled on slave)
Compile server	3xx10	No	No

Table 5.1 Database Processes in SAP HANA

Each data-persistent process also has a volume ID that is unique within the database system. On the file system level, the volume ID is used in the directory names of data and log volumes. Unfortunately, these volume IDs may differ from system to system. You have to look them up in monitoring view M_VOLUMES. Only the name server has a fixed volume ID (ID 1).

This chapter will introduce you to data and log volumes and the backups based on them as well as disaster recovery setups. In addition, we will present database snapshots and system replication, leaving you with a broad overview of the topic of persistency in SAP HANA.

5.1 Log and Data Volumes: The Data Image on Disk

We will start this discussion with the disk-based persistence of the database contents, that is, with the data and log volumes. As we have described in Chapter 3, any SAP HANA database installation needs dedicated file systems to provide space for data and log writing. This part of the chapter is about the content of these file systems.

We will start with a look at the relationship between memory and disk, introducing the major topics for the following section. The more detailed discussion starts with an insight into page management in SAP HANA before progressing to transaction logs and data volumes. We'll conclude with a discussion of how the system start procedure affects the data image.

5.1.1   Memory and Disk

As an in-memory database, SAP HANA uses RAM to store the primary image of data, and it tries to keep all data in the main memory to speed up data manipulation and data retrieval. Given the known volatility of RAM, additional ways of storing data are required in order to provide durability.

The main storage methods used in the SAP HANA system to achieve durability of the content of the database system are depicted in Figure 5.1 and discussed ahead:

▶ **Transaction logs**

Any write transaction, that is, any modification of the data content of the database system, will be written to a file-based transaction log at the latest when the write transaction is committed (unless the write transaction affects temporary tables that do not have disk-based persistence).

Log writing is optimized for high data throughput so that the duration of the commit phase can be minimized.

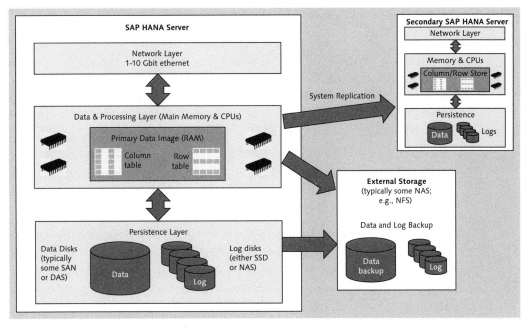

Figure 5.1 Persistence Components of SAP HANA Setups

▶ **Data files**

One could in principle simply rely on the transaction logs as nonvolatile

159

persistence. These logs are, however, not optimized for retrieving data or reconstructing the database image in the course of a (re)start of the system. This is why SAP HANA—like other databases—also has data files.

The data files are primarily optimized for the task of rebuilding the in-memory data image following a system start. Writing to the data files is handled in an asynchronous background process named *savepoint*. Unless the data or log volumes are damaged, the full database image can at any point in time be reconstructed from the data files and those transaction log entries that are more recent than the latest savepoint operation.

▶ **Data and log backups**
Did you notice the word "unless" in the previous paragraph? That is the main reason for having the data and log backups. In case the stored database content gets damaged by human error or software or hardware failures, you need a way to restore it consistently. Data backups are snapshots of the entire database content at a given point in time, and log backups are needed to roll forward the recovery to a more recent state than the point of creating the data backup.

▶ **System replication**
In order to protect your database system from large-scale disruptions (catastrophes) and to minimize downtime in case of system failure, you may implement redundancy in the form of a disaster-tolerant setup. In the case of SAP HANA, the database's native method for implementing such redundancy is called *system replication*. With this mechanism, the primary database system also writes any data change synchronously or asynchronously to a remote system with (almost) identical hardware specifications.

It should be noted for completeness that there are also disaster-tolerant setups available that rely on data replication on the storage level. From the point of view of the database, these are hardware, not software, solutions.

The mentioned persistence technologies exist in order to protect against the loss of data changes. There are, however, further data manipulations that do not change the data content. The database system might, for example, change the internal representation of a given data set. For readers who are already familiar with SAP HANA, we can mention the delta merge as an example of such a manipulation. The database can perform these operations entirely on the primary data set—that is, on the in-memory representation of the data—without having to take care of immediate nonvolatile persistence. In the case of a system disruption, the outcome of the operation might be lost. This is, however, not problematic, because the data content is independent from the way it is represented in the database, and the data manipulation can be repeated at any later point in time. Changes to the internal data representation are eventually also reflected in the data file, but the corresponding I/O operations can be deferred to some asynchronous process, for example, to the next savepoint operation.

5.1.2 Page Management

The content of the data files is organized in pages provided and managed by the persistence layer. Pages are also used to exchange data between the persistence layer and the in-memory stores. Some of these stores internally organize their data in pages (for example, the *row store*), whereas others have their own concept of memory organization. The column store, for example, relies on organizing table data in contiguous memory areas for optimal efficiency in accessing the data. For such data stores, memory pages of the persistence layer are only used for the data exchange between the in-memory store and the persistence layer. The disk representation in the data files, however, is always organized in (physical) pages—regardless of the in-memory store.

The page concept is mostly hidden from end users and administrators, so we will not spend much time on the topic. It is, however, important for one central component of the persistence layer called the *converter*.

The converter is that part of the persistence layer that maps the logical pages of the database stores to the physical pages of the data volumes in the so-called converter table. This mapping is essential, because at any given time multiple physical pages may exist for one logical page, and the converter table is needed to reconstruct a consistent database image. We will refer to the converter table when describing the savepoint, data backup, and snapshot operations.

The database supports multiple different page sizes, from 4 KB up to 16 MB. For a given object, the page size is chosen by the database, depending on object type, object size, and other criteria. Information on pages and the converter can be obtained from system views M_DATA_VOLUME_PAGE_STATISTICS and M_CONVERTER_STATISTICS.

5.1.3 Transaction Logs

Any write transaction in the database system will trigger the writing of a redo log entry in the database's transaction logs. An administrator will mostly be interested in two properties of the log system: the database's way of managing log files and the general role of logs in write transactions. We cover both aspects in the following sections.

Log Volumes and Log Segments

Each data-persisting process has a log volume containing the log files (named *log segments* in SAP HANA). Those volumes are located in the file system path *<log_path>/<SID>/mnt<node_ID>/hdb<volume_ID>/*. In a standard installation, the <log_path> is */hana/log/*. The <node_ID> is the ID of the given node in a scale-out cluster (00001 in a single-node system), and the <volume_ID> is the unique identifier of the process's persistence volumes that can be looked up in monitoring view M_VOLUMES.

> **Note**
>
> The term *node ID* is not used in the SAP HANA software or its documentation, nor is the term *node* itself clearly defined. In this book, we use *node* to refer to the process configuration and the data content of one worker host of a scale-out system. In a failover situation, the node will be moved to a configured standby host. The SAP HANA documentation will sometimes use the term *storage partition* to refer to the persistence part of what we call *node ID* here.
>
> See also the more detailed discussion in Chapter 6.

The log segments are individual files within the log volumes, named logsegment_<partition>_<segment_number>.dat. The <partition> may in the future be used for parallel writing to multiple log segments within one log volume. According to the *SAP HANA Administration Guide* for SPS 8, this technology is not yet in use, so <partition> always has the value "000".

Log segments are preallocated and preformatted files with a fixed size that is determined by the parameter [persistence] • log_segment_size_mb of the configuration file of the corresponding service. The default values of the log segment sizes for all process types are given in Table 5.2.

System Component	Service	Default Log Segment Size
Name server	nameserver	64 MB
Index server	indexserver	1024 MB

Table 5.2 Default Sizes for Log Segments

System Component	Service	Default Log Segment Size
Statistics server	statisticsserver	64 MB
SAP HANA XS	xsengine	8 MB
Script server	scriptserver	8 MB

Table 5.2 Default Sizes for Log Segments (Cont.)

The database will write into one given segment until it is full (until its preallocated size is reached) or has been backed up—whatever happens first. When the switch to the next log segment must occur, the new file will already have been prepared by the database in order to avoid wait situations arising from log file creation.

Log segments are kept for as long as needed—that is, until all information contained in the log segment has been transferred to the data file by a savepoint operation—and until the log segment has been backed up (if log backup is enabled). As soon as these operations have happened, the log segment can be marked as free for future re-use. In this way, log segments can be cyclically overwritten by the database system. We include a detailed discussion of the different modes of managing logs offered by SAP HANA later in this section.

In addition to the log segments, each log volume (directory) also contains a catalog of the log segments in a file named logsegment_<partition>_directory.dat; again, the value of <partition> is always "000" in the current release level. The log segment directory contains information used by the database in the start process to most quickly figure out which of the available log files contain information that is needed in addition to the data file.

Information on the log segments is available from the Volumes Monitor in SAP HANA Studio (see Figure 5.2). You can open this monitor by selecting the VOLUMES tab, shown in ❶, of the Administration Editor.

This monitor is divided into two screen areas: in the upper half, shown in ❷, a summary is presented of all data and log volumes of all data-persistent processes. The process entries can be expanded to reveal a breakdown into data and log volumes. You can mark any line in this table to display details of all data and/or log files of the service in the DETAILS table, as shown in ❸.

In Figure 5.2, we configured the display to include the VOLUME ID, as shown in ❹. You can right-click on the background, shown in ❺, of the upper table, and select CONFIGURE TABLE... from the context menu to change the fields being displayed.

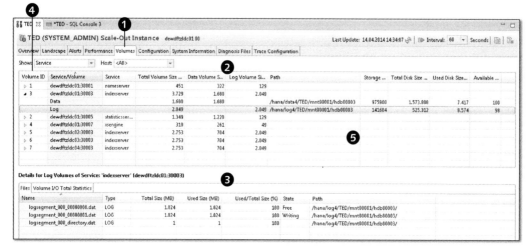

Figure 5.2 Volumes Monitor in the Administration Editor of SAP HANA Studio

Instead of using the predefined interface in SAP HANA Studio, you can also retrieve log volume information from the monitoring view M_LOG_SEGMENTS (Listing 5.1). In that listing, we add the process (service) name via a join to the M_VOLUMES monitoring view.

```
SELECT a.host AS hostname, b.service_name, a.volume_id,
    a.segment_id, a.file_name, a.state, a.in_backup,
    a.used_size/1024 AS "USED_SIZE [MB]",
    a.total_size/1024 AS "TOTAL_SIZE [MB]", a.min_position,
    a.max_position, a.hole_position
FROM m_log_segments AS a INNER JOIN m_volumes AS b
  ON a.host = b.host AND a.port = b.port
ORDER BY hostname ASC, service_name ASC, state DESC;
```

Listing 5.1 SQL Query to Display Log Segment Information

If you run the query from Listing 5.1, you might wonder about the meaning of the state field. This field is at the heart of our discussion on log modes and log housekeeping in the following sections.

Log Modes and Log Backup

There are two database parameters that govern how log segments are managed. Both parameters can be found in the [persistence] section of the global.ini configuration file. As the file name suggests, these parameters impact all processes of the entire database system.

Parameter `log_mode` may have the values `overwrite` or `normal` (log mode `legacy` is not available anymore, starting with SPS 7). Log mode `normal` is the recommended log mode for production systems and any other system that you may want to recover to arbitrary points in time. How log segments are managed in this log mode depends on the setting of the parameter `enable_auto_log_backup`, which can either be `yes` or `no`. Next, we summarize the different log-management settings:

▶ **Log mode overwrite**
In log mode `overwrite`, the database system will mark log segments as `Free` as soon as all contents of the log segment have been transferred to the data file. Free log segments will be cyclically overwritten. This log mode is only adequate for systems in which you will *never* need to recover the database to the latest consistent state or to arbitrary points in time. You will *only* be able to recover the database to a specific data backup. Automatic log backup is not possible in log mode `overwrite`.

▶ **Log mode normal without automatic log backup**
If you operate the database in log mode `normal` but do not enable automatic log backup, the database will mark log segments as `Free` as soon as their contents have been written to the data file, or until `log_backup_timeout_s` has been reached. The timeout is also defined in the [persistence] section of global.ini and has a default value of 900 seconds, that is, 15 minutes. Even an idle database will therefore create new log segments of the sizes given in Table 5.2 every 15 minutes.

With this database configuration, log segments in state `Free` will not be cleaned up or overwritten by the database. That means that the log volume will fill up gradually, and you will need to free log segments manually (see the "Housekeeping for Log Segments" section).

▶ **Log mode normal with automatic log backup enabled**
If automatic log backup is enabled in log mode `normal`, the database system will back up any log segment that is `closed`, that is, to which the database no longer writes. A log segment is closed either when it is full or when the `log_backup_`

`timeout_s` has been reached. In both cases, the database will switch to the next log segment.

Log segments that have been backed up and are not needed for system restart anymore are set to state `Free` and the database will overwrite them. Therefore, log full situations are very unlikely in log mode `normal` with automatic log backup.

> **Note**
>
> The log backup mechanism only becomes functional after the first data backup has been performed. Before this first data backup has occurred, log segments will be overwritten by the database without log backup as soon as they are not needed for restart; that is, the database will de facto operate in log mode `overwrite`.

See the sections on savepoint operation (Section 5.1.4) and log backup (Section 5.2) for more information.

Housekeeping for Log Segments

Under normal circumstances, there is no need to interfere with the database system's mechanisms to create and re-use log segments. There can, however, be situations that lead to the log disk filling up to close to 100%. Examples of such situations are:

▸ **Massive data loads**
If you optimize data loads for maximum throughput but leave log-writing enabled, you can easily produce hundreds of GB of logs between two savepoints.

▸ **Interruption of the log backup mechanism**
This can occur, for example, because of a full backup disk or an unavailability of a BackInt-connected backup system.

Because the database will not remove log segments of its own accord, these situations will create hundreds of free log segments, and they can even lead to disk-full events.

The database offers a safe mechanism to remove such free log segments. In order to understand this mechanism, we must first take a look at the state that a log segment can be in.

> **Note**
>
> Under no circumstances should you delete log files manually from the file system. Always use the SQL syntax provided by the database system. See the "Treating Disk-Full Situations of the Log Volumes" section.
>
> If the log segments on disk do not match the information in the log segment directory file, the system will not restart, and also point-in-time recovery will no longer be possible.

These log segment states are given in Table 5.3. From the table, we can deduce the typical lifecycle of a log segment: it has to be created, that is, a formatted file of the configured size has to be generated (state Formatting). The database aims to prepare the log files before they will be used (state Preallocated), but at some point in time the file will be filled (state Writing). Once the file is full—or when the log backup mechanism decides to switch to the next log segment—the file is closed.

State	Definition
Formatting	Segment is being prepared but not yet ready for use.
Preallocated	Segment is ready for use but not yet in use.
Writing	Segment is in use (being written to).
Closed	Segment is closed, still needed for system restart, and not yet backed up.
Truncated	Segment is closed, no longer needed for restart, but has not yet been backed up.
BackedUp	Segment is closed and backed up but still needed for system restart.
Free	Segment is closed, backed up (or log_mode is overwrite), and no longer needed for system restart. It can be reused or removed.

Table 5.3 Possible States of Log Segments

Now two things need to happen: The savepoint operation must transfer all data manipulations recorded in the log segment from main memory to the data file (see Section 5.1.4), so that it is no longer needed for system restart, and if log backup is enabled (log mode normal), the log segment has to be backed up. All four combinations of the states of these two events are reflected in the log segment states Closed, Truncated, BackedUp, and Free.

Only log segments in state Free can be removed from the database. If you removed segments in states Writing, Closed, or BackedUp, you would not be able to restart the database system any longer, because a consistent state cannot be created if 100% of the required data is not available. Deleting a segment in state Truncated would render any older database backup obsolete (as it could not be used any longer for full or arbitrary point-in-time recovery).

> **Note**
>
> If you test the log segment states programmatically (e.g., to test the number of free segments), be aware that the entries are case sensitive with capitalization, as given in Table 5.3.

If you have detected an exceedingly large number of log segments, and if you have understood and eliminated the root cause for this accumulation, you can instruct the database to remove all free log segments. The only correct way to do this is to issue the command:

```
ALTER SYSTEM RECLAIM LOG
```

Issuing this command will remove all log segments in state Free across all processes of all hosts of the database system.

> **Privilege Information**
>
> In order to remove free log segments, an administrator needs the system privilege LOG ADMIN.

Treating Disk-Full Situations of the Log Volumes

In our experience, disk-full situations mainly arise either from a combination of using log mode legacy with improper manual log management or from a malfunctioning log backup system (disk full on the log backup system or another reason that prevents the creation of log backups). In both cases, log segments will accumulate and not be removed automatically by database processes, eventually filling up the log volume(s).

Once the log volume is full and the last log segment is filled, the database has no way to write transaction logs; because even the creation of a new database session requires the writing of log entries, you will not be able to work with the database anymore.

If the disk is full but there is still free space in the log segments, you will be alerted to the situation by the statistics service. In order to treat the situation, you must understand whether it is the database or files created by other processes that is using up space. The database's volume monitoring helps you here; on the OVER-VIEW tab of the Administration Editor, the DISK USAGE indicator for your log volume (Figure 5.3) will show how much disk space is used by the database (LOG VOLUME SIZE, shown in ❶), how much is used on the disk in total (TOTAL DISK USAGE, shown in ❷), and the total size of the volume (TOTAL DISK SIZE, shown in ❸). In our example from a scale-out system, the database only uses about 8 GB, but all 513 GB of the log volume are occupied.

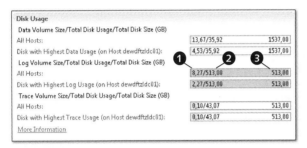

Figure 5.3 Full Log Volume Shown in Administration Editor

Next, you must free up space on the log disk so that the database can be set to an active state again, and you can clean up the log volume with the tools of the database.

If the disk is filled up by processes other than SAP HANA, remove these third-party files. If it is in fact database files filling the disk—namely, log segments—then your situation will be much more difficult, because you will damage the database if you try to manually delete files from the disk.

If the system is still working, and if there are many log segments in state `Free`, you can have the database remove these log segments by using the command `ALTER SYSTEM RECLAIM LOG`. In the rest of this section, we will assume that this is not possible and that you are facing a system that is not responding anymore.

> **Note**
>
> Never, ever manually delete log segments, not even in a disk-full event. You will not be able to start the database once you have manually deleted the segments.

What can you do in order to free up space? One possibility might be to enlarge the log volume file system. Depending on your storage system setup, this may or may not be possible. Assuming that enlarging the log volume file system is not possible, there is a safe recovery procedure to switch the database to a different log volume with sufficient space:

1. Identify a target storage volume on your SAP HANA server that is larger than the original log volume. Let us assume that this volume can be accessed with file system path *<temp_log>*.

   In the next steps, you will move all existing log segments to this location, and the database will need some additional space to create new log segments while you are cleaning up the system. The location *<temp_log>* should have a free space of at least 100 GB plus the total size of the original log volume.

2. Shut down the database. If you manipulate the log volume on disk while the database is online, you are very likely to create inconsistencies.

3. If possible and appropriate, create a disk copy of the database (copy data volumes, log volumes, and installation path; in typical installations, these are */hana/data/<SID>*, */hana/log/<SID>*, and */hana/shared/<SID>*. This is your emergency copy in case the recovery procedure fails.

4. On the Linux OS of the database server, move all log segments from the original log position *<log_path>* to the larger, temporary log space *<temp_log>*:
   `mv <log_path>/* <temp_log>/`

5. Change the database configuration to use *<temp_log>* as log position; because the database is probably no longer available, you will have to edit the configuration files manually.

   ▸ Make backup copies of the database configuration files (see Section 4.2.1 in Chapter 4 for details on the locations of these files).

   ▸ Make sure to verify the correct configuration in the system-wide and host-specific configuration files. Change the value of parameter `global.ini` • `[persistence]` • `basepath_logvolumes` to *<temp_log>*.

6. Start up the database. Make sure that no large data manipulations (e.g., data provisioning) will occur.

7. Check if there is a large number of log segments in state `Free` with a query against system view `M_LOG_SEGMENTS`. If yes, continue with the next numbered step. If not, you need to get the system to mark log segments as free:

   ▸ In log mode `legacy` (which should not be used!), all log segments not needed for restart should be always be marked as free. If you are in this log

mode and there are many log segments, but most of them are not in state
`Free`, forcing a savepoint (requires system privilege `SAVEPOINT ADMIN`)
might help: use the `ALTER SYSTEM SAVEPOINT` command.

▶ In log mode `overwrite`, it is virtually impossible to run into log-full situations, unless you have other processes than your SAP HANA instance filling up the log disk. The savepoint operation *might* have been prevented by a lock situation. This situation should have been resolved with the system restart, so that the database will list log segments as free.

▶ In log mode `normal` with log backup enabled, the log backup must be functioning. If there are issues preventing the database from backing up log segments, you must address these issues first. If you have many log segments in state `Truncated`, this hints at issues with the log backup system.

▶ In log mode `normal` without log backup enabled, the behavior is similar to log mode `legacy`.

8. Remove `Free` log segments using the SQL command

   `ALTER SYSTEM RECLAIM LOG`

   Monitor that log segments are indeed deleted from the disk.

9. Shut down the database.

10. Reverse the change of log volume—that is, move back the log segments to the original *<log_path>*—and change the related database configuration back to its original state (if you made changes to other system parameters, such as the log mode, you cannot simply install your backup copy of the configuration files).

11. Start the database.

12. Implement provisions to avoid future log-full situations. For example:

    ▶ Enable log backup.

    ▶ If log backup is not possible, evaluate whether log mode `overwrite` is acceptable.

    ▶ Implement regular monitoring and housekeeping of the log volumes and the log backup location.

Tip

You probably realized how much work it is to free space on the log volume if all space is occupied by log segments, and you probably never want to be in a situation in which you need to follow the preceding procedure.

The simplest way to achieve this goal is to place a *dummy file* of sufficient size into the log volume. If you run into a log-full situation, you can buy some time to clean up the situation by deleting the dummy file.

This file should therefore allocate sufficient disk space to give you, say, 30 minutes of working time. Let us assume that 50 GB of log space will be appropriate in your case. Then you can create the dummy file on the Linux operating system using the command:

```
dd if=/dev/zero of=<log_path>/dummy_allocator bs=1G count=50
```

where *<log_path>* must be replaced with the actual file system path to your log volume. The command will create a file consisting of `count=50` blocks of size 1 GB, filled with ASCII NUL characters.

Writing to the Log Segments

Every write transaction writes redo log entries to the log buffers provided by the database's logging system. For each process, the database provides a number of log buffers, configured in parameter `log_buffer_count`. Each log buffer has a size determined by parameter `log_buffer_size_kb`. Log buffers are queued for writing to the log segment when they are full, but at latest when a write transaction is committed.

Because transactional durability requires that data is written to disk before a write transaction ends, log buffers will often be half full when they are flushed to disk. At the same time, I/O optimizations of the database may allow the writing of commit records of multiple transactions with the same log buffer—given fitting I/O queuing and commit timing.

Each log entry consists of a unique log position, an indicator for the type of log entry (insert, update, delete...), an identifier of the write transaction, and additional information depending on the log entry type.

The database does not write undo information to the transaction logs. The technical handling of rolling back uncommitted information that may have been written to the data file is discussed in Section 5.1.4.

Relevant System Views for Transaction Logs

The system views in Table 5.4 can be used to retrieve information on log segments, log buffers, and related components.

View Name	Description
M_LOG_SEGMENTS	Display all log segments with state, size, log position, and so on.
M_LOG_PARTITIONS	Various performance statistics for each log partition (for the time being, this is equivalent to "each log volume").
M_LOG_BUFFERS	Information about the in-memory log buffers, such as sizes and wait counts.
M_VOLUMES	Displays all data and log volumes for all database services that persist data.
M_VOLUME_IO_TOTAL_STATISTICS	File access statistics for all data and log volumes.
M_DISKS	Disk configuration and usage statistics for all data, log, trace, and backup file systems.

Table 5.4 System Views Related to the Transaction Logs

For the full documentation of these views, refer to the SAP HANA SQL and System Views Reference available at *https://help.sap.com/hana_platform*.

Relevant Database Parameters for Transaction Logs

The most important parameters governing the log-writing mechanism of the SAP HANA database are listed in Table 5.5.

Parameter	Section	File	Description
log_mode	[persistence]	global.ini	Governs how the database handles transaction logs
enable_auto_log_backup	[persistence]	global.ini	Governs whether or not log backups are created in log mode "normal"
log_backup_timeout_s	[persistence]	global.ini	Time after which the database will close the currently open log segment and back it up
logsegment_size_mb	[persistence]	global.ini – override in service's ini	Fixed size of log segments of a given service (if not specified for service, value from global.ini is taken)

Table 5.5 Database Parameters Related to the Transaction Logs

Parameter	Section	File	Description
log_buffer_count	[persistence]	global.ini	Number of log buffers per service
log_buffer_size_kb	[persistence]	global.ini	Size of log each log buffer

Table 5.5 Database Parameters Related to the Transaction Logs (Cont.)

5.1.4 Data Volumes and the Savepoint Operation

The log-writing mechanism is required for achieving transactional durability, but it is not optimized for retrieving data, and restoring the database from the log entries is a complex and time-consuming process. Also, log segments are not compressed.

For these reasons, the SAP HANA database—like other database systems—stores its data image in data files. The process of writing to these files is what we'll discuss now.

Data Volumes and Data Files

Each data-persistent process has a data volume containing one data file. The data volumes are located in the file system path *<data_path>/<SID>/mnt<node_ID>/hdb<volume_ID>/*. In a standard installation, the <data_path> is */hana/data/*. The <node_ID> is the ID of the given node in a scale-out cluster (00001 in a single-node system—again, sometimes referred to as *storage partition* in the SAP HANA product documentation), and the <volume_ID> is the unique identifier of the process' persistence volumes that can be looked up in monitoring view M_VOLUMES.

The file name of the data file is datavolume_0000.dat. The only process whose data volume has two files with relevant information is the active master name server, whose persistence is always in volume 00001 of node 00001. This name server process also writes a file with the landscape ID of the database system.

The Savepoint Operation

From the point of view of the persistence layer, the database content is organized in pages. Any write transaction will modify one or multiple pages, and it is the task of the savepoint operation to write such changes to the data files.

Simply speaking, the savepoint operation will make sure that all pages listed in the current converter table are contained in the data file. That is, all pages that have been modified but not yet written to disk since the last savepoint will be written to the data file. Internally, the savepoint operation has three phases:

▸ **Phase 1**
During this phase, the database writes all changed pages to disk. Write transactions are allowed during this phase, and all page changes occurring during phase 1 will also be part of the savepoint.

▸ **Phase 2**
This is the phase that ensures that the savepoint refers to a unique state of the database. This state is identified by one particular log position so that during database restart the processing of transaction logs can start at precisely the right log position. The savepoint determines this log position by acquiring a process-wide exclusive change lock. This lock ensures that during phase 2 no page changes can happen and that no transactions can be started or finished. The database can now write the current log position as savepoint log position into the data file, together with a list of open transactions. While the exclusive lock is held, the database determines the list of all pages that have been modified in phase 1. The writing to disk of these modified pages is submitted to an asynchronous I/O process. As soon as this asynchronous process is triggered, the exclusive consistent change lock can be released, and normal transaction processing continues.

Phase 2 is named CRITICAL_PHASE in system views M_SAVEPOINTS and M_SAVEPOINT_STATISTICS.

▸ **Phase 3**
During this phase, the pages modified during phase 1 are written to disk. Write transactions are allowed again during this phase, but any page changes will no longer be part of the current savepoint.

The list of all pages that make up the database image at the time of the savepoint—including the mapping of these pages to the physical data pages in the data file—is also stored in the data file. This list is called the *converter table* of the savepoint.

By its design, the savepoint will contain committed and uncommitted data changes. For any uncommitted data change, undo information will be included in the savepoint.

Savepoints are automatically performed by the database in intervals determined by parameter `global.ini` • `[persistence]` • `savepoint_interval`. The default value of 300 seconds should normally not be changed.

It may come as a surprise that a regular savepoint operation is not synchronized across all processes of the database system. Instead, each process performs savepoints by its own schedule. This minimizes the potential wait times when the system acquires the consistent write lock. The restart procedure of the database acknowledges this behavior when replaying or rolling back distributed transactions.

Further Mechanisms That Write to the Data Files

The savepoint is the operation that ensures consistent and fast restore of the database during system restart. In order to minimize the amount of data that needs to be written to disk in the course of the savepoint operation, several database processes may write to the data file independently from the savepoints.

The best known of these processes is the delta merge operation of the column store (see Chapter 9). This operation will not change the information stored in the database but only the internal representation of the information. A delta merge will replace the entire database image of the table being merged so that massive amounts of data space will be modified. If the database waited for the next savepoint before writing the new table representation to disk, this would not only cause massive I/O operations in the course of the savepoint, but it would also allocate copious amounts of page buffers to hold the modified pages available for the savepoint. A delta merge can therefore write the new main store of the table directly to the data file without waiting for the next savepoint.

When writing into a column store table, the database will fill the delta store in main memory, and it will write transaction log entries (unless log writing is disabled). At the same time, the delta store is represented as a list of pages by the persistence layer, and these pages will be written to the data file with the next savepoint.

In the course of a delta merge, the in-memory representation of the table is completely rebuilt; a new main store is constructed from the contents of the previous main and delta stores, and a new delta store is set up. This changes all data pages of the table, and it is these new data pages that may be written to the data file directly in the course of the delta merge operation. Because the delta merge operation does not change the data content of the table, there is no need to write transaction log entries.

In the worst case, the database may crash before the result of the delta merge is written to disk. After restart, the database will then read the unmerged table representation from the data file and log segments, and the delta merge can be repeated at a convenient point in time.

The second prominent operation that may trigger writing to the data files outside of savepoint operations is the eviction or unloading of columnar tables or parts of them from main memory. If a table is evicted that has been modified since the last savepoint operation, the new or modified data pages belonging to that table will be written to the data file in the course of this table unload.

Undo Information and Shadow Pages

Undo information is required during system restart, because the database image on disk—in the transaction logs and in the data files—also contains data from uncommitted transactions that have to be treated properly during the start procedure. Uncommitted information in the transaction logs can be rolled back based on the nonexistence of a commit record.

The rollback of uncommitted data in the data files is slightly more complicated. The database has two different mechanisms for treating the rollback, depending on whether the uncommitted data has been written to the data file in the course of the last savepoint or by other processes after the last savepoint.

If uncommitted data is written to the data file as part of the savepoint information, undo information is also written to undo pages of the persistence layer so that the database can explicitly roll back the changes.

For information written since the last savepoint, the database makes use of the efficient concept of shadow pages; as we said before, the persistence layer organizes the entire database content in pages. Each table consists of a set of pages of the persistence layer, called *logical pages*. Each of these pages has a counterpart in the data file, called a *physical page*.

Every time the database creates a consistent image of its data content, this image comes with a converter table, mapping the logical pages of this consistent image to the physical pages of the data file. In order to reflect multiple states of the database in one data file, the database can maintain multiple versions of physical pages. Whenever a logical page, L1, is modified and written to disk after the last savepoint, the persistence layer does not overwrite the savepoint version, P1, of the page. Instead, the savepoint version is set to state Free after savepoint— thus turning P1 into a shadow page. A new physical page, P1', is assigned to the new version of the data file.

If the database now crashes before the next savepoint is completed, the database will open the converter table from the last savepoint. In this converter table, the logical page, L1, is mapped to the savepoint version, P1, of the data. The new page version, P1', will be ignored because it is unknown to the savepoint's converter table, thus effectively rolling back any uncommitted data changes contained in P1'. Committed information in P1' will be reconstructed from the transaction log.

Delta merges that have not yet been written to the data file will be rolled back in the same way, which is, of course, an undesired side effect. Remember, however, that a regular database shutdown will include a final savepoint, so under normal circumstances a delta merge will not be lost.

Managing Free Space within the Data Files

SAP HANA does not have a concept similar to the table spaces of other database systems. Because the primary data image is that in RAM, the database size is determined by the amount of main memory. The disk space for the data files is simply restricted by the available space in the data volume(s).

The database automatically allocates as much space for the data file as it needs. In order to avoid fragmentation and also reduce I/O wait times, the system will always keep the data files larger than is currently needed; that is, there will always be free blocks in the data files, so small write operations, such as a savepoint, will normally not need to allocate disk space.

Therefore, any data file will always have a total size that is larger than its payload. You can monitor the total size and the used size in system view M_VOLUME_FILES, or in the VOLUMES tab of the Administration Editor in SAP HANA Studio, as shown in Figure 5.4. If you select the data volume of a given service, as shown in ❶, the table in the lower half of the screen will show details of the data file in that volume. Next to the TOTAL SIZE (MB), shown in ❷, which reflects the size of the data file on the file system, you can also see the USED SIZE (MB), shown in ❸, that is, the payload of the data volume. As you can see, in our example this payload only makes up 45% of the allocated file size, as shown in ❹.

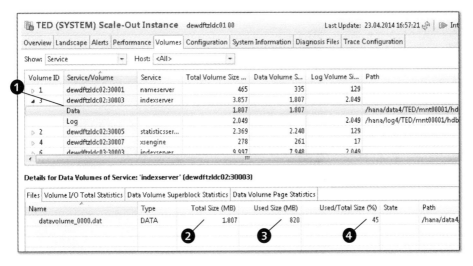

Figure 5.4 Monitoring the Usage of Data Volumes

In our situation, the overall size of the data volume is small, so there is no need to worry. But you may find yourself with a data volume size of a terabyte or more, with a similarly small usage percentage. The typical reason for such situations is either the deletion of very large tables or intensive data-load operations. If you load large amounts of data in a short timeframe, the column store's delta mechanism can lead to large amounts of free space in the data files. The reason is simply that first the delta store is written to the data file, and then a new table structure is built during the delta merge. This new table structure will also be written to the file, before the pages occupied by the delta store can be marked as free.

If there is a large amount of unused space in the data file, the database will of course occupy this space with new data pages before allocating more disk space. So in most cases, you do not need to worry about free space in the data file. If, however, you are operating multiple database instances on the same hardware, these instances typically share the same data volume, so the large and sparse data file of one instance might take away data volume space that another instance needs.

In this or a similar situation, you can shrink the data volume by using the syntax given in Listing 5.2. In that listing, the optional parameter `host:port` identifies the database process whose data file will be shrunk. The port is the internal port of the process, for example, `3<instance>03` for an index server (see Table 5.1). If the parameter is not specified, the database of all processes will be shrunk. The mandatory parameter `<perc>` gives the intended size of the data file as a percentage of the file's payload. One should always leave some free blocks in the data file; an overhead of about 20% of the payload is a good value. This leads to a value for `<perc>` of 120% of the payload.

> **Privilege Information**
>
> You need system privilege RESOURCE ADMIN in order to reclaim free space in the data volumes.

```
// Generic syntax:
ALTER SYSTEM RECLAIM DATAVOLUME [host:port] <perc> DEFRAGMENT;
// To leave an additional 20% of the payload for the index
// server process of host hana01, instance number 42, use:
ALTER SYSTEM RECLAIM DATAVOLUME 'hana01:34203' 120 DEFRAGMENT;
```
Listing 5.2 Releasing Free Space in the Data Volume

The shrinking will also defragment the data files, moving all occupied pages to the front of the data file.

> **Note**
>
> Freeing space in the data volume is an I/O-intensive process that can take several minutes, impacting system performance during this time.

Disk-Full Events of the Data Volumes

If the data volumes are full, that is, all disk space of the data volume is occupied, then the database system will alert you to a disk-full event. In the DISK USAGE section of the ADMINISTRATION CONSOLE of SAP HANA Studio (Figure 5.5), a DISK-FULL EVENT, shown in ❶, is displayed. Because it is possible that different data volumes are located on different storage devices, there can in principle be multiple disk-full events at the same time related to different storage devices. This is why there is also a counter, shown in ❷, for active disk-full events, and all events must be acknowledged individually once you have removed the root cause.

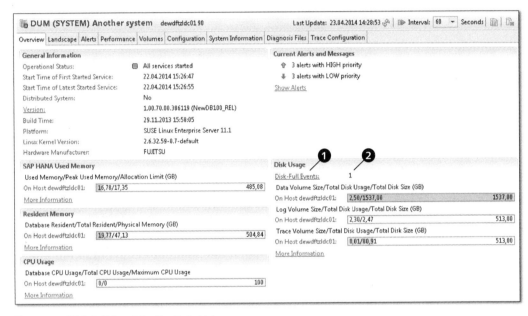

Figure 5.5 Disk-Full Event for the Data Volume

The statistics service will also alert you to disk-full events with messages as shown in Figure 5.6, see ❶, and you can find all disk-full events in monitoring view M_ EVENTS.

Even with a disk-full event, the database will still be operational as long as there are free pages in the data file so that you can monitor the database system, stop data provisioning processes, and so on.

If the data disk is full, the recovery procedure is similar to that of a full log volume, covered in Section 5.1.3. Typically, you will either be able to remove alien files from the data volume file system or you will be able to enlarge the data volume file system.

> **Note**
>
> You may be tempted to try and free (reclaim) unused space in the data file in order to resolve the disk-full event. This will, however, not be successful, because the data file will temporarily grow a little when you attempt to reclaim space in the data volume file system.

Once you have freed up space on the data volume file system, you can get the database into an operational state again by acknowledging the disk-full event and setting it to handled. The database offers SQL commands, as given in Listing 5.3.

```
// acknowledge the event:
ALTER SYSTEM SET EVENT ACKNOWLEDGED '<host>:<port>' <id>;
// mark the event as handled:
ALTER SYSTEM SET EVENT HANDLED '<host>:<port>' <id>;
```

Listing 5.3 Acknowledging Disk-Full Events and Marking them as Handled

The event IDs can be obtained from system view M_EVENTS.

> **Privilege Information**
>
> System privilege MONITOR ADMIN is required in order to mark events as acknowledged or handled.

Alternatively, you can click on the DISK-FULL EVENTS link in the Administration Editor of SAP HANA Studio. A pop-up window opens, as shown in Figure 5.6; see ❷. Use the check boxes, shown in ❸, to identify which events you have handled, and click OK.

After you have successfully resolved a disk-full situation of your data volumes, there are three things you should do: check if large portions within the data files are unused, and reclaim this space if appropriate; create dummy files of a fitting size to reserve disk space in the data volumes (see our proposal for the log volumes); and revise and improve your proactive monitoring and alerting setup to avoid future disk-full events.

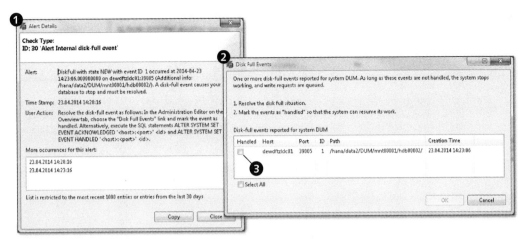

Figure 5.6 Disk-Full Alert and Handling Disk-Full Events

Relevant System Views for Data Volumes and Savepoint

The system views in Table 5.6 contain information on the data files and savepoint operations. In addition, the volumes- and disk-related views from Table 5.4 are also of interest here.

View Name	Description
M_DATA_VOLUMES	File names and sizes of data volumes
M_VOLUME_FILES	Total and used size of data and log volumes
M_DATA_VOLUME_SUPERBLOCK_STATISTICS	Number of allocated and used super blocks per data file
M_DATA_VOLUME_PAGE_STATISTICS	Usage statistics on pages and superblocks
M_SAVEPOINTS	Information on savepoint operations since system start, including duration, number of pages written, or resulting size of data file
M_SAVEPOINT_STATISTICS	Aggregated information from view M_SAVEPOINTS
M_EVENTS	Details of current disk-full events

Table 5.6 System Views Related to Data Volumes and Savepoint

For the full documentation of these views, refer to the SAP HANA SQL and System Views Reference available at *https://help.sap.com/hana_platform*.

Relevant Database Parameters for Data Volumes and Savepoint

The savepoint operation is an entirely automatic process for which no user inter-action or customizing is foreseen. The only potentially interesting parameter for database administrators is `savepoint_interval_s`, as given in Table 5.7.

Parameter	Section	File	Description
savepoint_ interval_s	[persistence]	global.ini	Time between two regular savepoint operations

Table 5.7 Database Parameters Related to the Transaction Logs

5.1.5 System Start Procedure

When the database system starts, it needs to rebuild the database image from the information stored on disk. The goal is not to have 100% of the data loaded into main memory immediately; this would lead to unreasonably long startup times. Instead, the database will only perform such steps that are essential for its func-tionality before making its external interfaces available to client programs. Once the database has started, the data content in main memory will be gradually filled up during the warm-up phase.

Start Procedure

We summarize here with some simplifications the essential startup steps that lead to a fully functioning SAP HANA database system. All data-persistent processes will follow this procedure using their respective data file and log segments.

1. **Open the data volume file.**
   The process opens its data volume file and reads restart information from a dedicated restart section of the file.

2. **Load the converter table from the last completed savepoint.**
   With the converter table, the system builds the mapping of logical pages to physical pages in the data file as it existed at the end of the critical phase of the last completed savepoint. This reflects the database contents at the savepoint log position.

3. **Load the list of open transactions from the last completed savepoint.**
   This information will be needed to enable rolling back uncommitted data from the savepoint.

4. **Load row store tables.**
   As of SAP HANA SPS 7, all row store tables must be completely in main memory at all times. Depending on the size of the row store, this step can have a significant duration. On standard storage devices without any attempts at optimization, we have seen throughput rates of about 250 MB/s to 300 MB/s, that is, load times of about five minutes for a row store of 100 GB.

5. **Replay redo log entries.**
   Redo log entries are read starting with the savepoint log position. The system creates multiple log replay queues into which the redo log entries are distributed while being read. Within boundaries set by the requirement to respect consistency, the system can process the replay queues in parallel. The number of queues created is equal to the number of logical CPUs of the database host. On a server with 32 physical CPU cores and Hyper-Threading enabled, 64 log replay queues will be created.

   Following a regular shutdown of the database, nothing will happen during this step, because the system writes a savepoint during shutdown.

6. **Roll back uncommitted transactions.**
   The system determines all transactions that were marked as unfinished in the savepoint and also for which no commit records exist in the transaction logs as well as those transactions for which start records but no commit records are found in the transaction logs. This is the set of all unfinished transactions in the database at time of shutdown, and these transactions are now rolled back by using undo information.

7. **Perform a savepoint.**
   The savepoint ensures that the restored consistent state of the database is fully recorded in the data files.

The database is now fully restored and operational. Client programs can connect to and interact with the database system while the in-memory representation of columnar tables is being built up in the background.

Warm-Up Phase

After restarting the database system, no column tables are in memory. Whenever the database needs to operate on a columnar table, however, the relevant portion of the table needs to be in RAM. Typically, this is a set of columns (in partitioned tables—from one or several partitions) of the table.

Any operation requesting data that is not yet loaded into main memory will trigger the corresponding load operation. Because this I/O work will impact the transactions, the database automatically loads columnar tables into main memory as follows:

- **Tables marked for preload**
  Columnar tables can be entirely or partially (on a per-column level) marked for preload. These tables or columns will be loaded first upon system start.

- **Tables that were loaded before the last shutdown**
  Next, the database starts loading those tables or table columns into main memory that were loaded before the last shutdown. The sequence of data loading is not based on usage statistics. If you would like to suppress this automatic loading, you can set parameter [sql] • reload_tables of the indexserver.ini configuration file to false.

- **Other tables**
  Other tables or columns are only loaded into main memory on request.

Tables are always loaded into memory column-wise. You can control the degree of parallelism for these load processes via parameter [parallel] • tables_ preloaded_in_parallel of the file indexserver.ini.

Trace File Information Related to the Start Process

The index server process writes interesting and comparatively easy to read information into its trace file. If you check the file */hana/shared/<SID>/HDB<instance>/ <hostname>/trace/indexserver_<hostname>.<port>.<max_counter>.trc* during or after system start, you will find information like the time needed for steps such as loading column store tables, replaying the redo logs, rolling back indoubt (uncommitted) transactions, and more. Some of these are regularly updated with progress information (e.g., the amount of data to still be rolled back).

This information is useful for troubleshooting problems that may occur during system start, and it also helps to derive an estimate for the probable system start time as row store data volumes grow.

5.2   Log Backup

For the purpose of recovering the database from a data backup to its latest consistent state, all redo logs are required that have been created since the data backup.

Depending on the quantity of write transactions that have occurred in the meantime, the amount of log segments may exceed the storage space available in the log volume.

Because most of these log segments will not be required for system restart, their content can be moved away from the log volume as long as this movement happens in such a way that the database can still access the moved log entries if needed.

The related database process is named "log backup" and is executed by all data-persistent processes. We cover in this section the creation and managing of log backups. Other aspects, such as the role that log backups play during database recovery, are discussed in Section 5.4 when we describe data backup and recovery.

5.2.1 Log Backup Procedure

If enabled, log backups are executed by all database processes autonomously whenever a log segment is closed—either because it is full or because the segment has been in state `Writing` for `log_backup_timeout_s` seconds.

Instead of moving the closed log segment to the log backup destination, the database creates a log backup file and copies the payload of the log segment into that file. For any log segment that is closed because the time limit has been exceeded, the payload can be much smaller than the allocated size of the log segment, so log backups usually need significantly less disk space than the original segments.

Log Backup Location and File Names

If file-based backups are used, the log backups are written to the location configured with parameter `global.ini` • `[persistence]` • `basepath_logbackup`; by default this is the location */usr/sap /<SID>/HDB<instance>/backup/log*. You can change this location, but for the sake of supportability we feel it is a good idea to keep the default location. You may either use it as a mount point for the network storage that you hopefully use as a backup drive, or you can turn it into a symbolic link to the actual mount point of your backup storage.

In a scale-out system, the log backup base path must exist on all hosts of the setup. It is recommended but not required that the path points to the same shared location on all hosts.

SAP HANA also offers a backup mechanism based on network streams called *BackInt*. If a third-party backup tool supporting the BackInt for SAP HANA interface is used for the management of log backups, then the backup is written into named pipes at file system location */usr/sap/<SID>/SYS/global/hdb/backint*.

The file names of log backups contain an identifier of the log volume, the log partition, the redo log positions of the first and last log entry contained in the backup, and a unique identifier of the backup: *log_backup_<volume_ID>_<partition_ID>_<first_redo_log_position>_<last_redo_log_position>.<backup_ID>*.

Log Backups and Log Segment States

While the log backup is being written, the state of the log segment is either Closed (if the segment is still needed for system restart) or Truncated. As soon as the log backup file has been written, an entry is added to the backup catalog, and the state of the log segment is updated to either BackedUp (if the segment is still required for system restart) or Free.

5.2.2   Enabling Log Backups

There are three requirements for enabling automatic log backup in SAP HANA:

▶ You must set the log mode to normal (parameter [persistence] • log_mode of global.ini).

▶ You must allow automatic log backups (parameter [persistence] • enable_auto_log_backup in the same location must be set to yes).

▶ You must have created at least one data backup.

The first two settings are set correctly for enabling log backup in the default configuration of the database. As long as no data backup has been performed, the system will display a related alert with high priority, signaling that you can neither create log backups nor recover the database in this state. As soon as you create the first data backup, the system will start backing up the log segments automatically.

5.2.3   Managing Log Backups

Although log backups allow you to keep the log volumes from filling up the log volume file system completely, you have only deferred the task of active housekeeping from the log volume file system to the log backup location. In case your log backup location fills up, any subsequent log backups will fail. As a consequence, log segments remain in state `Truncated` and cannot be reused or removed.

Compared to log segments, log backups have the advantage that you can delete them directly from the file system without damaging the database. You must be careful not to remove any log backups that may be required to recover the database from the oldest data backup that you intend to keep available.

It is also possible to move log backups to a different location. The recovery procedure allows you to enter additional log backup destinations.

The SAP HANA database offers an SQL command to remove any data and log backups that are older than a given data backup safely from the database, and this technique should be used for the housekeeping of your data and log backups. We introduce this technique in Section 5.4.8.

5.3   Snapshots

Before we can describe data backups, we need to introduce a fundamental concept, the *snapshot*, that is at the heart of data backups and other operations in the database.

A database snapshot is simply a consistent state of the entire database system that is frozen in the data files so that the physical pages belonging to this state cannot be removed, overwritten, or altered as long as the snapshot exists.

If you remember the converter table that we described as part of the savepoint operation, you will probably guess that a snapshot is described by its own converter table. When you create a snapshot, the database performs a global savepoint, that is, a synchronized savepoint operation is executed by all database processes. As is the case for a regular savepoint operation, only those pages that have been modified since the last savepoint will be written to the disk for creating the snapshot. This creation process is called *preparation* in the context of snapshots and typically only takes fractions of a second.

This section will walk you through the basics of snapshots in SAP HANA. We explain their purpose and lifecycle and three of the major tasks associated with them: creating a snapshot, recovering the database from a snapshot, and managing snapshots with SQL.

5.3.1   The Purpose of Snapshots

Database snapshots are sometimes used implicitly by primary processes such as data backups or system replication. In these cases, you do not need to actively manage the snapshot.

You can, however, also create database snapshots explicitly. The most common purpose of this operation is to create a storage copy (*storage snapshot*) of the data volumes that can be used to restore or copy the database. Only with such a snapshot can the consistency of the data files throughout the database system be guaranteed.

Another purpose can be the possibility of resetting the database to a database snapshot that is active (prepared) in the data files. This is very appropriate in training systems that need to be reset to the same initial state after each instance of the training.

As opposed to a database backup, the internal consistency of a snapshot is not verified by the database kernel at creation time. For this reason, snapshots should only be regarded as an additional measure in a backup concept that should also include regular creation of data backups.

5.3.2   Lifecycle of a Snapshot

The life of a database snapshot is influenced by two events; first a database snapshot needs to be created, and when it is not needed anymore it needs to be released or abandoned.

The screen elements in SAP HANA Studio use the terminology PREPARE STORAGE SNAPSHOT to signal that generating a database snapshot is a necessary preparatory step for creating a storage snapshot. We will use the terms "create" and "prepare" equivalently.

Preparing a snapshot triggers a global, synchronized savepoint of the database system. All physical pages from this savepoint are marked as belonging to the snapshot. The snapshot also consists of a converter table that maps logical pages of the persistence layer to their physical pages in the data files. This relationship is indicated in Figure 5.7 by the dotted line, shown in ❶, that encloses the logical and physical pages at the time of snapshot creation.

While the snapshot exists in the database, its pages cannot be overwritten. Of course, the database is still fully operational, and again the shadow page concept is used. In the example of Figure 5.7, a write transaction modifies logical page, L1, of a given table. With the next savepoint operation, the page modification needs to be reflected in the data file. There, the original physical page, P1, is kept unchanged but turned into a shadow page (S1). The modified logical page, L1', is written to a new physical page, P1'. The savepoint, shown in ❷, contains all physical pages, including P1' but not the shadow page S1, whereas the snapshot, shown in ❸, now does not contain P1' but instead contains the shadow page S1.

If the database snapshot has been created as preparation for a storage snapshot, you can now copy the data volumes on the file system level.

As soon as the storage snapshot is finished, you can and should release the database snapshot. There are two options for releasing the snapshot, and they only differ semantically:

▶ You can confirm the database snapshot and thus indicate to the database that a storage snapshot has been created that contains the database snapshot.

▶ Or, you can abandon the database snapshot, indicating that no storage snapshot has been created.

With this differentiation, the backup catalog can also contain information on the availability of database/storage snapshots for the purpose of recovering the database.

> **Note**
>
> At the release level of SPS 8, SAP HANA database only supports a single active snapshot at any point in time. Because database backups are based on snapshots, in most systems it is mandatory to release snapshots as soon as they have fulfilled their purpose in order to not interfere with regular backup operations.

When a snapshot is released, all of its shadow pages (those that are not also in state `Free after savepoint`) are set to `Free` and can be reused by the persistence layer.

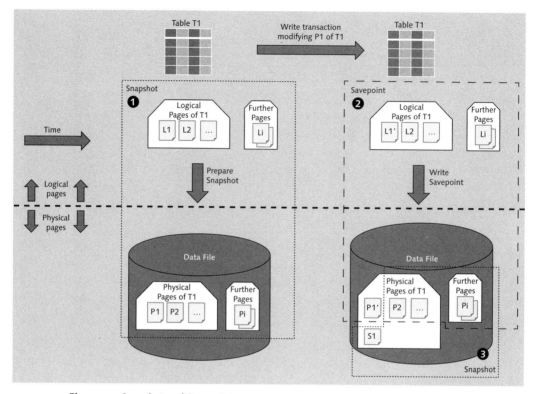

Figure 5.7 Snapshot and Savepoint

Even if you do not create a storage snapshot, the database snapshot can be used to restore the database to its state at snapshot creation. This is only possible if the snapshot has not been released. We show this procedure in Section 5.3.4.

Note

Database snapshots become invalid if at least one process with persistence is restarted. Thus, a prepared snapshot cannot be used any longer if the database or single processes has been restarted or crashed. If a database snapshot will be used to copy or recover the database, it is advisable to create the storage snapshot of the data volumes immediately.

You will not be able to confirm a database snapshot if it has been invalidated. Storage snapshots with a database snapshot that cannot be confirmed may contain a corrupt database snapshot and should therefore be disregarded immediately.

5.3.3 Creating a Database Snapshot in SAP HANA Studio

A database snapshot in SAP HANA can be created from the Backup Editor of SAP HANA Studio (Figure 5.8). On the right-hand side of the Overview tab, shown in ❶, you find the (SAP HANA Studio for SPS 7) section Prepared Storage Snapshot, shown in ❷, containing information and tooling for managing database snapshots. By clicking on the Storage Snapshot... button, shown in ❸, you can enter a wizard that allows you to create and release database snapshots.

The UI elements have changed in SAP HANA SPS 8 (lower half of Figure 5.8); the dedicated section for database snapshots has been removed. Instead, database backup and database snapshot are jointly handled in the left-hand side of the Backup Editor.

It is also possible to start the Storage Snapshot wizard directly from the navigator tree in the Systems view of SAP HANA Studio; if you right-click either on the top node or on the Backup node of the navigator tree, you can choose Storage Snapshot... from the context menu.

SPS 7:

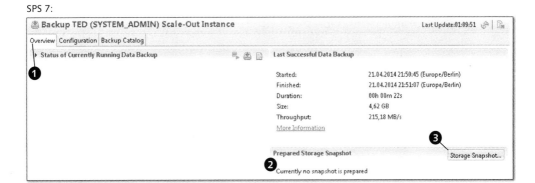

SPS 8:

Figure 5.8 Storage Snapshot Options in the Backup Editor

Privilege Information

You need system privilege BACKUP ADMIN or BACKUP OPERATOR to manage database snapshots; for using the snapshot wizard, system privilege CATALOG READ is also required.

In the STORAGE SNAPSHOT wizard (Figure 5.9, left-hand side; see ❶), the SNAPSHOT DETAILS area, shown in ❷, shows whether or not a snapshot is currently prepared. If there is no active snapshot, then you can create one by clicking the PREPARE button, as shown in ❸.

SAP HANA Studio now asks you to enter a comment for the snapshot, as shown in ❹. This comment will be added to all entries in the backup catalog that are related to the snapshot. In order to unambiguously identify a particular snapshot, it is best to choose unique names for each snapshot, for example, by including a time stamp or similar details.

As soon as you confirm the snapshot comment by clicking the OK button, as shown in ❺, the database snapshot will be created. The duration of this operation is under normal circumstances very close to the time required to create a database savepoint; typically we are talking about time periods of the order of magnitude of one second.

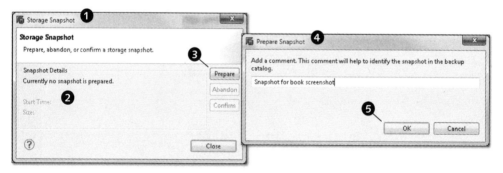

Figure 5.9 Preparing a Storage Snapshot

If the snapshot has been successfully prepared, then the snapshot wizard displays information on its size (Figure 5.10) in the SNAPSHOT DETAILS section, shown in ❶. The size of a snapshot is the sum of the sizes of all pages in the data file that belong to the snapshot. In SPS 8, the snapshot will be prepared asynchronously, the STOR-AGE SNAPSHOT wizard will close, and the Backup Editor will be updated with information on the prepared snapshot (as shown in the lower half of Figure 5.8). If you intend to create a storage snapshot based on this database snapshot, you should do this as soon as possible.

Once a snapshot is prepared, you can ABANDON it, as shown in ❷, or CONFIRM it, as shown in ❸, depending on whether or not you have also created a storage snapshot. In both cases, you can and should again enter a comment, as shown in ❹, which will also be reflected in the backup catalog of the database.

When confirming, the purpose of the comment is to document the relationship between the logical database snapshot and the physical storage snapshot, for example, by entering the ID or path name of the storage snapshot. When abandoning, you may, for example, enter the reason for abandoning the snapshot.

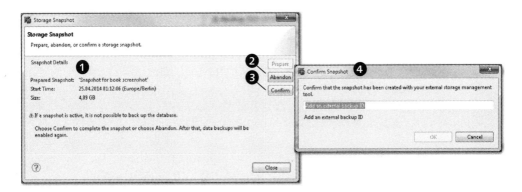

Figure 5.10 Snapshot Wizard with Information on Prepared Snapshot

We include information on retrieving the snapshot information from the backup catalog in Section 5.4.8.

5.3.4 Recovering the Database from a Snapshot

If a database snapshot is still active (prepared) within the data file of the database, you can reset the database to the data image reflected in the snapshot. Otherwise, if a storage snapshot has been created from the data volumes while a database snapshot was active, you can recover the database from the storage snapshot. This recovery will require that you replace the original data files with the version from the storage snapshot. Next, we will walk you through an example of creating a storage snapshot and recovering the database from it.

Creating a Storage Snapshot

In order to create the storage snapshot, you must first prepare it by creating a database snapshot, as described in Section 5.3.3. After the snapshot has been prepared, you can create the copy of the data volumes. If you plan to make use of storage snapshots regularly, your storage system will probably provide tools for efficient block-device replication or similar functions. Because these techniques depend on your storage hardware and tooling, we simply use the generically available but inefficient file system copy mechanism.

In the example shown in Listing 5.4, we have prepared a file system for storage snapshots in */hana/storage_snapshots/<SID>*. In this location, we will create a directory *snapshot_01* and copy the entire content of the data volume into this directory.

```
# Prepare snapshot location for our database system TED:
mkdir /hana/storage_snapshots/TED/snapshot_01
# Copy data volumes of system TED:
cp -rp /hana/data/TED/* \
    /hana/storage_snapshots/TED/snapshot_01/
```
Listing 5.4 Creating a Storage Snapshot by Copying the Data Volumes

When the copy is finished, we have created our storage snapshot. We now have to confirm it. In the confirmation dialog from Figure 5.10, shown in ❹, we could enter the file path *"/hana/storage_snapshots/TED/snapshot_01"* as EXTERNAL BACKUP ID.

Recovering the Database from the Snapshot

Now, we can recover the database. As a prerequisite, we need to shut down the SAP HANA system and replace the data volumes with the version from our storage snapshot. In our simple example, we will perform the actions given in Listing 5.5 after verifying that all database processes are in fact shut down.

```
# Check that all database processes are stopped. You should
# only see the sapstartsrv and HDB info itself:
HDB info
# Remove the data volumes of the database:
```

```
rm -r /hana/data/TED/mnt*
# Copy the data volumes from the storage snapshot:
cp -rp /hana/storage_snapshots/TED/snapshot_01/mnt*
   /hana/data/TED/
```

Listing 5.5 Copying Back the Data Volumes from the Storage Snapshot

Once the operation of copying back the storage snapshot has finished, we can start the actual snapshot recovery, which is supported in SAP HANA Studio by the same wizard as recovery from regular data backups. To open this wizard, right-click on the database entry for the system to recover and select RECOVER... from the context menu. Unless the credentials of operating system user <sid>adm are saved in the Eclipse secure store, you will be asked to enter them now.

> **Note**
>
> In our example, we have explicitly shut down the database before recovery. If the database is still online when you start the recovery wizard, it will be shut down. You can also replace the data volumes with the data files from the storage snapshot after the recovery wizard has stopped the database system.

In the recovery wizard, choose the recovery type, as you would with a data backup (see Section 5.4 for a full discussion). If you use the storage snapshot to copy the database, you can only recover the database to the full backup represented by the snapshot. If—as in our case—you recover the database from its own snapshot, and if log segments and log backups are available and undamaged, then point-in-time recovery is also possible, including restoring the database to its latest consistent state.

In our example, we are choosing to restore the database to its latest consistent state, as can be seen from the third step of the recovery wizard in Figure 5.11, which contains an indicator for the SELECTED POINT IN TIME, shown in ❶. The system has detected that a snapshot is available in the data files, as shown in ❷, and it has found the EXTERNAL BACKUP ID, shown in ❸, that we entered in the backup catalog.

During recovery, the system will load the converter table from the snapshot, then roll forward redo logs, starting from the log position of the snapshot. Redo logs will be read from log backups and log segments as required.

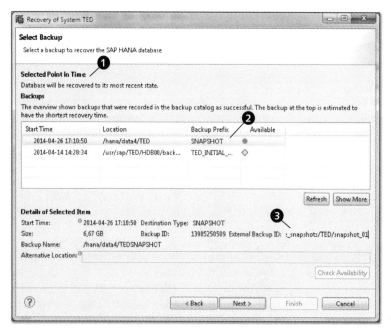

Figure 5.11 Recovering the Database from a Storage Snapshot

5.3.5 SQL Syntax for Managing Database Snapshots

In addition to using the Backup Editor of SAP HANA Studio, you can also manage snapshots through SQL commands. The syntax for creating, confirming, and abandoning a snapshot is given in Listing 5.6.

```
// Create a snapshot with comment 'Test Snapshot':
BACKUP DATA CREATE SNAPSHOT COMMENT 'Test Snapshot';
// Read the BACKUP_ID of the snapshot from the backup catalog:
SELECT backup_id, comment FROM "PUBLIC"."M_BACKUP_CATALOG"
  WHERE entry_type_name - 'data snapshot'
    AND state_name='prepared';
// Confirm the snapshot with external ID 'Abcd1234' and
// backup ID as determined in the above query:
BACKUP DATA CLOSE SNAPSHOT BACKUP_ID '<backup_id>'
  SUCCESSFUL 'Abcd1234';
// Abandon the snapshot, adding the comment 'Not needed':
BACKUP DATA CLOSE SNAPSHOT BACKUP_ID '<backup_id>'
  UNSUCCESSFUL 'Not needed';
```

Listing 5.6 SQL Syntax for Managing Storage Snapshots

5.4   Data Backup and Recovery of the SAP HANA Database

Data backups are the first and most rudimentary step towards protecting the database against the loss of information in case of incidents such as damage to the data volumes. They contain an image of the database at one point in time in a dedicated set of files.

In combination with log backups and log segments, data backups can be used to restore the database to any state between the point in time of backup creation and the latest consistent state preceding the recovery. Data backups can also be used to copy the database by recovering the database backup in a different (but compatible) database instance. This section will walk you through the most important aspects of data backup and recovery in SAP HANA.

5.4.1   Supported Backup Mechanisms

SAP HANA supports two fundamentally different backup mechanisms. Through *file-based backups*, the system writes into backup files located on a file system that is mounted in the database server(s). This backup location can and should be on a network file system or similar location. Nevertheless, from the point of view of the database it creates backup files locally.

SAP HANA also offers a backup mechanism based on network pipes. The system comes with an interface named BackInt for SAP HANA, which allows the execution of data backups, shipping of log backups, retrieving of backup information, and managing backups. Third-party backup tools can implement this interface and will then act as a middle layer between the database and the backup storage system, as shown in Figure 5.12.

When third-party backup tools are used, the responsibilities in the backup system are shared between multiple parties. SAP delivers the SAP HANA database, including its BackInt interface, as shown in ❶. The backup tool vendor needs to provide a backup agent to run on the SAP HANA database server. This agent must implement the BackInt interface and will communicate with the vendor's backup system (backup tool). The backup agent and tool are in the responsibility of the backup tool vendor, as shown in ❷. The backup tool will be connected to a backup storage system of some type, as shown in ❸, and manages the data transfer between the SAP HANA database and that storage system.

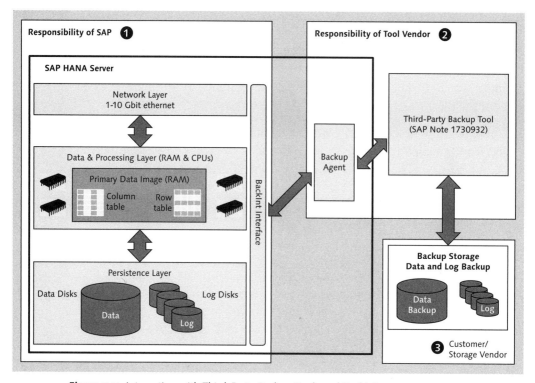

Figure 5.12 Integration with Third-Party Backup Tools and BackInt

If an SAP HANA system is configured to use the BackInt interface, then data and log backups will be sent to named pipes of the BackInt interface. Storage snapshots will not be managed by BackInt; you always have to use SAP HANA Studio or the SQL syntax for storage snapshot management, regardless of the mechanism used for database backups.

Because backup administration using third-party backup tools heavily depends on the chosen tool, we only discuss here file-based backups managed via SAP HANA Studio or SQL syntax. Information on third-party backup tools that have been certified for use with SAP HANA is contained in SAP Note 1730932.

All generic information in this section applies to both backup mechanisms, so reading on will also be helpful for users of third-party backup tools.

5.4.2   Properties of Data Backups in SAP HANA

A data backup in SAP HANA is a full online copy of one particular consistent state of the entire database system in dedicated backup files. The state is defined by the log position of the database at the time of executing the data backup. Technically, the data backup is very similar to a snapshot, with the major difference that all physical pages mapped by the converter table of the data backup are written to dedicated backup files instead of simply freezing the snapshot's pages in the data files of the database.

Internally, the database performs a database snapshot in order to map all relevant pages. Then, all physical pages from the snapshot's converter table are copied into backup files. The snapshot is automatically released as soon as all pages have been written to the backup files.

The log position of the data backup is thus the current log position at the time of the exclusive consistent change lock that is acquired in order to create the snapshot. Any database modification happening after this point in time is not reflected in the data backup.

Note that there is no offline data backup option for SAP HANA. As every data backup can be used to recover the database into a consistent state, there is simply no need to shut down the system for a consistent copy.

We give a schematic visualization of the data backup process in Figure 5.13. This figure is based on the data snapshot creation discussed in Section 5.3.2 and shown in Figure 5.7.

Assume that the database snapshot, shown in ❶, for the data backup has been prepared. The system will start writing all pages of the snapshot to the backup file. Write transactions are allowed, so modifications of the database content may occur, which means that a logical page, L1, gets modified, represented by new state L1', and this modification is reflected in the data file after the next savepoint operation, as shown in ❷. Page P1 from the snapshot is marked as a shadow page, S1, and a new physical page, P1', is created that contains the new content of L1'.

The write operation of the backup process will only transfer the snapshot content to the backup file. To reflect the fact that there are no shadow pages in a data backup, the original page P1/S1 from the snapshot is named P1 in the data backup file, as shown in ❸.

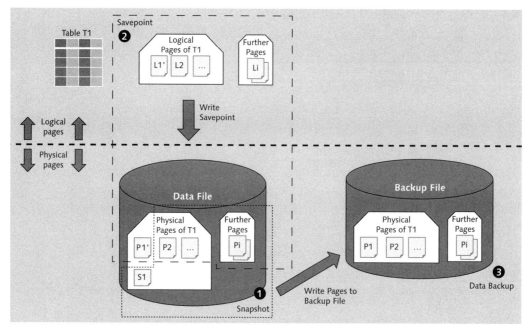

Figure 5.13 Creating a Data Backup

Contents of Data Backups

In SAP HANA, a data backup is always a full backup. There is no mechanism for incremental backups yet. Therefore, every database backup will contain all physical pages of the current database image.

In scale-out systems, the data backup contains all data from all processes on all hosts of the system. The consistency of the data backup in such distributed systems is guaranteed by the global savepoint that is part of the database snapshot on which the data backup is based.

In the course of creating the data backup, only the physical pages of this snapshot are copied to the data files. That is to say, the data backup will only contain the current payload of the data files. Unused blocks or other versions of physical pages that exist due to the shadow page concept will not be copied. A data backup is therefore always smaller than the data files (at the time of backup creation).

Note that data backups *do not* include the configuration files of the database. It is good practice to create backup copies of the customizing in the system-wide and host-specific layers of the database configuration and to store these copies with the data backups. With the exception of the customizing of running services in the daemon.ini file, successful database recovery will not depend on the database configuration.

Size of Data Backups

The best estimate of the expected size of a data backup can be obtained from a query to the system view M_CONVERTER_STATISTICS, as shown in Listing 5.7. That listing also includes an SQL example to check whether there is sufficient disk size available on the file system containing the configured data backup location (parameter [persistence] • basepath_databackup of the file global.ini). Note that the BACKUP CHECK command will also resolve environment variables of the <sid>adm operating system user, such as $(DIR_INSTANCE), which expands to /usr/sap/<SID>/HDB<instance>.

```
// Query the total size (in bytes) of all allocated pages
// that define the current data image:
SELECT SUM(allocated_page_size) FROM m_converter_statistics;
// Let us assume the answer is 6 487 576 576 bytes. We can
// now check if the data backup file system has enough free
// space (let's add an extra GB for safety):
BACKUP CHECK
  USING FILE ('$(DIR_INSTANCE)/backup/data')
  SIZE 7487576576;
// Generically, the statement syntax is:
BACKUP CHECK USING FILE ('<path_name>') SIZE <size_in_bytes>;
```

Listing 5.7 Checking Free Disk Space in the Data Backup Location

The BACKUP CHECK query will return successfully if there is sufficient disk space available, or it will return error code 14 (cannot allocate enough disk space) if not.

If you would like to automate the backup check, you can create a stored procedure or some other program following the example we give in Listing 5.8. That procedure will determine the estimated size of the data backup and add an extra GB for safety. It will then check whether a data path has been customized (which can only be a system-wide setting). Depending on the outcome of the check, it will read the value of parameter basepath_databackup either from the SYSTEM or from the DEFAULT layer of global.ini. Finally, it executes the BACKUP CHECK command with backup location and estimated backup size as determined earlier.

The procedure does not have a return value. Instead, it will either complete successfully (sufficient disk space) or with error code 14 (insufficient disk space).

```
CREATE PROCEDURE check_backup_space ()
  LANGUAGE SQLSCRIPT
  AS
    v_backup_size BIGINT;
    v_backup_path NVARCHAR(256);
    v_found       INTEGER := 0;
    v_statement   NVARCHAR(512) := '';
BEGIN
  /* Determine estimated backup size */
  SELECT SUM(allocated_page_size) INTO v_backup_size
    FROM m_converter_statistics;
  /* Add 10^9 bytes (ca. 950 MB) for extra safety */
  v_backup_size := v_backup_size + 1000000000;
  /* Check if there is a system-wide customized backup path */
  SELECT COUNT (*) INTO v_found FROM m_inifile_contents
    WHERE file_name='global.ini' AND layer_name='SYSTEM'
    AND section='persistence' AND key='basepath_databackup';
  IF :v_found = 0 THEN
    /* If not: read DEFAULT value of basepath_databackup */
    SELECT value INTO v_backup_path FROM m_inifile_contents
      WHERE file_name='global.ini' AND layer_name='DEFAULT'
      AND section='persistence' AND key='basepath_databackup';
  ELSE
    /* Otherwise, read SYSTEM-layer value */
    SELECT value INTO v_backup_path FROM m_inifile_contents
      WHERE file_name='global.ini' AND layer_name='SYSTEM'
      AND section='persistence' AND key='basepath_databackup';
  END IF;
  /* Assemble and run the check statement.*/
  v_statement := 'BACKUP CHECK USING FILE ('''  ||
    :v_backup_path || ''') SIZE ' || :v_backup_size;
  EXEC v_statement;
END;
```

Listing 5.8 Procedure for Automatic Backup Space Check

Naming of the Backup Files

A database backup of an SAP HANA system always consists of multiple backup files. Each data-persistent process will create one backup file (the master name server creates two). All files will be written to the same file system path defined in the parameter [persistence] • basepath_databackup.

Data backup file names are built from three components according to the pattern `<basepath_databackup>/<prefix>_<suffix>`. In this file name, `<prefix>` is an identifier for a particular data backup that can be chosen by the backup administrator when creating the backup. The system generated `<suffix>` has three parts: `<suffix>` = `databackup_<source>_<count>`, where `<source>` is the volume ID of the data volume whose backup is being created. The system topology is written to the backup file with `<source>` = 0. The size of data backup files can be limited, so that for one process there may be multiple files with consecutive values of `<count>`, starting with `<count>` = 1 for the first file.

A typical backup file for the index server process (which may have volume ID 3) of database system WUP with instance number 42, in the default backup file location, and with backup prefix "Monday_20140230", would thus be */usr/sap/WUP/HDB42/backup/data/Monday_20140230_databackup_3_1*.

Consistency Checks of Data Backups

Data backups of the SAP HANA database contain consistency check information both on the level of the backup files and on the level of individual data pages. The backup consistency can be verified at any time by using tools delivered with the database software. See Section 5.4.5 for more details on the consistency checks and especially the test tools.

5.4.3   Creating Data Backups

Data backups can manually be created within the Backup Editor of SAP HANA Studio. Users with the required privileges can start this editor by double-clicking the BACKUP item in the navigator tree of the SAP HANA system in the SYSTEMS view of SAP HANA Studio.

Privilege Information

In order to create data backups with the Backup Editor, the database user must have system privilege BACKUP ADMIN or BACKUP OPERATOR and also system privilege CATALOG READ.

In the Backup Editor (Figure 5.14), you can start the data backup by clicking on the OPEN BACKUP WIZARD button, shown in ❷, of the OVERVIEW tab, shown in ❶. It is also possible to start the backup wizard directly from the navigator tree in the

Systems view of SAP HANA Studio (the same privileges are required); if you right-click either on the top node or on the Backup node of the navigator tree, the you can choose Back Up... from the context menu.

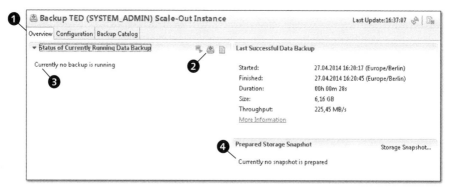

Figure 5.14 Starting a Data Backup from the Backup Editor

Prerequisites for Running a Data Backup

Data backups can only be created while the database is online. This requires that all processes of the database are running. In distributed systems with failover nodes, a data backup can be created in a failover situation as long as all data volumes are assigned to active services.

A data backup is also only possible when no other data backup is running and no snapshot is prepared. You should check the Status of Currently Running Data Backups, as shown in ❸, and of Prepared Storage Snapshots, as shown in ❹, in the Backup Editor before starting the backup.

Finally, there must be sufficient disk space on the backup storage.

While a data backup is being written, the database can be used as usual. The log backup system is also not affected by writing data backups.

Running the Backup

In the data backup wizard (Figure 5.15, left-hand side; see ❶), you can configure properties of the backup to be created. If the system is configured to use the Back-Int interface with a third-party tool, you can choose Destination Type (shown in ❷) File or BackInt. With file-based backups (as in our case), you can customize the Backup Destination, shown in ❸, for the backup to be written. That is, you can change the target directory for writing the backup. The configuration value of parameter `basepath_databackup` is prefilled.

Typically, the most important input field is that of the BACKUP PREFIX, shown in ❹. Here, you should choose a term that helps you identify the data backup later on. A time stamp and/or an indicator for the reason you are creating the backup are good choices.

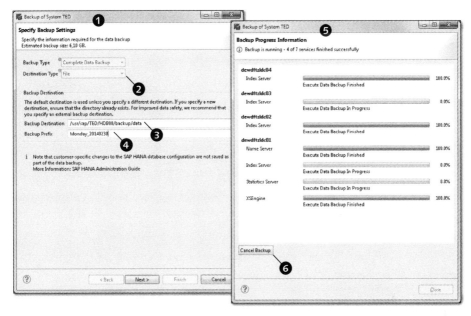

Figure 5.15 Running a Data Backup

Before you can start the actual backup, you have to proceed to the second screen of the backup wizard which will display a summary of the backup to be created. If you click the FINISH button on that screen, the database backup will be started.

You can monitor the backup progress within the wizard. A screenshot from a running backup is shown in the right-hand side (shown in ❺) of Figure 5.15. The wizard displays the progress for the data volumes of all data-persistent processes.

The same information is available on the OVERVIEW tab of the Backup Editor; see Figure 5.16. The editor displays the overall progress of the data backup in a single indicator, shown in ❶. The progress for individual data volumes can be viewed by expanding the DETAILS section, as shown in ❷. In this way, administrators can monitor the progress of ongoing database backups, regardless of how and by whom the backup was started.

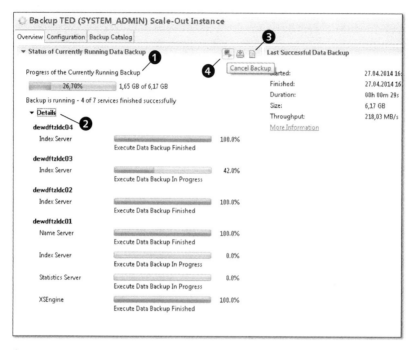

Figure 5.16 *Monitoring and Cancelling a Backup in the Backup Editor*

Once the data backup is finished, the wizard displays a success (or error) message and offers viewing the log of the backup operation. You can also view the backup log at any later point in time. The database collects log information for the creation of all log and data backups in the backup.log file, which is located in the database server's trace directory (in a scale-out system, with the trace files of the master node). From the OVERVIEW tab of the Backup Editor, the log file is available via the OPEN LOG FILE button, shown in ❸.

Cancelling a Running Data Backup

Running data backups can be cancelled in multiple ways:

▶ If you started the data backup from the Backup Editor of SAP HANA Studio, then you can cancel it directly in the backup wizard. At the bottom of the progress monitor, you can find a CANCEL BACKUP button (item ❻ in Figure 5.15).

- Any database user with the `BACKUP ADMIN` system privilege can cancel a running data backup from the Backup Editor in SAP HANA Studio. On the OVERVIEW tab of the Backup Editor, there is a CANCEL BACKUP button in the top-right corner of the status section (item ❹ in Figure 5.16). This button is only active while a data backup is running.
- Finally, you can cancel running backups by using an SQL syntax, which we introduce in Section 5.4.10.

Performance of Writing Data Backups

We have not attempted to run any performance tests or create benchmark information in the course of writing this book. It is, however, interesting for administrators to at least have a ballpark figure of the performance they can expect when writing data backups.

In simple tests, we have found the write performance of data backups to be of the order of about 500 GB/h when writing to a local storage system and without applying any optimizations. If your backup storage is connected to a network file system or similar system, I/O throughput may be limiting backup performance, depending on your hardware setup.

If you can ignore I/O throttling, then the performance of writing data backups in scale-out systems will not be influenced by the number of hosts, because all hosts will write their data backups in parallel. That is, a scale-out instance with 10 worker nodes, each managing 500 GB of data, may write its entire 5 TB data backup within one hour if the I/O system provides sufficient throughput.

5.4.4 Concepts of Database Recovery

Database recovery is the process of building new data files of the database from a data backup (or storage snapshot), the log backups, and the log segments. A recovery always applies to the whole database system; it is not possible to recover individual schemas or objects from a backup.

The recovery procedure supports multiple modes of recovery, depending on the state (or point in time) to which the database shall be recovered:

- **Recovery to most recent state (last consistent state)**
  In this mode, the database will be recovered to the state represented by all committed transactions before the last shutdown or crash.

The recovery procedure requires a data backup or database snapshot (the more recent, the better) and all redo log entries from the log position of data backup or snapshot onwards. In most cases, redo logs will be replayed from log backups and log segments.

Recovery to the last consistent state is the typical recovery mode in case the data volumes of the database have been damaged or corrupted.

▶ **Recovery to a specific data backup**
In this mode, only the information from the backup files will be restored. This technically resets the database to the log position from the snapshot on which the database was based.

For recovery, only a data backup or storage snapshot is required. The log area contents will be erased. That is, you will irreversibly delete any information in the database that is more recent than the data backup to which you are recovering. The log area will be initialized implicitly—which means that all existing log segments will be removed, and new ones will be created.

Recovering a system to a specific data backup is most useful for system copies. In regular operations, it is a rather unlikely option.

▶ **Arbitrary point-in-time recovery**
With arbitrary point-in-time recovery, you can recover the system not to a logical state (e.g., "last consistent" or "specific backup") but to the state it was in at a particular point in time.

The recovery generally has the same requirements as recovery to the most recent state.

▶ Typically this option is used for forensic purposes; if you know that data was corrupted by a user action, a data load process, or similar, you can reset the database to a state before the corruption happened. We will not discuss forensic recovery methods here, as they will be heavily dependent on the applications that were running on the database.

▶ **Recover to a specific log position**
The recovery to a specific log position is a technical recovery method that *should only be used by SAP Support*. It will basically recover the database to a specific point in time, but this point will be chosen not by a time marker but by a log position. Because it is very difficult to map log positions to events in the physical world, this recovery mode is only meaningful to database experts.

Note that in typical usage scenarios the SAP HANA database or the application running on it will be connected to other systems. Setting back the state of the database independently from those connected systems will create an inconsistency that cannot be fixed by means of database administration. If you decide to recover a production database to any other than the most recent state, make sure to consult SAP Note 434645 and SAP Note 434647 to understand the implications to the system landscape.

Recovery Sequence

The exact sequence of a database recovery will depend on the chosen recovery mode. Generally, a recovery consists of the steps depicted in Figure 5.17. The recovery will transfer the database from its initial state, shown in ❶, to the new state, shown in ❷. In the course of the recovery, the data files, shown in ❸, will be rebuilt.

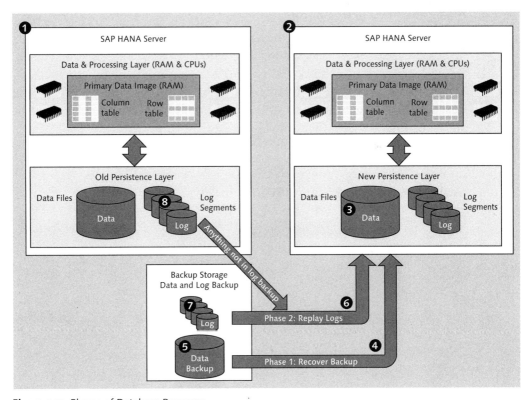

Figure 5.17 Phases of Database Recovery

There are three phases to the recovery process: In the first phase, shown in ❹, a data backup (or snapshot), shown in ❺, is recovered. Technically, new data files, shown in ❸, are created in the data volumes, and all physical pages from data backup or snapshot are copied into these data files. This phase will occur in any recovery mode.

In the second recovery phase, shown in ❻, redo logs are replayed. The system will determine the log position of the data backup or snapshot and locate all log back-ups, shown in ❼, and log segments, shown in ❽, containing more recent log entries. The system will replay either all redo log entries (last consistent state) or all entries until the selected point in time or log position is reached. Phase 2 will be skipped when recovering to a specific backup or snapshot.

In the third phase—not depicted in Figure 5.17—the database system is restarted. At the end of this phase, the database system will again be fully available.

Initializing the Log Area

When a system is recovered from its own data backup to its last consistent state or an arbitrary point in time, the recovery process offers you the option to initial-ize the log area. If you choose this option, no redo log entries from the log seg-ments will be replayed. At the end of the recovery process, all existing log seg-ments in the log volumes will have been deleted, and new segments will be created as if the system were newly installed.

Initializing the log area might be necessary if the segments are rendered unusable, for example, by a file system corruption. In this case, you can only recover the database to the latest committed state in the log backups.

> **Note**
>
> Under normal circumstances, you should not explicitly initialize the log area when recovering the database from its own data backup.

In some situations, initializing the log area is not optional. One such situation is recovery to a specific data backup or snapshot. In this recovery mode, the system will always initialize the log area.

The log area must also be initialized when you recover a data backup into a dif-ferent database, for example, for a system copy.

If the log area is not initialized, the contents of the log segments can be used in the course of database recovery. Once recovery is finished successfully, the log segment contents are not needed anymore, because the new data files contain all the data of the recovered state. The log segments will remain on disk in state Free and can be re-used for writing log entries.

5.4.5   Recovering the Database

The actual process of recovering an SAP HANA system is supported by a recovery wizard in SAP HANA Studio. We will guide you through this wizard for the different recovery modes.

Prerequisites for Recovery

The database system to recover and the data backup used in the recovery process must fulfill several requirements in order for recovery to be possible:

▶ **Correct number and type of processes**
A database backup contains backup files for all data volumes, that is, for all data-persistent processes of the source system. The target system of the recovery must have the same process configuration, that is, the same number of index servers, XS servers, script servers, and so on. It is possible to start multiple processes of the same type—for example, multiple index servers—on one host, so that the number of hosts does not matter.

We include examples of resolving incompatibilities in the topology between source and target system of backup/recovery in Section 5.4.7.

▶ **Database version**
The software version of the target system must be at least as high as that of the source system. You cannot recover a backup into a system with a lower release level (revision number).

Exceptions may occur when the source system of the backup is on a maintenance revision level and the target is a support package release; see SAP Note 1948334.

▶ **Credentials**
The person executing the recovery procedure must know the password of the <sid>adm user of the target database system.

Checking Backup Consistency

It is possible to check the backup files before a recovery. For this purpose, SAP provides two Linux tools named hdbbackupcheck and hdbbackupdiag, which are installed as part of the database software.

With the hdbbackupcheck tool, you can check backup files one by one for correctness. The check tool supports both file-based backups and the BackInt interface. You need to run the tool individually for each file (part) of a given data backup; there is no built-in option to check all files of a given backup.

The parameters tested include simple checks, such as verification of the file size, and internal information that requires database kernel knowledge, such as the check of page-wise checksums. However, the check does not perform an actual recovery.

In order to test a given backup file, including printout of test information, use the syntax given in Listing 5.9.

The hdbbackupdiag tool, on the other hand, allows you verify that all data and log backup files needed for a particular recovery are available in the specified locations. The most important usage options for this case are also given in Listing 5.9.

If not all data and log backups are available in the configured locations, you can specify a directory in which to search for the latest backup catalog and additionally one alternative location for the data backup as well as multiple alternative locations for log backups.

The return value of the tool is 0 if the check is successful or 1 if errors occurred. There is also comprehensive text output that in case of issues indicates why a recovery with the given backup locations would not be successful.

```
# Generic syntax for hdbbackupcheck
hdbbackupcheck -v <full_backup_filename>
# Specific example for hdbbackupcheck:
hdbbackupcheck -v \
  /usr/sap/WUP/HDB42/backup/data/COMPLETE_DATA_BACKUP_0_1
# Generic syntax for hdbbackupdiag
hdbbackupdiag --check -u <timestamp> -d <catalog_directory> \
  [--dataDir <data_backup_directory>] \
  [--logDirs <log_backup_directory_1>,<log_backup_dir_2>,...]
```

Listing 5.9 Using the hdbbackupcheck and hdbbackupdiag Tools

Further information on the tool usage is given in SAP Note 1869119 for `hdbback-upcheck` and SAP Note 1873247 for `hdbbackupdiag`.

Starting the Recovery Process

A database recovery can be started in SAP HANA Studio from the navigator tree of the system to recover. Right-click on the top node of the navigator tree, and choose RECOVER... from the context menu. It does not matter whether the system is online or offline at this point.

If the system is online, you will be asked to confirm system shutdown. Clicking CANCEL in this step will abort the recovery procedure and leave the system undisturbed.

Once the system is shut down, you are presented with the first screen of the recovery wizard (Figure 5.18). This screen offers all four recovery types, with recovery to a specific log position only available after clicking the ADVANCED button, shown in ❶. If you choose to recover to a specific point in time or a specific log position, you will have to enter details accordingly.

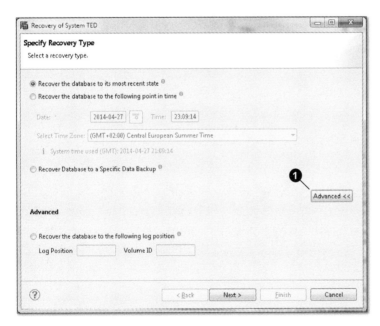

Figure 5.18 Recovery Wizard: Choosing the Recovery Type

In our detailed example, we will choose to recover to the most recent state. The recovery sequence in this mode is the same as that for point-in-time recovery or recovery to a specific log position. Recovery to a specific data backup has a different, but simpler, workflow.

After choosing the recovery type and progressing to the next screen, you have to enter the locations of the log backups (Figure 5.19). You may wonder why you are not asked for the data backup location first, and the explanation is simply that the backup catalog (a list of all data and log backups; see Section 5.4.8) is maintained together with the log backups. From the backup catalog, the database can determine a list of all data backups that may potentially serve in a recovery scenario.

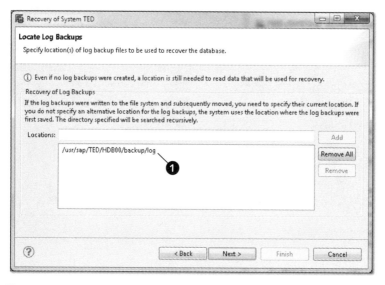

Figure 5.19 Recovery Wizard: Entering the Log Backup Location

As location, the wizard initially suggests the content of the `basepath_logbackup` parameter, shown in ❶. In case you have moved some or all log segments after they were created, you can enter additional locations. You can also use the `hdb-backupdiag` tool to list all data and log backup files required for a recovery; this is especially useful if you have moved backup files to a different storage location and need to copy them back for the recovery. See Section 5.4.7 and SAP Note 1821207 for details.

> **Note**
>
> If you have changed the value of the `basepath_logbackup` parameter since creating the most recent data backup but have not moved any log backups from their initial location,

then you do not have to change any entry here; the system will find the most recent backup catalog in the current log backup location. This backup catalog contains the initial location of each log backup, so the database will be able to locate all log backups.

You really only need to enter other locations here if the most recent backup catalog is not in the location specified by `basepath_logbackup` (e.g., when copying a database) and/or if log backups have been moved from their initial locations.

When you progress to the next step, the system will look for the most recent version of the backup catalog and read information on all available backups that may be used to recover the database. These backups are listed on the third screen of the recovery wizard (Figure 5.20). You can select an individual backup to display details, shown in ❶, such as the time of backup creation, its size, and the file system location as recorded in the backup catalog. If the data backup has been moved to a different location, you can enter the new file system path.

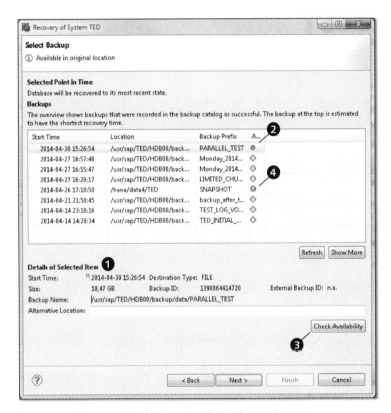

Figure 5.20 Recovery Wizard: Choosing the Backup to Recover

The system does not automatically check if the listed backups are available in the recorded location. Backup availability is indicated by the colored icons behind each data backup, such as the green icon shown in ❷. To check a given backup, highlight it in the table and click the Check Availability button, shown in ❸.

Backups are listed in ascending order of estimated recovery time, where the estimate is based on the amount of log entries that will need to be replayed. As can be seen, the system also shows database snapshots. The snapshot indicated in ❹ is not available, showing that it has already been released.

On the next screen of the wizard, you can choose selected additional options (Figure 5.21). The first option allows you to check for the availability of all required log backups before the actual recovery starts. It is highly recommended to enable this option. The system can check on the file system or in a third-party backup system using the BackInt interface.

The most dangerous option is the option to initialize the log area (see the discussion in Section 5.4.4). This option is required when copying the database or if the log volumes are corrupted. In other circumstances, it will probably not be a good choice to initialize the log area.

Note

If you initialize the log area in combination with an attempt to recover the database from its own data backup to its most recent state (or a state more recent than the last log backup and savepoint), then you will lose data, because only log backups will be replayed.

If you copy the database using a data backup or storage snapshot, the target system will need to be equipped with a new license key. If you already have a license key available, you can choose to install it as part of the recovery process, thus eliminating the possibility that you might forget about license key installation later. You can also install the new license key within the first 90 days after recovery.

The final screen of the recovery wizard presents a summary screen of the recovery to perform. Check the information on this screen carefully before you progress, because an incorrect recovery might lead to permanent loss of data (e.g., if you inadvertently choose to initialize the log area, use the wrong recovery type, etc.).

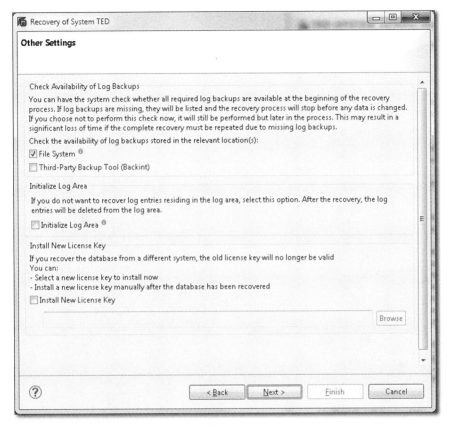

Figure 5.21 Recovery Wizard: Further Options

Monitoring a Database Recovery

The first and best place to monitor a database recovery is the recovery wizard, which will show the recovery progress for all processes of the database individually in each of the three phases (data recovery, log recovery, and restart), as shown in Figure 5.22. The recovery phase is shown at in the header area, shown in ❶, of the wizard.

More detailed information for the ongoing recovery process is written into the backup.log file that is located with the diagnosis files of the master node—typically */usr/sap/<SID>/HDB<instance>/<hostname>/trace/backup.log*. If interested, you can monitor this file, for example, by using the `tail` command on the operating system or by using the Diagnosis Files Editor in diagnosis mode.

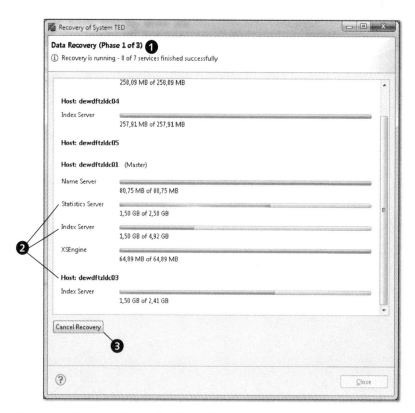

Figure 5.22 Recovery Wizard: Monitoring the Recovery Progress

Performance of Database Recovery

As you can see from the monitor (Figure 5.22, shown in ❷), the recovery is sched-uled and performed for all services and all hosts in parallel. Therefore, the speed of recovery does not depend on the number of hosts in a scale-out system as long as the I/O system provides sufficient throughput. Ignoring the influence of the I/O system, the data recovery of a 10-node scale-out instance can be as fast as the data recovery of a single node of the same host size. This, of course, assumes that data is uniformly distributed across all nodes and that the amount of data in the single-node system is equal to the average amount of data per node in the scale-out sys-tem.

In basic tests, we have observed a data recovery speed that was similar to the per-formance of writing the data backup.

In the next recovery phase—log recovery—parallelization can be limited by inter-host dependencies of distributed transactions that need to be replayed.

Cancelling a Database Recovery

The recovery monitor in Figure 5.22 also contains a CANCEL RECOVERY button, shown in ❸. If you cancel the recovery process, the database system will be left in an inconsistent state and cannot be started normally any longer. The same is true if the recovery process cannot finish successfully for any other reasons.

If recovery of a database system has been interrupted, then you will need to fix the underlying issue and repeat the recovery process—maybe by using a different data backup or storage snapshot or a different recovery type—in order to restore the database system to a working state.

5.4.6   Technical Recovery Scenarios

There can be different situations that require a database recovery (full recovery will not be possible in all cases):

▶ **Data area unusable**
The data may be unusable because of a file system corruption, human error, or other reasons that either render the data files unusable or lead to the deletion of at least one data file.

In this situation, the database can be recovered to its most recent state if a data backup is available and all log entries are available, starting from the log position of the data backup. The log entries may partially reside in log backups or entirely in the log segments, depending on system settings and timing.

▶ **Log area unusable**
If the log area is rendered unusable—which may be caused by something as small as the manual deletion of a single log segment—the database cannot be recovered to its most recent state any longer. If a data backup and log backups are available, you can recover to the most recent state contained in log backups by starting a recovery to most recent state and choosing to initialize the log area.

Unless you are operating a disaster-tolerant database with system replication, SAP HANA does not offer a means to write log entries to multiple physical locations at once. You can try to protect against loss of the log area by setting up mirroring of the log volumes with storage technology.

▶ **Data and log area unusable**
The situation is identical to an unusable log area.

▶ **Recent data or log backups corrupted**
If you notice that recent data or log backups are corrupted, then you should create a new data backup as soon as possible. If you know that there is a corruption in the log backups, then you should also remove all affected (and older) log backups so that nobody can attempt a database recovery using these files.

5.4.7 Copying an SAP HANA System Using Database Backups

In addition to its use in recovering a system in case of a corruption of the database persistence, homogenous system copy is a potential use case for copying the database. In the terminology used by SAP, a homogenous system copy in SAP HANA is one from an SAP HANA database to another SAP HANA database (as opposed to copying the contents of a different database into an SAP HANA database).

The act of copying the database using backup and recovery is trivial in itself. We use the topic to also discuss how you can resolve typical incompatibilities between the system topologies of the source and target systems. The two situations we will discuss are summarized in Table 5.8. In the first case, we are copying a single-node system, and in the second, we are copying a scale-out instance.

Case	Property	Source System	Target System
1	hostname	ld9506	dewdftzldc01
	SID	WUP	CPY
	Instance	42	78
	Statistics Service	Integrated in Name & Index Server	Dedicated Process
	AFL	Installed	Not Installed
2	SID	TED	DUP
	# Nodes	4+1	3+0

Table 5.8 Cases for System Copy

> **Note**
>
> Database copy using data backups is only supported with file-based backups (release level SPS 8). The BackInt interface does not yet include functionality for database copy.
>
> If you manage your database backups with third-party tools that implement the BackInt interface, then you can still use storage snapshots for database copies.

Preparations for a System Copy

Before you start the recovery process for a system copy, make sure to check the following prerequisites on the target system of the copy:

▶ **Database versions**
The target database must already be installed, and its software version must be at least the same as the software version of the target system.

▶ **Number of processes with persistence**
The number of processes of each type in the target system must match the configuration of the source system. It is best to configure the correct number of instances in the target system before starting the recovery.

▶ **Shut down the target system**
The target database must be shut down before you can continue with the next preparatory steps.

▶ **Remove data and log backups of target system**
The configured locations for data and log backups (basepath_databackup and basepath_logbackup) of the target system must be empty. Otherwise, you may by mistake choose a backup of the target system for recovery or run into other difficulties. You must delete the data and log backup files (if there are any) or move them to a different location if you assume that you might need these backups again.

▶ **Provide data and log backups for recovery**
For the system copy, you can recover either to a specific data backup or to a specific point in time, up to the most recent state reflected in the log backups of the source system. Depending on the state you want to copy, you need to provide either a data backup or a data backup and log backups. See ahead for an efficient way to determine required backups.

▶ **Location of data and log backups to recover from**
By default, the recovery process will search for data and log backups in the configured locations (basepath_databackup and basepath_logbackup) of the target system. We recommend providing the backup files in a different directory and pointing the recovery process to this location.

Choosing the Required Data and Log Backups

Depending on your system setup, you may have to copy the backup files from the source system to the target system. In this case, you will be happy to learn that the `hdbbackupdiag` tool can list all data and log backup files required for system recovery.

The tool will check the backup catalog and locate the most recent data backup. Based on that backup, it will determine all log backup files that are needed for either a full recovery or recovery until a specified point in time.

The output is the list of all backup files needed for the recovery (not including path names). The syntax for creating this list is given in Listing 5.10, and further documentation is available in SAP Note 1821207 and SAP Note 1873247.

```
# Generic syntax:
hdbbackupdiag -f -d <log_backup_directory> [-u <timestamp>]
# Example invocation for full recovery (most recent state):
hdbbackupdiag -f -d /usr/sap/WUP/HDB42/backup/log
```

Listing 5.10 Determining Required Backup Files with hdbbackupdiag

Copying the System

The actual system copy is a standard database recovery with a number of exceptions:

▶ In the recovery wizard of the target database, select the appropriate recovery mode. Note that point-in-time recovery as well as recovery to the most recent state will only include log backups. The log segments of the source system cannot be used in a system copy.

▶ When you have to enter the log backup location, remove the proposed default location, and add the path to the log backups that you want to recover from. As in regular recovery, the database will determine possible recovery paths from the most recent backup catalog that it finds in this location.

▶ The next important exception comes when you have to choose the data backup to base the recovery on. As in any recovery, the system will assume that the data backup resides in the location obtained from the backup catalog. In a system copy, this will most probably not be the correct location. Before checking the availability of the backup, you must therefore enter the actual backup location as ALTERNATIVE LOCATION.

▶ Another exception occurs on the OTHER SETTINGS screen of the recovery wizard; here you must choose to initialize the log area. The system does not make this choice automatically.

▸ In the course of the recovery, the database will erase the license information of the target system. Because the license key of the source system will not be valid in the target, the system will be left in a state without a license key. If there was a license key installed in the target system prior to the recovery, you can reinstall this license key. Otherwise, you will have to generate a new license key following the recovery.

If all requirements are met, your system copy will be finished after the successful recovery. We will, however, now discuss typical problems that may occur if your source and target systems do not match perfectly.

Resolving Typical Problems: Case One

In case one from Table 5.8, the aspect that will cause trouble in the course of recovery is the statistics server. In the source system, it has been embedded into the index and name server processes as described in SAP Note 1917938. In the target system, it is a standalone process. If you do not realize this before starting the recovery process, the recovery will abort immediately with an error message, as shown in Figure 5.23.

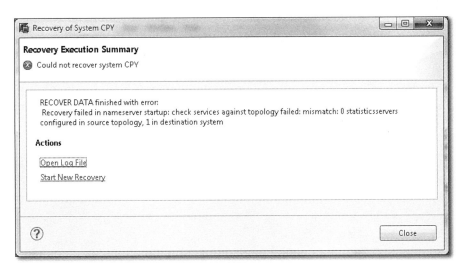

Figure 5.23 Recovery Failing with Wrong Number of Processes

Because you have already started the actual system recovery, the system cannot be started normally any longer. You will first need to perform a successful recovery.

In our case, this can rather easily be corrected by applying the configuration changes described in SAP Note 1917938. While the database is offline, you cannot use the recommended tools to modify the configuration files. Instead, you will have to edit the configuration files manually.

> **Note**
>
> You should check the compatibility of the system landscape prior to starting the recovery. In this case, you can change the configuration with SAP HANA Studio or other recommended tools. Our procedure should only be used in an emergency.

Enabling the statistics service in the name server is a system-wide configuration. You therefore have to enter the file nameserver.ini in the file system path */usr/sap/<SID>/SYS/global/hdb/custom/config/*, and make sure the file contains a [statisticsserver] section with parameter active = true, as shown in Figure 5.24.

Figure 5.24 Enabling the Statistics Server in File nameserver.ini

Next, you must set the number of statistics server processes to zero. To do this, edit the daemon.ini file of your database server (master host in scale-out systems) in the directory */usr/sap/<SID>/<instance>/<hostname>/*. In that file, remove the entire [statisticsserver] section, including the parameter instances = 1. After making these adjustments to the configuration files of the target system, you can simply restart the recovery process.

In the reverse situation, that is, a service missing on the target system, you can simply add the service to the daemon.ini configuration file of the host. In the case of the statistics server, you also have to adjust the nameserver.ini file.

Note that the recovery process will leave the instance number and SID of the target system unchanged. Also, the installation of add-ons, such as the AFL package, does not matter. In our case, the AFLs were not installed on the target system prior to the recovery, and they still will not be afterwards, but they can of course be installed in the usual way.

Resolving Typical Problems: Case Two

In our second test case, we copy a scale-out system to a system with a smaller number of worker nodes. Our source system has four worker nodes and one failover node, whereas the target system only has three worker nodes and no failover node.

This situation can be resolved, because SAP HANA allows running multiple instances of the index server process for one database system on the same host. The relevant number is the number of index server worker processes; we can ignore any failover nodes.

In order to add a second index server on a given host, you need to modify the daemon.ini file of that host. In section [indexserver.c], set parameter instanceids = 40. This will add a new index server process that communicates on internal port 3<instance>40.

You can also add multiple additional index server processes on one host. In this case, set parameter instanceids to a comma-separated list of values starting at 40 with a spacing of 2. For adding three index servers on one host, set parameter instanceids = 40,42,44 in section [indexserver.c] of the host's daemon.ini.

> **Note**
>
> For the index server process, there are two key sections in the daemon.ini file: [index-server] is the section for the one mandatory instance of the process on any SAP HANA host. You must not make changes to that section. [indexserver.c] is the section for additional instances of the process on a given host. In the host-specific configuration files in */usr/sap/<SID>/<instance>/<hostname>/daemon.ini*, this section typically does not exist. When editing the file manually, you can add an entry
>
> ```
> [indexserver.c]
> instanceids = 40
> ```
>
> As before, if you realize the mismatch before starting the recovery, you should make the necessary changes in the target system by using the Configuration Editor of SAP HANA Studio.

After applying this configuration change, the recovery can be performed in the usual way. The recovery process will assign all index server volumes to the configured index server processes. A progress monitor for such a recovery is shown in Figure 5.25. You can see the recovery progress of two index server processes, shown in ❶, on the second host.

Figure 5.25 Recovery with Multiple Index Servers on One Host

5.4.8 Managing Backups: The Backup Catalog

The set of information that helps the database keep track of all historical data and log backups is maintained in the so-called backup catalog. It consists of two lists: the list of all backups that have been performed (including metadata, such as time or volume IDs, as well as success information) and the list of all backup files that have been created. Through the unambiguous BACKUP_ID, each backup can be linked to the list of files it consists of. In the case of log backups, this is a 1:1

relationship (each log backup represents the backing up of exactly one log segment). In the case of data backups, the single backup process creates multiple files.

> **Note**
>
> If a data backup is overwritten (i.e., if you create another data backup with the same name in the same location), then the entry of the overwritten backup will be deleted from the backup catalog.
>
> This is only applicable for file-based backups. When using the BackInt interface, the naming of backups is delegated to the third-party backup tool.

In the database, the backup catalog is exposed through two system views: M_BACKUP_CATALOG contains the list of all performed backups, and M_BACKUP_CATALOG_FILES reveals all data and log backup files. The views can be joined via field BACKUP_ID.

In the database persistence, the backup catalog is backed up to the configured location for log backups (configured in parameter basepath_logbackup) every time that the database writes a data or log backup. In this way, it is available independently from the data files and log segments, making sure that as long as the backup files themselves are available the backup catalog also can be accessed.

The file name of the backup catalog is *log_backup_0_0_0_0.<backup_id>*. With every data or log backup, a new version of the backup catalog is written, and old versions are not deleted automatically.

Because the backup catalog is written also when data backups are created, the system will create log backup files (of the backup catalog) even when automatic log backup is not enabled (e.g., in log mode overwrite).

The backup catalog is used in the recovery process, allowing the database to determine the best data backup to recover from, and all log backups required for replaying log entries. It is also essential for housekeeping of the backup files.

Housekeeping: Deleting Data and Log Backups

At some point in time, you will want to start removing old data and log backups that are no longer needed. You might think that you can simply erase those files from their storage locations, and technically there is nothing stopping you from doing this. You should, however, consider the following implications of such deletions:

- **Incorrect information in the backup catalog**
  Because the database does not know that you are deleting files, the information on available backups in the backup catalog is not updated. The system may therefore present recovery options that are no longer available.

- **Size of the backup catalog**
  For the same reason, the amount of entries in the backup catalog will continue growing, making the backup catalog large and potentially slow to search. Remember that the backup catalog is located in the log backup area and that a new version is written with every single backup process. A large backup catalog will waste significant disk space.

- **Danger of deleting needed files**
  If you try to manually determine the backup files to remove, you may wrongly delete files, for example, log backups that you originally intended to keep for the purpose of potential recoveries.

The good news is that the database comes with a built-in mechanism for safely deleting old data and log backups, including the necessary operations on the backup catalog. For automation, there is an SQL syntax, which we include in Section 5.4.10. Here, we introduce the easy-to-use wizard provided in SAP HANA Studio.

The Backup Editor of SAP HANA Studio (Figure 5.26) gives access to the backup catalog on its BACKUP CATALOG tab, shown in ❶. In the screen section BACKUP CATALOG, shown in ❷, all available data backups and storage snapshots are listed. AVAILABLE means that the data backup has not been deleted from the backup catalog. In the default view of the table, the backups are sorted by age, with the most recent backup at the top. If you highlight a data backup, details such as backup size, original location, file names, and more are shown in the BACKUP DETAILS area, shown in ❸.

In the rather typical situation in which there is one oldest data backup that you want to retain, including all options for recovery from this data backup, you can remove any older data and log backups through a simple procedure:

1. Right-click on the oldest data backup that you want to keep. From the context menu, shown in ❹, choose DELETE OLDER BACKUPS.... This will open a wizard that will allow you to manage the deletion of all backups that are still listed in the backup catalog and that cannot be used for a recovery of the backup that you selected.

2. In the dialog that opens (Figure 5.27, left-hand side; see ❶), you can determine whether you want to only remove the backup information from the backup catalog or whether you also want to physically remove the backups. Physical deletion works for both file-based backups and for third-party tools that implement the BackInt interface.

3. Once you have made your choice, the system lists all data and log backups (including backups of the backup catalog) that will be deleted, as shown in ❷. If you click FINISH, the system will remove all entries related to these backups from the backup catalog. If you chose to also physically remove the backup files, this deletion will be performed asynchronously.

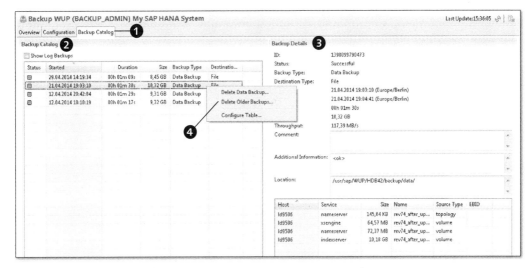

Figure 5.26 Managing Backups and the Backup Catalog in SAP HANA Studio

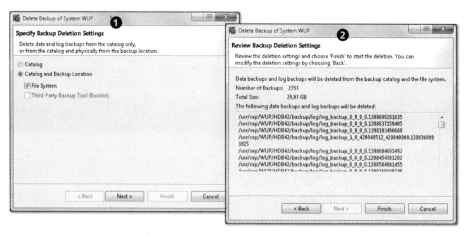

Figure 5.27 Deleting Older Backups

5.4.9 Sizing the Backup Storage

We can only give a little generic advice on sizing the storage system for your database backups. Simply speaking, the disk space requirements for data backups will depend on the database size, that is, the payload of the data files, the frequency of creating data backups, and the retention time of these backups.

The math involved is simple, as can be seen from an example: If you intend to perform daily data backups and you always need to keep the backups from the last 30 days, then you will have to plan for approximately 30 times the database payload.

If you already have a database installed with a relevant payload, then you can calculate the expected size of a data backup as shown in Listing 5.7. For proper sizing, you should also have a solid estimate of the database growth in the relevant timeframe. If the database is not yet filled, your best estimate is that the size of a data backup will be the same as the expected data size of the database.

The more difficult part is the sizing for log backups, because this depends on the amount of data changes that occur in the database, which in turn is a unique quantity for each system and timeframe.

When loading data, we have observed that the disk size of log entries created is typically at least twice the size of the loaded data after compression in SAP HANA; that is, if you create a column table with data so that the table size in memory is about 10 GB, then the write process will create log entries amounting to at least 20 GB.

At the same time, in a practically idle single-node database system approximately 10 GB of log backups were created in the course of a week.

5.4.10 SQL Syntax for Database Backups

Those administrators who manually manage the backup system will find the wizards offered in SAP HANA Studio very convenient. In most production operation scenarios, of course, most administrators will prefer to automate the tasks of creating and managing backups as much as possible.

If you are already using a backup management solution (backup tool) that supports the SAP HANA BackInt interface, there can be no doubt: The best choice is to integrate your SAP HANA databases into your regular backup operations with this tool.

For all those who are not that lucky, the database offers SQL syntax to create and manage database backups. In the following short sections, we introduce the typical usage of these SQL commands. The full documentation is available in the *SAP HANA Administration Guide* (and, as of SPS 8, not in the *SAP HANA SQL Reference*).

In our syntax examples, we will focus on file-based backups only. The SQL syntax also supports the BackInt interface.

Creating Data Backups

For creating data backups, the system offers the BACKUP DATA statement. The most important parameter for the statement is the name of the backup to create. You can choose to either create backup names with the standard file name *<file_path>/<prefix>_<suffix>* or with a dedicated directory for each backup set, leading to file names *<file_path>/<suffix>*. In the latter case, the *<file_path>* becomes the custom part of the backup file names. If a backup of the same name already exists, it will be overwritten.

Syntax examples for both ways of creating data backups are given in Listing 5.11.

```
// Generic syntax
BACKUP DATA USING FILE ('<prefix>') [ASYNCHRONOUS]
// Example one: creating files in the configured path
// <basepath_databackup>, with file names
// "BACKUP_NAME_databackup_X_Y"
BACKUP DATA USING FILE ('BACKUP_NAME')
```

```
// Example two: creating file with the same name, but in a
// specific directory "/hana/backup":
BACKUP DATA USING FILE ('/hana/backup/BACKUP_NAME')
// Example three: creating files with names databackup_X_Y in
// the directory /hana/backup/BACKUP_ONE/ (if the directory
// does not exist yet, it will be created):
BACKUP DATA USING FILE ('/hana/backup/BACKUP_ONE/')
```
Listing 5.11 Creating Data Backups Using SQL

While a data backup is running, you can cancel it with the BACKUP CANCEL command, as shown in Listing 5.12. In order to cancel the backup, you need to know its backup ID, which you can determine from the backup catalog. In system view M_BACKUP_CATALOG, you have to find the entry with ENTRY_TYPE_NAME = 'complete data backup' and STATE_NAME = 'running'.

```
// Determine the BACKUP_ID of the running data backup:
select BACKUP_ID from M_BACKUP_CATALOG where
  entry_type_name = 'complete data backup' and
  state_name='running'
// Cancel that backup (e.g., ID = 123456789 (integer)):
BACKUP CANCEL 123456789
```
Listing 5.12 Cancelling a Running Data Backup

Deleting Data and Log Backups

The functionality of the backup catalog wizard in SAP HANA Studio is also available in SQL; if you have identified the oldest data backup that you want to keep for the purpose of recovering the database, you can delete all older data and log backups from the backup catalog and optionally from the file system.

Assuming that the oldest data backup that you want to retain has backup ID 123456789, the SQL syntax needed for deleting any older data backups and any log backups not required to recover the data backup is given in Listing 5.13.

```
// Remove all backups "older" than the data backup with
// backup ID 123456789, including physical file deletion
BACKUP DELETE ALL BEFORE BACKUP_ID 123456789 COMPLETE
```
Listing 5.13 Deleting Backups

Technically, the data and log backups to be deleted can be determined as follows: For data backups and backups of the backup catalog, all backups can be deleted for which the backup ID is smaller than the ID of the backup to be retained.

For log backups, the system first needs to read the log position of the data backup from the backup catalog. It then finds all log backups for which the highest log position is smaller than the log position of the data backup. This needs to be done independently for each data volume, because all volumes have their own log sequences. An SQL query to determine all log backups that may be deleted (again, with respect to the data backup 123456789) is given in Listing 5.14.

```
SELECT DISTINCT
   l.destination_path FROM m_backup_catalog_files AS l,
   (SELECT * FROM m_backup_catalog_files
      WHERE backup_id = 123456789) AS d
   WHERE l.destination_type_name = 'file'
      AND ((l.last_redo_log_position IS NOT NULL
            AND l.source_id = d.source_id
            AND l.last_redo_log_position < d.redo_log_position)
         OR (l.source_type_name = 'catalog'
               AND l.backup_id < d.backup_id))
   ORDER BY l.destination_path asc;
```

Listing 5.14 Finding All Log Backups That May Be Deleted

Automating Backup Management

With the SQL syntax for backup management, it is easy to automate the creation and management of database backups. One simple way is to use some external scheduling mechanism to invoke the hdbsql tool in order to create, list, or delete backups.

An example of such a backup management system is provided and documented in SAP Note 1651055. That solution uses a bash script for orchestrating data backups and log backup management. It can be scheduled using the cron daemon of the Linux operating system of the SAP HANA database server.

5.4.11   Relevant System Views and Parameters for Backups

The system views in Table 5.9 contain information on the backup system.

View Name	Description
M_BACKUP_CATALOG	List of all data backups, log backups, snapshots, and backup catalog backups
M_BACKUP_CATALOG_FILES	List of all individual backup files

Table 5.9 System Views Related to Data Volumes and Savepoint

For the full documentation of these views, refer to the *SAP HANA SQL and System Views Reference* available at *https://help.sap.com/hana_platform*.

Multiple parameters are relevant for the configuration of the backup system, as shown in Table 5.10. For full documentation of these parameters, refer to the *SAP HANA Administration Guide* available at *https://help.sap.com/hana_platform*.

Parameter	Section	File	Description
basepath_databackup	[persistence]	global.ini	Default file system path for data backups
basepath_logbackup	[persistence]	global.ini	File system path for log backups
enable_automatic_log_backup	[persistence]	global.ini	Whether or not to write log backups in log mode normal
log_mode	[persistence]	global.ini	Must be normal to enable log backups
log_backup_timeout_s	[persistence]	global.ini	Maximum wait time before the system automatically backs up a log segment in state Writing
data_backup_max_chunk_size	[persistence]	global.ini	Limit the file size of individual files in a data backup (leads to automatic splitting); value in MB

Table 5.10 Database Parameters Related to the Transaction Logs

5.5   Disaster Recovery Setups and System Replication

SAP HANA offers technologies to increase the availability of the database system if this is required by the SLAs of the IT department. Such availability enhancements usually serve at least one and typically both of the following purposes:

▶ **Protect against loss of data**
Data may be lost through physical damage of the system's hardware components, including disasters that may disable entire data centers; by human actions that affect entire data files (file deletion or similar); or even through maleficent manipulation, destruction, or theft.

▶ **Minimize business downtimes of the IT landscape**
There can be planned downtimes (updates, other maintenance, etc.) and unplanned downtimes (emergency updates, software or hardware failures, etc.).

In general, there are three techniques available in the world of SAP HANA to address some or all of these requirements, as shown in Table 5.11. The primary intention of such setups is the protection against so-called disasters, which also explains the terms *Recovery Point Objective* (RPO: How many hours of database content may be lost in a disaster case?) and *Recovery Time Objective* (RTO: What is the expected downtime of a single incident?). In Table 5.11, we distinguish between the technical downtime that ends as soon as the database system is available again for clients and the business downtime that ends as soon as business applications can operate again with acceptable performance. In most availability solutions, the business downtime is significantly higher than the technical downtime because of the need to load columnar tables into the main memory in order to reach good performance.

Option	Protects against	RPO	RTO
Standby setup with backup shipment	Loss of data	A few hours	Up to about one hour
Storage replication	Loss of data, unscheduled downtimes	Zero (synchronous), a few seconds (asynchronous)	Close to zero (technical downtime), tens of minutes (business downtime)
System replication	Loss of data, scheduled and unscheduled downtimes	Zero (synchronous), a few seconds (asynchronous)	Close to zero (technical and business downtime)

Table 5.11 High-Availability Options in SAP HANA Systems

Of the availability techniques in Table 5.11, the standby setup with backup shipment is a trivial setup, and we will not discuss it further. The other two options will be introduced in the following two sections. Because the topic is relevant only for a rather small fraction of systems, we will be comparatively brief, with a clear focus on system replication. A generic overview of the two techniques is shown in Figure 5.28. Both are based on two mostly identical SAP HANA servers in two different data centers, of which the primary one is active, that is, currently in use, whereas the secondary is on standby, receiving data updates from the primary system.

In SAP HANA system replication, shown in ❶, the SAP HANA software of the primary system not only writes committed data to its own transaction logs but also sends them to the secondary database, either synchronously or asynchronously. In regular intervals, the primary system also sends snapshot deltas, that is, collections of all changes since the last delta shipment. This solution is a feature of the SAP HANA software, independent from the choice of hardware partner.

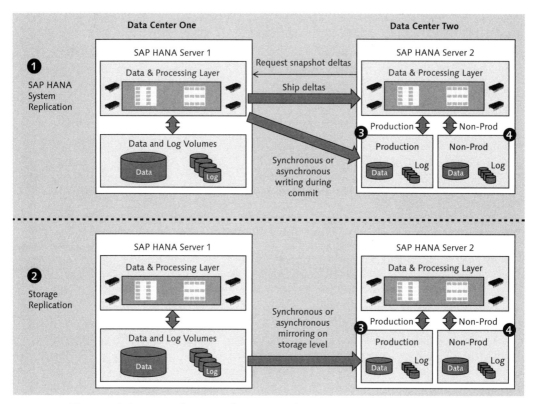

Figure 5.28 System Replication and Storage Replication

In storage replication, shown in ❷, the data replication is achieved by means of storage mirroring independently from the database software. Several hardware partners offer certified solutions for storage replication.

In both setup types, it is possible to not only use the database server in Data Center Two as a standby system (which is going to be idle most of the time); you can also implement an additional set of storage volumes, which can be used for operating nonproduction systems. In normal operation, while the SAP HANA server in Data Center One is in production use, the production data will be replicated to the primary storage volumes, shown in ❸, of the database in Data Center Two. Nonproduction database instances will be using the secondary storage volumes, shown in ❹. In a failover situation, the nonproduction instances in Data Center Two must be shut down, and the production instance must be started.

5.5.1 Storage Replication

Storage replication is a technology in which two identical SAP HANA database servers are located in two data centers that are sufficiently far apart to protect against disasters affecting both of them but close enough to allow synchronous mirroring of the storage systems. Typical rules of thumb limit the distance somewhere in the range of 50 km to 100 km (30 to 60 land miles). In early 2014, the first hardware setups with asynchronous storage replication were made available; they overcome the latency problem at the cost of an RPO greater than zero (which is an intrinsic property of any asynchronous replication method). All validated hardware solutions for storage replications are listed in SAP Note 1755396.

In this system, one side (arbitrarily called DC 1) is fully active, that is, the database is online and used in production. In the other data center (DC 2), the database is not online. The storage systems of the two databases are connected with some kind of mirroring technology, either on a file system or on a block device level. The precise setup depends on the choice of hardware partner.

In a disaster case that disables DC 1, a switchover procedure must be executed in which the SAP HANA database in DC 2 is started and all client applications are redirected to using the database in DC 2.

5.5.2 System Replication

The fundamental design difference between SAP HANA system replication and storage replication is that the former is a software solution that is part of the SAP HANA database software, whereas the latter is based on storage technologies. System replication therefore works independently from the chosen hardware technology. It is recommended (and required in order for the system to be supported by SAP) to add dedicated network components for the cross-site data shipment, but technically this is not necessary to set up a working system.

The basic working principle of system replication is based on two different types of data shipment from the primary to the secondary system:

▶ **Snapshot shipments**

In regular intervals, the primary system creates a snapshot and sends those pages that have been modified since the last snapshot (a delta snapshot) to the secondary system. These delta shipments are used to update the in-memory data image of the secondary system.

Snapshot shipping is also used for the initial data transfer.

▶ **Log shipments**

Whenever transactions are committed in the primary system, the log entries are also sent to the secondary system. These log entries are written to the disk of the secondary system, but they are not replayed in memory. Therefore, the in-memory image of the secondary system is always as current as the latest delta snapshot. In a failover situation, the log entries received since the last delta snapshot shipment need to be replayed.

Three different replication modes are supported, with the following behavior during the commit phase:

▷ Synchronous on disk (mode name `sync`): In order for a commit to be successful, data must be written to disk on the primary system and on the secondary system. This mode has the highest risk protection, but also highest latency in the commit phase.

▷ Synchronous in memory (mode name `syncmem`): The secondary system acknowledges the commit as soon as it has received the log entries but before writing them to disk. This mode can reduce the latency by a tiny fraction at the added cost of reduced risk protection.

▷ Asynchronous (mode name `async`): The primary system sends the log entries to the secondary system but does not wait for a response. This mode is necessary to achieve acceptable commit times when the distance between the two data centers is too big—usually larger than 100 km/60 miles.

In SPS 8, a fully synchronous mode was introduced in which a commit will be on hold until the secondary site has acknowledged it—without the time-out that exists in the synchronous modes `sync` and `syncmen`. Details are given in the *SAP HANA Administration Guide*.

In addition to providing a standby system with failover capabilities—which is by and large similar to the functionality provided with storage replication—system replication creates further options to increase the system availability.

It is possible but not mandatory to operate system replication in `warm standby` mode, in which the regular snapshot shipment is used to update the in-memory data image on the secondary system. In this way, the business downtime can be minimized, because very close to 100% of the data is already loaded into the memory of the secondary system at any point in time and the phase of memory warm-up is usually negligible.

If the secondary system is on warm standby, then there is also a procedure for performing near-zero-downtime upgrades of the database software by updating the secondary system, performing a planned failover, registering the former primary as the new secondary, and upgrading it.

With the release of SAP HANA SPS 7, the first steps have been made to support multiple secondary systems. In SPS 7, a chain consisting of a primary system with one synchronously coupled secondary and an asynchronously coupled tertiary system is possible.

Hardware Prerequisites for System Replication

System replication requires two fully functional SAP HANA servers, which should have the same hardware characteristics. In most cases, customers will install two identical servers.

System replication works with single-node instances as well as scale-out systems. In a scale-out system, the number of worker hosts has to be identical in both data centers. It is not possible to operate system replication with multiple index servers installed on one host.

The number of failover hosts in a scale-out setup is technically irrelevant for the functionality of system replication. You can build setups with one or more failover hosts on the primary site and no failover hosts on the secondary. This will, however, mean that no failover host is available in the "disaster" case, so you will have to fall back to the original primary site as soon as possible for optimal availability. If you plan to operate the primary system alternatingly in data centers one and two, both systems should be identical.

A crucial setup aspect is the network connection between the two data centers. In synchronous mode, network latency can significantly impact commit times and therefore write performance. The network connectivity should best be realized using a dedicated line with as few network hops as possible. SAP formulates no generic requirement for the network throughput that can be reached on this line. Instead, it is recommended that the network throughput be sufficient to perform the initial data shipment within one day. For 1 TB of data content, you will need a sustained network throughput of about 15 MB/s.

For a detailed discussion of the network setup, please refer to the documentation in the *SAP HANA Administration Guide* available at *https://help.sap.com/hana_platform/* and the related SAP how-to guide at *https://scn.sap.com/docs/DOC-47702.*

Software Requirements for System Replication

System replication can only be set up between two installed SAP HANA instances that meet the following requirements:

- Both instances must have the same SID.
- Both instances must have the same instance number, <i>.
- Instance number <i>+1 must be free on all involved hosts.
- The host names of all SAP HANA hosts in the setup must be unique.
- The software version of the secondary system must be the same as or higher than the software version of the primary system.
- A valid license must be installed on the primary system. License information will be replicated to the secondary system.
- The configuration of both systems must be the same. This is particularly important for the list of configured processes (embedded statistics service, enabled script server, scaled XS engine, etc.). If the configuration of one instance is changed, then the changes must be manually applied on the other instance as well.
- An initial data backup must have been created on the primary side.

From these prerequisites, it follows directly that it is not possible to set up system replication between two database instances installed on the same host.

Setting Up System Replication

The initial configuration of system replication consists of only a small sequence of steps. For the process, you will need to enter the credentials of the <sid>adm Linux user of the primary and secondary SAP HANA instances.

There are command-line tools for setting up system replication and performing failover actions, and the functionality has also been integrated into SAP HANA Studio. In our examples, we will make use of the SAP HANA Studio interface, showing system replication between two scale-out systems. The command-line syntax is given in the *SAP HANA Administration Guide* available at *https://help.sap.com/hana_platform/* and the excellent how-to guide on system replication that is available on SCN at *https://scn.sap.com/docs/DOC-47702*.

Before you start setting up system replication, you can shut down the secondary system. The overall setup procedure then consists of the following steps:

▶ **Create data backup on primary side**
It is generally recommended to create a data backup on the primary site directly before setting up system replication. If, however, no data backup has ever been made for the primary system, then you must create one now.

▶ **Start the system replication wizard**
Right-click on the system entry of the primary system in the SYSTEMS view of SAP HANA Studio, and choose SYSTEM REPLICATION... from the context menu.

▶ **Enable system replication on the primary site**
This step makes the necessary definitions on the primary site so that the SAP HANA system can be part of a system replication setup. In the wizard (Figure 5.29), choose ENABLE SYSTEM REPLICATION, as shown in ❶. In the next step of the wizard, shown in ❷, you must enter a logical name for the primary system. Typically, this might be the location or name of the primary data center.

The final screen of the wizard shows a summary, and you can start registration by clicking the FINISH button. Registration of the primary system will take a few seconds, after which the wizard will be closed.

Figure 5.29 Enabling System Replication on the Primary Site

▶ **Register the secondary system**

If the secondary system is still online, you must stop it now.

Restart the system replication wizard (again, for the primary system), and choose REGISTER SECONDARY SYSTEM. In the wizard (Figure 5.30), you have to enter a logical name, as shown in ❶, for the secondary data center, and choose the replication mode, as shown in ❷ (synchronous, synchronous in memory, or asynchronous). You also need to configure the host name of the secondary system, as shown in ❸ (in scale-out systems, the name of the master host), and enter the user name and password of the <sid>adm user on the secondary system, as shown in ❹.

Registration will only set up the secondary system so that it will be part of the system replication setup as soon as it starts; the registration itself will not transfer any data. This data transfer happens as soon as you start the secondary system. It is normally a good choice to automatically start the secondary system after registration, by selecting the checkbox shown in ❺.

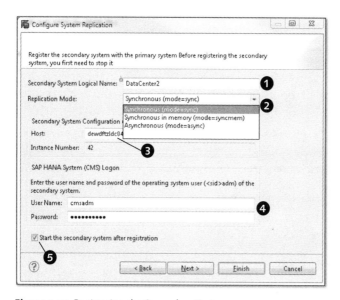

Figure 5.30 Registering the Secondary System

When you click the FINISH button, the registration, system start, and initial data shipment will be executed. From this time on, system replication between the two systems will be active.

> **Note**
>
> Setting up system replication will overwrite the entire contents of the secondary system. This includes all database users. Also, the password of the SYSTEM user in the secondary system will be changed to the one in the primary system.

While system replication is active, the secondary system is started in replication mode and cannot be accessed on its application interfaces, such as the SQL port. Communication between primary and secondary system happens on a set of ports reserved for system replication. Administration actions, such as stopping the secondary system, can be performed via the SAP Host Agent on the secondary system, so this type of functionality is also available in SAP HANA Studio.

Monitoring System Replication

The entire system replication setup can be monitored from the primary system. A simple status overview is given on the OVERVIEW screen of the Administration Editor for the primary system, as shown in Figure 5.31.

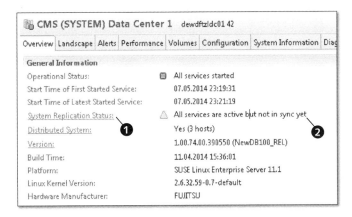

Figure 5.31 Overview Screen Showing System Replication Status

Our screenshot shows the SYSTEM REPLICATION STATUS, as shown in ❶, during the phase of initializing the secondary system, that is, during the initial data transfer, so that not all services are synchronized already, as shown in ❷. If you click on the link for SYSTEM REPLICATION STATUS, as shown in ❶, forward navigation takes you to the SYSTEM REPLICATION area of the LANDSCAPE tab in the Administration Editor.

This monitoring area simply displays the contents of system view M_SERVICE_REP-LICATION. With this view, you can monitor the progress of the initial data shipment (Figure 5.32), and you can find aggregated information on the data shipment between the primary and secondary systems.

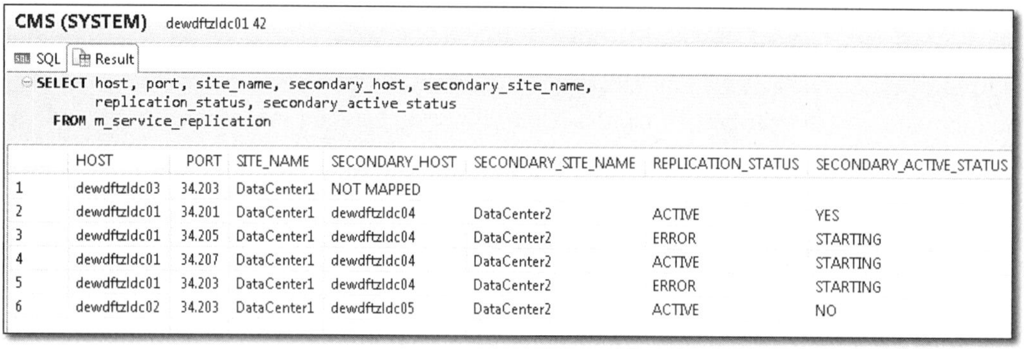

```
CMS (SYSTEM)    dewdftzldc01 42

SQL   Result

SELECT host, port, site_name, secondary_host, secondary_site_name,
       replication_status, secondary_active_status
  FROM m_service_replication
```

	HOST	PORT	SITE_NAME	SECONDARY_HOST	SECONDARY_SITE_NAME	REPLICATION_STATUS	SECONDARY_ACTIVE_STATUS
1	dewdftzldc03	34.203	DataCenter1	NOT MAPPED			
2	dewdftzldc01	34.201	DataCenter1	dewdftzldc04	DataCenter2	ACTIVE	YES
3	dewdftzldc01	34.205	DataCenter1	dewdftzldc04	DataCenter2	ERROR	STARTING
4	dewdftzldc01	34.207	DataCenter1	dewdftzldc04	DataCenter2	ACTIVE	STARTING
5	dewdftzldc01	34.203	DataCenter1	dewdftzldc04	DataCenter2	ERROR	STARTING
6	dewdftzldc02	34.203	DataCenter1	dewdftzldc05	DataCenter2	ACTIVE	NO

Figure 5.32 Monitoring Replication during Initialization

In order to support automatic detection of a system status that requires a takeover, SAP provides a Python tool called landscapeHostConfiguration.py, located in the file system path *${DIR_INSTANCE}/exe/python_support* on the database server. The <sid>adm user on the primary system can invoke this script and interpret the return value. To invoke the script, use the commands given in Listing 5.15.

```
# Run the landscapeHostConfiguration.py script:
python ${DIR_INSTANCE}/exe/python_support \
       /landscapeHostConfiguration.py
# Output the return value:
echo $?
```

Listing 5.15 Using Python Scripts to Monitor System Replication

A takeover is only necessary if the return value is 1, indicating error. Because this tool will not be able to detect all types of situations requiring a takeover, SAP recommends always using third-party tools for availability monitoring of system replication setups.

On the command line, you can check the system replication status with the command hdbnsutil -sr_state (execute as <sid>adm Linux user on the name server master host of the current primary system).

Working Principles and Parameterization of System Replication

At the heart of system replication are two methods of providing data to the secondary system: log replication and delta snapshot shipping. We will discuss these two processes in more detail, including the available parameterization options.

Unless stated otherwise, configuration parameters that we will mention in the following are located in the section [system_replication] of the global.ini configuration file.

Replication Mode

In order to guarantee full data redundancy between the primary and secondary systems, all write transactions must be replicated to the secondary system upon commit at the latest. This log replication can be performed synchronously or asynchronously, as determined by the replication mode.

This replication mode can be modified after the initial setup without requiring a new initialization. This configuration must be made on the secondary system; it will be automatically applied on the primary. Even though it is maintained in the database configuration, on the secondary system you must not change it in the usual way (editing the configuration with SAP HANA Studio or a similar method). Instead, the command-line utility hdbnsutil has to be used as follows:

▶ Determine the host of the secondary system that is currently home to the master name server. You can see it in the LANDSCAPE • HOSTS view of the Administration Console in SAP HANA Studio, or you can retrieve this host name with the following SQL query:

```
SELECT host FROM m_landscape_host_configuration
  WHERE nameserver_actual_role = 'MASTER'
```

▶ Log on to the Linux OS of that this master name server host of the secondary system with the <sid>adm user.

▶ Stop the current secondary system, for example, by using the sapcontrol command:

```
/usr/sap/hostctrl/exe/sapcontrol -nr <instance> -function StopSystem HDB
```

▶ Set the replication mode on the secondary system; execute the following command:

```
hdbnsutil -sr_changemode --mode=sync|syncmem|async
```

▶ Start the secondary system again, for example, by using the sapcontrol command:

```
/usr/sap/hostctrl/exe/sapcontrol -nr <instance> -function
StartSystem HDB
```

Note that the replication mode must always be configured on the secondary system, from which the setting will be propagated to the primary.

Log Replication Timeouts

If log replication is temporarily interrupted, for example, by a network disconnect, the system does not wait indefinitely in any of the replication modes. Instead, there is a timeout configured in parameter `logshipping_timeout` with a default value of 30 seconds. After this timeout, write transactions will continue without log replication.

> **Note**
>
> Unless, that is, the fully synchronous version of synchronous replication is used, in which case transactions on the primary system will be blocked when log replication fails. See the how-to guide on SCN at *https://scn.sap.com/docs/DOC-47702*.

The system will test the network connectivity automatically in intervals specified by the parameter `reconnect_time_interval` (the default value is 30 seconds). As soon as the secondary system is reachable again, a new delta snapshot will be shipped to the secondary system, and log replication will be resumed.

Snapshot Shipping

With SPS 8, SAP HANA does not replay the shipped log entries on the secondary site. In order to provide memory preloading on the secondary site and also to most efficiently build the data volumes there, delta snapshots of the data image are shipped in regular intervals from the primary site. These shipments must be requested by the secondary site.

The decision to request such a delta shipment is based on two parameters. A delta snapshot is obtained at the latest after `datashipping_min_time_interval` seconds (default value 600 seconds). If, however, a high log volume has accumulated since the last delta shipment, the secondary will request a snapshot earlier. The threshold value for the log volume is determined in the parameter `datashipping_logsize_threshold` (the default value is 5368709120 bytes, or 5 GB).

Delta snapshots are requested by all processes on the secondary system individually so that not all shipments will happen at the same time.

A data snapshot for system replication can maximally remain valid for the time specified in the parameter `datashipping_snapshot_max_retention_time` (the default value is 120 minutes). For more details on the implications, see our discussion in the "Performing a Takeover" section.

Preloading Tables on the Secondary System

Depending on your requirements, you may choose to preload tables in the secondary system's memory or not. Strictly speaking, this only applies to column tables, as the row store will always be preloaded on the secondary system.

If you set `preload_column_tables` to true on the primary and secondary system, then the primary system will include information on the `loaded` state of column tables with the delta snapshot shipments, and the secondary system will keep these tables loaded in its memory. This behavior is particularly important for use cases in which more data may be loaded in the database than fits into the main memory (e.g., SAP BW on SAP HANA with hot and warm data management).

Performing a Takeover

If a system takeover must be performed, you need to execute the following steps:

- **Perform a takeover on the secondary system**
  In SAP HANA Studio, right-click on the secondary system in the SYSTEMS view, and choose SYSTEM REPLICATION... from the context menu. In the system replication monitor, choose PERFORM TAKEOVER, as shown in ❶.

  On the next screen of the wizard, shown in ❷, it is usually a good choice to stop the original primary system (if it is still online), because this makes it most probable that you can successfully register the old primary as the new secondary without needing to perform a full initial data load. If you choose to stop the old primary system, you will have to enter the credentials of its <sid>adm Linux user.

  Once you click the FINISH button, the secondary system will start up in normal mode and be fully available for applications to connect. If the old primary is not stopped, it will remain online.

- **Make the old primary system operational again**
  If the takeover was triggered because of an error situation on the old primary system, the you will have to find the root cause of the error situation and solve the problem.

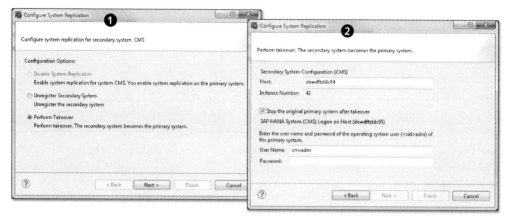

Figure 5.33 Performing a Takeover

▶ **Register the old primary as the new secondary system**
If the old primary system is still online, you must stop it now.

Using the system replication wizard of the new primary system, register the old primary as the new secondary system.

Note that in this step you also have to the set the replication mode again; the originally chosen value is not remembered.

Probably the most interesting question about the registration of the old primary as the new secondary system is whether or not the data area of the old primary system can be used as a basis for delta shipments. The answer to this question will have severe implications on the time needed for this registration.

The good news is that in many situations you will be able to continue using the original data image in the old primary system. We need, however, to distinguish the following different situations:

▶ If the data volumes of the old primary system have been corrupted, then a full initialization is required.

▶ If the old primary system has remained online following the takeover, re-use of its data area might be possible; the snapshot from the last delta shipment before the takeover must still be available, because any delta shipment can only be based on that snapshot. The snapshot will remain active for the time period configured in the parameter [system_replication] • datashipping_snapshot_max_retention_time from the configuration file global.ini, which defaults to

120 minutes. Hence, if you register the old primary system within this time period you will be able to reuse the last snapshot for new delta shipments.

▸ If the old primary system has been shut down in the course of the takeover and is not restarted before the system is registered as the new secondary, then you will always be able to reuse its data image for new delta shipments.

▸ If the old primary is stopped after takeover but restarted before being registered as the new secondary, the snapshot is invalidated if it is older than `datashipping_snapshot_max_retention_time`. The time is measured from the time of snapshot creation, even if the system was offline for most of the time.

▸ If you have disabled system replication on the old primary system following the takeover, the snapshot will be dropped with the next system start.

You can check whether or not the original data image is re-used in the trace files of the index server processes of the new secondary. Among the entries written during the first system start following registration as secondary, look for an entry like the one given in Listing 5.16.

```
PersistenceManag PersistenceManagerImpl.cpp(01821) : replication
snapshot is compatible with primary -> sync primary and secondary
with delta shipping!
```

Listing 5.16 Trace File Entry if Data from Old Primary Can Be Reused

To enable a seamless reconnect of client applications, the recommended methods are IP redirection or DNS redirection, depending on your network configuration.

Near-Zero-Downtime Upgrades with System Replication

A system replication setup can be used for updating the database software with close to zero downtime. On a very high level, the procedure consists of updating the secondary system, performing a takeover, stopping the old primary, updating the old primary, and re-registering the old primary as the new secondary system. There are, however, a few important details to take care of:

▸ **Preparation: Create user store entries**
For reasons we will explain in one of the following items, the database must not be restarted automatically in the course of the update of the old primary system. Instead, it should only be started when the old primary is registered as the new secondary. This means that one step that is usually part of the update

procedure will now automatically be performed as part of the restart after registration as the new secondary. This step is the importing of delivery units into the database, and for this step the SYSTEM user password is required. The system replication process will intrinsically make use of the hdbuserstore to obtain these credentials with a user store key named SRTAKEOVER. We need to install this key with the SYSTEM user credentials on all hosts of the system replication setup.

Log on to each host of the setup with the <sid>adm user, and run the following command:

```
hdbuserstore SET SRTAKEOVER <host>:<port> SYSTEM <password>
```

<host> must be the external hostname of the host; <port> is the SQL port of the index server: 3<instance>15; and <password> is the password of the SYSTEM user.

▶ **Preparation: Enable column table preload**
Although not strictly necessary in a purely technical sense, having the column tables preloaded is a requirement for minimizing the business downtime during the upgrade.

▶ **Update the secondary system**
Run this update in whatever way you prefer. Our personal choice would be the hdblcm/hdblcmgui tool. It is acceptable and recommended to restart the secondary system as part of the update procedure.

▶ **Wait until secondary is in sync again**
The update of the secondary system causes a downtime of this system. After its restart, the system will be synchronized again with the primary. Wait until this process has finished, for example, by using monitoring view M_SERVICE_REPLI-CATON or the command hdbnsutil -sr_state.

▶ **Perform a takeover**
Perform a takeover on the secondary system, and make sure to shut down the old primary in the course of the takeover.

▶ **Upgrade the old primary without restart**
Upgrade the old primary system. You have to absolutely make sure not to restart the old primary as part of the update. When using the hdblcm/hdblcmgui tools, the command-line option --hdbupd_server_nostart suppresses the restart. Restarting the system before it is registered as the new secondary might invalidate the data image so that system replication can only be resumed after

a full initialization. Depending on the database size, such a full initialization might last an unacceptably long time.

▶ **Register the old primary as the new secondary and restart it**
This brings the system replication setup to fully functional replication again.

For full zero-downtime upgrades, the client connections must not be terminated when the takeover happens. Recent SAP NetWeaver systems (SAP NetWeaver 7.40 SP 5 or higher, with SAP Kernel 7.41 or higher) offer such a connectivity suspend feature, described in SAP Note 1913302 and a document at *www.saphana.com/docs/DOC-4358*.

Further Landscape Options

In addition to the standard setup involving one primary and one secondary system, there are further landscape configurations possible with system replication. We mention these here for completeness but without further discussion. Details can again be obtained from the *SAP HANA Database Administration Guide* at *https://help.sap.com/hana_platform/* and the how-to guide on SCN at *https://scn.sap.com/docs/DOC-47702* ("How to Perform System Replication for SAP HANA").

In *multitier replication*, three systems can be connected in a chain, with synchronous replication between the primary and secondary system and asynchronous replication from the secondary to a tertiary.

It is also possible to operate *nonproduction systems* (e.g., development or test systems) on the secondary hardware. In this case, a fraction of the resources (about 10%) will still be needed for the system replication, but the remainder is available for nonproduction instances. Dedicated storage volumes are required for the data and log files of the additional instances; they cannot use the production storage system.

When using the secondary site for nonproduction instances, column tables must not be preloaded on the secondary system. In a takeover situation, the nonproduction instances must be shut down. Depending on the overall setup, you might make provisions to operate these instances on either side of the setup.

System Views and Parameters for System Replication

In SAP HANA SPS 8, the only relevant system view for system replication is M_SERVICES_REPLICATION, which offers information on the replication state of each process/volume as well as aggregated statistics on the log and snapshot data shipments.

The most important parameters for system replication are given in Table 5.12. All of these parameters must be set to equal values on both sides of the setup in order to ensure seamless operation following a takeover.

Parameter	Section	File	Description
`logshipping_timeout`	`[system_replication]`	global.ini	Maximum wait time for response from secondary during commit (in seconds).
`reconnect_time_interval`	`[system_replication]`	global.ini	Time interval for trying to reconnect after communication failure (in seconds).
`datashipping_min time_interval`	`[system_replication]`	global.ini	Minimum time interval between two delta snapshot shipments (in seconds).
`datashipping_logsize_threshold`	`[system_replication]`	global.ini	If the log volume since the last delta snapshot exceeds this quantity (in bytes), a new delta snapshot will be requested.
`datashipping_snapshot_max_retention_time`	`[system_replication]`	global.ini	Maximum retention time in the primary system of the last delta snapshot (in minutes).
`preload_column_tables`	`[system_replication]`	global.ini	Whether or not column tables shall be preloaded on the secondary system for warm standby (values `true` or `false`).

Table 5.12 Relevant Parameters for System Replication

5.6 Summary

Having finished this chapter, you have gained insight into how SAP HANA protects your data and ensures durability. As with any other database platform, implementing and monitoring an effective backup strategy is key to protect against data loss and is the most important duty of any DBA.

The largest single server you can buy may not contain enough main memory to hold all your data. To allow growing beyond the limits of single servers, SAP HANA offers a concept for setting up distributed database systems called "scale-out."

6 Scale-Out Systems and High Availability

In SAP HANA, you can create database systems that span multiple physical servers (hosts), as shown in Figure 6.1. These hosts are interconnected with a dedicated internal network, and they all access a common file system on which the data and log volumes for all database processes of all hosts are located.

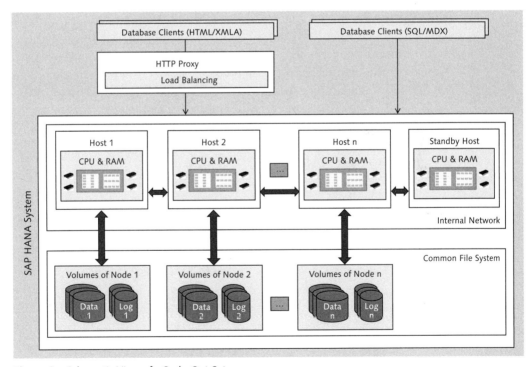

Figure 6.1 Schematic View of a Scale-Out Setup

The hosts of a scale-out system are built from the same core components (e.g., CPU generation) as those of single-node systems. The overall server form factor of scale-out systems, however, is usually different from that of single-node systems of the same hardware vendor (as always, there are exceptions).

The scale-out architecture is completely transparent to connecting client applications; they simply interact with one database system. Distributed execution and initial data distribution are handled internally by the database. Application developers or warehouse architects will often prefer to influence the data distribution in order to optimize the overall system performance (see the discussion in Chapter 9), but for the basic functionality, not even this is absolutely necessary.

When outlining the architecture of SAP HANA systems in Chapter 1, we invested a number of pages in explaining fundamental concepts involved in scaling SAP HANA systems. We encourage you to flip back to Chapter 1 and browse again through Section 1.5 to refresh your memory of the foundation of scale-out instances.

In the current chapter, we will discuss aspects of database monitoring and administration that are specific to scale-out systems, with the exception of installation/update (discussed in Chapter 3) and data distribution (discussed in Chapter 9). We will start with some more details of the architecture of distributed systems, including related monitoring aspects, followed by information on adding or removing hosts. The last two sections are dedicated to high-availability features and specific aspects of client connectivity in scale-out systems.

6.1   Scaling Out SAP HANA Systems

If an SAP HANA system is scaled out, then the database functionality is stretched across all worker nodes in the setup. Therefore, all fundamental database processes must be available on all worker nodes. By fundamental processes, we refer to those processes that are essential to provide the core database functionality of managing and processing data, that is, the index server process with related processes (compile server and preprocessor, as well as script server if enabled in the system) and the name server. The daemon process is also active on each host to enable the start and, if required, automatic restart of the database processes. In Figure 6.2, we show the process configuration for all types of nodes in a scale-out system, indicating in **bold** if a process is optional on some node or may have different roles on different nodes of the setup.

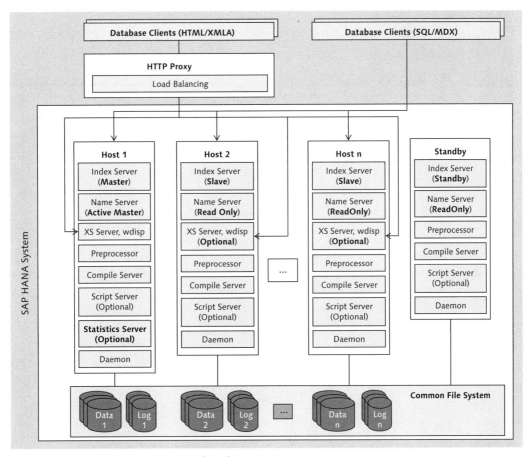

Figure 6.2 Database Processes in a Distributed System

With this process-distribution pattern in mind, we now look into how this can be broken down and applied to your installation. In this section, we will discuss conceptual aspects, such as the different types of nodes, the special role of the name server, and distributed persistence as well as the practical questions of adding and removing hosts to the database. Understanding these topics will allow you to successfully manage SAP HANA scale-out systems.

6.1.1 The Different Nodes of a Scale-Out System

In a scale-out system, there are three different types of nodes, determined by the role of the index server process. Two of these, the master and slave nodes, are classified as worker nodes, because they play an active role in the database operation, whereas the standby nodes only come to action in the case of component failures.

▶ **Master node**

In each scale-out system, there is exactly one master node (Host 1 in Figure 6.2). This is the node with the master index server. The initial location of the master node is determined at the install time of the system; it is located on the "first" host of the system—the host on which the installation program was started. Any hosts added during the installation are added as slave or standby nodes.

The master index server has a number of special responsibilities, such as managing the metadata of the database catalog, being the master transaction manager, or owning the row store (in all common usage scenarios).

▶ **Slave nodes**

All additional worker nodes (Hosts 2 through n in Figure 6.2) in a scale-out system are so-called slave nodes, with an index server running in slave mode. The term *slave* should not be misunderstood as signaling data redundancy or anything similar. It simply means that the node does not have the master index server and thus does not manage metadata or master transactions.

▶ **Standby nodes**

In order to address the increased likelihood of component failures in a scale-out system, redundant hardware can be added in the form of standby hosts with a standby node. See Section 6.2 for a detailed discussion of this concept.

The mapping of nodes to hosts can change during the lifetime of a scale-out system, as will be explained in Section 6.2. At any point in time, the configuration and current state of the system landscape can be monitored in the Administration Editor of SAP HANA Studio (see Figure 6.3). On the LANDSCAPE tab, as shown in ❶, of the Administration Editor, choose the HOSTS subtab, as shown in ❷.

This view shows all the hosts in the database system with the CONFIGURED, as shown in ❸, and ACTUAL, as shown in ❹, INDEX SERVER ROLE. In the same way, the CONFIGURED, shown in ❺, and ACTUAL, shown in ❻, NAME SERVER ROLES are displayed; see Section 6.1.2 for an explanation of these roles. CONFIGURED refers to the settings made during system installation. Strictly speaking, however, this configuration can also be modified in a wizard that can be accessed by clicking the CONFIGURE HOSTS FOR FAILOVER SITUATION button, shown in ❼. Under normal circumstances, it will not be necessary to modify this configuration.

The INDEX SERVER ROLE (ACTUAL) section, shown in ❹, indicates the present situation, which may be different from the configured one if a failover has happened since the last system restart.

At the front of the table, column ACTIVE, shown in ❽, shows whether the processes of the database instance on the given hosts are all active (YES) or in another state, such as STARTING or STOPPING.

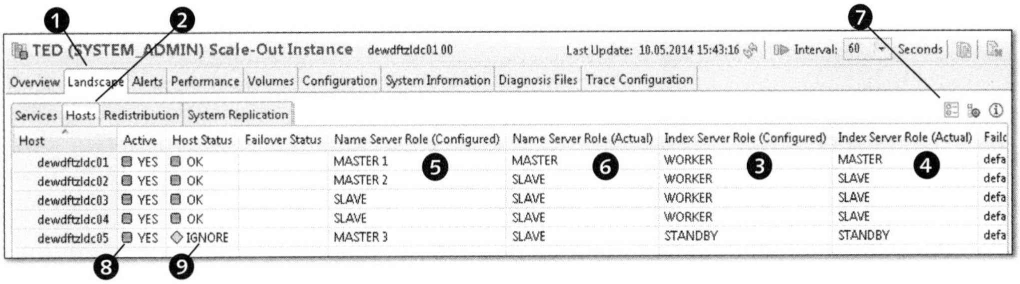

Figure 6.3 Host Information in a Scale-Out Instance

In the terminology of hosts and nodes that we introduced earlier, we can interpret the meaning of the column HOST STATUS, shown in ❾, as follows: This column indicates whether or not the node on the given host fulfills the configured role of a worker node (OK), a different role than configured (INFO), a standby role (IGNORE), is nonoperational but expected to be operational pending a failover or startup (WARNING), or is not operational at all (ERROR). The system is fully operational if all hosts are in state OK, INFO, or IGNORE.

The same information is exposed by the monitoring view M_LANDSCAPE_HOST_CON-FIGURATION. See the *SAP HANA SQL and System View Reference*, which is available at *https://help.sap.com/hana_platform/*, for a definition of all fields in this table.

6.1.2 The Master Name Server Concept

Several vital aspects of a scale-out system are controlled by the name server process. Most importantly, the name server maintains the *system topology*, which is the description of the database landscape (hosts, nodes, ports, hostnames, and many more aspects) as well as details of the object distribution (which database object is located on which node). This topology is needed for any query execution in a distributed landscape. The name server also controls the availability of all processes in the database instance and will trigger host failovers if necessary.

This crucial role justifies special availability measures for the name server in a distributed system. First, only one name server is allowed to modify the topology at any point in time. This name server is the active master name server, and its ACTUAL NAME SERVER ROLE is MASTER. All other name servers will have actual role SLAVE, meaning that they only have read access to a copy of the topology replicated from the active master name server.

Second, there are *three* name servers that have a configured master role (if there are less than three hosts in the system, then the number of master name servers will equal the number of hosts). At system startup, the active master name server is located on the system's configured master host. The other configured master name servers will continuously monitor the active master for its availability. If they detect that the active master has become unavailable, one of the remaining configured masters will be made the active master.

The availability of the active master name server will be verified in multiple ways. One test is based on the master.lck file that can be found in the data path for the master node (in directory *<basepath_datavolumes>/mnt00001/*; typically the file is at */hana/data/<SID>/mnt00001/master.lck*). This file contains two pieces of data: the hostname of the current active master name server and a random number that is changed every ten seconds. Even if the other name servers find that the active master cannot be reached over the network, they will not take over its role if they observe changes to the master.lck file.

There is no automatic failback of the master name server functionality. That is, if the original active master fails and another host assumes the role of active master name server, the original master will be in state SLAVE once it becomes available again.

6.1.3   Distributed Persistence

The layout of the data and log volumes in a scale-out system can be confusing at first sight. We try to shed some light on these in Figure 6.4, which only shows the data volumes; the log volumes are structured identically underneath the directory configured in parameter `basepath_logvolumes`. The figure matches the processes of a master node, shown in ❶, and a slave node, shown in ❷, to their respective data areas, shown in ❸ and ❹. All processes that do not necessarily exist on a node are marked as optional, and their data volumes are placed in brackets.

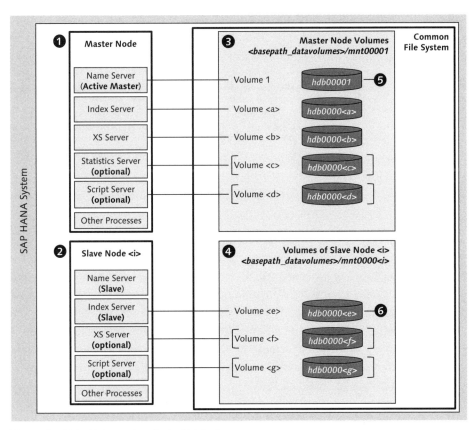

Figure 6.4 Data Volumes in a Scale-Out System

In the default configuration of a scale-out instance, only the master node has more than one data volume. Of all the processes normally active on slave nodes, only the index server, shown in ❻, has its own persistence. The name server only has a data volume, shown in ❺, on the master node, and the statistics server can only exist on the master node (if it is configured as a separate process at all).

You may have started additional processes with persistence on the slave nodes, for example, if you enable the script server (always a system-wide setting) or if you scale the XS server so that there also can be multiple data volumes for slave nodes. A standby node, on the other hand, *never* has data volumes.

Of the volume IDs, only the ID for the name server persistence is hard coded in the database software; this data volume, shown in ❺, always has the ID 1. The volume IDs of all other processes are allocated by the software at installation or configuration time and can change from database to database. This is indicated by the place holders <a> through <g> for the volume IDs in Figure 6.4.

In order to find the volume ID for a given process, you can query monitoring view M_VOLUMES.

In the file system, data files are located in a directory structure as follows:

▶ All data volumes of the system are placed within the directory configured in configuration parameter basepath_datavolumes.

▶ For each node, there is a subpath *mnt<node_ID>*, where <node_ID> is a five digit number starting with 00001 for the master node. At any point in time, you can monitor the current assignment of these node-specific subpaths to hosts in monitoring view M_DISKS.

It should be noted that the SAP HANA software does not make use of the term *node ID*, nor does the product documentation. In fact, there is no well-defined node-ID-like entity in SAP HANA. The entity coming closest to a node ID is the field STORAGE_PARTITION, for example, in monitoring view M_LANDSCAPE_HOST_ CONFIGURATION. We use the term node ID in this book because we feel that it is a good fit and simplifies the explanations.

▶ For each data volume, there is a subdirectory named *hdb<volume_ID>* within *<basepath_datavolumes>/mnt<node_ID>*, where <volume_ID> also is a five-digit identifier. The list of all volumes and their assignment to hosts is given in monitoring view M_VOLUMES.

6.1.4 Adding Hosts to a Scale-Out System

Adding a new host to a scale-out system is simple, as long as the host itself is prepared properly (hardware and operating system) and the shared file systems are already mounted. In particular, the SID and instance number of the database must not yet be in use on the host to be added, and the user ID of the Linux operating user <sid>adm must still be available (the <sid>adm user has to have the *same* user ID on all hosts of a scale-out system). Also, the group ID of the sapsys group must be the same on all hosts of the system.

No specific privileges are required, but you must know the passwords of the Linux operating users <sid>adm and sapadm (and of the root user when using the command-line tools hdbaddhost or hdblcm).

There are two and a half options available for adding a host. Up to and including SPS 7, the most prominent one was to use SAP HANA Lifecycle Manager (HLM). The other one is the `hdbaddhost` command-line tool, the functionality of which has in SPS 8 been integrated into the `hdblcm`(`gui`) command-line tool. The latter is the official and recommended variant as of SPS 8.

Using SAP HANA Lifecycle Manager (HLM)

After starting LIFECYCLE MANAGEMENT for the database system from the SYSTEMS view in SAP HANA Studio, choose the option to ADD ADDITIONAL HOSTS.

On the first screen of the wizard, you can specify the network to use—either the global network of the SAP HANA system or, preferably, the internal communication network (if it has been set up).

On the second screen (Figure 6.5), you must specify properties of the host to be added, most importantly the HOSTNAME (if the internal and external host names are different, this entry is for the internal host name). The system also needs the password of the sapadm Linux user to set up supporting system components. If applicable, the external host name also must be provided.

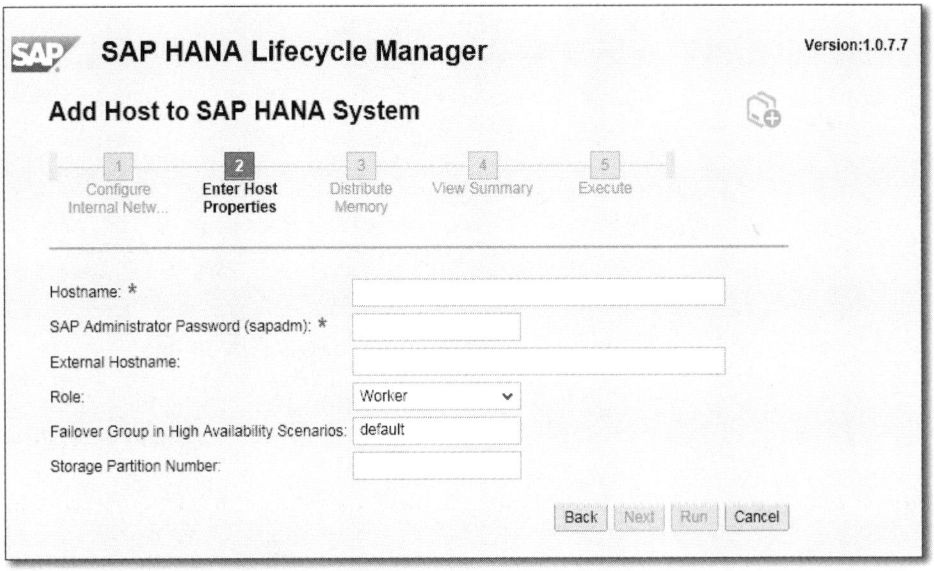

Figure 6.5 Defining Properties of the Host to Add

The host can be added as a WORKER or STANDBY host, and it must be assigned to a failover group (see Section 6.2.1). The storage partition number is only relevant when operating a system that uses the storage API.

On the third screen, you can view and if needed modify the memory distribution on the host to be added, in case you have multiple database systems making use of this host.

The add host functionality of HLM has been removed in SPS 8.

Using the Command-Line Tool hdbaddhost

The `hdbaddhost` program is part of the LCM tools that are installed with any SAP HANA database installation. Each system has its own copy of the tool. For a database system <SID>, the `hdbaddhost` tool is located in the file system path *install_path>/global/hdb/install/bin*. In a standard installation, the <install_path> is */hana/shared/<SID>*.

The program must be started by the root user on the host to be added. Because the shared file systems are already mounted, the <install_path> also will be in place on that host.

The tool can be used interactively, in which case you are prompted for all required values. If you intend to use the tool in batch mode, the full list of command-line options is given in the tool's documentation in the *SAP HANA LCM Tools Reference Guide* available at *https://help.sap.com/hana_platform/*.

Using the hdblcm(gui) Tool

The `hdblcm(gui)` tool is the official way to add hosts as of SPS 8 (the `hdbaddhost` tool is still available, though). You should use the resident version of the tool, that is, the one installed in */hana/shared/<SID>/hdblcm/* (default naming).

The tool must be started as the root user on any host of the system (one that is already part of the system or the host to be added), and you can add multiple hosts in a single procedure.

You can run both tools fully interactively, choosing the action to add a host at run time. With the command-line tool `hdblcm`, you can also include the option `--action=add_hosts` to immediately go into add-host mode, and you need to specify the `--addhosts=<host>` parameter. The value <host> of this parameter must include the host name and may optionally include the role and the failover group of the host, for example:

```
./hdblcm --action=add_hosts
         --addhosts=hana04:role=worker:group=ha_group2
```

If you omit the failover group specification, the host will be added to the default group.

Full information on adding hosts with the hdblcm(gui) tool is given in the *SAP HANA Administration Guide* at *https://help.sap.com/hana_platform/*.

> **Note**
>
> The documentation lists as a prerequisite for adding a host with hdblcm that the system has been installed with hdblcm. Hence, if your system has been installed by other means (e.g., Unified Installer) and if it is on the release level of SPS 8 (revision 80) or higher, you will have to use the hdbaddhost program.

In all three methods of adding a host, the database software on the new host will be started automatically, by which time the database system has been successfully extended.

After adding a new host, you will usually need to re-evaluate the table distribution (see Chapter 9), which is far more complex than adding the host itself.

6.1.5 Removing Hosts

Removing a host refers to configuring the database software so that the host to be removed will no longer be part of the scale-out cluster. It is not necessarily related to the physical removal of a host from the database hardware.

> **Note**
>
> If you need to physically replace a host (e.g., because of a hardware fault), it is not necessary to remove the host from the system configuration. Instead, you can use the hdbreg program (starting with SPS 8, you can also use the hdblcm program). We cover the task of exchanging hardware in material that can be downloaded from the book's page at *www.sap-press.com*.

The removing of hosts is not a simple task, owing to the fact that before you can remove a host you must make sure that no data is located on that host. After this is accomplished, you can safely remove the host from the system, which is done using HLM (up to SPS 7) or `hdblcm(gui)` (starting with SPS 8). We discuss these processes next.

Marking the Host for Removal: Data Relocation

The safe and recommended way of removing all data from a host is to mark the host for removal in SAP HANA Studio (see Figure 6.6). In the Administration Editor of SAP HANA Studio, go to tab LANDSCAPE, shown in ❶, then to HOSTS, shown in ❷, right-click on the host to be removed, and choose REMOVE HOST..., as shown in ❸, from the context menu. Carefully read the text in the pop-up window, as shown in ❹, and if you are certain that you do indeed want to remove the host, click YES to confirm.

Privilege Information

In order to mark a host for removal, you need system privileges CATALOG READ, DATA ADMIN, RESOURCE ADMIN, and SERVICE ADMIN. In addition, you need the EXECUTE privilege on a stored procedure in the SYS schema: SYS.UPDATE_LANDSCAPE_CONFIGURATION.

The actual removal will be delegated to an asynchronous process that will reorganize the database contents as required. You can monitor the progress of this reorganization on the LANDSCAPE • HOSTS tab of SAP HANA Studio. Only when the field REMOVAL STATUS of that table indicates that the reorg is finished or not required can you progress to the next step and actually remove the host.

Once the host is successfully marked for removal, you can remove it from the system configuration. There are different tools available for this task, depending on the version of SAP HANA that you are using; up to and including SPS 7, the tool of choice was the HLM tool. Starting with SPS 8, the functionality has been removed from HLM and added to the `hdblcm(gui)` tool.

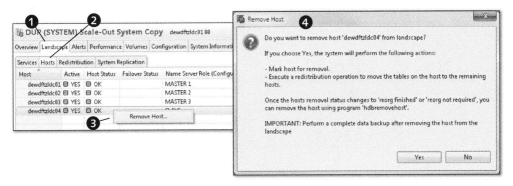

Figure 6.6 Marking a Host for Removal in SAP HANA Studio

Removing the Host with HLM (Up to SPS 7)

Up to and including SPS 7, you can remove hosts with the SAP HANA Lifecycle Manager (HLM). In the HLM tool, select REMOVE ADDITIONAL HOST, choose the host to be removed, and click RUN. Optionally, you can decide not to remove the <sid>adm Linux user from the host, and in case there are multiple database instances active on the host you may want to redistribute the host's memory among the remaining instances.

> **Note**
>
> Removal of the host in HLM will start *but fail* if you did not mark it for removal as outlined previously, leaving the system in an inconsistent state.
>
> When testing such a removal without preparation, we found that after the failed removal attempt the entry for the scale-out system was missing in the file */usr/sap/sapservices* on the host we tried to remove. After adding the entry back to the file (you can copy the entry from another host and adjust the host name) and starting the database services on the host, we could successfully mark the host for removal and actually remove it. We cannot, however, guarantee that this remedy procedure will always work in such situations.

Removing the Host with hdblcm(gui) (Starting with SPS 8)

Starting with SPS 8, hosts should be removed with the hdblcm(gui) tool. The resident copy of this tool should be used, which is installed in the file system path */hana/shared/<SID>/hdblcm/*.

Whether in GUI mode or on the command line, you can use the tool fully interactively, choosing to remove hosts from the system at runtime. The command-line flavor can also be started with parameter `--action=remove_hosts`.

See the documentation in the *SAP HANA Administration Guide* for further details.

> **Note**
>
> The documentation states as a prerequisite for removing a host with the `hdblcm(gui)` tool that this tool has already been used for system installation. If the system has been installed in a different way (e.g., with the Unified Installer) and if the system is on the SPS 8 release level (revision 80) or higher, you will have to use the `hdbremovehost` tool. This tool is documented in the *SAP HANA LCM Tools Reference* at *https://help.sap.com/hana_platform/*.

6.2 High Availability with Host Autofailover

In order to understand the relevance of host autofailover, we first have to develop a feeling for the impact of a fatal component failure on an arbitrary host of a scale-out system. The following two considerations will guide us to the answer:

▶ SAP HANA scale-out is based on a *shared-nothing* architecture, meaning that any element of the database content is at any time managed by just one system host. If a host fails within this system, the fraction of the database content managed by this host and the services provided by this host will become unavailable. In effect, such a single-host failure renders the entire database system inconsistent and thus unavailable; if a request needs data or a service from the failing host, then it will terminate with an error message. We will explain how this can be prevented in this section.

▶ In any scale-out system, the likelihood that one of the components fails within a given time frame will increase as the number of hosts in the system grows.

Putting these two insights together, it becomes evident that the probability of the database system becoming unavailable grows with the number of hosts in the scale-out cluster.

This problem can be solved by using the host autofailover functionality, which is a feature to increase the availability of a scaled SAP HANA instance. This feature makes it possible to define a *standby host* that will be activated in the event of a failing worker host. The standby host will then assume the role of the failing host.

The autofailover function is built upon three concepts, failover groups, host failover, and failback which are explained in this section.

6.2.1 Failover Groups

In distributed systems with a large number of hosts, you can define multiple standby hosts. It is also possible to configure disjoint groups of worker hosts with one or more dedicated standby hosts for each of these so-called *failover groups*. The standard failover group is named "default," and all hosts are placed into that group unless you explicitly choose differently.

The failover group configuration can already be implemented in the process of installing the system or when adding hosts, and it can also be changed at a later point in time. To see the current configuration, go to the LANDSCAPE • HOSTS tab in SAP HANA Studio (Figure 6.7) or query the monitoring view M_LANDSCAPE_HOST_ CONFIGURATION.

In our example, the SAP HANA system has five hosts in total, and two failover groups, shown in ❶, named DEFAULT and HA_GROUP2. As can be seen from the INDEX SERVER ROLE (ACTUAL), shown in ❷, each of the groups has one dedicated standby host. In failover group DEFAULT, there are two worker hosts; one of them is the actual index server and name server master. In failover group HA_GROUP2, there is just one worker node.

In this configuration, if one of the worker hosts in failover group DEFAULT fails, the standby host of this group will take over the role of the failing host. Likewise, if the worker host in failover group HA_GROUP2 fails, its standby host will take over.

It must be noted, however, that host failover will only happen within one failover group. Therefore, if both worker nodes in group DEFAULT fail at the same time, then the system will become unavailable, because the standby host can only take over the workload of one worker host.

In column NAME SERVER ROLE (CONFIGURED), shown in ❸, you can see that the standby host of failover group DEFAULT is also configured as one of the three master name servers (currently operating in slave mode). This may seem surprising at first sight, but it does make sense; the name server process is *always active*, including on standby hosts, and the failover of the name server master functionality to a standby host will generally be faster than the failover to a worker host. For this reason, the database system will automatically set up a standby host as the name server master during installation of a scale-out system.

S21 (SYSTEM) Failover Groups dewdftzldc05 23   Last Update: 13.05.2014 14:39:07   Interval: 60 ▾ Seconds

Overview | Landscape | Alerts | Performance | Volumes | Configuration | System Information | Diagnosis Files | Trace Configuration

Services | Hosts | Redistribution | System Replication

Host	Active	Host Status	Failover Status	Name Server Role (Configured)	Index Server Role (Actual)	Failover Group (Configured)	Failover Group (Actual)
dewdftzldc01	YES	IGNORE		SLAVE	STANDBY	ha_group2	ha_group2
dewdftzldc02	YES	IGNORE		MASTER 3	STANDBY	default	default
dewdftzldc03	YES	OK		SLAVE	SLAVE	ha_group2	ha_group2
dewdftzldc04	YES	OK		MASTER 2	SLAVE	default	default
dewdftzldc05	YES	OK		MASTER 1	MASTER	default	default

Figure 6.7 System Landscape with Two Failover Groups

To change the failover group configuration, you can click the CONFIGURE HOSTS FOR FAILOVER SITUATION button, shown in ❹. This opens a configuration wizard (Figure 6.8), which displays the configured and actual failover configuration in a table. Within this table, you can directly modify the configuration in columns CONFIGURED ROLE, shown in ❶, and CONFIGURED GROUP, shown in ❷.

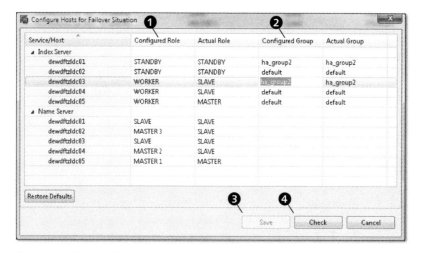

Figure 6.8 Changing the Failover Configuration

In this wizard, you can also define new failover groups, simply by giving a new group name to at least one worker or standby host. It is possible to create failover groups that consist only of worker hosts (but no standby) or vice versa. This obviously does not make sense, but the wizard will not stop you from making such configurations. It is therefore very important that you check the spelling of your failover group configuration carefully.

Note that you can change not only the index server role but also the name server role.

Before you can actually SAVE your configuration, as shown in ❸, you must CHECK it for consistency, as shown in ❹. The consistency check will (in the release level of SPS 8) not detect the previously mentioned questionable configurations of failover groups without worker or standby hosts.

From a purely statistical point of view, having just one failover group with multiple standby hosts provides higher availability than having multiple failover groups with one standby host each (in a given system with <x> worker and <y> standby hosts). Depending on the hardware setup, there may be technical reasons, such as optimized failover times, for having a dedicated standby host within a given set of hosts.

6.2.2   Host Failover

In order for a host failover to happen, the system must first detect that a worker host is unavailable. It is important the failover action is not triggered too quickly. If, for example, an index server process is manually stopped or crashes, the daemon process will immediately trigger the restart of this service. It is more efficient to wait for the index server to start up again than to failover to a standby host.

If the system determines that the worker host is indeed unavailable, it will trigger a failover to an available standby host. In the course of the failover, the following steps are performed by the system:

▶ The configuration of database processes on the standby host is adjusted to match the configuration of the failing host. Most processes are configured in any case on the standby host, but there are exceptions. One is the XS server, which in a standard configuration is active only on the master host. If the master host fails, the XS server must also be started on the standby.

  In some cases, such as after an asymmetric system copy, the failing host might have multiple index servers configured. On a standby host, there is only one configured index server process, but the additional ones will be started as required in a failover situation.

▶ The database processes on the standby host must assign the data volumes of the failing host.

▶ All processes with persistence will reconstruct their data image from the data and log files in the same way as during regular system start. This also includes loading of row store tables and preloading of columnar tables.

It is difficult to predict the time it will take until a standby host becomes available in a failover situation. Depending on the type of failure, it might be detected in a matter of seconds or a few minutes. The actual failover itself is usually a quick process, taking mere seconds.

As in regular system startup, the reconstruction of the data image in memory can take significantly longer. If the failing host carried a sizable amount of row store data, the index server startup can take several minutes. Once the index server is online, the columnar tables are still not loaded yet.

6.2.3 Failback

There is no automatic failback once the original worker host becomes available again. Instead, the original worker host will be configured as the new standby host, as indicated in Figure 6.9. This avoids having to go through the failover procedure once again and thus increases the overall availability of the database system.

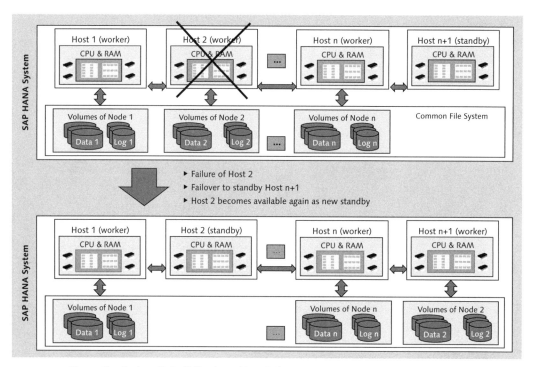

Figure 6.9 System State Following a Host Failover

In this way, the actual roles of the hosts can become different from the configured roles over time. If the entire database system is restarted, all hosts will again assume their configured roles.

6.3   Client Connect in Distributed Systems

In a distributed system, the database clients (JDBC/ODBC) will automatically distribute connections in a round-robin manner to all worker hosts of the database. It is not necessary to specify all hosts of the setup in the client connection string in order for this mechanism to work; it is sufficient to specify the master host.

The client software will establish the initial database connection to the master host and retrieve the list of all worker hosts. Starting from that point, sessions can be distributed in a round-robin fashion.

In the event that the master host may be unavailable when a client tries to connect for the first time, the connect attempt will fail. For such situations, it is possible to specify multiple hosts in the connection string. In Figure 6.10, we show the configuration of the corresponding connection strings in the connection setup for SAP HANA Studio, as shown in ❶, and the MS Windows ODBC registration, as shown in ❸.

Note that in SAP HANA Studio the different host entries must be separated by a semicolon, as shown in ❷, whereas the MS Windows ODBC Data Source Administrator user interface expects a comma-separated list, as shown in ❹.

In applications that use the JDBC or ODBC driver, you always have to use a semicolon-separated list of host names in the connection string, as shown in Listing 6.1.

```
JDBC:
Connect URL: jdbc:sap://<host1>:<port>;<host2>:<port>/
ODBC
Connect URL: "DRIVER=HDBODBC32;UID=<user>;PWD=<password>;SERVER-
NODE=<host1>:<port>;<host2>:<port>;<host3>:<port>;"
```

Listing 6.1 Connection Strings for Applications That Use JDBC or ODBC

In all of these connection strings, you have to enter <hostname>:<port> for each host, <port> being the external SQL port of the index server on the host.

273

It is sufficient to only specify all configured master name servers, because at least one of them must be operational for the system to be available at all.

Even if multiple hosts are defined in the connection string, sessions that are connected to the failing host at the time of failure will be disconnected, so end users may have to reconnect or restart applications.

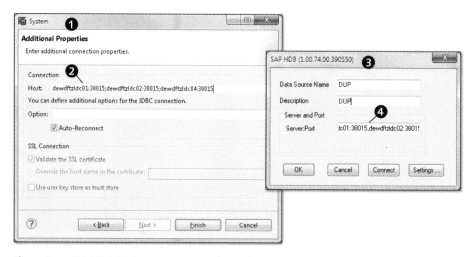

Figure 6.10 JDBC/ODBC Connection String for Scale-Out Systems

6.4   Summary

In most practical aspects, a scale-out system functions just like a single-node system, especially when it comes to simple interaction with the database, most monitoring tasks, and so on.

After reading this chapter, you should be aware of the most important design aspects of scale-out systems, such as the different node types (worker nodes—which are divided into one master and multiple slaves—and standby nodes) and the role of the name server in distributed systems. You should also be able to modify the system landscape by adding or removing hosts.

Last but not least, you should be aware of the host autofailover functionality that improves overall system availability in scale-out systems. Related to this topic is the configuration of the connection information for client applications, which in a scale-out system should always be set up to allow connections in a failover situation.

In order to work with a database, one needs an understanding of the objects the database can contain. This chapter will define the concepts behind each of these objects and then give examples of how the objects are used in SAP HANA.

7 Objects

If we look at what is stored in an SAP HANA database, we will find items such as tables, views, sequences, and so on. These entities are called *objects*. For every object in the database, we find additional metadata that specifies it. Also, each object type has some functional relevance in the database and can do what none of the other object types can do.

The object types we will discuss in this chapter are listed in Table 7.1 together with a short description and a reference to the catalog view that describes all objects of the given type.

Object Type	Short Description	Catalog View
Table	The basic container to store data in the database	TABLES
Trigger	A program that is executed when certain actions are performed on a table	TRIGGERS
SQL view	Standard database view	VIEWS where IS_COLUMN_VIEW ='FALSE'
Column view	SAP HANA-specific type of view, used, for example, in modeling	VIEWS where IS_COLUMN_VIEW ='TRUE'
Sequences	A customizable number generator	SEQUENCES
Procedures	Programming element with multiple input and output parameters (scalar or table type)	PROCEDURES

Table 7.1 List of Object Types

Object Type	Short Description	Catalog View
Functions	Programming element with exactly one output parameter, either scalar or table type	FUNCTIONS
Synonyms	Shortcuts for object name resolution— similar to file system links	SYNONYMS

Table 7.1 List of Object Types (Cont.)

Although the majority of the chapter is devoted to providing some basic information about these object types, we will start by discussing object properties that are common to all objects.

7.1 Common Properties of Database Objects

Before we dive into the different types of objects you'll find residing in an SAP HANA database, let's start by outlining some basic principles of objects in general. In this section, we'll introduce you to the following concepts: the database catalog; object naming; users, schemas, object ownership, and dependencies; object definitions; and system limits.

7.1.1 The Database Catalog

A very useful feature of basically every DBMS is that the databases are self-describing. This means that within every database there are tables or views that contain information about the objects stored in the database. In SAP HANA, these views are named *catalog views*, and they make up the *catalog* of the database.

As an example, SAP HANA provides a system view simply called TABLES that holds one record for every table created in the database. This catalog view also provides information on specific attributes of each table, for example, whether or not the automatic merge is active for the table (AUTO_MERGE_ON) or the compression settings will automatically be optimized (AUTO_OPTIMIZE_COMPRESSION_ON). Whenever a table is created, altered, or dropped, SAP HANA will automatically update the TABLES view so that it will always contain the current state of the tables in the database.

The TABLES view actually acts like a directory of tables in the database. There are similar views for all other object types listed in Table 7.1—and also for objects we will not cover in this chapter, such as the views SCHEMAS, USERS, ROLES, and PRIV-ILEGES. All database objects are also listed in a type-independent view that is simply named OBJECTS.

The catalog also keeps track of an internal unique ID for each object created: the OID. Depending on the object type, this OID sometimes can show up as OBJECT_OID, TABLE_OID, VIEW_OID, and so on. Usually, the OID is not relevant, but it can become useful for troubleshooting and problem analysis.

All the database catalog views are accessible to all database users that have the PUBLIC role assigned to them. As this is the default role for *every* database user (with the exception of the restricted users introduced in SPS 8), *every* database user in turn has the required privileges to access the catalog views. For all system catalog views, public synonyms are created by default, making it unnecessary to specify a schema name, such as SYS or SYSTEM, when accessing the catalog views.

In order to avoid confusion, we will dedicate a short paragraph to a part of the database system that does *not* belong to the catalog but still deals with objects: the repository.

The Repository

The catalog contains a description of all of the currently present objects in the database. It does not contain any information about objects that are not (yet) present and in the database; these are typically the design-time objects that are stored in the repository (consequently, they are also referred to as *repository objects*). Such design-time representations are available for many—but not all—object types. In short, the repository stores and manages all of the development artifacts and information models created in the MODELER or DEVELOPMENT perspective of SAP HANA Studio or in the web IDE. Only when those objects are activated will the corresponding catalog objects (also called *runtime objects*) be created. For information about the repository, see Chapter 11.

Note

The SAP HANA database catalog also contains special system views called monitoring views. We cover monitoring views in more detail in Chapter 16.

7.1.2 Object Naming and Identifiers

SAP HANA, like most DBMS, has two ways to handle the names of tables, columns, and objects in general. The default option is used when the object names or identifiers are written without double quotes (" "). (The SAP HANA SQL reference documentation refers to identifiers without double quotes as *undelimited* identifiers.) With this option active, SAP HANA converts lowercase characters to uppercase and prevents the use of characters that are not alphanumeric. Also, the first character of the object name cannot be a number.

> **Example**
>
> SALES is allowed as an undelimited object name, but 11-2007/ElephantSales would be rejected.

However, you may have good reasons to choose a "fancy" table name, and you can do this by enclosing the name in double quotes. This is the second option to handle identifiers. Including the name in double quotes prevents any automatic conversion, so "Sales", "SALES", and "sales" are three different names!

Whenever objects with such a delimited identifier need to be accessed, you must use the exact spelling and the double quotes again. Otherwise, an unknown identifier or syntax error error message will be returned. In SAP BW systems, a classic example of this is the SQL access to the database tables in the SAP BW schema. Although it is not supported by SAP, it is technically possible to directly read data from those tables, if you have a database user account with the appropriate privileges. An often encountered difficulty in such a case is that the table names in the SAP BW schema typically look similar to this: /BIC/ASALES01.

Let's look at some examples for the usage of object naming.

Listing 7.1 shows a common mistake that developers used to the ABAP environment make. Leaving out the double quotes and the capitalization of the table name works in ABAP but not in SQL.

```
SELECT count(*) FROM /bic/asales01;

SAP DBTech JDBC: [257] (at 22):
sql syntax error: incorrect syntax near "/": line 1 col 22 (at pos 22)
```

Listing 7.1 Wrong, but Easy to Type

Listing 7.2 shows a similar mistake. Using uppercase letters and leaving out the dashes does not work, either.

```
SELECT count(*) FROM BIC ASALES01;

SAP DBTech JDBC: [259] (at 21):
invalid table name: Could not find table/view BIC in schema LARS: line
1 col 22 (at pos 21)
```
Listing 7.2 Different, but Still Wrong

Listing 7.3 shows the correct way. The whole object name, including the dashes, needs to be in uppercase and enclosed in double quotes.

```
SELECT count(*) FROM "/BIC/ASALES01";

COUNT(*)
42
```
Listing 7.3 Correct, but Added Keyboard Deterioration

7.1.3 Users, Schemas, Object Ownership, and Dependencies

Users, schemas, object ownership, and dependencies are overlapping aspects of managing objects in a DBMS. Basic functions, such as a functional dependency between two objects (consider a view using a base table), require a dependency concept. Introducing a namespace concept like *a schema* requires tracking another kind of dependency. Finally, assigning ownership of objects in different namespaces adds another angle into the mix.

Next, we look into the most important aspects of these topics.

Users

The SAP HANA database can be accessed by providing a user name and a logon. The user account here really is a mechanism to handle object ownership and privileges. Every command in the SAP HANA database is executed in the context of a session (see Chapter 10 for more details), and in turn every session has exactly one user account linked to it. This links every command to the user account and in turn to the effective privileges that apply to the account at the time of command execution.

Another use for this linkage between user account and command execution is to audit the database. Whenever a command is issued to the database, the audit manager can associate the command with the session details and with the user name.

Schemas

A schema is a *namespace*. It is a way to group objects together by addressing them with the same group name. Schemas do not carry any security features. Every user has a *default schema* assigned, which is named after the user account name. Whenever a user tries to access a database object and does not provide a schema name, SAP HANA uses the default schema as a fallback. When looking up an object in the default namespace does not succeed, SAP HANA will try to find the object requested in the PUBLIC schema.

The order of object name resolution therefore is:

1. The provided schema
2. The current schema
3. The public schema

Whenever a matching object name is found in one of the steps, no further evaluation is done. If a schema name is provided (fully qualified object reference), then no further evaluation steps are performed in cases where the object cannot be found.

This evaluation process leaves it to the developers to specify the fully qualified object reference in their SQL commands—leading to an absolute object reference that does not allow any ambiguities—or to only specify the object name and rely on the evaluation logic that provides additional flexibility for the actual schema name. A useful technique for a database developer is, for example, to map commonly shared objects into an application user schema via a synonym.

As object names only need to be unique within a given schema, it is possible that multiple schemas contain, for example, tables with the same name. In fact, this is quite common. Sometimes, this behavior can lead to false impressions about which object is currently referenced when no explicit schema name is given. The easiest way to find this out is to use the EXPLAIN PLAN command, as demonstrated in the following example.

As a first step, two schemas, s1 and s2, are created, and in each of the schemas a table, t1, is created and filled with some sample data, as shown in Figure 7.1.

```
SQL  Result  Result
 1   create schema s1;
 2   create schema s2;
 3
 4   create column table s1.t1 (id integer primary key, name varchar(20));
 5
 6   create column table s2.t1 (id integer primary key, name varchar(20));
 7
 8   insert into s1.t1 values (1, 'Test');
 9
10   insert into s2.t1 values (1, 'DUCK');
11   insert into s2.t1 values (2, 'BIRD');
12   insert into s2.t1 values (3, 'BAND');
13
14   select * from s1.t1;
15   select * from s2.t1;
16
```

Figure 7.1 Schema Example Table Setup

Checking the table contents leads to the output shown in Figure 7.2.

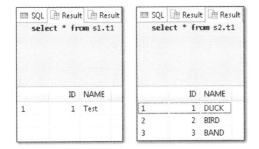

Figure 7.2 Content of Table T1 in Schemas S1 and S2

Now, if you try to access the table without specifying the schema name it results in an error message, as Figure 7.3 shows.

```
16
17   select * from t1;
18
19
       ◂                                                          ▸

Started: 2014-04-06 16:25:13
Could not execute 'select * from t1' in 356 ms 230 μs .
SAP DBTech JDBC: [259] (at 14): invalid table name: Could not find table/view T1 in schema
LARS: line 1 col 15 (at pos 14)
```

Figure 7.3 Invalid Table Name Error Due to Missing Schema Name

In order to be able to access the tables without having to specify the schema name all the time, SAP HANA provides the SET SCHEMA <SCHEMA_NAME> command.

> **Warning**
>
> A warning for administrators who frequently use the SQL editor in SAP HANA Studio: In the default setting SAP HANA Studio uses automatic reconnect when the connection to the database is lost for any reason. In this case, a new session will be started, and the current schema is back to the default schema for this user.

Finally, you can use the EXPLAIN PLAN command to check what table from what schema is used for the query. What this looks like is shown in Figure 7.4.

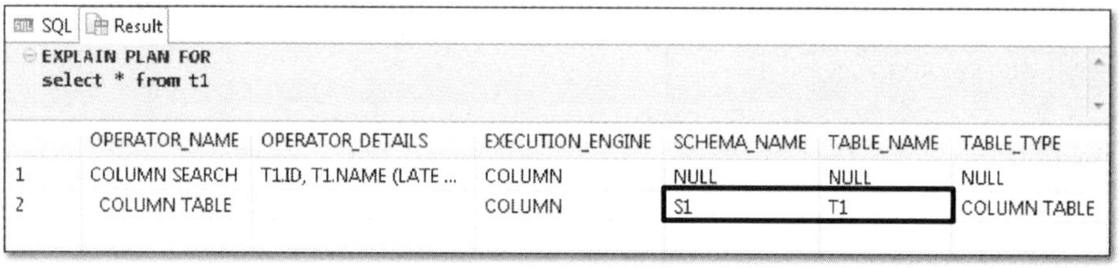

Figure 7.4 Schema and Table Reference Visible in EXPLAIN PLAN

Another handy use for schemas is that it is possible to use them as a dynamic way to affect many single objects in one go. For example, when the SELECT privilege for a schema is assigned to a user or a role and new objects in the schema are created, the SELECT privilege on the schema will automatically include the newly created objects. Exporting an entire schema is usually much easier than exporting single selected tables and other such items.

The relevant catalog view from which to find out about schemas is the SCHEMAS view, which lists all schemas, the schema owner, and whether the current user has any privileges on the schemas. Also, nearly every specific object type view (TABLES, VIEWS, INDEXES, SEQUENCES, etc.) provides a SCHEMA_NAME column to indicate the schema that the respective object belongs to.

It is not possible to directly change the schema of an object, just as it is not possible to change the owner once an object has been created. To still get the desired effect, that is, to have the objects in a different schema and/or with a different owner, the object needs to be recreated in the target schema by the user account that should be the owner of the objects. An easy way to achieve this is to export the objects with the EXPORT command or the Catalog Objects Export Assistant in SAP HANA Studio, and import the objects with the RENAME SCHEMA option. Be aware that to do this the user needs to have the IMPORT system privilege assigned.

In any case, schema design should be considered *before* the first objects are created. Although SAP HANA Studio displays schemas in the navigator window similar to how it displays file system folders, it is not easy to copy/move objects between schemas or users.

Ownership

We have seen that the schema of a table determines if and how the table will be found by SAP HANA during query execution. From a developer point of view, tables that belong together should be stored in the same schema. This makes it a lot easier to maintain security on the tables and provides a common grouping for administration tasks, for example, to export all tables of an application.

One aspect not covered by schemas is the ownership of objects. Objects are always owned by the user that created them, even if they are created in a different schema than the user's own schema. The only exception to this is with schemas, for which the desired owner can be provided with the CREATE SCHEMA <schema name> OWNED BY <owner> command.

Attention needs to be paid if a schema will be deleted via SAP HANA Studio, because the DELETE schema dialogue starts off with the CASCADE option as the default setting and does not provide a list of the affected objects (see Figure 7.5 for an example).

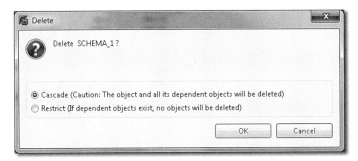

Figure 7.5 Delete Schema Dialogue with Dangerous Default Setting

As we have seen, using different schemas and object owners can lead to setups that are rather complex and in which supposedly simple commands can have the unexpected effect of dropping objects that were not meant to be deleted. This is especially true for SQL console usage, where no double checks and confirmations are requested from the user.

283

Before we wrap up our discussion of object ownership, let's look at a brief example to illustrate an important rule: When multiple developers create catalog objects in a shared schema, it is typically desirable to use a shared user to create the objects in the target schema. This shared user should only be used as the object owner and does not even need to be able to log on to the system. Instead, a shared procedure could be written that runs any provided `create` object command in the schema owners' session and grants access to the newly created object back to the calling user.

The following code illustrates how this can be done:

1. Create a user account for the shared user:

```
create user DEVSCHEMA password AllMy1000Objects;
grant create schema to DEVSCHEMA;
```

2. Logged in as the DEVSCHEMA user, create the proxy procedure and grant execution privilege to the developer users or roles:

```
create procedure proxyCreateObjectInOtherSchema
                (IN ddlCMD varchar(2000)
                ,IN grantCMD varchar(2000))
language SQLSCRIPT
sql security DEFINER
as
begin
    exec :ddlCMD;
    exec :grantCMD;
end;

grant execute on proxyCreateObjectInOtherSchema to USER_A;
grant execute on proxyCreateObjectInOtherSchema to USER_B;
```

3. Now, deactivate the DEVSCHEMA account so that it cannot be used to connect to the SAP HANA database any longer:

```
alter user DEVSCHEMA deactivate;
```

4. The development user USER_A now can call the proxy procedure to create objects as DEVSCHEMA:

```
call devschema.proxyCreateObjectInOtherSchema
'create column table ATAB3 (aaa_i int, aaa_v varchar (20))'
, 'grant all privileges on ATAB3 to USER_A');
```

5. Now, let's check which schema the object is in and who owns it:

```
select schema_name, table_name
from tables where table_name ='ATAB3';
```

```
SCHEMA_NAME TABLE_NAME
DEVSCHEMA   ATAB3

select * from ownership where object_name ='ATAB3';

SCHEMA_NAME OWNER_NAME OBJECT_NAME OBJECT_TYPE OBJECT_OID
DEVSCHEMA   DEVSCHEMA  ATAB3       TABLE       186287
```

If you now to try to log on to the database as the DEVUSER, logon is denied and indicated as shown in Figure 7.6.

Figure 7.6 Deactivated User Notification

A very similar technique is used by the information modeler during object activation. All runtime objects in the catalog are owned by the deactivated user _SYS_REPO and assigned to the _SYS_BIC schema. However, this only applies if developers want to create objects directly via SQL DDL instead of using the development artifacts for objects in the SAP HANA DEVELOPMENT perspective. When the SAP HANA DEVELOPMENT REPOSITORY is used, then the objects are always created in the assigned schema and are owned by _SYS_REPO, just like activated information models.

> **Note**
>
> DROP SCHEMA and DROP USER must acquire exclusive locks on the objects that should be dropped before the object can actually be dropped. That means that open transactions can potentially hold shared or intentional exclusive locks, which makes it impossible for the DROP SCHEMA/DROP USER command to get the exclusive locks on these objects. In such a case, the session hangs and waits until either the lock timeout has arrived or the exclusive lock has been granted.

Object Dependencies

SAP HANA tracks dependencies between objects, and eventually ensures that dependent objects get invalidated or deleted when the main object is modified. But how can SAP HANA possibly know which objects depend on others? This information is gathered during the creation of objects in the database and kept up-to-date over the lifetime of database objects. The database developer does not need to take care of this.

To review the dependency information kept in the catalog, SAP HANA provides a system view called OBJECT_DEPENDENCIES. This view contains the schema, object name, and object type for any base object for which there are dependent objects and the same set of information for the dependent object.

It contains one row per dependent object, and for each entry an additional column, DEPENDENCY_TYPE, is maintained. This column can contain values of 1 or 2, where 1 denotes a direct dependency and 2 any indirect dependency (e.g., a view that references a synonym that references a table; in such a case, the dependency synonym-to-table would be direct and the dependency view-to-table would be an indirect reference).

Reading the view directly can be a bit cumbersome, as shown in Figure 7.7.

```
select * from object_dependencies
where current_user in ( base_schema_name , dependent_schema_name)
```

	BASE_SCHEMA_NAME	BASE_OBJECT_NAME	BASE_OBJECT_TYPE	DEPENDENT_SCHEMA_NAME	DEPENDENT_OBJECT_NAME	DEPENDENT_OBJECT_TYPE	DEPENDENCY_TYPE
1	EFASHION	SHOP_FACTS	TABLE	LARS	TOP_TEN_ARTICLE_ID	VIEW	2
2	EFASHION	TOP_TEN_ARTICLES	VIEW	LARS	TOP_TEN_ARTICLE_ID	VIEW	1
3	LARS	TOP_TEN_ARTICLES	SYNONYM	LARS	TOP_TEN_ARTICLE_ID	VIEW	1
4	SYS	DUMMY	TABLE	LARS	MV	VIEW	2
5	SYS	HAS_NEEDED_SYST...	VIEW	LARS	MV	VIEW	2
6	SYS	M_DELTA_MERGE_...	VIEW	LARS	MV	VIEW	1
7	SYS	M_DELTA_MERGE_...	MONITORVIEW	LARS	MV	VIEW	2
8	LARS	TEST3	TABLE	_SYS_BIC	lars/DECTABTEST/CV	VIEW	1
9	LARS	TEST1	TABLE	_SYS_BIC	lars/DECTABTEST/CV	VIEW	1
10	LARS	CTINY	TABLE	_SYS_BIC	lars/TINYDDM	VIEW	1
11	LARS	CSMALL	TABLE	_SYS_BIC	lars/SMALLDIM	VIEW	1
12	LARS	CSMALL	TABLE	_SYS_BIC	lars/AV_DOUBLE_CONCAT	VIEW	1
13	LARS	CTINY	TABLE	_SYS_BIC	lars/AV_DOUBLE_CONCAT	VIEW	1
14	LARS	CBIG	TABLE	_SYS_BIC	lars/AV_DOUBLE_CONCAT	VIEW	1
15	LARS	TEST2	TABLE	_SYS_BIC	lars/AVTEST	VIEW	1
16	LARS	TEST1	TABLE	_SYS_BIC	lars/AVTEST	VIEW	1
17	LARS	TEST1	TABLE	_SYS_BIC	lars/MULTITABUSE	VIEW	1
18	LARS	TEST3	TABLE	_SYS_BIC	lars/MULTITABUSE	VIEW	1
19	LARS	TEST2	TABLE	_SYS_BIC	lars/MULTITABUSE	VIEW	1
20	LARS	DFACT	TABLE	_SYS_BIC	lars/AVTEST2	VIEW	1
21	LARS	TEST2	TABLE	_SYS_BIC	lars/AVTEST2	VIEW	1
22	LARS	TEST3	TABLE	_SYS_BIC	lars/AVTEST2	VIEW	1
23	LARS	TEST1	TABLE	_SYS_BIC	lars/AVTEST2	VIEW	1
24	LARS	COBJECTS	TABLE	_SYS_BIC	lars/TESTSQL	VIEW	1
25	LARS	TEST1	TABLE	_SYS_BIC	lars/DECTABTEST/CV/bisc	VIEW	2

Figure 7.7 Reading Directly from the OBJECT_DEPENDENCIES View

Although this view contains all of the required information, it is difficult to use it to answer the question "what objects depend on any object in my current schema?"

Rewriting the SQL a little bit, as shown in Listing 7.4, provides a more readable answer.

```
select   BASE_OBJECT_TYPE
       , '"'||BASE_SCHEMA_NAME ||'"."'
         || BASE_OBJECT_NAME||'"' AS BASE_OBJECT
       , ' === is '|| map (dependency_type, 1, 'directly',
                                          2, 'indirectly')
               ||' referenced by ==> ' AS REF_TYPE
       , DEPENDENT_OBJECT_TYPE
       , '"'|| DEPENDENT_SCHEMA_NAME || '"."'
         || DEPENDENT_OBJECT_NAME || '"'
        AS DEPENDENT_OBJECT
from ( select * from object_dependencies
       where current_user in
            ( base_schema_name , dependent_schema_name))
order by base_schemaSELECT count(*) FROM “/BIC/ASALES01”;

COUNT(*)42_name, base_object_name, dependency_type;
```

Listing 7.4 Using View OBJECT_OWNERSHIP

The output produced by this query is a lot easier to read, as shown in Figure 7.8.

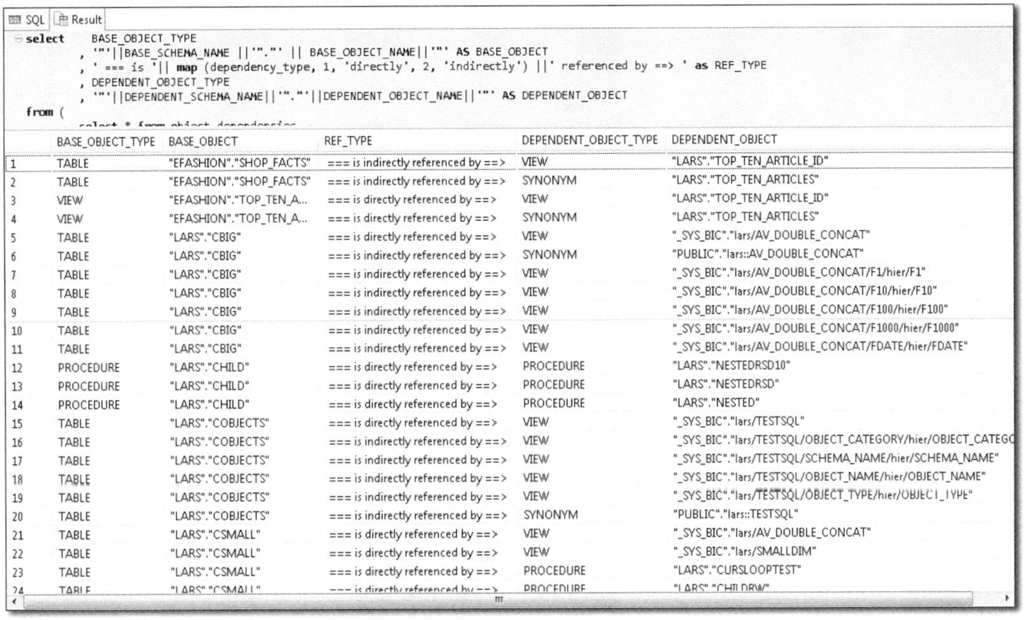

```
select   BASE_OBJECT_TYPE
       , '"'||BASE_SCHEMA_NAME ||'"."' || BASE_OBJECT_NAME||'"' AS BASE_OBJECT
       , ' === is '|| map (dependency_type, 1, 'directly', 2, 'indirectly') ||' referenced by ==> ' as REF_TYPE
       , DEPENDENT_OBJECT_TYPE
       , '"'||DEPENDENT_SCHEMA_NAME||'"."'||DEPENDENT_OBJECT_NAME||'"' AS DEPENDENT_OBJECT
  from (
```

	BASE_OBJECT_TYPE	BASE_OBJECT	REF_TYPE	DEPENDENT_OBJECT_TYPE	DEPENDENT_OBJECT
1	TABLE	"EFASHION"."SHOP_FACTS"	=== is indirectly referenced by ==>	VIEW	"LARS"."TOP_TEN_ARTICLE_ID"
2	TABLE	"EFASHION"."SHOP_FACTS"	=== is indirectly referenced by ==>	SYNONYM	"LARS"."TOP_TEN_ARTICLES"
3	VIEW	"EFASHION"."TOP_TEN_A...	=== is directly referenced by ==>	VIEW	"LARS"."TOP_TEN_ARTICLE_ID"
4	VIEW	"EFASHION"."TOP_TEN_A...	=== is directly referenced by ==>	SYNONYM	"LARS"."TOP_TEN_ARTICLES"
5	TABLE	"LARS"."CBIG"	=== is directly referenced by ==>	VIEW	"_SYS_BIC"."lars/AV_DOUBLE_CONCAT"
6	TABLE	"LARS"."CBIG"	=== is indirectly referenced by ==>	SYNONYM	"PUBLIC"."lars::AV_DOUBLE_CONCAT"
7	TABLE	"LARS"."CBIG"	=== is indirectly referenced by ==>	VIEW	"_SYS_BIC"."lars/AV_DOUBLE_CONCAT/F1/hier/F1"
8	TABLE	"LARS"."CBIG"	=== is indirectly referenced by ==>	VIEW	"_SYS_BIC"."lars/AV_DOUBLE_CONCAT/F10/hier/F10"
9	TABLE	"LARS"."CBIG"	=== is indirectly referenced by ==>	VIEW	"_SYS_BIC"."lars/AV_DOUBLE_CONCAT/F100/hier/F100"
10	TABLE	"LARS"."CBIG"	=== is indirectly referenced by ==>	VIEW	"_SYS_BIC"."lars/AV_DOUBLE_CONCAT/F1000/hier/F1000"
11	TABLE	"LARS"."CBIG"	=== is indirectly referenced by ==>	VIEW	"_SYS_BIC"."lars/AV_DOUBLE_CONCAT/FDATE/hier/FDATE"
12	PROCEDURE	"LARS"."CHILD"	=== is directly referenced by ==>	PROCEDURE	"LARS"."NESTEDRSD10"
13	PROCEDURE	"LARS"."CHILD"	=== is directly referenced by ==>	PROCEDURE	"LARS"."NESTEDRSD"
14	PROCEDURE	"LARS"."CHILD"	=== is directly referenced by ==>	PROCEDURE	"LARS"."NESTED"
15	TABLE	"LARS"."COBJECTS"	=== is directly referenced by ==>	VIEW	"_SYS_BIC"."lars/TESTSQL"
16	TABLE	"LARS"."COBJECTS"	=== is indirectly referenced by ==>	VIEW	"_SYS_BIC"."lars/TESTSQL/OBJECT_CATEGORY/hier/OBJECT_CATEG
17	TABLE	"LARS"."COBJECTS"	=== is indirectly referenced by ==>	VIEW	"_SYS_BIC"."lars/TESTSQL/SCHEMA_NAME/hier/SCHEMA_NAME"
18	TABLE	"LARS"."COBJECTS"	=== is indirectly referenced by ==>	VIEW	"_SYS_BIC"."lars/TESTSQL/OBJECT_NAME/hier/OBJECT_NAME"
19	TABLE	"LARS"."COBJECTS"	=== is indirectly referenced by ==>	VIEW	"_SYS_BIC"."lars/TESTSQL/OBJECT_TYPE/hier/OBJECT_TYPE"
20	TABLE	"LARS"."COBJECTS"	=== is indirectly referenced by ==>	SYNONYM	"PUBLIC"."lars::TESTSQL"
21	TABLE	"LARS"."CSMALL"	=== is directly referenced by ==>	VIEW	"_SYS_BIC"."lars/AV_DOUBLE_CONCAT"
22	TABLE	"LARS"."CSMALL"	=== is directly referenced by ==>	VIEW	"_SYS_BIC"."lars/SMALLDIM"
23	TABLE	"LARS"."CSMALL"	=== is directly referenced by ==>	PROCEDURE	"LARS"."CURSLOOPTEST"
24	TABLE	"LARS"."CSMALL"	=== is directly referenced by ==>	PROCEDURE	"LARS"."CHILDRW"

Figure 7.8 Formatted Output of System View OBJECT_DEPENDENCIES

With this approach, a simple impact analysis of object drops/invalidations can be quickly performed.

7.1.4 Object Definition

When it comes to working with objects, an often required functionality is to be able to recreate the DDL command that can create a given object that is active in the catalog. For repository objects, this is fairly simple, because the complete actual information that was used to create the object is explicitly stored in the repository.

For catalog objects, this is somewhat more difficult, because the original DDL command is not stored in SAP HANA. To ease the task of picking each relevant piece of information from the catalog views, SAP HANA comes with a built-in shared procedure called GET_OBJECT_DEFINITION. By calling the procedure with the schema name and the object name, we can easily create a DDL command that could create a similar object with the same attributes and settings. This is shown in Figure 7.9.

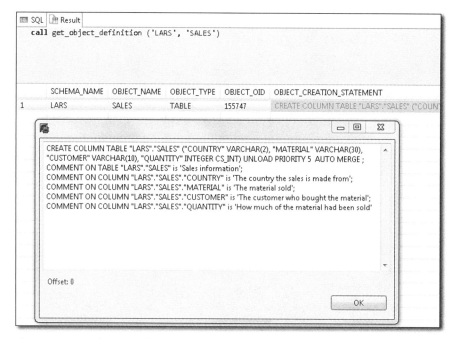

Figure 7.9 Example Output for Procedure GET_OBJECT_DEFINITION

One thing to keep in mind with this procedure is that it takes the current actual version of the object as it is present in the database right now. It does not show us the actual original version nor can it find out which alterations have been performed on the object since its creation.

As an alternative to this procedure, it is also possible to simply open the definition of any catalog object by double-clicking its entry in the SAP HANA Studio navigator and then clicking the EXPORT SQL button in the upper-right corner.

7.1.5   System Limits

Let's wrap up our discussion of the common properties of database objects with another element common to most database objects: the technical limits built into SAP HANA. "How many indexes can I create on a table?" "How many columns can a primary key have?" These questions and more can be answered by checking the system view M_SYSTEM_LIMITS, which is shown in Figure 7.10.

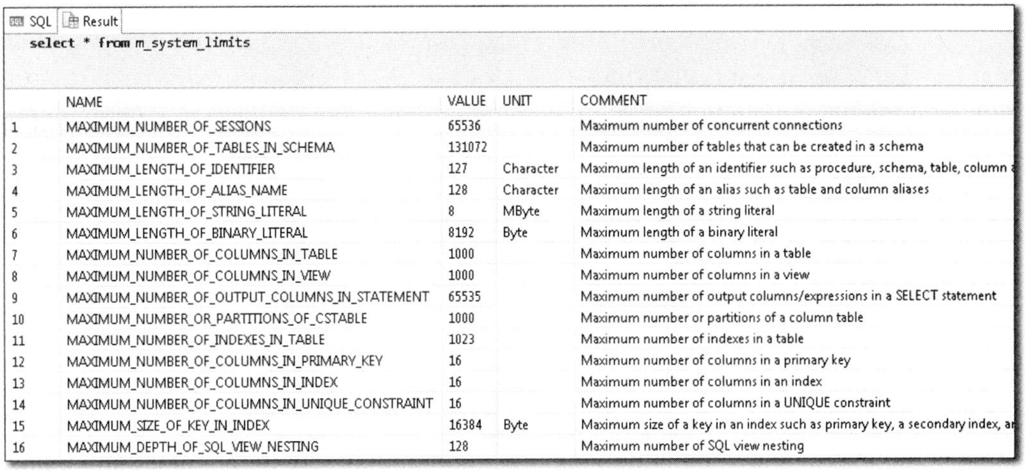

```
SQL   Result
  select * from m_system_limits
```

	NAME	VALUE	UNIT	COMMENT
1	MAXIMUM_NUMBER_OF_SESSIONS	65536		Maximum number of concurrent connections
2	MAXIMUM_NUMBER_OF_TABLES_IN_SCHEMA	131072		Maximum number of tables that can be created in a schema
3	MAXIMUM_LENGTH_OF_IDENTIFIER	127	Character	Maximum length of an identifier such as procedure, schema, table, column a
4	MAXIMUM_LENGTH_OF_ALIAS_NAME	128	Character	Maximum length of an alias such as table and column aliases
5	MAXIMUM_LENGTH_OF_STRING_LITERAL	8	MByte	Maximum length of a string literal
6	MAXIMUM_LENGTH_OF_BINARY_LITERAL	8192	Byte	Maximum length of a binary literal
7	MAXIMUM_NUMBER_OF_COLUMNS_IN_TABLE	1000		Maximum number of columns in a table
8	MAXIMUM_NUMBER_OF_COLUMNS_IN_VIEW	1000		Maximum number of columns in a view
9	MAXIMUM_NUMBER_OF_OUTPUT_COLUMNS_IN_STATEMENT	65535		Maximum number of output columns/expressions in a SELECT statement
10	MAXIMUM_NUMBER_OR_PARTITIONS_OF_CSTABLE	1000		Maximum number or partitions of a column table
11	MAXIMUM_NUMBER_OF_INDEXES_IN_TABLE	1023		Maximum number of indexes in a table
12	MAXIMUM_NUMBER_OF_COLUMNS_IN_PRIMARY_KEY	16		Maximum number of columns in a primary key
13	MAXIMUM_NUMBER_OF_COLUMNS_IN_INDEX	16		Maximum number of columns in an index
14	MAXIMUM_NUMBER_OF_COLUMNS_IN_UNIQUE_CONSTRAINT	16		Maximum number of columns in a UNIQUE constraint
15	MAXIMUM_SIZE_OF_KEY_IN_INDEX	16384	Byte	Maximum size of a key in an index such as primary key, a secondary index, a
16	MAXIMUM_DEPTH_OF_SQL_VIEW_NESTING	128		Maximum number of SQL view nesting

Figure 7.10 System View M_SYSTEM_LIMITS

Although the system limits are also documented in *SAP HANA SQL and System Views Reference* in Chapter 19 (see *https://help.sap.com/hana/SAP_HANA_SQL_ and_System_Views_Reference_en.pdf*), using this view can be handy to check the limitations that apply to the current system.

With that, we have covered a great deal about general database objects in SAP HANA. The rest of this chapter will shed light on the specifics of each of the different types.

7.2 Tables

Tables are the central object in any RDBMS, and SAP HANA is no different. Because tables are covered in depth in Chapter 8 and Chapter 9, this section focuses only on the basic aspects of tables.

Obviously, database tables exist to store data. From a consumer or client point of view, how the data is stored and retrieved is completely transparent. This decoupling of the conceptual data structure table (the table definition) from the actual implementation contributed to the enormous success of relational database management systems. Tables can be seen as a data storage and retrieval API with SQL as the interface description.

Application developers who want to use the database can focus on the application logic and do not need to know how and where the data is stored, what is done in order to guarantee transactional consistency, or how the database caters for protection against data loss. Moreover, using a relational database freed developers from writing code to navigate within the database. Whatever the data model looks like, developers can use SQL to specify conditions that the result data needs to fulfill, and SAP HANA will find all matching records. All that matters to the developer are the table definition and the commands that can be used on it. These are most often SQL commands, but SAP HANA also offers APIs, such as *MDX*, *CE_-functions*, and so on.

To be very clear on this point, because this is often a topic of concern when column-oriented databases are used by developers for the first time, there is *no change* whatsoever in the SQL that can be used with column store tables compared to row store tables, with the exception of table-management statements such as `MERGE DELTA OF <COLUMN_STORE_TABLE>`. Programming is always done against the conceptual table, not against the data structure maintained by SAP HANA (or any other DBMS).

Tables in general consist of at least one column, and every column needs to have a distinct name in this table. Across tables, column names can be used multiple times with different data type definitions and meanings, so attention has to be paid during the design phase to keep column names clear, short, and expressive. Although the actual table name does not have any functional relevance, choosing good names can make all the difference when it comes to understanding your application and the data design.

SAP HANA provides catalog views for both logical and physical tables. TABLES and TABLE_COLUMNS refer (mostly) to the logical table and provide an overview of the table structure that is present in the database. They also cover the rather fixed attributes of the table implementation. For example, we find information about whether or not a specific column's store table should be considered by the automerge functionality in the TABLES system view (TABLES.AUTO_MERGE_ON).

Information about the current runtime data and the internal implementation data structures, often called *physical tables*, can be found in catalog views M_CS_TABLES, M_CS_COLUMNS, M_CS_ALL_COLUMNS, M_CS_PARTITIONS, M_CS_UNLOADS, M_RS_TABLES, M_RS_MEMORY, and M_RS_TABLE_VERSION_STATISTICS.

Physical Tables vs. Logical Tables

Clearly, physical tables are no more or less real to the physical world than the conceptual or logical tables. Both things exist as electronic states in computer memory. They are simply two different things; the physical table is the data structure to keep and retrieve data, and the logical table defines a data interface to it.

A sometimes overlooked standard feature of SQL tables and columns (and views) is the option to add comments to provide documentation. This can easily be done with the COMMENT ON TABLE|VIEW|COLUMN <object_identifier> IS <comment text> command. Any comment entered will be visible in the respective system view (column COMMENT). In addition, the comments are used by the MODELER perspective in SAP HANA Studio to display long description texts for tables and columns. When tables are replicated from an SAP NetWeaver system via SLT, the long description text is used to create comments in SAP HANA.

Note

A little oddity of comments is that there is no command available to delete an object comment. In order to get rid of an existing comment, the only option is to set it to an empty string value.

7.3   Triggers and Constraints

Although tables are the central object in SAP HANA, there are, of course, others. The topic of this section is objects that can effect actions in the database when the contents of a table are changed. The most obvious action is that of a trigger, which will perform data changes in the background depending on other activities performed on tables.

Constraints, on the other hand, can be used to specify additional conditions that must be fulfilled for a data manipulation to be successful. Such constraints can be internal to the table (e.g., a uniqueness constraint), or they may even refer to the contents of another database table (referential constraints).

In this section, we will briefly look at both concepts in SAP HANA. Although these objects only exist dependent to tables and not in their own right, they are relevant and should be familiar to SAP HANA DBAs.

7.3.1   Triggers

Triggers are, to be very blunt, the administrator's nightmare and should be avoided whenever possible.

Triggers are small SQLScript programs that are executed whenever the trigger condition is fulfilled. Such a condition could be the insertion of a row into a table or the update of a set of rows or the deleting of several otherwise independent rows. The trigger defined on any of these actions will then be automatically executed without further notice.

This is exactly the problem with triggers; if you do not specifically look them up, then it is impossible to know about triggers being in place when using the database. Although the potential for problems might be small as long as the trigger performs small, side-effect free operations, a common mistake of database developers is to embed application logic into triggers. Often, this is done in order to implement certain "if this, then that" business rules, and triggers seem to be the right tool for this. As with all nontrivial rule sets, it is virtually impossible to comprehend the exact consequences of cascaded rules to the full extent. Chained rules are typically created when employing triggers for application logic. Given a sufficiently large set of tables fitted with triggers that refer to other tables and taking into account that there is no way to control the order of trigger execution (it is only guaranteed that the triggers will have been completed after COMMIT), it is easy to envision quite unexpected activity due to what was supposed to be a simple INSERT into a "harmless" table. In addition to these problems, triggers also do not provide many administration options.

However, triggers are part of the SQL standard and as such supported by SAP HANA. Also, SLT replication uses triggers in the source system to keep track of table data changes so that changed data will be replicated.

Triggers are created by the CREATE TRIGGER command. You can disable and enable triggers via the ALTER TABLE <table_name> ENABLE|DISABLE TRIGGER [<trigger_name>] command. When no <trigger_name> is provided, all triggers on the table will be enabled or disabled.

> **Note**
>
> There are no monitoring options available that provide insight into the performance characteristics of the trigger execution. This makes it rather difficult for the SAP HANA administrator to estimate the additional overhead for (data manipulation language) DML execution that triggers create.

The main use case for triggers in SAP HANA currently is to implement logging-like functionality without complex logic. Although it is possible to chain trigger execution (by default, up to eight chained triggers get executed), doing so is highly discouraged. This would impact the system performance and can easily create unpredictable side-effects, because, as mentioned earlier, the order of trigger execution is not controllable.

Be aware that triggers cannot be executed on partitioned tables for which the partitions reside on different hosts and also not on the "slave" parts of replicated tables.

7.3.2 Constraints

SAP HANA does provide limited support for SQL constraints. Constraints in SAP HANA exist only as attributes of the tables they are defined on. This means that there are no database-wide constraints available. Furthermore, constraints in SAP HANA are not handled as objects on their own, which is why we do not find them in the OBJECTS system table.

We mention constraints here in the context of triggers because triggers may also be created implicitly when creating a referential constraint between two tables. Although the column store natively supports referential constraints and the propagation logic that comes with them (the UPDATE rule and the DELETE rule), row store tables implement these features by the means of triggers.

These triggers get automatically created when a foreign key constraint is set up between two tables. Notable here is that the referential constraint checking for column store tables is not actually performed by the triggers but by the column store itself. In this case, the triggers are technically superfluous but cannot be manually removed or modified.

For the administrator, it is useful to know that although SQL standard allows choosing explicit names for referential constraints (or constraints in general, for that matter), but does not require it, common practice is to let the database system choose a name for the constraint automatically. In Listing 7.5, we provide an example for this and demonstrate how to find the system-generated constraint name.

```
ALTER TABLE efashion.shop_facts ADD FOREIGN KEY (shop_id)
REFERENCES efashion.outlet_lookup (shop_id)
ON UPDATE RESTRICT;

select constraint_name from referential_constraints
WHERE (schema_name, table_name) = ('EFASHION', 'SHOP_FACTS');

CONSTRAINT_NAME
_SYS_CONSTRAINT_159651_#24_#F0
```

Listing 7.5 Referential Constraint Definition

Due to this common practice, checking the CONSTRAINTS or REFERENTIAL_CONSTRAINTS system views in SAP HANA therefore typically results in lists of generated constraint names, as shown in Figure 7.11.

The name-generation pattern for this is rather obvious: All system-generated constraint names begin with _SYS_, followed by the type of the constraint (e.g., TREE_ CS or CONSTRAINT). The next piece indicates whether the table upon which this constraint is defined is a row store or a column store table, (_RS_/_CS_), followed by the table object ID and the column number in the table (for multicolumn constraint, a so-called concatenated column will be created, and the constraint then will refer to this internal column).

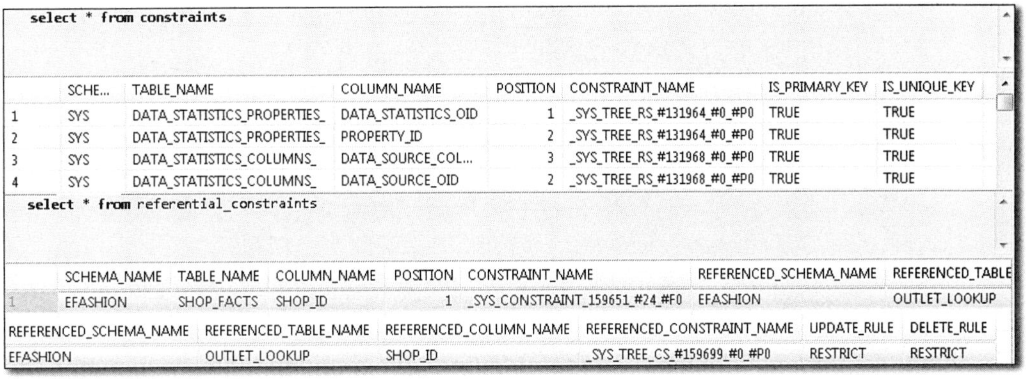

```
select * from constraints
```

	SCHE...	TABLE_NAME	COLUMN_NAME	POSITION	CONSTRAINT_NAME	IS_PRIMARY_KEY	IS_UNIQUE_KEY
1	SYS	DATA_STATISTICS_PROPERTIES_	DATA_STATISTICS_OID	1	_SYS_TREE_RS_#131964_#0_#P0	TRUE	TRUE
2	SYS	DATA_STATISTICS_PROPERTIES_	PROPERTY_ID	2	_SYS_TREE_RS_#131964_#0_#P0	TRUE	TRUE
3	SYS	DATA_STATISTICS_COLUMNS_	DATA_SOURCE_COL...	3	_SYS_TREE_RS_#131968_#0_#P0	TRUE	TRUE
4	SYS	DATA_STATISTICS_COLUMNS_	DATA_SOURCE_OID	2	_SYS_TREE_RS_#131968_#0_#P0	TRUE	TRUE

```
select * from referential_constraints
```

	SCHEMA_NAME	TABLE_NAME	COLUMN_NAME	POSITION	CONSTRAINT_NAME	REFERENCED_SCHEMA_NAME	REFERENCED_TABLE
1	EFASHION	SHOP_FACTS	SHOP_ID	1	_SYS_CONSTRAINT_159651_#24_#F0	EFASHION	OUTLET_LOOKUP

REFERENCED_SCHEMA_NAME	REFERENCED_TABLE_NAME	REFERENCED_COLUMN_NAME	REFERENCED_CONSTRAINT_NAME	UPDATE_RULE	DELETE_RULE
EFASHION	OUTLET_LOOKUP	SHOP_ID	_SYS_TREE_CS_#159699_#0_#P0	RESTRICT	RESTRICT

Figure 7.11 Example Output from System Views CONSTRAINTS and REFERENTIAL_CONSTRAINTS

From the example in Listing 7.5, we retrieved constraint name _SYS_CONSTRAINT_ 159651_#24_#F0. We can tell that this is a system-generated constraint name for the table with table ID 159651 on column number 24 of this table. The #F0 indicates that this is a foreign key constraint.

Noteworthy as well is that primary key and unique key constraints are implemented as types of indexes on both row store and column store tables. This means that the constraint name can be used to look up the corresponding index in the INDEXES system view, as demonstrated in Figure 7.12.

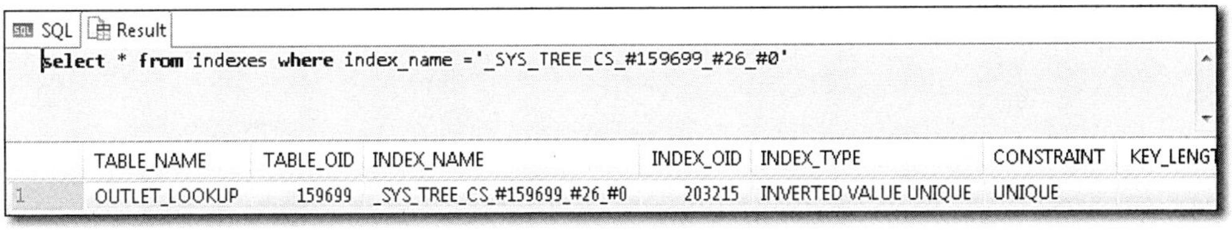

```
select * from indexes where index_name ='_SYS_TREE_CS_#159699_#26_#0'
```

	TABLE_NAME	TABLE_OID	INDEX_NAME	INDEX_OID	INDEX_TYPE	CONSTRAINT	KEY_LENGT
1	OUTLET_LOOKUP	159699	_SYS_TREE_CS_#159699_#26_#0	203215	INVERTED VALUE UNIQUE	UNIQUE	

Figure 7.12 Index Corresponding to a Unique Constraint

7.4   SQL Views

Although tables are the database objects for storing data, views are there to define reusable access paths to these tables. SQL views, or simply views, are exactly what the name implies: a way to look at the data. Although the physical data model—the tables—is rather fixed by the table design, views allow you to access the same data in different ways without storing the data multiple times. There is no option to create indexes, triggers, or statistics and the like on a view.

> **Note**
>
> The SQL standard actually specifies triggers on views, but SAP HANA does not provide this feature.

From a developer standpoint, views are useful because they can be used to wrap complex SQL logic, lengthy queries, and recurring join constructs into a single object that can then be used like ordinary tables in queries. Technically, SQL views are stored SELECT commands, which are executed every time data in a view is accessed.

A very handy aspect of views is that they allow you to selectively grant access to only some of the columns of a table or to aggregated data without providing access to the base objects of the view (tables and maybe other views).

As an example, we look at a simple setup. A table called SHOP_FACTS contains sales information, and we want to provide information on the top-selling articles without allowing access to the single transactions data.

The table data looks like that shown in Listing 7.6.

```
SELECT article_id, color_code, shop_id, amount_sold, quantity_sold FROM
shop_facts;

ARTICLE_ID|COLOR_CODE|SHOP_ID|AMOUNT_SOLD|QUANTITY_SOLD
166544    |711       |64     |199.0      |1
166544    |902       |110    |199.0      |1
166544    |902       |185    |199.0      |1
166544    |902       |268    |199.0      |1
155939    |902       |261    |199.0      |1
144940    |902       |185    |199.0      |1
166544    |210       |197    |199.0      |1
144940    |723       |268    |199.0      |1
166544    |210       |3      |199.0      |1
166544    |210       |268    |199.0      |1
. . .
```

Listing 7.6 SHOP_FACTS Table

By accessing the table directly, we see every transaction, along with information that we are not interested in (e.g., AMOUNT_SOLD).

A select statement to provide a list of the top-ten most sold articles/color combinations could look like Listing 7.7.

```
select top 10
    article_id, color_code, sum(quantity_sold) as TOT_QUANT_SOLD
from shop_facts
group by article_id, color_code
order by sum(quantity_sold) desc;
```

```
ARTICLE_ID|COLOR_CODE|TOT_QUANT_SOLD
166544    |902       |6620
166544    |7008      |6346
177264    |902       |4879
177264    |1103      |4604
166544    |1300      |4591
177264    |731       |4543
155939    |902       |3553
155939    |702       |3453
166699    |902       |2990
177264    |308       |2956
```

Listing 7.7 Aggregation Select Statement on Table SHOP_FACTS

The obvious problem here is that each user would have to run this statement to get the correct information. Also, the users would need to have direct access to the SHOP_FACTS table, which may not be wanted (think of shop managers who are entitled to see their own shops' data and the aggregated top-ten information but not the data of other shops).

In such a case, an SQL view can be handy, as it encapsulates the data access and the query logic. This is shown in Listing 7.8.

```
create view top_ten_articles as
select top 10
    article_id, color_code, sum(quantity_sold) as TOT_QUANT_SOLD
from shop_facts
group by article_id, color_code
order by sum(quantity_sold) desc
with read only;
```

Listing 7.8 SQL View TOP_TEN_ARTICLES

After its creation, the view can be accessed like any other table, as shown in Listing 7.9.

```
select * from top_ten_articles;

ARTICLE_ID|COLOR_CODE|TOT_QUANT_SOLD
166544    |902       |6620
166544    |7008      |6346
177264    |902       |4879
177264    |1103      |4604
166544    |1300      |4591
177264    |731       |4543
155939    |902       |3553
155939    |702       |3453
166699    |902       |2990
177264    |308       |2956
```

Listing 7.9 SQL View TOP_TEN_ARTICLES Results Set, Including Aggregated QUANTITY_SOLD Column

Note that you did not need to provide any aggregate function or order by command to get the top-ten list. The SELECT privilege on a view is sufficient to read from the view; it is not necessary to explicitly grant SELECT on the underlying tables. This is shown in Listing 7.10.

```
-- As different user:
select * from shop_facts

Could not execute 'select * from top_ten_articles' in 49 ms 447 μs .
SAP DBTech JDBC: [258]: insufficient privilege: Not authorized

select * from efashion.top_ten_articles;

Statement 'select * from efashion.top_ten_articles'
successfully executed in 61 ms 170 μs  (server processing time: 24 ms
313 μs)
Fetched 10 row(s) in 0 ms 85 μs (server processing time: 0 ms 0 μs)
```

Listing 7.10 SELECT Privilege on SQL View vs. Table

When working with SQL views, database developers must be aware of several inherent properties of these objects. We will discuss in detail the dependency between a view and its base objects, as well as performance considerations for SQL views.

7.4.1 View Dependencies

An important aspect of views is that they are technically dependent on the objects they refer to. If, for example, a view is based on a table and the definition of the table is changed (for example, a column gets dropped), then all dependent objects, including views, will be marked as invalid. Invalid views can be dropped, edited, and recreated, because SAP HANA does not provide an ALTER VIEW command. To check the current state of a view, system table VIEWS can be used.

We show an example of this in Listing 7.11 through Listing 7.14.

```
create synonym lars.top_ten_articles
      for efashion.top_ten_articles;

create view top_ten_article_id as
    select article_id
    from top_ten_articles
with read only;
```
Listing 7.11 Definition of an SQL View Referring a Synonym

In Listing 7.11 we defined an SQL view that refers a table via a synonym and not directly. This is the starting point for our example in which we will check what happens when we drop or change the synonym used in the view. In Listing 7.12, we check the current state of the SQL view in catalog view VIEWS.

```
select schema_name, view_name, is_valid
    from views where view_name='TOP_TEN_ARTICLE_ID';

SCHEMA_NAME VIEW_NAME           IS_VALID
----------- ------------------- --------
LARS        TOP_TEN_ARTICLE_ID  TRUE
```
Listing 7.12 Current State of the SQL View

Now, we drop the synonym used in the view and check the state of the view again, as shown in Listing 7.13.

```
drop synonym lars.top_ten_articles;

SCHEMA_NAME VIEW_NAME           IS_VALID
----------- ------------------- --------
LARS        TOP_TEN_ARTICLE_ID  FALSE
```
Listing 7.13 Drop Synonym and Check View

As we see, the SQL view now is marked as invalid, because the synonym it used to refer to the table is no longer available. The view cannot be executed any longer.

Finally, you can recreate the synonym and check the state of the view again, as shown in Listing 7.14.

```
create synonym lars.top_ten_articles for efashion.top_ten_articles;

SCHEMA_NAME VIEW_NAME              IS_VALID
----------- -------------------    --------
LARS        TOP_TEN_ARTICLE_ID     TRUE
```

Listing 7.14 Recreate Synonym and Check View State

As we have seen, sometimes it is not required to actually drop and recreate a view after dependent objects have been modified. In fact, this is something that should be avoided, because dropping a view, just like dropping any other object, also removes the privileges granted on it. After the re-creation of the objects, the privileges would need to be regranted, which could easily be a difficult and time-consuming task, as will be explained in Chapter 13.

7.4.2 Performance of SQL Views

A common misunderstanding about SQL views is that they are inherently slow performing. In fact, this is not the case, because the SAP HANA query optimizer automatically includes the SQL command that defined the view in the overall SQL statement and optimizes the total of it.

For the simple example shown in Listing 7.11, the SAP HANA SQL query optimizer would internally transform the statement from the following:

```
select * from efashion.top_ten_articles
to
select * from (select top 10
    article_id, color_code, sum(quantity_sold) as TOT_QUANT_SOLD
    from shop_facts
    group by article_id, color_code
    order by sum(quantity_sold) desc)
```

We see that the SQL optimizer replaces the reference to the view TOP_TEN_ARTI-CLES (Listing 7.11) with the SELECT statement that defines the SQL view; this is called *inlining*.

This yields the same result set and the same execution path (the EXPLAIN PLAN output has been edited for readability) as selecting from the TOP_TEN_ARTICLES view, as we show by using the EXPLAIN PLAN function in Listing 7.15 and Listing 7.16.

```
select * from (select top 10
               article_id, color_code,
               sum(quantity_sold) as TOT_QUANT_SOLD
               from shop_facts
               group by article_id, color_code
               order by sum(quantity_sold) desc);
```

```
OPERATOR_NAME              OPERATOR_DETAILS
COLUMN SEARCH             SHOP_FACTS.ARTICLE_ID,
                         SHOP_FACTS.COLOR_CODE,
                         TOT_QUANT_SOLD (LATE MATERIALIZATION)
   LIMIT                 NUM RECORDS: 10
      ORDER BY           SUM(SHOP_FACTS.QUANTITY_SOLD) DESC
         AGGREGATION     GROUPING: SHOP_FACTS.ARTICLE_ID,
                                   SHOP_FACTS.COLOR_CODE,
                         AGGREGATION:
                         SUM(SHOP_FACTS.QUANTITY_SOLD)
. . .
```

Listing 7.15 EXPLAIN PLAN for Inlined SQL Statement

```
select * from top_ten_articles;
```

```
OPERATOR_NAME              OPERATOR_DETAILS
COLUMN SEARCH             TOP_TEN_ARTICLES.ARTICLE_ID,
                         TOP_TEN_ARTICLES.COLOR_CODE,
                         TOP_TEN_ARTICLES.TOT_QUANT_SOLD
                         (LATE MATERIALIZATION)
   LIMIT                 NUM RECORDS: 10
      ORDER BY           SUM(SHOP_FACTS.QUANTITY_SOLD) DESC
         AGGREGATION     GROUPING: SHOP_FACTS.ARTICLE_ID,
                                   SHOP_FACTS.COLOR_CODE,
                         AGGREGATION:
                         SUM(SHOP_FACTS.QUANTITY_SOLD)
. . .
```

Listing 7.16 EXPLAIN PLAN for SQL View Statement

7.4.3 Changing Data through SQL Views

A final fact about SQL views that is often left unnoted is that it is possible to run INSERT, UPDATE, UPSERT, and DELETE statements against an SQL view. As long as the view definition allows for mapping the action back to individual records, then the commands are propagated to the base table(s). Typically, usage of aggregate functions, outer joins, and dynamically computed columns prevent data manipulation through a join, which makes it a rather seldom-used option in SQL databases. However, SAP HANA supports this SQL standard feature as well, which also implies that DML object privileges are available for SQL views, too.

7.5   Column Views

One of SAP HANA's big promises is to reduce the requirement to store transformed versions of data in tables in order to use them for further reporting. For example, on classic DBMSs the aggregation of data to certain levels could be so time intensive that it would be only done in batch runs, and the results would be stored in separate result tables. Obviously, the data in those result tables would only be accurate as long as the base data is not changed. But typically this is exactly the data we want to see changing, because it is data about business processes (sales, production, invoices, etc.).

With SAP HANA, on the other hand, transformations such as aggregations, currency transformation, master data alignment, assignment to organizational units, and more can be done on the fly. The tools for this in SAP HANA are column views, which have a flexible computation model.

Figure 7.13 schematically shows how complex data transformations are stacked on top of each other via column views (in this case, calculation views) and how the final result can be consumed via SQL or used in further transformations. In the example calculation view, C1 performs a join of tables A and B. Calculation view C2 takes the result from C1 and performs an aggregation and a currency conversion. Finally, calculation view C3 uses the output of C2 and processes it in some SQLScript code.

Column views are a database object type specific to SAP HANA. They basically provide the SQL interface to the column store engines in SAP HANA (Join Engine, OLAP Engine, and Calculation Engine). Although this generally means that only column store tables can be used in column views, there are exceptions to this rule. For example, scripted calculation views can access row store tables, virtual tables (tables in other databases and made accessible via smart data access [SDA]), or data sets returned by an R-procedure call.

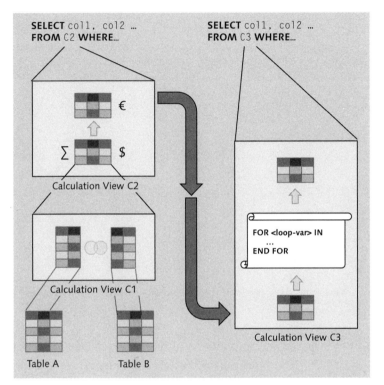

Figure 7.13 Example of Complex Stacked Transformations in Calculation Views

Column views are typically not created via SQL DDL statements, although this is technically possible. Instead, they are created during the activation of SAP HANA information models.

Because all activated information models are stored in the _SYS_BIC schema, that is where the columns views can be found, via the object navigator CATALOG • _SYS_ BIC • COLUMN VIEWS.

It is possible to display the definition for column views, but the actual coding is stored in unformatted JSON format, as seen in Figure 7.14.

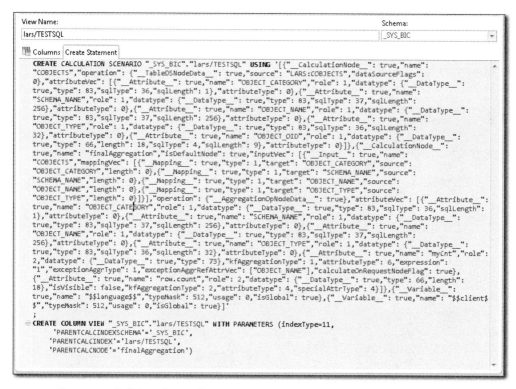

Figure 7.14 Definition for a Column View

An additional option to inspect the column views in the _SYS_BIC schema is the
JOIN VIEWER (see Figure 7.15), which is available in the context menu when a column view of type OLAP has been selected. Despite being possibly interesting in
order to review the actual join setup in the active version of an analytic view and
to compare it to the design-time setup, the JOIN VIEWER has not yet played any significant role for SAP HANA administrators.

From a consumer's perspective, column views can be used like SQL views. The
main difference is that column views actually don't adhere to SQL formalism and
structure, and this has led to several misunderstandings about the expected result
sets for column views. For a more detailed description on the somewhat odd
workings of column views, especially calculation views, please refer to SAP Note
1764658, SAP Note 1764662, and SAP Note 1783880.

The reason for the nonrelational behavior of calculation views is that, unlike SQL
views, column views are not merely wrappers around an SQL statement. Instead,

more or less complex data transformation and access logic is saved in a calculation scenario. The scenario itself is not reachable via SQL, but, as shown in Figure 7.14, with every calculation scenario a column view gets created. This column view is what is accessible to SQL and therefore the interface to the calculation scenario.

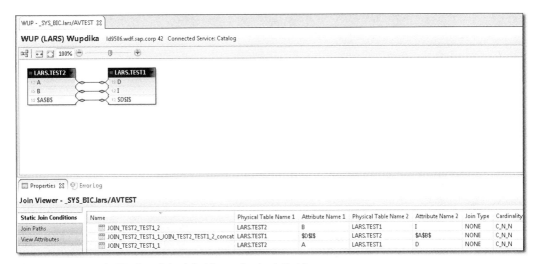

Figure 7.15 Example Display of the Join Viewer for Analytic Views

As soon as the column view is queried, the calculation scenario is invoked. Again, unlike SQL views, calculation scenarios take into account what output has been requested every single time they are called and may remove parts of their calculation logic from the processing steps when they are technically not required. Depending on the kind of operation at hand, this might lead to a reduced result set.

Typically, there are no actions or responsibilities present concerning column views for the administrator. Column views of all types are fully managed by the repository or the application that creates them (e.g., SAP BW on SAP HANA uses column views).

7.6   Sequences

Sequences generate nonrepeating number sequences in a high-performance, lock-free manner with the possibility for gaps between two numbers. If you are asking yourself what that means, then read on.

Imagine you want to store records in a table, and each record should get its own unique ID number. This can be implemented in many different ways, but it typically would involve application logic similar to this:

1. SELECT the current lowest/highest number from a table, and add an offset to it, for example, 1. As other sessions might also want to do the same, the SELECT needs to be completed with the FOR UPDATE option to set an exclusive lock. All other sessions that now want to do the same have to wait for the lock to be released.

2. Now the record gets inserted or updated in the application table with the number retrieved in the previous step. After the successful INSERT or UPDATE, this number also has to be stored back in the numbers table. Just in case the INSERT/UPDATE operation went wrong for any reason (ironically, for example, a duplicate key or a check constraint error), the current transaction has to be rolled back. For the number table, this means that the current number does not get changed and that the exclusive lock is released.

The reason for storing the increased new number only after the actual use of the number is simply a matter of optimization. If the number table was updated right after the number was retrieved, then the number table would be modified regardless of whether or not the transaction is later rolled back. That in turn could generate unnecessary undo and redo information in the (hopefully) rather seldom event of a ROLLBACK.

The problem with this home-brew number dispenser table is that due to the necessary locking, parallel running sessions will have to wait for each other, which can become a very constraining aspect for systems that need to handle a high number of parallel transactions. Also, every transaction that wants to use the number table needs to ensure that it follows the access pattern correctly and only fetches new numbers with the use of the exclusive lock. Otherwise, numbers potentially would get used multiple times.

The positive aspect of this technique, however, is that due to the lock-per-use-and-update-afterwards approach, there cannot be gaps between two subsequentially generated numbers. Depending on your application requirements, that might be required (although not very often), and if this is the case, the locking cannot be avoided.

Now, how can sequences help here? Sequences provide this number dispenser service out of the box. Transactions only need to ask for the next number (`<sequence_name>.nextval`), and the sequence object performs all necessary steps automatically. Internally, sequences check the highest number currently stored in monitoring table `M_SEQUENCES` upon first usage since system startup.

The following example demonstrates most options for sequences.

Start by creating a dummy table for which you need a unique ID. We will use a sequence called `things_id_spiller` for that. It will deliver values in steps of 10 and cache 100 values. Upon system restart, the current value will be looked up in the dummy table. Listing 7.17 shows the commands used for that.

```
create column table things
(id integer primary key,
name varchar(30) default 'UNKNOWN');

CREATE SEQUENCE things_id_spiller
    START WITH 1
    INCREMENT BY 10
    NO MAXVALUE
    NO CYCLE
    CACHE 100
RESET BY (select ifnull(max(id), 0) + 1 from things );
```
Listing 7.17 Sequence Definition Example

To fetch the next number, you simply select from the sequence as if it had a function called `.nextval`, as shown in Listing 7.18.

```
select things_id_spiller.nextval from dummy;

THINGS_ID_SPILLER.NEXTVAL
1
```
Listing 7.18 Using the .nextval Function of a Sequence

Once we have selected from `.nextval` in our session, we can always go back and review the last provided number with `.currval`, as demonstrated in Listing 7.19. Be aware that `.currval` does not return anything if `.nextval` has not been executed in the current session:

```
select things_id_spiller.currval from dummy;
```

```
THINGS_ID_SPILLER.CURRVAL
1
```
Listing 7.19 Using the .currval Function of a Sequence

Trying to use .currval in a second session in fact leads to the error message shown in Listing 7.20.

```
select things_id_spiller.currval from dummy;
```

```
ERROR:
Could not execute 'select things_id_spiller.currval from dummy' in 186
ms 522 μs .
SAP DBTech JDBC: [326]: CURRVAL of given sequence is not yet defined in
this session:
cannot find currval location by session_id:300513, seq id:203224, seq
version:1
at function __currval__()
```
Listing 7.20 Using .currval Function of a Sequence without a Prior .nextval Call

Of course, fetching the next value in the second session works and delivers the next value in line (1 + 10 = 11), as shown in in Listing 7.21.

```
select things_id_spiller.nextval from dummy;
```

```
THINGS_ID_SPILLER.NEXTVAL
11
```
Listing 7.21 Using .nextval from a Second Session

In order to use the sequences as an ID generator for our table, we can use INSERT from a subquery command (Listing 7.22). Alternatively, we would have to select the ID into a variable beforehand and then insert the value in a second step.

```
insert into things (ID) (select things_id_spiller.currval from dummy);
```
Listing 7.22 Insert Command with Subquery that Calls the .currval Function of Sequence Spilller

After repeating the insert, the table contents look like Listing 7.23.

```
select * from things;

ID  NAME
1   UNKNOWN
11  UNKNOWN
```

Listing 7.23 Table Data after Using the Different Ways to Insert Records with Sequence-Generated IDs

Our ID is indeed unique and can serve as a primary key. However, it is only guaranteed that no two numbers provided will ever be the same. It is not guaranteed that there won't be any gaps between the numbers or that no numbers had been skipped. If this is not acceptable, then other ID-generating mechanisms need to be employed.

In order to reinitialize the sequence, that is, to get rid of the currently cached values and get a new set of numbers into the cache, all the administrator has to do is to run the ALTER SEQUENCE <sequence_name> command without additional parameters, as shown in Listing 7.24.

```
alter sequence things_id_spiller;

select things_id_spiller.nextval from dummy;

THINGS_ID_SPILLER.NEXTVAL
1001
```

Listing 7.24 Reinitialize a Sequence

In case the database or the indexserver process gets restarted, the current value is reinitialized by the select statement we provided earlier. Right after the restart, in this case, we get 12 from the .nextval function and the same result by using the RESET BY statement (Listing 7.25). Note that the IFNULL() expression is there to cater to truly empty tables, for which the max() function would yield NULL.

```
select things_id_spiller.nextval from dummy;

THINGS_ID_SPILLER.NEXTVAL
12

select ifnull(max(id), 0) + 1 from things;

IFNULL(MAX(ID),0)+1
12
```

Listing 7.25 Simulating the Restart Value for Sequence Reinitializaion

309

In case the table used in the RESET BY clause is not available during system startup, the sequence cannot be initialized, and trying to access it will fail, as we see in Listing 7.26.

```
rename table things to things_2;
```

```
>>> restart indexserver
```

```
select things_id_spiller.nextval from dummy;
```

ERROR:
```
Could not execute 'select things_id_spiller.nextval from dummy' in 590
ms 40 µs .
SAP DBTech JDBC: [313]: invalid sequence: RESET BY query is invalid
```
Listing 7.26 Error in Sequence Reinitialization Due to Table Renaming

In Listing 7.27, we show how changing the RESET BY statement for the sequence fixes this problem easily.

```
alter sequence things_id_spiller reset by select ifnull(max(id), 0) + 1
from things_2;
```

```
select things_id_spiller.nextval from dummy
```

```
THINGS_ID_SPILLER.NEXTVAL
12
```
Listing 7.27 Updating the RESET BY Clause of a Sequence

Whereas M_SEQUENCES provides a view on the current state of the sequences, catalog table SEQUENCES contains the definition for every sequence.

As we see, sequences also provide the option to do the following:

▶ Limit the possible numbers to an interval between MIN_VALUE and MAX_VALUE (in M_SEQUENCES, these are oddly named differently: START_VALUE and END_VALUE).

▶ Set the step size in which the sequence should be increased (INCREMENT_BY) with every call of .nextval.

▶ Define whether the sequence should wrap around in case it reaches the value limits (IS_CYCLED).

- Specify an SQL query that should be used to determine a new start value when the sequence gets reset (RESET_BY_QUERY) during system restart. This is especially useful when sequences are transported between different systems, in which case the current value might be very different.

- Define a CACHE_SIZE parameter. This parameter holds the size of the sequence cache as number of cached values. Setting up a sequence cache can lead to better performance in scenarios in which many numbers are fetched in a very short period. As sequence access typically is not a major performance problem, the recommendation for this is to use the cache conservatively (e.g., 500 values) and to measure the effect before using larger caches. If a cache has been specified, SAP HANA will fill the cache with numbers generated by the sequence, and the following SQL statements will retrieve the .nextval from the cache. In this way, no waiting for the update of the M_SEQUENCES view is required. In the case that the server node that holds the cache crashes, the numbers within the cache are "lost," and SAP HANA will restart the sequence with the current high/low number. This means that if using the cache is necessary and no large chunks of numbers can be lost, the RESET BY QUERY should be set so that the restart is done based on the table values.

- In addition to these features, the ALTER SEQUENCE statement provides some handy tools to work with sequences. For example, a sequence can be increased by a given value so that it is not required to call .nextval in the loop to get to a specific number (Listing 7.28).

```
alter sequence things_id_spiller restart with 5000;
select things_id_spiller.nextval from dummy;

THINGS_ID_SPILLER.NEXTVAL
5000
```

Listing 7.28 Setting a Sequence to a Specific Number

As we have seen, sequences provide a conveniently packaged object type that encapsulates many handy functions of a general number dispenser that otherwise would need to be encoded in the application logic. On top of that, the fact that sequences are proper catalog objects makes them just as manageable as tables. They can be exported and imported, monitored via a common monitoring table (M_SEQUENCES), and protected by SQL privileges (SELECT ON <sequence_name>).

7.7 Procedures and Functions

Although most of the objects discussed up to this to point are simply the functionality built in by SAP HANA developers, procedures and functions allow the database developer to extend built-in functionality. In this way, application logic can be implemented directly on the database level. Stored procedures and functions can contain SQLScript code, allowing for procedural/functional processing of data. Both of them use direct input parameters and can access other input data, such as common tables during runtime.

A main purpose of these procedural objects is to encapsulate application logic and make it reusable throughout the system. Very similar to subroutines in other development environments, it is typical to find hierarchies of procedures calling other procedures or functions and so forth. Given this, the same rules and heuristics for system decomposition apply as in any other development language (e.g., "a function should do one thing and only one thing"); how to implement this is of course left to the developer. SAP HANA does not enforce design restrictions on that matter.

The major difference between procedures and functions is the use case and the form in which each type is actually used. Functions are meant to be used directly within SQL statements to solve recurring processing requirements. They come in two different flavors: scalar functions (functions that return a single value of a specific data type) or table functions (functions that return a single table-type value).

Scalar functions can be used like common functions in SQL statements, for example, `SELECT myfunction_add10percent(salary) as new_salary FROM employees`. Table functions, meanwhile, can be used like tables, as shown in Figure 7.16. From an administration point of view, this difference does not matter, because there is only one function object type in SAP HANA.

Procedures are similar to functions, but they provide the option to return multiple result values via `OUT` or `IN/OUT` parameters and possibly multiple result sets. In addition to that, it is possible to assign a result view to a procedure so that it can be executed and so that the result can be worked with as if the procedure was an SQL view. Just like for SQL views and column views, the source code for functions and procedures is stored in the database catalog and can be reviewed in the respective catalog views `FUNCTIONS` and `PROCEDURES`.

```
SQL   Result
SELECT e.name,
       e.salary_group,
       e.salary,
       f.uplift_factor,
       e.salary*f.uplift_factor as new_salary
  FROM
       employees e
       join myfunction_ulfactors(org_unit => 'DIVIDE&CONQUER')  f
  on e.salary_group = f.salary_group
```

	NAME	SALARY_GROUP	SALARY	UPLIFT_FACTOR	NEW_SALARY
1	CLAUDIUS	2	3200.00	1.15	3680
2	RICHARD	1	2500.00	1.1	2750
3	AUGUSTUS	1	1800.00	1.1	1980
4	CAESAR	3	4500.00	1.2	5400

Figure 7.16 Example for a Table Function

Although this is true for both catalog and activated repository objects, it is highly recommended to use the repository for function and procedure development, because catalog objects cannot be debugged with the SQLScript debugger, they cannot be transported, and no version management for catalog objects is provided. When creating functions or procedures directly in the catalog, it is unfortunately required to drop the existing version of the object before a newer version can be created, which also is handled automatically when activating the repository versions.

Besides the usual execute permission management, there are no administration tasks present for procedures or functions. Currently, in SPS 8, SAP HANA provides no usage statistics on the object level for functions or procedures that would allow for system-wide analysis of, for example, impact on the system load.

7.8   Synonyms

Synonyms and public synonyms are other kinds of objects in SAP HANA. They are shortcuts for the object name resolution in the database and work very much like file system links in a computer's file system. In order to access any object, it is necessary to provide the name and the schema of the object. Depending on where the object is stored logically, this fully qualified object name can become very long and impractical to work with.

Synonyms can be created not only for tables or (SQL and column) views but also for functions and procedures. They cannot be created for users, schemas, or other synonyms. They have two main use cases:

▶ **Indirect object access**
Using synonyms, it is easy to redirect object access from, for example, a table to a view so that no direct table access is performed. Alternatively, one could switch between development and test objects that are present in the same SAP HANA instance.

▶ **Framework or database management objects**
Public synonyms are database-wide indirections and valid for all sessions and users in the database. If the name resolution does not find the addressed objects in the current schema, then the PUBLIC namespace is searched, and with that the public synonyms are accessed. Due to this database-wide effect, public synonyms typically are used for framework or database management object—such as the SAP HANA system views, for each of which a public synonym is present.

A good use case for synonyms in SAP HANA is to create shorter names for catalog objects created through the activation of repository content. For example, a table name such as `"mycompany.myapp1.componentXYZ::THINGS"` is still a short name for a table that has been designed with SAP HANA Core Data Services (CDS). As the table name follows a specific pattern (`"<schema_name>"."<full.package.hierarchy>"::"<table_name>"`), the resulting table names can be very long.

In order to easily access such tables, synonyms can be created, as shown in Figure 7.17. 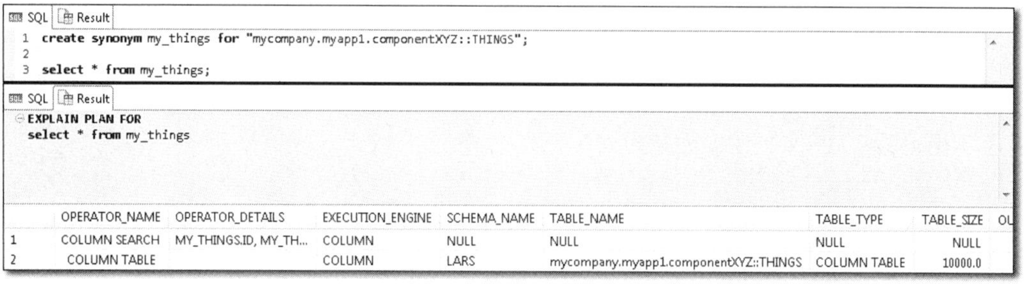

Figure 7.17 Example for a Table Synonym

314

A little-known specialty of synonyms is that DROP SYNONYM can also drop dependent objects when called with the CASCADE option. The default option RESTRICT would simply invalidate any dependent object, which can be views, procedures, triggers, functions, and so on: basically every object that can refer to a synonym. An example of this is shown in Table 7.2. Here, we can see that the CASCADE option actually drops the dependent view, thereby removing it from the catalog view VIEWS.

DROP SYNONYM	DROP SYNONYM (with CASCADE)
create synonym my_things for "mycompany.myapp1.compo-nentXYZ::THINGS";	create synonym my_things for "mycompany.myapp1.compo-nentXYZ::THINGS";
CREATE VIEW myView as SELECT * FROM my_things;	CREATE VIEW myView as SELECT * FROM my_things;
DROP SYNONYM my_things;	DROP SYNONYM my_things CASCADE;
SELECT view_name, is_valid FROM views WHERE view_name = 'MYVIEW';	SELECT view_name, is_valid FROM views WHERE view_name = 'MYVIEW';
VIEW_NAME IS_VALID MYVIEW FALSE	Fetched 0 row(s)

Table 7.2 Cascade Option for DROP SYNONYM

7.9   Summary

In this chapter, we looked at all relevant database objects that can be found in the catalog of the SAP HANA database. The main takeaway should be to have an idea of the purpose of every object type and likewise where to find information about the objects of any specific object type.

You should also remember that the catalog in SAP HANA is where every session can find information about the database and the current state of the system. This catalog is represented by a set of system views, including a dedicated system view for each object type. As we have seen, the catalog handles objects that are already present and available for use, but not design-time objects.

Although SAP HANA supports different types of data storage objects, relational tables by far are the most important way to structure and store data.

8   Table Types

Tables are the most fundamental data structure in any relational database. Even though tables are made up of a set of columns, these columns could not exist in the database on their own; they can exist only in the compound of a table. In fact, the whole relational design approach is based on relations that are later mapped to physical tables, leaving columns as mere attributes of the relations.

SAP HANA, like most other database systems, offers multiple different types of tables. These types differ in the way the tables are represented internally in the database. These differences in the internal representation have an impact on certain aspects of interactions with the table, such as performance for a given kind of data manipulation or data-retrieval process (that is, for a given type of workload). It is, therefore, important for a database developer or database administrator to be able to optimally match table types to different processes or workloads within their applications. In SAP NetWeaver systems, this matching is taken care of by the application developers at SAP.

There are two natural choices for the internal representation of tabular data in a relational database management system (RDBMS): The data may be stored by row or by column. Most RDBMS use one of these types, and row store data representation is the most common choice.

SAP HANA is an exception to this rule, allowing for either a row store or a column store representation for its tables as well as for the conversion of a table from one type to the other. Virtually all application data in SAP HANA systems will be stored in tables of these two basic types, and we devote the majority of this chapter and Chapter 9 to introducing the concepts and principles of working with these objects.

There are several other types of tables available in the system for special use cases, such as temporary tables, flexible schema tables, or history tables. These special types are based on the basic types (there are, for example, temporary row store tables and temporary column store tables) but behave very differently from the basic types in certain aspects. We will spend a few pages working out the special features of these additional types of tables, but first we will talk about those aspects of tables that are common to all types.

8.1   Common Properties of All Tables

All database tables describe relations between columns, that is, their structure or definition consists of a set of columns or fields, and each column has a unique name within the table and a specific data type. Usually, the table definition also contains semantic information, such as uniqueness constraints (duplicate values are not allowed in column <x>), primary key definitions, and so on.

A second common concept of all tables is that of a row (also commonly referred to as a *record* or *tuple*). Each data entry in the database contains of a row, that is, one value for each field. If a table has a primary key, then each row in the table can be uniquely identified by the values of the primary key fields.

Applications can interact with database tables by using the interfaces and languages supported by the database system. The most common language in database systems is SQL, but other languages may be available. SAP HANA does, for example, offer interfaces for the well-known MDX or OData standards as well as for SAP HANA-specific APIs, such as CE-functions, that are part of SAP HANA's SQLScript syntax for stored procedures.

Regardless of the type of table, interactions of applications with a given table are based on the table definition. That is to say, an application does not need to know whether a table is a row store table or a column store table in order to read data from the table. The SQL command to retrieve a certain data set from a table is thus independent from the type of the table.

It is, therefore, useful to speak of the table definition as the *logical table* — basically, the API offered to applications for interacting with the data represented by the table — and to refer to the internal representation of the table within the database as the *physical table*.

8.2   Row Store Tables

The DBMS has to store records that are inserted into a table in some form in the main memory. The classic approach for relational databases, in which the data is stored in table form, is to store the data in a form resembling the logical table structure. Every record is saved as one concatenated chunk of values for every column in memory. A visual representation of this is shown in Figure 8.1.

Exception

The exceptions to the above rule are long records and columns with very large data types, for example, LOB (large objects) columns. For such data types, typically some sort of special storage implementation is provided in most DBMS, and SAP HANA is no different.

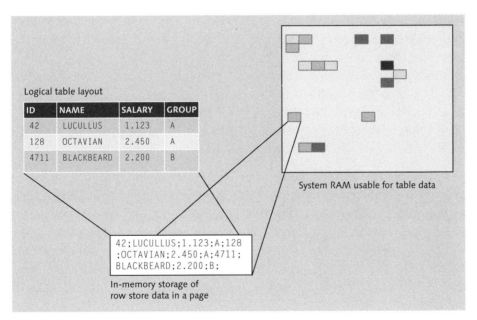

Figure 8.1 In-Memory Data Storage of Row Store Tables

In the following sections, we will guide you to the most important aspects of row store tables for the database developer and the administrator. We first talk about the advantages and drawbacks of row store table representation in general and in SAP HANA. Then, we introduce two specific details of row store tables in SAP

HANA: The implementation of multiversion concurrency control allows for lock-free data access and manipulation while maintaining transactional consistency, and indexes are a technique for optimizing data access that is also relevant in the row store of SAP HANA.

8.2.1 Properties in SAP HANA

This design has the obvious benefit of a very direct mapping of the logical table layout and the operations performed against it to the actual data manipulation that happens in memory. It is easy to program for the DBMS developer and easy to understand for the DBA.

A disadvantage here is that structuring the data representation by rows is not very effective for many typical operations on a relational database. One of the more obvious inefficiencies in the row-oriented storage is that every value is stored again for every occurrence of the value within the table. Even with normalized data models, this repetition of data, especially for very common values, cannot be prevented, because the foreign key references need to be stored. On top of this, the reference needs to be resolved during processing by joins, which adds to the computational effort required in this situation. The less obvious but far more important issue is that the DBMS cannot directly access a specific column of a table. Instead, whole data pages need to be transferred to the CPU to scan through the stored rows in order to identify where values for a specific column are stored.

This data movement from the system's main memory to the CPU caches—the memory areas on the chip that CPUs can actually work with—is what impacts performance the most, especially for mass data processing, such as data warehouse queries and analytics. For a completely different workload, though—namely, the access of a single or a few records with all of their columns—this storage method is beneficial, because the required data transformation from the internal storage to the external representation (also called a projection) to the database client is minimal.

> **Note**
>
> When records are most often accessed with all columns, and mass data processing and analysis do not play any role, then row store tables can show better performance than column store tables.

SAP HANA row store tables do come with some important limitations, though:

▶ Row store tables cannot be partitioned, which limits the possible total size of all row store tables to the memory available on the single server that the tables are located on. The exception to this is table replicas; these appear as partitions of the table they are defined upon.

▶ SAP HANA offers no compression for row store tables.

▶ Columns in row store tables cannot be accessed independently and in parallel. That does not mean that row store tables won't be processed in parallel, though. In fact, many operations, such as sorting, grouping, index creation, and window function processing, can be heavily parallelized.

▶ Row store tables cannot be displaced from memory. All row store tables need to be present in memory all the time while the system is up and running. Therefore, the tables are automatically loaded into memory during system startup, which might take some time. This in turn prolongs the system startup time, for example, after a crash or after offline maintenance.

▶ When row store tables cannot be fully loaded into memory, the system can no longer be started up.

▶ Row store tables cannot be directly used as data sources in most types of SAP HANA information models.

Considering the mentioned limitations of row store tables, we recommend using column store tables as the default choice. Row store tables should only be used when column store tables cannot be used.

> **Note**
>
> In order to prevent accidental creation of row store tables, the initialization file parameter `indexserver.ini` • `[sql]` • `default_table_type` should be set to `COLUMN`. This will cause all tables that are created without an explicit table type to be created as column store tables.

For SAP NetWeaver systems running on SAP HANA, SAP defines which tables shall be row store tables. Upon installation or migration of an SAP NetWeaver system to an SAP HANA database, the correct assignment is performed automatically. Over time—with the experience gained—this standard assignment of tables gets updated with newer versions of SAP NetWeaver-based applications. To check the current assignment in your system and see if you need to update it to the current version, please see SAP Note 1659383 and SAP Note 1815547.

8.2.2 Multiversion Concurrency Control

Multiversion concurrency control (MVCC) is a well-known technique to allow parallel access to the same bits of information to multiple sessions, even when one or more sessions are actively changing this information. This is accomplished by keeping copies of the original version of the record and presenting each session with the version appropriate to the sequence of system changes (COMMITs) that the session had been exposed to.

For the SAP HANA user or developer, this happens automatically, and no additional care or precautions need to be taken. However, the column store and the row store implement this feature in quite different ways, each bringing different consequences for the administrator with it.

For tables placed in the row store, each changed page is copied first and placed into a chain of page versions with each version reflecting the state of data for a specific commit point. These page chains are saved in virtual container structures in memory called undo cleanup files. Monitoring view M_UNDO_CLEANUP_FILES provides detailed information on these internal virtual file container structures, but usually it is not necessary for the DBA to look into these. The garbage collector thread will automatically take care of getting rid of old, unrequired information so that more main memory is available for current data processing. Be aware that this will not necessarily lead to more free or usable memory immediately.

> **Note**
>
> Because of the way data pages of row store tables are managed, the row store may become fragmented in rare circumstances. It is possible to reorganize the row store data (see SAP Note 1813245), but this operation should be treated with great care.

One aspect of this garbage collection is, however, important to the DBA; the garbage collector can only remove those old versions of a record for which the update transactions have been finished (committed or rolled back). In the case of a transaction modifying tens of thousands of records without committing them, you may end up in a situation in which large amounts of redundant row store data need to be kept in main memory, because there will be tens of thousands of record locks and new active record versions kept in the database.

This situation can be visualized in the load diagram of SAP HANA Studio in ADMINISTRATION CONSOLE • PERFORMANCE • LOAD by displaying the key figures ACQUIRED RECORD LOCKS, ACTIVE TRANSACTION ID RANGE, and ACTIVE VERSIONS. A situation with 100,000 changed records is shown in Figure 8.2.

Because situations like this can become problematic, SAP HANA provides several alerts and warnings that notify the DBA in case the garbage collection is impaired; see also SAP Note 1833835.

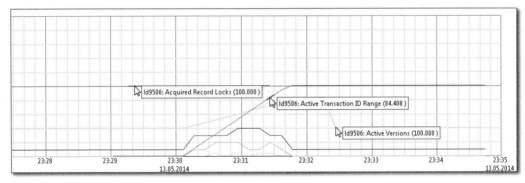

Figure 8.2 Load Diagram Example for Long-Time-Open Change Transactions

More information on MVCC and the related monitoring and administration tasks are provided in Chapter 10.

8.2.3 Indexes

Like any other DBMS, SAP HANA provides indexes to speed up record access on tables. The row store of SAP HANA is specifically designed to work in memory only, so the internal data structure including the possible secondary indexes are optimized for that.

For row store tables, two different index types are available: a classic b-tree index implementation and a cpb+-tree index. The latter stands for "compressed prefix b-tree index" and is an index structure that is highly optimized to handle character-based index keys in memory. It uses partial keys to store and navigate within the index structure.

Although it is possible to specify which index type shall be used for a specific index on a row store table, typically it is not necessary to do so. SAP HANA will use the cpb+-tree for all indexes that are defined on columns or combinations of columns that are of string, binary string, or decimal types. For all other data types, the classic b-tree index will be used.

To review runtime information of indexes on row store tables, monitoring view M_RS_INDEXES can be used. Indexes on row store tables are not saved to the persistency but rebuilt when the table is loaded into memory. This happens during index server process startup and can potentially prolong the startup process as can be observed in the trace file entries written by the index server process during startup.

8.3   Column Store Tables

Column store tables are the major table data structure used in SAP HANA. Much of SAP HANA's high-performing analytical and mass data processing happens thanks to the benefits of the column store.

Although we cannot completely cover all relevant details of the column store, this section explains the most important aspects of it. This section covering SAP HANA's implementation of column store tables starts with a discussion on how data is stored and retrieved and how data updates are managed. Then, we advance to data compression and space usage. We close this section with a view on indexes and multiversion concurrency on column store tables.

8.3.1   Data Storage and Retrieval

The column store, as the name implies, stores the table record data column by column and not row by row over many pages. As the information is already stored in separate data structures, SAP HANA can directly access the columns requested by an SQL query without needing to read and decode other column data. This also means that a lot less data needs to be transported from the RAM to the CPU caches, which, again, saves a lot of time. In addition, multiple CPU cores can work on several columns at the same time—all due to the separate in-memory data structures.

The next benefit lies in the efficient default data storage in column store tables. Very often, columns contain repetitive data. Information such as material numbers, ZIP codes, or customer IDs are referenced over and over again, which is no wonder, because the tables should store what business events occurred with these items. Knowing that, it seems to be logical to store each different value only once and refer to it when it is used again. This is precisely what SAP HANA does; each different value of a column is kept in the so-called dictionary of the column and is assigned an internal value ID.

> **Note**
>
> The benefit of having the columns stored separately also comes at a price; when SAP HANA returns complete records, it needs to recombine the correct column data entries that make up all of the records in the table. We will see how this is done in a very efficient way later in this section.

This value ID currently (as of SPS 8) is a variable-length integer of a maximum 4-byte integer size. This leads to a maximum of 2,147,483,648 different possible values that can be stored in any column dictionary. SAP HANA column store tables actually can only store about two billion records per partition or table, depending on whether the table is partitioned or not. To store the actual values per record, only the value IDs are stored one after the other in a contiguous memory area. Literally, this is a very long string of zeroes and ones that represents the actual information itself. To know which value belongs to which record, the offset of the ID is used.

We can see this in Figure 8.3 for the column GROUP. The column contains two distinct values, A and B. The first two records in the table refer to group A, whereas the third one refers to group B. This is exactly what we find in the main vector of the column: The first two entries reference the dictionary entry with value ID 1, and the third one references value ID 3. By using only the references instead of the actual values, many base operations on table data—for example, finding records that contain a specific value—can be immensely sped up, because the task can be delegated to the CPU cores and their ability to perform operations on arrays and vectors of data (single instruction, multiple data: SIMD).

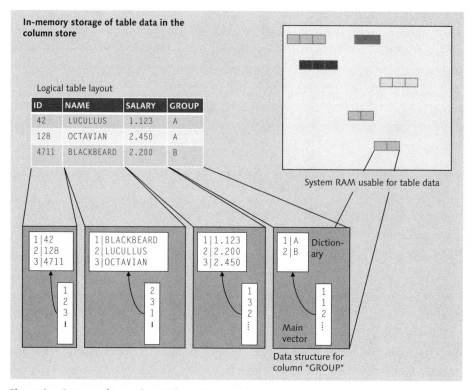

Figure 8.3 Storage of Records in Column Store Tables

Figure 8.4 provides an example of how data is accessed in the column store. To find the record that matches the WHERE condition ID = 4711, SAP HANA reads the dictionary of the column ID and retrieves the stored valueID for value 4711. Here, it is valueID 3. Next, the main vector is scanned completely for all occurrences of valueID 3. The offset of the occurrence is the offset to be used when reading from the other columns.

The preliminary result set is created by reading the columns NAME and SALARY at the offset position found in ❷ of Figure 8.4. In order to make the result set readable, the actual values for NAME and SALARY now need to be looked up in the column's dictionaries.

As we can see, the column GROUP was never touched during this query execution. Although this access mechanism looks a lot more complex than the one used for the row store table, splitting it up into so many substeps allows for several important optimizations:

▶ **Cache usage**

The dictionary data from ❶ can fit completely into the CPU cache of one core. To find the matching record, it is not required to scan through the full table.

▶ **Benefitting from SIMD instruction sets**

In ❷, instead of scanning through the full table, an SIMD operation on the column's main vector delivers the matching row within a few CPU cycles.

▶ **Parallelization**

With the offset information, the next two columns can be accessed in parallel by two CPU cores to build the preliminary result set in ❸.

▶ **Parallel materialization**

Finally, in ❹, the materialization can be performed in parallel.

▶ **Late materialization**

For mass data, SAP HANA supports a bulk materialization that also uses SIMD CPU instructions to resolve the `valueID`s to actual values (late materialization).

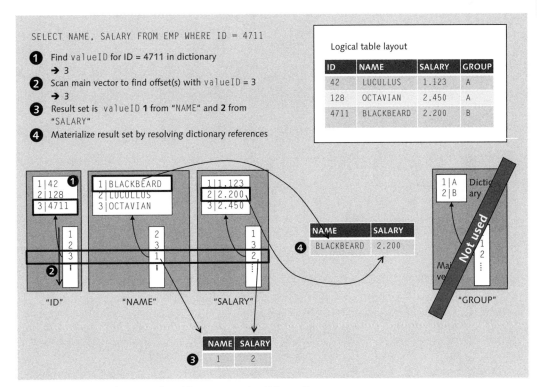

Figure 8.4 Example for a Simple Table Access in the Column Store

▶ **Intrinsic sorting**

Another improvement for read performance is that the entries in the dictionary are sorted so that in order to find a specific value—for example, the filter condition provided in the WHERE clause of an SQL statement—SAP HANA can easily perform a binary search in the dictionary.

A side effect of the dictionary encoding is that for most of the data that is usually stored in columns it works like a compression algorithm that saves storage space for repeated values. On top of this "accidental" compression—obviously the dictionary encoding does achieve compression on columns with unique values, such as primary keys or GUIDs—SAP HANA can compress the main vector data very effectively. SAP HANA uses several different possible compression algorithms that are automatically selected for the best efficiency based on the data distribution and clustering in the main vector.

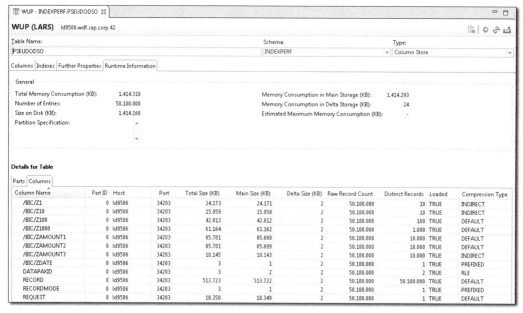

Figure 8.5 Column Store Runtime Information in SAP HANA Studio

Note
The type of compression actually applied on any column can be reviewed in the M_CS_ COLUMNS monitoring view or in the Runtime Information tab of the SAP HANA Studio Table Editor, as shown in Figure 8.5.

> **Warning**
>
> When checking for the memory usage of any column store table, it is important to make sure that the table is loaded fully to memory (in monitoring view M_CS_COLUMNS, column LOADED = 'TRUE').

8.3.2 Changing Data: Inserts, Updates, and Deletes

The picture of performance improvement radically changes when we try to change data in the column store structures. Because the column dictionaries may need to be sorted after, for example, the INSERT of new values into the column, the new value must be placed right into the dictionary, and a new ID has to be assigned. Eventually, this means that the dictionary needs to be resorted. To enable good INSERT and UPDATE performance, the column store provides a separate data structure for changed data: the *delta store*.

The delta store is a data container structure in memory that is optimized for high INSERT performance, as this is the only operation allowed for the delta store. UPDATEs and DELETEs are handled by marking old entries as invalid and creating new entries. This is what makes the delta store the insert-only data structure in the column store.

The advantages in the INSERT speed come at the price of high memory consumption (because no compression takes place in the delta store) and lower read-access performance. To compensate for this, the delta store is regularly used to update the optimized columnar data structure of the table, named the *main store*. This operation is called *delta merge*. The important key takeaway here is to realize that data from column store tables is changed or written only in one structure, the delta store.

On the other hand, reading the data always happens on both the delta and the main store. Because this is done by SAP HANA automatically, the application developer or end user does not have to take care of this—but it does carry some consequences. For example, it is possible to insert new data into a column store table without loading the already existing records in the main store first. As all inserts are performed in the delta store, only the internal ROWID column needs to be in memory for the INSERT operation. Of course, any column involved in a unique or primary key constraint that should be enforced needs to be in memory, too.

8.3.3 Redo Logging and the Delta Store

A misconception that occurs quite often is to assume that the delta store is used during the recovery process of the database. After all, it contains data change information just as the redo log does. In reality, the delta store is not persisted at all. It is a pure in-memory structure that is not represented in the persistency. For more on persistency in SAP HANA, refer back to Chapter 5.

Figure 8.6 provides an overview of the persistency access for the column store memory containers.

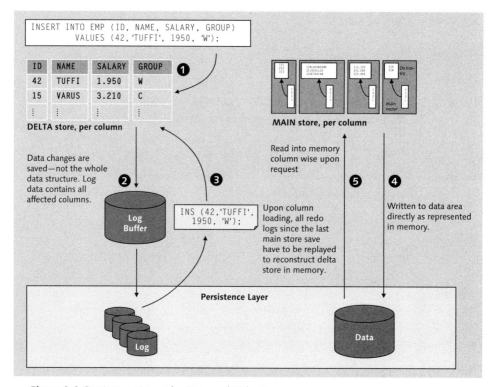

Figure 8.6 Persistency Access by Main and Delta Store

Although each column of the table has its own delta store, for data change purposes all delta stores for all columns of a table are handled as one combined unit so that the delta store of the table is at any point in time either entirely loaded into main memory or not loaded at all.

When new data is inserted, as shown in ❶, the values for all columns of the new tuple are inserted into the delta store: each value into its corresponding column-related delta store.

Once the data has been written to the delta store, a log entry is written into the log buffer, as shown in ❷, and eventually to the log file in the disk persistence. When logging is disabled, this is the processing step that is omitted. In the case of a system crash, the data in the delta store will be lost.

Because the delta store itself is never written to the data volume files, it has to be reconstructed following a table unload or a restart. To this end, SAP HANA has to read and replay all of the data changes that occurred to the table since the main store was last written to persistency.

> **Note**
>
> Because all data changes have to be performed again in the same sequence they had followed originally, this might take a long time.

Once the changed data is written into the delta store, it is available for processing. But due to lack of compression, the data-access performance is a lot worse than for the data in the main store.

Also, the high memory consumption of the delta store entries might impact the rest of the system, where memory could be put to better use. So, eventually the data in the delta store should be transferred into the main store. This is done during the delta merge operation. We go into more detail about delta merges in Chapter 9.

The process of redo logging is largely different for the main store; here the data is stored to persistency exactly as it looks in memory, as shown in ❹. Each column can be loaded, unloaded, and written to disk independently from the other columns. Once a column is requested, SAP HANA only needs to read the data for this specific column and transfer it into memory, as shown in ❺.

Obviously, being able to just read the data as is from the persistency saves a lot of time compared to the sequential approach of the delta store. Thus, tables with only main-store data or very little data in the delta store typically load much more quickly than those with a lot of data in the delta store.

8.3.4 Data Compression

As mentioned earlier, SAP HANA provides additional compression on the column store main vector structures. Depending on the order of dictionary references in a main vector, SAP HANA can apply different compression algorithms to it.

The system picks the best compression algorithm for any given sort order automatically based on the present order of values in the main vector of any column. This means that the compression is affected by the order in which the data gets loaded into the main vector. To achieve better compression factors, we need to reorder the table records—but sorting the table affects all columns and may worsen the compression of other columns when the sort order is altered. Finding the best possible sort order for a table can become a difficult optimization problem.

Fortunately, DBAs or developers do not need to manually choose the compression for each column. Instead, SAP HANA does this during *compression optimization*, a processing step that is automatically applied after an automatic delta merge or smart merge if the table contents have been changed substantially since the last compression optimization. The thresholds for the optimization compression to kick in are defined as parameters, as shown in Table 8.1.

Parameter Name	Default	Description
`Active`	YES	Compression optimization status
`min_change_ratio`	1.75	Minimum required changed row count (ratio)
`min_hours_since_last_merge_of_part`	24	Minimum hours since the last merge of a part
`min_rows`	10240	Minimum required rows

Table 8.1 Thresholds for Optimization Compression

These default settings mean that the table compression will only be executed if:

▸ The last delta merge was at least 24 hours ago (`min_hours_since_last_merge_of_part`) in order to prevent compression optimization runs that are too frequent.

▸ At least 10,240 rows (`min_rows`) are stored in the table (for small tables, the overall space savings effect typically does not rectify a compression optimization run).

▸ The ratio *#of total rows/#of changed rows* is smaller than or equal to 1.75 (`min_change_ratio`) (it is assumed that the data distribution will be only be impacted by large-scale data changes).

▸ The compression optimization is actually active (`active`).

Compression optimization is an operator-free process of the SAP HANA column store. However, in cases in which table compression rates are not satisfying, it is possible to find out about the details of the storage space utilization of column store tables. We cover this next.

> **Further Resources**
>
> A more detailed discussion of compression optimization can be downloaded from the book's page at *www.sap-press.com/3506*.

8.3.5 Space Usage and Internal Columns

A very common request for SAP HANA DBAs is to investigate memory usage of tables, especially for tables in the column store. When looking into this, it becomes obvious that the runtime information shown in the Table Editor of SAP HANA Studio does not give you the complete truth; adding up the sizes of all of the columns of the table will result in a number that is lower than what is reported as the total memory consumption. The reason for this deviation is that SAP HANA uses additional hidden internal columns for various purposes on column store tables. See SAP Note 1986747 for a technical explanation and a reference to detailed examples. The internal columns that get created can be reviewed in the monitoring view `M_CS_ALL_COLUMNS` but unfortunately not in the runtime information overview of the Table Editor.

The following table gives an overview of the different types of internal columns and their major uses. Please note that even though columns with unique values such as `$rowid$` or `$trexexternalkey$` can consume a lot of memory, especially for large tables, it is not possible to drop these columns, because they are an integral part of the table data structure in SAP HANA.

Column Type	Column Name	Description
ROWID	$rowid$	Row pointer, unique identifier of a record, internal, cannot be deleted
TREX_UDIV	$trex_udiv$	Transaction and visibility management, internal, cannot be deleted
TREX_EXTERNAL_KEY	$trexexternalkey$	Multicolumn primary key index
CONCAT_ATTRIBUTE	$<col1>$<col2>$...$	Multicolumn index, join indexes

Table 8.2 Types of Internal, Hidden Columns of the SAP HANA Column Store

Rather unknown but particularly important types of hidden columns are the concat attributes. Up to SPS 7, SAP HANA was not able to efficiently join column store tables when the join condition spanned multiple columns. To overcome this and in order to allow using the single-column join algorithms, concatenated columns were created. These CONCAT_ATTRIBUTE columns consist of the concatenated data of the involved join columns, as shown in Figure 8.7.

The problem here is that up to SPS 7 these columns were created automatically whenever a multicolumn join was executed for the first time. The CONCAT_ATTRIBUTE columns then were kept and maintained, but never automatically dropped again, so that they would be available for later reuse.

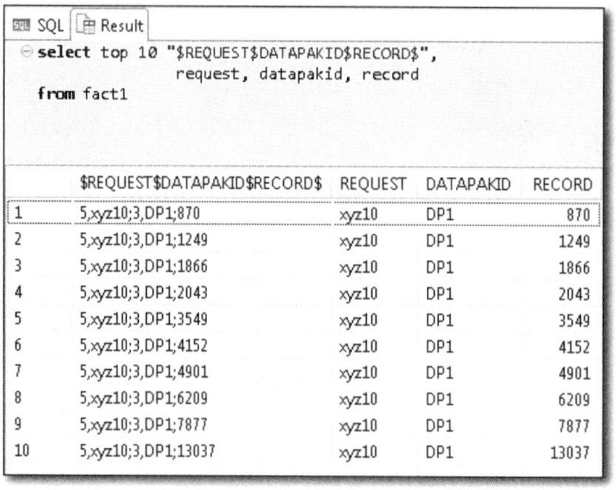

Figure 8.7 Contents of CONCAT_ATTRIBUTES

As of SPS 7, SAP HANA supports multicolumn joins without `CONCAT_ATTRIBUTE` columns along with further decreased usage (and implicit creation) of concatenated attributes in SPS 8. The already existing concat attributes can be reviewed and dropped if required. To do so, use the script `HANA_Tables_ColumnStore_TableColumns` from the SQL statement collection available in SAP Note 1969700. The script lists all columns, including the internal columns, links the `CONCAT_ATTRIBUTE` columns back to their origin (multicolumn secondary index or information model view), and provides the correct SQL syntax to drop the `CONCAT_ATTRIBUTE` column if this is possible.

If the performance advantage of `CONCAT_ATTRIBUTE` columns is important to your application, then the recommendation is to explicitly create secondary indexes on the set of columns that should be used to perform the join. This makes these columns much more visible as what they really are (join indexes) and allows for easy dropping and transport.

8.3.6 Indexes

It is frequently stated that in columnar databases indexes are not required for optimizing the performance of data retrieval. Although this is true in most situations, it is possible to find constellations that can greatly benefit from the creation of inverted indexes on columnar tables. One such example is that of searching for a small number of records identified by a single value or few values out of a table column with billions of unique entries—a typical requirement in OLTP scenarios. Finding these records requires a search on the dictionary for the value(s) and then scanning the main vector for all occurrences of the value ID(s). The time for this scan will increase linearly with the number of entries in the column.

An inverted index for a given column is a list of all individual values in a column with pointers to all positions at which a given value occurs in the column (Figure 8.8). These pointers will greatly reduce the cost of the previously mentioned main vector scan.

Inverted indexes are created simply via the `CREATE INDEX` command. Because the column store does not support different index types like the row store does, SAP HANA creates column store indexes regardless of the provided index type. Inverted indexes are also automatically created when a primary key or unique constraint is defined on column store tables.

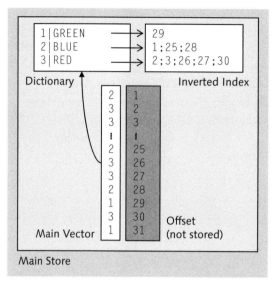

Figure 8.8 Inverted Index in SAP HANA Column Store

The inverted index for a column will typically require approximately as much space in main memory as the main vector of the column, as can be verified with a check on monitoring view M_CS_ALL_COLUMNS. As is the case with any other index structures, inverted indexes buy access speed performance with memory consumption. More important than the relative speedup factor for a given query is that the access time for the inverted index will stay stable regardless of how many records are stored in the table. The scan access without the index, on the other hand, will take longer and longer to perform this lookup as more data is loaded into the table.

Given the high costs of inverted indexes, questions arise: "When is it sensible to create indexes?" and of course "On which columns should indexes be created?" Let's look at some of the more common reasons to use indexes in a classic row store RDBMS and see if these reasons are also applicable in the SAP HANA column store:

▶ **Create indexes in order to enable an index-only access strategy and thereby avoid touching the table.**
This does not make any sense for the SAP HANA column store, as inverted indexes are part of the column data structure. Reading from the index is working on the volume of data; the data is simply organized in a different way.

▸ **Create indexes to speed up min/max queries.**
Inverted indexes do not help here, because this issue can already be addressed efficiently via the column dictionary.

▸ **Create indexes to speed up reading data in a sorted way.**
Because data must be read from the delta log as well and the index exists in the main part only, a separate sorting step is required regardless.

It should also be considered that inverted indexes are recreated in memory at the loading time of the column. This means that there is an additional delay for the first use after loading.

All of this sounds rather negative and against using inverted indexes, and in fact the actual use cases for secondary indexes are much rarer than in classic RDBMS. This is one of the big sales arguments in favor of SAP HANA as a database platform: being able to get rid of indexes and stored precomputed results.

What then is a good indicator for when to create indexes on column store tables? For SAP Business Suite on SAP HANA, the following approach has been used:

▸ The application performs many selective lookups on large tables. Even though the table is large, the result set is rather small.

▸ SAP Note 1794297 delivers an ABAP report to create secondary indexes in SAP NetWeaver systems based on the following heuristic:

  ▸ Single-column secondary indexes (inverted indexes) are created on column store tables for tables up to 500,000 records (*small tables*) when the column to be indexed has at least 10,000 distinct values, and on tables larger than 500,000 records (*large tables*) when the column to be indexed has least 1,000 distinct values.

  ▸ There are no indexes on time fields, because they are almost always selected with ranges with poor selectivity.

  ▸ Multicolumn indexes are not created, because the penalty of additional memory occupation will outweigh the usually small performance gain that can be achieved with multicolumn indexes.

▸ The *(#of records/#of distinct values)* of the column to be indexed needs to be smaller or equal 10,000, as the filtered result set shouldn't be larger than 10,000 records.

> **Note**
>
> Inverted indexes do not need to be rebuilt or optimized in any way. The inverted index structure is created once and only once during the delta merge. After that, as a part of the main store, the index is not going to be changed ever again. This makes it possible to employ a very dense data structure—especially compared to b-tree indexes that commonly have only 50% space usage.

8.3.7 Multiversion Concurrency Control

Like row store tables, the SAP HANA column store supports multiversion concurrency. This way, no read will ever block another reader or writer in the system, allowing for much higher parallel throughput.

The way this feature is implemented for column store tables is rather straightforward. New versions of records are not stored in a separate data structure. Instead, every new version is placed in the delta store together with validity information on a transaction level. Once the new version of the record is committed, the last valid version is provided with end-of-validity information. The new record version now is the current version, and the old version is only visible to those transactions that started before the new version became valid. The invalid record versions will be removed during the delta merge if no active transaction is still able to access the record in its old version.

All of this happens automatically, and the DBA does not need to take action to trigger the garbage collection. Because the handling of multiversion concurrency is so deeply embedded into the core data structures of the column store, there is no additional data structure to monitor or reorganize.

8.4 Special Types of Tables

In addition to the two basic types of tables we have covered so far, SAP HANA offers several other types for special use cases. The columnar structure of flexible schema tables can be extended dynamically as the table is being used by an application. Temporary tables are there for data that is not needed beyond the context of a session or transaction and thus does not need to be written to the persistence layer. History tables allow running transactions against the state of the table at a time in the past. Finally, the DUMMY table is an auxiliary table in the database for the convenience of database developers. We will walk you through the use of these types of tables.

8.4.1 Flexible Schema Tables

SAP HANA provides the option to create *schema flexible* tables, which are tables that enable you to store data in a table for which the structure is not known completely in advance. This could be useful, for example, for an inbound data-staging layer.

In classic DBMS, a common workaround design for such problems is to use generic data models in which the actual physical data model contains metadata tables to describe the current data model and large shared tables that contain every value for every record. Although ultimately flexible, such models lead to severe problems with performance, constraint checking, and access permission handling, to name just a few.

With flexible schema tables, such a design could be avoided, because the table adapts to the data that is put into it. Tables with schema flexibility can contain up to 64,000 columns, whereas standard tables can contain a maximum of 1,000 columns. At least one column needs to be fixed.

> **Note**
>
> One assumption for flexible schema tables is that the flexible created columns are sparsely populated—which makes perfect use of the column store, because no data is saved in columns for rows that do not contain values for this column.

Tables with a flexible schema need to be handled differently by the application using them. Because the table structure is not known when the application is written, SQL statements have to be dynamically generated to work with the present data.

Unlike classic key:value modelling approaches in fixed schema tables, it is not necessary to read from the same few columns of the table over and over in an eventually recursive fashion. Instead, a record in a flexible table can be used as if it was a common table, and access to specific keys (columns) is as fast as with normal tables.

As new flexible columns are defined during INSERT/UPDATE/UPSERT commands, it is not possible to specify the exact data type at that point. However, the data type can be changed later via `ALTER TABLE <table_name> ALTER COLUMN (<column_name> <data_type>)`.

To make the concept of flexible schema tables more tangible, we provide the following example. Start with the creation of a table with schema flexibility, as shown in Listing 8.1.

```
create column table flex_log (id integer, log_name varchar(20))
        WITH SCHEMA FLEXIBILITY;
select table_name, HAS_SCHEMA_FLEXIBILITY from tables
where table_name ='FLEX_LOG';


TABLE_NAME  HAS_SCHEMA_FLEXIBILITY
FLEX_LOG      TRUE
```
Listing 8.1 Creating a Table with Schema Flexibility

You just created a table with schema flexibility; now, enter some data. Note that the columns you insert the data into in Listing 8.2 do not exist yet.

```
insert into flex_log (id, log_name, MACHINE_START_TS)
        values  (1, 'START_MACHINE', current_time);

insert into flex_log (id, log_name, LOGON_NAME)
        values  (2, 'SYSTEM LOGON', cast('LARS' as varchar) );

insert into flex_log (id, log_name, MACHINE_STOP_TS)
        values  (3, 'STOP_MACHINE',
                    cast (current_timestamp as timestamp));
```
Listing 8.2 Entering Data for Columns That Do Not Yet Exist in the Table

When you select from the table now in Listing 8.3, you will find that the columns have been created automatically.

```
select * from flex_log;


ID  LOG_NAME       MACHINE_START_TS  LOGON_NAME  MACHINE_STOP_TS
1   START_MACHINE  13:48:49          NULL        NULL
2   SYSTEM LOGON   NULL              LARS        NULL
3   STOP_MACHINE   NULL              NULL        13:56:33
```
Listing 8.3 Selecting Data from the Dynamically Added Columns

Checking the data type, as shown in Listing 8.4, reveals that all columns that had been created on the fly are of the type `character`, which allows them to accept most values without any data type–matching issues.

```
select column_name, data_type_name, length, scale, HAS_SCHEMA_FLEXIBIL-
ITY
 from table_columns
where table_name ='FLEX_LOG';
```

COLUMN_NAME	DATA_TYPE_NAME	LENGTH	SCALE	HAS_SCHEMA_FLEX.
ID	INTEGER	10	0	FALSE
LOG_NAME	VARCHAR	20	NULL	FALSE
LOGON_NAME	NVARCHAR	5000	NULL	TRUE
MACHINE_START_TS	NVARCHAR	5000	NULL	TRUE
MACHINE_STOP_TS	NVARCHAR	5000	NULL	TRUE

Listing 8.4 Checking the Data Types of the Dynamically Added Columns

8.4.2 Temporary Tables

Storing data safely and securely in a fully recoverable fashion according to ACID requirements is key to most databases, and, of course, the same is true for SAP HANA. There are, however, use cases in which it is fully acceptable, even desirable, for data to be only available for a limited time. Such use cases could include, for example, an intermediate result set that should be put into a table structure for further use (e.g., to join it with another table) or storing intermittent system information, such as application server session states, in a database table.

SAP HANA provides three different table constructs for temporary tables: global temporary tables, local temporary tables, and no logging tables. Global and local temporary tables can be used with both row and column storage, but no logging tables can only be used with column storage.

Global Temporary Tables

Global temporary tables are tables for which the table definition is shared with all sessions, just like normal tables. The content of the table, however, is only visible to the current session; as soon as the session ends, the content will be removed. Global temporary tables can be created both as row or column store tables. Join-

341

ing the table with a column store table will be more efficient when the temporary table is a column store table as well.

Although the table and its structure show up in system tables such as TABLES, TABLE_COLUMNS, and the monitoring views for tables, no runtime-specific data, for example, the number of records in the table, is visible outside of the session that owns the data.

A common use case for global temporary tables is the recurring exchange of result sets between SQLScript procedures without table parameters. The structure of the result set data has to stay fixed in this scenario.

Local Temporary Tables

Local temporary tables are pretty much the same as global temporary tables with the exception that the entire table existence is limited to the session that the table was created in. There is a naming convention for local temporary tables: The table name has to start with a hash sign (#).

No Logging Tables

Column store tables can be created or altered with the NO LOGGING option. The full option parameter set is:

```
CREATE COLUMN TABLE ...
      NO LOGGING [RETENTION <retention_period>]
```

This will create a standard column store table, but none of the changes will be logged. The table's delta store will work the same way as usual but without writing redo log entries into the log buffer. This means that only the table content stored in the main store can possibly be available after a system restart.

On top of that, it is possible to provide a retention time for the data in the table. In case the index server process faces memory shortage, it should drop NO LOGGING tables after a retention time of n seconds, specified as the <retention period>.

Because the existence of this table as well as its contents is not at all reliable, this kind of table should only be used for cache-like structures of the application using the database. For example, SAP BW hierarchy information used during query processing could be implemented with such tables.

> **Note**
>
> DBAs familiar with other DBMS platforms probably know NO LOGGING tables and assume that SAP HANA NO LOGGING tables work the same way. This is not the case. In order to simply disable the creation of redo log entries on column store-tables, use:
>
> ALTER TABLE <table_name> DISABLE DELTA LOG
>
> To disable redo log generation for the whole database, including row store tables, use:
>
> ALTER SYSTEM LOGGING OFF
>
> In both cases, the system needs to be backed up after mass data loading, because none of the data changes will be recoverable.
>
> Also note that for SAP HANA systems, due to the hardware system specifications, writing out log data to the log volumes typically is not a major performance bottleneck when loading data.

8.4.3   History Tables

One of the features that had been advertised more heavily in the early days of SAP HANA is history tables, which give the option to see what the data looked like at some point in the past. With history tables the SAP HANA user can deliberately choose to not have old, now-invalid records removed from the column store table. History tables have two additional internal columns—$validfrom$ and $validto$—that store commit IDs if the update transaction from and to a record was valid. During an automerge operation, the outdated records are then moved to a second set of main and delta stores: the history main and history delta. To manually trigger this data movement, the MERGE HISTORY DELTA OF <table_name> command is available.

In order to review the old state of a history table, it is necessary to use a session with AUTOCOMMIT disabled. Then, you can set a session-wide point in time to go back to. The point in time is specified by a UTC timestamp or an SAP HANA internal commit ID. The timestamps and commit IDs that had been used for changes in history tables in the system can be checked in the system table TRANSACTION_HISTORY.

The semantic here is to be able to look at a specific *point* in time; access to a *period* of time is not possible with currently supported standard SQL. That means that it is not possible to review the change history of a specific record or to compare what changed in past versions. Because the commit IDs stored in the history tables are specific to the SAP HANA system on which the commit ID occurred, it is not possible to export and import history tables. This is especially true when the export is done on a different system than the import. Although no error will be thrown, the historic data will be incorrectly assigned to commit IDs or timestamps or will simply point to nonexisting commit IDs.

Due to these limitations, most application use cases for time-related databases cannot be properly handled with history tables—which is why we cannot recommend using them.

8.4.4 Special Table DUMMY

Table DUMMY is a convenience object for the SQL developer. It is used throughout the system, especially by internal SQL commands, for example, from the statistics server or statistics service. The table is defined to consist of a single character column, DUMMY, that holds a single record with value X, as shown in Listing 8.5.

```
select * from dummy;
DUMMY
X
```

Listing 8.5 Table DUMMY

On first sight, surely you might ask: "What is so useful about this table?" The answer is that it is useful to generate result sets with only one record, like the one in Listing 8.6.

```
SELECT current_time FROM dummy;

CURRENT_TIME
11:20:32
```

Listing 8.6 Using Table DUMMY as a Row Generator

Here, the actual content of table DUMMY is not interesting at all. What is important is the number of records (1), because the function current_time is evaluated for every record in the result set.

Because SQL functions such as current_time cannot be evaluated out of thin air but only on records, the DUMMY table can be used to overcome this limitation. DUMMY is present in every SAP HANA database and is SELECTable by every user. To retain the special setup of the one-row/one-column table, no user has INSERT, UPDATE, DELETE, or TRUNCATE privileges, nor can the table be altered.

Similar tables exist in other DBMS platforms, such as Oracle (DUAL), SAP MaxDB (DUAL), or IBM DB2 (DUAL). Still other platforms, such as MS SQL Server or SAP (Sybase) Adaptive Server Enterprise (ASE), support SELECT statements without a FROM clause and evaluate functions anyway.

In scale-out systems, the table exists once in the row store of each indexserver, statisticsserver, and xsengine process of the system. This leads to a slightly odd situation when querying system table TABLES for table DUMMY, because it will report not one record but the sum of one record per DUMMY table in the system.

8.5   Summary

SAP HANA offers multiple types of tables to choose from. After reading this chapter, you should know the basic properties and appropriate usage scenarios for all types of tables.

An unusual feature of the database is that it has not just one but two conceptually different basic types of tables: the row store table and the column store table. Of these, the most important one for most practical purposes is the column store table, and we have spent the majority of this chapter discussing its most prominent features. For special purposes, the database also supports temporary tables—the content of which are not written to disk persistence—flexible schema tables with a flexible column layout, and other types.

Having introduced the types of tables conceptually, the next chapter is all about administration tasks related to database tables.

Now that you understand the basics of the types of tables in SAP HANA, this chapter will teach you what you need to do with them.

9   Working with Tables

There is a wealth of functionality available in SAP HANA for working with database tables. For this chapter, we have picked out those items that are most important for database administrators in order to understand what is happening in the database system and how to optimally manage the tables in the system.

We will start with basic functionalities of the column store, such as loading and unloading columns to and from memory and performing and monitoring delta merges. Next, we will cover arguably the most difficult topic, namely, the partitioning of tables and the distributing of tables in scale-out systems, including a discussion of optimizing this process. We'll conclude the chapter with discussions of importing/exporting tables and checking tables for consistency.

9.1   Loading Tables to and from Memory

The algorithms for processing data in SAP HANA are optimized for in-memory data management. It is therefore mandatory that all data that is being worked with is contained in the main memory. Understanding the mechanism for loading and unloading data into/from memory is particularly important in two respects:

▶ At system start time, most database tables are not yet loaded into the main memory. This is to minimize the time needed for the system start. It is therefore important for the DBA to understand if and how tables can be loaded into the main memory.

▶ In some situations, even with proper sizing, the main memory available in the database system may not be sufficient to store all table data and at the same time accommodate dynamic memory demands for ongoing requests in the system. In such cases, the database may decide to explicitly evict tables or parts of tables from the main memory.

In this section, we will tell you about all features around modifying the presence of tables in the main memory. We will start with the manual or automatic loading and unloading of data before handling the special case of large object columns and the rather new feature of page-wise loading of columns. We'll conclude with a discussion of the hot and cold data concept.

9.1.1 Loading and Unloading of Columns

As an in-memory database, SAP HANA's main memory is the primary storage for tables and columns. However, at some point there likely will be more data in the database then what would fit into memory. Although SAP HANA's in-memory storage provides immense benefits in terms of database schema simplicity, processing speed, and flexibility, it is not as easy to add more memory to a SAP HANA server as it is to add more disk space to a classic database.

SAP HANA employs different mechanisms to handle data loading to memory and data removal from memory. The most prominent feature is the column load/unload mechanism. The way this works is that, after system restart, no column of any column store table will be loaded to memory. But as soon as an SQL statement requires access to a specific column, SAP HANA will load this column (plus at least the $rowid$ and $udiv$ internal columns, as those are required for consistent data access) from disk into memory.

Once in memory, the column will stay in memory until a column unload is triggered. Then, the column unload stores the current state of the column to disk and releases the SAP HANA internal memory container back to the memory management facility.

Note

Even though columns are unloaded from memory and the memory is returned to the memory management system, this does not mean that the memory will be released on the operating system level.

Instead, the SAP HANA memory management system can now reuse the freed memory internally, for example, for different columns that need to be accessed now, for intermediate result sets, for delta merge working memory, and so on.

Table-column unloads can be triggered either automatically—when the memory management finds that this is the only way to free up some memory to satisfy current requests—or manually with the UNLOAD command.

The UNLOAD command always triggers the UNLOAD of the complete table, whereas with the counterpart command LOAD it is possible to selectively load single columns (LOAD <table_name> (<column #1>, <column #2, ...)).

> **Note**
>
> Historically, the MERGE DELTA and LOAD/UNLOAD commands have evolved from the parameterized UPDATE statement, like UPDATE <table_name> WITH PARAMETERS ('OPTIMIZE_COMPRESSION' = 'FORCE').
>
> In versions up to SAP HANA SPS 8, this is still visible in the fact that the required privilege to execute any of those commands to a table is the UPDATE TABLE privilege. This means that every DBA who should be able to perform any of these commands against production tables needs to have UPDATE privileges on the tables. Obviously, this is a highly undesirable situation.
>
> As a workaround, very similar to the workaround for the object ownership problem discussed in Chapter 7, stored procedures can be implemented to prevent unwanted data being updated through DBAs or developers.

In addition to the manual unloading of column store tables, SAP HANA can also automatically unload tables when memory shortage occurs. There is no specific threshold of memory usage that once reached would lead to table unloading. Instead, SAP HANA tries to keep tables in memory as long as possible. Only when a memory request from a session cannot be satisfied from the currently available memory will SAP HANA try to free up memory.

In a first step, possible fragmented free memory will be defragmented so that a memory request for, say, 10 MB of contiguous memory can be satisfied after merging two free segments of, say, 7 MB and 4 MB. If there is still not enough free memory available after memory compaction, then table columns will be unloaded.

In order to not get rid of column that are currently in use or that had been recently used, SAP HANA employs a least recently used (LRU) list of the columns internally. After temporary tables and resources have been unloaded first, columns that have not been touched for the longest time will be unloaded, followed by the more recently used columns. The unloading will proceed until enough memory is free and available to fulfill the memory request that kicked off the unloading.

Now that we have covered loading and unloading columns, we will dive a bit deeper and look into three aspects of this topic that are of special interest to the SAP HANA DBA. The ability to monitor the unload of columns is important in order to understand system performance and sizing. As possible remedies for excessive column unloading or reduced query performance after system startup, we cover unload priorities and column preloading.

Monitoring Column Unloads

Clearly, having columns constantly unloaded and loaded back to memory again will negatively impact the system's performance a great deal. In order to monitor the columns that had been unloaded and what had been the trigger event, the monitoring view M_CS_UNLOADS is available (Figure 9.1).

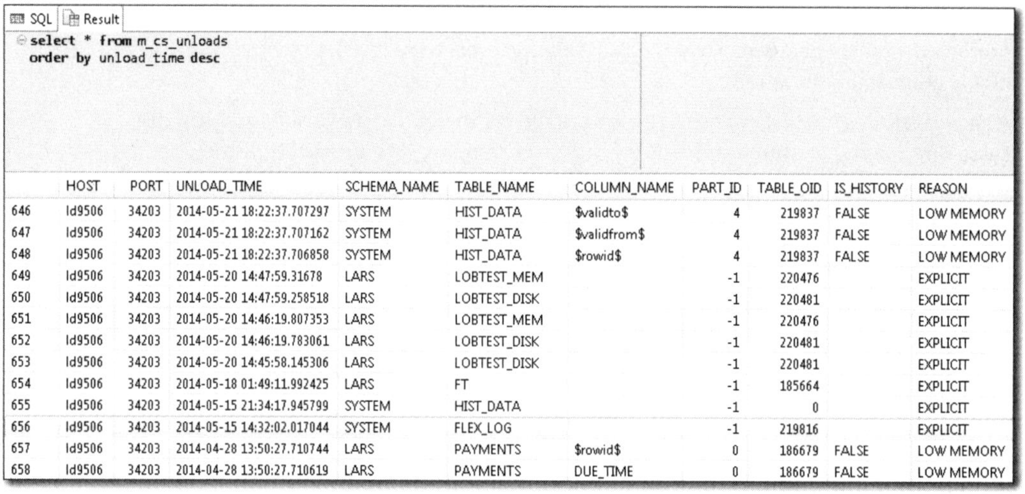

```
SQL  Result
select * from m_cs_unloads
 order by unload_time desc
```

	HOST	PORT	UNLOAD_TIME	SCHEMA_NAME	TABLE_NAME	COLUMN_NAME	PART_ID	TABLE_OID	IS_HISTORY	REASON
646	ld9506	34203	2014-05-21 18:22:37.707297	SYSTEM	HIST_DATA	$validto$	4	219837	FALSE	LOW MEMORY
647	ld9506	34203	2014-05-21 18:22:37.707162	SYSTEM	HIST_DATA	$validfrom$	4	219837	FALSE	LOW MEMORY
648	ld9506	34203	2014-05-21 18:22:37.706858	SYSTEM	HIST_DATA	$rowid$	4	219837	FALSE	LOW MEMORY
649	ld9506	34203	2014-05-20 14:47:59.31678	LARS	LOBTEST_MEM		-1	220476		EXPLICIT
650	ld9506	34203	2014-05-20 14:47:59.258518	LARS	LOBTEST_DISK		-1	220481		EXPLICIT
651	ld9506	34203	2014-05-20 14:46:19.807353	LARS	LOBTEST_MEM		-1	220476		EXPLICIT
652	ld9506	34203	2014-05-20 14:46:19.783061	LARS	LOBTEST_DISK		-1	220481		EXPLICIT
653	ld9506	34203	2014-05-20 14:45:58.145306	LARS	LOBTEST_DISK		-1	220481		EXPLICIT
654	ld9506	34203	2014-05-18 01:49:11.992425	LARS	FT		-1	185664		EXPLICIT
655	ld9506	34203	2014-05-15 21:34:17.945799	SYSTEM	HIST_DATA		-1	0		EXPLICIT
656	ld9506	34203	2014-05-15 14:32:02.017044	SYSTEM	FLEX_LOG		-1	219816		EXPLICIT
657	ld9506	34203	2014-04-28 13:50:27.710744	LARS	PAYMENTS	$rowid$	0	186679	FALSE	LOW MEMORY
658	ld9506	34203	2014-04-28 13:50:27.710619	LARS	PAYMENTS	DUE_TIME	0	186679	FALSE	LOW MEMORY

Figure 9.1 M_CS_UNLOADS Example Output

> **Note**
>
> The monitoring view is based on unload trace files. If the unload trace (indexserver. ini • [unload_trace] • enabled) is disabled, then unloads will not be captured.

As the unload trace information will eventually be overwritten in time, there is another option to gather unload information, the statistics server table _SYS_STA-TISTICS.HOST_CS_UNLOADS.

Unload Priority

Under certain conditions, there may be tables that should never get unloaded, regardless of the memory requests. Or, the other way around, there may be tables for which it is certain that they will not be used very often after some initial activity on them. An example for that would be the SAP BW persistent staging area (PSA) tables.

For such special requirements for unloading behavior, SAP HANA provides the option to set an unload priority per table. The unload priority is given as a number between 0 (never unload the table) and 9 (unload this table first). To specify the unload priority, the `ALTER TABLE <table_name> UNLOAD PRIORITY <priority>` command can be used. Alternatively, the unload priority can be provided at table-creation time. The default setting for unload priority is 5 and is used when no unload priority has been specified.

Preload of Columns

Depending on the use case, it might not only be desirable to keep specific tables from being unloaded but also to have them loaded to memory all the time, specifically immediately after an instance restart. This is done with the following command:

```
ALTER TABLE <table_name>
      PRELOAD ALL
      |PRELOAD (<column name #1>, <column name #2>)
```

Up to SAP HANA SPS 6, the preload of tables was performed before an SQL session could be opened with the database. This prolonged the restart time considerably when large tables were marked to be preloaded.

As of SPS 7, the preloading, together with the reloading, of tables happens asynchronously directly after the system restart has finished. That way, the system is again available for SQL statements that do not require the information of the columns that are still being loaded. Any statement that requires this information will have to wait until the column data is successfully loaded to memory.

9.1.2   Reload of Tables

The SAP HANA column store generally loads data into memory only when it is actually requested. That way, only the columns that really get used allocate space in memory, and the others are left on disk. A problem with this approach is that after a system crash or shutdown it may take a long time until all columns that are necessary for the application to work properly have been reloaded into memory. Setting up the important tables with the preload option does not particularly help here, because preload loads all marked tables into memory before SQL access is allowed. The system is practically unavailable during the table preload. In addition, it can be difficult to determine which tables or columns are actually required.

Since SPS 6, SAP HANA has had a more suitable feature available to get systems to a fully functional state after a restart: the table reload. During uptime, SAP HANA monitors and saves information on what tables and columns are currently in memory. This information is then used during database restart to asynchronously load those columns that had been in memory before the restart back into memory. Figure 9.2 gives an example of the parallel loading activity.

Host	Service	Connection ID	Thread ID	Calling	Caller	Thread Type	Thread Method	Thread Detail	Duration (ms)
ld9506	indexserver	-1	57114			SubmitThread-DATA-0			106.531
ld9506	indexserver	-1	57730	57740, 57757, ...		Assign	post_assign	open data+log volume 3 / preload tables	54.461
ld9506	indexserver	-1	57740	| 57744, 57794	57730	TableReload	reloading table	COPYTEST:CBIG03en	24.384
ld9506	indexserver	-1	57744		| 57740	LoadField		COPYTEST:CBIG03en RECORD	14.977
ld9506	indexserver	-1	57794		| 57740	LoadField		COPYTEST:CBIG03en $DATAPAKID$RECORD$REQUEST$	14.978
ld9506	indexserver	-1	57757		57730	TableReload	reloading table	LARS:CBIGen	24.384
ld9506	indexserver	-1	57760		57730	TableReload	reloading table	INDEXPERF:PSEUDODSOen	24.384
ld9506	indexserver	-1	57773	| 58099	57730	TableReload	reloading table	COPYTEST:CBIG01en	24.385
ld9506	indexserver	-1	58099		| 57773	LoadField		COPYTEST:CBIG01en $DATAPAKID$RECORD$REQUEST$	17.653
ld9506	indexserver	-1	57775	| 58096, 58108	57730	TableReload	reloading table	COPYTEST:CBIG02en	24.384
ld9506	indexserver	-1	58096		| 57775	LoadField		COPYTEST:CBIG02en RECORD	13.191
ld9506	indexserver	-1	58108		| 57775	LoadField		COPYTEST:CBIG02en $DATAPAKID$RECORD$REQUEST$	13.192

Figure 9.2 Example of Thread Overview during Asynchronous Table Reload after a Restart

You can activate or disable the table reload function with indexserver.ini parameter [sql] • reload_tables = true|false. Setting parameter [parallel] • tables_preload_in_parallel defines the maximum number of tables that will be preloaded and reloaded in parallel.

9.1.3   Large Object (LOB) Columns

When storing large data in the database, the binary large object (BLOB) and character large object (CLOB) data types are typically used. For the application developer, columns of this type can be used as containers for large chunks of data that belong to a specific record. Such columns can contain virtually anything, from pictures or video or audio files to PDF documents.

Up to SAP HANA SPS 6, LOB columns were handled like any other column. Once accessed via an SQL statement, the complete column was loaded into memory and kept there. Clearly, this strategy comes with the huge drawback that the content of these large object columns can of course be large. Loading and keeping several GB of LOB data in memory just to access a small piece of the data would require a lot of memory that otherwise could be put to better use.

To deal with this problem, SAP HANA introduced hybrid LOB columns with SPS 7. These can be used like any other column, but they will be unloaded early. Even more important is that every LOB value for every record can be independently loaded into memory. If just one record is selected, then only the corresponding LOB values are read into memory. The same is true for unloading LOB data from the memory. Hybrid LOB entries that have not been used recently will be unloaded while other values can stay in memory.

A special case within this scenario is the way that SAP NetWeaver uses LOB columns. Instead of actually storing large values, SAP NetWeaver has several tables in which the LOB data itself is rather small, but the table size in terms of the number of records is immense.

As of SPS 7, all LOB columns can be configured with a threshold value. As long as the actual data size in the LOB column is smaller than the threshold in bytes, the value will be stored in memory. Once the LOB data grows larger, it will be stored in a separate memory object that will be displaced onto disk immediately after use.

Further Resources

See SAP Notes 1994962 and 2007021 for more information on hybrid LOBs. These SAP Notes will also explain how to use scripts to perform a mass LOB conversion if you run a system that was installed on an earlier release of SAP HANA.

9.1.4 Paged Attributes

The option to load only parts of column data upon request and leaving the unrequested remaining part on disk is helpful not only for LOB columns but also — depending on the column size — for simple data types. As of SPS 7, SAP HANA supports this kind of chunk-wise loading of column data to memory with the *paged attribute feature*. As described in SAP Note 1871386, it is currently only possible to ALTER an existing column to switch to the page-wise loading. Only columns that are not part of the primary key and on which no UNIQUE constraint is defined can be marked as paged attributes.

The internal data structure of a paged attribute column consists of multiple chunks of data. These chunks require additional structural information, and accessing data across the chunks is less efficient than working on a contiguous data, main store structure. The only actual benefit of paged attributes arises when a very small number of records from of a very large table will be accessed individually. If the table is not yet in memory, accessing only some of the data chunks can allow for more efficient access to the data.

9.1.5 Hot/Cold Data Aging Concept

One of the major concerns with handling mass volume data in SAP HANA is determining what data will reside in the main memory. Ideally, all data would fit into the main memory, and enough free memory would be left to allow for data processing. In reality, however, the available amount of memory is constrained by the hardware or the SAP HANA license. To overcome this problem, SAP HANA systems and applications implement a data aging concept, also referred to as a *hot/cold data aging concept*.

The basic idea here is that data that is heavily used at the moment, such as bookings that are being processed right now, last weeks' sales, and so on, should be kept in main memory. This kind of data is considered to be *hot* data. Data that is no longer of interest for active data processing and that needs to be retained for purposes such as auditing and large-scale data analysis over a broader timeframe should be kept available, but not in memory. This kind of data is *cold* data.

Obviously, there is no way for the database engine to know which data can safely be considered to be cold, because it cannot foresee what data will be requested next by the application. Therefore, hot/cold data concepts are all driven by the application that uses it.

A classic data-aging concept for SAP NetWeaver is data archiving. Here, the application provides the logic for how to find related data that should be archived, and the archiving service of SAP NetWeaver manages to save the data in an archive and remove it from the database tables. To access the archived data, the archive has to be read into the application again.

SAP BW provides a more flexible approach, called nearline storage (NLS). Here, the retrieval of archived data is automated in the query processing. That way, an end user can specify if data stored in the NLS should be retrieved, and SAP BW automatically reads the NLS data during the query execution and incorporates it into the query result. These solutions are still available with SAP BW on HANA.

For SAP BW on SAP HANA, the current NLS implementation integrates with the SAP (Sybase) IQ database system, which allows a high query performance on archived data. SAP HANA can use smart data access to directly access the tables with the archived data in the SAP (Sybase) IQ database. At query time, SAP BW only needs to send the query to SAP HANA, and it will also automatically retrieve the archived data if requested. Writing into the SAP (Sybase) IQ database and deciding what records should be archived is done solely by SAP BW on SAP HANA. Another functionality used by SAP BW on SAP HANA is the early unload of column store tables for specific object types (PSA and write-optimized DataStore objects [DSO]). See SAP Note 1767880 for details on this. With these approaches, the application—SAP BW on SAP HANA in this case—needs to specify the data temperature on a table level and also needs to manage the access to archived data in an NLS.

Wouldn't it be nicer if the application could simply specify records as hot or cold, and SAP HANA could then keep the cold data out of memory? This is exactly what the data aging concept implemented in SAP NetWeaver 7.4 SP5 does. The tables for which data aging should be used are partitioned in a specific time-dependent scheme supported by SAP HANA (recognizable by the _DATAAGING column). SAP NetWeaver provides ABAP code to manage aged data, and the SAP NetWeaver database interface automatically adds specific extensions to the SQL commands— for example, WITH RANGE_RESTRICTION('CURRENT')—to signal to SAP HANA what group of data should be considered.

This partitioning scheme is managed by the SAP NetWeaver application and as of now is not released for custom development outside of SAP NetWeaver. In addition, every individual record is marked by the application to be either hot or cold and is stored in one of the partitions based on this marking. Current hot records are stored in a "current" partition that is kept in memory. All other records are moved to cold partitions that are unloaded from memory. SAP

HANA does not check key uniqueness on those cold partitions when data is modified in the hot partition, thereby circumventing the need to load the cold partitions into memory.

These examples for current data aging concepts should make it obvious that SAP HANA does not and cannot provide a generic data aging mechanism that works for all applications the same way. Whenever data aging or data lifecycle management should be part of the solution built on top of SAP HANA, this does require logic and development on the application level.

Further Resources

For more details on data aging features, we recommend the following:

https://help.sap.com/saphelp_nw74/helpdata/en/53/06a0995655488785175d57bef083da/frameset.htm

https://help.sap.com/saphelp_nw74/helpdata/en/60/cf63e1bbbb49429ee6c35e6ad03a45/frameset.htm

Although there are no specific activities for the SAP HANA administrator around data aging as of now, the topic should at least not be completely unknown. The functionality around data aging and data lifecycle management in general is still in its early stages but will most likely continue to gain importance and attention.

9.2   Running Delta Merges

Changing data in the main store of SAP HANA is very expensive, which is the reason for having a delta store. Consequently, SAP HANA does not provide any commands to change data in the main store directly. Instead, SAP HANA can only create a new main store based on the full set of input data. During the delta merge, this is exactly what happens: The data from the old main store and the delta store are read, and a new main store is created based on the combined data of both the old main and the delta stores.

If the design really was that simple, it would have the disadvantage that no data changes to the table would be allowed while the delta merge process is running, because otherwise operating the delta store would become very complex. As a solution to this, a simple yet effective mechanism is in place. Before the delta merge actually starts, the delta store is briefly locked against changes. A new delta store memory structure is then created and all data-changing commands fill the new delta store from there on. This new delta store is identified by delta2 in the documentation and in the system tables. All table accesses now have to read from the main store, delta store, and delta2 store to cover all records in the table.

Once the merge is completely finished, a second brief exclusive lock is acquired to redirect data access to the new main store. Afterwards, the old main and delta store are invalidated and the memory they allocated is returned to the memory management for further use.

In Figure 9.3, we see how read requests access the data stored in the original main store, the original delta store, and the new delta store. The new main store is not accessible yet to any SQL command. All data-changing operations, on the other hand, only access the new delta2 store.

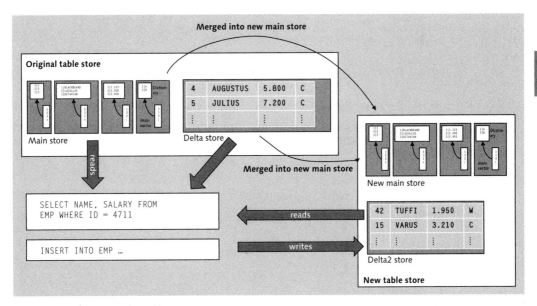

Figure 9.3 Delta Merge Data Movement

The diagrams in Figure 9.4 provide a conceptual overview of what data areas are used over the time during which the delta merge process is active. Also, we see how the memory usage develops, eventually climbing up to twice the memory that was required before the merge. Note that although all columns need to be loaded to memory during delta merge, not all columns will be worked on in parallel; instead, they will be worked on in sets of columns. This way, the delta merge operation is a little bit less CPU and memory resource hungry.

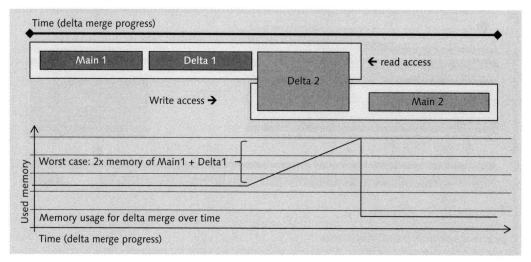

Figure 9.4 Data Access and Memory Usage during Delta Merge over Time

By default, the new main store will also be written to disk after the delta merge is finished. This is not done via a regular savepoint. Instead, the column store can perform the required I/O itself, writing out only the new main store and not any other data that had been changed in the meantime.

The delta merge functionality has several facets that we will discuss in the following sections. We will start with the default behavior of automatic merging and then treat different special merge mechanisms: the memory merge, smart merge, manual merge, and critical merge processes.

9.2.1 Automerge

Although knowing about how the delta merge mechanism works in SAP HANA is interesting, it is nothing that any user or developer of the database wants to think about. It clearly belongs to the responsibility of the DBMS to manage its internal data structures, and the end user should not need to take care of this.

To take care of an automatic merge of the delta stores of the column store tables, SAP HANA has two specific background threads: the MergedogMonitor and the

MergeAttributeThread. MergedogMonitor runs every 60 seconds and checks if tables need to be merged. In a scale-out environment, each node runs a separate MergedogMonitor thread. If a table should be merged, multiple MergeAttributeThreads are triggered by the MergedogMonitor.

The decision as to whether or not a table should be merged is made by evaluating the automerge decision function. This function is a configurable indicator function that allows you to fine tune the automerge process on a system-wide basis. It takes runtime parameters such as the current size of the delta store in MB (DMS) or rows (DRC) and the number of rows marked as deleted in the main store (DMR) as input and returns whether or not a table matches one of the conditions and should be merged. The relevant parameter is indexserver.ini • [mergedog] • auto_merge_decision_function.

Also, we want the system to ensure that not too many of those highly expensive delta merge operations are executed in parallel or too often. To cater to this, another set of parameters (token_per_table and *merge_priority_func) is available.

> **Note**
>
> Although Section 2.6.3 ("The Delta Merge Operation") of the *SAP HANA Administration Guide* covers the configuration of the decision and priority functions extensively, our advice is to not modify these settings; the majority of problems with the automerge that we have seen so far resulted from a faulty customization of these functions. This led to large tables that never got merged and in turn to overly high memory consumption and decreased performance.
>
> In addition to this, changing this system-wide setting for something as widespread as the automerge causes a rather big operational effort, because the changed setting needs to be consistent across the system landscape, typically spawning multiple systems.

The MergedogMonitor also writes out a warning into the indexserver.trc file when the size of a delta store exceeds the value of parameter max_delta_memsize in MB. In order to check on the MergedogMonitor thread, the THREADS tab in ADMINISTRATION CONSOLE • PERFORMANCE in SAP HANA Studio can be used. Because the default filter for the list of threads only shows the currently active threads (<active>), it is necessary to specifically include the MergedogMonitor process, as shown in Figure 9.5.

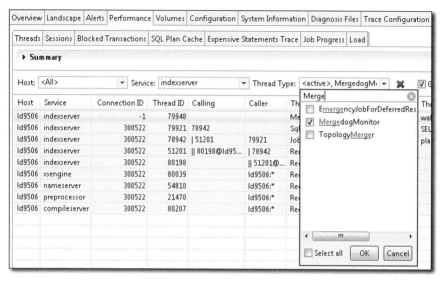

Figure 9.5 Including the MergedogMonitor Thread in the Thread Type Filter

Once the `MergedogMonitor` thread type is included, it is easy to observe the activity and the next scheduled check for tables to be merged. Figure 9.6 shows an example of this.

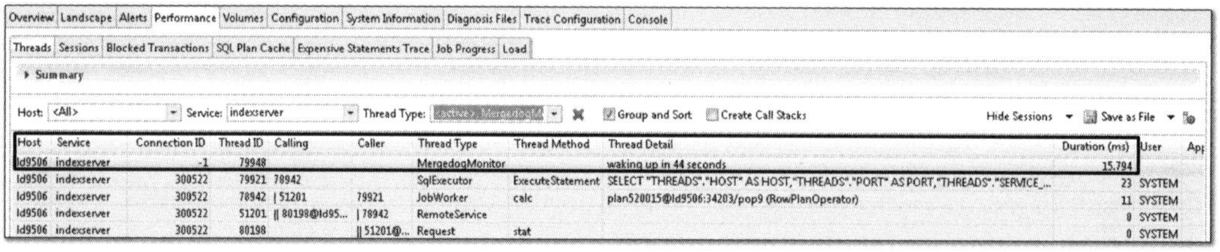

Figure 9.6 MergedogMonitor Thread in Threads Overview

As we can tell, the thread will resume its duty in 44 seconds. By refreshing the thread list, we can observe how the seconds are counted down.

If the `MergedogMonitor` thread does not appear in the list, the time until the next check is not counted down, or the time until the next check is much longer than a minute, it is important to check the [mergedog] parameter section for non-default values, indicated by a little gray diamond next to the parameter value in the SYSTEM or HOST column of the CONFIGURATION tab and reset them if required.

In the case that the `MergedogMonitor` is active but still shows tables that are marked for automerge (check system view `TABLES`, column `AUTOMERGE_ENABLED_ON = TRUE`), it is possible to get a detailed insight into the evaluation of the decision functions by setting the `indexserver` trace for the trace components `mergedog` and `mergedogmonitor` to level `INFO`. The resulting trace is quite comprehensive, as shown in Figure 9.7.

```
1324 i TraceContext     TraceContext.cpp(00702) : UserName=SYSTEM, ApplicationUserName=I028297, ApplicationName=HDBStudio
1313 i MergeMonitor     TableDeltaMerge.cpp(00926) : MergeMonitor reconfigured
2022 i MergeMonitor     TableDeltaMerge.cpp(01084) : merge token per table: 2
2030 i MergeMonitor     TableDeltaMerge.cpp(01093) : check compression flag for smart merge: 0
2034 i MergeMonitor     TableDeltaMerge.cpp(01095) : use cost function: true
2036 i MergeMonitor     TableDeltaMerge.cpp(01098) : reclaim delta decision function: DUV > 0 and DUV > 0.5*DRC
2038 i MergeMonitor     TableDeltaMerge.cpp(01099) : auto merge decision function: ((THM>=256000 and (((DMS>100 or DCC>100 or DLS>1000) and DRC > MR
2040 i MergeMonitor     TableDeltaMerge.cpp(01100) : auto merge priority function: 1 / (7 + MMS)
2042 i MergeMonitor     TableDeltaMerge.cpp(01101) : smart merge decision function: (MMS<1000 or DMS>1000 or DRC>0.1*MRC or DMR>0.1*MRC or DLS>5000)
2043 i MergeMonitor     TableDeltaMerge.cpp(01102) : smart merge priority function: 1 / (7 + MMS)
2045 i MergeMonitor     TableDeltaMerge.cpp(01103) : hard merge priority function: QDW
2046 i MergeMonitor     TableDeltaMerge.cpp(01104) : critical merge decision function: UPT > 43200  and ((MMS<10000 and DMS>1000 and TMD>86400) or T
2048 i MergeMonitor     TableDeltaMerge.cpp(01105) : memory merge decision function: 0
2049 i MergeMonitor     TableDeltaMerge.cpp(01106) : load balancing function: 1 + LCC * (AHM/THM) * (100-CLA)/100
2051 i MergeMonitor     TableDeltaMerge.cpp(01126) : delta merge statistics record limit: 100000
2056 i Mergedog         Mergedog.cpp(00392) : Mergedog reconfigured
2193 i Mergedog         Mergedog.cpp(00467) : active: 1
2197 i Mergedog         Mergedog.cpp(00468) : watch thread's sleep interval: 60000ms
2199 i Mergedog         Mergedog.cpp(00469) : watch thread's initial down time: 900000ms
2201 i Mergedog         Mergedog.cpp(00470) : maximum CPU load for merge: 95%
2203 i Mergedog         Mergedog.cpp(00471) : maximum CPU load for merge in parallel: 45%
2204 i Mergedog         Mergedog.cpp(00472) : number of parallel merge threads: 3
2206 i Mergedog         Mergedog.cpp(00473) : maximum delta mem size: 1000MB
2208 i Mergedog         Mergedog.cpp(00474) : maximum delta log size: 5000MB
2209 i Mergedog         Mergedog.cpp(00475) : maximum delay since last merge: 3601sec
2211 i Mergedog         Mergedog.cpp(00476) : maximum delta/main ratio: 0
2213 i Mergedog         Mergedog.cpp(00477) : maximum number of rows in delta: 0
2215 i Mergedog         Mergedog.cpp(00478) : maximum number of cells in delta: 800000000
2217 i Mergedog         Mergedog.cpp(00479) : min cid threshold: 1000000
2219 i Mergedog         Mergedog.cpp(00480) : check unused table: 0
2220 i Mergedog         Mergedog.cpp(00481) : check compression no automerge: 0
2222 i Mergedog         Mergedog.cpp(00482) : table list sync interval: 86000
 i TraceContext     TraceContext.cpp(00702) : UserName=
 i Mergedog         Mergedog.cpp(00531) : skip register local tables: sync interval=86000 sec, last sync elapsed time=9016 sec
 i Mergedog         TableDeltaMerge.cpp(00349) : STATISTICS_SCHEDULE: DUV > 0 and DUV > 0.5*DRC = 0, parameters: drc=0.359598[Mio] duv=0.177974[Mio]
 i Mergedog         TableDeltaMerge.cpp(00349) : STATISTICS_SCHEDULE: ((THM>=256000 and (((DMS>100 or DCC>100 or DLS>1000) and DRC > MRC/100) or (DM
 i Mergedog         TableDeltaMerge.cpp(00349) : STATISTICS_SCHEDULE: UPT > 43200  and ((MMS<10000 and DMS>1000 and TMD>86400) or TMD>604800) = 0, p
```

Figure 9.7 Example Trace Ouput for Mergedog and MergedogMonitor

The first place to check for missed delta merges, however, should always be the `M_DELTA_MERGE_STATISTICS` monitoring view, as shown in Figure 9.8.

	TYPE	SCHEMA_NAME	TABLE_NAME	MEMORY_MERGE	START_TIME	EXECUTION_TIME	MOTIVATION	SUCCESS	MERGED_DELTA_RECORDS	LAST_ERROR	ERROR_DESCRIPTION
1	MERGE	LARS	CBIG	FALSE	2014-05-14 03:12:52.221	29953	HARD	TRUE	0	0	
2	MERGE	LARS	CBIG	FALSE	2014-05-14 02:55:28.579	2	HARD	FALSE	0	2048	column store error: [2482] table optimization was nc
3	MERGE	LARS	CBIG	FALSE	2014-05-14 02:48:39.749	29548	HARD	TRUE	1000	0	
4	MERGE	LARS	CBIG	FALSE	2014-05-14 02:16:09.278	27786	HARD	TRUE	0	0	

Figure 9.8 M_DELTA_MERGE_STATISTICS View

In order to gain an overview of the delta merge activities in the system, SAP HANA Studio provides a monitoring statement in ADMINISTRATION CONSOLE • SYSTEM INFORMATION • DELTA MERGE ANALYSIS. (The output of this report requires a fixed-width character set to be properly readable; therefore, copy and paste the output to a text editor.) The overview information shown in Figure 9.9 allows you to easily spot when many delta merges were executed, how many errors were reported, what tables were merged the most often, and so on.

```
1   STATISTIC                                          VALUE
2   Merge statistics from ... to:                      2014-05-23 11:10:46 - 2014-05-23 14:55:42
3   No. of total merges (succ. / unsucc. / auto / hard) :   34(32/2/32/2)
4   Average No. of Merges per Hour:                    11
5
6   Details per hour:
7
8   Time            No. of merNo. of SucNo. of Err# auto    # hard   max time  min time  avg time  max rec   min rec   avg rec    max err   min err   avg err
9   2014-05-23 14   22      20      2       20      2        4038      0         3000      25165920  0         1143905    0         0         0
10  2014-05-23 12   1       1       0       1       0        1408300   1408300   1408300   327       327       327        0         0         0
11  2014-05-23 11   11      11      0       11      0        15        0         3         219878    120       22401      0         0         0
12
13  TOP 5 - No. of merges:
14  -----
15  20 - RLOG_TEST (LARS)
16  2 - GC_TEMP (LARS)
17  1 - HELPER_ALERT_CHECK_DISK_SPACE_LASTVALUES (_SYS_STATISTICS)
18  1 - HELPER_ALERT_CHECK_HOSTS_CPU_LASTVALUES (_SYS_STATISTICS)
19  1 - HELPER_ALERT_BLOCKED_TRANSACTIONS_PERCENTAGE_LASTVALUES (_SYS_STATISTICS)
20
21  TOP 5 - time (ms):
22  -----
23  1408300 - WIDE64K (LARS)
24  66008 - RLOG_TEST (LARS)
25  15 - STATISTICS_SCHEDULE (_SYS_STATISTICS)
26  4 - HELPER_ALERT_CHECK_DISK_SPACE_LASTVALUES (_SYS_STATISTICS)
27  3 - HELPER_ALERT_CHECK_HOSTS_CPU_LASTVALUES (_SYS_STATISTICS)
28
29  TOP 5 - No. of records merged:
30  -----
31  25165920 - RLOG_TEST (LARS)
32  219878 - STATISTICS_SCHEDULE (_SYS_STATISTICS)
33  10182 - HELPER_ALERT_COLUMN_TABLES_SIZE_GROWTH_LASTVALUES (_SYS_STATISTICS)
34  4494 - HOST_SERVICE_THREAD_SAMPLES_BASE (_SYS_STATISTICS)
35  3636 - HELPER_ALERT_CHECK_HOSTS_CPU_LASTVALUES (_SYS_STATISTICS)
```

Figure 9.9 Example Output for Delta Merge Analysis

9.2.2 Memory Merge

As explained before, SAP HANA saves the new main store after the delta merge operation is completed. This can be prevented by running the delta merge as a MEMORY_MERGE. The benefit of the memory merge is that it does not take as long and does not put I/O load during the merge onto the system. To trigger a memory merge, the following syntax has to be used:

```
MERGE DELTA OF <table>
    WITH PARAMETERS ('MEMORY_MERGE' = 'ON');
```

A possible scenario is high-volume data loading, for which it is not desirable to have the AUTOMERGE working on the table that is currently loaded. At the same time, the delta store of a table should not grow too big, for multiple reasons:

▸ A chunk of data consumes far more memory space in the delta store than it does in the main store.

▸ If the delta store grows very large, insert performance decreases.

▶ Read performance also suffers from large delta stores, because data must always be retrieved from the main and the (not-read-optimized) delta store.

▶ Delta merges run longer and need more resources if the delta is very large.

If you can control the process of a significant data load into a column table, then you can implement a procedure that alternates loading (without automerging) and explicit memory merges after each chunk. The steps for this are as follows:

1. Disable AUTOMERGE for the table to be loaded to.

2. Load data chunk #1.

3. Run MEMORY_MERGE.

4. Load data chunk #2.

5. Run MEMORY_MERGE.

6. ...

7. Load data chunk #X.

8. Run normal (persisted) MERGE.

9. Enable AUTOMERGE for the table.

It is also possible to change the automerge behavior to memory merge for selected tables. The command for this is

```
ALTER TABLE <table_name> DISABLE PERSISTED MERGE
```

This setting should be used with extreme care, because the new main store will only be written to disk when the table is unloaded from memory. In the case of a system crash, the main store has to be completely rebuilt by recovery of log information, which can take a long time.

9.2.3 Smart Merge

Another optimization to prevent overexcessive merging is the smart merge. The smart merge had been introduced for SAP BW on SAP HANA but is suitable for any application that loads data in a controlled way. The idea is that when the application manages all data loads (all INSERT, UPDATE, UPSERT, and DELETE commands), then the table really does not need to be monitored for automerge. Also, it is not desirable to have automerge running on tables that the application is currently loading data into. Instead, the application can tell SAP HANA whenever a data-load activity is finished.

SAP HANA then applies a separate merge-decision function to evaluate whether a merge is actually required and performs it if necessary. This way, the application does not need to know about the technical details of the table storage but is still able to flexibly indicate when a merge would not interfere with the application logic.

To use the smart merge in your own code, disable automerge for the tables in question: ALTER TABLE ... DISABLE AUTOMERGE.

Afterwards, the smart merge can be used for this table:

```
MERGE DELTA OF <table_name>
        WITH PARAMETERS ('SMART_MERGE' = 'ON');
```

If required, the smart merge parameter can also be combined with the memory merge parameter:

```
MERGE DELTA OF <table_name>
        WITH PARAMETERS ('SMART_MERGE' = 'ON',
                         'MEMORY_MERGE' = 'ON' );
```

9.2.4 Hard and Forced Merge

Despite automerge being active for most tables, sometimes we may want to manually trigger a delta merge. This can be done via the context menu for table entries in the object navigator tree in SAP HANA Studio (*note:* selecting multiple tables by holding the ⌈Ctrl⌋ key allows you to execute a delta merge for multiple tables). (Alternatively, we can simply use the MERGE DELTA OF <table_name> command without any parameters.)

For large partitioned tables, we may have a situation in which data was only changed in one partition. To prevent the merge activity on the other partitions (thereby loading those partitions into memory, if they were unloaded), we can specify the partition name with the merge delta command:

```
MERGE DELTA OF <table_name> PART <part_id>
```

Because retrieving the partition ID for this command requires you to check M_CS_ PARTITION or M_CS_TABLES, this command is mostly used for ad hoc merge requests.

Regardless of the different options we can supply for the merge commands, all of the variants reviewed so far can only request a merge. SAP HANA will then queue the request, evaluate the decision function, and only execute the request when the table matches the decision rules and when enough system resources are available. Other merge requests that had been queued up earlier will be processed earlier.

Although this is nice to have in an automated setup, sometimes we actually want to force a delta merge, for example, to review the data compression, even if the amount of data in the table does not yet indicate a merge. For this situation, which is seldom encountered and rather academic, and for other situations there exists the "do-it-now" version of the merge command: the forced merge.

```
MERGE DELTA OF '<table_name>'
              WITH PARAMETERS ('FORCED_MERGE' = 'ON').
```

9.2.5 Critical Merge

As we have seen, SAP HANA provides many options to tune the delta merge process by setting up rules and using special parameters for the merge commands. Unfortunately, rule-based systems have the tendency to truly stick to the rules and not to what was intended with the rule set. This is no different with the delta merge in SAP HANA, and situations could occur in which tables are not getting merged, which leads to massive memory consumption and in turn out-of-memory errors or crashes. To prevent such things from happening, there is another rule in place that will trigger the so-called *critical merge*.

The goal of the critical merge is to be a safety belt for tables with a delta store so large that a delta merge operation would require more memory than the system could provide. As the worst case for memory usage during the delta merge is twice the size of the unmerged main and delta store, the hard technical limit would be 50% of the available memory in a single indexserver process. Approaching that size of a table would require all other tables to be unloaded from memory—a situation that is practically system downtime.

The critical merge decision function is set by default and should not be changed.

9.3 Partitioning and Distributing Tables

SAP HANA is designed to process large amounts of data with high speed. All data resides in memory and is immediately accessible. Yet, the very well-known option to partition tables into smaller units of storage is not only available but vital to SAP HANA.

Table partitioning in SAP HANA can serve multiple purposes:

- ▶ Distributing data within one table over multiple nodes
- ▶ Improving data-loading speed (multiple partitions can be worked on at the same time)
- ▶ Allowing for easy disposal of data by the means of dropping partitions instead of deleting single records
- ▶ Avoiding the two-billion record limitation of column store tables
- ▶ Reducing the resource requirement for performing delta merges on recently changed data
- ▶ Allowing unused data to not be loaded into memory, leaving resources available to other uses
- ▶ Improving performance in queries by allowing additional parallel and partition pruning
- ▶ Improving performance of statements spanning multiple tables by keeping related partitions of different tables together on the same node

SAP HANA provides different ways to partition tables, of which each way supports one or more purposes, but no partitioning method supports all of them at once. As of SAP HANA SPS 8, the following partitioning schemes are available: round-robin partitioning, hash partitioning, range partitioning, and multilevel partitioning. In this section, we'll offer a discussion of each. We'll conclude with discussions of three other major concepts related to portioning: partition pruning, repartitioning, and colocated partitioning.

9.3.1 Round-Robin Partitioning

Round-robin partitioning occurs when INSERT data is distributed over all partitions by simply storing every record in a different partition than the record before. Partitions are not necessarily filled sequentially. Instead, data gets distributed more evenly the more data is inserted.

There are a few disadvantages to round-robin partitioning:

- ▶ Whenever records need to be retrieved, all partitions need to be accessed, because it is not possible to know upfront which partition holds the records we are interested in.

- It is not possible to determine which partitions do not contain the records without actually accessing the partitions.

- The table must not have a primary key constraint.

There is also one major advantage:

- The equal distribution of records over the partitions does not depend on the data that is inserted; even very monotonous data sets can be evenly spread over all partitions.

Round-robin partitioning is appropriate when data-loading performance is critical and the data, once loaded, will typically be used in its entirety for the queries.

In order to partition a table round-robin style, the CREATE TABLE or ALTER TABLE command must be used with an appropriate partition by clause as shown for ALTER TABLE in Listing 9.1.

```
// Partition table my_tab into four partitions with
// round-robin partitioning
ALTER TABLE my_tab PARTITION BY ROUNDROBIN PARTITIONS 4;
```

Listing 9.1 Example for Round-Robin Partitioning

As the round-robin partitioning is entirely independent of the data content, it is not necessary to specify a column on which to base the partitioning.

9.3.2 Hash Partitioning

Hash partitioning uses a group of columns, the partitioning key, to determine the partition into which any record should be stored. The trick here is that the partitioning key is evaluated by a hash function. This hash function guarantees that the same output for the same input will be generated every time and that only output values within a specific range of values will be generated. This means that the number of possible output values is guaranteed to be limited to the number of partitions.

A very simple example for a hash function is the modulo operator that returns the integer part of a remainder for a division. Using the mod function in SQL, we can easily check how data would be distributed with different column combinations for the partitioning key in a hash-partitioned table.

367

In the example shown in Figure 9.10, we use the `bintohex` function to turn the character data in column `BBB`, the column we want to use as the partitioning key, into a numeric value. This numeric value is then used with the `mod` function for the divisor 4, because we want to check the data distribution over 4 partitions. All values of `BBB` are equal, and therefore all records will be placed into the same partition. This is not the equal data distribution we wanted to achieve.

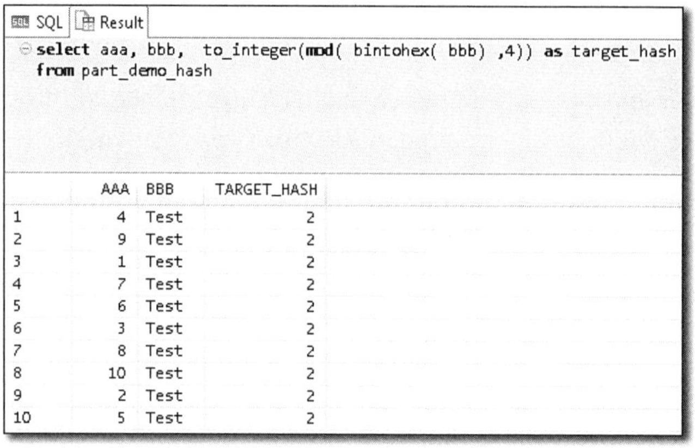

```
SQL  Result
select aaa, bbb,  to_integer(mod( bintohex( bbb) ,4)) as target_hash
from part_demo_hash
```

	AAA	BBB	TARGET_HASH
1	4	Test	2
2	9	Test	2
3	1	Test	2
4	7	Test	2
5	6	Test	2
6	3	Test	2
7	8	Test	2
8	10	Test	2
9	2	Test	2
10	5	Test	2

Figure 9.10 Simulating Hash-Partitioning Data Distribution with the mod() Operator

To have the data spread more evenly over all partitions, we need to include another column into the partitioning key, `AAA` in this case. Because `AAA` is a unique sequence, it will ensure that the data now will be spread over the partitions evenly, as shown in Figure 9.11.

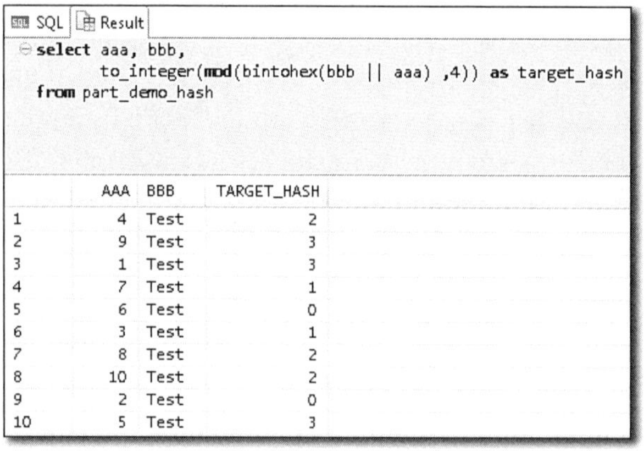

```
SQL  Result
select aaa, bbb,
       to_integer(mod(bintohex(bbb || aaa) ,4)) as target_hash
from part_demo_hash
```

	AAA	BBB	TARGET_HASH
1	4	Test	2
2	9	Test	3
3	1	Test	3
4	7	Test	1
5	6	Test	0
6	3	Test	1
7	8	Test	2
8	10	Test	2
9	2	Test	0
10	5	Test	3

Figure 9.11 Simulating Hash-Partitioning Data Distribution with Multicolumn Partition Key

By changing the SELECT statement of our simulation example a little bit, we can even get a prediction of how many records will end up in each partition (Figure 9.12).

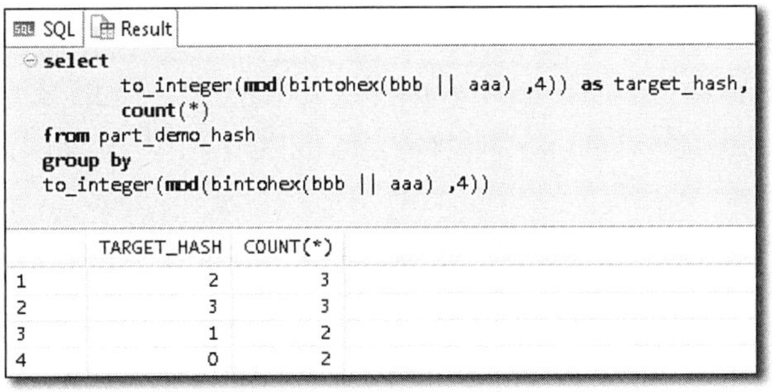

```
SQL  Result
select
        to_integer(mod(bintohex(bbb || aaa) ,4)) as target_hash,
        count(*)
  from part_demo_hash
  group by
  to_integer(mod(bintohex(bbb || aaa) ,4))

       TARGET_HASH  COUNT(*)
1              2        3
2              3        3
3              1        2
4              0        2
```

Figure 9.12 Simulating Hash-Partitioning Data Distribution, Record Count per Partition

Before actually performing the partitioning, it is recommended that you perform some analysis of the data distribution and simulate the outcome. Performing the partitioning on our example table shows that the simulation was not 100% accurate but close enough for all practical purposes. This is shown in Listing 9.2 and Figure 9.13.

```
alter table part_demo_hash
          partition by HASH (bbb, aaa) partitions 4;

select part_id, record_count
from m_cs_tables
where table_name = 'PART_DEMO_HASH';
```

Listing 9.2 Partitioning a Table with Hash Partitioning

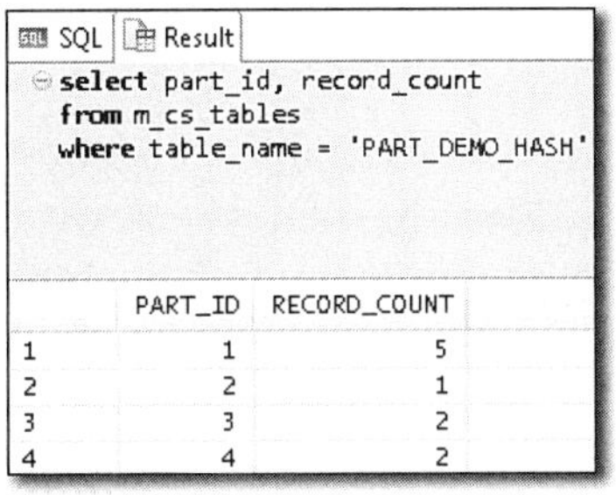

```
SQL  Result
select part_id, record_count
  from m_cs_tables
  where table_name = 'PART_DEMO_HASH'




       PART_ID  RECORD_COUNT
1         1           5
2         2           1
3         3           2
4         4           2
```

Figure 9.13 Actual Hash Partitioning Result

In addition, by applying the hash function to the partitioning key data, SAP HANA can compute in which partition the corresponding record is stored without having to access any partition. This can be very beneficial, especially when table partitions are spread across multiple nodes. Also, this feature is used during query execution to exclude partitions from processing that cannot contain the requested data (partition pruning).

As a downside, the hash function does not even-out skewed data to equally distribute data. Instead, if many records share the same values in the partitioning key columns, then these records will all be stored in the same partition.

9.3.3 Range Partitioning

With range partitioning, single values or value ranges of the partitioning key are explicitly assigned to a specific partition. This partitioning strategy allows for an indirect control of which partition a query should run on by providing a `where` condition that only includes values stored in the partition.

Also, with range partitioning, partition-level operations such as adding or dropping partitions can be directly mapped to application-level data. That way, it is easily possible to add a partition, for example, to store the data for sales transactions that are going to happen next quarter. The same is true for deleting, for example, the transaction data from ten years ago; simply dropping the corresponding partitions will remove that data from the table.

As with hash partitioning, the distribution of data over the partitions is completely dependent on the data distribution for the partitioning key. Typically, data clusters that make sense from an application point of view, such as time or date information, product groups, material types, sales channels, and so on, have skewed data distribution. Therefore, checking the data distribution of the partitioning key is important before implementing partitioning.

The syntax for range partitioning is shown in Listing 9.3. The partitioning must always be based on the values of the partition expression. This expression can be a column or one from a set of supported transformations of a column; in our case, we use the year calculated on the fly from a date field. A partition can either contain all entries for a single value of the partition expression or a range of values. You can optionally prepare a rest partition for all records that cannot be assigned to one of the partitions.

```
// Create the table for this example
CREATE TABLE my_tab_2 (
  CUSTOMER NVARCHAR(10),
```

```
    ARTICLE NVARCHAR(10),
    TX_DATE DATE,
    QTY_SOLD INTEGER,
    PRIMARY KEY (CUSTOMER, ARTICLE, DATE) );
// Partition the table by range partitioning on field YEAR.
// We create one partition for the years 2000 to 2012,
// one partition each for the years 2013 and 2014,
// and one partition for all other entries.
ALTER TABLE my_tab_2 PARTITION BY RANGE (YEAR(TX_DATE))
        ( PARTITION 2000 <= VALUES < 2013,
          PARTITION 2013,
          PARTITION 2014,
          PARTITION OTHERS);
```

Listing 9.3 Example for Range Partitioning

9.3.4 Multilevel Partitioning

A partial remedy to the mentioned limitations of the different partitioning options is *multilevel partitioning*, which is simply the combination of two different types of partitioning. Very often, the HASH-RANGE partitioning scheme is used when the data should be evenly spread across different nodes; a time-based condition is used most of the time the data is accessed. In multilevel partitioning, SAP HANA is able to skip the first level of partitioning and only evaluate the second level for a query—given that the selection criteria are provided in the right way.

We give an example of this partitioning type as the basis for the next topic: partition pruning.

9.3.5 Partition Pruning

One very important aspect of partitioning is that it allows the database to reduce the data set to be searched in a query, if the system can unambiguously determine from the query restrictions which partitions may return data and which ones may not. This so-called *partition pruning* is only possible for hash and range partitioning; in round-robin partitioning, the system is oblivious to the data content in the partitions.

Partition pruning can also be relevant for write operations if not all partitions of a table are loaded into main memory at the beginning of the write process. The database can selectively only load those partitions into main memory that are needed for this operation. The writing itself only touches the delta store. For the subsequent delta merge, the main store also must be loaded. Partition-wise loading works for both the main and the delta store.

In the following example, we use a table partitioned with HASH-RANGE multilevel partitioning to demonstrate partition pruning in write and read operations. We will also point out typical query patterns that may seem appropriate for enabling partition pruning but that will not lead to partition pruning by the database. First, create a table with hash-range partitioning (Figure 9.14). Column CCC is a date column that will be used for the second-level RANGE partitioning.

	AAA	BBB	CCC
1	1	Test	2014-07-01
2	5	Test	2014-11-01
3	8	Test	2015-02-01
4	7	Test	2015-01-01
5	10	Test	2015-04-01
6	4	Test	2014-10-01
7	6	Test	2014-12-01
8	3	Test	2014-09-01
9	2	Test	2014-08-01
10	9	Test	2015-03-01

Figure 9.14 HASH-RANGE Partition Example Initial State

The partitioning is done by the statement given in Listing 9.4, assigning 4 HASH partitions on level 1 based on column AAA and three RANGE partitions on the YEAR component of the date column CCC. Partition OTHERS is there to cater for data of other years; we do not have separate partitions for them yet.

```
alter table part_demo_hash_range
    partition by HASH (aaa) partitions 4,
                    RANGE ( YEAR(ccc) )
                        (PARTITION VALUE = '2014',
                        PARTITION VALUE = '2015',
                        PARTITION OTHERS);
```

Listing 9.4 Example of Multilevel Partitioning

The next step in our example is to unload all partitions and to insert one record (Listing 9.5). We then verify that not all partitions need to be loaded into main memory when inserting data into the table (Figure 9.15).

```
unload PART_DEMO_HASH_RANGE;

insert into PART_DEMO_HASH_RANGE
```

```
     values (12, 'TESTDATA', date'2014-06-01');
// Now, we check which partitions had been loaded to
// memory in order to store the record
select part_id, record_count, loaded
from m_cs_tables
where table_name = 'PART_DEMO_HASH_RANGE';
```

Listing 9.5 Testing Partition Pruning for Data Insertion

```
▦ SQL  ⊟ Result
⊝select part_id, record_count, loaded
  from m_cs_tables
  where table_name = 'PART_DEMO_HASH_RANGE'


        PART_ID   RECORD_COUNT   LOADED
1          1              1      NO
2          2              0      NO
3          3              0      NO
4          4              1      NO
5          5              1      NO
6          6              0      NO
7          7              0      NO
8          8              2      NO
9          9              0      NO
10         10             5      PARTIALLY
11         11             1      NO
12         12             0      NO
```

Figure 9.15 HASH-RANGE Partition Example: Partition-Loading State after INSERT

As you can see, only one partition has been touched by the INSERT. This also means that later on only this partition will have to perform a delta merge. After unloading the partitions again, we now SELECT the record that we inserted by specifying the whole partitioning key set; the where clause of our query restricts data retrieval in such a way that the database can determine which partitions may contain data to be returned and which ones cannot. We call this a *fully qualified* SELECT. Our query will retrieve exactly one record, which will obviously be in just one partition. The interesting question is whether or not the partition pruning will work, that is, whether or not the system will in fact only load this one partition into main memory. Our test query is given in Listing 9.6, and the loaded state of the partitions after running the query is shown in Figure 9.16.

```
select * from PART_DEMO_HASH_RANGE
where aaa = 12
and ccc = date'2014-06-01';
```

Listing 9.6 Fully Qualified SELECT to Test Partition Pruning

```
SQL  Result
 select part_id, record_count, loaded
   from m_cs_tables
   where table_name = 'PART_DEMO_HASH_RANGE'
```

	PART_ID	RECORD_COUNT	LOADED
1	1	1	NO
2	2	0	PARTIALLY
3	3	0	PARTIALLY
4	4	1	NO
5	5	1	NO
6	6	0	PARTIALLY
7	7	0	PARTIALLY
8	8	2	NO
9	9	0	PARTIALLY
10	10	5	PARTIALLY
11	11	1	NO
12	12	0	PARTIALLY

Figure 9.16 Verifying Partition Loading after Test Query

This time, it seems that a lot more partitions have been touched. But do not be fooled; only empty partitions have been touched in addition to the actual relevant partition (PART_ID 10). We can use the PlanViz tool (see Chapter 15) to verify that only data from partition 10 has been accessed, as shown in Figure 9.17; the query execution contains searches on partition 10 and its delta store.

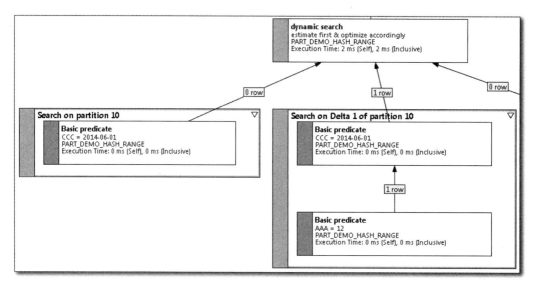

Figure 9.17 HASH-RANGE Partition Example: PlanViz Output for Fully Qualified SELECT

As an additional check on the partition pruning functionality, it is possible to activate the PARTITIONING trace with trace level INFO or DEBUG. For our example, this generates the (reformatted) output shown in Listing 9.7.

```
d partitioning      Pruning.cpp(00510) :
Pruning for index LARS:PART_DEMO_HASH_RANGE (760):
considering part(s) 10 only.
Partition spec is HASH 4 AAA; RANGE year(CCC) 2014,2015,*.
Query values are (((<UNKNOWN> == 12)
              AND (<UNKNOWN> == 2014-06-01)).
```

Listing 9.7 Result of Partition Trace for Fully Qualified SELECT

You can see that partition pruning works efficiently when all the partition key information is available. Next, let's perform a partly qualified selection just based on the year of the records and check which partitions are touched this time (Listing 9.8). Again, we have unloaded the partitions first.

```
select * from PART_DEMO_HASH_RANGE
where
year(ccc) = 2014;
```

Listing 9.8 Partly Qualified SELECT

This time all partitions have been touched (Figure 9.18), which can also be confirmed with PlanViz (not shown) and the PARTITIONING trace (Listing 9.9). This is surprising, as only four partitions can contain data for the selected year.

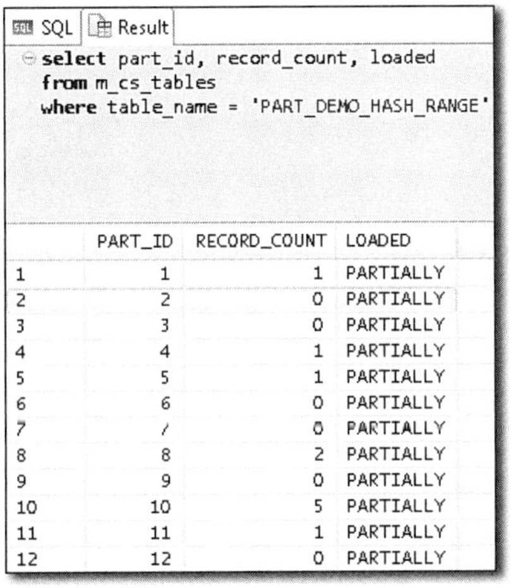

Figure 9.18 Checking Partition Loading after Partly Qualified SELECT

```
d partitioning      Pruning.cpp(00490) :
Pruning for index LARS:PART_DEMO_HASH_RANGE (760):
all parts have to be considered.
Partition spec is HASH 4 AAA; RANGE year(CCC) 2014,2015,*.
Query values are .
Starting inlist-pruning for LARS:PART_DEMO_HASH_RANGE (760).
Skipping inlist-pruning since no inlist is provided..
```
Listing 9.9 Partition Trace for Partly Qualified SELECT

The difficulty for the partition pruning function within the SAP HANA optimizer here is the function expression YEAR(CCC). As of SPS 8, SAP HANA is not able to figure out that the YEAR(CCC) in the partitioning definition and the YEAR(CCC) in our query's where clause are actually the same. To enable the system to skip the first partition level, we need to provide the date range in a different form, as shown in Listing 9.10.

```
select * from PART_DEMO_HASH_RANGE
where
 CCC between date'2014-01-01' and date'2014-12-31'
```
Listing 9.10 Rewritten Partly Qualified SELECT

The PARTITIONING trace proves that this time only the relevant partitions are touched (Listing 9.11).

```
d partitioning      Pruning.cpp(00510) :
Pruning for index LARS:PART_DEMO_HASH_RANGE (760):
considering part(s) 1, 4, 7, 10 only.
Partition spec is HASH 4 AAA; RANGE year(CCC) 2014,2015,*.
Query values are ((2014-01-01 <= <UNKNOWN> >= 2014-12-31)).
```
Listing 9.11 Verifying Partition Pruning for Rewritten Partly Qualified Query

Care must also be taken concerning the data type used in the where clause. To be on the safe side, ensure that the data type matches the data type used in the partitioning function. Something as similar to the working example shown previously as the following can lead to much worse partition pruning, as shown in Listing 9.12.

```
// Partly qualified query with not matching data type in where
// clause:
select * from PART_DEMO_HASH_RANGE
where
 CCC between to_timestamp('2014-01-01') and '2014-12-31'
```

```
// Output in partitioning trace:
d partitioning     Pruning.cpp(00510) :
Pruning for index LARS:PART_DEMO_HASH_RANGE (760):
considering part(s) 1, 3, 4, 6, 7, 9, 10, 12 only.
Partition spec is HASH 4 AAA; RANGE year(CCC) 2014,2015,*.
Query values are ((<UNKNOWN> <= 2014-12-31)).
```

Listing 9.12 Partly Qualified Query with Unmatching Data Type in Where Clause

This time, only partitions 2, 5, 8, and 11 could be eliminated, because only the upper border condition of the range made it to the pruning operation.

Whatever your primary objective is that you want to achieve with partitioning, make sure to check the data distribution of your source data first and to check the actual query processing with PlanViz (see Chapter 12) or the PARTITIONING trace on trace level INFO or DEBUG.

9.3.6 Repartitioning

Repartitioning of tables simply means changing the partitioning schema of a table. For most partitioning schemes, this is achieved with an ALTER TABLE ... PARTITION statement that describes what the new partitioning scheme should look like. For RANGE partitioning schemes, it is possible to specifically DROP or ADD partitions.

Typically, SAP HANA creates the new partitioning scheme by copying the whole table into a new table structure with the new partition layout. This can easily take a lot of time and uses a lot of system resources. Luckily, there are two exceptions to this that improve the situation for the most critical scenarios.

In case the number of HASH partitions needs to be increased—for example, because new hosts have been added to the scale-out cluster—it is important to always specify the new number of partitions as a multiple of the old number of partitions. That way, new partitions will be created colocated with the source partition, and the data copy does not need to transport data via the network. The same principle applies when reducing the number of partitions.

Technically, it is also possible to create partitioned tables with only one partition—a common situation when the partitioning specification uses the GET_NUM_SERVERS function and the table was created on a single node system. In order to turn those tables into proper unpartitioned tables, the command ALTER TABLE <table_name> MERGE PARTITIONS is used.

A caveat here is that for HASH-partitioned tables with only one partition, the command will return an error, as shown in Listing 9.13.

```
alter table part_demo_hash merge partitions;
```

```
Could not execute 'alter table part_demo_hash merge partitions' in 37 ms 12 µs .
SAP DBTech JDBC:
[2048]: column store error: fail to alter partition:
[2593] Error during split/merge operation;
Source and target partition spec are identical.
Aborting execution.,object=LARS:PART_DEMO_HASHen
```

Listing 9.13 Merge Error for Hash-Partitioned Tables with Only a Single Partition

The workaround for this is to set the number of partitions to two first, and execute the `merge partitions` afterwards.

Alternatively, the table data could be copied into a table without partitioning; afterwards the original table could be dropped and the new table renamed to the name of the original table. This will typically be quicker than the workaround, because the data has to be copied only once, but all dependent objects of the original table will either be dropped or invalidated and will eventually require reactivation.

9.3.7 Colocated Partitions and Table Replicas

With scale-out systems and the shared nothing approach—a table or table partition is always only present on one node at any given time—that SAP HANA uses to distribute the database over many nodes, a new kind of problem can occur. What if a query accesses a table that had been partitioned and distributed over all the nodes and needs to join to another partitioned table? It would be great if SAP HANA could run a partition-wise join, computing the join results locally between the partitions on each node. A similar scenario would be the join between a partitioned, distributed table with a nonpartitioned table. It would be great to be able to process the join locally, especially when partition pruning would allow running the query execution on a single node anyway. SAP HANA provides two features to help with these scenarios.

Colocated Creation of Dependent Tables

If two or more tables are partitioned by the same partitioning key and the data processing should happen partition-wise, then the tables should be created within the same transaction (AUTOCOMMIT = OFF). SAP HANA will recognize the shared partitioning pattern and place every matching partition of each table on the same node.

Listing 9.14 provides an example of the creation of colocated partitioned tables.

```
-- Start an SQL session with AUTOCOMMIT OFF.
create column table header
       (head_id integer primary key, header_info varchar(30))
        partition by HASH (head_id) partitions get_num_servers();

create column table line_items
       (head_id integer, line_seq integer, line_info varchar(30),
                                   primary key (head_id, line_seq))
        partition by HASH (head_id) partitions get_num_servers();
commit;

select table_name, part_id, host,port
from m_cs_tables
where table_name in ('HEADER', 'LINE_ITEMS',)
order by part_id;
```

Listing 9.14 Creation of Colocated Partitioned Tables

In Figure 9.19, it is easy to see how each partition of table LINE_ITEMS is placed on the same node as the corresponding partition of table HEADER.

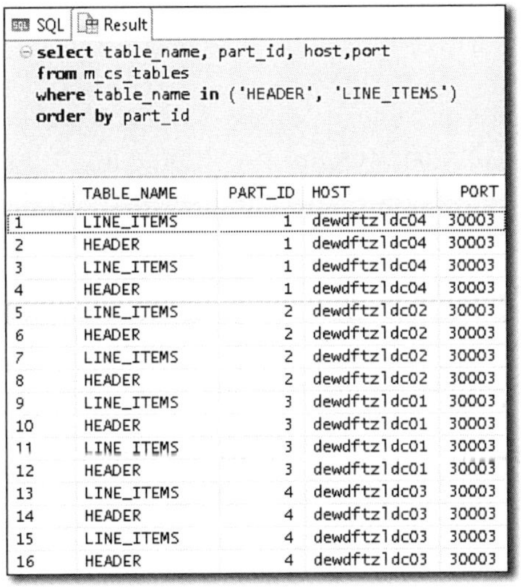
SQL | Result

```
select table_name, part_id, host,port
from m_cs_tables
where table_name in ('HEADER', 'LINE_ITEMS')
order by part_id
```

	TABLE_NAME	PART_ID	HOST	PORT
1	LINE_ITEMS	1	dewdftzldc04	30003
2	HEADER	1	dewdftzldc04	30003
3	LINE_ITEMS	1	dewdftzldc04	30003
4	HEADER	1	dewdftzldc04	30003
5	LINE_ITEMS	2	dewdftzldc02	30003
6	HEADER	2	dewdftzldc02	30003
7	LINE_ITEMS	2	dewdftzldc02	30003
8	HEADER	2	dewdftzldc02	30003
9	LINE_ITEMS	3	dewdftzldc01	30003
10	HEADER	3	dewdftzldc01	30003
11	LINE_ITEMS	3	dewdftzldc01	30003
12	HEADER	3	dewdftzldc01	30003
13	LINE_ITEMS	4	dewdftzldc03	30003
14	HEADER	4	dewdftzldc03	30003
15	LINE_ITEMS	4	dewdftzldc03	30003
16	HEADER	4	dewdftzldc03	30003

Figure 9.19 Example for Colocated Table Creation

After inserting some dummy data, you can now try and see if the node local join would work; see Listing 9.15.

```
select
    h.head_id, l.line_seq, l.line_info
from
    header h inner join line_items l
    on h.head_id = l.head_id
where h.head_id = 1;
```

Listing 9.15 Selecting Data from Colocated Partitioned Tables

As PlanViz clearly shows (Figure 9.20), only the first partition of each table, residing on the same node, is touched for this join.

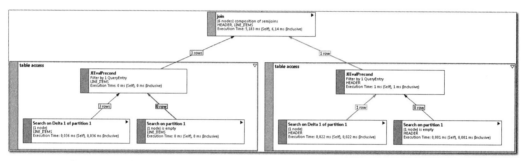

Figure 9.20 PlanViz Output for Partition-Wise Join of Colocated Tables

Table Replicas

We can easily extend our example with another table, MASTERDATA, that cannot be partitioned by the same pattern. In fact, this table is not partitioned at all but needs to be joined to the LINE_ITEMS table. In order to avoid cross-node join execution, table replicas replicate the same table data to each node. That way, the MASTERDATA table is available locally on every node and the joins can be performed locally.

To set up table replicas for tables, the following command can be used:

```
ALTER TABLE <table_name> ADD REPLICA AT ALL LOCATIONS
```

The replicas will show up as partitions in the monitoring views but will contain the same data on all nodes.

Table replicas come with some important restrictions that need to be considered before using them:

▸ Because the replication is performed synchronously at the time at which the data is changed, the update/insert/delete performance on the replicated table will be decreased.

▸ The overall memory consumption will increase, because every replica is a full copy of the original table.

▸ Table replication does not work for partitioned tables; thus tables with replicas can contain a maximum of two billion rows.

▸ SAP BW on SAP HANA does not support table replication for SAP BW tables.

9.4   Optimizing Table Distribution and Partitioning

To ease the handling of table distribution and partitioning, SAP HANA provides the landscape redistribution function. In order to illustrate working with the landscape redistribution, we walk through a simple example. The setup of our example is simple and consists of four tables in two groups. For our example, the actual table structure does not matter, so all of the tables share the same structure. This is shown in Listing 9.16.

```
create schema tabledist;
set schema tabledist;

create column table fact_cube_1
("REQUEST"      NVARCHAR(30) DEFAULT '' NOT NULL ,
 "DATAPAKID"    NVARCHAR(6) DEFAULT '000000' NOT NULL ,
 "RECORD"       INTEGER  DEFAULT 0 NOT NULL ,
 "RECORDMODE"   NVARCHAR(1) DEFAULT '' NOT NULL ,
 "/BIC/Z1"      NVARCHAR(2) DEFAULT '0' NOT NULL ,
 "/BIC/Z10"     NVARCHAR(8) DEFAULT '00000000' NOT NULL ,
 "/BIC/Z100"    NVARCHAR(8) DEFAULT '00000000' NOT NULL ,
 "/BIC/Z1000"   NVARCHAR(8) DEFAULT '00000000' NOT NULL ,
 "/BIC/ZDATE"   NVARCHAR(8) DEFAULT '00000000' NOT NULL ,
 "/BIC/ZAMOUNT1" DECIMAL(17,3)  DEFAULT 0 NOT NULL ,
 "/BIC/ZAMOUNT2" DECIMAL(17,3)  DEFAULT 0 NOT NULL ,
 "/BIC/ZAMOUNT3" DECIMAL(17,3)  DEFAULT 0 NOT NULL ,
 PRIMARY KEY ("REQUEST", "RECORD"));
```

```
create column table fact_cube_2 like fact_cube_1;
create column table dso_cube_1 like fact_cube_1;
create column table dso_cube_2 like fact_cube_1;
```
Listing 9.16 Creating the Tables for the Example

The idea of this example is that there are two different kinds of tables in our application: fact tables and DSO tables. For each kind, we want to be able to define different rules for automatic distribution and repartitioning.

However, even though the tables are of different kinds, they might belong to the same object group in the application. We could, for example, say that the dso_cube_1 table and the fact_cube_1 table belong together, because they both belong to the objects that make up cube_1, including the data flows.

Because we expect data flows from table dso_cube_1 to fact_cube_1, it might be good to keep partitions of those tables together on the same SAP HANA node. To indicate that the tables belong to certain groups and types, SAP HANA provides extended ALTER TABLE SQL syntax. This is shown in Listing 9.17.

```
alter table dso_cube_1 set group type "CUSTOM_DSO";
alter table dso_cube_1 set group name "CUBE_1";

alter table dso_cube_2 set group type "CUSTOM_DSO";
alter table dso_cube_2 set group name "CUBE_2";

alter table fact_cube_1 set group type "CUSTOM_FACT";
alter table fact_cube_1 set group name "CUBE_1";

alter table fact_cube_2 set group type "CUSTOM_FACT";
alter table fact_cube_2 set group name "CUBE_2";
```
Listing 9.17 Defining Groups and Types for the Tables

Because we have chosen the group types and group names arbitrarily, we need to tell SAP HANA what rules should apply to tables with these group types and names. This is done by inserting the rule definition into system table _SYS_RT.TABLE_PLACEMENT, as shown in Listing 9.18. A complete description of the different parameters available for this table can be found at *https://scn.sap.com/community/hana-in-memory/blog/2013/09/03/sap-hana-landscape-redistribution-with-sp6* ("SAP HANA Landscape Redistribution with SP6").

```
-- rule for  fact tables
UPSERT "_SYS_RT"."TABLE_PLACEMENT"
( SCHEMA_NAME, TABLE_NAME, GROUP_NAME, GROUP_TYPE, SUBTYPE, MIN_ROWS_FOR_
PARTITIONING, INITIAL_PARTITIONS, REPARTITIONING_THRESHOLD, LOCATION )
VALUES
('TABLEDIST', '', '', 'CUSTOM_FACT', '', 500000, 3, 500000, 'all')
WHERE SCHEMA_NAME = 'TABLEDIST'
AND TABLE_NAME = ''
AND GROUP_NAME= ''
AND SUBTYPE = '';

-- rule for dso tables
UPSERT "_SYS_RT"."TABLE_PLACEMENT"
( SCHEMA_NAME, TABLE_NAME, GROUP_NAME, GROUP_TYPE, SUBTYPE, MIN_ROWS_FOR_
PARTITIONING, INITIAL_PARTITIONS, REPARTITIONING_THRESHOLD, LOCATION )
VALUES
('TABLEDIST', '', '', 'CUSTOM_DSO', '', 10000, 3, 10000, 'all')
WHERE SCHEMA_NAME = 'TABLEDIST'
AND TABLE_NAME = ''
AND GROUP_NAME= 'CUBE_1'
AND SUBTYPE = '';
```

Listing 9.18 Defining Distribution Rules for Custom Table Groups

Wherever we enter an empty string or a NULL into the rule record, it indicates a match on all tables, so we do not, for example, have any restriction on the actual table name in our example. The rules we set up here are:

▶ For tables in schema TABLEDIST with the group type CUSTOM_FACT, the minimum number of records the table can have before it gets partitioned into more than one partition is 50,000. When the table gets partitioned, an initial number of three partitions will be created, irrespective of whether or not the actual number of records fills up these partitions. Later partitions will be added when existing partitions reach the 50,000 records mark.

▸ For tables with the group type CUSTOM_DSO, the minimum number of records in the table is 10,000, and for each subsequent 10,000 records a new partition will be created.

▸ These are of course just dummy values in order to demonstrate the feature. SAP BW and SAP Business Suite on SAP HANA typically use much larger values, as explained in SAP Note 1899817, SAP Note 1781986, and SAP Note 1908075.

> **Note**
>
> Up to revision 74 of SAP HANA Studio, there is no option to review the TABLE_GROUP data via the UI.

SAP HANA comes with a set of default database parameters for the redistribution; however, SAP Note 1958216 provides revision-dependent recommendations on how to set the parameters. For our revision 70 scale-out system, the commands to setup the parameters are shown in Listing 9.19.

```
ALTER SYSTEM ALTER CONFIGURATION ('indexserver.ini','system') SET ('table_
redist','balance_by_execution_count') = 'false' WITH RECONFIGURE;
ALTER SYSTEM ALTER CONFIGURATION ('indexserver.ini','system') SET ('table_
redist','balance_by_execution_time') = 'false' WITH RECONFIGURE;
ALTER SYSTEM ALTER CONFIGURATION ('indexserver.ini','system') SET ('table_
redist','balance_by_memuse') = 'false' WITH RECONFIGURE;
ALTER SYSTEM ALTER CONFIGURATION ('indexserver.ini','system') SET ('table_
redist','balance_by_part_id') = 'false' WITH RECONFIGURE;
ALTER SYSTEM ALTER CONFIGURATION ('indexserver.ini','system') SET ('table_
redist','balance_by_partnum') = 'true' WITH RECONFIGURE;
ALTER SYSTEM ALTER CONFIGURATION ('indexserver.ini','system') SET ('table_
redist','balance_by_partnum_weight') = '1' WITH RECONFIGURE;
ALTER SYSTEM ALTER CONFIGURATION ('indexserver.ini','system') SET ('table_
redist','balance_by_rows') = 'true' WITH RECONFIGURE;
ALTER SYSTEM ALTER CONFIGURATION ('indexserver.ini','system') SET ('table_
redist','balance_by_rows_weight') = '2' WITH RECONFIGURE;
ALTER SYSTEM ALTER CONFIGURATION ('indexserver.ini','system') SET ('table_
redist','balance_by_table_classification') = 'false' WITH RECONFIGURE;
ALTER SYSTEM ALTER CONFIGURATION ('indexserver.ini','system') SET ('table_
redist','balance_by_table_subclassification') = 'false' WITH RECONFIGURE;
```

Listing 9.19 Redistribution Parameter Setup

Note that all of the parameters relevant to the redistribution are found in the same area of the configuration files: indexserver.ini • [table_redist].

To start the example, all you need to do is provide some data for the tables. Because the actual data does not matter here, generate some random data for one table first and copy different volumes of that data over to the other tables (Listing 9.20).

```
create sequence demoseq cache 5000;

insert into FACT_CUBE_1  (
    select top 1500000
    'xyz10', 'DP1', demoseq.nextval, 'X',
    to_nvarchar(to_integer(rand() *10)),
    to_nvarchar(to_integer(mod(rand() * 100000, 10))   ),
    to_nvarchar(to_integer(mod(rand() * 100000, 100))  ),
    to_nvarchar(to_integer(mod(rand() * 100000, 1000)) ),
    '20121001',
    to_decimal (rand()*10, 17,3),
    to_decimal (rand()*10, 17,3),
    to_decimal (rand()*10, 17,3)
    from
        objects cross join objects cross join objects
    );
insert into FACT_CUBE_2 (select top 1000000 * from  FACT_CUBE_1);
insert into DSO_CUBE_1 (select top 15000000 * from FACT_CUBE_1);
insert into DSO_CUBE_2 (select top 1000000 * from  FACT_CUBE_1);
```

Listing 9.20 Dummy Data Creation

Note that the column REQUEST has a constant value; this will be important towards the end of this example. We can now manually check the locations of the four tables as well as their assignments to table group types and group names, as shown in Listing 9.21 and in Figure 9.21.

```
select * from table_groups;
```

SCHEMA_NAME	TABLE_NAME	GROUP_TYPE	SUBTYPE	GROUP_NAME
TABLEDIST	DSO_CUBE_1	CUSTOM_DSO	NULL	CUBE_1
TABLEDIST	FACT_CUBE_2	CUSTOM_FACT	NULL	CUBE_2
TABLEDIST	FACT_CUBE_1	CUSTOM_FACT	NULL	CUBE_1
TABLEDIST	DSO_CUBE_2	CUSTOM_DSO	NULL	CUBE_2

Listing 9.21 Checking on the Table Group Configuration

```
SQL  Result
select * from m_cs_tables where schema_name = 'TABLEDIST'
order by table_name
```

	HOST	PORT	SCHEMA_NAME	TABLE_NAME	PART_ID	MEMORY_SIZE_IN_TOTAL	MEMORY_SIZE_IN_MAIN	MEMORY_SIZE_IN_DELTA
1	dewdftzldc02	30003	TABLEDIST	DSO_CUBE_1	0	39917389	39892885	24504
2	dewdftzldc02	30003	TABLEDIST	DSO_CUBE_2	0	29740679	29716175	24504
3	dewdftzldc02	30003	TABLEDIST	FACT_CUBE...	0	44886773	44862269	24504
4	dewdftzldc02	30003	TABLEDIST	FACT_CUBE...	0	29739839	29715335	24504

Figure 9.21 Column Table Runtime Information, Including the Table Location (HOST)

To conveniently review the table distribution over the different nodes in a scale-out setup, SAP HANA Studio provides the SHOW TABLE DISTRIBUTION dialog. Right-clicking on the SCHEMA or TABLES entry in the navigator shows the menu in Figure 9.22.

Figure 9.22 Show Table Distribution Menu Entry

The TABLE DISTRIBUTION view itself is straightforward. Each table is represented by a row in the upper half of the list. For each host in the SAP HANA system, one column exists. In the cross-section of the table rows and the host columns, we either find - (no partition of this table on this host), x (the complete table with less than two partitions is located on this host), or a list of partition numbers of this table that are located on this host.

In Figure 9.23, we can easily see that all of the tables for this example are not partitioned, and all of them are located on the same host (`dewdftzldc02`).

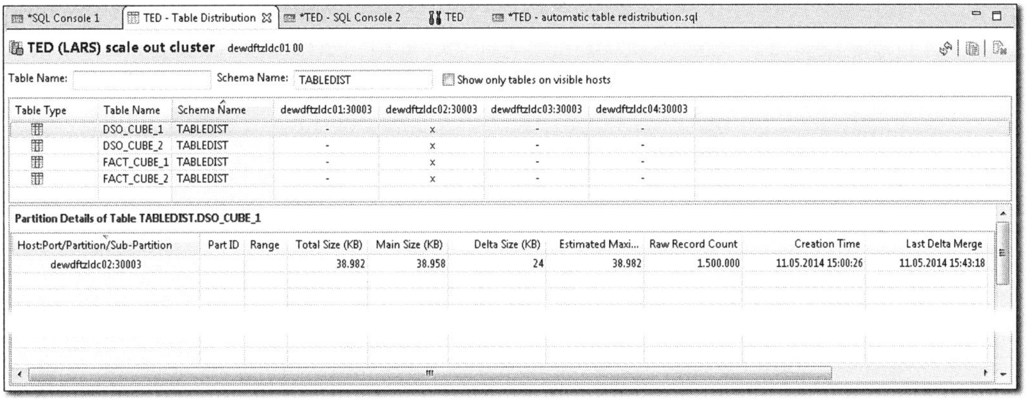

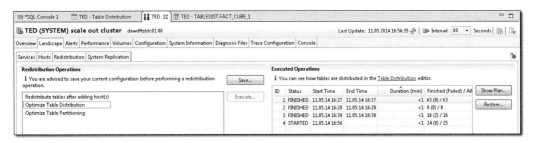

Figure 9.23 Table Distribution View

To manually partition the tables or to relocate them to a different host, we could use the context menu by right-clicking on any table in the upper list and choosing either PARTITION TABLE ... or MOVE TABLE.... This time, however, we want to leave this to SAP HANA.

The UI for the landscape redistribution can be found in SAP HANA STUDIO • ADMINISTRATION CONSOLE • LANDSCAPE REDISTRIBUTION. The view looks like that shown in Figure 9.24.

Figure 9.24 Landscape Redistribution View

The left-hand side provides the options to OPTIMIZE TABLE DISTRIBUTION, OPTIMIZE TABLE PARTITIONING, or SAVE the current setup (Figure 9.25). This last option is very important; it basically provides an undo option to the last optimization run.

That way, in case something did not work as expected, it is easy to restore the old setup.

Optimize Table Distribution will try to place the tables equally over the hosts according to the specified rules. Optimize Table Partitioning checks if tables need to be split into more partitions, given their current number of rows as a main function, but it will also move tables if specified in the rule sets.

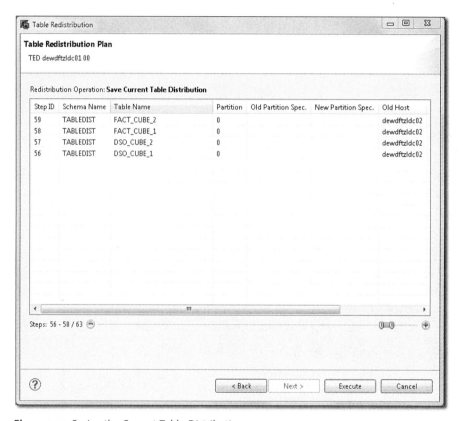

Figure 9.25 Saving the Current Table Distribution

After saving the current setup, run the Optimize Table Partitioning function to reach the dialog shown in Figure 9.26.

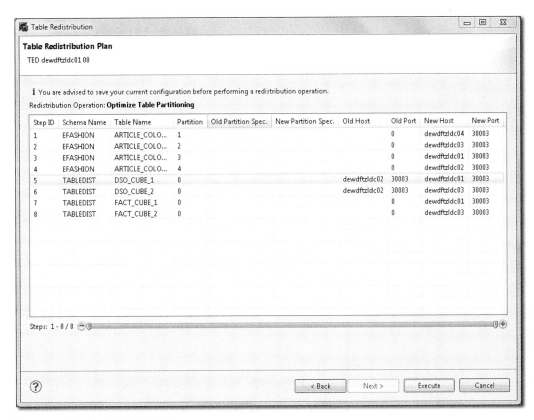

Figure 9.26 Optimize Table Partitioning

Note that the slider on the lower end of the list view only limits and selects the displayed tables in the list. It does not affect which tables are going to be processed.

The observant reader will notice that the only action the dialog is about to perform is to move tables DSO_CUBE_1 and DSO_CUBE_2 to two different hosts. No change concerning the partitioning is performed.

After clicking EXECUTE, you will find that the tables are now on different hosts (see Figure 9.27).

389

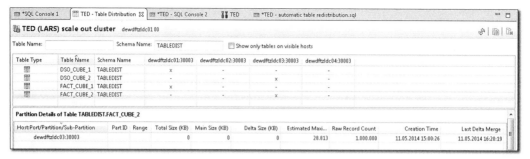

Figure 9.27 Moved but Still Nonpartitioned Tables

To have your tables partitioned and the partitions then distributed over the different hosts, you need to set up the partitioning scheme first. It is sufficient to specify just one partition for now, because you will want to use the automatic feature to create additional partitions later (Listing 9.22).

```
alter table fact_cube_1 partition by hash (REQUEST) partitions 1;
alter table fact_cube_2 partition by hash (REQUEST) partitions 1;
alter table dso_cube_1 partition by hash (REQUEST) partitions 1;
alter table dso_cube_2 partition by hash (REQUEST) partitions 1;
```

Listing 9.22 Adding an Initial Partition

Note that by creating the tables with only a single initial partition, the runtime information in M_CS_TABLES looks exactly the same as it would if a table were *not* partitioned. In order to check if a table is indeed partitioned, M_TABLES.IS_PAR-TITIONED is the relevant indicator column.

Choose the HASH-partitioning function here, because you want to achieve a rather equal distribution of data over the partitions. Also, you should expect new data loads to come in their own requests, just as in data load requests in SAP BW, so the expectation is that every other load request will be stored into a different partition. Adding the partitioning information with just one partition does not actually change the data structures in memory, so this step is finished in an instant.

Now you can restart OPTIMIZE TABLE PARTITIONING again and find that new partitions will be created (see Figure 9.28).

Step ID	Schema Name	Table Name	Partition	Old Partition Spec.	New Partition Spec.	Old Host	Old Port	New Host	New Port
1	TABLEDIST	DSO_CUBE_1			MERGE DELTA		0		0
2	TABLEDIST	DSO_CUBE_1		HASH 1 REQUEST	HASH 3 REQUEST		0		0
3	TABLEDIST	DSO_CUBE_1	1				0	dewdftzldc04	30003
4	TABLEDIST	DSO_CUBE_1	2				0	dewdftzldc03	30003
5	TABLEDIST	DSO_CUBE_1	3				0	dewdftzldc03	30003
6	TABLEDIST	DSO_CUBE_2			MERGE DELTA		0		0
7	TABLEDIST	DSO_CUBE_2		HASH 1 REQUEST	HASH 3 REQUEST		0		0
8	TABLEDIST	DSO_CUBE_2	1				0	dewdftzldc01	30003
9	TABLEDIST	DSO_CUBE_2	2				0	dewdftzldc02	30003
10	TABLEDIST	DSO_CUBE_2	3				0	dewdftzldc02	30003
11	EFASHION	ARTICLE_COLOR_LOOKUP_REP	1				0	dewdftzldc03	30003
12	EFASHION	ARTICLE_COLOR_LOOKUP_REP	2				0	dewdftzldc04	30003
13	EFASHION	ARTICLE_COLOR_LOOKUP_REP	3				0	dewdftzldc01	30003
14	EFASHION	ARTICLE_COLOR_LOOKUP_REP	4				0	dewdftzldc02	30003
15	TABLEDIST	FACT_CUBE_1	0				0	dewdftzldc04	30003
16	TABLEDIST	FACT_CUBE_2	0				0	dewdftzldc01	30003

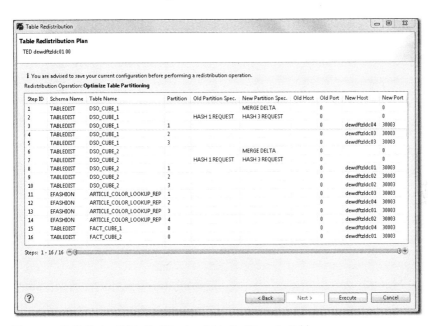

Figure 9.28 Optimize Table Partitioning Adds Partitions to Tables

Checking the result (Figure 9.29) of this run reveals that new partitions have been created, but unfortunately the new partitions are not already distributed to the planned hosts.

Table Type	Table Name	Schema Name	dewdftzldc01:30003	dewdftzldc02:30003	dewdftzldc03:30003	dewdftzldc04:30003
	DSO_CUBE_1	TABLEDIST	-	-	2, 3	1
	DSO_CUBE_2	TABLEDIST	1	2, 3	-	-
	FACT_CUBE_1	TABLEDIST	-	-	-	x
	FACT_CUBE_2	TABLEDIST	x	-	-	-

Host:Port/Partition/Sub-Partition	Part ID	Range	Total Size (KB)	Main Size (KB)	Delta Size (KB)	Estimated Maxi...	Raw Record Count	Creation Time	Last Delta Merge
dewdftzldc02:30003									
dewdftzldc01:30003									

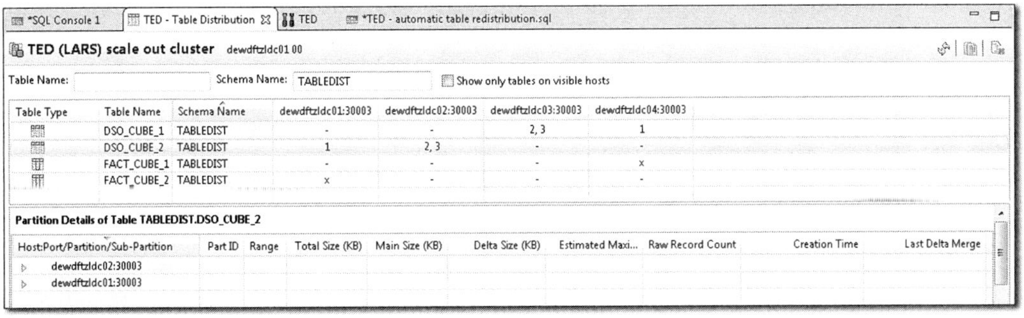

Figure 9.29 Table Partitioning and Distribution after Partitioning Optimization

To fix this, run the Optimize Table Distribution function (Figure 9.30).

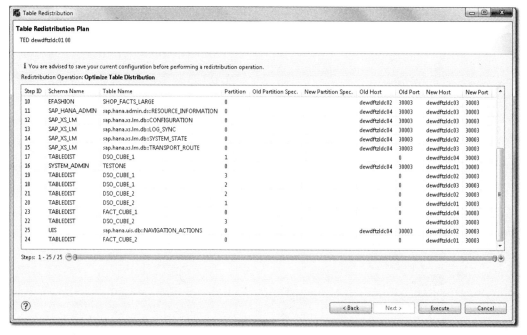

Figure 9.30 Optimize Table Distribution

After this step is finished successfully, you can review the result again (Figure 9.31). Now, the tables are partitioned, and the partitions are located on different hosts. On each of the four hosts of the example, you will find two tables or table partitions.

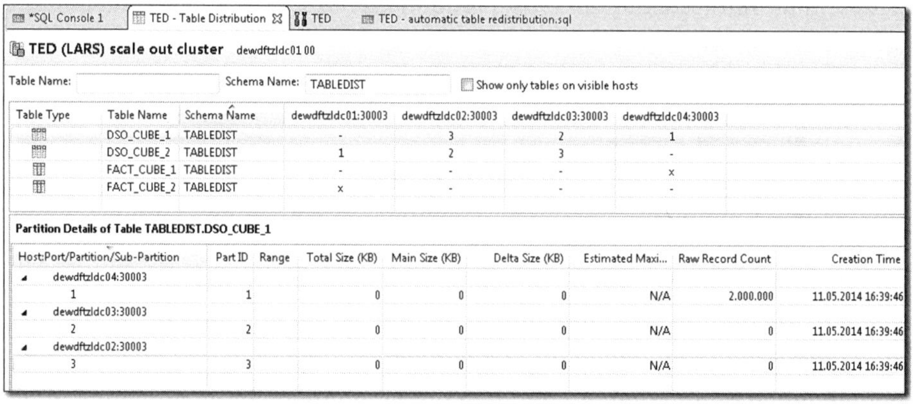

Figure 9.31 Final Table Partitioning and Distribution

Although the data seems equally distributed, it is not. Currently all our data is stored in just one of the partitions, because the data we inserted at the beginning of this example is constant for the partitioning key (REQUEST). It is as if only one large request had been loaded so far. Due to this, the result of the HASH-partitioning function for all records is the same and directs all records to the same partition. By clicking on the table row for DSO_CUBE1 on the list in the TABLE DISTRIBUTION overview, we can review the actual data distribution in the lower list.

This shows that the actual data distribution has tremendous impact on the effect of partitioning and needs to be evaluated before assumptions about what the data looks like are made. SAP HANA Studio provides a very useful tool for this: the DATA PREVIEW function, which is available in the context menu of tables in the navigator tree.

Figure 9.32 shows how conveniently one can click-through the columns of any table and review the data distribution without writing any SQL code. This is a very easy way to quickly double-check if your assumptions about data distribution in columns match reality.

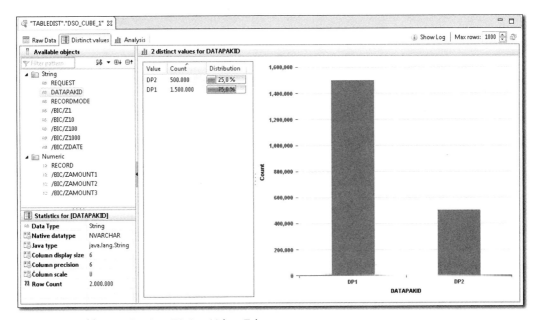

Figure 9.32 Table Data Preview, Distinct Values Tab

> **Note**
>
> Although it can be tempting to use an automatic feature like table distribution and partitioning optimization (it sounds like carefree mass data handling), we recommend that you carefully plan and test the results of using the tool.
>
> As long as not too many tables—maybe around 150 or so—are involved, it might be more efficient to manually check the memory usage on the available hosts and decide how to redistribute the table partitions based on that information.

Finally, all optimization runs can be reviewed later on, because they are stored in the SAP HANA database, as shown in Figure 9.33.

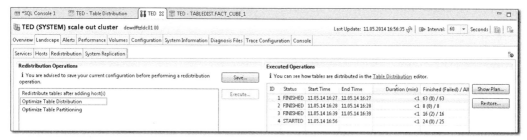

Figure 9.33 Stored Information on Past Optimization Runs

What we have done so far was to evenly distribute the available tables over all available hosts based on a specific schema. The primary goal of this is to prevent an overallocation of resources on one host while other hosts are barely used.

Optimizing the data and table distribution for query or data manipulation performance is not what the table distribution and partitioning function does. Finding the optimal partitioning scheme depends on the access pattern to the table data, for example, which columns are typically in the where clause, what the actual data distribution looks like, and so on. However, in many cases, having a consistent strategy for distributing the data over the available nodes in a more or less automatic fashion is more important than tuning the partition setup toward a very specific query scenario.

> **Further Resources**
>
> More information on table distribution and placement can be found in the *SAP HANA Administration Guide*.

For more detailed information on the setup of redistribution rules and database parameters, please see SAP Note 1958216, SAP Note 1908075, SAP Note 1899817, SAP Note 1950099, SAP Note 1819123, SAP Note 1908073, SAP Note 1908082, and SAP Note 1899817, depending on the scenario and application you are using on top of SAP HANA.

9.5   Importing and Exporting Tables

Like any other DBMS, SAP HANA offers functionality to export and import data. Technically speaking, SAP HANA can export data in two formats:

▸ Comma-separated text files (CSV)

▸ Binary files that represent the internal structures of a column store table

For row store tables, only the CSV file export is available; although it is possible to specify binary as the export type, the data will be saved as a CSV file.

The export and import can either be managed from SAP HANA Studio via a GUI or from the SQL console. When using SAP HANA Studio, the data can be exported and imported to and from the client running SAP HANA Studio, whereas the SQL console option only allows server-side export or import of target files. We recommend importing and exporting tables via the GUI from SAP HANA Studio, so that is the focus of this section. For more information about how to do this using SQL, we recommend consulting the SAP HANA SQL reference documentation, which is available at *http://help.sap.com/hana_platform/*.

9.5.1   Exporting Data

Exporting tables is straightforward with SAP HANA. The main goal is to be able to export the current state of a set of tables with or without dependent objects, that is, to move a fully working model, including data, to another SAP HANA system. (The function is not meant to substitute for proper system integration; such use cases should be addressed with tools such as SAP SLT, SAP Data Services, and the like.)

Apart from the SCRAMBLE (making the exported CSV file harder to read) and the STRIP (leaving out objects that can be generated, such as generated columns or concat attributes) options, the wizard provides a GUI for all EXPORT options (Figure 9.34).

Figure 9.34 Export Catalog Object Example: Export Options

After selecting the objects to export—just one table in this example—you can choose the export format, whether only the DDL or also the data should be exported, and if dependent objects, such as SQL views, procedures, or information models, should be included in the export.

When choosing the export format, you need to consider what should be done with the exported data. If the only purpose is to restore the exported objects into the same system again, then choosing binary will allow for the best export and import performance. In this case, the actual internal table structure will be serialized and saved into the export files. With a binary export file, the import can only be done as a create-or-replace import. It is not possible to add the rows of the exported table to an existing table. Also, the table structure must be exactly the same as the source table structure.

We also need to specify the EXPORT LOCATION. When using EXPORT TO CURRENT CLIENT, all we have to provide is an empty folder in the file system. The exported data will then be read in over the network via the JDBC connection of SAP HANA Studio and written into the files. The EXPORT TO CURRENT CLIENT function is limited to the export of files up to 2 GB. For larger exports, use the EXPORT ON SERVER function.

With EXPORT ON SERVER, you have to specify an existing folder on the SAP HANA server that is writable for the <sid>adm user that runs the `indexserver` process. The folder has to be present before the export is started, and it either needs to be empty or the REPLACE EXISTING EXPORT... checkbox needs to be selected. Also, in a scale-out setup, the target folder must be located on a shared mount, because all `indexserver` processes will write locally into the same file system path.

Specifying the NUMBER OF PARALLEL THREADS provides an option to export multiple tables in parallel. Be aware that this setting does not have any effect when only one table is exported. The export will work on multiple columns of any exported table in parallel.

Clicking the FINISH button starts the export. As long as the export is running, a progress dialog is shown in SAP HANA Studio, along with a button to keep the export running in the background (Figure 9.35).

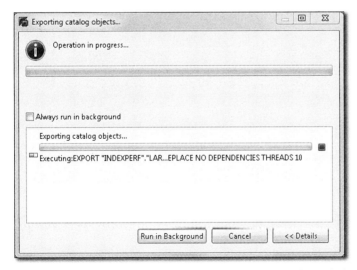

Figure 9.35 Export Catalog Object Example: The Progress Dialog with the Run in Background Button

While the export is running in the background, it is possible to monitor the process either in the THREADS overview of the PERFORMANCE tab in SAP HANA Studio (see Figure 9.36) or by querying system table `M_EXPORT_BINARY_STATUS` (Figure 9.37).

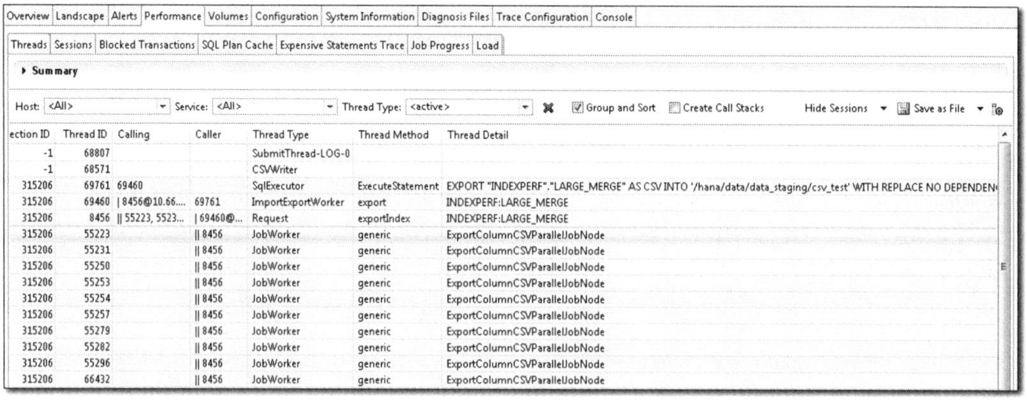

ection ID	Thread ID	Calling	Caller	Thread Type	Thread Method	Thread Detail
-1	68807			SubmitThread-LOG-0		
-1	68571			CSVWriter		
315206	69761	69460		SqlExecutor	ExecuteStatement	EXPORT "INDEXPERF"."LARGE_MERGE" AS CSV INTO '/hana/data/data_staging/csv_test' WITH REPLACE NO DEPENDEN
315206	69460	| 8456@10.66....	69761	ImportExportWorker	export	INDEXPERF:LARGE_MERGE
315206	8456	|| 55223, 5523...	| 69460@...	Request	exportIndex	INDEXPERF:LARGE_MERGE
315206	55223		|| 8456	JobWorker	generic	ExportColumnCSVParallelJobNode
315206	55231		|| 8456	JobWorker	generic	ExportColumnCSVParallelJobNode
315206	55250		|| 8456	JobWorker	generic	ExportColumnCSVParallelJobNode
315206	55253		|| 8456	JobWorker	generic	ExportColumnCSVParallelJobNode
315206	55254		|| 8456	JobWorker	generic	ExportColumnCSVParallelJobNode
315206	55257		|| 8456	JobWorker	generic	ExportColumnCSVParallelJobNode
315206	55279		|| 8456	JobWorker	generic	ExportColumnCSVParallelJobNode
315206	55282		|| 8456	JobWorker	generic	ExportColumnCSVParallelJobNode
315206	55296		|| 8456	JobWorker	generic	ExportColumnCSVParallelJobNode
315206	66432		|| 8456	JobWorker	generic	ExportColumnCSVParallelJobNode

Figure 9.36 Export Catalog Object Example: Export Threads in Thread Overview

In the screenshot in Figure 9.36, we can easily see that even though only one table is exported, multiple threads are working on the export.

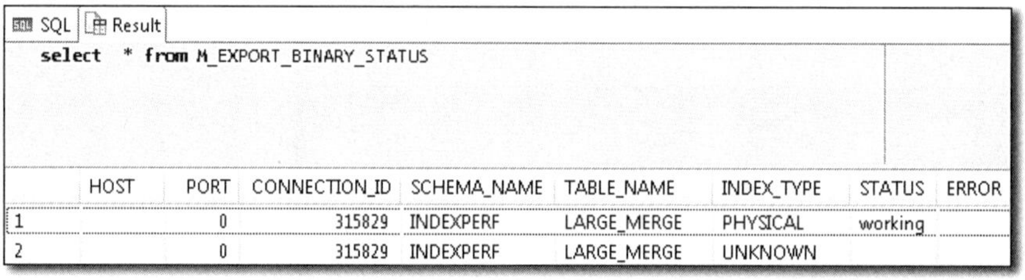


```
select * from M_EXPORT_BINARY_STATUS
```

	HOST	PORT	CONNECTION_ID	SCHEMA_NAME	TABLE_NAME	INDEX_TYPE	STATUS	ERROR
1		0	315829	INDEXPERF	LARGE_MERGE	PHYSICAL	working	
2		0	315829	INDEXPERF	LARGE_MERGE	UNKNOWN		

Figure 9.37 Export Catalog Object Example: Export Status in System Table M_EXPORT_BINARY_STATUS

Checking monitoring table `M_EXPORT_BINARY_STATUS` usually is only beneficial if multiple objects get exported, because the status for every row is noted as `queued`, `working`, `skipped`, `done`, or `failed`, but you do not see how far the export for a large table, for example, has progressed. Also, the system table gets emptied once the export process is finished, which makes it only useful during long, ongoing exports.

After the successful export, you will find the directory structure in the target file system folder. Listing 9.23 and Listing 9.24 explain this directory structure in more detail.

```
<target folder>

+ export
  + <schema name>
    + <first two letters of object name>
      + <object name>
        + create.info
        + create.sql
      + more object folders with the same two starting letters...
    + more two letter folders...
  + more schema folders...

+ index
  + <schema name>
    + <first two letters of object name>
      + <object name>
        + create.sql
        + data.csv
        + data.ctl
        + data.err
        + data.info
        + table.xml
        + lobs
          + xx_xx_xxxxxxxxxxxx.lob
          + ...
      + more object folders with the same two starting letters...
    + more two letter folders...
  + more schema folders...
```

Listing 9.23 Directory and File Structure of CSV Exports

In the above listing:

▶ + export only exists for nontable objects, e.g., views.

▶ + create.info is a text file describing the exported object.

▶ + create.sql is a text file with a DDL command to create the object.

▶ data.csv is the actual data in CSV format.

▶ data.ctl is the control file for the IMPORT FROM command.

▶ data.err is the import error file, which is empty for export.

▶ data.info is the general runtime information (number of records, etc.).

▶ + table.xml is an XML representation of the object.

▶ lobs is the folder for LOB column data.

In the case of a binary export, the object folder in the index hierarchy contains a different set of files.

```
+ index
  + <schema name>
    + <first two letters of object name>
      + <object name>
      + attributes
        + attribute_201.bin
        + more attribute_xxx.bin files
        + attributeStore.js
      + create
      + create.sql
      + $delta$.log
      + freeUdivStore
      + RuntimeData
      + table.xml
      + lobs
        + xx_xx_xxxxxxxxxxxx.lob
        + ...
      + more object folders with the same two starting letters...
    + more two letter folders...
  + more schema folders...
```

Listing 9.24 Export Object File System Hierarchy

In the above listing:

▶ + attributes is a subfolder with the binary export of the table columns.

▶ + attribute_201.bin is a binary export file.

▶ + attributeStore.js is a text file with information about the attribute_xxx.bin files in JSON format.

▶ + create is a binary file with an internal command to create the table.

▶ + create.sql is a text file with a DDL command to create the table.

▶ + $delta$.log is a binary file containing the delta log data.

▶ + freeUdivStore is a text file containing record validity data.

▶ + RuntimeData is a text file with runtime information like M_CS_TABLES.

▶ + `table.xml` is an XML representation of the object.

▶ + `lobs` is the folder for LOB column data.

Be aware that when exporting column store table data to CSV files, it is typically difficult to predict the size of the export in the file system. The `UNCOMPRESSED_SIZE` information in `M_CS_COLUMNS` can only be used to approximate the expected export size. Also, the size of LOB columns needs to be gathered separately.

9.5.2 Importing Data

Once data has been exported, you can import it into SAP HANA again. Two commands are available for this: `IMPORT` and `IMPORT FROM`.

IMPORT

`IMPORT` is used to import data exports generated by `EXPORT` straightaway with little or no modification. The command syntax is pretty simple, and not too many options need to be specified. The command requires only information about where to look for the export file structure.

```
IMPORT <object_name_list>
FROM <path>
[WITH <import_option_list>]
[AT [LOCATION] <indexserver_host_port>]
```

To import the data from the earlier example, all you need to type is the following:

```
IMPORT ALL FROM '/hana/data/data_staging/csv_test'
```

With the `AT LOCATION` clause, you can specify the `indexserver` node that the import should run on (in scale-out systems).

The `WITH` clause allows you to specify how many tables can be imported at the same time, whether the table data or only the definition will be imported, and—very usefully—the option to change the schema for the imported tables.

IMPORT FROM

Although the `IMPORT` command also includes a `FROM` keyword, the command is quite different from the more versatile `IMPORT FROM` command. `IMPORT FROM` is meant to help with loading external data and offers several ways to specify the input data format, the loading behavior, and error logging either directly in the command parameters or via a control file (CTL).

The control file itself contains an import statement (IMPORT DATA INTO TABLE), a source file specification, and a description of the input data format. Note that a strict one-record-per-line structure is expected; the line delimiter, however, can be freely defined to support text fields containing carriage returns or line feed characters. Complex data record structure layouts, for example, EDI-conforming layouts or dynamic data sets such as XML, cannot be imported directly with the IMPORT or IMPORT FROM command.

Note

Although the IMPORT FROM command of SAP HANA is sometimes recommended as the fastest way to load data from external sources, the recommendation for that should be to rely on proper data-loading tools, such as SAP Data Services. The CSV file import of IMPORT FROM makes aggressive use of the CPU cores, which may hamper the overall system performance. It also lacks proper error handling and does not support LOB data types.

Because importing data via the standard interfaces (JDBC, ODBC, or SQLDBC) can leverage performance features such as BULK insert/update, statement routing, and client-based record image creation (not JDBC), it is usually possible to set up data loading with similar or better performance than is achieved by using the IMPORT FROM command.

A common question about data imports in migration or demo situations is how to improve the import speed. For that, two parameters are available: THREADS and BATCH.

With THREADS, the maximum number of objects that are imported in parallel can be specified. Note that this does not determine how many indexserver threads will be active working on a single table. If only one table will be imported, the parameter does not have any effect on the import performance and can be ignored. When more tables are going to be imported, it is important to not overload the server. The larger the tables and the more columns they have, the lower the number of THREADS should be chosen. A good starting point may be 10 THREADS, further tuning the number to the actual system thereafter.

The BATCH parameter sets the number of records after which IMPORT should send a commit. The more often commit is performed, the longer the wait time for the import (because commits are processed synchronously, the session has to wait until it is finished). In some cases, the import performance can be considerably improved by partitioning the target table, because doing so will allow for parallel insert into the different partitions.

9.5.3 Custom Excel File Import

A final convenience option to import data has been introduced with SAP HANA SPS 7: the MS Excel file import in SAP HANA Studio. This function allows you to directly read from files compatible with MS Excel (CSV, XLS, or XSLX formats) and either match the file structure to an existing table or create a new table during the import. The main goal for this option is to enable quick data imports to play around with the data in SAP HANA or to kick off development activities. The function is not supposed to be a high-performance import interface for recurring or ongoing data imports. It should simply make the on-board toolset of SAP HANA Studio a little bit more complete for typical development and implementation scenarios.

The whole import is wizard driven. To illustrate it, let's start off with a little MS Excel spreadsheet that contains membership data for some kind of club (Figure 9.38).

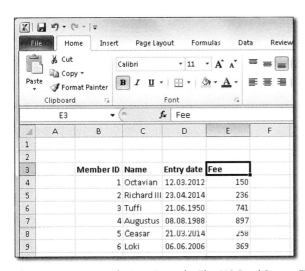

Figure 9.38 Import File Data Example: The MS Excel Source File

To open the import wizard in SAP HANA Studio, navigate to File • Import... • SAP HANA content • Data from Local File, as shown in Figure 9.39.

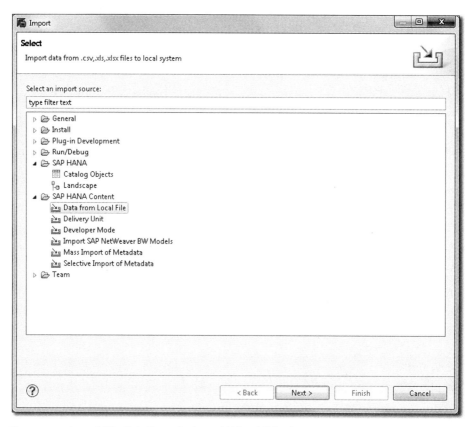

Figure 9.39 Import File Data Example: Import Wizard Selection

The next wizard window (Figure 9.40) allows you to select the file to be imported, as shown in ❶. If the file is an MS Excel format file, then you can choose which worksheet should be imported, as shown in ❷.

Next, you can specify whether the file contains a header row, as shown in ❸. Typically, it is very helpful to have a header row in order to easily identify the columns during import.

If you want to import only a selection of lines from the file, you can specify the line range, as shown in ❹, or choose IMPORT ALL DATA. This will import all the lines after the header row until the first completely empty line is reached.

Having specified all the import options, you need to define the target table next, as shown in ❺. This can either be an existing table or a new table. Be aware that the data will be appended to an existing table during the import. If you want to import the data into a new table with the same structure as an existing one, you have to create the target table manually before the import.

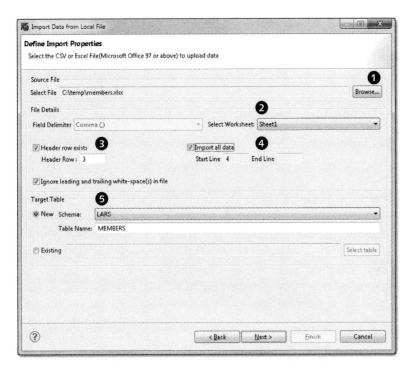

Figure 9.40 Import File Data Example: Import from Local File Options

Figure 9.41 shows the MANAGE TABLE DEFINITION AND DATA MAPPINGS wizard page. In the lower part of the screen, as shown in ❶, you will see a data preview that helps you to decide which columns should be mapped and how. By resizing the dialog window, more lines can be displayed.

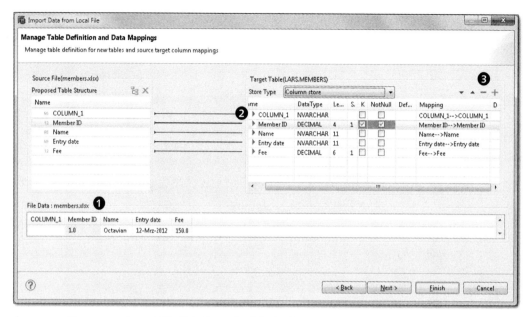

Figure 9.41 Import File Data Example: Edit the Source to Target Mapping

The target table structure has been automatically derived from the input file. The column names are taken from the header line in the source file, and the data types are best guesses based on the first couple of lines. Therefore, it is typically required that you adapt the target data types to what you want the table to actually look like. In the example, you will see that the Entry date column is automatically mapped to an NVARCHAR column—but DATE might be the more appropriate data type.

In this example, the first column of the input file COLUMN_1 is actually empty and should not be imported. Therefore, we need to select the corresponding column in the TARGET TABLE column list, as shown in ❷, and delete it with the – button, as shown in ❸.

The empty COLUMN_1 now is no longer mapped to any target table column and will be skipped during import, as shown in Figure 9.42.

When you click NEXT or FINISH, the import is started, and you are presented with a SUMMARY dialog (Figure 9.43).

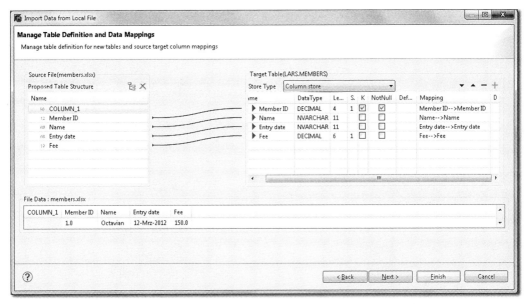

Figure 9.42 Import File Data Example: Final Mapping of the Input File to the New Table Structure

Figure 9.43 Import File Data Example: Summary View of Imported Data

Click FINISH again to save the data in the target table, and then you can review the import JOB DETAILS messages (Figure 9.44).

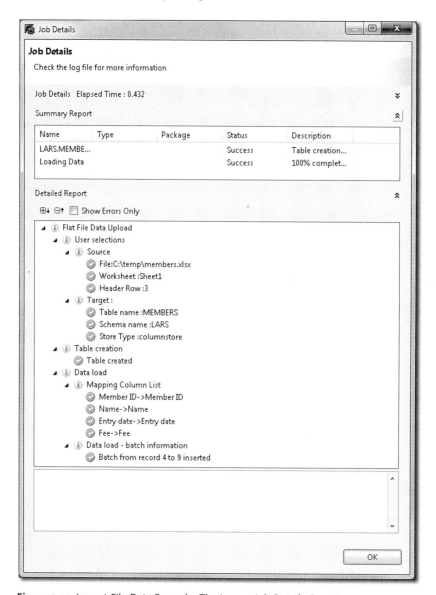

Figure 9.44 Import File Data Example: The Import Job Details Overview

After the import, the data is available for use in your newly created target table, as shown in Figure 9.45.

	Member ID	Name	Entry date	Fee
1	1.0	Octavian	12-Mrz-2012	150.0
2	2.0	Richard III	23-Apr-2014	236.0
3	3.0	Tuffi	21-Jun-1950	741.0
4	4.0	Augustus	08-Aug-19...	897.0
5	5.0	Ceasar	21-Mrz-2014	258.0
6	6.0	Loki	06-Jun-2006	369.0

Figure 9.45 Import File Data Example: The Imported Data in the SAP HANA Table

9.6 Checking Tables for Consistency

Just like any other data storage and processing system, SAP HANA cannot assume that it will never face any kind of data inconsistency or corruption. Faulty hardware, software bugs, or the sheer complexity of interconnected system components nearly guarantee that corruptions will occur at some point.

There are two general aspects of coping with corruptions:

▸ Finding or identifying database corruptions

▸ Removing the corruption/recreating the correct state of data

Most DBMS platforms provide functionality to check for the consistency and the proper working of the storage containers of the database (tables, table partitions, files, etc.). SAP HANA is no different: It provides a set of stored procedures that allow you to test for specific corruptions. CHECK_CATALOG_CONSISTENCY performs checks of the database catalog, whereas CHECK_TABLE_CONSISTENCY performs checks of the actual table data. Both procedures take the same input parameters: ('<check_action>', '<schema>', '<table>'). (If <schema> or <schema> and <table> are omitted, then the command will be executed against the whole schema or the whole database, respectively.)

To find out which check actions are available, an auxiliary procedure, GET_CHECK_ACTIONS, exists and provides output as shown in Figure 9.46.

409

SQL | Result

```
CALL GET_CHECK_ACTIONS('CHECK_TABLE_CONSISTENCY')
```

	ACTION	DESCRIPTION
1	CHECK_PRIMARY_KEY	Column Table: Check the consistency of the primary key
2	CHECK_VALUE_INDEXES	Column Table: Check the consistency of the internal value indexes
3	CHECK_ROWID	Column Table: Check the consistency of the internal $rowid$ column
4	CHECK_COMBINED_KEY_COLUMN	Column Table: Check the key columns against the combined key column
5	CHECK_PARTITIONING	Column Table: Check the meta data of table partitioning
6	CHECK_PARTITIONING_DATA	Column Table: Check the assignment of rows to partitions
7	REPAIR_PARTITIONING_DATA	Column Table: Repair the assignment of rows to partitions
8	CHECK_REPLICATION	Column Table: Check the meta data of replicated tables
9	CHECK_REPLICATION_DATA_LIGHTWEIG...	Column Table: Perform a lightweight check to assure that all replica store the same data
10	CHECK_REPLICATION_DATA_FULL	Column Table: Perform a full check to assure that all replica store the same data
11	CHECK_NULLITY	Row Table: Check the nullity of the not-null fields
12	CHECK_LENGTH	Row Table: Check the actual data length of each variable length field
13	CHECK_VSLOT_SANITY	Row Table: Check the sanity of the logical pointers
14	CHECK_INDEXES	Row Table: Check the consistency of the indexes
15	CHECK_METADATA_SEGMENT_SEPARATI...	Row Table: Check if metadata and userdata are stored separatedly from each other
16	CHECK_DUPLICATE_VSLOT_POINTER	Row Table: ~~~~~~~~~~~~~~
17	CHECK_VARIABLE_PART_BINDING	Row Table: Check the correctness of vslot binding

Figure 9.46 Output of the GET_CHECK_ACTIONS Procedure

The procedures can be called interactively in SAP HANA Studio, and the check result is returned in the form of a result table. In the case that data corruptions have been found, the return table will contain the schema_name, table_name, object_type, error_code, and the error_message. Some corruption may be repaired via the REPAIR_ procedures, but it is highly recommended that you get in touch with SAP Support to get help with the analysis and remediation of the problem.

Currently, the checks are performed in a single thread and can put considerable load on the system by loading columns that should be checked into memory. In their current form, this makes them unsuitable for production system usage. Thus, SAP recommends running the checks on copied systems. This is good advice, because the DBA is primarily interested in knowing that it is possible to recover any lost or corrupted data. Thus, proving that a system that has been restored to a different SAP HANA hardware setup is corruption free is typically more important than finding corruptions in the production system.

To the seasoned DBA, this may not sound ideal; there is certainly space for improvement in the area of consistency checks and corruption handling. However, it is worth mentioning that, due to the main memory-centric architecture, SAP HANA systems do not suffer as often from disk or file system-based corruptions as disk-oriented systems.

Further Resources

For further information on consistency checks and corruption handling, please see the *SAP HANA Administration Guide* as well as the SAP Note 1977584, SAP Note 1660125, and SAP Note 1666976.

9.7   Summary

After reading this chapter, you should understand some of the most important table-related features of SAP HANA systems: loading tables to and from memory, running delta merges, and partitioning and distributing tables. In addition to these three fundamental concepts, you should also know how to export and import tables and should be aware of the consistency check mechanisms that the database offers.

Sessions and transactions are the very basic system elements that enable us to communicate with SAP HANA and to process data. Understanding how the database guarantees correct access to shared data and automatically enables parallel query processing is essential.

10 Sessions and Transactions

This chapter is all about the dynamic interaction of database clients such as SAP NetWeaver Application Server, MS Excel, or SAP HANA Studio with the SAP HANA database. We look into the definition of core topics such as sessions, transactions, commands, processes, and threads and how these relate to each other. We also cover how to transfer these concepts into monitoring and actions for the SAP HANA administrator.

We will start our discussion by following the lifecycle of a database session and describing the important metadata information of the session context. We then cover the relationship between sessions and transactions of the database to processes and threads of the operating system. Having covered these fundamental principles, we can dive into a discussion of the monitoring of sessions and transactions. Finally, we will finish up with the complex topics of concurrency and parallelism and the related notions of locks and blocking situations.

10.1 Introduction to Sessions and Transactions

To use SAP HANA as a database management system (DBMS), it is necessary that users or programs log on to SAP HANA and create a session. The *session* is the vehicle for the communication between the database client and SAP HANA in which all data exchange and processing takes place. It can be understood as the ongoing conversation between client and server. This conversation provides the framework for all data processing. For example, the user account and the privileges assigned to it are part of this context, so all data processing that is performed during this session takes the user's privileges into account.

A *transaction*, on the other hand, is the bracket in which a single command or multiple commands are executed together as a unit. Either all of the commands are successfully executed or none are. This is what makes a transaction *atomic*, which means that either all data changes that are performed within a transaction are successfully stored in the database or none of them are.

Finally, *commands* are the most granular element of client-server interaction in SAP HANA. Throughout this chapter, we will use the term *command* instead of *SQL statement*, because SQL statements really are just a special type of commands, and there are other types, such as MDX statements, that are processed in a similar fashion. However, very often we can find that an SQL statement will map directly to a command.

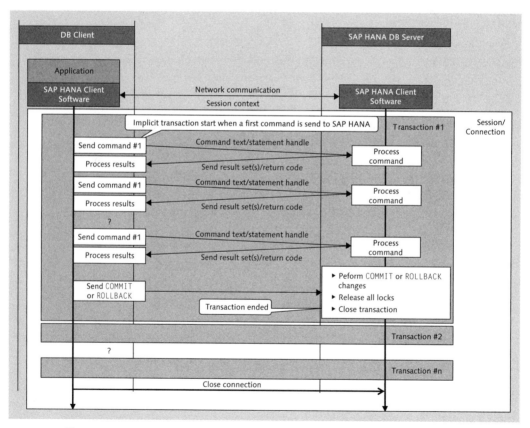

Figure 10.1 DB Sessions, Transactions, and Commands in SAP HANA

A session can consist of one or more transactions (within one session, transactions are processed one after the other), and each transaction can consist of one or more commands (again, within one transaction, the commands are executed one after the other). Figure 10.1 shows a graphical representation of the dependencies between sessions, transactions, and commands.

As you can see, all commands are executed within a transaction. Each transaction is identified with a transaction ID that is unique only for the session, as read-only transactions don't require global uniqueness. When commands are executed that could potentially change data, then the transaction is set to be an update transaction and gets assigned a system global update transaction ID. To distinguish different sessions from each other, each session is assigned a connection ID (sessions are sometimes referred to as *logical connections*). This can be easily monitored with the M_TRANSACTIONS system view, as shown in the following example.

Start a session with AUTOCOMMIT = OFF. The default for connections in SAP HANA Studio and hsql is to execute a commit after each command. This would not allow you to run multiple commands in one transaction, which is why you need to change to AUTOCOMMIT OFF.

The current_connection function returns the ID for your current session/connection:

```
select current_connection from dummy;

CURRENT_CONNECTION
303232
```

You can use it to find information belonging to your session in several system views.

System view M_TRANSACTIONS contains detailed information on transactions:

```
select transaction_id, update_transaction_id
from m_transactions
where connection_id = 303232;
```

TRANSACTION_ID	UPDATE_TRANSACTION_ID
105	0

Here, you only need to look at the TRANSACTION_ID and the UPDATE_TRANSACTION_ID. You will see that the initial connection is a read-only connection, because

UDPATE_TRANSACTION_ID is 0. Running a read-only command such as SELECT does not change the transaction mode:

```
select * from cpoints;
```

```
| NAME   | POINTS         |
| ------ | -------------- |
| Carol  |           7.20 |
| Paul   |           2.40 |
| Lars   |           7.10 |
| Louise |           4.50 |
```

The transaction still is a read-only transaction, because UPDATE_TRANSACTION_ID is still 0:

```
select transaction_id, update_transaction_id
from m_transactions
where connection_id = 303232;
```

```
| TRANSACTION_ID | UPDATE_TRANSACTION_ID |
| -------------- | --------------------- |
| 105            | 0                     |
```

However, now change a record:

```
update cpoints set points = 42 where name ='Paul';
```

Now you can see that the transaction has become an update transaction:

```
select transaction_id, update_transaction_id
from m_transactions
where connection_id = 303232;
```

```
| TRANSACTION_ID | UPDATE_TRANSACTION_ID |
| -------------- | --------------------- |
| 105            | 829360                |
```

Finally, roll back all changes and end the transaction:

```
rollback;
```

Typically, a client application will open a session with SAP HANA and re-use it as long as the application is active. Because creating a session takes quite some time for resource allocation on the client and server sides, network communication, authentication, and so forth, it is usually best to keep the connection open. In addition to that, inactive or idle sessions don't require CPU resources and require only a small amount of memory in the SAP HANA server.

Within the session, the application will then run multiple commands in one or more transactions. Once the client application no longer requires database access, the connection is closed, and with it all open transactions are terminated.

Now that you understand the basics of sessions and transactions, the rest of this section will provide a few more details. In Section 10.1.1, we walk you through the lifetime of a session; in Section 10.1.2, we give you a bit more detail on the session context.

10.1.1 Lifetime of a Session

In order to understand how sessions are used in client programs, see Figure 10.2.

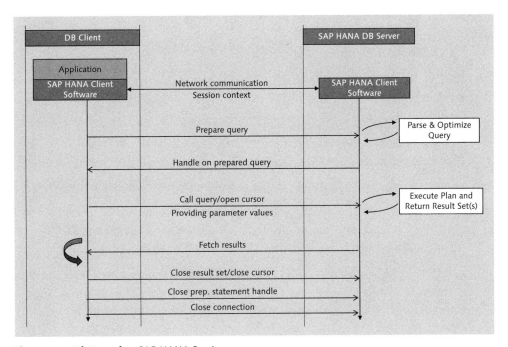

Figure 10.2 Lifetime of an SAP HANA Session

Like most other DBMS, SAP HANA uses the client-server communication model. In this model, the application that will use the database is the database client, and SAP HANA takes on the role of the database server.

> **Note**
>
> Important to note here is that client and server in this communication model refer to the roles of the system components. Although the terms "client" and "server" are also used to refer to specific pieces of hardware, this is not what we are talking about here.

To connect to SAP HANA, the client application has to use the SAP HANA client software. It provides the functionality to communicate with the SAP HANA server via the network so that the application programmer doesn't need to implement this. For that, the client software needs to be installed on the same machine on which the client application runs. The client software consists of dynamic loadable libraries or shared objects (DLL libraries on MS Windows systems, SO files on Linux) that are loaded by the client program. The client libraries provide the application programming interfaces (APIs) for different programming environments to communicate with the SAP HANA database. Most often, the standard APIs JDBC (Java database connectivity) and ODBC (open database connectivity) are used, but there are also APIs for other environments available (see the *SAP HANA Developer Guide* for details on this).

For SAP NetWeaver ABAP systems, the database connectivity is created via a separate software component, the database interface (DBI). The ABAP DBI basically consists of two parts:

▸ The functionality provided to the ABAP work processes, including features such as buffered tables, OpenSQL, and handling of multiple database connections

▸ The DBMS vendor-specific database shared library (DBSL, dbhdbslib.dll or dbhdbslib.so)

The DBSL acts as a conversion layer between the ABAP world and the vendor-specific database commands and features.

Just like for any other supported DBMS platform, SAP provides a DBSL for SAP HANA (see SAP Note 1600066). The DBSL in turn uses the SAP HANA client software, more specifically the SQLDBC driver (e.g., libSQLDBCHDB.dll on MS Windows systems) that provides the proprietary SAP HANA client API.

Figure 10.3 provides an overview of how the SAP NetWeaver Application Server ABAP uses the SAP HANA client.

As you can see, even though the SAP NetWeaver Application Server acts as a server for your business users, with the database it takes on the role of the client.

> **Note**
>
> To sum up: Whenever a client application wants to connect to SAP HANA, it needs to use the SAP HANA client software.

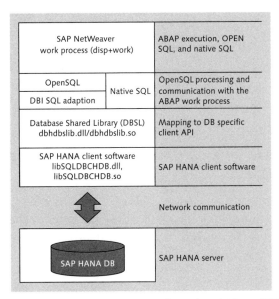

SAP NetWeaver work process (disp+work)	ABAP execution, OPEN SQL, and native SQL
OpenSQL / DBI SQL adaption — Native SQL	OpenSQL processing and communication with the ABAP work process
Database Shared Library (DBSL) dbhdbslib.dll/dbhdbslib.so	Mapping to DB specific client API
SAP HANA client software libSQLDBCHDB.dll, libSQLDBCHDB.so	SAP HANA client software
	Network communication
SAP HANA DB	SAP HANA server

Figure 10.3 SAP NetWeaver Database Shared Library (DBSL)

With this background information, you're now ready to learn about each of the major actions that determine the lifecycle of a session. We discuss each in more detail next.

Connecting to the SAP HANA Database

The very first step in starting a session is to connect with the SAP HANA database. To do so, a logon is provided by the client. This needs to be done by one of the supported authentication methods. See Chapter 12 for details on this.

Once the logon has been processed successfully, SAP HANA will reserve some memory for the conversation between the client and itself. By this time, the network connection is also chosen, which will be used for subsequent communications between the server and the client. The SAP HANA client will now receive information about the system landscape, for example, what other nodes are available in the case of a scale-out system.

You can check the session and connections that are used by different database users by looking into the monitoring views M_CONNECTIONS and M_CONTEXT_MEM-ORY. See Section 10.3 for examples of using these system views.

Preparing a Query

After a session has been created and a session connection and context have been assigned, the client application can send queries to the SAP HANA database and wait for the results of the commands.

These queries are sent as text strings to the database; whether the text is SQL, MDX, or some other query language does not matter at this point in time. The database receives a text string and needs to analyze it so that it can process it. The process of analyzing a command string is called *preparing a statement*.

During statement preparation, SAP HANA:

- Breaks the command string into single tokens
- Checks the tokens against the SQL/MDX command grammar
- Creates an internal tree of query expressions and predicates
- Transforms and rewrites the query based on built-in heuristics (e.g., un-nesting of subqueries, pulling out common expressions, etc.)
- Optimizes the statement on the SQL level
- Produces an internal list of operations that need to be performed to create the result set of the query (called the execution plan)

Figure 10.4 provides a close-in view of the query preparation part of the session lifetime.

Later on, when the query should be executed, the execution plan is used by the different execution engines to process the request and to deliver the requested result set(s). There can be more than just one result set to a query, for example, if a stored procedure returns multiple result sets or if an SQL query uses GROUPING

SETs (see the SAP HANA SQL reference documentation for the SELECT command for details on grouping sets).

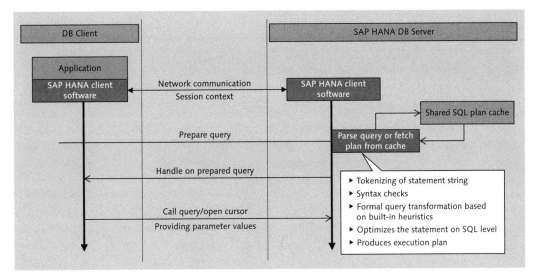

Figure 10.4 Query Parsing and Optimizing

All of these preparation steps can take some time. If the same statement needs to be executed more than once, it would be nice to save the prepared statement for later. This is done in the SQL plan cache, where SAP HANA stores the SQL statement text, the generated plan, and the aggregated runtime statistics once the statement is executed.

This cached SQL plan will be reused once a client wants to prepare or execute a query with the exact same query text string. Similar statements or statements that only differ a little bit would require a new preparation run, though. In Table 10.1, two examples for similar statements are presented that make reparsing necessary.

Example	

SELECT * FROM
    product_texts
WHERE product_id = '031';
SELECT /* find product texts*/ * FROM
    product_texts
WHERE product_id = '031';
	The two query strings are different, and each one will be parsed, even though the only difference is the comment and doesn't change the result set.

Table 10.1 Examples for Nonmatching SQL Statement Strings

Example

`SELECT * FROM product_texts`
`WHERE product_id in ('031', '032');`
`SELECT * FROM product_texts`
`WHERE product_id in ('031', '032', '031');`
	The two query strings are different, and each one will be parsed, even though the only difference is the number of values in the `in` clause.

Table 10.1 Examples for Nonmatching SQL Statement Strings (Cont.)

Executing a Query

After a statement has been prepared (or found in the Shared SQL cache), a handle on this statement is sent to the client. The client application can now use the handle to execute the statement over and over again.

By now, we see that an SQL query is very much like other computer program queries: It needs to be compiled before it can be executed, the compiled form of the statement is stored to speed up subsequent usages of the same query, and it can take input variables to perform the same computation for different values. These input variables are called *parameters* in SAP HANA queries. The query parameters are denoted by question marks in the SQL statement text.

Example

This is an SQL statement without parameters:

```
select * from user_parameters where user_name='LARS'
```

This is an SQL statement with parameters:

```
select * from user_parameters where user_name= ?
```

The benefits of using parameters for queries that will be executed the exact same way for different search values are as follows:

▸ The statement will only be parsed once, because the statement text doesn't change for different search values. This can save a huge amount of time if the statement is going to be executed over and over again by the application (e.g., select the line items of an order record). "Parse once, execute often" is the key phrase here.

▸ The prepared statement will be stored only once in the Shared SQL cache, thereby saving memory.

▸ The usage of query parameters prevents SQL injection attacks, because the value of the parameter can never be interpreted as part of the SQL command.

▸ For programmers, the use of the parameter requires explicit typing on the client side, which also prevents coding errors.

Because the client program receives a handle on the prepared statement from SAP HANA to execute it, it is not even necessary to send the command text to the database again. Instead, the client program can keep the handle in a variable or an array and reuse it with different parameter values later on.

As long as handles for a statement are not closed, they cannot be removed from the Shared SQL cache.

> **Note**
>
> The SAP NetWeaver DBSL automatically takes care of preparing queries, setting parameter values, and keeping the prepared statement handles. In order to speed up database access, every work process keeps up to 1,000 handles and reuses them when required.

To execute the parameterized query, the client needs to provide the parameter values. In SAP HANA Studio, the SQL Editor provides an input mask for parameterized queries, as shown in Figure 10.5.

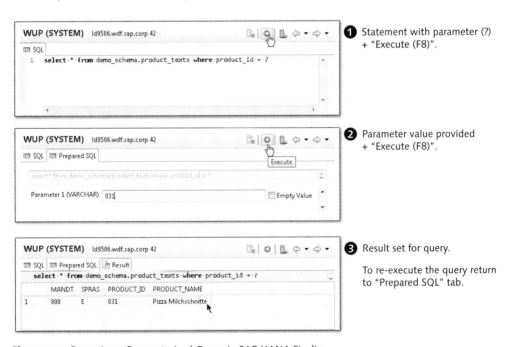

Figure 10.5 Executing a Parameterized Query in SAP HANA Studio

Fetch Result Sets and Close Cursor

Once the query has been executed, the client application retrieves or fetches the result record. Because the result set can be larger than the amount of data that can be sent in one network roundtrip, the records are transferred in chunks to the client.

Although it is possible for the client to not fetch all result records, for example, to list only the first ten records, usually it's best to specify the desired number of rows in the SQL query with the LIMIT n or TOP n clause. Remember that the whole result set will be materialized in the SAP HANA server's memory, so requesting more records than are required is wasting system resources in multiple system components.

Close Handle on Prepared Statements

The Shared SQL cache keeps reference counter for each statement. Closing the handle for a parsed statement decreases this counter. Once the reference counter reaches zero, the statement is a candidate for removal from the Shared SQL cache (plan eviction).

Close Connection

The last action during the lifetime of a session is to close the connection. This will implicitly rollback any open transactions, release all SQL locks, and close all pre-pared query handles and all other resources allocated by the session.

10.1.2 The Session Context

The session context sets the general conditions for all data processing that happens within a session. The context contains information on the database host to which the session is connected (important in scale-out systems) and on the database user as well as on the client host from which the session originated (client IP, process ID of the client program, etc.). It also describes important parameters for transaction handling, such as the autocommit mode. Finally, the context includes key-value pair variables that can be freely set for the lifetime of a session. Any session can set up to 50 of these variables.

Unlike information stored in tables, the context variables are not persisted by the database and can only be set by the session they belong to. Nevertheless, other sessions can read them without requiring further privileges except to read the M_CONTEXT_VARIABLES monitoring view.

> **Warning**
>
> Never store private or sensitive information in the context variables, as the content is accessible to all database users!

A major use case for session context variables is to provide additional metadata information about the current session to the database. The following subsections explain the most important standard context variables.

Session Context LOCALE/LOCALE_SAP Variables

Using context variables can provide additional functionality to your SAP HANA applications or information models. The logon language and locale information, for example, is stored via session context variables LOCALE and LOCALE_SAP. Language-dependent information models can use the value of these variables to filter data based on the selected language (either by specifying a text join or an equality filter for the $$language$$ variable). A common use case for this is that information models use language-dependent master data.

The difference between LOCALE and LOCALE_SAP here is simply the locale encoding scheme. Whereas LOCALE follows the ISO-3166 encoding standard (e.g., de_DE for German, en_GB for British English, and so on), the LOCALE_SAP contains the SAP internal single-byte encoding for languages. The SAP HANA server automatically takes care of filling the LOCALE variables with the correct values based on the locale settings provided with the logon string that was used to connect to the database. It is also possible to specify the default locale for a user using ALTER USER <user_name> PARAMETER SET PARAMETER 'LOCALE' = '<value>'. This value will then be used when no locale is set in the logon string.

This means that as an SAP HANA user or application developer you don't need to care about mapping between both language encodings.

Session Context CLIENT Variable

In SAP HANA, every database user can have a special user parameter, CLIENT, assigned that can also be used for content filtering in information models or in your own SQL/SQLScript code (filter variable `$$client$$`). The client as a data-modeling element has been taken over from the SAP NetWeaver database model design. To separate the data sets of different application user groups, called clients, each client-dependent table contains a special column (`CLIENT`, `MANDT`) that contains a three-digit number to denote the client for each record.

The user parameter can be assigned either by using the `ALTER USER <user_name>` `PARAMETER SET PARAMETER 'CLIENT' = '<value>'` command or via the User Editor in SAP HANA Studio, as shown in Figure 10.6.

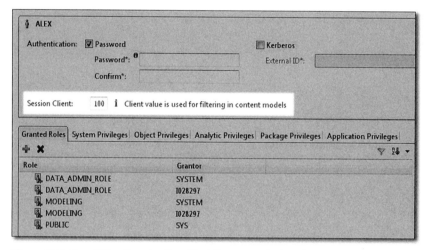

Figure 10.6 User Editor Showing the Client Parameter Assigned to a User Account

Internally, the user parameters are stored in system view `USER_PARAMETERS` and can be checked as shown in Listing 10.1.

```
select * from user_parameters where user_name ='ALEX';

USER | PARAME | VAL
ALEX | CLIENT | 100
```

Listing 10.1 Reading from System View USER_PARAMETERS

Session Context APPLICATION* Variables

Information such as the `CLIENT` and the `LOCALE` variables has a direct impact on how SAP HANA works with queries; the information models can be used in a flexible manner, without the need for additional development effort.

Another functional aspect of session context variables is to provide information that helps to monitor and troubleshoot an application. The APPLICATION* variables can contain information about the database client application that is otherwise not available on the server side. This information includes the actual user name of the frontend user (APPLICATIONUSER), the name of the client program (APPLICATION), the current source code position for the client program (APPLICATIONSOURCE), and the version of the client program (APPLICATIONVERSION).

Although this metadata information may not seem to be of great interest at first, it is extremely useful for monitoring and problem analysis. The values of these variables for each current session can be checked in the monitoring view M_SESSION_CONTEXT. By filtering the content to the current session, you can display the context variables that are currently set for your session.

Listing 10.2 is the output from the SQL statement in the SAP HANA command-line client tool hdbsql.

```
select connection_id, key, value
> from m_session_context
>  where connection_id = current_connection;
| CONNECTION_ID | KEY              | VALUE       |
| ------------- | ---------------- | ---------- |
|        254669 | CILENT           | 800         |
|        254669 | PROTOCOL_VERSION | 4.1 (1, 4) |
2 rows selected (overall time 163,006 msec; server time 50,364 msec)
```

Listing 10.2 HDBSQL Output

Compare this with the output of the same SQL statement executed from an SAP HANA Studio session, as seen in Figure 10.7.

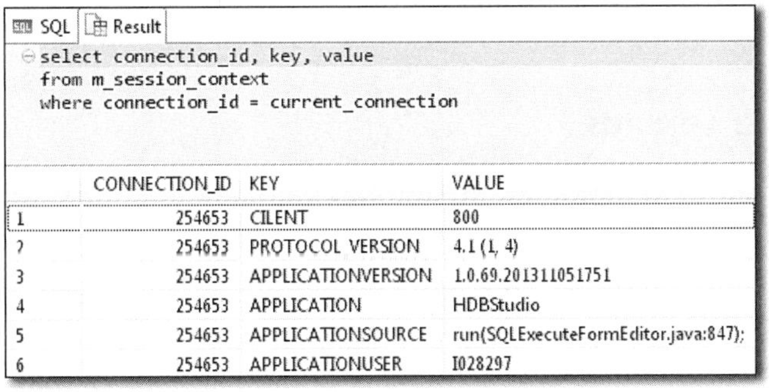

Figure 10.7 SAP HANA Studio Context APPLICATION* Variables

As you can see, SAP HANA Studio makes good use of these variables and sets all values according to the usage convention; `hdbsql`, on the other hand, doesn't set any of the `APPLICATION*` variables.

> **Note**
>
> Context variables have to be set by the client application after a session has been created. The SAP NetWeaver DBSL fills `APPLICATIONUSER` with the user that runs an ABAP report and `APPLICATIONSOURCE` with the current ABAP module and source code line number. This way, it's easy to find the SAP NetWeaver session that triggered a specific command or that uses an SAP HANA session.

If you want to make use of the context variables in your own programs, you can either use the `SET/UNSET` commands to set or delete the key-value pair variables or use the `CLIENTINFO` methods of the JDBC or ODBC drivers.

One of the most important steps during database problem analysis is to find out which of the sessions currently present on the server belongs to the client application in question. The SESSIONS monitor in SAP HANA Studio (or in Transaction DBACOCKPIT) answers exactly this question, as Figure 10.8 shows.

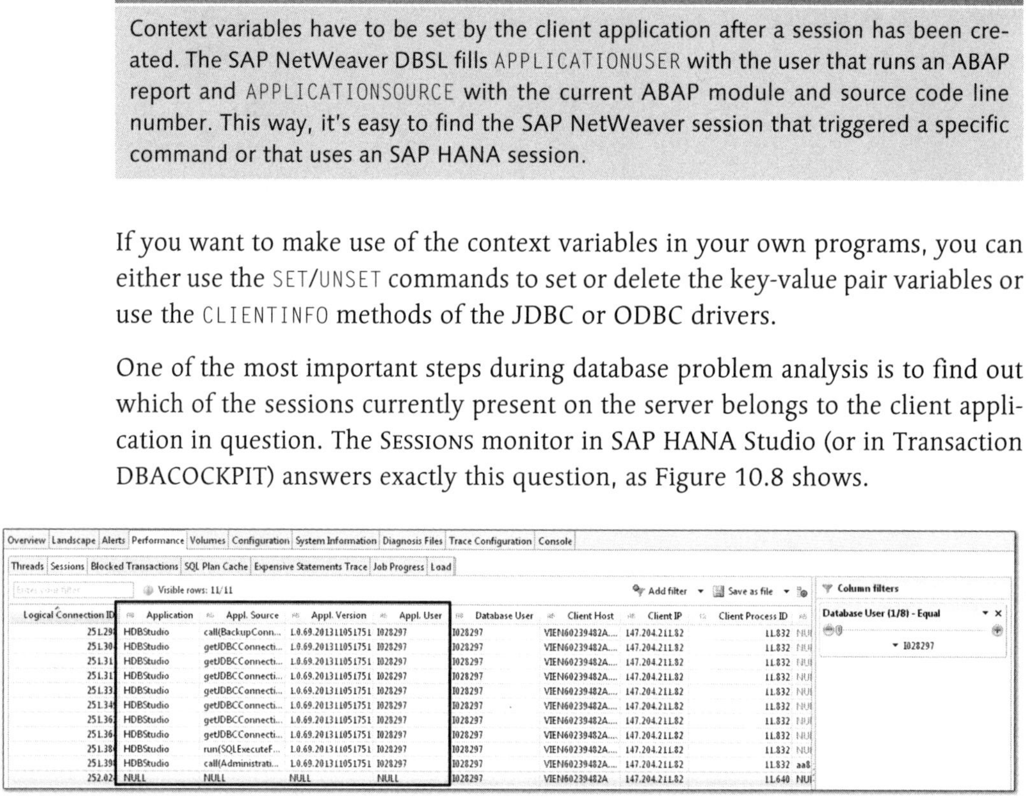

Figure 10.8 Sessions Overview in SAP HANA Studio displaying APPLICATION* Variables

10.2 Processes and Threads

As you have seen, sessions are the basis for every command execution and provide the context in which these commands are executed. Sessions and connections are all about the conversation between the SAP HANA client and server. They do not determine how the SAP HANA server actually performs its computations and processes the requests; the actual execution of command requests is performed by specialized worker threads that are part of the `indexserver` process.

To review the processes that belong to an SAP HANA instance, you can use SAP HANA Studio ADMINISTRATION PERSPECTIVE • LANDSCAPE • SERVICES. The processes are listed there as services. On the Linux command-line level, you can use the command `HDB info` to get this information, as seen in Figure 10.9.

```
ld9506:/usr/sap/WUP/HDB42> HDB info
USER        PID    PPID %CPU     VSZ     RSS COMMAND
wupadm    33282   33221  0.0   93228    2156 sshd: wupadm@notty
wupadm    33283   33282  0.0   54336    2136   \_ /usr/lib64/ssh/sftp-serve
wupadm    33220   33216  0.0   95436    2416 sshd: wupadm@pts/0
wupadm    33223   33220  0.0   14652    2740   \_ -sh
wupadm    33317   33223  0.0   13668    1688       \_ /bin/sh /usr/sap/WUP/
wupadm    33340   33317  0.0    4748     868         \_ ps fx -U wupadm -
wupadm    18728       1  0.0   19812    1456 sapstart pf=/usr/sap/WUP/SYS/
wupadm    18820   18728  0.0  848184  301812   \_ /usr/sap/WUP/HDB42/ld950
wupadm    18839   18820  6.2 29339324 2433948     \_ hdbnameserver
wupadm    19203   18820  0.0 7751540  400024     \_ hdbpreprocessor
wupadm    19206   18820  0.0 7071696  412700     \_ hdbcompileserver
wupadm    19233   18820 17.4 30621752 22172936     \_ hdbindexserver
wupadm    19236   18820  6.1 13777980 2211712     \_ hdbxsengine
wupadm    20632   18820  0.0  203192   72304       \_ sapwebdisp_hdb pf=/us
wupadm    38530       1  0.0  222252   74500 /usr/sap/WUP/HDB42/exe/sapsta
ld9506:/usr/sap/WUP/HDB42> █
```

Figure 10.9 Example Output of the HDB Info Command

On the operating system level, a *process* is the shell in which every program can run. All resources of the computer, such as CPU time, memory, or I/O devices, although shared amongst all processes that run in parallel, appear to every process as if that process was the only one using the resource. This way, all processes are isolated (or better insulated) from each other.

To allow parallel execution of parts of a program within a program, *threads* are available as a lightweight option for the operating system scheduler. One program, while still running as a single process on an operating system level, can start (or "spawn") several threads that then run as part of itself. With threads, different parts of the program can now run virtually at the same time and access the same memory.

Threads see CPU time as if they were the only ones ever running (of course, because they don't "see" anything when they are not running), but they do share the same system memory and all other resources. A program with multiple threads can actively run on multiple CPU cores at the same time, or threads that are currently waiting for resource accesses (e.g., disk I/O or network transport) can let go of the CPU time (yield) and let other threads use the CPU. This shared access of resources, specifically main memory, is a huge performance benefit of threads compared to processes.

In Figure 10.10, we see how threads can run in parallel and how they can access the same memory areas and resources within their process. However, the memory access is limited to what every process "sees." Accessing the memory of another process is prevented by the operating system.

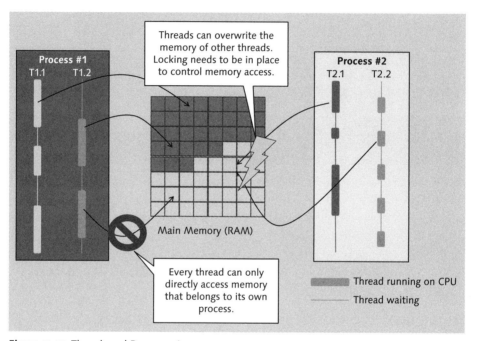

Figure 10.10 Threads and Resource Access

Therefore, when you want to have multiple processors working on the same data, threads are a good implementation choice, because they can easily "see" all the memory of their process. All the threads need to ensure is that they do not accidentally overwrite parts of the memory that other threads were just working on. This is usually done by some form of access regulation, such as locking, critical regions, or the like.

This in fact is one of the bigger problems to deal with in multithreaded programs: managing the access to the common memory of threads within a process. Especially when high-performance computing needs to occur that optimizes speed by reducing CPU cache line invalidation (something that would make it necessary to transport memory back and forth between CPU and RAM and thus take time), locks, latches, and mutexes are often not the best choice. To address this while still retaining the performance benefit of running multiple CPU cores at the same time, lock-free algorithms are implemented in SAP HANA in certain areas.

We see that although threads allow for better performance, they are not as robust as single processes, because the memory access is not separated. For example, one thread could fail and write garbage into the memory. Because the same memory will then be accessed by the other threads, the garbage data will immediately affect them, eventually leading to their failure.

> **Note**
>
> SAP NetWeaver, for example, uses separate `disp+work` processes that can be stopped and started independently from each other. These `disp+work` processes are single threaded.

We will now explain the multithreaded nature of SAP HANA. We begin with the relation between threads on the one hand and sessions and database requests on the other. This relationship also has implications for the stopping of requests, sessions, and threads, which we cover next. We conclude with a discussion of difficulties that may occur when cancelling statements.

10.2.1   Sessions Running in Threads

As mentioned before, the session itself does not permanently map to a specific process or thread in SAP HANA. This is quite different from many other DBMS supported by SAP NetWeaver. Very often, these DBMS implement a session to be bound to a specific process or thread, which makes it easy to follow up on which SAP NetWeaver work process is using which session on the database and in turn which process or thread of the DBMS.

Figure 10.11 shows an example of this mapping of threads to a user session.

The session with `ConnectionID 300288` started to work on the create `column table ... with data` command. The purpose of this command is to copy an existing table with the records stored in it. To process the command, the connection got assigned to an `SQLExecutor` thread with `Thread ID 12533`.

Figure 10.11 Session Spawning JobWorker Threads

Because SAP HANA is a column store database, the task of copying the table can be split into copying each column. Each column can independently be copied, which means that it can be done in parallel. To work on the columns in parallel, a thread for each column is required. Also, these worker threads need to be controlled and coordinated.

The `SQLExecutor` thread creates `JobWorker` threads and delegates work to them. One of these `JobWorker` threads gets to be the coordinator (thread method `generic`), whereas the remaining `JobWorker` threads actually perform the data-copy work.

In the THREADS overview, you can observe this dependency by checking the CALL-ING and CALLER columns. Once a `JobWorker` is done with its share of data shoveling, it reports back to the coordination thread and then terminates. The coordination thread waits until all the `JobWorker` threads are finished and then reports back to the `SQLExecutor` thread that called it initially. The `JobWorker` processes are created upon demand, and their number is automatically determined by SAP HANA's internal job management. This is different from the `SQLExecutor` threads, which are typically kept and then reassigned to other connections. This multi-leveled work-scheduling setup allows for fast assignment of `SQLExecutor` threads to incoming commands from open connections as well as dynamic parallelization.

With SAP HANA, this mapping is not fixed. Instead, every session is kept in a session pool and stays there idle until the client sends commands to be executed. SAP HANA employs a set of network listener threads that receive and dispatch the client requests to the corresponding sessions.

> **Note**
>
> One of the design goals for SAP HANA is to provide as many processing resources as possible to any query so that even complex queries that consist of many processing steps can be executed quickly. The internal job management via threads is the technical implementation towards this goal.

SAP HANA not only handles multiple sessions with multiple threads, it also uses multithreading for parallelized processing of the workload in one session. We will now explain this important mechanism before showing how you can monitor threads on the operating system.

Parallel Processing of Requests

To process requests, sessions get assigned to one of the threads (SQLExecutor) from a thread pool in SAP HANA. As most of the request can be broken down into smaller pieces of work, SAP HANA can assign multiple JobWorker threads to one request and thereby reduce the total runtime of a statement.

As an end user or developer, you do not have to worry about this, because SAP HANA automatically finds the maximum possible parallelization for every processing step. Note that some of the processing steps may not allow for indefinite parallel processing due to design of algorithms or loss of efficiency (when coordinating the parallel threads consumes more CPU time than what is saved by executing the query in parallel).

For a summary of the session assignment and query execution mechanism in SAP HANA, see Figure 10.12. Every client process, for example, the disp+work processes of an SAP NetWeaver instance or a Java program connecting via JDBC, is logged on to a session in the database server.

When queries need to be executed, the session is assigned to one of the free SQLExecutor threads. The SQLExecutor threads are created upon SAP HANA startup (the number created is usually twice that of the CPU cores, because SAP HANA employs Hyper-Threading) and are not terminated under normal circumstances. As we mentioned, these threads can execute the query, but they can also create JobWorker threads and then hand work off to them. These JobWorker threads are created and terminated as required.

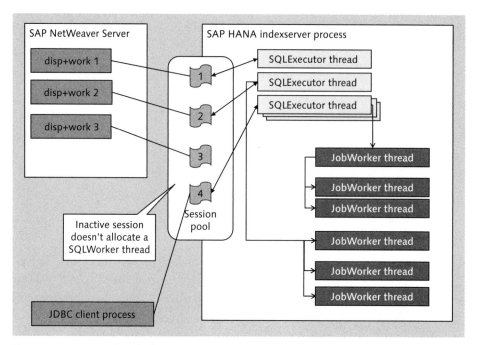

Figure 10.12 Session Thread Allocation

Note that there are many other thread types present and running in any SAP HANA instance. These threads usually are designated to special background tasks, such as writing out changed data to disk or creating log backups. Typical administration tasks for SAP HANA do not involve managing these background tasks, so we leave discussion of them aside for now.

Watching Threads on OS Level

Sometimes, it can be interesting to look at the SAP HANA processes and threads on an operating system level. For example, you could realize that the server host on which SAP HANA is running uses around 700% CPU, and you might wonder how that could be.

The first thing to understand in this situation is the math behind this CPU usage number. Technically, what tools like top do is read CPU usage cycles per interval (say, every second) and compare this against the total number of CPU cycles during this period. Because the CPU normally does not stop when there is no work to do, the cycles are still performed, but the usage accounting groups the cycles into time spent for user programs/in user mode (%us); which basically means all application code; system mode (%sy), which usually covers larger parts of the core operating system and device drivers; and idle time (%id). There are more categories available, but for our example it's sufficient to know these three.

When top is started, the initial screen may look like Figure 10.13, and the figures are updated every second.

```
top - 21:52:33 up 6 days, 14:21,  2 users,  load average: 0.52, 0.29,
Tasks: 2130 total,   1 running, 2129 sleeping,   0 stopped,   0 zombi
Cpu(s):  1.1%us,  0.5%sy,  0.0%ni, 98.5%id,  0.0%wa,  0.0%hi,  0.0%si
Mem:    969321M total,   951272M used,    18048M free,    1842M buff
Swap:    32767M total,    1464M used,    31303M free,   557509M cach

  PID USER      PR  NI  VIRT  RES  SHR S %CPU %MEM     TIME+ COMMAND
68160 wrladm    20   0  345g 323g 169g S  107 34.2  93537:36 hdbindex
97383 omgadm    20   0  135g 121g 663m S   17 12.8 754:16.20 hdbindex
97386 omgadm    20   0 23.9g 8.4g 439m S   10  0.9 439:27.24 hdbstati
19233 wupadm    20   0 29.2g  21g 1.1g S    7  2.2 128:39.24 hdbindex
97389 omgadm    20   0 9740m 2.4g 419m S    7  0.3 393:58.95 hdbxseng
93696 wrgadm    20   0 11.8g 4.7g 658m S    7  0.5 590:13.15 hdbindex
99459 htgadm    20   0 15.2g 8.2g 650m S    6  0.9 575:01.30 hdbindex
18839 wupadm    20   0 28.0g 2.3g 549m S    6  0.2  46:10.17 hdbnames
57164 wrladm    20   0 31.8g  15g 408m S    6  1.6 628:20.41 hdbstati
97076 omgadm    20   0 28.4g 3.8g 549m S    6  0.4 395:12.42 hdbnames
19236 wupadm    20   0 13.0g 2.1g 414m S    6  0.2  45:41.20 hdbxseng
56854 wrladm    20   0 27.6g 3.0g 489m S    6  0.3 510:36.67 hdbnames
57161 wrladm    20   0 23.5g 3.7g 374m S    6  0.4 493:18.60 hdbscrip
57167 wrladm    20   0 23.4g 3.8g 375m S    6  0.4 498:03.00 hdbnames
99462 htgadm    20   0 10.8g 4.3g 440m S    5  0.5 385:03.11 hdbstati
99465 htgadm    20   0 10.6g 2.7g 415m S    5  0.3 348:49.72 hdbxseng
93702 wrgadm    20   0 10.9g 3.0g 422m S    5  0.3 390:56.86 hdbxseng
99151 htgadm    20   0 27.5g 2.4g 549m S    5  0.3 339:55.13 hdbnames
93394 wrgadm    20   0 27.6g 2.4g 548m S    5  0.3 347:05.52 hdbnames
```

Figure 10.13 Example Output of the top Tool (Unfiltered)

On our server, several SAP HANA instances are running, so we see multiple hdbindexserver processes. Therefore, we need to focus on one of them, which we can do by either specifying the -p <process id> parameter or the -u <user name> parameter when starting top. Let's use top -u wupadm to look at only get the processes belonging to our user (Figure 10.14).

With only the processes included in the output that belong to our system, we already find something noteworthy: The total CPU usage in user mode (SAP HANA code runs in user mode) currently makes up for 1.0% of the total host CPU usage. However, looking at the %CPU column for our hdbindexserver process, we see a number around 107%.

```
top - 22:00:39 up 6 days, 14:29,  2 users,  load average: 4.46, 2.58,
Tasks: 2131 total,   1 running, 2130 sleeping,   0 stopped,   0 zombi
Cpu(s):  1.0%us,  0.4%sy,  0.0%ni, 98.6%id,  0.0%wa,  0.0%hi,  0.0%si
Mem:   969321M total,   957544M used,   11777M free,    1842M buff
Swap:   32767M total,    1464M used,   31303M free,  557514M cach

  PID USER      PR  NI  VIRT  RES  SHR S %CPU %MEM    TIME+  COMMAND
19233 wupadm    20   0 37.9g  27g 1.1g S  107  2.9 140:14.47 hdbindex
18839 wupadm    20   0 28.0g 2.3g 549m S    6  0.2  46:39.54 hdbnames
19236 wupadm    20   0 13.0g 2.1g 414m S    5  0.2  46:10.40 hdbxseng
33475 wupadm    20   0 14920 7420  876 R    2  0.0   0:10.64 top
33220 wupadm    20   0 95436 2536 1500 S    0  0.0   0:00.05 sshd
18728 wupadm    20   0 19812 1456  824 S    0  0.0   0:00.00 sapstart
18820 wupadm    20   0  828m 294m 267m S    0  0.0   0:01.01 hdb.sapW
19203 wupadm    20   0 7569m 391m 111m S    0  0.0   0:13.71 hdbprepr
19206 wupadm    20   0 6905m 403m 108m S    0  0.0   0:20.68 hdbcompi
20632 wupadm    20   0  198m  70m  59m S    0  0.0   0:01.50 sapwebdi
33223 wupadm    20   0 14652 2744 1536 S    0  0.0   0:00.03 sh
33282 wupadm    20   0 93228 2156 1160 S    0  0.0   0:00.00 sshd
33283 wupadm    20   0 54336 2136 1560 S    0  0.0   0:00.00 sftp-ser
38530 wupadm    20   0  217m  72m 3144 S    0  0.0   0:47.85 sapstart
```

Figure 10.14 Example Output of top Tool, Filtered for User WUPADM

Which number is correct here? In fact, both. However, they show different aggregation levels.

The number in the header section shows the average CPU usage of every logical CPU core in the system. This host runs on 80 physical CPU cores with Hyper-Threading enabled (allowing it to run two processes in parallel on a single CPU core), which means that the number is probably calculated in the following way:

$$\frac{(CPU1 : (100\% us) + CPU2 : (7+6+5+2\% us) + CPU3...CPU160 : 0\% us\,)}{(\# \text{ of logical CPUs } (160))}$$

$$\approx \frac{(114\% us + 0\% us)}{160}$$

$$= 0,7125\% us$$

The second number (%CPU), however, is simply the sum of all CPU usage percentages used by the hdbindexserver process. Because SAP HANA makes heavy use of running parallel workload through threads, it is easily possible to use more than one CPU core (1 CPU core = 100%) at a time. In this case, apparently roughly four of the 160 possible logical CPU cores have been used, or, to be more precise, the total number of CPU cycles spent in user mode by the hdbindexserver process (and all of its threads) was worth 400% of the standardized single CPU cycles over the whole system.

> **Note**
>
> To keep things simple, you can think about it like this: There is 1 CPU core for every 100% in the list output.

Now, it would be interesting to get at least an idea of what the `hdbindexserver` process is doing. With `top`, it is possible to switch the display to threads mode by pressing [Shift] + [H]. The list then displays single threads and their respective thread IDs (although the column header still reads `PID`).

```
top - 22:55:13 up 6 days, 15:24,  2 users,  load average: 4.04, 4.06,
Tasks: 8015 total,   5 running, 8010 sleeping,   0 stopped,   0 zombi
Cpu(s):  2.6%us,  0.4%sy,  0.0%ni, 97.0%id,  0.0%wa,  0.0%hi,  0.0%si
Mem:    969321M total,   952384M used,    16936M free,     1833M buff
Swap:    32767M total,     1469M used,    31298M free,    540520M cach

  PID USER      PR  NI  VIRT  RES  SHR S %CPU %MEM    TIME+  COMMAND
12270 wupadm    20   0 47.4g  38g 1.1g R   58  4.1  2:17.44 JobWrk00
12212 wupadm    20   0 47.4g  38g 1.1g R   58  4.1  1:22.50 JobWrk01
12200 wupadm    20   0 47.4g  38g 1.1g R   57  4.1  2:20.95 JobWrk01
12477 wupadm    20   0 47.4g  38g 1.1g S   57  4.1  2:39.97 PoolThre
12212 wupadm    20   0 47.4g  38g 1.1g S   22  4.1  2:17.19 JobWrk01
12220 wupadm    20   0 47.4g  38g 1.1g S   13  4.1  2:26.62 JobWrk01
12223 wupadm    20   0 47.4g  38g 1.1g S   13  4.1  1:10.05 JobWrk01
12233 wupadm    20   0 47.4g  38g 1.1g S   13  4.1  2:19.61 JobWrk01
12246 wupadm    20   0 47.4g  38g 1.1g S   12  4.1  2:22.17 JobWrk00
12263 wupadm    20   0 47.4g  38g 1.1g S   11  4.1  2:20.77 JobWrk01
12266 wupadm    20   0 47.4g  38g 1.1g S    9  4.1  2:18.78 JobWrk00
19502 wupadm    20   0 47.4g  38g 1.1g S    7  4.1  2:29.57 JobWrk00
19523 wupadm    20   0 47.4g  38g 1.1g S    7  4.1  2:18.28 JobWrk00
19616 wupadm    20   0 47.4g  38g 1.1g S    6  4.1  2:18.41 JobWrk01
34109 wupadm    20   0 14852 7360  876 R    6  0.0  1:57.38 top
19577 wupadm    20   0 47.4g  38g 1.1g S    5  4.1  2:16.97 JobWrk01
19483 wupadm    20   0 47.4g  38g 1.1g S    4  4.1  2:39.04 JobWrk00
19515 wupadm    20   0 47.4g  38g 1.1g S    2  4.1  2:17.53 JobWrk00
19490 wupadm    20   0 47.4g  38g 1.1g S    1  4.1  2:18.00 JobWrk00
```

Figure 10.15 Example Output of the top Tool, Filtered for User WUPADM in Threads Mode

As we can tell by the thread names shown in the COMMAND column, there are Job-Worker threads actively running in parallel as well as a PoolThread. This information can be easily matched against the THREADS overview in SAP HANA Studio, as shown in Figure 10.16.

Comparing the THREAD ID numbers, we find that the PoolThread (12477) in the top output is our SqlExecutor (12477) thread that runs our SQL command and that the JobWorker threads have been spawned to parallelize the work.

Overview	Landscape	Alerts	Performance	Volumes	Configuration	System Information	Diagnosis Files	Trace Configuration	Console

| Threads | Sessions | Blocked Transactions | SQL Plan Cache | Expensive Statements Trace | Job Progress | Load |

▸ **Summary**

Host: `<All>` ▾ Service: `indexserver` ▾ Thread Type: `<active>` ▾ ✖ ☑ Group and Sort ☐ Creat

Service	Connection ID	Thread ID	Calling	Caller	Thread Type	Thread Method	Thread Detail
indexserver	301751	12477	12070		SqlExecutor	ExecuteStatement	insert into cbig (select * from indexperf.p...
indexserver	301751	12070	| 12200, 12212, ...	12477	JobWorker	calc	plan400280@ld9506:34203/pop0 (JERequ...
indexserver	301751	12200		| 12070	JobWorker	execute	execute
indexserver	301751	12212		| 12070	JobWorker	execute	execute
indexserver	301751	12220		| 12070	JobWorker	execute	execute
indexserver	301751	12223		| 12070	JobWorker	execute	execute
indexserver	301751	12233		| 12070	JobWorker	execute	execute
indexserver	301751	12246		| 12070	JobWorker	execute	execute
indexserver	301751	12263		| 12070	JobWorker	execute	execute
indexserver	301751	12266		| 12070	JobWorker	execute	execute

Figure 10.16 Threads Overview with Parallel Running Threads

10.2.2 Stopping Processes and Threads

As explained previously, the operating system manages how much CPU time each process and each thread can use, but it tracks memory access only on the process level. Within the memory area of a process, threads can use the memory freely, and the operating system cannot know which memory belongs to which thread. This means that the operating system can easily cut off any process from CPU time and release all of its allocated resources, but it cannot know how to remove a thread from a running process safely without knowledge of the internal data structures of the program. For example, what if the thread that is about to be killed just modified some data and is in between two calculation steps? How should the operating system's task or process manager know how to clean this up properly? The answer is that the operating system cannot know, and thus when a thread needs to be ended it needs to be done by the process the thread belongs to.

For a multithreaded application, the process that started the thread in the first place needs to take the necessary steps to stop the thread. The big benefit of this approach is that the resource cleanup can happen close to where the resource consummation happened, so no other piece of code needs to learn how to clean up this thread's resource usage. Unfortunately, this comes at a price; for the thread to be able to perform a kind of self-destruction, it needs to check whether it should end itself every now and then. The programmer of the thread code needs to include these checks into the application code, which would look similar to Listing 10.3.

```
 1 BEGIN
 2    IF cancelFlag == SET THEN EXIT;
 3    CREATE LIST l;
 4    FOR each row r in table t LOOP
 5          IF r MATCHES CONDITION
 6                ADD r TO LIST l;
 7          END IF;
 8          IF cancelFlag == SET THEN BREAK;
 9    END LOOP;
10    FREE LIST l;
11    EXIT;
12 END
```

Listing 10.3 Pseudocode for Request Cancellation

The pseudocode in Listing 10.3 gives an example of how a thread could check for cancellation. The first instruction in the procedure (line 2) checks whether the global cancelFlag is set and exits the procedure correctly with no work done if the flag indeed is set. The next step is to allocate memory for some result, a LIST in this case.

The procedure then loops over all records of a table and adds those records that match certain criteria to the result list. In line 8, the cancelFlag is checked again and the loop will be quit if the flag is set. Below the loop, the list is deleted and the memory it allocates is freed. If everything is working as it should, the code will execute nicely, probably not taking too much time, and it finally will release the memory it used back to the system.

Now, imagine that this thread crashes or that it is killed during the execution of the loop. In this case, the LIST would be in an unknown state and the memory could not be properly returned to the system. To address the stopping problem, the procedure regularly checks for the cancelFlag and cleans up the used resources. As nice as this approach is, there are two problems:

▶ The programmer needs to decide in advance where the code should be cancellable. Making this decision can be difficult, because one only wants to check in situations that could potentially take a long time or hinder other threads from working. Also, it is very easy in a complex system like a DBMS to fail to foresee what part of the code could take a long time or block others.

▶ Checking for the `cancelFlag` can be a costly operation that has a severely negative impact on performance. Especially in SAP HANA, many so-called cache-conscious algorithms are used that provide high-performance characteristics and that leverage the CPU internal data-caching structures to work very quickly on large amounts of data (e.g., scanning a table column). Introducing cancellation check code like the example in Listing 10.3 into such optimized code can easily destroy the performance benefit, so cancellation checks need to be placed very carefully.

We see that enabling multithreaded code to gracefully stop leads to a tradeoff among performance, code maintainability, and system stability. The more often the flag is checked, the easier it is to stop "bad" threads, but the slower the system will be in total.

This leads us to an important administration topic.

10.2.3 Canceling a Running SQL Command

Long-running commands or sessions that block other statements from proceeding can be a problem in database management systems. This is because these commands can affect other sessions by using CPU and memory resources or by keeping locks on records that need to be changed by the other sessions. In the worst case, this could render the whole system unresponsive.

Fortunately, SAP HANA provides commands to stop the execution of running statements or to disconnect a session. The first command is:

```
ALTER SYSTEM CANCEL [WORK IN] SESSION <session_id>
```

This command can be executed by any user for sessions that belong to this user. To cancel other users' sessions, the system privilege SESSION ADMIN has to be granted prior to running the command.

In Figure 10.17, we see that the user DTX is running an SQL statement in the right-hand window. As the SQL Editor window is waiting for the statement to finish and to retrieve the result set, we cannot run the ALTER SYSTEM CANCEL SESSION command in this window.

Therefore, we use the left SQL Editor window to find out the connection id of the other running session; in this case, it is connection id 381561.

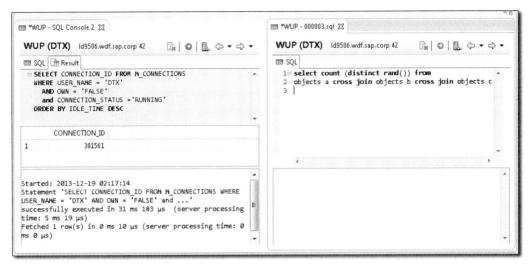

Figure 10.17 Statement Cancellation Example

Figure 10.18 shows the result of the ALTER SYSTEM CANCEL SESSION command. It took a couple of seconds for the cancellation request to be recognized by the specific part of the SAP HANA code that was currently running, but then the running operation was gracefully cancelled and the open transaction was rolled back.

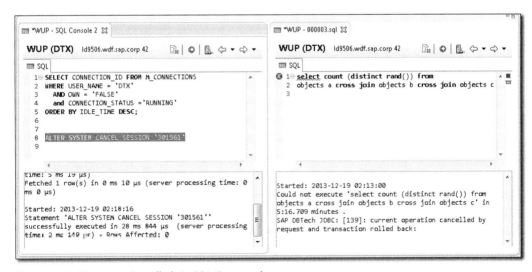

Figure 10.18 Statement Cancelled via SQL Command

This works because the user who tries to cancel the other session is the same as the user running the session to be cancelled. If you tried to cancel any other users' sessions without the ADMIN SESSION privilege, you would get error message [258]: insufficient privilege: Not authorized.

Clearly, this is a cumbersome way to just abort a running statement. Luckily, SAP HANA Studio offers an easier way to cancel a running statement that was started from the SQL Editor, as depicted in Figure 10.19. To provide this functionality, SAP HANA Studio uses the statement.cancel() method of the JDBC driver that allows other threads in a Java client application to retrieve the connection id and to send the cancellation command.

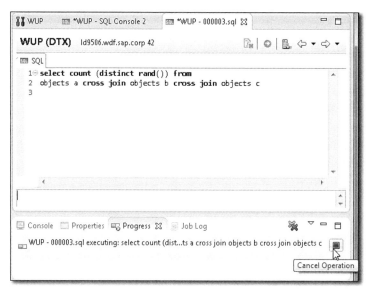

Figure 10.19 Cancel Operation Button for SQL Editor

Although this functionality is handy, it unfortunately cannot be used for statements that were not started from SAP HANA Studio and that run in a different user context—which is a common scenario with statements that should be cancelled. Finding the exact correct connection id for such a session on a heavy-duty SAP HANA system with hundreds of sessions simply by using the SQL commands shown previously is difficult and error prone.

The THREADS monitor in SAP HANA Studio (ADMINISTRATION CONSOLE • PERFORMANCE • THREADS) is much easier to use. There, we can simply right-click on the session we want to cancel and select CANCEL OPERATION from the context menu, as shown in Figure 10.20.

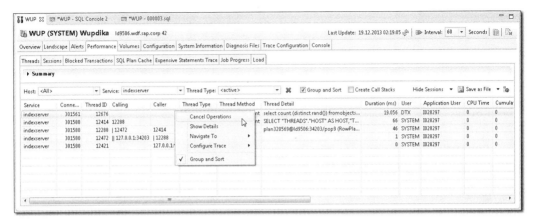

Figure 10.20 Cancel Operation in the Threads Monitor

10.2.4 Killing a Session

Sometimes it might be desirable to not only cancel a currently running statement of a session but to disconnect the session completely. The command for this is ALTER SYSTEM DISCONNECT SESSION '<CONNECTION ID>' and can be used similarly to the CANCEL SESSION command. The difference between this and the CANCEL WORK command simply is that not only will the current command be cancelled but the session itself will be terminated.

> **Note**
>
> Disconnecting the session is not a "stronger" way to force the termination of a long-run-ning command. With either option, the running command first needs to recognize the cancellation flag and then the transaction rollback must be performed, which also can take a considerable amount of time. If the CANCEL WORK command did not succeed to stop a running command, then there is no point in trying DISCONNECT SESSION.

10.2.5 Problems with Session Cancellation

As you have seen, the ability to stop running commands and disconnect sessions relies on the idea that the session that should be cancelled actively checks for the cancellation flag to be set. This approach has the drawback that there are situa-tions in which the session cannot check the flag and thus can never be cancelled.

For example, a session could open a transaction and update a table but not commit the update. Instead, the session no longer does anything and therefore just holds a lock on the changed record (e.g., think of a user having a data-entry mask open and unsaved leaving for lunch). If other sessions now need to change this record as well, they need to wait until the first session releases the lock.

In this situation, a CANCEL SESSION on the lock holder session does not help, because the session is currently not running any code that could check for the cancellation flag. This situation, in which the session is IDLE, can only be resolved by disconnecting the session.

The problem with this is obvious: What if the client application is currently legitimately processing the data and should write the results back to the database? In this case, the work is lost and the session needs to be restarted. Therefore, it is important to try to find out why the session is currently inactive while a transaction is open and decide on a case-by-case basis whether or not to disconnect the session. (We will see how to find out who is running a session in Section 10.3.)

A second problem is that sometimes it takes several minutes until the rollback of a session is performed and the cancellation is successfully finished. During that time, there are no visible signs, in the THREADS monitor, for example, that the specific thread is flagged for termination. This might lead to DBAs trying to run the CANCEL SESSION command over and over again until it works. Clearly, this is futile.

To double-check whether the session control commands have been understood, you can examine the index server trace file in Listing 10.4.

```
[...]
[12351]{301610}[-1/-1] 2013-12-19 03:03:05.410801 i SQLSessionCmd
    Statement.cc(03254) :
        session control command is performed by 301610,
        user=LARS, application user=I028297,
        application source=csns.sql.editor.SQLExecuteFormEditor$1$1
                        .run(SQLExecuteFormEditor.java:796);
        , query=ALTER SYSTEM CANCEL SESSION '301611'
[...]
```

Listing 10.4 Index Server Trace File Excerpt

In the case that a statement or session cancellation does not succeed at all, it could be that SAP HANA currently executes a routine that does not check (yet) for the cancelFlag. To find these routines and to improve them, SAP HANA development needs to know about them. Such information can be gathered by the means of a runtime dump. SAP Note 1951590 covers this.

In such a case, unfortunately, the only chances to stop the running session are to trigger the client to release the lock (if that is possible), to stop the client process, or, as a very last resort, to stop and restart the whole indexserver process, which will also end all other sessions.

Therefore, before taking this very last step, consider if the cancellation can wait until, for example, the majority of users has logged off and important jobs have finished. Also, you should open an incident with SAP Support for this situation and make sure to collect the runtime dump so that the root cause can be analyzed even though the system was restarted. In short, do not rush to cancel threads by restarting the system!

10.3 Monitoring Sessions and Transactions

We have already covered some important concepts of sessions and threads in SAP HANA. Now, it is time to see how these concepts can be applied to monitoring the database. We will begin with the session monitor in SAP HANA Studio and then introduce you to the monitoring views of the database that are underlying this monitor.

10.3.1 Using the Session Monitor

To access the session monitor, navigate to ADMINISTRATION CONSOLE • PERFOR-MANCE • SESSIONS. Figure 10.21 shows most of the functions of the session monitor at once.

Typically, the list of sessions will be rather large and overwhelming. Therefore, it is important to filter the list down to the interesting entries. SAP HANA Studio provides two independent options to filter lists:

▶ The QUICK FILTER box on the left side of the screen just above the list

▶ The list of column filters that can be set by clicking on the FILTERS… button

With the QUICK FILTER, you can just type in the search term by which you want to filter the list. The list will then be searched over all columns, and only those rows will be displayed that match the search term in any column. Also, the QUICK FILTER will highlight the found search term by using a bold typeface in the list display. With that ability, the Quick Filter is suitable for quick and simple filtering of the session list.

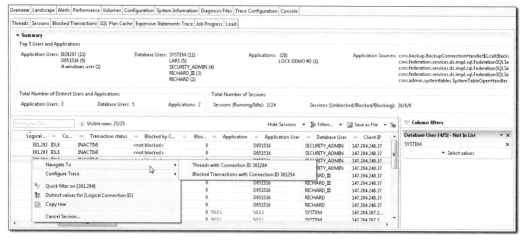

Figure 10.21 SAP HANA Studio Session Monitor

For more complex filters that can include several columns with different filter conditions, the Filters... button can be used. The filter conditions are applied with a logical AND operation (all filter conditions are applied) so that the list can be reduced to the interesting sessions effectively.

The summary section shown in Figure 10.21 is initially hidden, but it can be shown by clicking on the triangle symbol next to the word Summary. Note that the filters set up for the list are not applied to the summary section.

The context menus for the list rows provide options to cancel a session, to apply quick filters based on the table cell that was right-clicked, to create a Distinct Values report for the current column (see Figure 10.22), and also to navigate to other displays in SAP HANA Studio, for example, to the Threads overview.

Typical questions that can be answered from the Sessions overview include:

▶ Which sessions are currently active or have open transactions? See columns Connection Status and Transaction Status.

▶ Which user triggered this command logged on as DB user SYSTEM? Check column Application User.

▶ How many sessions are created from a specific client computer? Add a filter on the CLIENT IP ADDRESS or HOST NAME and check the VISIBLE ROWS counter.

To filter out noise from SAP HANA Studio sessions, the HIDE SESSIONS button provides built-in filters that remove idle sessions, all SAP HANA Studio sessions (based on the APPLICATION context variable), or just the Administration Editor sessions (based on the APPLICATION and APPLICATIONSOURCE context variables.)

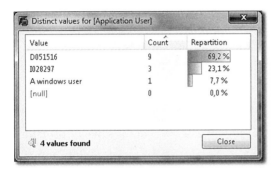

Figure 10.22 Distinct Values Report for the Application User Column

10.3.2 Using the Monitoring Views via SQL

As mentioned earlier, all information about sessions and connections can be found in the monitoring view M_CONNECTION. To provide a starting point for using the view, let's see what information is available in it.

Running SELECT * FROM M_CONNECTIONS will deliver all information at once, but its output is barely useful; we would drown in data without being able to understand what we see. Luckily, the view comes with a column OWN that indicates the record that contains information about the session that is currently executing the select command.

By simply executing SELECT * FROM M_CONNECTIONS WHERE OWN = 'TRUE', you just get back one record, which serves as a starting example. In hdbsql, the result of the preceding statement looks like Listing 10.5.

```
select * from m_connections where own = 'TRUE';
HOST,PORT,CONNECTION_ID,TRANSACTION_ID,START_TIME,IDLE_TIME,CONNECTION_
STATUS,CLIENT_HOST,CLIENT_IP,CLIENT_PID,USER_NAME,CONNECTION_
TYPE,OWN,IS_HISTOR
Y_SAVED,MEMORY_SIZE_PER_CONNECTION,AUTO_COMMIT,LAST_ACTION,CURRENT_
STATEMENT_ID,CURRENT_OPERATOR_NAME,FETCHED_RECORD_COUNT,AFFECTED_
```

```
RECORD_COUNT,SENT_
MESSAGE_SIZE,SENT_MESSAGE_COUNT,RECEIVED_MESSAGE_SIZE,RECEIVED_MESSAGE_
COUNT,CREATOR_THREAD_ID,CREATED_BY,IS_ENCRYPTED,END_TIME,PARENT_
CONNECTION_ID,C
LIENT_DISTRIBUTION_MODE,LOGICAL_CONNECTION_ID,CURRENT_SCHEMA_
NAME,CURRENT_THREAD_ID
"coe-he-084",32003,206178,265,"2013-11-28 15:17:13.852639000",0,"RUN-
NING","VIEN60239482A","147.204.250.248",10040,"RDP361_
0","Remote","TRUE","FALSE",7
248,"TRUE","ExecutePre-
pared","885529776966318","",5,0,9824,20,4208,21,16010,"Ses-
sion","FALSE",?,0,"STATEMENT ROUTING",206178,"RDP361_0",16010
1 row selected (overall time 610,884 msec; server time 16,777 msec)
```
Listing 10.5 Output from M_CONNECTIONS

Clearly, this output is far from readable, and even looking at the same information in the grid view in SAP HANA Studio does not improve the situation much, as you can see in Figure 10.23.

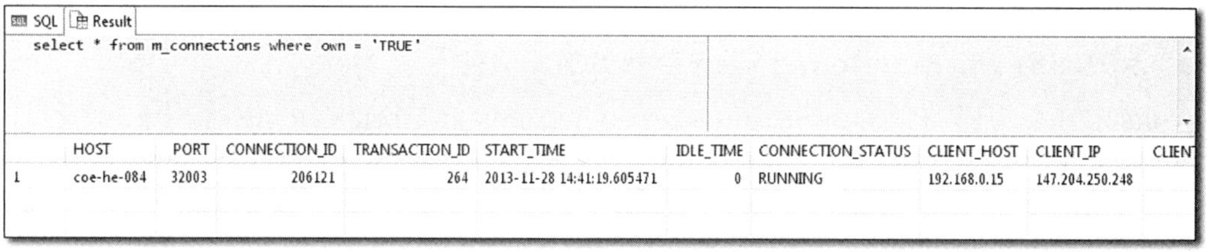

Figure 10.23 Query Result from M_CONNECTIONS System View in SAP HANA Studio

You would need to horizontally scroll all the way over to the right to review all columns. To make the result easier to read, you need to transpose the columns to rows, for example, via MS Excel or a text editor (Table 10.2).

Column	Value
HOST	coe-he-084
PORT	32003
CONNECTION_ID	206178
TRANSACTION_ID	265
START_TIME	2013-11-28 15:17:13.852639000

Table 10.2 Transposed Information from M_CONNECTIONS

Column	Value
IDLE_TIME	0
CONNECTION_STATUS	RUNNING
CLIENT_HOST	VIEN60239482A
CLIENT_IP	147.204.250.248
CLIENT_PID	10040
USER_NAME	RDP361_0
CONNECTION_TYPE	Remote
OWN	TRUE
IS_HISTORY_SAVED	FALSE
MEMORY_SIZE_PER_CONNECTION	**7248**
AUTO_COMMIT	TRUE
LAST_ACTION	ExecutePrepared
CURRENT_STATEMENT_ID	**885529776966318**
CURRENT_OPERATOR_NAME	[blank]
FETCHED_RECORD_COUNT	5
AFFECTED_RECORD_COUNT	0
SENT_MESSAGE_SIZE	9824
SENT_MESSAGE_COUNT	20
RECEIVED_MESSAGE_SIZE	4208
RECEIVED_MESSAGE_COUNT	21
CREATOR_THREAD_ID	16010
CREATED_BY	Session
IS_ENCRYPTED	FALSE
END_TIME	?
PARENT_CONNECTION_ID	0
CLIENT_DISTRIBUTION_MODE	STATEMENT ROUTING
LOGICAL_CONNECTION_ID	206178
CURRENT_SCHEMA_NAME	RDP361_0
CURRENT_THREAD_ID	16010

Table 10.2 Transposed Information from M_CONNECTIONS (Cont.)

Now, with this readable output, it's easy to find information about the session.

At the very moment of the query execution, the `MEMORY_SIZE_PER_CONNECTION` was only 7,248 bytes (302 KB). The connection itself is identified via its `CONNECTION_ID`, which also can be found in, for example, the trace files.

Even with this approach to reading the data, it's still not very comfortable to manually transpose single rows. Also, interesting additional information, such as the actual SQL command text that was last executed, would be nice to see; right now, all we see is the `CURRENT_STATEMENT_ID`, which we could use to query the `M_PREPARED_STATEMENTS` monitoring view.

Fortunately, SAP HANA Studio provides several displays that are much more comfortable to use and that combine these system views for us. For every row in the THREADS overview (ADMINISTRATION CONSOLE • PERFORMANCE • THREADS), a DETAILS window can be opened, either by double-clicking on the row or via the context menu SHOW DETAILS. Figure 10.24 shows an example of the THREADS DETAILS window listing combined information about the connection, the current transaction, threads, and the SQL statement. With this set of information, although presented in a rather long list, we get a comprehensive overview of what a given thread is currently doing.

Figure 10.24 Thread Details Window

10.4 Concurrency and Parallelism

SAP HANA's advantage in speed is rooted in many aspects of the design of the system. One of these aspects is that single commands can be internally broken down into smaller pieces of work and processed in parallel on the many CPU cores of an SAP HANA server.

In Section 10.2.1, we discussed how SAP HANA processes commands in SQLExecutor threads that can span JobWorker threads to parallelize the work of a single statement. In the next four subsections, we shed light on the impact of such parallelism on the transaction management of the database.

We will begin by working out the different types of parallelism offered in the database system. Certain kinds of parallel processing can lead to locks or blocking situations, and we cover these items next, including the closely related timeouts. Finally, we explain the database system's multiversion concurrency control mechanism that enables the database to avoid locks in reading transactions.

10.4.1 Types of Parallelism

First, it is good to get an idea of the different types of parallelism that can be used with SAP HANA:

- **Interquery parallelization**
  This means that multiple separate statements can be executed in parallel. This seems to be an obvious feature, but it is important to understand how this is implemented. For each statement that should run at the same time as other statements, there has to be one SQLExecutor thread available. When more sessions want to run commands in SAP HANA than there are SQLExecutor threads, the requests need to be queued and the sessions have to wait until an SQLExecutor thread is available again.

  This of course does not mean that an SAP HANA system with, for example, 160 logical CPUs can only handle 160 sessions that are connected at the same time, but it does mean that only 160 of these sessions can process a request at the same time. Should more requests need to be processed in parallel than that, more logical CPUs need to be available. This can either be done by scaling up the host to a platform that supports more CPUs or CPUs with more cores or by scaling out to multiple SAP HANA nodes.

▶ **Intraquery parallelization**
This means that single processing steps for a query can be executed in parallel, because these steps don't depend on each other. For example, reading data from multiple columns of one table could be done by two threads on two separate CPU cores. Or, in case the involved table is partitioned, each table partition could be worked on by a separate thread. The actual decision about the degree of parallelism is taken by the SAP HANA query optimizers upon query execution. That way, the developer or DBA does not need to care about dynamic system-load situations, but it also means that the actual degree of parallelism for a given query cannot be controlled.

To monitor the current interquery parallelization, SAP HANA Studio provides the overview sections of the THREADS and SESSIONS monitors, as shown in Figure 10.25.

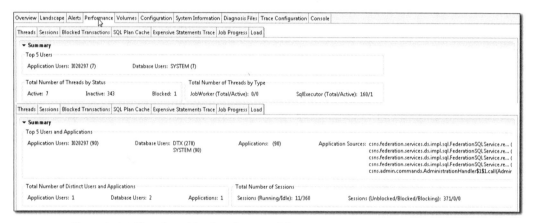

Figure 10.25 Threads and Sessions Summary Views

Checking on the intraquery parallelization is somewhat more difficult, because it depends on the current system-load situation. However, it's possible to trace and visualize a query execution with the Plan Visualizer (PlanViz) tool and to analyze parallel processing steps for a query (or an SQLScript procedure) with it.

We will look into this tool in more detail in Chapter 15.

10.4.2 Locks and Blocking

Another aspect of parallelism is *concurrency* or the use of the same resource by more than one session at a time. Resources for our commands could be any database objects, such as schemas, tables, views, or indexes, as well as records in tables. SAP HANA employs a locking mechanism to ensure that no session changes data that is currently worked upon in another session.

For practical matters, there are two relevant lock types, table locks and row locks, to consider. Depending on the command that will be executed, the locks can be set in different modes, allowing or preventing other locks of the same type to be set.

Table 10.3 provides an overview of lock types and lock modes. In this table, DML stands for *data manipulation language*, which includes all SQL statements that change data. DDL stands for *data definition language*, which includes all SQL statements that define or modify the structure of the database, tables, views, etc.

Lock Type	Lock Mode	Comment
Table lock	IX (intentional exclusive)	Set by DML commands: INSERT, UPDATE, UPSERT, DELETE, SELECT FOR UPDATE, and MERGE DELTA
	X (exclusive)	Set by LOCK TABLE command and DDL commands like ALTER TABLE, DROP TABLE, CREATE/ DROP INDEX, and TRUNCATE TABLE
Row lock	X (exclusive)	Set by DML commands: INSERT, UPDATE, UPSERT, DELETE, and SELECT FOR UPDATE.

Table 10.3 Overview of Lock Types and Modes

There are several noteworthy things in this table. First of all, there is no shared lock mode present. Typically, a shared lock would be used to allow multiple sessions to read the same record at a time but prevent any session from changing this record. This can be necessary to guarantee the consistent read of records when multiversion concurrency (MVCC) is not available. SAP HANA never sets shared locks on records.

Key Takeaway

Reading table rows never sets a lock in SAP HANA.

The next surprising element is the table lock mode IX (intentional exclusive). This lock mode practically behaves like a share lock. There can be multiple IX mode locks present on a table at any given time, but no X (exclusive) lock can be set. The idea here is that the commands that intentionally set an exclusive lock on a row also need to make sure that the table cannot be locked exclusively by some other session. This is achieved by the IX lock that is implicitly set when an exclusive row lock is acquired.

What may not be obvious with IX locks is that these are acquired on the command level, whereas the records locks are acquired for each single, affected record. In other words, it is perfectly possible that an UPDATE command acquires an IX lock on the table but sets no X lock on any record when the WHERE condition does not fit to any existing record in the table.

Also, we find that running a delta merge on a column store table only sets an IX lock, which means that other commands that also only need an IX lock can be executed while the delta merge is running. The table tells us that this includes all DML commands. Short and simple: Rows can be inserted, updated, deleted, and selected while the delta merge is running. However, even though an unrestricted DELETE is possible during a delta merge, a TRUNCATE command would have to wait, because it requires an X lock.

We also see that creating an index on a table requires an X lock as well, which means that, for example, INSERT statements on a large table have to wait until the CREATE INDEX command has been completed. Depending on the importance of the table for business transactions, this could lead to serious wait situations in the business application and eventually block business transactions from being committed. Therefore, be careful when creating indexes on large tables in production systems!

Releasing Locks

A common question from new DBAs is "How can we release a table or record lock?" To do so, there are two transaction control commands: COMMIT and ROLL-BACK. Because SQL locks are crucial for the DBMS in order to guarantee transactional consistency, the only way to release locks is by ending the transactions that acquired them in the first place. Session management commands such as ALTER SYSTEM END SESSION or ALTER SYSTEM DISCONNECT SESSION implicitly trigger a rollback and release the locks of the affected session.

Monitoring Locks

To monitor locks, SAP HANA offers two basic monitoring views, M_OBJECT_LOCKS and M_RECORD_LOCKS, that contain information about current locks, as shown in Listing 10.6.

```
update cpoints set points =4.0 where name ='Louise';
select * from m_object_locks;


HOST                                 1d9506
PORT                                 34203
LOCK_OWNER_TRANSACTION_ID            463
LOCK_OWNER_UPDATE_TRANSACTION_ID     1861041
ACQUIRED_TIME                        21.12.2013  03:32:37.92126
SCHEMA_NAME                          LARS
OBJECT_NAME                          CPOINTS
OBJECT_TYPE                          TABLE
LOCK_MODE                            INTENTIONAL EXCLUSIVE


select * from m_record_locks;


HOST                                 1d9506
PORT                                 34203
LOCK_OWNER_TRANSACTION_ID            0
LOCK_OWNER_UPDATE_TRANSACTION_ID     1861041
ACQUIRED_TIME                        21.12.2013  03:32:37.923777
RECORD_ID               OID=0x000001ea, PARTID=0x0, OFFSET=0x60f7203f
SCHEMA_NAME                          LARS
TABLE_NAME                           CPOINTS
LOCK_MODE                            EXCLUSIVE
```

Listing 10.6 Example Output from Lock-Monitoring Tables

We can find that a single UPDATE command for a single row creates two lock entries, one for the table and one for the record itself. By comparing the ACQUIRED_TIME information of both entries, we find that the record lock (... 37.923777) was set a tad later than the table lock (...37.92126). This is due to the fact that the IX table lock is set for the command first and only thereafter are rows matching the WHERE condition locked.

> **Note**
>
> Unfortunately, the RECORD_ID from M_RECORD_LOCKS does not provide a way to find out the actual row that the lock belongs to without internal development knowledge.

Although these system views can be very useful for learning about ongoing locking situations, typically a DBA will be interested in locks when they cause blocking sessions. For that, the THREADS monitor in SAP HANA Studio provides an easy-to-use user interface. To see what this looks like, let's consider the following example. The update command in Listing 10.7 will create an exclusive record lock in addition to the intentional exclusive table lock that was shown in Listing 10.6.

```
update cpoints set points =4.0
where name ='Louise';
```

Listing 10.7 Start DB Session #1 with Autocommit OFF

Executing the statement again from a second session (Listing 10.8) will make this session wait for the lock and thus hang, because it is blocked by the transaction from session #1.

```
update cpoints set points =4.5
where name ='Louise';
```

Listing 10.8 Start DB Session #2 with Autocommit OFF

This leads to the display in SAP HANA Studio ADMINISTRATION CONSOLE • PERFORMANCE • THREADS shown in Figure 10.26.

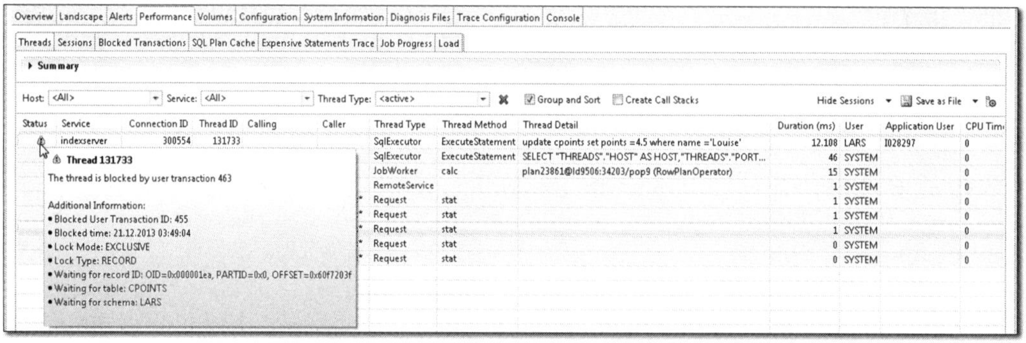

Figure 10.26 Blocked Transaction Information in Threads Monitor

Because the first session has already successfully updated the row and is now idle, you will not find an entry for it in the list of active threads (the THREADS monitor is filtered to <ACTIVE> threads by default). Remember, an idle session does not have any threads assigned to it.

The blocked session is marked with an alert icon, and the tooltip information shows you which transaction is currently holding this lock (463).

You could manually query M_TRANSACTIONS with the TRANSACTION ID, but there is an easier way; the context menu provides a NAVIGATE TO submenu. There, we find the option to navigate to the SESSIONS monitor with our current transaction as a filter or to the BLOCKED TRANSACTION tab. The latter brings us to the display in Figure 10.27.

Overview | Landscape | Alerts | Performance | Volumes | Configuration | System Information | Diagnosis Files | Trace Configuration | Console

Threads | Sessions | Blocked Transactions | SQL Plan Cache | Expensive Statements Trace | Job Progress | Load

Enter your filter · Visible rows: 2/2 · Hide Sessions ▾ Save as File ▾

Connection ID	Blocking Update Transaction ID	Blocked Update Transaction...	Transaction ID...	Lock Owner Transaction ID ...	Blocked Time Stamp	Thread Detail
300.624	1.861.041	1.861.374	463		21.12.2013 03:49:04.171664	
300.554	1.861.041	1.861.374	455	463	21.12.2013 03:49:04.171664	update cpoints set points =4.5 where name ='Lo

Figure 10.27 Blocked Transactions Overview

Going back to the THREADS monitor, the context menu also shows CANCEL OPERATION (ALTER SYSTEM CANCEL SESSION <ID>). Because the current waiting thread is still active and can check for the cancellation flag, we could cancel the waiting thread this way.

> **Note**
>
> It is possible to cancel threads waiting for locks, but it is not possible to cancel an inactive/idle holder of a lock.

As the lock holder is still holding the lock, the situation has not much improved. In most cases of blocking threads, it is necessary to first understand which session is holding the lock and why it is required. Then, you can decide how to release the lock again.

More information on the analysis of lock wait situations can be found in SAP Note 1858357 and the *SAP HANA Administration Guide*.

10.4.3 Timeouts

Because long-held locks and transactions that had been open for a long time can have negative effects, such as blocking other sessions or allocating system resources, SAP HANA provides timeout thresholds for such situations.

▸ **Idle session timeout**

For idle sessions (sessions that do not have any transactions open), the default timeout is 1,440 minutes (60 × 24). Sessions that stay idle longer than this timespan will be disconnected.

This timeout can be configured via parameter `indexserver.ini` • `[session]` • `idle_connection_timeout`. A value of `0` disables the timeout mechanism.

▸ **Idle cursor timeout**

Cursors (see the "Executing a Query" section) that are open over a long period of time allocate system resources and could potentially block garbage collection in SAP HANA. This timeout parameter (defaulting to 60 × 12 = 720 minutes) leads to disconnect of the session that opened the cursor.
The parameter to be set is `indexserver.ini` • `[transaction]` • `idle_cursor_ timeout`.

▸ **Lock wait timeout**

To prevent sessions waiting too long to acquire a table or a record lock, this timeout is used. After exceeding the timeout threshold, the waiting transaction will be rolled back and error message `131: transaction rolled back by lock wait timeout` will be returned. The parameter for this timeout is `index- server.ini` • `[transaction]` • `lock_wait_timeout` and is given in milliseconds (!). It defaults to 1,800,000 milliseconds or 180 seconds (three minutes).

To specify the maximum wait time for locks for a specific transaction, as of SPS 7 it is possible to specify the desired timeout via `ALTER SYSTEM SET TRANSACTION LOCK WAIT TIMEOUT`.

10.4.4 Multiversion Concurrency Control

We have already seen that reading records in SAP HANA never set locks on the record or the table that is read. This is done by keeping old versions of records in the system as long as any transactions could possibly need them. Changing records does not overwrite the old one; instead, a new version of the record is created and used from then on.

Depending on the isolation level active for the data-reading transaction, the old version of the record can be released after the `SELECT` statement has finished (isolation level `READ COMMITTED`) or after the reading transaction has finished (isolation levels `REPEATABLE READ` and `SERIALIZABLE`).

SAP HANA manages version management automatically without user interaction. Technically, preserving old versions of records is done differently for row store and column store tables. We discuss this briefly next.

MVCC Row Store

The internal data organization of the row store in SAP HANA is very similar to classic DBMS. Records are stored on pages and inserts and updates and deletes are performed in place. To allow for multiversion concurrency control (MVCC), a before image of the page needs to be stored before any data is changed. This before image is kept in memory in SAP HANA, just as all table data is.The before image is also included in the regular savepoints and data backups of SAP HANA so that during recovery of rolled-back transactions the original records can be recreated.

To monitor the multiversion concurrency control for row store tables, SAP HANA provides two system views: M_VERSION_MEMORY (Listing 10.9) and M_MVCC_TABLES.

```
select allocated_memory_size as allocated_mem,
       used_memory_size as used_mem,
       reclaimed_version_size as reclaimed_vers,
       free_memory_size as free_mem
  from
         m_version_memory vm
    join m_services s
    on (vm.host, vm.port) = (s.host, s.port)
where s.service_name ='indexserver'
order by vm.host;


ALLOCATED_MEM|USED_MEM|RECLAIMED_VERS|FREE_MEM
1474560      |1376256 |65536         |32768
```

Listing 10.9 Output of M_VERSION_MEMORY

In many system views, data is listed for all services on all hosts of a multinode system. For SQL processing, only the indexserver process is interesting; therefore we filter M_VERSION_MEMORY by joining against the M_SERVICES system view.

Once old record versions are not required any longer, they are not immediately removed from the version management. Instead, garbage collection is performed asynchronously by a background task (MVCCGarbageCollector). This garbage collection is referred to as *reclaiming version memory* and can also be triggered manually via the ALTER SYSTEM RECLAIM VERSION SPACE command. This is typically not required, and SAP HANA delivers alerts and error messages in the index server trace file. These regular checks are performed by the background task MvccAnti-AgerChecker (see Listing 10.10[1]).

```
 [131520]{-1}[-1/-1] 2013-12-22 22:07:52.068900 e Statement
mvcc_anti_ager.cc(01075) :
long running uncommitted write transaction detected:
 CONNECTION_ID = 301362, LOGICAL_CONNECTION ID = 301362,
 CONNECTION_STATUS = IDLE, HOST = 1d9506:34203,
 TRANSACTION_ID = "60", TRANSACTION_TYPE = "USER TRANSACTION",
 UPDATE_TRANSACTION_ID = "1912012", MIN_MVCC_SNAPSHOT_TIMESTAMP = -1,
 TRANSACTION TOTAL EXECUTED TIME = 19449 sec,
 CLIENT_HOST = VIEN60239482A, CLIENT_PID = 3656,
 CURRENT_STATEMENT = "null",
LAST_STATEMENT = "SELECT VERSION FROM SYS.M_DATABASE"

[131520]{-1}[-1/-1] 2013-12-22 22:07:52.438525 e Statement
mvcc_anti_ager.cc(01505) :
 M_MVCC_TABLES HOST = 1d9506:34203,
                NUM_VERSIONS = 23,
                MAX_VERSIONS_PER_RECORD = 3,
                MIN_SNAPSHOT_TS = 492205889,
                GLOBAL_TS = 492205889,
                MIN_READ_TID = 1912011,
                NEXT_WRITE_TID = 1918844
```

Listing 10.10 Index Server Trace File Excerpt for Long-Running Statement Detection

The second line in the trace file message shown in Listing 10.10 refers to another system view that we already mentioned: M_MVCC_TABLES. Although the alert refers to a condition that is only valid for row store tables, it will fire for all transactions, because a transaction can span multiple statements that use both row store and column store tables.

The information to look out for is the total number of versions kept in the version memory (NUM_VERSIONS) and the maximum number of records of any versioned

---

1 Yes, SAP HANA actually provides antiaging features...!

record (MAX_VERSIONS_PER_RECORD). In general, values below 1,000,000 for NUM_VERSIONS are not of concern.

To get a better understanding of the view's content, let's consider an example. First, let's copy the CPOINTS table to the row store table RPOINTS, including the stored data:

```
create row table rpoints like cpoints with data;
```

As you can see, the data was copied over to the row store table:

```
select * from rpoints;
```

```
| NAME    | POINTS         |
| ------  | -------------- |
| Carol   |          7.20  |
| Lars    |          7.10  |
| Louise  |          4.50  |
| Paul    |         44.00  |
```

Now let's update two records from the same transaction:

```
update rpoints set points=12.2
where name ='Paul';
update rpoints set points=4.1
where name ='Lars';
```

Unlike most other system views, M_MVCC_TABLES presents data in a key-value fashion, which means that for every value there is separate row in the table instead of a separate column (see Listing 10.11).

```
select * from m_mvcc_tables;
```

```
HOST   |PORT  |NAME                    |VALUE
1d9506|34203|NUM_VERSIONS            |2
1d9506|34203|NUM_INSERT_VERSION      |0
1d9506|34203|NUM_UPDATE_VERSION      |2
1d9506|34203|NUM_DELETE_VERSION      |0
1d9506|34203|NUM_GROUP_INSERT_VERSION|0
⋮
```

Listing 10.11 Example Output for M_MVCC_TABLES

This is the reason for the slightly more complex SQL statement used to read this view.

We have also joined the TABLES system view just for the row that contains the
TABLE ID so that we see for which table the most versions are held (Listing 10.12).

```
Select
    mv.host, mv.name, mv.value,
    case
    when 'TABLE_ID_OF_MAX_NUM_VERSIONS'= mv.name
    then (select max(schema_name||'.'||table_name)
        from tables
        where table_oid = to_number(mv.value)
        )
    else null
    end as table
from
    M_MVCC_TABLES mv
    join M_SERVICES s
    on (mv.host,mv.port) = (s.host, s.port)
where s.service_name ='indexserver'
and mv.name in ('NUM_VERSIONED_RECORDS'
                ,'MAX_VERSION_PER_RECORD'
                ,'AVG_VERSIONS_PER_VERSIONED_RECORD'
                ,'TABLE_ID_OF_MAX_NUM_VERSIONS')
order by mv.host, mv.name;^
```

```
HOST  |NAME                                      |VALUE |TABLE
1d9506|AVG_VERSIONS_PER_VERSIONED_RECORD|1.0     |NULL
1d9506|NUM_VERSIONED_RECORDS                     |2     |NULL
1d9506|TABLE_ID_OF_MAX_NUM_VERSIONS       |158534|LARS.RPOINTS
```

Listing 10.12 M_MVCC_TABLES Output with Joined table_name

In the example in Listing 10.12, we see that currently two records have been versioned and that on average just one version is kept. Note that this view only
shows the current state and does not provide historical information.

MVCC Concurrency in the Column Store

Unlike the row store, in which records are overwritten upon update or delete, the
column store is designed as an insert-only data structure. Every time a change is
made to a record, the new version of the record is stored in the delta store of the
table together with the information for what transaction onwards the new version

is valid. Once this transaction is committed, the record becomes visible for other sessions and will be used as the most current version. The old versions of the record, however, are not yet overwritten or deleted; they keep on existing in the main or the delta store. SAP HANA will remove the outdated records automatically during a delta merge operation. By storing the old record versions in the same column table data structures, no additional memory monitoring or administration is required.

To illustrate this, we have the following example, starting with Listing 10.13. Start by looking at the runtime details of a column store table CBIG. For that table, the system view M_CS_TABLES provides all the necessary information.

To start off, it is important for this experiment that the table be completely loaded into memory; otherwise, the MEM_SIZE_TOTAL figure will change in an unexpected way.

```
load cbig all;

select MEMORY_SIZE_IN_TOTAL as MEM_SZ_TOTAL
     , RECORD_COUNT as REC_CNT
     , RAW_RECORD_COUNT_IN_MAIN as RAW_RECS_MAIN
     , RAW_RECORD_COUNT_IN_DELTA as RAW_RECS_DELTA
from m_cs_tables
where table_name ='CBIG';


MEM_SZ_TOTAL|REC_CNT  |RAW_RECS_MAIN|RAW_RECS_DELTA
3918973946  |50100000 |50100000     |0
```

Listing 10.13 Total and Raw Record Entries for Example Table CBIG

Execute this statement throughout this example to check the data modifications. Right now, the table is fully merged. All records are stored in the main store, and the number of current rows (RECORD_COUNT) equals the number of all rows in the main store (RAW_RECORD_COUNT_IN_MAIN). This means that no rows have been marked as invalid.

To prevent automerge from kicking in during our experiment, turn it off quickly for this table:

```
ALTER TABLE CBIG DISABLE AUTOMERGE;
```

First, delete some rows and check the table data structure again (Listing 10.14).

```
delete from cbig where record in
        (select top 100000 record from cbig order by record);
```

```
MEM_SZ_TOTAL|REC_CNT |RAW_RECS_MAIN|RAW_RECS_DELTA
4128578266  |50000000|50100000     |0
             ^^^^^^^^
```

Listing 10.14 Table CBIG after Deleting 10,000 Records

Notice that there is a change in the number of currently valid records (decreased) and the total memory size (increased), but the total number of all records remains unchanged. Also, the delta store does not contain any changed records.

This makes sense, because writing delete records into the delta store would be wasteful and unnecessary. To mark records in the main store as deleted or invalid, it is sufficient to change visibility flags for the records in the main store. Although the main store is otherwise write protected, setting the visibility flags is both possible and crucial. It is counterintuitive that deleting records could increase the memory consumption, so it is best to remember that the DELETE command always only hides the records from transactions.

As a next test, update some records and check the data structure again (Listing 10.15).

```
update cbig set recordmode ='-' where record in
        (select top 100000 record from cbig order by record);
```

```
MEM_SZ_TOTAL|REC_CNT |RAW_RECS_MAIN|RAW_RECS_DELTA
4310429526  |50000000|50100000     |100000
                                    ^^^^^^
```

Listing 10.15 Table CBIG after Updating 10,000 Records

Once again, the total memory size increased, but the total number of records and the number of visible records stayed the same. What changed is the number of records in the delta store, which now contains the new, valid versions of the records.

Finally, trigger the merge operation to see if this cleans up the old versions (20,000 records are no longer valid) and whether memory gets released (Listing 10.16).

```
merge delta of cbig;

MEM_SZ_TOTAL|REC_CNT |RAW_RECS_MAIN|RAW_RECS_DELTA
3924672171   |50000000|50000000     |0
              ^^^^^^^^^^^^ ^^^^^^
```

Listing 10.16 Table CBIG after Performing a Delta Merge

As you can easily see, memory was released, and the total number of records equals the number of visible records again.

For the sharp-eyed reader: The reason for the now higher memory requirement than before the start of the experiment is that the compression of the new main store after the merge is slightly less efficient. By introducing a new value to the recordmode column, the overall compression for this column decreased. This is not a bug; it is the direct consequence of the way the column store works. The table is still compressed.

10.5 Summary

In this chapter, we covered a broad range of topics, all of which are fundamental for understanding database request processing in SAP HANA. We showed how all sessions are mapped to SQLExecutor threads (one thread for each logical CPU core) and how multiversion concurrency works in practice.

We also described how many monitoring and analysis steps can be performed conveniently via the SAP HANA Studio graphical user interface and that all information is available in system views. This makes SAP HANA not just easy to use for beginners and for day-to-day routine monitoring tasks but it also allows for data analysis on the raw data for the experts.

Finally, we analyzed memory consumption for multiversion concurrency control for both row- and column store tables and explained where deleted and changed record versions are stored.

The repository of SAP HANA offers capabilities to store and manage development artifacts. This chapter describes the SAP HANA repository and the principles of managing repository content.

11　Working with the Repository

The persistence and lifecycle management of SAP HANA development artifacts—for example, for data models, stored procedures, or SAP HANA XS—is handled by the repository. The repository offers functionality such as content organization in packages, versioning, export and import, or content transport. It is the technical foundation of the development capabilities of the SAP HANA system.

In this chapter, we will give a technical introduction to the repository itself, including the package structure, the concept of delivery units, and the repository's persistence in the database. We will then deal with repository contents, starting with the creation and deletion of objects and touching on object versioning and generic techniques for the import and export of objects before describing SAP HANA's built-in mechanism for content transports in a system landscape.

11.1　Properties of the SAP HANA Repository

The most obvious characteristic of the SAP HANA repository is that it provides a hierarchical structure for organizing content. In this section, we will first describe the options for accessing the SAP HANA repository and then introduce the package mechanism and define the term *repository content*. We will then show you how the repository itself is persisted inside of the SAP HANA database. Finally, we'll offer a brief statement about the ownership of repository objects.

11.1.1　Accessing the Repository

For most administrators and developers in SAP HANA systems, the primary tool to access the repository is SAP HANA Studio, which offers comfortable editors for most common development objects, such as data models, stored procedures, and more. The functionality in SAP HANA Studio embraces the needs of developers and in part that of administrators who are also responsible for the development platform of the SAP HANA system.

With SPS 7, a web-based development IDE was introduced, which offers simple access to SAP HANA repository objects for developers but lacks features compared to the functionality in SAP HANA Studio. In addition, an application for managing the lifecycle of SAP HANA content has existed since SAP HANA SPS 6; it is usually referred to as SAP HANA Application Lifecycle Management (HALM).

Whatever tool you use, there are two privileges needed to access the SAP HANA repository:

▶ **Execute on the repository stored procedure**
The repository's functionality is exposed in the database through the stored procedure REPOSITORY_REST in schema SYS. Developers and administrators require the EXECUTE privilege on this procedure.

▶ **Package privilege REPO.READ on at least one package**
In order to see *any* content in the repository *at all*, a user will need the package privilege REPO.READ on *at least one* repository package (which may be located anywhere within the package hierarchy).

The SAP HANA XS applications for working with the repository come with predefined roles for developers and administrators. These roles contain the EXECUTE privilege on the REPOSITORY_REST procedure, but for obvious reasons they might not contain the package privileges required for your particular development project.

The actual steps for accessing the repository differ slightly based on the tool being used. We'll discuss the specifics of each next.

Accessing the Repository in SAP HANA Studio

In SAP HANA Studio, the repository is integrated into the Systems view (Figure 11.1) as the Content node, shown in ❶. You can expand this node to show the repository tree. Expand individual packages to navigate to the intended location. The properties of the presently selected package, as shown in ❷, are shown in the generic Properties view, shown in ❸, of SAP HANA Studio.

In Figure 11.1, we show the situation as you will find it in the ADMINISTRATION or MODELER perspective of SAP HANA Studio. When using the DEVELOPMENT perspective, the workbench also offers the REPOSITORIES view, in which you can see the repository workspaces that you have set up for your development projects.

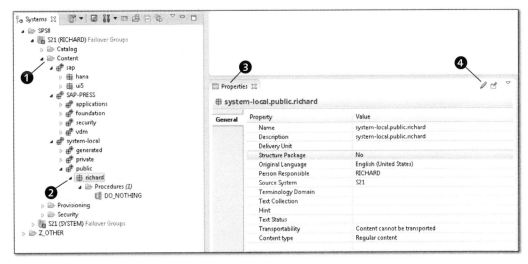

Figure 11.1 Accessing the Repository in SAP HANA Studio

Accessing the Repository in the Web IDE

The HTML5-based IDE for SAP HANA development can be reached on any SAP HANA system with the URL *http://<host>:<port>/sap/hana/xs/ide/*. In this URL, <host> denotes a host in your SAP HANA system on which the XS server is running. <port> is the external communication port of the XS server, usually 80<instance> (or 43<instance> for HTTPS).

Privilege Information

A user in the SAP HANA database is required to log on to the web IDE. This user must have one of the roles `sap.hana.xs.ide.roles::Developer` or `sap.hana.xs.ide.roles::EditorDeveloper` that come preinstalled with your SAP HANA system.

Within the web IDE, you can click the EDITOR icon to start the EDITOR tool (Figure 11.2), which shows the CONTENT tree and an editor area. If you select objects in the repository, the editor area will either show a generic editor or—for certain recognized object types, such as stored procedures—an object-specific editor. The editor also allows drag and drop to add objects to the selected repository package. If you have, for example, the text file representation of an SAP HANA data model on your local computer, then you can drag that file from Windows Explorer into the MULTI-FILE DROP ZONE and release it (which will implicitly attempt to activate the object; only if this activation is successful will the object be added to the repository).

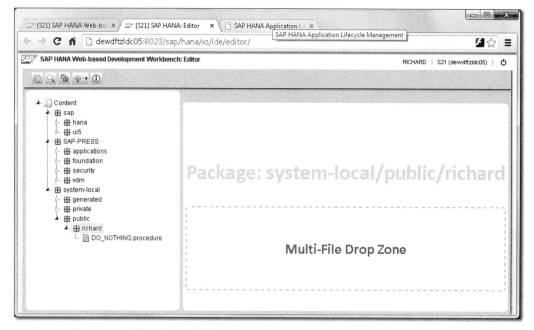

Figure 11.2 Editor of the SAP HANA Web IDE

Accessing the Repository with the SAP HANA Application Lifecycle Manager

The third tool to access the repository is the SAP HANA Application Lifecycle Manager (HALM). The HALM XS application is available via the URL *http:// <host>:<port>/sap/hana/xs/lm/* with the definition of <host> and <port> as stated earlier.

From the HOME screen of the application (Figure 11.3), a multitude of actions is available. The tiles of this screen act as shortcuts to entries from the application menu at the top of the screen. Of these tiles, the ones marked with ❶ in Figure 11.3 are related to managing the repository structure or its contents, whereas the ones marked with ❷ are related to transporting, exporting, or importing contents.

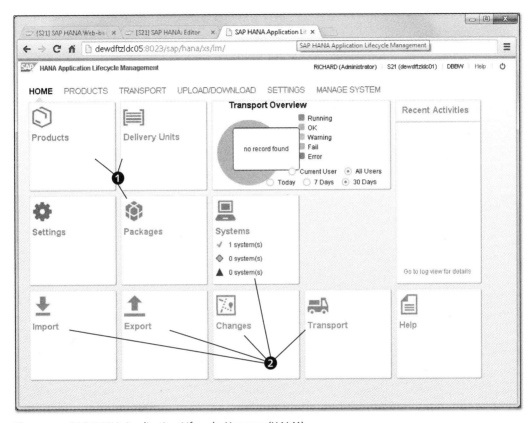

Figure 11.3 SAP HANA Application Lifecycle Manager (HALM)

11.1.2 The Package Structure of the Repository

The package structure of the repository is mainly self-explanatory, so we only need to highlight a couple of little-known aspects.

Structural Packages

Packages in the repository can be structural or not. A structural package is a package that can contain only packages and no content objects. When you create a new package (regardless of the tool used), it will always be created as a nonstructural package; you will not be given a choice to influence this property in the creation process (as of SPS 8). Only SAP HANA Studio allows you to change the package to a structural one, as shown in Figure 11.4; within the CONTENT tree of the SYSTEMS view, select the package and edit its details. You can access the wizard to edit the package details in two ways: Either right-click on the package and choose EDIT from the context menu, or highlight the package and click on the EDIT icon in the properties view (in Figure 11.1, we have labeled this icon as ❹).

Back to Figure 11.4, you can immediately see in SAP HANA Studio whether a package is structural or not from its icon within the CONTENT tree. For example, the `sap` and `system-local` packages, shown in ❶, are structural, whereas our newly created package `system-local.public.richard`, shown in ❷, is nonstructural. Unfortunately, the web-based tools do not show whether a package is structural or not.

Figure 11.4 Structural Packages

Structural packages are very useful to manage the repository structure. You can define a basic organization-wide repository structure based entirely on structural packages and create further structural packages for development projects. If members from the development teams only have write access to their respective project packages, this is the first step to a well-managed repository.

Delivery Units

Packages in the repository can be assigned to entities called *delivery units*. A delivery unit is a logical collector for packages that belong together, for example, for the purpose of transporting. A package can at any time only belong to one delivery unit, but one delivery unit may contain multiple packages.

Delivery units are a fundamental principle for controlled export/import of repository contents, especially for content transports. We therefore postpone a more elaborate discussion of this topic until Section 11.4.2.

Native and Imported Packages

The SAP HANA repository further differentiates between native and imported packages. An imported package is one that came into the system by means of a delivery-unit import. Such imports may be executed manually for server- or client-side imports of delivery units, or they may be implicitly executed as part of a content transport. In any of these cases, packages originating from such an import are treated as imported. Any other packages in the database are native packages. They are usually created either manually in SAP HANA Studio or in other tools, or they originate from a developer-mode import.

A package (whether native or imported) can technically contain a mixture of native and imported content. Such mixing of imported and natively created objects is, however, not good practice in our eyes (there may be justifiable exceptions).

In the CONTENT tree in SAP HANA Studio, imported packages are marked with a little blue arrow (for example, in Figure 11.4, see the sap.hana package, shown in ❹).

Privileges on Packages

Privileges on packages are discussed in detail in Chapter 13. Here, we only want to highlight two properties of package privileges that are important for setting up the package structure in a manageable way:

▶ **Package privileges are recursive**
If a user has a package privilege on a given package, then the privilege extends to all subpackages.

▶ **There are individual privileges for imported and native content**
Except for the REPO.READ privilege, all package privileges exist in one flavor for native and another for imported objects. This makes it possible to have read-only imported content within a portion of the repository hierarchy that developers otherwise have write access to.

Defining the Package Structure

Before you start a development project, you should carefully design your package structure, taking into account not only the intended development projects but also considerations of manageability and security.

SAP recommends that each organization that develops SAP HANA content (typically referred to as "vendor" in the related documentation) create one package in the repository root folder with package name <vendor>. Underneath this package, the vendor may create whatever they like.

In Chapter 14, we give some advice about setting up the development environment, including the fundamental package structure.

Special Packages

SAP HANA is delivered with two existing packages. The sap package contains all SAP-provided content, that is, it is the <vendor> package used by SAP. Naturally, in a development project started at an organization other than SAP, nobody should be working in the sap package. Developers may, of course, choose to take a look at some of the applications provided by SAP to derive ideas about structuring an application project in the repository.

The second special and pre-installed package is the system-local package. This package is supposed to be used for test purposes only, that is, it is a sandbox in which developers can experiment. The most important special property of the system-local package is that the package and all of its contents are not transportable. It is technically not possible to assign the system-local package or any subpackage to a delivery unit.

This restriction has been implemented on purpose so that the usually weakly governed test artifacts cannot be propagated to a production system. The system-local package is structural, and it comes with two structural subpackages; generated is intended for automatically generated content and private for sandbox packages that are dedicated to individual developers or groups of developers. We propose adding a third structural subpackage named public in which everyone can work freely without having to request a private test package. Again, see the discussion in Chapter 14.

11.1.3 Repository Content

Repository content is our umbrella term for any type of object that can be stored in the packages of the SAP HANA repository. All repository content objects have in common that they are design-time descriptions (think "source code") that can be activated to generate a runtime object in the database catalog.

In the following lists, we group the different types of content objects by usage area. Some content types are relevant for multiple use cases and will thus be listed more than once.

- **Modeling artifacts**
  The best known (and oldest) type of repository content, the objects relevant for data modeling in SAP HANA, include (as of SPS 8):

  - Attribute views: These typically represent master data objects in multidimensional data models.

  - Analytic views: These represent multidimensional join models similar to InfoCubes. They usually join multiple attribute views to a fact table in the so-called data foundation.

  - Calculation views: Generic data models that offer the highest modeling flexibility.

  - Stored procedures: Subroutines in the database system that can be used in SQL queries.

  - Decision tables: Objects for a special modeling technique that allows you to represent certain types of logical decision in a data model.

  - Analytic privileges: Privileges that define row-based restrictions for reading from data models (see the detailed discussion in Chapter 13).

- **Security artifacts**
  Several types of security-related objects can be designed as repository objects:

  - Repository roles (also known as design-time roles)—the recommended representation of database roles unless you are using an identity management solution supporting SAP HANA (see the discussion in Chapter 13)

  - Analytic privileges

- **Schemas and other database objects**
  You can also define typical database catalog objects, such as schemas, tables, SQL views, sequences, procedures, and more, in the SAP HANA repository.

This is a way to create transportable catalog object definitions. For many of these objects, SAP HANA offers two ways of defining them. One way is to create individual development objects for each entity to be created, for example, an `.hdbtable` file that defines a database table.

Alternatively, the Core Data Services (CDS) infrastructure that has existed in SAP HANA since SPS 7 comes with a data definition language (DDL), which you can use to describe data models, that is, data types, tables, and table associations.

For more details about both methods of creating database objects, see the *SAP HANA Developer Guide*, which is available at *https://help.sap.com/hana_platform/*.

▶ **Applications**
The most complete use case of the SAP HANA development platform is the creation of entire applications. The tooling provided for this purpose adds to the previously mentioned development artifacts an engine to execute server-side JavaScript code, web-based data access using OData or XMLA, and the creation of HTLM5 user interfaces with the SAPUI5 development toolkit.

For details on these development tools, see the *SAP HANA Developer Guide* at *https://help.sap.com/hana_platform/*.

In one package, all object types supported by the SAP HANA repository can be mixed. For the manageability of the development environment, it is of course recommended that you create a package structure that separates different types of development artifacts.

11.1.4 The Persistence of the Repository within the Database

The repository itself is stored in tables of the `_SYS_REPO` schema in the database. All repository functionality is exposed via a REST API that is implemented by SAP HANA Studio and the other tools that can access the repository. This API is not published for use outside of SAP.

> **Note**
>
> By no means should the contents of the `_SYS_REPO` schema be modified manually, for example, by using SQL commands to change the contents of the repository tables. With such actions, there is a risk of creating inconsistencies in the repository or damaging the repository contents.

This absence of a published API implies that customers cannot presently generate or manage repository contents programmatically.

11.1.5   Ownership of Repository Objects

The design-time objects created in the repository do not have owners in a strict sense. The repository tracks the name of the user who modifies a given object mostly for the purpose of documentation. Design-time objects can be modified by any database user that has the REPO.EDIT_NATIVE_OBJECTS (or REPO.EDIT_IMPORTED_OBJECTS) privilege on the package containing the object—regardless of who created the object.

Upon activation, most repository objects are turned into runtime objects of the database (exceptions include, for example, server-side JavaScript programs for SAP HANA XS or SAPUI5 elements). These runtime objects always belong to the _SYS_REPO user, regardless of which database user triggered the object activation.

11.2   Creating and Editing Objects in SAP HANA Studio

Data models in SAP HANA can simply be created using the SAP HANA MODELER perspective. In that perspective, you can right-click on a package in the repository and choose to create the intended object. This will open the dedicated editor for the object type you want to create.

> **Privilege Information**
>
> The prerequisite for creating or editing objects in a given package is the REPO.EDIT_NATIVE_OBJECTS package privilege on that package or a parent package. In order to edit objects that have been imported via a delivery unit import or transported into the system, the package privilege REPO.EDIT_IMPORTED_OBJECTS on the package or a parent package is required.

All other repository-based development in SAP HANA Studio—XS application, design-time roles, or other development artifacts—requires the creation of a development project in the Developer Workbench. In this workbench, you will work with development projects and repository workspaces. Development projects allow you to manage your development.

This section focuses on the creation and editing of objects in SAP HANA Studio. (Repository objects can also be created during an import or a transport; see Section 11.4 and Section 11.5 for details.) Because administrators may need to make use of the Developer Workbench—for example, for creating and managing repository roles—we will briefly walk you through the process of setting up a development project, creating objects, and checking out a project. We will then tell you what you need to know about concurrent development.

Creating Objects with the Web IDE

An alternative to SAP HANA Studio-based development is the web IDE that was introduced with SPS 7 of SAP HANA. The web IDE allows you to edit all types of repository content without needing to create development projects. It is thus easier to set up and more welcoming to the occasional developer. At the same time, the editors provided by the web IDE are not yet equivalent to those in the Developer Workbench. This includes graphical editors for special objects such as data models, syntax highlighting, auto completion, and more.

For details on using the web IDE, see the *SAP HANA Developer Guide* at *https://help.sap.com/hana_platform/*. In our view, the web IDE is presently still inferior to the SAP HANA Studio editors in many aspects, so we will focus our discussion on SAP HANA Studio-based development.

11.2.1 Setting up a Development Project

In order to work with the Developer Workbench, you must create a development project. This project will be the central place for managing any development artifacts of the project. These artifacts will be stored in a local directory of your computer. By sharing the project with a repository workspace, you can commit objects into the SAP HANA repository.

There are three main steps involved in setting up a development project. We discuss these next.

Prepare the Repository

You must set up repository packages to work with. For a project, there are two options: You can either set up the package hierarchy, including the root package of the project to be created, or you can create the hierarchy up to the parent of the project's root package. In the latter case, the system will create a new package with the name of the project and make it the project root.

In our example, we will be creating a project named MY_PROJECT. The aim of this project is to define persistence objects in a package named SAP_PRESS.persistence.lector. Because the name of the project and its root package are not identical, we have prepared the package hierarchy, including the project's root package. Note that this root package must not be structural.

Create the Repository Workspace

Connect your SAP HANA Studio with the database user for your development and open the DEVELOPMENT perspective. Switch to the REPOSITORIES tab, as shown in Figure 11.5, marked with ❶.

Figure 11.5 Creating the Repository Workspace

On this tab, click on the CREATE REPOSITORY WORKSPACE button, as shown in ❷, to start a wizard for setting up the workspace. The most important choice here is to select the correct system entry, as shown in ❸ (SAP HANA database system and database user), for the development project.

The choice of WORKSPACE ROOT directory, as shown in ❹, determines the folder on your local hard drive in which the local copies of development artifacts from your project will be stored. The suggestion made by SAP HANA (in SPS 8) will be acceptable in most situations: In the user's home directory, a new directory named *hana_work* will be created, and in this directory there will be a folder of which the name specifies database system, instance number, and user name: <SID>_<instance>_<user>.

You can share multiple projects with the same repository workspace, so workspaces do not need to have a name.

Creating and Sharing the Project

With your development user, switch to the PROJECT EXPLORER tab, as shown in Figure 11.6, marked as ❶. On that tab, create a new project by following the menu path FILE • NEW • OTHER... • SAP HANA • APPLICATION DEVELOPMENT • XS PROJECT. Instead of using the main menu, you can right-click on the background, shown in ❷, of the PROJECT EXPLORER view and choose accordingly from the context menu.

This opens a wizard for creating the project. On the first screen of the wizard, shown in ❸, you only need to enter a project name. Remember that depending on how you choose to set up the repository package structure, the project name may become part of the repository path name of your application; in the case of an XS application, this path name will define the application URL. Therefore, choose the project name wisely, or manually create the project's root package (this is what we will do here).

On the second screen of the wizard, shown in ❹, you have to choose the repository workspace to connect to. In case you have multiple workspaces defined in your instance of SAP HANA Studio, it is important to select the right workspace.

If you have already manually created the root package for the project, uncheck the ADD PROJECT FOLDER AS SUBPACKAGE checkbox, as shown in ❺.

Finally, you can choose the repository package that will contain the project or (as in our case) the project contents. After you click the FINISH button, the project will be created locally on your hard disk and immediately shared with the repository. The automatically generated initial project files are thus automatically transferred to the SAP HANA repository.

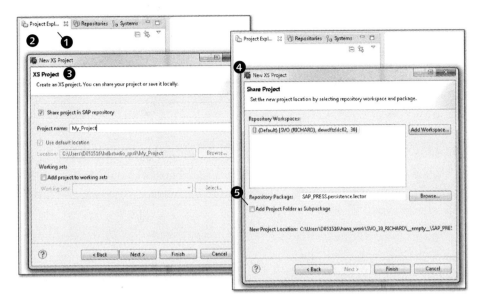

Figure 11.6 Creating and Sharing the Project

After the project is shared, you can see these newly created repository objects in your REPOSITORY WORKSPACE (Figure 11.7, left-hand side, shown in ❶). These objects are not displayed in the CONTENT tree of the SYSTEMS view, shown in ❷. The reason is that the SYSTEMS view by default only shows objects that can be edited outside of development projects, that is, modeler objects.

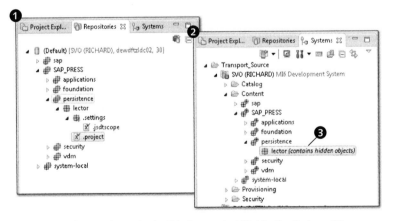

Figure 11.7 Objects Shown in the Workspace but Not in the Systems View

481

You can switch on the display of those hidden objects in the SAP HANA Studio preferences: Follow the menu path Window • Preferences • SAP HANA • Modeler •
Content Presentation, and select the checkbox Show all objects. From now on,
you will see entries for nonmodeler objects in the repository representation of the
Systems view, but you will not be able to open, edit, activate, or remove such
objects from here.

11.2.2 Creating Objects in the Developer Workbench

We will show the general workflow of creating repository objects through the
Developer Workbench by using the example of the most simple development
object: a database schema.

Create the Empty Object File

To create an object in the Developer Workbench, switch to the Project Explorer
view and choose from the menu or context menu the path New • Other.... In the
wizard that opens (Figure 11.8), you must in the first step, shown in ❶, choose the
type of object to create. If you know the type name, you can search for it in the
input field Wizards, shown in ❷. In the second step, shown in ❸, you have to
enter the file name. In most cases, the file name must be the same as the object
name, including capitalization. The wizard adds the correct file extension automatically. In our case, the extension is .hdbschema.

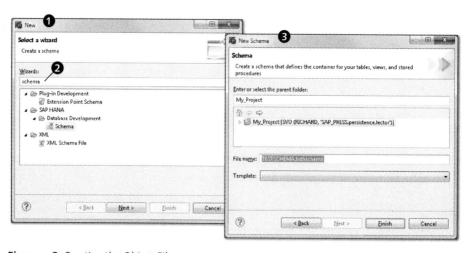

Figure 11.8 Creating the Object File

Implement the Object

Once the object file is created, we have to fill it with content. The details of this process will depend on the type of object to be created. In the case of our database schema, a simple text editor is opened (right-hand side of Figure 11.9) in which we have to enter the name of the schema to be created; remember that the schema name must exactly match the file name of the .hdbschema file.

You have now created and activated a repository object. In the SYSTEMS view, you can verify that in fact a runtime object has been created during the activation.

You can save the object using the SAVE button in SAP HANA Studio or by typing the key combination $\boxed{\texttt{Ctrl}}$ + $\boxed{\texttt{S}}$. This will store the object locally on your hard drive and (in the default configuration of SAP HANA Studio) also commit it to the repository.

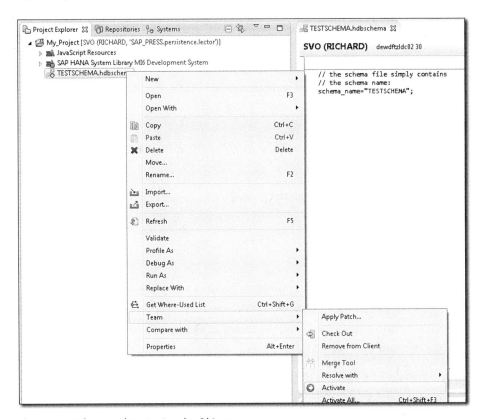

Figure 11.9 Editing and Activating the Object

483

Activate the Object

To create the corresponding runtime object, you have to activate the object. Right-click on the object, and choose TEAM • ACTIVATE from the context menu.

> **Note**
>
> If you reproduce our example, you may find that the newly created database schema is not visible to your database user, because SAP HANA Studio will usually only show those schemas that your database user has object privileges for.
>
> To disable this implicit filtering, right-click on the CATALOG node in the SYSTEMS view and choose FILTERS... from the context menu. In the pop-up box, select the checkbox DISPLAY ALL SCHEMAS and click OK.

11.2.3 Checking Out a Project

If multiple database users need to work on the same project or if contents of a transported project must be edited in the target system of a transport, then the project must be checked out from the repository. To check out the project, you must first create a development workspace for the database user.

> **Note**
>
> A project can only exist once in an SAP HANA Studio workspace (not to be confused with a repository workspace). Therefore, a project cannot be created and checked out in the same instance of SAP HANA Studio.
>
> If the same person needs to work on a project of the same name in multiple systems (e.g., source and target of a transport landscape), then this person will have to set up an additional SAP HANA Studio workspace for importing the project.

In the newly created development workspace, navigate to the package containing the project (Figure 11.10, left-hand side, shown in ❶), and select CHECK OUT AND IMPORT PROJECTS..., shown in ❷, from the context menu. In the wizard, shown in ❸, select the project to check out, as shown in ❹ (the selected package hierarchy may contain multiple projects).

The project has now been successfully checked out, and you can start working with its contents in the PROJECT EXPLORER view of the Developer Workbench.

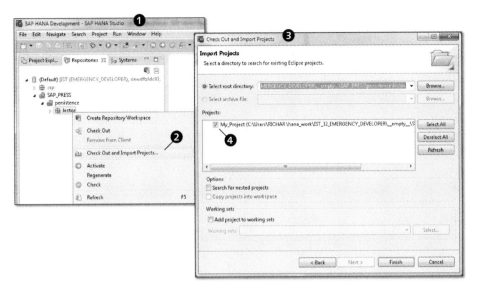

Figure 11.10 Importing a Project

11.2.4 Concurrent Development

When you check out development objects from the repository into your Developer Workbench or start editing an object in the SAP HANA modeler or the web IDE, these objects are not locked. This means that multiple database users may concurrently edit the same repository object.

Whenever a user saves a modified version of an object to the repository, the system checks whether the present version in the repository is identical to the one that the user checked out or started editing. If the version in the repository has been changed in the meantime, the user will be presented with a warning and asked to manage the situation actively.

The development tools offer version comparison and support for merging changes, as shown in Figure 11.11 for the example of SAP HANA Studio's Developer Workbench. In SAP HANA Studio, this tool is available via the context menu of the object being modified: TEAM • MERGE TOOL. You can also see all past versions in the object history, which you can access from the context menu of the object: COMPARE WITH... • LOCAL HISTORY.

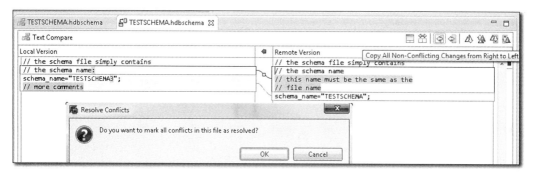

Figure 11.11 Merge Tool in the Developer Workbench

In the web IDE, you can view version history and compare versions by selecting the Versions entry from the context menu of the object.

11.3 Deleting Development Objects in SAP HANA Studio

The most important rule about deleting development artifacts is that they must always be deleted from the repository. This deletion will also trigger the deletion of the corresponding runtime objects that have been created when the development object was activated. If you simply delete the runtime object, its design-time representation will remain in the repository so that the next activation will create the runtime object again.

We have to differentiate two different ways of deleting objects: from the Systems view and from a development project. We discuss these next.

> **Deleting Objects in the Web IDE**
>
> It is also possible to delete objects in the web IDE. As opposed to the Systems view in SAP HANA Studio, the web IDE does not check for object dependencies. You can thus delete objects even if they are used within other objects without receiving a warning.
>
> If there are existing dependencies, the object may still show up after deletion in the repository tree of the web IDE. In such cases, you will have to activate the containing package in the Systems view of SAP HANA Studio to clean up the situation.
>
> In addition, the web IDE allows the recursive deletion of packages, including all of their contents.

Given the behavior of the web IDE, we must advise you to be very careful when using it. If you are certain that a given mass deletion is required, then the web IDE is easier to use than the SAP HANA Studio deletion mechanisms.

11.3.1 Deleting Objects from the Systems View in SAP HANA Studio

Data modelers will most probably not be using the Developer Workbench; they will most likely manage their development objects directly in the SYSTEMS view of SAP HANA Studio.

You can only delete an object from the repository if there are no other objects depending on it (using it). If you attempt to remove an object that is being used by other objects, then the deletion will fail, and a notification will be shown in the JOB LOG of SAP HANA Studio.

For any object, you can open the WHERE-USED list from the context menu of that object.

You can delete multiple objects by marking them all with the mouse (hold down the Ctrl key while selecting the individual objects).

It is not possible to delete entire packages if they still contain objects or subpackages.

11.3.2 Deleting Objects from a Development Project

If an object is part of a development project, then the leading entity for all related development is the project. You therefore also must delete the object from the PROJECT EXPLORER. If you delete the object here, it will only be removed from the project—and thus also from your local file system—but it will remain in the repository, and the runtime object will continue to exist in the database catalog.

The development workbench does *not* execute a dependency check; if the object you delete is used by other repository objects, you will *not* be warned about this.

In order to complete the deletion, you must now activate a parent container of the object. This might be a containing folder within your project or the project itself. After this deletion, all object representations will be deleted from your local file system, the database repository, and the database catalog.

If the parent container that you activate in this step contains objects that depend on the deleted object, you will receive related error messages in the activation process.

11.4 Mechanisms for Exporting and Importing Objects

SAP HANA offers two fundamentally different mechanisms for exporting and importing repository contents. Developer-mode exports are not well controlled. In fact, they simply require the same privileges that are needed to perform typical development tasks in a given repository package, and thus they may be regarded as yet another option for locally creating content objects.

Delivery-unit exports, on the other hand, are the technical foundation for content transports within a system landscape and content provisioning from external vendors, such as SAP.

11.4.1 Developer-Mode Export and Import

Any developer who has at least the privileges needed to read the contents of a given repository package can export these contents into a directory structure on their client computer. Similarly, the import is available to all database users who have the privileges needed to create and activate the repository objects contained in the import.

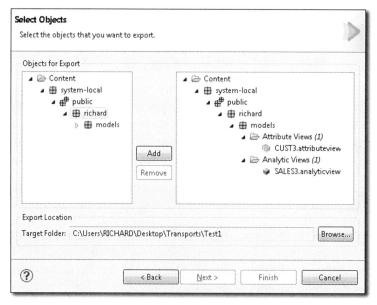

Figure 11.12 Choosing Objects and the Target Folder for Developer-Mode Export

Developer-mode export is available from the SAP HANA Studio menu path FILE • EXPORT • SAP HANA CONTENT • DEVELOPER MODE. In the wizard, select the system and database user to export from, and then choose the objects to export. Here, you can select individual objects or entire packages (Figure 11.12). You must also specify a file system location as the target for the export. Within the selected folder, a directory hierarchy will be created that reflects the package hierarchy for all repository objects to be exported. Once you click FINISH, the export will be started. The outcome can be monitored in the JOB LOG of SAP HANA Studio.

Developer-mode imports work the same way as exports.

11.4.2 Delivery-Unit Export and Import

Delivery-unit exports are the method of choice for any kind of export that needs to happen in a controlled way, and it may be performed by an administrator as opposed to a developer.

A standard manual delivery-unit export will contain all objects in those packages that are assigned to the delivery unit. It is also technically possible to only include those objects that have been changed since a given time stamp; for most practical use cases, however, this option does not seem useful.

Exporting Delivery Units

You can create delivery unit exports in the following way:

1. **Create a delivery unit**
   Delivery units can be managed in two places: either in the QUICK LAUNCH window of the MODELER perspective in SAP HANA Studio or in the HALM application.

Privilege Information

You need system privilege REPO.MAINTAIN_DELIVERY_UNITS in order to manage delivery units.

In SAP HANA Studio, the QUICK LAUNCH window opens automatically when you switch to the MODELER perspective. Alternatively, while using the MODELER perspective you can open this window from the menu path HELP • QUICK LAUNCH. In this window, you must first make sure to work with the correct user in the right system. Click the Select System... button to choose the system and user to work with.

Once the correct connection is chosen, you can click on the Delivery Units... link of the Quick Launch window to open a wizard in which you can create delivery units.

In the HALM application, you can find an entry to manage delivery units directly on the home screen.

Finally, the `hdbalm` program that is part of the client package for all operating systems contains functionality to create and manage (but not to deploy) delivery units.

> **Note**
>
> Delivery units can only be created if the `[repository]` • `content_vendor` parameter of file indexserver.ini is set.

2. **Assign packages to the delivery unit**

   The wizards for creating and managing delivery units (either in Quick Launch or in HALM) also offer functionality to add packages to the delivery units.

   Alternatively, you can edit packages in the Systems view of SAP HANA Studio, and choose the delivery unit for the package from a dropdown menu.

3. **Export the delivery unit**

   In SAP HANA Studio, follow the menu path File • Export • SAP HANA Content • Delivery Unit.

   In the HALM application, delivery-unit exports can be reached via the Import button of the home screen or the Upload/Download menu entry.

   The entries to be made in both wizards are self-explanatory.

The result of a delivery-unit export is a single Linux TAR archive compressed with the `gzip` command, that is, a TGZ file. If you choose a server-side export, the file will be located in the file system path */hana/shared/<SID>/HDB<instance>/backup*.

Importing Delivery Units

Delivery units can be imported by using the corresponding import wizards in SAP HANA Studio. Alternatively, if a delivery unit is located on the file system of the

SAP HANA server, then there is a command-line tool to load the delivery unit into the database.

This tool is named `hdbudrep` and is located in the file system path */hana/shared/<SID>/global/hdb/install/bin*. This tool is documented as part of the *SAP HANA LCM Tools Reference Guide* on *https://help.sap.com/hana_platform/*. You can also get usage hints by starting the tool with the option `--help`. The syntax for using the tool for the import of a given delivery unit is shown in Listing 11.1.

```
# Create a user store entry named RICHARD for database user
# RICHARD—so that the password does not need to be specified
# in the call to hdbupdrep
hdbuserstore -i SET <host>:3<instance>15 RICHARD
# As <sid>adm user, change to the location of the hdbupdrep
# tool:
cd /hana/shared/<SID>/global/hdb/install/bin
# Run the tool, specifying a delivery unit "/tmp/du.tgz" and
# using the database user RICHARD
./hdbupdrep --delivery_unit=/tmp/du.tgz
    --user_store_key=RICHARD --system_user=RICHARD
```

Listing 11.1 Loading a Delivery Unit with the hdbupdrep Program

Privilege Information

The database user provided to the `hdbupdrep` program needs three privileges: system privilege `REPO.IMPORT`; object privilege `EXECUTE` on procedure `SYS.REPOSITORY_REST`; and object privilege `SELECT` on table `_SYS_REPO.DELIVERY_UNITS`.

Support Mode Transports

A special type of transport is the *support mode transport*. This is a transport of an individual content object—for example, a data model—with all content and catalog objects it depends on. It is particularly useful for support incidents related to a content object. Behind the scenes, the content objects are transported like a delivery-unit export, and the catalog objects are transported as a binary export (see Chapter 9).

11.5   Change Recording and Transports

If you have a system landscape consisting of a development system, a production system, and typically one or more tiers in the middle for testing, quality assurance, or other purposes, then you will need a way to safely propagate content through this system landscape.

SAP offers three different methods of managing SAP HANA content:

- If SAP HANA content is closely coupled to ABAP developments in an SAP NetWeaver system, you can encapsulate a delivery unit inside of a regular CTS transport. This mechanism is called SAP HANA Transport Container (HTC), and more information is available at *https://scn.sap.com/docs/DOC-43035* ("How to Transport ABAP for SAP HANA Applications with HTC").

- If you are already using the Extended Change and Transport System (CTS+) for transports of non-ABAP content, then you can easily integrate SAP HANA content transports into your CTS+ setup, as described in *https://scn.sap.com/docs/DOC-8576* ("Resources on CTS+") in the section titled "SAP HANA."

- For all others, there is also a native transport application shipped with any SAP HANA system, starting with SPS 6 of the database. This XS application is SAP HANA Application Lifecycle Manager (HALM), and it can be reached at the URL *http://<host>:<port>/sap/hana/xs/lm/*.

In the following sections, we will only discuss the HALM application. The HALM transports (as well as CTS+ transports of SAP HANA content) can be used in two fundamentally different modes: You can either transport entire delivery units with each transport—that is, in a transport the active version of all objects within the delivery unit will be transported—or you can enable change recording and only transport released changes.

In the following, we will first describe how to enable change recording, before giving a brief introduction to setting up transports of either mode in the HALM application.

11.5.1 Change Recording

Content transports that are based on delivery units will always transport the entire delivery unit. In many cases, this will be inappropriate. Imagine, for example, a situation in which one object in a given package is finished and ready for transport. A second object within the same package has been modified since the last transport, but current testing shows that these modifications have in fact broken the object's functionality. Because of some emergency, you now must transport the first object into the production system. A full delivery-unit transport will also transport the current development version of the second object into your production system.

Problems like these can be avoided with change recording. This feature provides the following functionality:

▶ Objects can be attached to a logical entity called *change*.

▶ The first time an object is activated following a transport involving this object, the object must be attached to a new change.

▶ Objects within the same package do not need to be attached to the same change.

▶ Objects can be moved from one change to another.

▶ If change recording is enabled in a system, the only transportable entities are changes; delivery unit transports are no longer available.

▶ Individual objects can be transported by attaching them to a dedicated change.

▶ A change must be explicitly released before it can be transported.

▶ A change can only be released after all contributing developers have approved their respective contributions.

▶ If required, a developer may approve *foreign contributions*—for example, if another contributor is presently not available to approve their contributions.

> **Privilege Information**
>
> The system privileges `REPO.MODIFY_CHANGE`, `REPO.MODIFY_OWN_CONTRIBUTION`, and `REPO.MODIFY_FOREIGN_CONTRIBUTION` are related to change management.

Change recording is a system-wide setting; it is either enabled for all development activities or for none.

11.5.2 Transporting with the SAP HANA Application Lifecycle Manager

The HALM application offers an easy-to-use yet powerful transport mechanism. On a high level, the following steps are required in order to set up transports between a source and a target system:

▶ Prepare a transport user on the source system. This user must have the prede-livered role `sap.hana.xs.lm.roles::Transport`.

- Prepare a transport management user on the target system. This user must have the predelivered role `sap.hana.xs.lm.roles::Administrator`.

- You may define a less privileged user to execute the actual transports. Again, this user must be set up on the target system and needs the privileges from the role `sap.hana.xs.lm.roles::ExecuteTransport`.

- Start the HALM application on the target system—*http://<host>:<port>/sap/ hana/xs/lm/*—and log on with the transport management user.

- In the application menu, navigate to TRANSPORT • SYSTEM. Here, you can create an HTTP destination to the source system. This destination will use the transport user on the source system to assemble and provide the transport content.

- Once the destination is set up, go to the TRANSPORT • TRANSPORTS menu entry. Create a new transport route. A transport route connects the HTTP destination with one or several delivery units of the source system. In addition, the transport route contains a definition of the type of transport. In general, the options FULL for full delivery-unit exports and CHANGE for transporting of changes are available.

- At this point, you have set up one complete transport route that can from now on be used to transport the content objects within the delivery units (or the changes associated with those delivery units).

Even with change recording, packages must be assigned to delivery units, and transport routes must be tied to delivery units, so for a given transport route only those changes will be offered for transport that contain objects of the delivery unit.

For full details on managing change recording and transports, see the *SAP HANA Developer Guide* available at *https://help.sap.com/hana_platform/*.

11.6 Summary

The repository in SAP HANA offers the technical foundation for managing development artifacts. Even though this book is not about developing in SAP HANA, administrators must have a basic understanding of the related principles, because they will be confronted with database developers and development objects in the course of their work.

We introduced the three most common tools for accessing the repository:

- SAP HANA Studio, which offers two modes of working with the repository: the MODELER perspective, which allows you to work directly in the CONTENT node of the SYSTEMS view; and the Development Workbench, which features a project-based approach
- The SAP HANA Application Lifecycle Manager (HALM), which offers managing capabilities, most notably a transport functionality
- The web IDE, which gives quick access to all types of content objects in the repository

You should now also understand how the repository is organized with packages and delivery units. Most importantly, you should have an idea of why it is important to define an appropriate package structure in your development system and what such a structure might look like.

We also spent some time on creating, editing, and deleting objects in the repository with SAP HANA Studio.

You will need to get content out of a system and into a system—either as a single export or as a transport for regular content shipments. In the last two sections of this chapter, we introduced the capabilities offered by SAP HANA for exporting and transporting development artifacts.

The SAP HANA database has its own mechanisms for managing security in the areas of authentication, user management, object ownership, and audit logging. When setting up the security concept for an SAP HANA-based project, an understanding of the specifics in these areas is essential.

12   User Management and Security

The contents of their database systems are typically among corporations' most valuable assets, and one of the key features of a database system is to secure this data. This requires administrators to take responsibility for three dimensions of the database:

▶ Proper authentication and authorization for database users

▶ Auditing actions and events happening in the database

▶ Securing the infrastructure of the database system, that is, the operating system of the database server and especially the network interfaces of the server

In this chapter, we will give you more than just an introduction to all these aspects of database security. We will explain the main concepts behind security in an SAP HANA system and then give examples of how to perform the administration tasks related to these concepts. The topic of authorizations, with discussions of roles and privileges, will be addressed in Chapter 13.

> **Note**
>
> The terms *user* and *account* are often used synonymously in the SAP HANA database and related product documentation. At the time of writing of this book, database user and database account cannot be separated in the SAP HANA database.
>
> In SAP HANA's SQL syntax as well as the corresponding elements of the administration tools, SAP has chosen the term *user*. We will therefore always employ the term *user* when referring to database users or accounts. That is to say, in this book the user has a name, a password (or other credentials), privileges, and roles, and the user also owns objects.

12.1 Essential Security-Related Concepts

Before we dive into any details, we want to make you aware—on a high level—of two essential concepts in SAP HANA: catalog object ownership and stored procedures. Understanding these concepts will make it much easier for you to follow all the intricacies we are going to throw your way in the following sections.

12.1.1 Object Ownership

Strictly speaking, we are talking about catalog objects here (tables, views, stored procedures, etc.). Such objects in an SAP HANA database are always owned by their creator. There is no ownership relationship between a catalog object and the schema it is located in.

There are a few basic additional object ownership rules you should understand:

▶ Users can—assuming they have the necessary privileges—create catalog objects in database schemas owned by other users.

▶ Users can own multiple schemas; a schema does not necessarily belong to a database user of the same name. (If, however, a database schema and owner with identical names exist, the schema belongs to the database user. If schema <x> already exists and is owned by user <y>, it is not possible to create user <x>.)

▶ Objects cannot exist without an owner, and it is not possible to change object ownership.

▶ Any catalog object created through the activation of a development artifact in SAP HANA's repository is owned by the _SYS_REPO user.

12.1.2 Stored Procedures in Definer Mode

A stored procedure in an SAP HANA database can be created in so-called definer mode. In this case, there will be an implicit change of user context when a procedure is executed. Regardless of who calls the procedure, the code within the procedure body will be executed by and with the rights of the user that created the procedure.

12.2 Database Users

End users can interact with SAP HANA in multiple ways and for multiple purposes. The purposes span widely from database administration, through development in the database or modification of the contents of the database, to information retrieval. The means of interaction includes direct entering of SQL statements in an SQL editor, interaction through client tools, execution of custom-developed programs, or access through application servers. Any such interaction happens in the context of a database user and is limited by the privileges granted to the user.

In order to establish a database session, one must authenticate with the database, that is, one must specify valid database credentials. These credentials identify the database username and a means of verification, such as a password or the token of an external user repository.

In this section, we'll explain the basic tasks an administrator will have to perform with respect to database users: creating, modifying, deactivating and locking (or undoing deactivating and locking), and dropping. We'll then introduce you to two specific categories of users: built-in users and restricted users.

12.2.1 Creating Database Users

There are several ways in which you can create users in an SAP HANA database. For creating a small number of individual users, SAP HANA Studio is typically the tool of choice. For creating larger numbers of users following very simple rules, direct creation via SQL syntax is a good option (e.g., for preparing participant accounts for a classroom exercise, for which all accounts have the same password and the same set of privileges).

For more complex user management, integration into corporation-wide user-management processes is necessary. Such integration may be easy, if identity management software is used that either supports the SAP HANA database or that can easily be extended to include functionality for the SAP HANA database; or it can require significant development effort.

When creating a user in the SAP HANA database, you must specify at least one mechanism for authentication (see Section 12.3). For simplicity, our examples will be using name/password authentication.

In the following sections, we are going to demonstrate how to create users with SQL statements and in SAP HANA Studio.

Privilege Information

Database users in an SAP HANA database can only be created by users that have the USER ADMIN system privilege.

SQL Syntax for Creating Users

In our experience, the SQL syntax for creating and managing database users is more frequently used than the graphical user interface in SAP HANA Studio. There are multiple reasons, partly to do with the ability to automate user-management tasks.

Therefore, we first introduce the CREATE USER statement. When creating a user, there are two mandatory attributes that need to be provided: the username and a means of authentication. However, the CREATE USER SQL statement also offers multiple other optional arguments, as listed in Table 12.1.

Parameter	Usage
Username	Name of the database user to be created. Input is converted to all uppercase characters.
Means of authentication	This has to be at least one of the following: ▶ Password (for name/password authentication), following the password policy defined in the system ▶ Kerberos Principle Name (for delegated Kerberos ticket authentication) ▶ Mapped user name for a given SAML provider ▶ Subject distinguished name for X.509 authentication
Validity specification	To create users with a limited validity span. The user will not be able to log on (but not be removed) outside of the validity range. Restriction: The beginning of the validity period must be a time stamp in the future, i.e., at least 1 second after the execution of the CREATE USER statement. It is possible to create the validity period as an open interval: ▶ Only FROM clause: User is valid from begin date and never expires. ▶ Only UNTIL clause: User is valid from time of creation until specified end date.
Additional user parameters	Add metadata to the account. The following user parameters exist: ▶ CLIENT: Specify the SAP client for implicit filtering in queries against activated data models that include the SAP client field. In order for this filter to be active, the CLIENT parameter of the data model needs to be set to dynamic. See the *SAP HANA Modeling Guide* for details.

Table 12.1 Parameters for the CREATE USER Command

Parameter	Usage
	▸ LOCALE: Specify the default locale for the user. The locale setting can be used by applications in or on SAP HANA.
	▸ TIME ZONE: The time zone of the user; not used within the database but may be used by applications.
	▸ EMAIL ADDRESS: Like TIME ZONE, this is offered to applications as metadata information. In the future, EMAIL ADDRESS might be used for authentication, and thus the system accepts only unique values.

Table 12.1 Parameters for the CREATE USER Command (Cont.)

In Listing 12.1, we create a user named "RICHARD_III" with name password authentication valid throughout the year 2015 and the setting parameters CLIENT and EMAIL ADDRESS.

```
CREATE USER RICHARD_III
   password Mickey1928
   VALID FROM '2015-01-01 00:00:00' UNTIL '2015-12-31 23:59:59'
   SET PARAMETER CLIENT='800',
                EMAIL ADDRESS='richard3@dead_kings.gov'
```

Listing 12.1 Example CREATE USER Statement

Starting January 1, 2015, one can log on to this SAP HANA database with the newly created user RICHARD_III. The initial password that was given by the administrator may or may not need to be changed on first logon, depending on the system's password policy settings (see Section 12.3.1).

> **Note**
>
> In SAP HANA SPS 8, so-called restricted users have been introduced (see Section 12.2.6). These users can be created with the CREATE RESTRICTED USER command, which otherwise has the same syntax as the CREATE USER command.

Creating Users in SAP HANA Studio

SAP HANA Studio offers an editor to create and modify database users. The editor can be accessed from the SAP HANA SYSTEMS view in the ADMINISTRATION, MODELING, and DEVELOPMENT perspectives (in some perspectives, this view is simply called SYSTEMS). The steps in this process are as follows:

1. In the navigator, identify the system/user combination of your database user for user administration. In our example, this user is named "USER_ADMIN".

2. Expand the navigator tree to reach the location SECURITY • USERS, and right-click the USERS folder. Select NEW USER from the context menu (Figure 12.1).

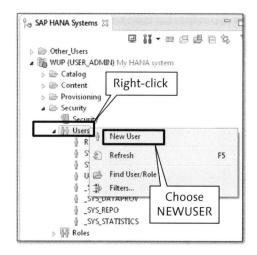

Figure 12.1 Creating a New User in SAP HANA Studio

The User Editor of SAP HANA Studio (Figure 12.2) offers input fields for the username, all authentication options, and the `CLIENT` user parameter. There are no screen elements to set other user parameters. If these extended properties must be set, use the SQL syntax.

3. Enter username and specify authentication details, for example, the initial password of the user. Then, click the green DEPLOY arrow, as shown in ❷, or the SAVE button, as shown in ❶, or press either the ⌨F8⌨ key or the key combination ⌨Ctrl⌨ + ⌨S⌨, or use the menu path FILE • SAVE.

Starting with SPS 8, one can mark the user as RESTRICTED USER, as shown in ❸, which means that the user will be created without the PUBLIC role and will thus have no privileges assigned to it initially. It can be interesting to work with restricted users if system security plays a particularly important role; see the discussion in Section 12.2.6.

Once you have successfully created the new user, it is listed under SECURITY • USERS in the SAP HANA SYSTEMS view. The newly created user might only appear after refreshing the SECURITY • USERS folder.

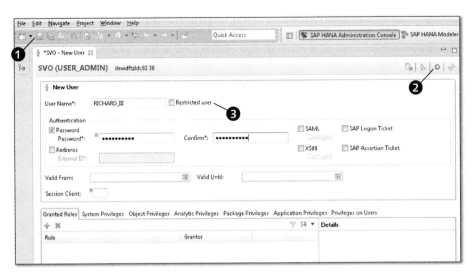

Figure 12.2 The User Editor in SAP HANA Studio

12.2.2 Modifying Database Users

SAP HANA allows you to modify database users in many different aspects, as listed in Table 12.2. Of the possible user modifications, all except for the granting and revoking of roles and privileges are technically handled with the ALTER USER statement. The User Editor in SAP HANA Studio offers functionality for a subset of the options of the ALTER USER statement—see Table 12.2—and it offers functionality for granting and revoking roles and privileges.

As can be seen from the column "Alter Self?" in Table 12.2, users cannot modify themselves in critical aspects, with the exception of granting and revoking privileges—and these risks can easily be mitigated through the creation of a few simple stored procedures (see discussion in Section 14.3.2 of Chapter 14).

Task	In Studio?	SQL Syntax	Alter Self?
Change password	Yes	ALTER USER <name> PASSWORD <password>	Yes
Force password change	No	ALTER USER <name> FORCE PASSWORD CHANGE	No

Table 12.2 The Different Reasons to Modify a User

Task	In Studio?	SQL Syntax	Alter Self?
Exempt user from password lifetime rule	No	`ALTER USER <name> DISABLE PASS-WORD LIFETIME`	No
Change authentica-tion options	Yes	Variants of the `ALTER USER` and other statements; see Section 12.3	No
Change validity date range	Yes	`ALTER USER <name> VALID FROM '<timestamp>' TO '<timestamp>'`	No
Change user para-meter `CLIENT`	Yes	`ALTER USER <name> SET PARAMETER CLIENT='<client>'`	No
Change other user parameters	No	`ALTER USER <name> SET PARAMETER <parameter_name>='<value>'`	Yes
Deactivate	Yes	`ALTER USER <name> DEACTIVATE [USER NOW]`	No
Activate	Yes	`ALTER USER <name> ACTIVATE [USER NOW]`	No
Unlock (reset connect attempts)	Yes	`ALTER USER <name> RESET CONNECT ATTEMPTS`	No
Remove history of connect attempts	No	`ALTER USER <name> DROP CONNECT ATTEMPTS`	No
Grant role or privilege	Yes	SQL `GRANT` statement or appropriate stored procedure call	Partially
Revoke role or privilege	Yes	SQL `REVOKE` statement or appropriate stored procedure call	Partially

Table 12.2 The Different Reasons to Modify a User (Cont.)

Privilege Information

All user modifications that can be triggered with an `ALTER USER` statement require the issuer of the statement to hold the `USER ADMIN` system privilege.

For database users to modify themselves (e.g., to change an initial password), the `USER ADMIN` system privilege is not required.

12.2.3 Deactivating and Locking Users

In SAP HANA, users can be deactivated or locked. If a user is locked or deacti-vated, that user will not be able to establish new database sessions. Existing ses-sions with this user will, however, not be affected.

The reasons for deactivation or locking are as follows:

▶ **Deliberately deactivating a user**
A database administrator with the USER ADMIN system privilege can deactivate a user.

  ▶ In SQL, the command ALTER USER <user_name> DEACTIVATE will deactivate the named user.

  ▶ In the User Editor of SAP HANA Studio, the user can be deactivated by clicking the DEACTIVATE USER... button in the top-right corner of the editor, as shown in Figure 12.3.

  ▶ SAP provides helper procedures to deactivate all users in the database system (except for administrators identified by certain system privileges or users from a white list). These procedures are delivered and documented in SAP Note 1986645.

▶ **Automatic locking because of too many failed connect attempts**
If someone has tried too many times consecutively to logon with the wrong credentials for a given user, this user will be locked (for details of the configuration, see Section 12.3.1).

▶ **User is outside of its validity specification**
Starting with SPS 6 of SAP HANA, users can be created with limited temporal validity. Outside of this validity range, a user will not be able to establish new database sessions. The validity range can be defined and changed in the User Editor of SAP HANA Studio or via the CREATE USER or ALTER USER commands.

In most cases, it requires administrator action to unlock or reactivate a database user. A user that has been deliberately deactivated can only be reactivated by a database admin with the USER ADMIN system privilege, and there the admin has two choices:

▶ **Reactivate the user**
In SQL, use the syntax ALTER USER ACTIVATE <user_name>. Or, in the User Editor of SAP HANA Studio use the button that has now turned into ACTIVATE USER..., also depicted in Figure 12.3.

▶ **Set a new password**
This option is appropriate for users with authentication method name/password. This is also possible if multiple authentication methods are enabled for the user, as long as name/password is among them.

Users that have been locked automatically because of too many invalid connect attempts are automatically unlocked after the configurable lock period (which may be indefinite). Users that are outside of their validity period can only be activated by modifying their validity period appropriately.

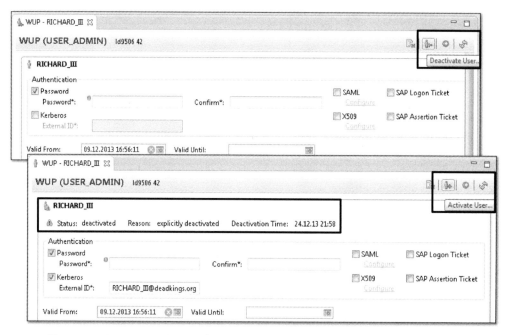

Figure 12.3 Deactivating (Top) and Reactivating (Bottom) a User in SAP HANA Studio

12.2.4 Dropping Database Users

One of the most powerful and most critical actions in an SAP HANA database is the dropping (deletion) of database users.

The criticality lies in the side effects of dropping users. These side effects are related to object ownership and to the transitivity in the behavior of granting user privileges. Before demonstrating the dropping of database users in SAP HANA, we first give an example of the mentioned side effects.

Object ownership is discussed in detail in Chapter 7 and the dependencies for privilege granting are discussed in Chapter 13.

Privilege Information
Any database user holding the USER ADMIN system privilege may drop database users.

When you drop a database user, all objects owned by the user must be dropped as well. The database verifies whether or not the user to be dropped owns database objects. If there are objects owned by the user, one must drop the user with the cascade option, thus explicitly approving the removal of these objects.

The less obvious side effect relates to privileges granted by the user being dropped. We will illustrate both side effects with a simple example, starting with the transitive behavior of granting.

Let us assume that there are three users, A, B, and C, and two catalog roles, R1 and R2. Initially, A has permission to grant both roles to other users. Then, the grant actions listed in Table 12.3 occur.

Grantor	SQL Statement	Comment
A	GRANT R1 TO B	A grants role R1 to user B.
A	GRANT R2 to B WITH ADMIN OPTION	A grants role R2 to user B, allowing B to grant the role to others.
B	GRANT R2 to C	B grants R2 to C.

Table 12.3 Example: Granting of Roles with ADMIN OPTION

The situation can be easily understood from the result of a query against the system view PUBLIC.GRANTED_ROLES, which shows role assignments, including grantor information; see Figure 12.4.

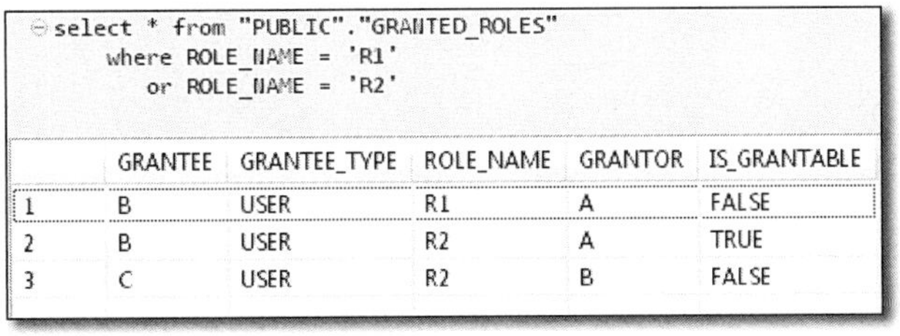

```
select * from "PUBLIC"."GRANTED_ROLES"
    where ROLE_NAME = 'R1'
    or ROLE_NAME = 'R2'
```

	GRANTEE	GRANTEE_TYPE	ROLE_NAME	GRANTOR	IS_GRANTABLE
1	B	USER	R1	A	FALSE
2	B	USER	R2	A	TRUE
3	C	USER	R2	B	FALSE

Figure 12.4 Example: Result of a Query against PUBLIC.GRANTED_ROLES

507

Now we drop user A. In our example, A was explicitly created as a user that does not own any objects in the database system; hence, we can simply drop the user.

Rerunning the same query against the PUBLIC.GRANTED_ROLES view shows that roles R1 and R2 have been revoked from users B and C.

The reason for this behavior is that user B only was assigned to those roles because user A had granted them. With user A removed from the system, the authority that gave roles R1 and R2 to user B does not exist anymore. SAP HANA reacts to this situation by revoking the role from user B, and with the same logic also from user C.

> **Note**
>
> In our example, catalog roles (also referred to as *runtime roles*) have been used explicitly. The described behavior does not appear if repository (design-time) roles are used; see Chapter 13 for details.
>
> With repository roles, granting and revoking of roles is performed by means of stored procedures. These procedures abstract the end-user management of roles from the technical implementation at the heart of the database, allowing a more application-friendly role management.

As with creating database users, there are two ways to drop them: via SQL and via SAP HANA Studio. We discuss both options next.

SQL Syntax for Dropping Users

Users can be dropped with the DROP USER SQL statement. The statement accepts an option that can either be RESTRICTED or CASCADE, defaulting to RESTRICTED. This default is the safe way of deleting users, as it will result in an error message if the user owns database objects that would be dropped together with the user.

For illustration, we will extend the previous example involving users A, B, and C a little further with the actions listed in Table 12.4.

User	SQL Statement	Comment
A	CREATE COLUMN TABLE "T_A1" (F_1 VARCHAR(3) PRIMARY KEY);	User A creates a table T_A1 in his own home schema.

Table 12.4 Example: Creation of Objects in Various Schemas

User	SQL Statement	Comment
A	CREATE SCHEMA "SCHEMA_A2"; GRANT CREATE ANY ON SCHEMA "SCHEMA_A2" TO B;	User A creates a new schema, SCHEMA_A2, and grants the CREATE ANY privilege on that schema to user B.
B	CREATE COLUMN TABLE "SCHEMA_A2"."T_B1" (F_1 VARCHAR(10) PRIMARY KEY);	User B creates a table T_B1 in this schema, SCHEMA_A2.
C	GRANT CREATE ANY ON SCHEMA "C" TO A;	User C allows user A to create objects in C's home schema.
A	CREATE COLUMN TABLE "C"."T_A2" (F_1 VARCHAR(5) PRIMARY KEY);	User A creates a table T_A2 in user C's home schema.

Table 12.4 Example: Creation of Objects in Various Schemas (Cont.)

In this state, user A owns two database schemas, namely the user's home schema A and the newly created schema SCHEMA_A2. User A also created and thus owns a table T_A1 in schema A and a table T_A2 in schema C. User B created and thus owns table T_B1 in schema SCHEMA_A2. This situation is depicted in Figure 12.5.

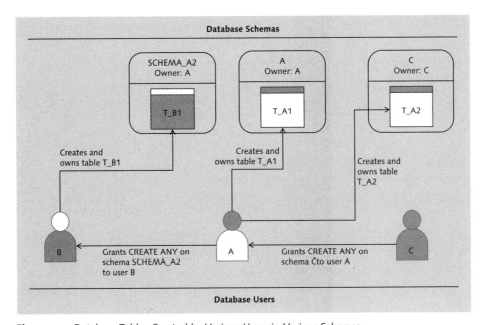

Figure 12.5 Database Tables Created by Various Users in Various Schemas

To attempt to delete the user without deleting depending objects, we use the simple SQL statement:

```
DROP USER A
```

This SQL statement will result in an error message, because user A owns objects other than empty database schemas.

To see the objects that will be deleted if user A is dropped with the CASCADE option, we need to combine two pieces of information:

▶ All objects directly owned by A, including database schemas owned by A

▶ All objects owned by any arbitrary database user in a schema owned by A

We can retrieve this information in a single SQL query, as shown in Listing 12.2.

```
(
SELECT  "SCHEMA_NAME",
        '' AS "OBJECT_NAME",
        'SCHEMA' AS "OBJECT_TYPE",
        "SCHEMA_OWNER" as "OWNER_NAME"
  FROM "PUBLIC"."SCHEMAS"
  WHERE SCHEMA_OWNER = 'A'
UNION ALL

SELECT  "SCHEMA_NAME", "OBJECT_NAME",
        "OBJECT_TYPE", "OWNER_NAME"
  FROM "PUBLIC"."OWNERSHIP"
  WHERE
     "SCHEMA_NAME" IN
       ( SELECT "SCHEMA_NAME" from "PUBLIC"."SCHEMAS"
           WHERE "SCHEMA_OWNER" = 'A' )
     OR "OWNER_NAME" = 'A'
) ORDER BY "SCHEMA_NAME" ASC, "OBJECT_NAME" ASC;
```

Listing 12.2 Query to Retrieve All Objects That Will Be Deleted When Dropping a User

In our example, this query yields the expected result set, as shown in Figure 12.6. Note that dropping user A would delete objects owned by other users as well as objects from schemas owned by other users!

Note

The system view "PUBLIC"."OWNERSHIP" typically only reveals information for objects that the querying user has explicit privileges on. An administrator carrying only the USER ADMIN privilege will therefore generally not see the correct list of objects that would be deleted if a given user was dropped from the system.

It is therefore advisable to also give the system privilege CATALOG READ to user administrators, because this will give unfiltered read access to the ownership view.

```
(select SCHEMA_NAME, '' as OBJECT_NAME, 'SCHEMA' as OBJECT_TYPE,
        SCHEMA_OWNER as OBJECT_OWNER
   from "PUBLIC"."SCHEMAS" where SCHEMA_OWNER = 'A'
 UNION ALL
 select SCHEMA_NAME, OBJECT_NAME, OBJECT_TYPE, OWNER_NAME
   from "PUBLIC"."OWNERSHIP"
   where SCHEMA_NAME IN (
      select SCHEMA_NAME from "PUBLIC"."SCHEMAS" where SCHEMA_OWNER = 'A')
   OR OWNER_NAME='A'
) order by SCHEMA_NAME asc, OBJECT_NAME asc
```

	SCHEMA_NAME	OBJECT_NAME	OBJECT_TYPE	OBJECT_OWNER
1	A		SCHEMA	A
2	A	T_A1	TABLE	A
3	C	T_A2	TABLE	A
4	SCHEMA_A2		SCHEMA	A
5	SCHEMA_A2	TB_1	TABLE	B

Figure 12.6 Overview of All Objects That Would Be Deleted if User A Was Dropped

After checking which objects will be deleted when we drop user A and verifying that it is okay to do so, we can finally drop user A:

```
DROP USER A CASCADE
```

Note

Dropping user A in our example also deleted objects owned by other users (table T_B1 owned by user B), and it deleted objects located in schemas owned by other users (table T_A2 in schema C owned by user C).

Dropping Users in SAP HANA Studio

Like user creation, the dropping of users is supported by a wizard in SAP HANA Studio. Again, the editor can be accessed from the SAP HANA SYSTEMS view in the ADMINISTRATION, MODELING, and DEVELOPMENT perspectives, and again we have to work with a database user that has the USER ADMIN system privilege. The steps in this process are as follows:

1. Expand the navigator tree in the SAP HANA Systems view to expand the Security • Users folder, and right-click on the user to be deleted. Select Delete from the context menu (Figure 12.7). If there are many users in the system, locate your user via the Find User/Role entry, which is available in the context menus of the Users and Roles folders.

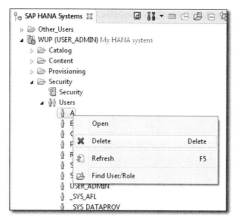

Figure 12.7 Deleting a User in SAP HANA Studio

2. In the wizard that appears, you can choose whether to drop the user with option Restrict or Cascade. Choose Cascade to check if the user owns any objects (Figure 12.8). You can still abort deletion.

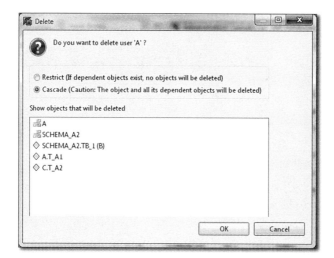

Figure 12.8 The Drop User Dialog in SAP HANA Studio

After selecting the CASCADE radio button, the wizard is updated to show all objects that will be deleted if user A is dropped.

3. Confirm deletion of the user and objects by clicking the OK button, or abort deletion by clicking the CANCEL button.

> **Note**
>
> It may take some time for the system to assemble the information on all objects that will be deleted.

12.2.5 Built-in Database Users

SAP HANA comes with a set of built-in database users that is not intended to be used in regular database operations; with the exception of one, these users are not even foreseen for database logon.

All users whose name begins with _SYS are built-in users (sometimes referred to as *internal users*). These users are not enabled for logon. We will list these users in alphabetical order:

▸ **_SYS_AFL**
Objects of the Application Function Library—that is, the PAL and the BFL objects) are installed into a schema _SYS_AFL owned by a user _SYS_AFL. Access to these objects is granted through roles delivered with the libraries.

▸ **_SYS_DATAPROV**
SAP HANA offers a way to model data flows for real-time replication technologies. The only one such technology partially supported in SPS 7 is SAP Landscape Transformation (SLT).

The data flow modeler comes with a number of dedicated objects in schema _SYS_DATAPROV owned by user _SYS_DATAPROV.

▸ **_SYS_EPM**
A very useful demo model comes with SAP HANA; it is called SAP HANA Interactive Education (SHINE) and it is based on the well-known Enterprise Procurement Model (EPM) from SAP NetWeaver. Catalog objects of the SHINE demo model belong to user _SYS_EPM and are located in schema _SYS_EPM.

▸ **_SYS_REPO**
The _SYS_REPO user is the owner of all repository content as well as the catalog schema _SYS_REPO, which contains the persistence objects of the SAP HANA repository.

▸ **_SYS_STATISTICS**
Finally, _SYS_STATISTICS is the user who owns all statistics server data and executes all periodic checks of the statistics server.

> **Note**
>
> In early versions of the database, it was possible to change the passwords of these technical _SYS_* users and use them for logging on to the system. This option was removed around SPS 6. We have never encountered a situation in which this option would have been necessary. Conceptually, in a properly managed SAP HANA database, you must never do this, even if your database is so old that you *can* do it.

The SYS User

The most special user in SAP HANA database is named SYS and is basically the owner of the database itself. In the history of SAP HANA, it has always been impossible to log on with the SYS user.

All objects in schema SYS belong to the user of the same name. Those objects that are of interest to users, administrators, or developers in the database are exposed via public synonyms. Most other objects are only accessible to the SYSTEM user (who cannot grant this privilege to others) or to the holder of the SAP_INTERNAL_HANA_SUPPORT role.

The SYSTEM User

The best-known and most frequently abused built-in user is the SYSTEM user. It is the only logon-enabled user among the built-in users, and its password is chosen at the install time of the database. In principle, SYSTEM is just a regular database user.

The purpose SAP assigns to the SYSTEM user is to bootstrap the database system, that is, to create the initial system setup—a list of objects, users, and roles plus initial system configuration—that is sufficient to then operate the entire database system without ever needing the SYSTEM user again.

Therefore, as soon as the bootstrapping is finished, the SYSTEM user is supposed to be deactivated and only reactivated in case of emergencies.

Reality shows, however, that virtually no customer team has ever deactivated the SYSTEM user. It is one intention of this chapter and the next two to give you all the information you need to successfully run your SAP HANA database as a free administrator without guiltily switching to SYSTEM every now and then. In Chapter 14, we include a bootstrapping sequence that will help you get rid of the SYSTEM user quickly.

12.2.6 Restricted Users

Regular database users are automatically assigned to the PUBLIC role when they are created. With this role, they have a number of privileges that may be considered harmful, such as the ability to create objects within their own user schema (and thus potentially fill up the database). It is also not possible to disallow logging on via the SQL interface, even if certain users will only need to log in via the HTTP interface of SAP HANA XS.

In SPS 8, restricted users have been introduced that initially come without any privileges. These users are therefore not even able to log on to the database. You can create restricted users either by selecting the corresponding checkbox in the User Editor or by using the SQL command CREATE RESTRICTED USER.

> **Note**
>
> Whether or not a user is restricted is a choice made at creation time. This property cannot be changed at a later point in time. It is also not possible to grant the PUBLIC role to a restricted user.

Restricted users can always log on to the database using HTTP (but you can control access to the XS applications for each user). If you want to allow them to create via the JDBC or ODBC interface, you need to grant the RESTRICTED_USER_JDBC_ACCESS or RESTRICTED_USER_ODBC_ACCESS roles, respectively. These roles are part of the database software starting with SPS 8. In addition to these roles, you must grant use-case specific privileges to the users in order for them to work with the database.

Restricted users are primarily intended for end-user accounts, for example, for people who are supposed to only interact with SAP HANA through BI tools. These users will not need to be able to browse the database catalog or to perform other actions that will be relevant to developers or administrators.

12.3 Authentication Methods

SAP HANA supports a multitude of standard authentication methods, both on the SQL interface (standard database access via ODBC/ODBO/JDBC) as well as on the HTTP/HTTPS interface (SAP HANA XS).

An overview of these authentication methods is given in Table 12.5, and some further information is provided in the following sections. Due to the complexity of most of the authentication methods, these topics cannot be covered here in full depth.

Method	SQL (JDBC/ODBC)	HTTP(S) (HANA XS)
Name/Password	Yes	Yes (basic authentication, form-based login)
Kerberos	Yes	Yes (SPNEGO)
SAML 2.0	Yes (bearer token)	Yes
SAP Logon/Authentication Assertion Tickets	Yes	Yes
X.509	---	Yes

Table 12.5 Overview of Authentication Methods in SAP HANA Database

12.3.1 Name/Password Authentication

The most basic form of authentication is by user name and password and is appropriate if single sign-on is not possible or not required. SAP HANA comes with a password policy concept of medium complexity that will in most cases be sufficient to comply with your requirements and not confuse you with too many options that you are not going to need.

Configuring the Password Policy

The password policy can technically be configured in the configuration files of the database. However, beginning with SPS 6, SAP HANA offers a security editor with a comfortable UI for this purpose.

> **Privilege Information**
>
> The INIFILE ADMIN system privilege is required in order to make changes to the password policy.

You can enter into the Security Editor from the SYSTEMS view of SAP HANA Studio. In the navigation tree of your database system, navigate to the SECURITY folder and double-click the SECURITY icon therein. The password policy is on the second tab of the editor; see Figure 12.9.

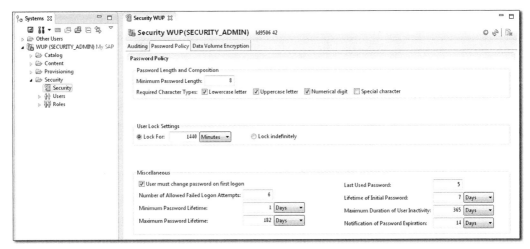

Figure 12.9 Defining the Password Policy in SAP HANA Studio

In the editor, one can configure the following properties:

▶ Requirements with respect to password strength: minimal password length and required character groups.

▶ The requirement to change an initial password on first logon. Whenever an administrator changes the password of another user, this password is considered initial.

Even if you switch off the requirement for users to change an initial password on first logon, the password lifetime rules stay intact as well as the lifetime of initial passwords. Hence—depending on the other parameters of the password policy—users may still have to change initial passwords.

▶ LIFETIME OF INITIAL PASSWORD: If this is exceeded before the user sets his own password, the user is locked and a user administrator must set a new initial password.

▶ MAXIMUM PASSWORD LIFETIME: The time span after which a user needs to change their password. If a user does not change his passwords in time, the next logon attempt will fail, and if the application used to connect to the database interprets the error code appropriately, the user will be asked to change his password.

▶ NOTIFICATION OF PASSWORD EXPIRATION: Users can receive a warning upon logon if their password is about to expire within the specified time span.

▶ LAST USED PASSWORDS: This specifies the number of previously used passwords that the user is not allowed to reuse.

▶ MINIMUM PASSWORD LIFETIME: This can be set to prevent users from circumventing LAST USED PASSWORDS. It is the amount of time that has to pass after the last password change before a user is allowed to change their password again.

▶ NUMBER OF ALLOWED FAILED LOGON ATTEMPTS is not quite named appropriately: The parameter specifies the number of consecutive failed logon attempts at which a user will be locked. The default setting of six allows five consecutive failed logon attempts. Upon the sixth consecutive failed logon attempt, the user will be locked and must be unlocked via an ALTER USER <name> RESET CONNECT ATTEMPTS statement.

▶ USER LOCK SETTINGS: Locked users are unlocked automatically after the specified amount of time. Starting with SPS 7, one can also lock users indefinitely.

▶ MAXIMUM DURATION OF USER INACTIVITY: Specifies the amount of time after which a user's password will be invalidated if the user does not log on to the database. To enable the user again, a user administrator must set an initial password.

Exempting Users from the Password Policy

It is not possible to completely exempt users from the password policy. For example, the password layout rules apply to all password changes of all users, including the SYSTEM user.

The SYSTEM user will, however, never be locked because of too many failed logon attempts, and it is the only user in the system that can show this behavior. It is not possible to exempt other users individually from this rule.

Only the forced password change can be disabled for individual users, via the following SQL syntax:

```
ALTER USER <name> DISABLE PASSWORD LIFETIME
```

The password lifetime should only be disabled for technical users, for example, the connection user of an SAP NetWeaver Application Server or similar users.

Password Blacklist

In the lower half of the PASSWORD POLICY tab in the Security Editor, we can maintain a PASSWORD BLACKLIST (Figure 12.10). One can add individual entries to the PASSWORD BLACKLIST by using the green plus icon. An entry may represent either an entire password or a part of a password (at an arbitrary position within the password) and may or may not be case sensitive.

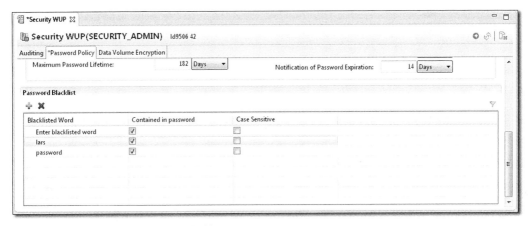

Figure 12.10 Editor for the Password Blacklist

At the time of writing (SPS 8 of SAP HANA), the Security Editor does not offer an import wizard to load, for example, CSV files into this table and the password list is not transportable.

> **Privilege Information**
>
> The password blacklist is maintained in database table _SYS_PASSWORD_BLACKLIST in the _SYS_SECURITY schema.
>
> In order to manage the blacklist via the SAP HANA Studio editor, a user needs the SELECT, INSERT, and DELETE privileges on this table.

When a large number of entries needs to be maintained in the blacklist, it is most sensible to insert the values from some data source via either a table import or some kind of programmatic insertion.

Table _SYS_SECURITY._SYS_PASSWORD_BLACKLIST has a simple layout, as can be seen from Listing 12.3, making it easy to prepare input for this table in an appropriate format. For your convenience, we included the data types for the table columns in that listing. The primary key spans all three columns.

> **Note**
>
> Direct inserts into the password blacklist table are not officially supported by SAP; the blacklist is supposed to be edited only through the official interface in the Security Editor.
>
> If you choose to maintain values in this table via direct insert, you should understand that there is a risk that the table might be renamed or its layout changed in the future.

```
SELECT * FROM _sys_security._sys_password_blacklist
===============================================================
BLACKLIST_TERM  |CHECK_PARTIAL_PASSWORD|CHECK_CASE_SENSITIVE
 [NVARCHAR(256)]|[NVARCHAR(6)]         |[NVARCHAR(6)]
----------------|----------------------|--------------------
password        |TRUE                  |FALSE
lars            |TRUE                  |FALSE
```

Listing 12.3 The Password Blacklist Table

12.3.2 Single Sign-On with Kerberos Authentication

SAP HANA supports Kerberos version 5 for Kerberos-based single sign-on with Active Directory or Kerberos authentication servers.

The database's ODBC and JDBC clients natively support the Kerberos Protocol, so applications using these clients can immediately use authentication based on domain users. SAP HANA Studio is an example of such a client application.

When using SAP HANA XS applications, Kerberos authentication is supported starting with SAP HANA SPS 7 by using the Simple and Protected GSSAPI Negotiation Mechanism (SPNEGO), which today is supported by all major web browsers.

Further Resources

For more information about SPNEGO, we recommend The Simple and Protected Generic Security Service Application Program Interface (GSS-API) Negotiation Mechanism by L. Zhu et al. (Network Working Group, October 2005): *https://tools.ietf.org/html/rfc4178*.

Kerberos can be used for direct client-server authentication (where the client is an application accessing SAP HANA and the server is the SAP HANA database server), as shown in Figure 12.11, or with Kerberos delegation through an intermittent application server, such as the SAP BusinessObjects BI server.

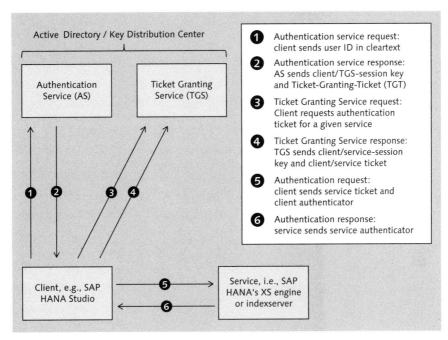

Figure 12.11 Schematic View of Client-Server Kerberos Authentication

Setting Up Kerberos Authentication

There are excellent guides available that describe the steps needed to implement Kerberos SSO with SAP HANA. The best end-to-end guide, which has been applied in multiple projects so far, is the how-to guide *Single Sign-On with SAP HANA® Database using Kerberos and Microsoft Active Directory*, which is available as an attachment to SAP Note 1837331.

The guide's instructions apply to SAP HANA SPS 5 (revision 45 or above) for Kerberos authentication on the SQL port and to SAP HANA SPS 7 (revision 70 or above) for the SPNEGO authentication for SAP HANA XS.

The procedures to set up Kerberos and SPNEGO are almost identical. If Kerberos authentication is already set up in your database and SPNEGO is to be added, only a small number of additional steps is required. All of these steps are discussed in the mentioned how-to guide.

SAP also provides a script to help validate many steps of the Kerberos setup on the SAP HANA database server. This script is made available as an attachment to SAP Note 1813724.

Setting up Kerberos requires support from network administrators and Kerberos/ AD administrators along with a good measure of familiarity with the concepts of ticket-based authentication in general and Kerberos between Linux Servers and Microsoft Active Directory in particular.

Registering Users for Kerberos Authentication

Users can authenticate using Kerberos if the user is valid and active and if it has been enabled for Kerberos authentication.

In SAP HANA Studio's User Editor (see Figure 12.12), select the checkbox for KERBEROS authentication, and enter the user's EXTERNAL ID into the input field; then save the user. Note that the EXTERNAL ID must match exactly the format <user>@<domain> as used in Active Directory, including capitalization.

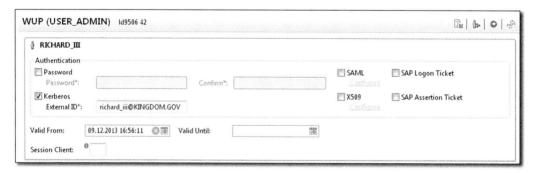

Figure 12.12 Setting up Kerberos Authentication in SAP HANA Studio

Alternatively, you can add the Kerberos External ID in the CREATE USER or ALTER USER commands. Listing 12.4 shows how to switch from name/password authentication to Kerberos authentication for the existing user RICHARD_III with domain user name richard_iii@KINGDOM.GOV.

```
// Add Kerberos authentication:
ALTER USER RICHARD_III
         ADD IDENTITY 'richard_iii@KINGDOM.GOV'
         FOR KERBEROS;
// Optional: Disable password authentication
ALTER USER RICHARD_III DISABLE PASSWORD;
```

Listing 12.4 SQL Syntax for Switching Authentication to Kerberos

12.3.3 Further Authentication Methods

In addition to name/password and Kerberos authentication, SAP HANA also offers authentication via other mechanisms, such as SAML or SAP Logon Ticket. These are not used as frequently in SAP HANA systems so far, and we only cover them very briefly.

Single Sign-On with SAML 2.0

Especially for web browser single sign-on, the XML-based SAML authentication protocol is popular. SAP HANA introduced support for the widely used SAML 2.0 protocol for HTTP access (SAP HANA XS) in SPS 6 of the software and added SAML 2.0 support for SQL access with SPS 7. A wizard to register SAML identity providers with the database has been added to the Security Editor in SPS 8.

A guide to setting up SAML-based SSO between SAP HANA and the SAP BI tools is included in SAP Note 1900023.

Authentication via SAP Logon/Authentication Assertion Tickets

Finally, SAP HANA also supports authentication by means of SAP Logon Tickets or SAP Authentication Assertion Tickets.

For database administrators, who certainly can be excused for not being familiar with these concepts, the SAP Help Portal offers information on both authentication mechanisms:

▶ For SAP Logon Tickets, see *http://help.sap.com/saphelp_nw73/helpdata/en/43/ 9d7bb1e08021b5e10000000a1553f6/content.htm?frameset=/en/85/ ba255812404f7b932a30bb309fd5bf/frameset.htm.*

▶ For SAP Authentication Assertion Tickets, see *http://help.sap.com/saphelp_ nw73/helpdata/en/85/ba255812404f7b932a30bb309fd5bf/content.htm.*

The differences between the two authentication methods are described on SCN at *scn.sap.com/thread/721203.*

12.3.4 Enabling Multiple Authentication Methods for One User

As can be seen in Figure 12.12 or Listing 12.4, it is possible to set up multiple authentication mechanisms for a given user. What authentication method will be used in a specific scenario will depend on the client application.

As an example, consider the dialog to register a new system or database user in SAP HANA Studio, as shown in Figure 12.13. In this dialog, you can switch between Kerberos authentication (AUTHENTICATION BY CURRENT OPERATING SYSTEM USER) and name/password authentication (AUTHENTICATION BY DATABASE USER). Depending on which option is selected, SAP HANA Studio will initiate authentication with the database following the corresponding protocol.

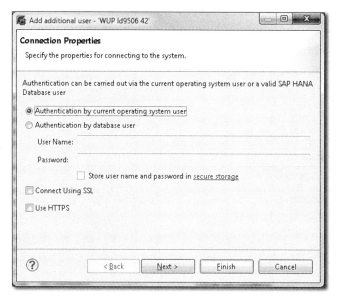

Figure 12.13 Registering a New User in SAP HANA Studio

12.4   Securing SAP HANA's Network Interfaces

Having reasonable user management and authentication as well as proper authorizations (see Chapter 13) set up is all good and well. However, if you do not take
care to secure the network connections into the database, then the overall system
will be vulnerable.

In this section, we will provide an overview of the most important internal and
external network connections of the database system and briefly touch on the
topic of encrypting network communication.

12.4.1   External Network Connections to an SAP HANA System

Communication with SAP HANA systems can have multiple purposes. There may
be external communication of some client with the database, and there is internal
communication between different parts of the database system.

External communication is that between a client and the database server. We will
define any external entity that communicates with the database as a client here;
for the sake of simplicity, we will apply this term to human beings and software
programs alike. In this sense, a client may be any of the following:

- An end-user application accessing the database on its SQL port in direct client-
  server communication. This would, for example, apply to users of SAP Business-
  Objects Analysis for Office or SAP Lumira Desktop.
- An end-user application accessing the database on its HTTP interface in direct
  client-server communication. An example of this interaction is the consump-
  tion of an SAP HANA XS application with an SAPUI5 interface.
- Communication through an application server, such as SAP NetWeaver or SAP
  BusinessObjects BI servers.
- Administration access for purposes of database monitoring, administration,
  lifecycle management, or SAP Support.

All typical connections of an SAP HANA system are displayed in Figure 12.14. In
this figure, we depict multitiered network landscapes with three tiers (database
layer, application layer, and end-user layer) and an additional administrator network. In the port numbers, "xx" denotes the two-digit instance number of the SAP
HANA system.

In the following sections, we will discuss end-user connections and administration connections separately.

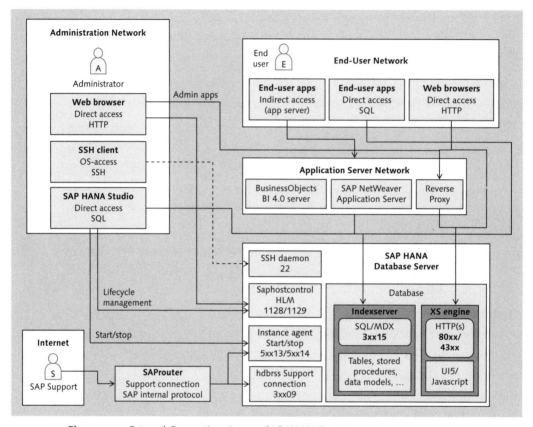

Figure 12.14 External Connections into an SAP HANA System

End-User Connections into an SAP HANA System

End users will typically use SAP HANA services provided via the SQL interface of the index server (port 3xx15), through the HTTP interface of the XS engine (ports 80xx and 43xx for HTTP and HTTPS, respectively), or indirectly through an application server of some sort.

The most usual application servers in the context of SAP HANA systems are SAP NetWeaver Application Servers and SAP BusinessObjects BI 4.0 servers. We added an HTTP reverse proxy in the application server network to show that this is a supported option, too.

The typical persona here is an end user who—depending on the scenario—consumes or even modifies data in SAP HANA. Especially in the nonproduction instances of a system landscape, you will also have developers in the picture.

The communication ports for end-user access are listed in Table 12.6. It must be noted that there are several end-user applications that run locally on an end-user device (desktop computer, notebook, mobile device, etc.) and access the database through its SQL interface. As there is no reverse SQL proxy, these applications require direct network access to the database server. The most common such applications in SAP HANA use cases are:

▸ SAP BusinessObjects Analysis, edition for Microsoft Office

▸ SAP Lumira Desktop

▸ SAP Crystal Reports 2008/2011

▸ For developers: SAP HANA Studio

> **Note**
>
> If you implement any of these applications in the context of your SAP HANA implementation, then you must open the database's SQL port to the end-user network.
>
> If there is a small (well-controlled) group of end users that needs such applications, then you may consider deploying the application on a WTS or a similar system.

Other common applications either use the HTTP(S) interface or intermediate application servers, so network layer segregation is usually possible.

Port	Communication Purpose	Protocol	Database Component	Communication Partners
3xx15	SQL communication with the database	SQLDBC (JDBC/ODBC)	indexserver	**Software:** Application servers, clients applications with direct DB access **Personas:** End user, developer

Table 12.6 External Ports for End-User Communication

Port	Communication Purpose	Protocol	Database Component	Communication Partners
80xx	HTTP communication with SAP HANA	HTTP	xsengine	**Software:** Either HTTP proxy/ load balancer or web browsers **Personas:** End-user, developer
43xx	HTTPS communication with SAP HANA	HTTPS	xsengine	Same as HTTP port 43xx

Table 12.6 External Ports for End-User Communication (Cont.)

Administration Connections in an SAP HANA System

For administrators, there is a wealth of network ports available—and the group of administrators will typically need all of the connections listed in Table 12.7.

Because SAP HANA Studio is the most important administration tool, administrators will need SQL access to the database.

Certain functionalities in SAP HANA Studio will access other ports than the SQL port:

▶ **Start/stop of the entire database system**
SAP systems are started through an instance agent (sapstartsrv) that can be remotely accessed via port 5xx13/5xx14 (without/with SSL encryption).

▶ **Using SAP HANA Lifecycle Manager**
For tasks such as upgrading the database, adding software components, changing the scale-out landscape, or deploying further instances, SAP HANA Lifecycle Manager (HLM) is the preferred option before SPS 8. On the SAP HANA server, the software listens on ports 1128/1129 (without/with SSL encryption).

In addition to SAP HANA Studio, SAP has started building administration applications using the XS engine that are exposed via the HTTP/HTTPS port. We expect to see more and more of these applications in the future. They especially are needed if you deploy end-user applications based on the XS engine.

Access to the operating system of the database server will typically be established using an SSH connection (port 22).

A very special (but highly recommended) connection type is the SAP HANA Studio service connection, as described in SAP Note 1592925. This connection allows SAP Support staff use their locally installed SAP HANA Studio to connect to a customer's SAP HANA database system through an SAProuter. It is the equivalent in the SAP HANA world to the well-known R/3 support connection.

Port	Communication Purpose	Protocol	Database Component	Communication Partners
3xx15	SQL communication with the database	SQLDBC (JDBC/ODBC)	`indexserver`	**Software:** Application servers, clients with direct DB access **Personas:** Administrator, in-house support
3xx17	SQL communication with the statistics server	SQLDBC (JDBC/ODBC)	`statisticsserver` (if installed as separate service)	Should not be required externally; all communication can go through `indexserver` port 3xx15
80xx	HTTP communication with SAP HANA	HTTP	`xsengine`	**Software:** Either HTTP proxy/load balancer or web browsers **Personas:** Administrator, in-house support
43xx	HTTPS communication with SAP HANA	HTTPS	`xsengine`	Same as HTTP port 43xx
3xx09	SAP Support connection	Internal SAP protocol	`hdbrss`	**Software:** SAProuter **Personas:** SAP Support staff
1128	SAP HANA Lifecycle Management	SQLDBC (JDBC/ODBC)	`saphostcontrol`	**Software:** SAP HANA Studio or web browser **Personas:** Administrators

Table 12.7 External Communication Ports Required by Administrators

Port	Communication Purpose	Protocol	Database Component	Communication Partners
1129 (SSL)	SAP HANA Lifecycle Management	SQLDBC (JDBC/ODBC)	saphostcontrol	Same as port 1128
5xx13	Start and stop SAP HANA instances	SQLDBC (JDBC/ODBC)	Instance agent (sapstartsrv)	**Software:** SAP HANA Studio **Personas:** Administrators
5xx14 (SSL)	Start and stop SAP HANA instances	SQLDBC (JDBC/ODBC)	Instance agent (sapstartsrv)	Same as port 5xx13
22	Operating system access	SSH	SSH daemon	**Software:** SSH clients **Personas:** Basis admins

Table 12.7 External Communication Ports Required by Administrators (Cont.)

12.4.2 Encrypting External Network Connections

All external network connections can be encrypted using SSL. Except for the SQL interfaces, different ports are used for the encrypted and the unencrypted connections.

Recommendation

SAP recommends using SAP's Common Cryptographic Library, CommonCryptoLib, for encrypting network connections to SAP systems. This software component is available for download on SAP Service Marketplace.

Alternatively, one can use OpenSSL or the older SAP Cryptographic Library. The latter is only supported for reasons of backwards compatibility.

Further Resources

The steps for setting up SSL encryption for the SQL port are described in the *SAP HANA Security Guide*:

https://help.sap.com/hana/SAP_HANA_Security_Guide_en.pdf
This process requires setup on the server as well as on the client or end-user devices. SSL encryption can also be used for the SQL connection between an SAP NetWeaver Application Server and the database.

For SSL encryption of HTTP connections, the *SAP HANA Administration Guide* lists the necessary steps in the context of SAP HANA XS administration tools (as of the documentation for SAP HANA SPS 8):

https://help.sap.com/hana/SAP_HANA_Administration_Guide_en.pdf

Finally, you can always find the documentation for previous Support Package Stacks on SAP Service Marketplace:

https://service.sap.com/hana/

Enforcing Encryption on External Network Connections

Since SPS 7 of SAP HANA, it is possible to enforce SSL encryption of SQL connections to HANA. For the other external connections, this feature is already available in earlier releases.

Encryption of SQL connections can be enforced by setting parameter [communication]•sslenforce in configuration file global.ini to TRUE.

Note

Only enforce encryption of SQL (JDBC/ODBC) access after you have migrated to the new implementation of the statistics service, in which case it is not running as a dedicated server any longer.

For enforcing encryption of HTTP connections, there are multiple options:

▶ **Global setting of the web server (SAP Web Dispatcher)**
HTTP services are offered through the SAP Web Dispatcher component of SAP HANA. The configuration of this component can be found in file */usr/sap/ <SID>/HDB<instance>/<hostname>/wdisp/sapwebdisp.pfl*. If SSL encryption of HTTP connections has been configured, you will find one entry each for HTTP and HTTPS connectivity in this file. Remove (by placing into a comment) the entry for HTTP connectivity:

```
icm/server_port_0 = PROT=HTTP
```

▶ **Firewall configuration**
Because different ports are being used for HTTP and HTTPS connectivity, you can simply use firewall techniques to disallow access to the HTTP port.

▶ **Application-specific setting**
Each SAP HANA XS application can be configured to allow communication with and/or without encryption. Details are, again, given in the *SAP HANA Administration Guide*.

12.4.3   Internal Network Connections

In certain setup types, you also have to consider internal network connections within your database system.

One scenario is the implementation of scale out, which enforces communication between the database services on the individual server nodes that when combined form the database system.

The other scenario is the implementation of disaster-tolerant (DT) setups using SAP HANA system replication. In this setup, the two database systems that form the DT cluster need to be able to communicate with each other.

Connections within a Scale-Out Cluster

Within a scale-out cluster, the services of SAP HANA on the different server nodes communicate with each other through dedicated internal ports. Of the ports listed in Table 12.8, not all of them exist in all systems. The scriptserver is an optional component, and since SPS 7 it is possible to migrate the statistics service to a new implementation that is integrated into the nameserver and indexserver processes. The "xx" notations in Table 12.8 denote the two-digit instance number of the database system.

Certified SAP HANA hosts for scale out come with dedicated, set-up network cards for internal communication. It is recommended to tie the internal communication ports to these network devices and to operate all hosts of a scale-out system in a dedicated private network.

Port	Service	Comment
3xx00	HDB daemon	—
3xx01	nameserver	—

Table 12.8 Internal Communication Ports of SAP HANA Systems

Port	Service	Comment
3xx02	preprocessor	—
3xx03	indexserver	—
3xx04	scriptserver	Optional
3xx05	statisticsserver	Optional since SPS 7
3xx07	xsengine	—
3xx10	compileserver	—
3xx40–3xx98	indexserver	Only relevant after n:1 recovery of data backup

Table 12.8 Internal Communication Ports of SAP HANA Systems (Cont.)

It is technically possible and supported to encrypt internal network communication. However, if all internal communication ports are tied to the dedicated network devices and only accessible within the cluster-internal network, this encryption will normally not be required. Because communication encryption adds an (ever so small) overhead, it is recommended that you do not encrypt the internal connections within one scale-out system unless you cannot isolate the internal network.

> **Note**
>
> In single-node setups, the ports for internal communication are bound to `localhost` and blocked for external access. It is strongly recommended that you do not change this setting.

Connections in Disaster-Recovery Setups Using System Replication

In a disaster-tolerant database system, you set up two (typically identical) systems in two data centers that are separated by tens, hundreds, or sometimes even thousands of kilometers. Naturally, the database systems in the two data centers must communicate with each other.

> **Note**
>
> It is not only possible but also strongly recommended to secure the database-internal communication between the data centers of a disaster-tolerant setup using SSL encryption. The necessary steps are described in the *SAP HANA Security Guide* available at *https://help.sap.com/hana_platform/*.

The ports used for internal communication in a system replication setup are given in Table 12.9. In that table, "xy" equals "xx+1"—that is, the instance number of the database system plus one.

Port	Service	Comment
3xy00	HDB daemon	—
3xy01	nameserver	—
3xy02	preprocessor	—
3xy03	indexserver	—
3xy04	scriptserver	Optional
3xy05	statisticsserver	Optional since SPS 7
3xy07	xsengine	—
3xy10	compileserver	—

Table 12.9 Internal Communication Ports Used for System Replication

12.5 Auditing in the Database

SAP HANA comes with a built-in audit logging mechanism that allows you to log security-relevant events of the core database layer and of the repository. All auditing settings are made available through the Security Editor of SAP HANA Studio, which can be accessed via SYSTEMS (or SAP HANA SYSTEMS) by double-clicking SECURITY.

The editor (see Figure 12.15) offers global audit settings in its upper section and the definition of those events that shall be monitored in the lower section (collected in so-called audit policies).

Privilege Information

In order to read or modify any information in the AUDITING tab of the Security Editor, system privilege AUDIT ADMIN is required.

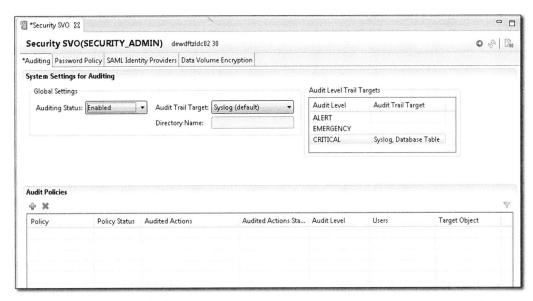

Figure 12.15 The Auditing Tab of SAP HANA Studio

12.5.1 Global Audit Settings

There are only two global audit settings available. Changes to these settings take effect after deploying them via the green arrow button or the ⌈F8⌉ key.

▶ AUDITING STATUS
Allows switching auditing on and off globally. Obviously, these are very important actions to audit; see Section 12.5.3 for details.

▶ AUDIT TRAIL TARGET
The dropdown box lets you choose between three targets for audit logging. Starting with SPS 8, multiple targets can be active at one time. In earlier releases, this was not possible.

  ▶ SYSLOG: The default audit target is the `syslog` daemon of the operating system. You may configure the `syslog` daemon itself to suit your auditing needs, for example, by forwarding any SAP HANA audit events to a remote audit server. In the default configuration of SUSE Linux Enterprise Server, the `syslog` output is only readable by the root user of the operating system.

  ▶ DATABASE TABLE: Logging into a database table is a new option that was introduced with SPS 7 of SAP HANA. If this target is chosen, audit events are written into a table in the SYS schema, to which no database user has direct access. The table is only exposed for reading through public view AUDIT_LOG. In addition, the database provides the ALTER SYSTEM CLEAR AUDIT LOG UNTIL <timestamp> command to delete from the audit log table (in order to control the table size).

▶ CSV TEXT FILE: For test purposes, this is the most comfortable audit target. However, because of the inherent insecurity of this target, this option is not supported (and obviously is not an appropriate choice) for production usage. The default target is a file in the trace-file directory of the database server, which is accessible in SAP HANA Studio's Administration Editor, tab DIAGNOSIS FILES. You can change the output file for this target in the text box DIRECTORY NAME.

Next to the dropdown box for AUDIT TRAIL TARGETS, there is a table in which you can configure AUDIT LEVEL TRAIL TARGETS, that is, different audit trail targets for different audit levels (see below for the audit level of an audit policy). This table has been newly introduced with SPS 8, and it is here that you can select multiple audit trail targets for each of the audit levels.

12.5.2 Audit Policies

Audit policies can be added or deleted by using the "plus" and "X" icons on top of the table of audit policies.

Audit policies are defined by multiple properties, each of which is represented by one column in the table of audit policies:

▶ POLICY
The name of the audit policy. Because the policy name is written to the audit trail with each event that is logged under the policy, it is a good idea to choose a useful name ("Policy 123" might be less informative than "Direct Granting of Privilege").

▶ POLICY STATUS
You can disable audit policies without deleting them. The status is either ENABLED or DISABLED.

▶ AUDITED ACTIONS
To add actions to the policy, click the small ... icon in the AUDITED ACTIONS cell of the policy. This brings up a selector for auditable actions, which is divided

into groups of actions that semantically belong together and can be added to the same audit policy (see Figure 12.16). It is not possible to mix actions from different groups in the same audit policy.

You can, however, create as many audit policies as you like, and they can all be active at the same time.

▶ AUDITED ACTIONS STATUS
Sometimes, you may want to only audit actions that were successful or that failed (for example, it may be of interest to audit all failed logon attempts with a technical user). Here, you can choose whether the audit policy will log all events of the selected action, only successful ones, or only failed ones.

▶ AUDIT LEVEL
The audit level only serves to structure the output. Each audit policy can have an administrator defined *criticality*. The available criticality levels are INFO, WARNING, ALERT, CRITICAL, and EMERGENCY.

All event messages of a given audit policy will contain the chosen criticality level, which enables administrators to define alerts based on the audit messages being logged or to filter the audit messages by criticality.

As an example, if you log all successful logons to the database, this would typically be level INFO, whereas direct granting of privileges might be CRITICAL and logon with the SYSTEM user might constitute an EMERGENCY.

In addition to adding semantics to the audit messages, the audit level plays a role if a given database event would be logged by multiple audit policies. In this case, only the policy with the highest criticality (in the order given previously) will log a message.

▶ USERS
Per default, an audit policy will log all events of the configured actions regardless of the user who triggered the event.

You can restrict the logging to a list of users, or you can exclude a list of users from the logging (failed connect attempts only for the SAP<sid> user of an SAP NetWeaver instance or granting of roles by anyone except for user administrators, for example).

Within one policy, you can either exclude or include users, but you cannot mix both.

▶ TARGET OBJECT

The logging of some auditable actions can be restricted to certain objects that might be involved in the action. This applies, for example, to the actions around DATA DEFINITION or DATA QUERY AND MANIPULATION.

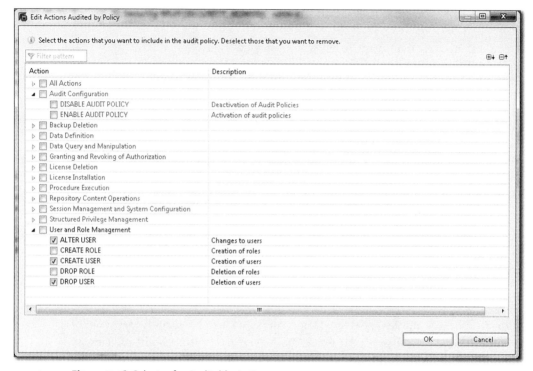

Figure 12.16 Selector for Auditable Actions

Modifications to the audit policies are deployed by clicking the green arrow button or clicking the F8 key.

12.5.3 Principles of Auditing in SAP HANA

In the following sections, we will discuss a number of important aspects of auditing in SAP HANA that will help you define appropriate audit policies. We will first discuss very generally what can be audited; after this, we give a brief introduction to the output structure of audit messages; then, we will warn you how very easy it is to have unrealistic expectations when restricting audit policies to individual users; and finally, we will tell you about mandatory audit policies.

What Can Be Audited?

It's most enlightening to start with events that *cannot* be audited. Anything that is not an execution of SQL statements cannot be audited.

SQL statements do not need to be executed by entering them into an SQL editor; activating or deploying something in SAP HANA Studio or running other applications that trigger SQL statement execution also can lead to auditable actions.

The execution of an SAP HANA XS application, however, or the recovery of a database backup is not auditable, nor is the changing of database configuration files with a text editor on the operating system of the database server, or the shutdown of the database using `SAPHostcontrol`.

Even if it comes to executing SQL commands, not all of them are auditable. The setting of a session parameter is such an example of a nonauditable event that is typically noncritical (but application developers had best not rely on sensitive information being maintained in a session variable). You will also find some non-auditable `ALTER SYSTEM` commands, such as the tracing and trace-file related commands or the commands related to the management of the data and log volumes.

Output Structure of Audit Messages

The most important aspect to be aware of about the output structure of audit messages is that it is documented in SAP's product documentation, specifically the *SAP HANA Security Guide*.

Second, the structure of the text-file-based audit trails (`syslog` and CSV text files) is different from the structure of the table-based audit trail, mostly because of a different ordering of the output fields.

Such minor differences notwithstanding, all three audit trails give information on the following aspects of an audited event (we list the corresponding columns of the `AUDIT_LOG` table with each aspect, without diving more deeply into details):

▸ **When and where (physically) did the event occur?**
  `TIMESTAMP`, `HOST`, `PORT`, `SERVICE_NAME`, `CONNECTION_ID`

▸ **Where (physically did the event originate from?**
  `CLIENT_HOST`, `CLIENT_IP`, `CLIENT_PID`, `CLIENT_PORT`

▸ **Who did it?**
  `USER_NAME`, `APPLICATION_USER_NAME`

▶ **Why do your security administrators want to log this event?**
AUDIT_POLICY_NAME, EVENT_STATUS, EVENT_LEVEL

▶ **What did or did not happen?**
EVENT_ACTION, STATEMENT_STRING

  ▶ Actions on catalog objects: SCHEMA_NAME, OBJECT_NAME

  ▶ Granting/revoking: GRANTEE, PRIVILEGE_NAME, ROLE_NAME, GRANTABLE, (and potentially object information)

  ▶ Configuration changes: FILE_NAME, SECTION, KEY, VALUE, PREV_VALUE (introduced with SPS 8)

Avoiding User-Specific Surprises

In some cases, the user triggering the execution of an auditable action might in the end not be the database user that actually executes the action. The most prominent audit-relevant example for such a situation is the granting (or revoking) of a repository role. Such roles are implicitly granted by the _SYS_REPO user; our database user only triggers this granting by running a stored procedure in definer mode. That is, our named user executes a procedure, but the code within the procedure (in particular, the GRANT command) is executed by _SYS_REPO.

Hence, for any granting of repository roles, the audit trails will list the _SYS_REPO user as USER_NAME. Fortunately for us, the audit trails include also the APPLICATION_USER_NAME, and if the application in question enters something meaningful here, we may still receive useful information.

For user-defined stored procedures in definer mode, the situation is similar. Consider the stored procedure in Listing 12.5, which simply reads something from the built-in pseudotable DUMMY.

```
CREATE PROCEDURE run_something(OUT MY_NAME VARCHAR(256))
  SQL SECURITY DEFINER
  READS SQL DATA AS
BEGIN
  SELECT SESSION_USER() INTO MY_NAME FROM DUMMY;
END;
```

Listing 12.5 Minimal Stored Procedure in Definer Mode

Let's assume that user RICHARD created this procedure, and user RICHARD_III executes it, for example, by running `CALL richard.run_something(?)`. In the audit trail, we will find two entries, as shown in Table 12.10.

Statement	USER_NAME
`SELECT "SESSION_USER"() FROM "DUMMY"`	RICHARD
`CALL richard.run_something(?)`	RICHARD_III

Table 12.10 Audit Log Entries for Stored Procedures in Definer Mode

Mandatory Audit Policies

If you decide to implement auditing in the database, there are certain events that need to be audited for the auditing to make any sense at all. These are the events involving the configuration of the audit mechanism.

For this reason, as soon as auditing is enabled, a built-in policy named `MandatoryAuditPolicy` is switched on and cannot be disabled. This policy will log any modification of the audit settings, that is, it will log disabling auditing, changing the audit trail targets, or adding, modifying, or deleting audit policies.

> **Note**
>
> Even if your audit trail target is the database table, truncating the table (`ALTER SYSTEM CLEAR AUDIT LOG UNTIL <timestamp>`) is not logged by the `MandatoryAuditPolicy`.

12.6 Summary

In this chapter, we have touched on the most important aspects of SAP HANA security—with the exception of role and privilege management, which is covered in Chapter 13. If you memorize the three core concepts we mentioned at the beginning of this chapter, you should be able to avoid at least half the pitfalls of user management or auditing that we covered.

SAP HANA database offers a complex toolbox for granting authorizations to database users. This chapter will help you find your way through the available options.

13   Roles and Privileges

In organizations, members have roles and the authorization to execute actions related to these roles. In software systems, organization members are represented by users and the roles they have in physical reality must be translated into actions and corresponding authorizations in the software system.

The numbers of privileges that exist in a software system such as the SAP HANA database can be overwhelming. Not only are there many different types of privileges but also a multitude of privilege instances of each type. The database therefore offers a concept for grouping privileges into database roles. In this chapter, we first talk about database roles in general before diving into the details of the different kinds of privileges SAP HANA has to offer.

The chapter then gives an overview of typical administration tasks in the database and the related privileges before closing with advice about troubleshooting authorization issues.

13.1   Database Roles

The SAP HANA database offers two different types of roles to collect privileges into containers. The basic type of role in the SAP HANA database is the so-called *catalog role*. These objects are sometimes also referred to as runtime roles, because they do not have a persistent design-time representation.

The other type of role is the repository role, sometimes referred to as design-time role, which is created as an object of the SAP HANA repository in the Developer Workbench and which needs to be activated in order to create the runtime representation (see Chapter 11 for a general introduction to the underlying concepts of the repository).

Next, we will introduce these two types of roles before discussing the differences between them in Section 13.1.3.

13.1.1 Catalog Roles

Catalog roles are simple containers for grouping multiple privileges and roles into a single grantable object. They are created either in the Role Editor of SAP HANA Studio or by using the CREATE ROLE SQL statement.

Any database user who wants to create or drop catalog roles needs the ROLE ADMIN system privilege. Privileges are granted to or revoked from catalog roles either in the Role Editor of SAP HANA Studio or by using SQL. When using the SQL syntax, you have to use either the GRANT/REVOKE statements or the corresponding stored procedures for privileges originating from objects developed in the SAP HANA repository, depending on the type and origin of the privilege. See Section 13.2.1 and Section 13.2.2 for details. The Role Editor handles these differences transparently so that when using the editor you do not need to take care of them.

Catalog roles are granted to users (or other catalog roles) by means of the GRANT statement and revoked via the REVOKE statement. Alternatively, one can employ the User or Role Editor of SAP HANA Studio.

The Role Editor can be started from within SAP HANA Studio's SYSTEMS view via the path <YOUR_HANA_SYSTEM> • SECURITY • ROLES (right-click) • NEW ROLE. The Role Editor is almost identical to the User Editor, but of course it does not offer authentication information. Figure 13.1 shows the editor for a role named DUMMY_ROLE. The Role Editor has different tabs for the different types of privileges that may be added to the role, such as further roles, system privileges, and so on.

Many privileges and roles can either simply be granted or can be granted with the option GRANTABLE TO OTHER USERS AND ROLES. For certain privileges, there is no such GRANT OPTION or ADMIN OPTION, for example, for analytic privileges or application privileges.

There is another category of privileges that do not have a GRANT OPTION or ADMIN OPTION and thus cannot be GRANTABLE TO OTHER USERS AND ROLES; privileges created by the activation of a repository object or privileges based on activated repository objects cannot be granted to a database user by including the GRANT OPTION or ADMIN OPTION. Instead, these privileges are always granted by using dedicated stored procedures; see Section 13.2.2.

Figure 13.1 Role Editor for Catalog Roles in SAP HANA Studio

Some privileges are not simple privileges but privileges based on database objects, for example, the SELECT privilege on a given table. In this case, one has to first choose the object itself and then include all required privileges on that object, as shown in Figure 13.2 for the SELECT privilege on table CUSTOMER_TEXTS in schema DEMO_SCHEMA.

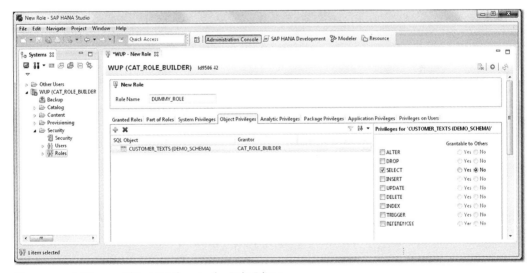

Figure 13.2 Adding an Object Privilege in the Role Editor

Changes to roles (or the creation of a new role) take effect after saving the role. You save a catalog role either by clicking the DEPLOY button in the top-right corner of the Role Editor (the green arrow), or by clicking the SAVE button (the floppy disk icon) in the top-left corner of SAP HANA Studio. The keyboard shortcuts are F8 or Ctrl + S, respectively.

13.1.2 Repository Roles

Repository roles can only be created as development objects in the SAP HANA Developer Workbench. Hence, creation and management of these roles requires setting up a development project (see Chapter 11 for details). The object that represents a role in the repository is a HDBROLE file, that is, a text file with the extension .hdbrole that contains the role definition in a specific syntax.

As of the writing of this book (release level SPS 8 of SAP HANA database), the editor for repository roles is purely text based, but it can be expected that there will be a UI-supported Role Editor soon.

In order to turn the HDBROLE file into a database object, the role needs to be activated. In the process of activation, the database system assembles a catalog role based on the role specification made in the HDBROLE file. This process is performed by the _SYS_REPO database user. In this process, all requirements for assembling a catalog role must be fulfilled. Most notably, the assembly of the role is technically a CREATE ROLE statement followed by GRANT statements for all privileges in the role and executed by the _SYS_REPO user.

> **Note**
>
> The fact that repository roles are assembled by the _SYS_REPO user implies that this user must be able to grant all privileges to be placed into repository roles, that is, _SYS_REPO must either be the owner of the privilege or the privilege owner must grant the privilege to _SYS_REPO, including GRANT OPTION or ADMIN OPTION (see Section 13.2.1).

Next, we'll outline the most common tasks with respect to repository roles: granting, editing, and deleting them. Then, we'll briefly discuss the syntax for assembling repository roles.

Granting Repository Roles

It is not possible to grant repository roles to or revoke them from database users or catalog roles via the GRANT or REVOKE statements. Instead, one must use the stored procedures delivered for this purpose: GRANT_ACTIVATED_ROLE (<role_name>, <grantee>) and REVOKE_ACTIVATED_ROLE (<role_name>, <grantee>). The User and Role Editors in SAP HANA Studio recognize the type of role being granted and transparently choose the correct mechanism for granting or revoking.

These stored procedures are owned by the _SYS_REPO user and defined in SQL security mode definer—meaning that regardless of who executes the procedure the actions defined in the procedure will be executed by the _SYS_REPO user. Thus, _SYS_REPO will implicitly be the grantor of the role. This makes role granting and revoking technically independent from the named user who triggered the grant/revoke action, avoiding complications that occur when using catalog roles.

Editing Repository Roles

It is not possible to grant privileges to the design-time representation of repository roles using the SQL GRANT statement or to extend such roles in the Role Editor (for catalog roles) of SAP HANA Studio. Unfortunately, however, you can technically grant privileges to the activated version of a repository role with the GRANT statement. Doing this leads to an inconsistency between the design-time and the runtime version of the role and hence should be avoided.

The correct way of modifying a repository role is to edit its design-time version in the repository and then to reactivate the role.

Deleting Repository Roles

You cannot simply delete a repository role by removing its runtime representation with a DROP ROLE command. The database will not permit this type of deletion; even if it did, the dropping of the runtime object would not remove the object in the repository.

Instead, you need to remove the role from within your development project in the SAP HANA repository. After deleting the role, you need to activate the package or project containing the role to actually perform the deletion. This will remove the design-time representation from the repository and also the runtime representation from the database catalog.

Syntax for Assembling Repository Roles

The syntax to be used in HDBROLE files is largely different from the syntax of the GRANT statement (which will be introduced in Section 13.2.1). Table 13.1 gives an overview of the syntax for all types of privileges that may be added to a repository role. Listing 13.1 shows a simple example of an HDBROLE file, including the syntax for including other repository or catalog roles.

```
-- Comments can be started with a double hyphen
// or with a double forward slash.
// Role hierarchies are built by extending other repository
// roles or catalog roles.
role <package_name>::<role_name>
  extends role <repository_role_1>[, <repository_role_2, ...]
  extends catalog role <cat_role_1>[, <cat_role_2>, ...]
{
  -- The role body contains privilege listings; see Table 13.1.
  -- We show here the inclusion of the SELECT and UPDATE
  -- privilege on a database table.
  -- All privilege definitions must end with a semicolon ";"
  catalog sql object "<schema>"."<table>": SELECT, UPDATE;
}
```

Listing 13.1 Example HDBROLE File of a Repository Role

One of the most common mistakes in the definition of repository roles is usage of incorrect capitalization, which will always lead to activation errors. The following general rules should help you to avoid these errors:

▶ The keyword for the privilege type (for example, the term catalog sql object in the example of Listing 13.1) must be in lowercase.

▶ The case of objects (schema name, table name, package name, etc.) must be exactly the case used in the definition of the actual objects.

▶ Finally, the privilege name (e.g., SELECT or CATALOG READ) must be in uppercase.

Another typical error source is incorrect quoting of objects on which privileges are granted. There is a simple rule that should help you to avoid such mistakes:

▸ Whenever directly referring to a catalog object, the schema name and object name must be individually enclosed in double quotes, as in `"schema"."object"`.

▸ When referring to repository objects, no double quotes are allowed, such as in `package.sub_package::object`.

Privilege	Repository Role Syntax
Privileges on Schemas, Objects, and Packages	

Privileges on a catalog schema, i.e., a schema created via SQL in the database catalog (not through activation of a repository object)	`catalog schema "<schema>": <privilege_1>` `[, <privilege_2>, ...];`
	
	 Example:
	 `catalog schema "my_schema": SELECT, UPDATE;`
	
	 Notes:
	 ▸ The schema name must be placed in double quotes.
	 ▸ Do not use this syntax for database schemas created through activation of a repository specification, e.g., an HDBSCHEMA file or through a core data services definition. For these cases, use the syntax for schema as stated in the following row.

Privileges on a schema created through activation of a schema definition in the repository (HDBSCHEMA file)	`schema <package>:<schema_name>.hdbschema:` `<privilege_1>[, <privilege_2>, ...];`
	
	 Example:
	 `schema project_1.objects:my_schema.hdbschema:` `SELECT, UPDATE;`
	
	 Notes:
	 ▸ Double quotes around the schema or object name are not allowed.
	 ▸ `.hdbschema` and `analytic privilege` are the only object types for which you cannot separate package and object by a double colon and for which you have to specify the file extension.

Privileges on a catalog object, e.g., `SELECT` on table
 	
 For objects created directly in the database catalog
	`catalog sql object "<schema>"."<object>":` `<privilege_1>[, <privilege_2>, ...];`
	
	 Example:
	 `catalog sql object "my_schema"."TABLE_1": SELECT,` `UPDATE;`

Table 13.1 Syntax for Adding Privileges to Repository Roles

Privilege	Repository Role Syntax
Privileges on Schemas, Objects, and Packages	
	Notes: ▸ Objects can be any type of object that can be placed into a database schema. The object type determines the available privileges. ▸ The double quotes around schema name and object name are mandatory. ▸ Do not use this syntax to grant privileges on objects created through activation of repository objects, because the privilege will vanish from the activated role whenever you reactivate the object in the repository. Instead, use the syntax for `sql object` as stated in the following row.

Privileges on a catalog object created through activation of the repository representation of
 	
▸ SAP HANA Modeler views (attribute view, analytic view, or calculation view)
 	
▸ Stored procedures
 	
▸ Sequences
 	
▸ Tables
	`sql object <package>::<object>:`
	`    <privilege_1>[, <privilege_2>, ...];`
	
	Example (grant `EXECUTE` right for the activated procedure named `do_something` in package `project_1.procs`):
	
	`sql object project_1.procs::do_something: EXECUTE;`
	
	Notes:
	
	▸ Double quotes are not only not needed but not even allowed.
	
	▸ There is a deprecated syntax that should not be used:
	
	`sql object <package>:<object>.<extension>:`
	`    <privilege_1>[, <privilege_2>, ...];`
	
	where <extension> can be .hdbtable, .hdbview, .hdbsquence, .attributeview, .analyticview, .calculationview or .procedure, depending on the object type.

Package privileges	`package <package_name>: <privilege_1>`
	`[, <privilege_2>, ...];`
	
	Example:
	
	`package project_1.procs: REPO.READ,`
	`REPO.ACTIVATED_NATVIVE_OBJECTS;`

Other Privileges	

System privileges	`system privilege: <privilege_1>`
	`[, <privilege_2>, ...];`
	
	Example:
	
	`system privilege: CATALOG READ, BACKUP ADMIN;`

Table 13.1 Syntax for Adding Privileges to Repository Roles (Cont.)

Privilege	Repository Role Syntax
Other Privileges	

Structured privileges created directly in the catalog through a `create structured privilege` call	`catalog analytic privilege: "<privilege_name>";`
	
	Example:
	`catalog analytic privilege: "my_ap_1";`
	
	Note:
	▸ The privilege name must be enclosed in double quotes.
	▸ Do not use this syntax for granting analytic privileges created through activation of a modeler/development object. Use the syntax for `analytic privilege` as in the following row.
	▸ Capitalization of the privilege name must match exactly the capitalization of the privilege's catalog object name.

Analytic privilege created through activation of an object from the Modeler or Development Workbench	`analytic privilege: <package>:<privilege_name>.analyticprivilege;`
	
	Example:
	`analytic privilege: project_1.privs:ap_1.analyticprivilege;`
	
	Note:
	▸ Double quotes around the package or privilege name are not allowed.
	▸ Capitalization of the privilege name must match exactly that chose during definition of the analytic privilege itself.
	▸ `Analytic privilege` and `.hdbschema` are the only object types for which you cannot separate package and object by a double colon and for which you have to specify the file extension.

Application privileges	`application privilege: <privilege_name>;`
	
	where
	`<privilege_name> = <application_schema>::<privilege>`
	
	Example:
	`Application privilege: project_1.app::Execute;`
	
	Note:
	▸ The capitalization of the privilege name (e.g., `Execute` in the example) must match the privilege definition in the XSPRIVILEGES file of the application.
	▸ Double quotes around package name, application name, or privilege name are not allowed.

Table 13.1 Syntax for Adding Privileges to Repository Roles (Cont.)

13.1.3 Catalog Roles vs. Repository Roles

In principle, one can set up an SAP HANA project using either type of role or even a mix of catalog and repository roles. In practice, however, there are such significant differences in the management of these two types of roles that the mixing should be avoided (at least in roles granted directly to database users).

The most compelling reason for choosing catalog roles may be the ability to create, modify, drop, grant, and revoke them via a simple and well-documented SQL syntax, which is not possible with repository roles. The other advantage is the availability of a user-friendly Role Editor, which does not yet exist for repository roles (as of SPS 8).

At the same time, catalog roles also have multiple properties that make life more complicated, so the list of arguments in favor of repository roles is quite extensive:

▶ All the side effects of managing privileges via the GRANT and REVOKE statements (Section 13.2.1) also apply to managing catalog roles, whereas they are avoided when using repository roles.

▶ Segregation of duties cannot be implemented with catalog roles unless one creates a dedicated application for the management of roles, including creation, modification, granting, and revoking of roles. In fact, you might consider repository roles a built-in application wrapped around catalog roles.

▶ Catalog roles are not transportable; repository roles, like any other object in the SAP HANA repository, can be transported.

▶ Starting with SPS 7, SAP HANA Studio offers a functionality to copy users, which does not work if catalog roles are granted to the user to be copied.

▶ SAP prefers usage of repository roles. More and more built-in applications are delivered with SAP HANA, and these applications come with predelivered repository roles.

In conclusion, we clearly recommend exclusive use of repository roles when setting up new SAP HANA projects.

You might still consider using catalog roles for projects with minimal security requirements in the database. This might be the case if SAP HANA is purely used as the database underneath an SAP NetWeaver Application Server and there is no intention to ever extend this usage to something that will require more extensive user management in the database.

Catalog roles are also an option if there is an identity-management solution available that can handle SAP HANA catalog roles. The mechanism for creating, modifying, granting, and revoking these roles is rather simple, so one can easily create in the course of a project an application for role management. When it comes to user management, SAP Identity Management and SAP GRC Access Control can handle catalog roles in SAP HANA.

13.2 Privileges in the Database Catalog and Repository

The User and Role Editors in SAP HANA Studio offer a uniform UI for granting all kinds of privileges. Technically, however, there are significant differences between the way granting works for different types of privileges. This especially impacts the SQL syntax that an administrator has to use when granting privileges of certain kinds.

In this section, we introduce two fundamentally different principles of privilege management that occur in SAP HANA: one for those managed in the catalog and one for those managed in the repository.

13.2.1 Privileges Managed in the Catalog of SAP HANA

Most privileges in SAP HANA are basic database privileges that only exist as runtime objects in the database catalog. This includes system privileges, which give access to functionalities of the database (such as creating users, running backups, etc.), and object privileges, which allow working with objects in the database (tables, views, procedures, etc.).

These privileges cannot be created; they simply exist. In the case of system privileges, they are a part of the database itself; in the case of object privileges, their existence is tied to the existence of the database object. In the example of a database table, as soon as the table is created, the SELECT, INSERT, UPDATE, or DELETE privileges for this table exist as well.

Each privilege in the database catalog is owned by exactly one database user. For object privileges, the owner of the privileges is the owner of the object. Taking the example of a database table, if user PLUTO owns the table, PLUTO also owns all object privileges related to this table.

We will now describe the granting and revoking of different types of privileges. In addition to the mere technicalities, we will also pay attention to side effects of revoking privileges, especially when making use of the GRANT or ADMIN options.

Granting Catalog Privileges

Privileges of the database catalog can be granted to database users or roles by using the GRANT SQL statement.

> **Note**
>
> In order to grant a privilege of the database catalog to some other user or role, one must either be the owner of the privilege or have explicit permission to grant that privilege (privilege granted with GRANT OPTION or ADMIN OPTION).

The syntax of the GRANT statement varies slightly, depending on the type of privilege being granted:

- **Granting a system privilege**

  ```
  GRANT <privilege name> TO <grantee> [WITH ADMIN OPTION]
  ```

  Grants the system privilege to a database user or a catalog role. If the addendum WITH ADMIN OPTION is included, the grantee also has permission to grant this privilege to other database users or roles.

  It is possible to grant multiple system privileges at once by specifying a comma-separated list of system privileges for <privilege name>.

- **Granting privileges on catalog objects**

  ```
  GRANT <privilege_name_1>[, privilege_name_2>, ...] on <object> to <grantee> [WITH GRANT OPTION]
  ```

  Grants the object privilege (e.g., SELECT) on the named object (e.g., a table) to the grantee. Permission to grant that privilege to other users can be given by specifying the GRANT OPTION.

  One can grant multiple object privileges at once by specifying a comma-separated list of object privileges for <privilege name>.

- **Granting privileges on catalog schemas**

  ```
  GRANT <privilege_name_1>[, <privilege_name_2> ...] ON SCHEMA <schema> TO <grantee> [WITH GRANT OPTION]
  ```

Behaves just like the granting of object privileges on catalog objects, but has an effect on the named schema and all objects therein.

▶ **Granting structured privileges**

`GRANT <structured privilege name> TO <grantee>`

Structured privileges are the catalog representation of analytic privileges. In rare cases, these objects will be created directly via SQL statements (as opposed to creation as design-time objects in the repository), and only for such rare cases is the SQL `GRANT` syntax applicable.

Note the absence of a `GRANT/ADMIN` option for structured privileges. This means that only the owner (creator) of the privilege can grant it.

> **Note**
>
> Analytic privileges—that is, the flavor of structured privileges that can be created by using the SAP HANA Modeler or the Developer Workbench—can only be granted (or revoked) by using the dedicated stored procedures `GRANT_ACTIVATED_ANALYTICAL_PRIVILEGE (<privilege>, <grantee>)` and `REVOKE_ACTIVATED_ANALYTICAL_PRIVILEGE (<privilege>, <grantee>)`.

▶ **Granting package privileges**

`GRANT <privilege_name_1>[, <privilege_name_2>, ...] ON <package> TO <grantee> [WITH ADMIN OPTION]`

Grants the named package privilege(s) (e.g., `REPO.READ`) on the named package to the grantee. The privilege is valid for the package itself and all subpackages. The `ADMIN` option can be used to allow for granting the privilege to others.

▶ **Granting catalog roles**

`GRANT <role_name> TO <grantee> [WITH ADMIN OPTION]`

This grants the given role to the grantee. If the `ADMIN` option is specified, then the grantee can grant the role to others.

Revoking Catalog Privileges

Revoking of privileges works very similarly to granting. Simply replace the term `GRANT` with `REVOKE` and `TO` with `FROM`. The `GRANT` and `ADMIN` options cannot be revoked explicitly, and the `REVOKE` statement does not offer related arguments.

The most important feature of the REVOKE statement is that only the grantor of a particular privilege (i.e., the database user that has granted the privilege to the user) can also revoke it; see the following discussions.

Side Effects of Revoking Privileges Using the REVOKE Statement

There are multiple possible side effects or surprising behaviors related to the revoking of privileges or roles using the REVOKE statement. The best known—and documented—side effect lies in the recursive revoking of privileges and is very similar to the matter we discussed previously in the context of dropping users: If one makes frequent use of the GRANT or ADMIN options, then there can be a complicated path from the owner of a privilege to an end user that has been granted that privilege.

Assume user A owns table T_1. User A grants the SELECT privilege on that table, including the GRANT option, to user B. User B grants this SELECT privilege to user C. We illustrate this situation in Figure 13.3.

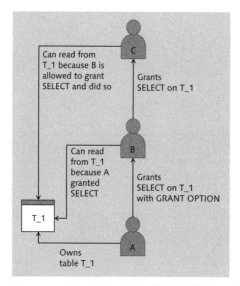

Figure 13.3 Illustration of the GRANT/ADMIN OPTION

In this situation, C has not been directly granted this privilege by the owner, A, but by another user, B.

If user A now revokes the SELECT privilege on table T_1 from user B, this will implicitly also revoke the privilege from all users that have been given the privilege by user B.

A less well-known side effect centers on the fact that the REVOKE statement in SAP HANA does not in fact revoke the privilege from a user but actually simply creates a database state in which the privilege has not been granted to the grantee by the user who attempts to revoke it. This plays a role if the same privilege or role has been granted to the same user by multiple grantors or if the user who revokes is not the grantor.

To extend our example, let us assume that users A and B both granted the SELECT privilege on table T_1 to user C, as illustrated in Figure 13.4.

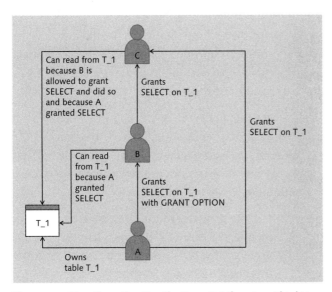

Figure 13.4 Two Users Granting the Same Privilege to a Third User

We can check the "PUBLIC"."EFFECTIVE_PRIVILEGES" view to verify that SAP HANA keeps track of both grant actions; see Figure 13.5.

```
⊖SELECT "GRANTOR", "GRANTEE",
       "OBJECT_TYPE", "SCHEMA_NAME", "OBJECT_NAME", "PRIVILEGE"
   FROM "PUBLIC"."EFFECTIVE_PRIVILEGES"
   WHERE "USER_NAME"='C' and "OBJECT_NAME"='T_1'
```

	GRANTOR	GRANTEE	OBJECT_TYPE	SCHEMA_NAME	OBJECT_NAME	PRIVILEGE
1	B	C	TABLE	A	T_1	SELECT
2	A	C	TABLE	A	T_1	SELECT

Figure 13.5 Granting of One Privilege to One User by Two Different Users

Now, user B revokes that privilege. The REVOKE call will return a success message. However, the system has revoked the action of granting the privilege to user C by user B, not the privilege itself. In order to remove the privilege from user C, both users A and B will have to revoke it.

> **Key Takeaway**
>
> The same privilege or role may be granted multiple times to the same user by different grantors. In such circumstances, each grantor will have to revoke the privilege explicitly from the grantee.

The somewhat surprising behavior of the REVOKE statement also means that the REVOKE statement can return a success message even if nothing is revoked at all. This happens if the user executing the REVOKE statement never granted the privilege to the grantee but technically is allowed to grant it.

The following example will illustrate this behavior. We are again working with users A, B, and C and table T_1 owned by user A. Again, user A has granted the SELECT privilege on table T_1 to user B, including the GRANT option, and user B has granted this privilege to user C. However, A has not granted this privilege to C directly. Hence, the situation is the same as in Figure 13.3.

Now, user A revokes the SELECT privilege directly from C. The statement execution is considered successful, because afterwards user C does not have the SELECT privilege on table T_1 granted by user A. However, nothing has changed in the system; user C still has the SELECT privilege, with user B as the grantor.

> **Key Takeaways**
>
> ▶ SAP HANA's interpretation of the REVOKE statement is different than the natural expectation of most human beings.

▸ It can happen that after successfully revoking a privilege from a database user or role the user or role still has this privilege.

▸ After revoking a privilege or role by using the REVOKE statement, you should check that the privilege has indeed been revoked successfully. Either query the system views "PUBLIC"."EFFECTIVE_PRIVILEGES" or "PUBLIC.EFFECTIVE_ROLES" or check the User Editor in SAP HANA Studio.

Considerations of the GRANT and ADMIN Options

All the above listed side effects around the revoking of individual privileges only play a role if the GRANT or ADMIN options are used, because only in this case can there be grantors different from the owner of the privilege.

The side effects also come to play if you use catalog roles and multiple users have the ROLE ADMIN privilege (which allows the granting of any catalog role in the system, i.e., it works similarly to an ADMIN option for all roles in the system).

The GRANT or ADMIN option is implicitly revoked if you revoke a given privilege. It is not possible to revoke the GRANT or ADMIN option explicitly. In other words: if you have granted a privilege and by mistake included the GRANT or ADMIN option, you have to revoke the privilege and grant it again without that option.

13.2.2 Privileges Managed in the Repository of SAP HANA

If you carefully read the section about managing privileges in the catalog of SAP HANA, you will probably conclude that the concept behind this privilege management is highly technical and not adequate for typical requirements in a development scenario or other scenarios that require more elaborate user and privilege management.

SAP HANA's repository offers more appropriate means to implement privilege and especially role management. In order to understand some aspects of this privilege management, we must first explain how the database handles the creation of database objects through the activation of repository objects.

In SAP HANA, one can maintain design-time versions of objects in the repository. These design-time objects can be activated in order to create runtime objects. The actual creation of runtime objects is performed by a technical database user named _SYS_REPO, who will then be the owner of the activated object.

All of these runtime objects are technically objects of the database catalog—but management of privileges for such activated objects needs to be handled in a special way, because it is not possible to log on with the _SYS_REPO user to use the GRANT statement for granting the privileges to other users.

In order to grant or revoke privileges on such activated objects, SAP HANA provides stored procedures that replace the corresponding flavor of the GRANT and REVOKE statements. Regardless of who triggers the execution of these stored procedures, they are run in the context of the _SYS_REPO user (in definer mode) so that the actual grant action is performed by the _SYS_REPO user.

We introduce these stored procedures in the next sections while discussing the different types of privileges available in the database.

> **Note**
>
> All privileges related to activated repository objects can simply be added to repository roles without the need for using these stored procedures.

13.3   Types of Privileges in SAP HANA

In SAP HANA, there are six different kinds of privileges, some of them coming in two different flavors, related to catalog and repository objects. In this section, we explain the purpose of each privilege type and also introduce the SQL syntax you have to choose when granting a given type and flavor of privilege.

We expect that after reading this section you might be confused, and you may be troubled by too many different privilege and syntax flavors. That's why, in Section 13.3.7, we explain that if you set up your system properly you can reduce the amount of relevant options by a large margin.

13.3.1   System Privileges

System privileges allow the execution of certain actions in the database, such as creating users, performing database backups, implementing a license key, or restarting database processes. Many system privileges allow the execution of significant database operations, and thus granting of system privileges should be controlled very carefully.

The following box gives the syntax for granting system privileges in SQL as well as for inclusion into repository roles. As with all of the following examples, we do not explicitly list the syntax for revoking the privileges, because it is self-explanatory. If in doubt, refer to the *SAP HANA SQL Reference*, which is available online at *https://help.sap.com/hana_platform/*.

Syntax for Granting System Privileges

In SQL, use the syntax:

```
GRANT <privilege_1>[, <privilege_2>, ...] TO <user_or_catalog_role_
name> [WITH ADMIN OPTION]
```

In repository roles, use the syntax:

```
system privilege: <privilege_1>[, <privilege_2>, ...];
```

Using the SQL GRANT statement, system privileges can only be granted by a database user who has been granted the privilege, including the ADMIN OPTION.

The SAP HANA database offers more than twenty system privileges, and in the past the list of privileges has been extended with each support package of the database. At any point in time, the current list of available system privileges is given in the context of the GRANT statement in the *SAP HANA SQL Reference*.

Further Resources

Instead of listing all available system privileges here, we have assembled a detailed list of typical administration tasks and all privileges required for these tasks. This material can be downloaded from the book's page at *www.sap-press.com*.

13.3.2 Object Privileges

Object privileges give a certain type of access to a database object such as a table, view, or stored procedure. What kind of access can be given depends on the type of the object at hand. The types of database objects that come with object privileges are database tables, views, procedures, functions, and sequences.

Syntax for Granting Object Privileges

SQL syntax for granting privileges on objects created directly in the catalog:

```
GRANT <privilege_1>[, <privilege_2>, ...] ON <schema>.<object> to
<user|role>
```

SQL syntax for granting privileges on objects created through activation of a design-time object in the SAP HANA repository:

```
CALL "PUBLIC"."GRANT_PRIVILEGE_ON_ACTIVATED_CONTENT" ( '<privilege>',
'"<package>::<object>"', '<user|role>' );
```

Note the required single-quote and double-quote placement! Because this can be confusing, we give an explicit example for an analytic view:

Grant SELECT on analytic view AN_DEMO_1 in package project_x.models to user PLUTO:

```
CALL "PUBLIC"."GRANT_PRIVILEGE_ON_ACTIVATED_CONTENT" ( 'SELECT',
'"project_x.models::AN_DEMO_1"', 'PLUTO');
```

Syntax for inclusion in repository roles if the object has been created directly in the catalog (note the mandatory double-quotes around <schema> and <object>):

```
catalog sql object "<schema>"."<object>": <privilege_1>[, <privilege_
2>, ...];
```

Syntax for inclusion in repository roles if the object has been created through activation of a design-time object in the repository:

```
sql object <package>::<object>: <privilege_1>[, <privilege_2>, ...];
```

Privileges on objects created in the database catalog can only be granted by the object owner (or someone who has the object privilege, including GRANT OPTION). To find the owner of a catalog object, use the SQL command:

```
SELECT * FROM "PUBLIC"."OWNERSHIP" WHERE "SCHEMA_NAME"='<schema>' AND
"OBJECT_NAME"='<object>'
```

Not all object privileges exist for all types of objects. We have compiled an overview of the available privileges for the different object types in Table 13.2.

Privilege	Schema	Table	View	Procedure/ Function	Sequence
ALL PRIVILEGES		X	X		
SELECT	X	X	X		X
INSERT	X	X	X*		
UPDATE	X	X	X*		
DELETE	X	X	X*		
DROP	X	X	X	X	X

Table 13.2 Map of Object Privileges for the Different Types of Objects

Privilege	Schema	Table	View	Procedure/ Function	Sequence
ALTER	X	X		X	
INDEX	X	X			
REFERENCES	X	X			
TRIGGER	X	X			
DEBUG	X		X**	X	
EXECUTE	X			X	
CREATE ANY	X				

Table 13.2 Map of Object Privileges for the Different Types of Objects (Cont.)

Table 13.2 Notes

* INSERT, UPDATE, and DELETE are only available for updatable views. See Section 7.4.3 in Chapter 7.

** Debugging is only available for calculation views (and stored procedures), not for SQL views, analytic views, or attribute views.

13.3.3 Schema Privileges

Schema privileges are very similar to object privileges. However, a schema privilege has an effect not on a single object but on all objects within the schema. For example, granting the SELECT privilege on a schema will permit read access to all tables, views, and sequences in that schema.

The syntax for granting schema privileges is slightly different from the syntax of granting object privileges.

Syntax for Granting Schema Privileges

SQL syntax for granting privileges on schemas created directly in the catalog:

```
GRANT <privilege_1>[, <privilege_2>, ...] ON SCHEMA <schema_name> TO
<user_or_role>
```

SQL syntax for granting privileges on schemas created by activating an HDBSCHEMA file in the repository:

```
CALL GRANT_SCHEMA_PRIVILEGE_ON_ACTIVATED_CONTENT ('<privilege>',
'"<schema_name>"', '<user_or_role>');
```

For inclusion in repository roles, if the schema was created directly in the database catalog:

```
catalog schema "<schema_name>": <privilege_1>[, <privilege_2>, ...];
```

For inclusion in repository roles, if the schema was created by activating an HDBSCHEM file in the repository (note that this only works if the schema name equals the file name of the HDBSCHEMA file, and it only works for one schema definition per HDBSCHEMA file):

```
schema <package_name>:<schema_name>.hdbschema: <privilege_1>[,
<privilege_2>, ...];
```

All object privileges except for ALL PRIVILEGES are available for schemas; see Table 13.2.

Privileges on schemas created in the database catalog can only be granted by the schema owner (or someone who has the schema privilege, including GRANT OPTION). To find the owner of a database schema, use the SQL syntax:

```
SELECT "SCHEMA_OWNER" FROM "PUBLIC"."SCHEMAS" WHERE "SCHEMA_NAME" =
'<schema_name>'
```

13.3.4 Package Privileges

Package privileges are privileges for developers that give access to areas of the repository (packages). Table 13.3 lists all available package privileges, including a short description. You will notice that most privileges exist in two flavors: one for so called native objects or native packages and one for imported objects or imported packages.

Native objects or packages have been created locally in the SAP HANA database. Such local creation can happen by means of:

▸ The SAP HANA Modeler

▸ The SAP HANA Developer Workbench

▸ The web IDE for development in SAP HANA

▸ Developer-mode import of packages (as opposed to imports of delivery units)

Imported objects, on the other hand, are objects that have been imported into the SAP HANA system by means of a delivery-unit import. Typically, you will encounter imported objects in the following:

- SAP-delivered repository content, such as applications and other repository packages shipped with the database, or SAP HANA Live content.
- Packages transported within a multitier SAP HANA system landscape. All SAP transport mechanisms for SAP HANA content are technically based on export/import of delivery units.

Package Privilege	Explanation
REPO.READ on <package>	Gives read-only access to the contents of <package>, including all subpackages. Basically, one can open the package contents in editors such as the SAP HANA Modeler or the editors of the Developer Workbench but cannot modify them.
Privileges on Native Objects or Packages	
REPO.EDIT_NATIVE_OBJECTS on <package>	Gives write access to all contents of <package>, including all subpackages. Read access is not included, so any developer will always need REPO.READ together with REPO.EDIT_NATIVE_OBJECTS.
REPO.ACTIVATE_NATIVE_OBJECTS on <package>	Activate any natively created object within <package> or its subpackages.
REPO.MAINTAIN_NATIVE_PACKAGES on <package>	Allows managing repository package <package>, including all subpackages. Management tasks include the following: - Everything in the edit dialog for packages, e.g., renaming the package, setting a package comment, or assigning a package to a delivery unit - Creating new subpackages or deleting subpackages underneath <package> Note that REPO.EDIT_NATIVE_OBJECTS is also needed to create new packages underneath <package> in addition to REPO.MAINTAIN_NATIVE_PACKAGES.
Privileges on Imported Objects or Packages	
REPO.EDIT_IMPORTED_OBJECTS on <package>	Same as REPO.EDIT_NATIVE_OBJECTS but only for packages that have been imported via delivery-unit import.

Table 13.3 Overview of All Available Package Privileges

Package Privilege	Explanation
Privileges on Imported Objects or Packages	
REPO.ACTIVATE_IMPORTED_OBJECTS on <package>	Same as REPO.ACTIVATE_NATIVE_OBJECTS but only for packages that have been imported via delivery-unit import.
REPO.MAINTAIN_IMPORTED_PACKAGES on <package>	Same as REPO.MAINTAIN_NATIVE_PACKAGES but only for packages that have been imported via delivery-unit import.

Table 13.3 Overview of All Available Package Privileges (Cont.)

Syntax for Granting Package Privileges
In SQL, use the syntax:
GRANT <privilege_1>[, <privilege_2>, ...] ON <package_name> TO <role/ user>
In repository roles, the syntax is:
package <package>: <privilege_1>[, <privilege_2>, ...];

Using the GRANT statement, package privileges can only be granted by users that have the package privilege, including the ADMIN OPTION.

13.3.5 Analytic Privileges

Analytic privileges are privileges associated with activated data models, such as attribute views, analytic views, or calculation views. They can be used to control the following:

▶ Object-level access to activated data models

▶ Row-level restrictions for accessing the content of activated data models

Analytic privileges are development objects that need to be created for all data-modeling projects, matching the security requirements of the individual project.

Note
Since SPS 6 of the SAP HANA database, use of analytic privileges for accessing data models is no longer mandatory. When creating data models, one can explicitly exclude the need for analytic privileges for the given data model; see APPLY PRIVILEGES in the top-right corner of Figure 13.6.

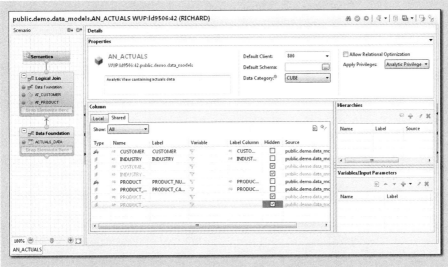

Figure 13.6 Analytic View with Apply Privileges Dropdown Box

If the data model is configured to require analytic privileges, any database user trying to consume data from the data model will need an analytic privilege that references this data model. Without such a privilege, the query will fail with an authorization failure message.

If the user holds an analytic privilege referencing the data model, their access to the content of the data model will be restricted to certain attribute values as defined in the analytic privilege.

These restrictions can be defined in two ways:

▶ Static restrictions mean that the particular restrictions of one user (or a group of users with the same restrictions) are hardcoded in the analytic privilege object. This requires the creation of one analytic privilege object for each user (or group of users) and data model.

▶ Dynamic restrictions allow for the creation of a single privilege object that offers the correct restrictions for all users. The actual restriction values for a user querying the data model are derived at runtime through a stored procedure. In nearly all cases, except for highly trivial ones, you will want to choose this option. An analytic privilege with dynamic attribute restrictions is often referred to as a dynamic analytic privilege.

Further Resources

If you are confused by the preceding descriptions, don't worry. We have prepared a detailed example with step-by-step instructions for creating an analytic privilege with dynamic restrictions. This material can be downloaded from the book's page at *www.sap-press.com/3506*.

Granting Analytic Privileges

It is not possible to grant a typical analytic privilege by using the SQL GRANT statement, because of two properties of analytic privileges:

▶ They are created in the SAP HANA repository, and thus the activated object (which is of object type *structured privilege*) belongs to the _SYS_REPO user. (It is technically possible to directly create structured privileges in the catalog, by using the CREATE STRUCTURED PRIVILEGE statement. We cannot, however, recommend making use of this option.)

▶ There is no GRANT OPTION or ADMIN OPTION for structured privileges, meaning that only the owner can grant them.

For granting activated analytic privileges in SQL, the database offers a dedicated stored procedure.

Syntax for Granting Analytic Privileges

In SQL, we always have to use the provided stored procedure for granting analytic privileges:

```
CALL "PUBLIC"."GRANT_ACTIVATED_ANALYTICAL_PRIVILEGE" ('"<package>/
<privilege>"', '<grantee>')
```

Here is an example for the sake of clarity: granting the analytic privilege named AP_DEMO_CUSTOMER_GROUP in package public.demo.privileges to user PLUTO:

```
CALL "PUBLIC"."GRANT_ACTIVATED_ANALYTICAL_PRIVILEGE"
('"public.demo.privileges:AP_DEMO_CUSTOMER_GROUP"', 'PLUTO');
```

In repository roles, use the syntax:

```
analytic privilege: <package>:<privilege>.analyticprivilege;
```

SQL-Based Analytic Privileges

In SPS 7, SAP introduced SQL-based analytic privileges. These privileges currently (as of SPS 8) only exist as runtime objects, that is, they cannot be designed in the repository yet. For this reason, use of SQL-based analytic privileges is not recommended for regular projects.

There is, however, one reason for mentioning them at least briefly: SAP BW 7.40 on SAP HANA can generate data models and corresponding SAP BW analysis authorizations into the SAP HANA system. For generating the analysis authorizations, the SAP BW system makes use of SAP HANA's SQL-based analytic privileges. In these privileges, the restriction can be formulated as an SQL query, allowing more complex restrictions than regular analytic privileges.

The syntax for creating SQL-based analytic privileges can be found in the *SAP HANA Security Guide* available at *https://help.sap.com/hana_platform/*.

On a single activated view (attribute view, analytic view, or calculation view), either regular analytic privileges or SQL-based analytic privileges can be enabled, but not both kinds at the same time. Within a hierarchy of views, the types of privileges can be mixed. It is, for example, possible to include a view generated by the SAP BW system (with SQL-based analytic privileges) in a calculation view and to enable this calculation view for regular analytic privileges.

13.3.6 Application Privileges

Application privileges are part of XS applications and can be used to give access to the entire application (execute the application) or to functionalities within the application. They are defined by the application developers. The technical name of application privileges is composed of the application name and the simple name of the privilege (e.g., `Execute`).

The SQL `GRANT` statement does not offer a syntax to grant application privileges. Instead, there are stored procedures available for granting and revoking application privileges.

Syntax for Granting Application Privileges
In SQL, we must use the system-provided stored procedure: ``` CALL "PUBLIC"."GRANT_APPLICATION_PRIVILEGE" ('<application_package>::<privilege>', '<user/role>') ```

In repository roles, use the following syntax:

```
application privilege: <application_package>::<privilege>;
```

13.3.7 Easing Your Mind

We did tell you that you'd be confused when you reached this point, and we assume that we did not disappoint you. It is time to take a step back and ask yourself: Do you really need to know all of these details?

And the answer is not an unequivocal "yes."

It is important to have an idea of what all of the different types of privileges do. As for all the different syntax flavors for granting different privileges, you will most likely not need them if you get one thing right, and this is highlighted in the following box.

> **The Most Important Rule of Privilege Management**
>
> The only type of privilege you should ever grant to database users is a repository role.
>
> Do not use catalog roles, and do not grant privileges directly to users—unless this privilege management is handled by an IDM solution.

If you stick to this rule, you will hardly ever need to run any SQL statement that grants anything to a user or role, and thus you will not have to worry about the syntax.

It is only during some preparation steps that you will need to actually grant individual privileges; remember that you can only place a privilege into repository roles if the _SYS_REPO user has this privilege (including GRANT OPTION or ADMIN OPTION). Thus, whenever you create, for example, a new database schema, the schema owner will need to grant the privileges on that schema to _SYS_REPO.

13.4 Critical Privileges and Privilege Combinations

As with any authorization system, there are certain privileges and privilege combinations in SAP HANA that are so powerful that their use should be avoided or—if that is not possible—controlled very strictly. Any such list will be subjective, so here is our personal recommendation of privileges to worry about.

13.4.1 Critical System Privileges

Although most system privileges enable powerful actions (e.g., SERVICE ADMIN, which allows for restarting database services), we consider the following privileges especially critical in terms of a security setup whose task is to secure the integrity of and access to some of your company's most important assets: its data.

USER ADMIN

This privilege would be sufficiently critical to warrant careful treatment if it only allowed the creation of database users. However, with USER ADMIN you can also drop database users and all catalog objects and schemas (including objects) owned by them.

Of course, use of the USER ADMIN privilege cannot be avoided, but it is a privilege worth tracking.

REPO.IMPORT

This might at first sight be surprising. However, REPO.IMPORT allows the import (including activation) of development objects without requiring further privileges on the repository, such as package privileges. Hence, the easiest way to slip modifications to developed objects—such as data models, roles, analytic privileges, or applications—into a system is the import of a delivery unit, which is allowed for any holder of this privilege.

In a development scenario, that is, a system landscape in which the SAP HANA Modeler or the SAP HANA Developer Workbench is being used, you should need the REPO.IMPORT privilege at least for one user, namely the account used for transporting repository contents. REPO.IMPORT is, for example, included in the role sap.hana.xs.lm.roles::Transport, which is part of the SAP HANA Application Lifecycle Management application sap.hana.xs.lm.

ROLE ADMIN

In short, ROLE ADMIN should not be granted in an SAP HANA system. It is not needed, with one single exception (discussed ahead) if you stick to our advice and only make use of repository roles (see Section 13.1.3).

ROLE ADMIN allows for creating and dropping catalog roles, and it allows granting of all catalog roles in the database system. This combination of create and grant rights will typically violate the requirements of segregation of duties.

The one single exception: There is one catalog role in the system that is predelivered with SAP HANA, will be required in exceptional circumstances, and cannot be included in a repository role. This is the powerful role SAP_INTERNAL_HANA_SUPPORT, whose name was chosen intentionally; it is a role that should only be given to SAP Support if requested by SAP Support—and if you care, we do encourage you to ask why it is requested. This role has a number of interesting properties:

▶ It can only be granted to one database user at a time (starting with SPS 8 to a limited, configurable number of database users).

▶ It cannot be included in other roles, neither catalog roles nor repository roles.

▶ It contains privileges that are only of value to people who know and understand the source code of the database and that are not available in any other way.

How do you grant this privilege to SAP Support if nobody in your database system has ROLE ADMIN? You also cannot grant it to your user admin with GRANT OPTION and then have your user administrators pass on the privilege to SAP Support.

The answer is simple: Create a stored procedure in definer mode, either in the repository or in the catalog with user SYSTEM. Make sure the EXECUTE permission for this procedure is given to your user admins.

This procedure should accept a user name as input parameter and simply grant SAP_INTERNAL_HANA_SUPPORT to the given user. The procedure definition itself is simple, as we demonstrate in Listing 13.2.

```
CREATE PROCEDURE "GRANT_SAP_INTERNAL_HANA_SUPPORT_ROLE"
  ( IN GRANTEE VARCHAR(128) )
  LANGUAGE SQLSCRIPT
  SQL SECURITY DEFINER
  AS
    v_statement VARCHAR(256);
    found INT := 0;
BEGIN
    -- Prepare error handling in case of invalid grantee
    DECLARE ERRCOND CONDITION FOR SQL_ERROR_CODE 10001;
    DECLARE EXIT HANDLER FOR ERRCOND RESIGNAL;
    -- Check input parameter
    SELECT COUNT(*) INTO found FROM "USERS"
```

```
        WHERE "USER_NAME" = :grantee;
    IF :found = 1 THEN
        v_statement :=
            'GRANT SAP_INTERNAL_HANA_SUPPORT TO ' || :GRANTEE;
        EXEC v_statement;
    ELSE
        SIGNAL ERRCOND SET MESSAGE_TEXT =
            'INVALID GRANTEE PROVIDED' ;
    END IF;
END;
```

Listing 13.2 Procedure for Granting Role SAP_INTERNAL_HANA_SUPPORT

Give the EXECUTE privilege on this procedure, including GRANT OPTION, to the _SYS_ REPO user, and from now on you can include this EXECUTE privilege in repository roles. Thus, your user administrators are empowered to grant the SAP_INTERNAL_ SUPPORT role to SAP Support without violating your security policies.

Again: Do not grant ROLE ADMIN to any user or role in your database, ever.

DATA ADMIN

This is an interesting privilege; it gives the holder the DROP and ALTER privilege on all catalog objects in the database without requiring any schema or object privileges, meaning that the holder of this privilege can drop any table in the system. Possibly even worse, they can modify all tables by adding or removing fields.

We believe that DATA ADMIN should not be granted to any user or role in your database.

INFILE ADMIN

A holder of this privilege can modify the database configuration, including backup locations, password policy, and other beautiful settings. You will need this privilege, and you want to be careful.

13.4.2 Critical Privilege Combinations

Sometimes, it is not a single privilege that is critical, but it is the combination of several privileges. This list could probably be infinitely long, but we just discuss our top three.

Grant Roles and Modify Roles

Nobody who has privileges to modify roles should be allowed to grant these roles. In a typical SAP HANA system in which only repository roles are used, you should thus avoid combining the following:

▶ EXECUTE ON "PUBLIC"."GRANT_ACTIVATED_ROLE", that is, the privilege to grant repository roles.

▶ REPO.EDIT_NATIVE_OBJECTS and REPO.ACTIVATE_NATIVE_OBJECTS (as well as the equivalents for imported objects) on any package in the repository. This in turn means that user administrators (who are allowed to grant activated roles) must not have development privileges in the SAP HANA repository.

Similarly, nobody should have permission to modify their own roles, which means that a person with roles from package <package_1> must not have developer rights on that package.

Grant Analytic Privileges and Create/Modify Them

Similar to the case of roles, but typically a tad less critical, because here we "only" speak of data access. The rule is this: Never grant EXECUTE ON "PUBLIC"."GRANT_ ACTIVATED_ANALYTICAL_PRIVILEGE" and system privileges CREATE STRUCTURED PRIVILEGE or STRUCTUREDPRIVILEGE ADMIN to the same user.

Unlike roles, we do not have to eliminate developing in the repository per se, because the (re)activation of analytic privileges is controlled by these system privileges.

You should also not combine EXECUTE with privileges that allow modification of stored procedures or look-up tables for restriction values used in dynamic value restrictions of analytic privileges.

Cross-Tier Development Rights

Finally, in the best of all worlds, no person should have developer rights in two systems of the same transport landscape, including developer rights in one system and transport rights into a higher-level system of the transport landscape.

13.5 Standard Roles for SAP HANA Systems

The SAP HANA system does not come with predelivered standard roles for the administrator, for user management, or for other typical tasks. Such a set of recommended roles has been published in a how-to guide on SCN at *https://scn.sap.com/docs/DOC-53974*.

That guide documents more than 40 roles for database administrators, security managers, developers, and support staff. The roles are intended as templates to help project teams set up a good set of roles for secure management of their database systems.

In Chapter 14, we refer to several of the roles proposed in the how-to guide when describing our proposal for setting up a database system.

Further Resources

If you need to build roles on your own, you will find our extensive list of administration tasks and related privileges helpful. This material can be downloaded from the book's page at *www.sap-press.com/3506*.

13.6 Troubleshooting Authorization Issues

For all software users, there will come a time when they try to do something and receive a message similar to "not authorized." If they don't like the message, they are likely to approach IT. In this section, we will give you some tips to make those folks happy.

There are two primary parts to this topic: knowing what authorizations a user has and finding what authorizations they are missing for the action they are trying to perform.

13.6.1 Finding Information on Granted Privileges and Roles

The SAP HANA database offers multiple views with information on privileges in the system. There are views that simply list all available roles and privileges in the database, and there are views that contain information on privilege granting. We will give you a brief introduction to all of these views.

The PRIVILEGES View

From the PRIVILEGES view, you can simply retrieve a list of all system privileges, package privileges, object privileges, and application privileges that exist in the database. Except for the application privileges, the view content is static, because the available system, object, and package privileges do not change.

Note that the object and package privileges listed here are simply the available privileges that can be granted on an object, for example, SELECT (object privilege) or REPO.READ (package privilege).

For an administrator, the most interesting piece of information in this view will probably be the list of all application privileges in the system.

```
SELECT "NAME", "TYPE" FROM "PRIVILEGES"
  WHERE "TYPE" = 'APPLICATIONPRIVILEGE'
```

Listing 13.3 Reading All Existing Application Privileges

The STRUCTURED_PRIVILEGES View

The list and definition of all analytic privileges (as well as structured privileges created directly via a CREATE STRUCTURED PRIVILEGE call) is available from the STRUCTURED_PRIVILEGES view.

The view contains multiple records for each analytic privilege, and each record lists one restriction of the privilege. A restriction can, for example, be one entry from the list of reference data models, one restriction value defined on one attribute, or so on.

This can easily be illustrated by an example query against the STRUCTURED_PRIVI-LEGES view and its output in Listing 13.4 and Figure 13.7, respectively.

```
SELECT "STRUCTURED_PRIVILEGE_NAME", "RESTRICTION_TYPE",
       "DIMENSION_ATTRIBUTE", "FILTER_TYPE",
       "OPERATOR", "OPERAND"
  FROM "STRUCTURED_PRIVILEGES"
  WHERE "STRUCTURED_PRIVILEGE_NAME" LIKE 'public.demo.%'
```

Listing 13.4 Reading from the STRUCTURED_PRIVILEGES View

The entries for one particular analytic privilege can be categorized by the field RESTRICTION_TYPE, where the two most interesting values are as follows:

- CUBERESTRICTION
  Each data model in the list of reference models will result in one entry of type CUBERESTRICTION.
- DIMENSIONRESTRICTION
  For each restriction value defined on an attribute field, there will be one entry of type DIMENSIONRESTRICTION. If the restriction values are obtained from the return value of a stored procedure, then the FILTER_TYPE is DYNAMIC and the procedure name can be found in the field OPERAND.

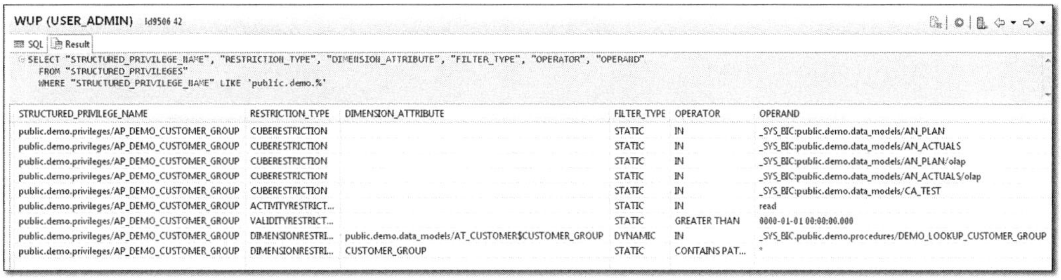

STRUCTURED_PRIVILEGE_NAME	RESTRICTION_TYPE	DIMENSION_ATTRIBUTE	FILTER_TYPE	OPERATOR	OPERAND
public.demo.privileges/AP_DEMO_CUSTOMER_GROUP	CUBERESTRICTION		STATIC	IN	_SYS_BIC:public.demo.data_models/AN_PLAN
public.demo.privileges/AP_DEMO_CUSTOMER_GROUP	CUBERESTRICTION		STATIC	IN	_SYS_BIC:public.demo.data_models/AN_ACTUALS
public.demo.privileges/AP_DEMO_CUSTOMER_GROUP	CUBERESTRICTION		STATIC	IN	_SYS_BIC:public.demo.data_models/AN_PLAN/olap
public.demo.privileges/AP_DEMO_CUSTOMER_GROUP	CUBERESTRICTION		STATIC	IN	_SYS_BIC:public.demo.data_models/AN_ACTUALS/olap
public.demo.privileges/AP_DEMO_CUSTOMER_GROUP	CUBERESTRICTION		STATIC	IN	_SYS_BIC:public.demo.data_models/CA_TEST
public.demo.privileges/AP_DEMO_CUSTOMER_GROUP	ACTIVITYRESTRICT...		STATIC	IN	read
public.demo.privileges/AP_DEMO_CUSTOMER_GROUP	VALIDITYRESTRICT...		STATIC	GREATER THAN	0000-01-01 00:00:00.000
public.demo.privileges/AP_DEMO_CUSTOMER_GROUP	DIMENSIONRESTRI...	public.demo.data_models/AT_CUSTOMER$CUSTOMER_GROUP	DYNAMIC	IN	_SYS_BIC.public.demo.procedures/DEMO_LOOKUP_CUSTOMER_GROUP
public.demo.privileges/AP_DEMO_CUSTOMER_GROUP	DIMENSIONRESTRI...	CUSTOMER_GROUP	STATIC	CONTAINS PAT...	*

Figure 13.7 Output of a Query against View STRUCTURED_PRIVILEGES

The ROLES View

The names of all database roles, together with the name of the role creator and the creation time, can be retrieved from the view ROLES. For most practical cases, the view is not particularly interesting. You can, for example, retrieve the list of all repository roles with a query such as the one in Listing 13.5 (note that there is no perfect way of doing this, because catalog roles also can in principle contain the pattern ::).

```
SELECT "ROLE_NAME", "CREATOR", "CREATE_TIME"
  FROM "ROLES"
  WHERE "ROLE_NAME" like '%::%';
```

Listing 13.5 Reading the List of all Repository Roles

The GRANTED_PRIVILEGES View

More interesting than just a listing of objects or roles is the question of who has granted which privilege to whom.

The view GRANTED_PRIVILEGES has a promising name, and for some purposes it may do what is needed: It shows details of each direct granting of a privilege to a user or a role.

The drawback of this view is that it cannot answer two typical questions: Which privileges does user <x> have? Which users carry privilege <y>? Soon, we will show you the view EFFECTIVE_PRIVILEGES, which answers the first question. For the second question, SAP HANA does not offer a simple generic answer.

Still, the GRANTED_PRIVILEGES view has its value. For example, you might want to know which users in your systems have some privileges that have been directly granted to them (as opposed to granted via a role). A query to answer this question that excludes all predelivered system users is given in Listing 13.6.

```
SELECT "GRANTEE", "GRANTEE_TYPE", "GRANTOR",
       "OBJECT_TYPE", "SCHEMA_NAME", "OBJECT_NAME",
       "PRIVILEGE"
  FROM GRANTED_PRIVILEGES
  WHERE "GRANTEE_TYPE" = 'USER'
    AND "GRANTEE" NOT IN ('SYSTEM', 'SYS', '_SYS_REPO',
                          '_SYS_STATISTICS', '_SYS_DATAPROV',
                          '_SYS_EPM', '_SYS_AFL')
```

Listing 13.6 Finding All Users That Have Privileges Granted Directly to Them

The GRANTED_ROLES View

Similar to GRANTED_PRIVILEGES, the view GRANTED_ROLES shows all role assignments in which one role has been granted directly to a user or another role. The similarity extends to the limited use of this view when it comes to asking the question of whether or not a user has been granted a certain role. After all, we can build unlimited role hierarchies in the database, and we cannot easily query this view in a way that resolves such hierarchies.

Of course, there are many other useful questions we can answer with the GRANTED_ROLES view, for example, the question of whether any user in our system has been assigned to catalog roles. Listing 13.7 contains an example query that will display any role assignment of a catalog role to users other than the predefined system users in the database.

```
SELECT "GRANTEE", "GRANTEE_TYPE", "GRANTOR", "ROLE_NAME"
  FROM "GRANTED_ROLES"
  WHERE "ROLE_NAME" NOT LIKE '%::%'
    AND "ROLE_NAME" != 'PUBLIC'
    AND "GRANTEE" NOT IN ('SYSTEM', 'SYS', '_SYS_REPO',
```

```
'_SYS_STATISTICS', '_SYS_DATAPROV',
'_SYS_EPM', '_SYS_AFL')
```

Listing 13.7 Finding All Users That Have a Catalog Role Granted to Them

The EFFECTIVE_PRIVILEGES View

If you do want to know all privileges that a given user has, either granted directly or indirectly through roles or hierarchies of roles, the view EFFECTIVE_PRIVILEGES is your friend.

> **Note**
>
> Resolving the potentially complex role hierarchies can be an expensive database query. In order to prevent excessively long-running and resource-hungry queries, it is mandatory to include a filter condition on field USER_NAME when querying the EFFECTIVE_PRIVILEGES view.

The field structure of the EFFECTIVE_PRIVILEGES view is almost identical to that of the view GRANTED PRIVILEGES. However, we now find a more complex structure around the grantee.

Consider the query in Listing 13.8 and the output of that query in Figure 13.8. In the query, we ask for all privileges granted directly or indirectly to user RICHARD_III. If you recall, we used this noble person in the testing of dynamic analytic privileges, granting the role reporting_demo_model and nothing else. In that role, we give the SELECT privilege on three activated data models and we grant one analytic privilege. We expect to retrieve this information from EFFECTIVE_PRIVILEGES.

In Listing 13.8, we have removed all privileges granted through the PUBLIC role for the sake of the clarity of the result.

```
SELECT "USER_NAME", "GRANTEE",  "GRANTEE_TYPE",
       "GRANTOR", "GRANTOR_TYPE",
       "OBJECT_TYPE", "SCHEMA_NAME", "OBJECT_NAME",
       "PRIVILEGE"
  FROM "EFFECTIVE_PRIVILEGES"
  WHERE "USER_NAME" = 'RICHARD_III'
    AND "GRANTOR" != 'PUBLIC'
    AND "GRANTEE" != 'PUBLIC'
```

Listing 13.8 Retrieving Privileges Granted to User RICHARD_III

A look at the result set of this query in Figure 13.8 may be confusing at first sight. For each privilege, you see two entries here: one for the privilege being granted to our role `reporting_demo_model` through the user _SYS_REPO and another one for the privilege being granted to user RICHARD_III through role `reporting_demo_model`. If we had a more complex role hierarchy, you would see even more entries for each privilege.

In addition to seeing all privileges granted directly or indirectly to our user, we can also see the entire role hierarchy through which the privilege has been granted. This can be very helpful when you have to traverse a complicated authorization setup.

If you are not interested in the entire role hierarchy, simply add the filter condition `WHERE "GRANTEE" = "USER_NAME"`.

```
SELECT "USER_NAME", REPLACE("GRANTEE", 'security.roles.reporting::', 'roles::') AS "GRANTEE", "GRANTEE_TYPE",
    REPLACE("GRANTOR", 'security.roles.reporting::', 'roles::') AS "GRANTOR", "GRANTOR_TYPE",
    "OBJECT_TYPE", "SCHEMA_NAME", REPLACE("OBJECT_NAME", 'public.demo.', '') AS "OBJECT_NAME", "PRIVILEGE"
    FROM EFFECTIVE_PRIVILEGES
    WHERE "USER_NAME" = 'RICHARD_III'
    AND GRANTOR != 'PUBLIC'
    AND GRANTEE != 'PUBLIC'
```

USER_NAME	GRANTEE	GRANTEE_TYPE	GRANTOR	GRANTOR_TYPE	OBJECT_TYPE	SCHEMA_NAME	OBJECT_NAME	PRIVILEGE
RICHARD_III	roles::reporting_demo_model	ROLE	_SYS_REPO	USER	ANALYTICALPRIVILEGE	?	privileges/AP_DEMO_CUSTOMER_GROUP	EXECUTE
RICHARD_III	RICHARD_III	USER	roles::reporting_demo_model	ROLE	ANALYTICALPRIVILEGE	?	privileges/AP_DEMO_CUSTOMER_GROUP	EXECUTE
RICHARD_III	roles::reporting_demo_model	ROLE	_SYS_REPO	USER	VIEW	_SYS_BIC	data_models/AN_ACTUALS	SELECT
RICHARD_III	RICHARD_III	USER	roles::reporting_demo_model	ROLE	VIEW	_SYS_BIC	data_models/AN_ACTUALS	SELECT
RICHARD_III	roles::reporting_demo_model	ROLE	_SYS_REPO	USER	VIEW	_SYS_BIC	data_models/AN_PLAN	SELECT
RICHARD_III	RICHARD_III	USER	roles::reporting_demo_model	ROLE	VIEW	_SYS_BIC	data_models/AN_PLAN	SELECT
RICHARD_III	roles::reporting_demo_model	ROLE	_SYS_REPO	USER	VIEW	_SYS_BIC	data_models/CA_TEST	SELECT
RICHARD_III	RICHARD_III	USER	roles::reporting_demo_model	ROLE	VIEW	_SYS_BIC	data_models/CA_TEST	SELECT

Figure 13.8 Result Set of the Query against the View EFFECTIVE_PRIVILEGES

The EFFECTIVE_ROLES View

The one thing that the view `EFFECTIVE_PRIVILEGES` does not show us in an entirely basic way is the list of roles that are granted directly or indirectly to a given user. Even if we did not mention it here, you would guess that there is an equivalent view called `EFFECTIVE_ROLES`.

This view behaves just like `EFFECTIVE_PRIVILEGES`, so we do not have to describe it in depth.

An example query is shown in Listing 13.9. In this case, we ask for roles granted to the SYSTEM_ADMIN user, who has been granted some slightly more interesting roles.

Note

The EFFECTIVE_ROLES view—just like EFFECTIVE_PRIVILEGES—can only be queried when filtering on field USER_NAME.

```
SELECT * FROM "EFFECTIVE_ROLES"
  WHERE "USER_NAME" = 'SYSTEM_ADMIN'
```

Listing 13.9 Query against the EFFECTIVE_ROLES View

From the result of this query (Figure 13.9), we can see that three roles have been granted directly to our user: the PUBLIC role and two repository roles named system_admin_generic and system_admin_preinstalled.

Both repository roles contain other roles. There are three roles included in system_admin_generic, and one role is included in system_admin_preinstalled.

USER_NAME	GRANTEE	GRANTEE_TYPE	GRANTOR	ROLE_NAME	IS_GRANTABLE
SYSTEM_ADMIN	SYSTEM_ADMIN	USER	SYS	PUBLIC	FALSE
SYSTEM_ADMIN	SYSTEM_ADMIN	USER	_SYS_REPO	security.roles.admin::system_admin_generic	FALSE
SYSTEM_ADMIN	security.roles.admin::system_admin_generic	ROLE	_SYS_REPO	security.roles.admin::backup_admin	FALSE
SYSTEM_ADMIN	security.roles.admin::system_admin_generic	ROLE	_SYS_REPO	security.roles.admin::basic_admin	FALSE
SYSTEM_ADMIN	security.roles.admin::system_admin_generic	ROLE	_SYS_REPO	security.roles.admin::persistence_admin	FALSE
SYSTEM_ADMIN	SYSTEM_ADMIN	USER	_SYS_REPO	security.roles.admin::system_admin_preinstalled	FALSE
SYSTEM_ADMIN	security.roles.admin::system_admin_preinstalled	ROLE	_SYS_REPO	sap.hana.admin.roles::Monitoring	FALSE

Figure 13.9 Result of the Query against the EFFECTIVE_ROLES View

13.6.2 Tracing Missing Authorizations

Being able to know which privileges and roles exist in the system and which ones are granted to a given user is good. However, a typical question that might be asked is, "Why does the system prevent me from working?"

If the user can explain clearly enough what he is trying to accomplish, you might have a hunch as to what privileges he is missing. But what if you have no idea what's wrong? The solution in this case is an authorization trace. We will show you how to trace a typical reporting authorization problem step-by-step on the next pages.

Setting the Scene

For this exercise, we will continue with user RICHARD_III and the data model, analytic privilege, and `reporting_demo_model` that we have introduced previously. The present wealth of privileges of that user was shown in our query to the view `EFFECTIVE_PRIVILEGES` in Section 13.6.1.

Let's assume that RICHARD_III attempts to report against another calculation view for which the poor chap does not have any privileges. For this purpose, we have built a simple calculation view, `CA_TEST_1`, in the package `public.demo.data_models`.

Our user runs the query and receives the error message shown in Listing 13.10. Of course, a typical end user would run the query not in an SQL editor but through some reporting frontend—and then the frontend would receive the error message from the database and should display it to the user.

```
select "CUSTOMER_description", SUM("SALES_VOLUME") as "SALES_VOLUME"
  from _SYS_BIC."public.demo.data_models/CA_TEST_1"
  group by "CUSTOMER_description"
-------------------------------------------------------------------
Could not execute 'select "CUSTOMER_description", SUM("SALES_VOLUME")
as "SALES_VOLUME" from ...' in 57 ms 113 µs .
SAP DBTech JDBC: [258]: insufficient privilege: Not authorized
```

Listing 13.10 Authorization Error in Query on view CA_TEST_1

Running an Authorization Trace

With this error message, RICHARD_III approaches IT support. Note that the error message mentions neither the object being queried nor the type of privilege missing.

The easiest and best way to find what's missing is to have the user repeat the action that fails while recording additional trace information related to authorizations, and the best way to run this trace is by enabling a USER-SPECIFIC TRACE.

Open the Administration Editor of the SAP HANA database system RICHARD_III is using. In this editor, you can configure the USER-SPECIFIC TRACE on tab TRACE CONFIGURATION; see Figure 13.10.

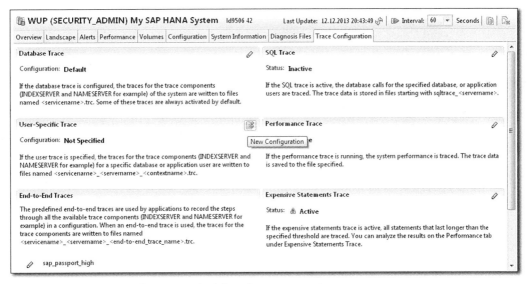

Figure 13.10 The Trace Configuration Tab of the Administration Editor

In the wizard for setting up the User-Specific Trace, make the following entries (see Figure 13.11):

▶ Context Name

This is an identifier for the trace and has to be unique. Only alphanumeric characters are allowed. The trace will create a dedicated output file, and the Context Name will be part of the file name. In our case, the Context Name is AUTHTRACER3.

▶ Database User

The name of the user whose actions we need to trace; you can only enter a single user name here.

▶ Trace Component

The component for authorization traces is called `authorization`, and we typically only need to trace the `indexserver` processes, even though it does not hurt to trace on ALL SERVICES.

Note that you will only find this component after selecting the checkbox Show All Components!

The best way to find the component (once the checkbox is selected), is to simply start typing the string "authorization" in the search box on top of the COMPONENT table.

▶ TRACE LEVEL

Useful and comparatively readable trace information is written if we set the trace level of this component to INFO.

Start the tracing by clicking FINISH.

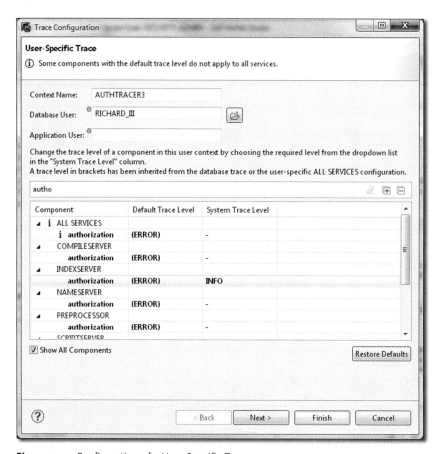

Figure 13.11 Configuration of a User-Specific Trace

While the trace is active, user RICHARD_III will have to re-execute the action that resulted in authorization issues.

As soon as the user-specific trace has recorded any information (i.e., as soon as RICHARD_III has encountered authorization issues), a new trace file will appear on the tab DIAGNOSIS FILES of the Administration Editor. You can most easily find the dedicated trace file by filtering on the CONTEXT NAME chosen during trace configuration; see Figure 13.12. Simply double-click the file to study its content. The trace output is shown in Listing 13.11, with the most important bits in **bold**.

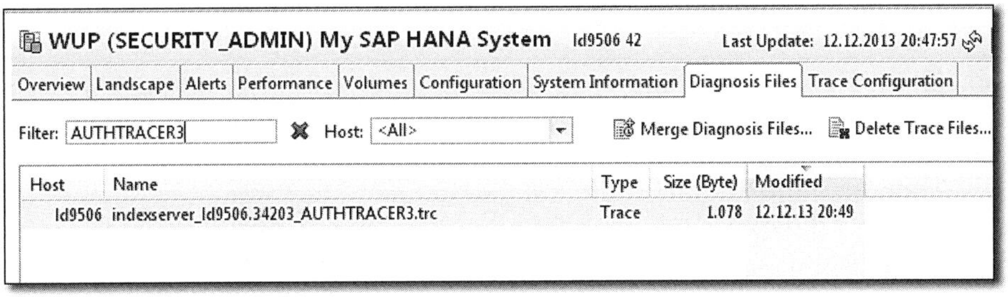

Figure 13.12 Finding the User-Specific Trace in Tab Diagnosis Files

You can see that an SQL_ACT_SELECT action was found to be not authorized. It would not be wrong to assume that this hints at a missing SELECT privilege on some object. The object has object ID 155111, and a bit further down you will find an entry VIEW-155111-public.demo.data_models/CA_TEST_1. This is all you need to know; your user is missing the SELECT privilege on the data model CA_TEST_1 in package public.demo.data_models.

```
[29078]{303404}[1597/-1] 2013-12-12 20:49:24.981332 i
  TraceContext       TraceContext.cpp(00699) :
  UserName=RICHARD_III, ApplicationUserName=D051516,
  ApplicationSource=csns.sql.editor.SQLExecuteFormEditor$1$1.
  run(SQLExecuteFormEditor.java:796);
[29078]{303404}[1597/-1] 2013-12-12 20:49:24.981151 i
  Authorization    SQLFacade.cpp(01181) : UserId(155772) is
  not authorized to do SQL_ACT_SELECT on
  ObjectId(3,0,oid=155111)
[29078]{303404}[1597/-1] 2013-12-12 20:49:24.981361 i
  Authorization    SQLFacade.cpp(01493) :
    system-action : none
    SCHEMA-140899-_SYS_BIC : {} , {SQL_ACT_SELECT}
       VIEW-155111-public.demo.data_models/CA_TEST_1 : {} , {SQL_ACT_
SELECT}
          COLUMN-155125-SALES_VOLUME : {SQL_ACT_SELECT}
          COLUMN-155121-CUSTOMER_description :
```

```
{SQL_ACT_SELECT}
[29078]{303404}[1597/-1] 2013-12-12 20:49:24.981432 i
  Authorization    query_check.cc(02440) : User RICHARD_III
  tried to execute 'select "CUSTOMER_description",
  SUM("SALES_VOLUME") as "SALES_VOLUME"
  from _SYS_BIC."public.demo.data_models/CA_TEST_1"
  group by "CUSTOMER_description"'
```

Listing 13.11 Output of the Authorization Trace

Add the SELECT privilege on the activated calculation view to the reporting role of user RICHARD_III, and let him repeat his query.

Unfortunately, it turns out that there is still something missing. The error message returned is slightly different. Perhaps a different type of privilege is missing; see Listing 13.12 and compare to the error message in Listing 13.10.

```
Could not execute 'select "CUSTOMER_description", SUM("SALES_VOLUME") as
"SALES_VOLUME" from ...' in 65 ms 298 μs .
SAP DBTech JDBC: [2048]: column store error: [2950] user is not authorized :
```

Listing 13.12 New Error Message in the Same Query Against CA_TEST_1

If the authorization trace is still running, then you can simply refresh the contents of the trace file to see if there is new information. Indeed, there are now a few lines added to the trace file, as shown in Listing 13.13. Again, we have set the interesting bits in **bold**. The trace tells you clearly that your user is missing an analytic privilege for this view.

```
[29078]{303404}[1597/-1] 2013-12-12 20:56:48.996832 i
  Authorization    ceAuthorizationCheck.cpp(00354) :
  AuthorizationCheckHandler::isAuthorizedToSelect (AP check):
  (Original) User RICHARD_III is not authorized on
  _SYS_BIC:public.demo.data_models/CA_TEST_1en due to XmlAP check
[29078]{303404}[1597/-1] 2013-12-12 20:56:48.997085 i
  Authorization    XmlAnalyticalPrivilegeFacade.cpp(01252) :
  UserId(155772) is missing analytic privileges in order to
  access _SYS_BIC:public.demo.data_models/CA_TEST_1
  (ObjectId(21,0,oid=3816)). Current situation:
  AP ObjectId(19,2,oid=167): Not granted.
```

Listing 13.13 New Output of the Authorization Trace

Bonus: Finding Analytic Privileges for an Activated Data Model

You could now ask RICHARD_III to apply for the missing privilege. However, you might want to know if there are analytic privileges existing in the system that would grant access to the calculation view in question.

You can use the `STRUCTURED_PRIVILEGES` view to find any such analytic privilege; see the example query in Listing 13.14. You simply have to look for entries with `CUBERESTRICTIONS` on the activated data model you are interested in.

```
SELECT "STRUCTURED_PRIVILEGE_NAME", "RESTRICTION_TYPE", "DIMENSION_
ATTRIBUTE", "FILTER_TYPE", "OPERATOR", "OPERAND"
  FROM "STRUCTURED_PRIVILEGES"
  WHERE "RESTRICTION_TYPE" = 'CUBERESTRICTION'
    AND "OPERAND" = '_SYS_BIC:public.demo.data_models/CA_TEST_1'
```

Listing 13.14 Searching for Analytic Privileges on a Given View

13.7 Summary

We did go to great lengths in this chapter in order to get a few simple messages across:

► **Only use repository roles**

Do not use catalog roles, and do not grant privileges directly to users.

Using catalog roles, you will face serious obstacles trying to implement reasonable segregation of duties in the areas of role management and user management.

If you grant privileges directly to users, and—against popular belief—also when using catalog roles, there are multiple difficult-to-control side effects of privilege management, especially to do with the revoking of roles and privileges.

Use of catalog roles can be acceptable if an appropriate IDM solution is being used.

► **Understand the privileges required for a given action**

When you set up your database users and their roles, especially administrators and developers, first decide on the tasks of the different user groups; then make a list of the database actions related to these tasks; and finally build database roles enabling these actions. Take note of the troubleshooting advice in Section 13.6; it can also help for assembling roles.

► **Be aware of critical privileges or privilege combinations**
We gave our view of critical privileges in Section 13.4. In any case, try to avoid the ROLE ADMIN and DATA ADMIN system privileges.

► **Create analytic privileges intelligently**
Analytic privileges with dynamic attribute restrictions help you minimize the number of analytic privilege objects that you have to build. The stored procedures used for restriction value lookup should be created through repository objects so that the analytic privilege and the procedure can both be transported.

Be aware of the combinatorics related to analytic privileges. Especially do not use the option APPLICABLE TO ALL INFORMATION MODELS!

If you are about to start a project involving SAP HANA, you need to pre-pare and set up the system properly to avoid complications during system operation. This chapter gives an overview of what you need to know.

14   Planning and Setting Up an SAP HANA System Landscape

In this chapter, we will combine a lot of what we have covered so far. We will cover the first steps in an SAP HANA project that will lead to a system that is well-prepared for production usage.

There are three main parts in this chapter. In the first part (Section 14.1), we will talk about sizing, the choice of single-node versus scale-out architectures, and other available form factors. In the second part (Section 14.2), we take a look at the system landscape from development to the production system and discuss the options you have for deploying SAP HANA on the different nodes of the land-scape. The third big block (Section 14.3) covers the actual setting up of the system after database installation. This bootstrapping process will include items such as creating database users for the administrator teams, enabling security-relevant features such as audit logging, and other steps that are necessary for reliable sys-tem operation.

We will try to develop the chapter in a way that it is useful for both the seasoned administrator who has already studied the preceding chapters and the project manager who will usually not have detailed knowledge across all areas. Where relevant, we will reference the deep-dive sections of previous chapters.

Throughout this chapter, we assume that you are planning an on-premise instal-lation, so some aspects of our discussion may not be relevant for customers pre-paring a cloud deployment.

14.1 Preparation: Sizing, Hardware Choices, and More

When you prepare a project involving SAP HANA, there are three main questions you will need to answer before you can set out to acquire the system hardware: What system size is required? Will you build a single-node or a scale-out system? Will it be an appliance or based on Tailored Data Center Integration?

There are further questions, such as the choice of hardware partner and self-managed system vs. hosting or cloud offerings, which we will not discuss here.

14.1.1 System Sizing for SAP HANA

As in probably all SAP systems, there are two critical aspects that need to be considered in the system sizing in SAP HANA: data volume and system workload. Translated to the hardware of the SAP HANA system, these aspects relate to the available main memory and the CPU power, respectively. Of these two quantities, the data sizing is by far easier to plan for.

Fortunately, in the vast majority of cases that we have seen, the system sizing has been and could be primarily based on data volume. The amount of CPU cores then follows automatically from the form factors offered within the appliance definition.

We will first discuss the generic sizing approach for SAP HANA memory and CPU sizing before pointing out specific considerations for typical use cases. Please note that the sizing procedure must be performed by qualified personnel. SAP Consulting and the SAP HANA hardware partners offer sizing services for SAP HANA.

Memory Sizing

To determine the RAM requirements for a new SAP HANA installation, the most crucial part is to estimate the memory consumption of the tables in SAP HANA. Once this figure is known, the memory requirements are easily calculated. To estimate the memory size of the tables to be loaded into SAP HANA, you must consider five steps, as visualized in Figure 14.1. SAP offers tools to support the sizing process. These tools handle those steps that can be automated, which is at least steps ❷ and ❺ of the following procedure. In some use cases, there is also partial support for steps ❸ and ❹. We cover these tools in the sections on the individual use cases that follow:

❶ Select the tables that will exist in the SAP HANA system

Setting up a new system or migrating an existing system to a new database offers great opportunities to think about waste. Removing or not transferring unnecessary tables or parts of tables is the most efficient way to reduce data volume. Your SAP HANA use case plays an important role in deciding what is waste and what is important.

If you plan for a data mart or another type of new system in which tables will be replicated from one or multiple source systems into your SAP HANA database, then you will have to carefully select the tables to transfer. It may also be sufficient to only transfer a fraction of the table contents, perhaps those determined by a transaction date.

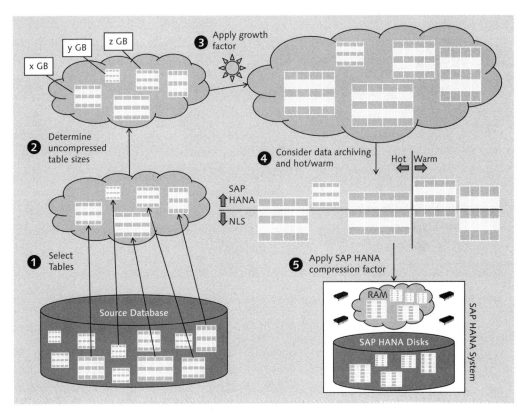

Figure 14.1 Memory Sizing for SAP HANA

If you migrate an SAP BW system to SAP HANA, there are usually two categories of tables that can easily be removed or reduced in size; aggregates and most secondary indexes are not needed as performance measures in SAP HANA, and they should therefore not be considered in your SAP HANA database sizing. In many SAP BW systems, you can also find copious amounts of old logging or other status information that should normally be cleaned up as part of regular housekeeping. In the course of a system migration, one will very often find that one could have been more efficient in this area.

In addition to these trivial ways of reducing the data volume, you may or may not plan to also modify your warehouse architecture, making use of the extended capabilities offered by SAP HANA (these capabilities are often summarized under the term *LSA++*, which stands for the new Layered Scalable Architecture with SAP HANA features). Such a redesign is entirely optional and can also be started at a later point in time.

Note

For more on LSA++, we recommend the following:
https://scn.sap.com/docs/DOC-35212

The situation is similar when migrating an SAP Business Suite system to SAP HANA: Most indexes will not be needed, some tables may not be required anymore, and housekeeping often offers room for freeing up some space.

❷ **Determine the uncompressed table sizes**

All database systems offer some way of compressing data. The effective compression rate depends on the type of database, even on the software version, on the data topology, and other factors. It is therefore not possible to define a general compression factor to compare the compressed size of data in arbitrary source databases and in SAP HANA.

Instead, one has to define a nominal data size that is independent from the source database system. This is the uncompressed size of a table, determined by the length of the table fields and the number of records in the table.

SAP offers sizing reports to determine these uncompressed sizes in existing SAP systems for different system types, for example, SAP BW systems or SAP Business Suite systems. We list the specific information sources in the corresponding dedicated sections.

If, on the other hand, you plan for an entirely new SAP system, you can follow the standard sizing procedures for the system in question to determine the uncompressed table sizes. See, for example, SAP QuickSizer at *https://service.sap.com/quicksizer*.

❸ **Estimate the data growth**
Your new SAP HANA system must provide resources to store and operate not only on the initial data volume; in most cases, the contents of a database system grow with time. You should include this growth in your system sizing.

❹ **Consider data archiving or hot-/warm-data concepts**
Depending on the SAP HANA use case, you might be able to integrate data volume-management techniques such as data archiving (e.g., nearline storage) or hot and warm data concepts. Both options are supported, for example, by SAP BW on SAP HANA, and SAP BW offers assistance if you plan to employ them. Hot/warm data is usually referred to as "nonactive data concept" in resources related to SAP BW on SAP HANA sizing.

If you build a custom data mart, you will not find any tool assistance for setting up a hot/warm data concept or implementing data aging using, for example, the Smart Data Access feature for data virtualization. We cannot recommend trying to implement these techniques in a custom data mart.

With hot/warm data in SAP HANA, there is the possibility of defining unload priorities for individual tables, so that some tables may be evicted from main memory very quickly. In SAP BW memory sizing, such tables are accounted for with a scale factor significantly smaller than 100%.

❺ **Apply the appropriate SAP HANA compression factor**
Up to this step, we have identified the uncompressed data volume that will be loaded into SAP HANA initially plus the projected growth over a reasonable time frame. The final step in the memory sizing is now to apply the compression factor that we can expect to reach.

Technically, the compression factor that can be reached depends primarily on the target in-memory store: Columnar tables generally have a much better compression than row store tables. The compression also can be strongly influenced by the data distribution within a table: Columns with a very high percentage of unique values will be compressed less efficiently than very sparse columns (see the discussion in Chapter 8). If an application creates data in a compressed format, the ability of the database to compress even further will be limited.

In practice, the tools supporting SAP HANA sizing for the individual use cases make different assumptions regarding the compression factor. The generic sizing tool assumes a typical compression factor of 7 for columnar tables, based on overall experience. The tool supporting sizing for an SAP BW migration to SAP HANA has different compression values for the different object types in an SAP BW system, based on intensive measurements performed by the development team. Similarly, the sizing tool for SAP Business Suite systems includes application knowledge to optimize the accuracy of the sizing approach.

Once you have determined the memory consumption of the database tables, the overall memory requirements of the database system generally follow from a simple rule of thumb: 50% of the database server's main memory can be used to store data, and the other half must be reserved for operating on that data, that is, for query executions and other workload. Hence, the total memory requirement <V_{DB}> for the database is twice the expected compressed data volume <V_{DATA}>.

The database server must be able to host more than just the database processes. There also needs to be RAM available for the operating system itself and typical auxiliary processes required on the server, such as monitoring agents, backup tools, and so on. The database system reserves space for such processes by limiting its own maximum memory allocation to the value of parameter global.ini • [memorymanager] • global_allocation_limit. The default limit is set at approximately 90% of the installed physical RAM. It follows that the installed main memory <V_{RAM}> of the system must at least be 1/0.9 times the memory requirement of the database processes: <V_{RAM}> = 1/0.9 x <V_{DB}> = 1.11 x 2 x <V_{DATA}>.

Once you have determined the quantity <V_{RAM}>, you can look up the available server form factors and choose from those servers whose installed memory is as big as <V_{RAM}> or higher. See Section 3.5 for the precise setting of global_allocation_limit.

> **Note**
>
> If you plan to operate multiple applications on the same SAP HANA database server, then you need to include all of these applications in the sizing process and add their respective RAM (and potentially CPU) requirements.
>
> The same is true if you operate an SAP NetWeaver Application Server on the database server, as described in SAP Note 1953429.

An additional complication arises if you need to size for a scale-out system. In this case, the required main memory must be split among multiple hosts of identical installed memory. If, for example, <V_{RAM}> = 2.3 TB (and the use case is not SAP

Business Suite on SAP HANA), then you may plan a scale-out system consisting of either five hosts with 512 GB of installed RAM each or three hosts with 1 TB of installed RAM each.

Depending on the use case, however, the master node of a scale-out system might be dedicated to "transactional workload" and only contain related tables, whereas application data underlying the OLAP workload will be distributed across the slave nodes. In these cases, the data separation between master and slave nodes must also be considered.

Finally, standby nodes do not play a role in the sizing. The memory requirements determined in the sizing procedure must be met by using the worker nodes. Standby nodes should then be added to optimize system availability.

CPU Sizing

The sizing procedure for CPU requirements is less well-defined than the procedure for memory sizing, because it is based on more ambiguous quantities. Generally speaking, it is assumed that an average active user will cause a certain workload on the system. (An *active user* is a user who is currently logged on to the system and from time to time triggers database transactions.)

SAP has established a performance standard for measuring system workload named SAPS (SAP Application Performance Standard). This standard provides a relationship between the hardware of a system and a typical quantum of workload. The computing power of an SAP-validated server is measured in SAPS, as is the CPU-requirement of SAP sizing procedures. Hence, if the input provided for CPU sizing is accurate, then the hardware vendors can easily find a system matching your CPU requirements.

> **Note**
>
> For more information about SAPS, we recommend the following:
> *https://global.sap.com/campaigns/benchmark/measuring.epx*

For the two major use cases of SAP HANA (SAP BW on SAP HANA and SAP Business Suite on SAP HANA), there is no specific guidance published regarding CPU sizing. In most circumstances, it will be sufficient to rely on memory sizing for these system types. Exceptions are mentioned in the sizing documentation for the particular use cases. We will therefore give details regarding CPU sizing only in the "Sizing for Generic SAP HANA Use Cases" section.

Sizing for SAP BW on SAP HANA

If you are planning to migrate an existing SAP BW system on "any database" to SAP BW on SAP HANA, SAP offers a very detailed sizing program that you can execute in your existing SAP BW system. This program presently (July 2014) has the following main features:

- Analyzes existing SAP BW system tables, including sampling of table contents
- Most accurate compression estimates, based on the different object and table types in an SAP BW system
- Automatically separates tables into row store and column store
- Considers nearline storage (extended table concept) and hot/warm classification of data
- Can account for data growth estimates
- Automatically adds required uplift for technical factors such as non-Unicode source systems
- Respects SAP BW-specific best practices for scale-out systems

The details of the SAP BW sizing procedure are constantly adjusted as the capabilities of SAP BW on SAP HANA are extended. We will not cover tool usage in detail but will refer you to the SAP Notes listed in Table 14.1 instead.

Note	Note Name	Comment
1637145	SAP BW on HANA: Sizing SAP In-Memory Database	Master note for sizing SAP BW on SAP HANA. Do not use the attachments to this note (use SAP Note 1736976 instead).
1736976	Sizing Report for BW on HANA	Contains a more accurate sizing report, and the most up to date documentation attachments for general SAP BW/SAP HANA sizing, as well as special considerations for scale-out in SAP BW on SAP HANA.
1767880	Non-Active Data Concept in BW on HANA	Information on the hot and warm classification of data in SAP BW on SAP HANA.

Table 14.1 SAP Notes Related to Sizing for SAP BW on SAP HANA

Note	Note Name	Comment
1702409	HANA DB: Optimal Number of Scale Out Nodes for BW on HANA	Special considerations for using SAP BW on a scale-out SAP HANA system.
1855041	Sizing Recommendation for Master Node in BW-on-HANA	Particular considerations for the master node in SAP BW on scale-out SAP HANA.
1666670	BW on SAP HANA—Landscape Deployment Planning	General consideration for SAP BW system planning, including options for operating additional applications on the same SAP HANA server.

Table 14.1 SAP Notes Related to Sizing for SAP BW on SAP HANA (Cont.)

If instead of a migration an entirely new SAP BW system is planned using SAP HANA as database, the entry point for SAP HANA sizing is the SAP QuickSizer.

CPU sizing for the SAP HANA database of an SAP BW system is considered unnecessary; the critical resource is in virtually all cases the main memory.

Sizing for SAP Business Suite on SAP HANA

Similar to SAP BW, the SAP Business Suite offers a sizing tool that will analyze the tables in an existing SAP Business Suite system and produce a sizing recommendation accompanied by detailed output regarding different table categories and so on.

The sizing report recognizes particular properties of the SAP Business Suite system such as large object columns (LOBs) that can be configured to reside mainly on disk since SPS 7 of SAP HANA. Similar to the report for SAP BW sizing, it includes rule sets for separating tables into row store and column store.

Details for the sizing procedure are published by SAP in the SAP Notes given in Table 14.2.

Note	Note Name	Comment
1793345	Sizing for SAP Suite on HANA	Master note for sizing the SAP HANA system for SAP Business Suite on SAP HANA.
1872170	Suite on HANA Memory Sizing	SAP Note providing the sizing report for memory sizing of the SAP HANA system, including a detailed FAQ document.

Table 14.2 SAP Notes Related to Sizing for SAP Business Suite on SAP HANA

Note	Note Name	Comment
1781986	Business Suite on SAP HANA Scale Out	Generic information regarding support of SAP HANA scale-out in the SAP Business Suite. See especially the SAP Notes referenced from here, which contain important technical details, e.g., regarding table distribution.
1825774	SAP Business Suite Powered by SAP HANA—Multi-Node Support	Restrictions for scale-out support in SAP Business Suite on SAP HANA.
1950470	Hardware Prerequisites for Business Suite on SAP HANA Scale Out	Specific hardware requirements for restricted ramp-up for SAP Business Suite on scale-out SAP HANA.
1826100	Multiple Applications SAP Business Suite powered by SAP HANA	Provides a white list of applications related to the SAP Business Suite that may be installed on the same database system.

Table 14.2 SAP Notes Related to Sizing for SAP Business Suite on SAP HANA (Cont.)

If no existing SAP Business Suite system is available to run the sizing report, SAP also gives a rule of thumb for deriving the SAP HANA sizing from the sizing for a regular disk-based database. See SAP Note 1793345 for the most up-to-date formula.

Note

At the time of writing (July 2014), SAP does not yet fully support SAP HANA scale-out for the SAP Business Suite. The only supported setup is a simple failover scenario consisting of one worker node and one standby node. Scale-out with multiple worker nodes is not yet generally available for SAP Business Suite on SAP HANA. See SAP Note 1825774 for details and possible changes. The note also contains information on how to contact SAP if you would like to participate in a restricted availability process for scale-out in SAP Business Suite on SAP HANA.

Load tests have shown that the mostly transactional workload of an SAP Business Suite scenario allows lowering the ratio of CPU/RAM on the SAP HANA server. Consequently, there are special hardware setups available for SAP Business Suite on SAP HANA that come with higher memory and storage configurations compared to the general-purpose hardware systems. You can find these hardware configurations in the SAP Product Availability Matrix (at *https://service.sap.com/pam/*) for systems based on the Westmere CPU family and on SCN ("SAP Certified Appliance Hardware for SAP HANA" at *https://scn.sap.com/docs/DOC-52522*) for systems based on the more recent Ivy Bridge CPU family.

SAP considers memory sizing sufficient for most SAP Business Suite use cases, with the exception of above-average usage of SAP HANA Enterprise Search (see SAP Note 1793345).

Sizing for Generic SAP HANA Use Cases

If you are not planning an SAP BW or SAP Business Suite system, then we consider your project a generic SAP HANA use case for the purpose of system sizing. The sizing guidelines in this section apply to custom data marts as well as accelerator applications and other use cases which do not come with a dedicated set of sizing rules.

In the generic use case, the database memory will normally be the limiting factor for system sizing. Such systems will often contain copies of data from other SAP systems, replicated into SAP HANA by a selection of the available data provisioning technologies. For such setups, SAP offers a generic sizing report that may be executed in the source system(s) to determine the approximate memory footprint in SAP HANA of the data to be replicated.

This sizing report, as well as up-to-date information about generic compression factors of row store and column store data, can be obtained from SAP Note 1514966. This SAP Note also contains general rules for CPU sizing.

If the sizing report cannot be used, an approximate sizing can be performed using SAP QuickSizer at *https://service.sap.com/quicksizer*.

14.1.2 Hardware Choices

When preparing to acquire your SAP HANA system, you will need to make a few decisions to determine the boundary conditions of your hardware purchase. The two most important ones are about binary choices: scale-up versus single-node and full appliance versus Tailored Data Center Integration. We discuss each of these two choice briefly. A third important choice concerns the hardware vendor for your database system, and naturally we will be impartial in this aspect.

Single-Node versus Scale-Out Systems

The first choice related to SAP HANA hardware is the choice between single-node and scale-out hardware. As a simple rule of thumb, we recommend choosing a single-node system whenever possible in order to avoid the added complexity that is inherent to a clustered system. This complexity starts with the hardware setup itself, touches on aspects of system administration, and ends with the topic of data partitioning and distribution for optimal overall system performance.

Hence, if the outcome of your sizing procedure leads to systems that can be built from a single-node server or a scale-out system, the single-node server should be preferred. Single-node systems can contain up to 6 TB of RAM for SAP Business Suite on SAP HANA and up to 2 TB of RAM for all other use cases.

The question is not as simple if the sizing indicates that the initial system will fit into a single-node server, but estimated data growth puts the system beyond this hardware limit. In this situation, you have three basic choices:

▸ Start with scale-out hardware to avoid the necessity of a hardware change in the foreseeable future.

▸ Confirm with your hardware vendor whether you can scale-out from hardware initially purchased as a single-node system.

▸ Start with a single-node system, and monitor resource consumption carefully. Be prepared for a hardware exchange to move your database to a scale-out system at a later point in time.

You must also keep in mind that not all SAP applications offer unrestricted support for SAP HANA scale out. The best support is offered by the SAP BW system, which also actively assists with the questions of optimal data distribution and partitioning. There are by now quite a few customers who successfully and mostly painlessly operate SAP BW installations with scale-out SAP HANA systems.

If system sizing puts you safely into the realm of single-node systems, you still have a choice to make: Do you buy the smallest available system that is big enough for initial sizing plus projected data growth? Or do you buy a larger system to make room for added SAP HANA usage—for example, adding further applications, unexpected data growth, and so on?

The choice can be made easy if your hardware partner offers SAP HANA servers that can easily be scaled up by adding additional RAM, CPU, and disk resources without the need to exchange the entire hardware.

If your hardware partner does not offer such systems, you will have to balance the cost of larger hardware against the probability of needing to scale up before the hardware is written off. In many cases, it will be most cost-efficient to go with the larger hardware system, at least as far as the hardware is concerned. On the licensing side, SAP offers multiple licensing models by now, of which the traditional memory-based sizing may be affected by a larger server system (see SAP Note 1704499). In this case, you may be able to license less memory than is physically installed and force the system to use at most the licensed amount of main memory by setting the `global_allocation_limit` parameter accordingly. We gladly refer you to your SAP sales representative and leave this book free from any further discussions related to the licensing topic.

Full Appliance versus Tailored Data Center Integration

As we mentioned in Chapter 1, SAP has opened up the hardware requirements to support hardware for SAP HANA that is based on prevalidated standard SAP HANA appliances in which customers may replace selected components, such as the storage system and the network layer, with existing components from their data center.

To make it simple, Tailored Data Centers allow customers to balance hardware cost against skills; a full appliance will probably come with a higher price tag, but it will have all hardware and database software already installed.

The (in most cases) more important aspect relates to the name Tailored Data Center Integration; depending on your data center setup, a standard appliance might simply not fit—either with your rules for acquiring hardware or with the setup of responsibilities in the data center. In such cases, Tailored Data Center Integration will allow you to tune the SAP HANA systems in a way that they can meet your requirements.

14.2   Planning the System Landscape

A typical SAP system landscape consists of at least three and often four or even more tiers. A four-tier landscape with development, test, quality assurance (QA), and production system, as depicted in Figure 14.2, can be regarded as a best-practice setup for typical requirements. In that figure, each tier of the focused system landscape <1> consists of an application server (which might be an SAP NetWeaver server, an SAP BusinessObjects BI server, or something similar) that interacts with an SAP HANA database system. There will usually be transports of content between neighboring system tiers. Depending on the use case, there may be application server content to be transported, SAP HANA content, or both.

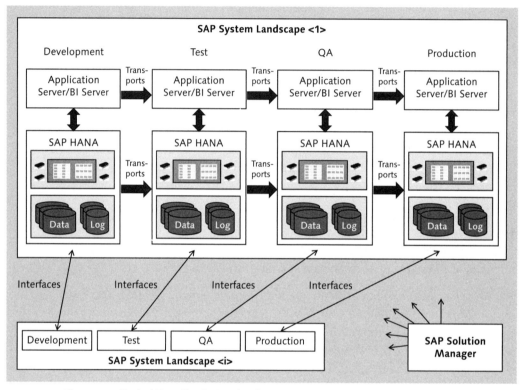

Figure 14.2 Typical Four-Tier System Landscape

One will hardly ever find an isolated system landscape. In most cases, multiple system landscapes will exist (e.g., an ERP landscape, an SAP BW landscape, a CRM landscape, and more), and there will be interfaces between these landscapes. In most cases, there will be one SAP Solution Manager system for certain administration aspects of the systems in all landscapes. In the following, however, we will ignore such external interfaces of a system landscape.

Even if we simply focus on one system landscape, we have a wide variety of topics to consider: deployment options and sizing for the SAP HANA systems in the different tiers of the landscape, deployment options for the applications in the different tiers, business continuity requirements in the different tiers, and also content transports.

14.2.1 Choosing SAP HANA Deployment Options

When planning the SAP HANA deployment, you have a multitude of options to choose from. You can install standard appliance hardware or go for Tailored Data Center Integration; you can install single-node or scale-out systems; you can install multiple database systems on a single physical server; you may operate the database on virtualized or physical hardware. And you can in principle choose differently on each tier of your system landscape. In the following subsections, we will help you sort out the majority of options.

Standard Appliance or Tailored Data Center Integration

As explained in Section 14.1.2, there are good reasons for choosing either a standard appliance or Tailored Data Center Integration. Whatever your choice is, it will very probably be the same for all tiers of a given system landscape. In any case, a reasonable QA system must have hardware that is comparable to that of the production system, and thus these two tiers should be based on the same type of hardware.

Single-Node or Scale-Out Server

For the production tier, you will in most cases not have a choice; your system sizing will determine whether the database can be a single-node server or has to be a scale-out cluster. Even if you plan your QA system smaller than the production one, we urgently recommend that both tiers be based on the same type of hardware—that is, they should both be either single-node or scale-out systems.

Multiple Databases on One Server

Again, this topic is rather easy to sort out. At the time of writing (July 2014), SAP does not support under any circumstances operating more than one database instance on a physical server that is host to a production instance. This limitation is also valid in the scenario of operating SAP HANA productively in virtualized environments on VMware vSphere 5.5.

On hardware that is not being used in production, you can set up as many database systems as you like, provided that the hardware is sized appropriately for the resource utilization of all instances combined.

For more details on virtualization choices and multiple databases, see the discussion in Chapter 1; the installation of multiple database instances on one server was covered in Chapter 3.

In a typical system landscape, you may consider placing all nonproduction systems except for the QA system on a single hardware server, as indicated in Figure 14.3. In that figure, the first nonproduction SAP HANA server, shown in ❶, hosts the development and test database instance, as well as other optionally existing systems, such as sandbox systems.

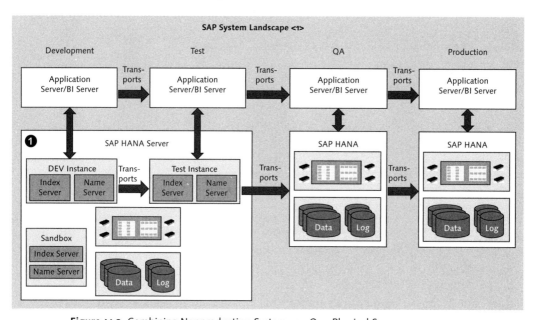

Figure 14.3 Combining Nonproduction Systems on One Physical Server

You may consider operating the QA system on the same hardware as other nonproduction systems. Whether or not this is acceptable will mainly depend on the existing practice in your data centers and the purpose of the QA system. If it is used for performance tests, load tests, or other tasks that aim at verifying production readiness of developments or other changes, it is best to operate the QA system on dedicated hardware in order to avoid negative impact through other non-production systems.

It should be noted that it is also possible to install multiple databases with different numbers of nodes on scale-out hardware. If you have a nonproduction multinode system that has free memory and CPU resources, then you can add single-node database systems on the different hosts of the scale-out hardware.

Physical or Virtualized Hardware

In May 2014, SAP announced support for production SAP HANA systems on virtualized hardware using VMware vSphere 5.5. With this announcement, two previous limitations were lifted, namely the exclusion of production systems and the missing support for features such as VMware VMotion.

With these changes, operating SAP HANA on virtualized hardware has become a very reasonable option in all tiers of your system landscape. You will of course pay a penalty in terms of performance, but you gain hardware abstraction, built-in availability features, and so on.

The main restriction of the present virtualization support is the limitation to single-node hardware with up to four CPU sockets, putting the memory maximum at 1 TB. If you need a larger system, virtualization is not yet an option. For the most up-to-date state of the offering, please refer to the virtualization roadmap published at *www.saphana.com/docs/DOC-3334*.

If there are no technical limitations in the way, the decision for or against virtualization will depend on your overall data center operation guidelines.

14.2.2 Application Deployment Options

SAP HANA hardware is not inexpensive, and each additional production system usually requires a number of dedicated preproduction servers, not to mention that any system comes with associated administration costs. It is therefore tempting to combine multiple applications (or use cases) on one database system instead of deploying individual database systems for each application.

Because operating multiple production database instances on one physical server is not supported, you can only run multiple production applications on one server if they all connect to the same database instance.

Multiple Applications in the Production Tier

As discussed in Chapter 1, SAP does not generally oppose the concurrent operation of multiple applications on the same production database system. The supported combinations of applications are, however, restricted by white lists that are maintained in SAP Note 1661202, SAP Note 1666670, and SAP Note 1826100.

These SAP Notes also mention possible drawbacks of this type of coexistence, for example, the fact that maintenance operations in the database—such as changes of the database configuration, system patching, or backup/recovery—will always affect all applications, even if the cause of the operation is related to one particular application. There is also no workload separation in the database for the different applications.

SAP is planning to increase the database functionality to better support multiple applications. For the time being, however, the existing limitations may represent a challenge in some data centers.

A typical case in which the limitations can be acceptable is an SAP NetWeaver-based primary application, for example, SAP BW or an SAP HANA accelerator, whose data set in SAP HANA is also used in a custom data mart. There are two main difficulties in this scenario that one has to pay attention to:

▶ **Security**
In typical SAP NetWeaver systems, there is seldom significant development happening in the database, and the security architecture relies on this characteristic. If you create an SAP HANA data mart on the database of the SAP NetWeaver system, you will introduce a good measure of database development, and you will have to make sure that this does not jeopardize the security setup of the primary application.

This means that you will have to exercise control over the development activities in those system tiers in which development is permitted and that you will have to implement content transports also for SAP HANA contents in such a way that you can operate the production system as read only.

▶ **Workload management**
SAP HANA data marts are usually created with the goal of allowing more agile report development and empowering the end users by giving them maximum flexibility. Both criteria will lead to comparatively little control over the work-

load generated by the end users of the data mart. In the absence of prioritization or separation of workload, there is a danger that the data mart may negatively impact the primary application.

The measures to take against this possibility are exercising control over the design of data models and reports to ensure they follow best practices; testing, testing, and testing before moving new data models and reports to production; and carefully monitoring the system workload, especially in times of high system load.

There is little risk in operating multiple SAP HANA accelerators (CO-PA accelerator, FI-CO accelerator, Customer Segmentation accelerator, etc.) on the same database system. All of these make use of the SAP HANA database in a similar way and without the need for database development, thus eliminating most security risks mentioned previously. They are usually not highly critical, because SAP HANA will only hold a redundant copy of the application data, and the applications remain operational even if the accelerator solution should fail.

In general, you should consider the criticality of the applications to coexist on SAP HANA. If one of them is highly critical, you must carefully evaluate whether any of the other applications may impact its security, stability, or availability. You may also include provisions for shutting down a less critical application if there are indications that it endangers other applications on the same database server.

Multiple Applications in Nonproduction Tiers

Even if you decide to operate applications on different individual production servers, you can cut costs by running the nonproduction instances of these applications on the same server. Without any doubt, the best option to run such a scenario is to operate multiple database systems on the nonproduction server, each database system supporting one application (and one landscape tier). We indicate such a possible system landscape in Figure 14.4.

In that figure, there are two applications, A and B, each of which operate on top of dedicated SAP HANA servers in the production and QA system tiers.

In the development and test tiers, however, there is only one SAP HANA server, shown in ❶, on which four database instances are installed: one database instance each for the development and test systems of applications A and B.

You may, of course, also operate a joint database server for the QA systems of both applications.

An option that should not be overlooked is the possibility of operating SAP HANA and SAP NetWeaver Application Server ABAP on the same server, as outlined in SAP Note 1953429.

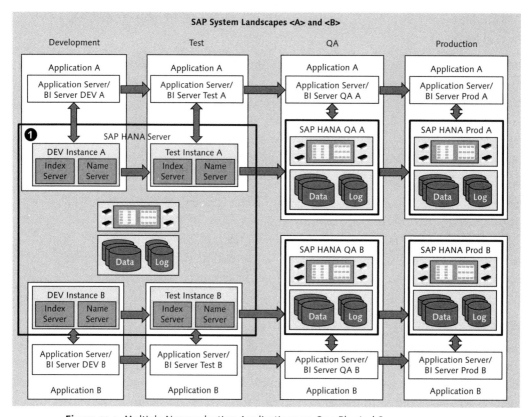

Figure 14.4 Multiple Nonproduction Applications on One Physical Server

14.2.3 Preparing for Business Continuity Requirements

The service level agreements for your data center operations will probably contain specifications with respect to business continuity. These requirements will be another influential factor in the design of your system landscape. The SAP HANA software comes with several built-in methods to increase system availability. We summarize these options in Table 14.3. The discussions in the following sections will help you choose the options needed for your situation.

Option	Protects Against	Recovery Point Objective (RPO)	Recovery Time Objective (RTO)
Process autorestart	System staying unavailable after individual process stops/crashes	Zero	Close to zero (technical downtime), up to tens of minutes (business downtime)
Host auto-failover	Downtime because of individual host failure in scale-out systems	Zero	Close to zero (technical downtime), tens of minutes (business downtime)
Standby setup with backup shipment	System outage, loss of data	Few hours	Up to about one hour (time to recover database)
Storage replication	System outage, loss of data, unscheduled downtimes	Zero (synchronous), few seconds (asynchronous)	Close to zero (technical downtime), tens of minutes (business downtime)
System replication	System outage, loss of data, scheduled and unscheduled downtimes	Zero (synchronous), few seconds (asynchronous)	Close to zero (technical and business downtime)

Table 14.3 (High) Availability Options for SAP HANA Systems

Process Autorestart

The first entry from this table, process autorestart, is a standard feature that exists in every SAP HANA system and therefore does not need to be given much thought when you plan your system. It describes the behavior of SAP HANA if one of the core database processes should fail. Such processes will be immediately and automatically restarted by the daemon process (see Chapter 1).

Host Autofailover

Host autofailover is a solution local to one data center. If you are operating a scale-out system, this mechanism lowers the likelihood of a total system outage by adding redundant hardware to the system in the form of one or multiple standby hosts, as discussed in Chapter 6.

Because the administration overhead of operating standby hosts is negligible and there is comparatively little added hardware cost, we cannot think of a reason to not implement standby hosts in a scale-out cluster. Or, to avoid the double negative, you definitely should include at least one standby host in a planned scale-out system.

Technically, it is possible to use the autofailover mechanism to establish a full failover mechanism for a single-node system. You should, however, always consider the alternative approach of setting up system replication between the primary host and the failover host.

Database Backups

Database backups are the most common form of protecting against loss of data. If you have this requirement, database backups should be part of your data protection strategy.

As we discussed in Chapter 5, SAP HANA offers two different ways of creating a copy of the database contents for the purpose of database recovery. Storage snapshots are quick but contain no provisions for checking the internal consistency of the snapshot with database kernel knowledge. Database backups do contain such consistency information, but are generally slower to create.

Any backup strategy should therefore incorporate regular database backups, preferably scheduled and managed by a dedicated tool (see the discussion related to the BackInt for SAP HANA interface in Chapter 5).

You may also create storage snapshots, for example, in a mixed scenario with frequent storage snapshots and less frequent database backups.

The optimal interval between two data backups will vary from customer to customer, influenced not only by generic rules in a given data center but also by recovery performance benchmarks. The time to recover from a data backup of a given age will be strongly impacted by the amount of log entries that need to be replayed for the recovery.

Acknowledging that recovery performance cannot easily be predicted, a good option is to start with a reasonable initial interval, and verify that it is adequate by running test recoveries under realistic circumstances (using data and log backups for a system copy on identical or at least comparable hardware).

> **Note**
>
> Do not forget to include backup storage in your system planning. The appliance hardware definitions do not cover dedicated storage technology.

If you need to safeguard against system outages that might, for example, be caused by incidents disabling an entire data center ("disasters") and if a recovery point objective (RPO) of a few hours is acceptable, then you may consider setting up a standby database server in a remote location and regularly ship database backups to this standby server.

The potential data loss in such a scenario is determined by the time it takes to write and transfer the database backup. You may reduce the maximum RPO by working with database snapshots at the cost of consistency checks in the backup files.

By also replicating log backups to the secondary setup as quickly as possible, you can reduce the RPO time even further, down to approximately the maximum log backup interval as specified in parameter `log_backup_timeout_s`.

Your SAP HANA hardware partner can advise you on suitable hardware setups that can be used to efficiently transfer backup files from the primary to the secondary system. Such provisions are not part of standard SAP HANA appliance definitions.

Because the hardware of the standby system is (mostly) identical to that of the primary system, the standby system can be used for nonproduction purposes-typically as a QA system—during regular operation.

Disaster Recovery with Storage Replication

If a recovery point objective that must be measured in hours rather than seconds is not acceptable, then you need to look for solutions that can replicate data as it is committed in the database. Synchronous replication will help you achieve an RPO of zero in most cases, but it only works for distances between primary and secondary systems of up to about 100 km. Asynchronous replication methods can not inherently achieve an RPO of zero, but they will work for larger distances between data centers.

Storage replication is the hardware-based method for replicating the data and log volumes of an SAP HANA system. Most hardware partners offer systems for synchronous replication, and the first asynchronous setups have recently been validated, too.

In most of these solutions, it is possible to operate nonproduction database instances on the standby site provided that there are dedicated storages available for data and log volumes of these additional systems.

Although storage replication can lead to an RPO of zero for most cases that would lead to a loss of data, the business downtime in a failover situation will be significant. The reason is that the secondary system is always on cold standby and has to perform a regular database start as part of the failover procedure. If you define the business downtime to include the time for loading the most important data sets into main memory, then this downtime can easily reach tens of minutes.

Disaster Recovery with System Replication

The most flexible disaster-recovery solution for SAP HANA is system replication (see Chapter 5). Not only does it offer synchronous and asynchronous replication independently from your choice of hardware partner, but you also have the option to operate the secondary system in warm standby mode, thus minimizing the need to load tables into the memory of the secondary system during a failover period.

With system replication, SAP also introduced near-zero downtime upgrades (provided that table preload on the secondary system is enabled) and similarly near-zero downtime hardware exchange.

If your SLAs require minimal downtimes in a situation necessitating a failover, then you need to keep column preload enabled on the secondary site and cannot use the standby setup for hosting nonproduction systems.

If, on the other hand, you can afford to switch off column preload, then you can install additional nonproduction instances on the secondary site. A typical choice would be a QA system, because primary and secondary servers of the replication cluster will consist of identical hardware. Such a landscape might look like the one depicted in Figure 14.5, in which two SAP HANA systems in different data centers are connected in one disaster-recovery cluster, as shown in ❶.

We have only sketched a cohabitation of QA and production system on the database server in Site B. Such a setup will make it necessary to fail back the production system to Site A as soon as that hardware becomes available again in order to continue operating the QA system. It is therefore recommendable to make plans for operating the nonproduction instances on either site of the DR cluster. You can then either set up system replication also for the QA system or prepare recovery of the QA system after a failover situation via database backups.

Even when you are operating a DR cluster, you must continue creating regular database backups to protect the system against failures that the DR method may not cover (e.g., misbehavior of the replication mechanism).

To keep the picture simple, Figure 14.5 only shows the DR setup of the database server. Naturally, the design of the application servers and other vital setup components must provide a comparable level of availability.

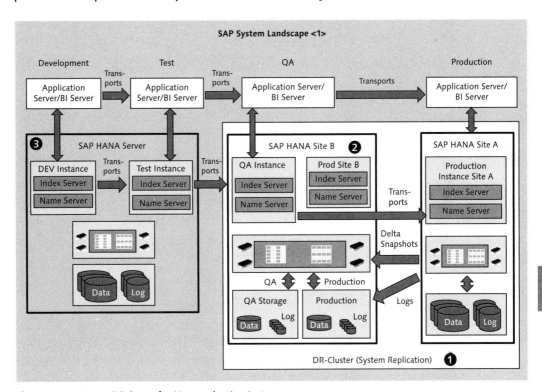

Figure 14.5 Using a DR Setup for Nonproduction Instances

14.2.4 Content Transport

Multitier system landscapes serve the purpose of separating the system used in production from development and testing. This separation requires that there are means for transporting modifications through the system landscape. Development can happen in different layers of the system architecture: There may be development on the application server side or on the database side. In the case of SAP HANA, the database side includes classical database development, such as database object definitions, data models, or stored procedures, but it also comprises application development, such as applications using SAP HANA XS and SAPUI5. Generally, all repository objects can be transported in SAP HANA (see Chapter 11).

For application development on top of SAP HANA, there can be different transport solutions depending on the application technology being used. In the SAP world, the transport mechanism will usually be either the classical Change and Transport System (CTS) for ABAP developments or the Extended Change and Transport System (CTS+) for other supported technologies, such as the SAP NetWeaver Java stack or the SAP BusinessObjects BI Platform.

For SAP HANA content transports, there are three solutions available. All of these are technically based on the export and import of delivery units. Each of these solutions has its own justification depending on the SAP HANA use case and your existing infrastructure:

▶ **SAP HANA Transport Container**
The SAP HANA Transport Container (HTC) is a collection of SAP HANA development content that can be embedded as a binary object into a classical ABAP transport request. This scenario is useful for transport of SAP HANA content that is only used in the context of an ABAP application. In this case, it makes sense to transport related SAP HANA and ABAP developments within the same transport request.

For more information on using HTC, see "How to Transport ABAP for SAP HANA Applications with HTC" at *https://scn.sap.com/docs/DOC-43035*.

▶ **Extended Change and Transport System**
The Extended Change and Transport System (CTS+) system offers transport of SAP HANA delivery units. This is the transport method of choice if you have SAP HANA developments such as data models or SAP HANA XS applications and if you already use CTS+ for other non-ABAP transports. In this case, you can easily include your SAP HANA database in your transport setup. Using

CTS+ is particularly recommended if your SAP HANA developments and other non-ABAP developments need to be transported synchronously.

For more information on using CTS+ with SAP HANA, see "Resources on CTS+" at *https://scn.sap.com/docs/DOC-8576#HANA*.

▶ **SAP HANA Application Lifecycle Manager**
If you do not use CTS+ yet, SAP HANA offers a built-in transport system named SAP HANA Application Lifecycle Manager (HALM). This system is based on an XS application that is part of the SAP HANA database server since SPS 6. Setting up HALM for content transports between your SAP HANA systems is a simple procedure and makes the most sense if you have no need to synchronize these transports with other non-SAP HANA developments.

The HALM tool is described in the SAP HANA Developer Guide, available at *https://help.sap.com/hana_platform/*.

As alternative to the CTS integration with the SAP HANA Transport Container, you may consider generating SAP HANA content programmatically within your ABAP applications and thus transporting the SAP HANA content implicitly with the transport of the generating ABAP code. This is in fact a technique used by SAP BW 7.40 (SP 5 or higher) to generate views in the SAP HANA repository that correspond to the SAP BW InfoProviders, as described in "SAP First Guidance—SAP NetWeaver BW 7.40 on HANA View Generation" at *https://scn.sap.com/docs/DOC-52790*.

Although technically possible, this method has the drawback that there exists no documented programmable API of the SAP HANA repository. The method is, however, very relevant if you intend to directly generate objects in the database catalog, such as tables, SQL views, or catalog roles.

14.3   Bootstrapping the System

Once your database hardware is delivered to your data center and the database software is installed, you can start taking possession of the system. There is a multitude of actions that you can and should execute now to make the system ready for regular usage. These actions include setting up administration user accounts, installing a license key, basic system configuration, initializing the backup system, and more.

There is no natural order in which to perform these steps. The bootstrapping process that we propose in this section is guided by the following principles:

▶ Set up administration accounts as quickly as possible.

▶ Minimize the number of actions to be performed by the SYSTEM user.

▶ Deactivate the SYSTEM user as soon as possible.

▶ Prioritize steps that lead to higher system security.

Even within these principles, the ordering of many steps is somewhat arbitrary, and the sequence can be changed without jeopardizing the overall procedure.

In our bootstrapping proposal, we assume that the SAP HANA system will be used in a way that demands database-side user management—for example, a data mart project or something similar, with named developers and end users in the database. If your project foresees a simpler usage of the database system, then there may be several steps that can be skipped. We do not include steps that are specific to an application, such as setting up the data-provisioning procedure.

> **Note**
>
> In an initially installed SAP HANA system, the log area will fill up gradually because the log mode is set to Normal, but the automatic log backup cannot yet be enabled. You should complete all steps in Section 14.3.2 and Section 14.3.3 quickly to avoid disk-full situations. At the end of these sections, you will have set up a functioning backup system, including log backups.

Our bootstrapping sequence contains the full procedure for one system. Many parts of the sequence must be performed on all tiers of the system landscape. The role development is an exception; because we create roles in the SAP HANA repository they are transportable, and you may choose to transport the roles into the other system tiers at the beginning of system setup there (see Section 14.3.9).

14.3.1 Preparing the Operating System

Of course, your operating system configuration should have been optimized for SAP HANA before the database software was installed. There are, however, a number of provisions that you should now take before you start working with your shiny new database system.

Create a Storage Copy of the Database System

Especially if your database system was shipped as a standard appliance, with the database software preinstalled by your hardware partner, we recommend that before you do anything else you create a storage copy of the entire database server—at least of the directories or mount points */hana/shared*, */hana/data*, and */hana/log* (assuming standard file system configuration), but preferably the entire file system. If you for any reason destroy the database software installation during the setup phase, you can restore the system from these copies without needing to perform a database installation.

The main reason for this recommendation is that SAP only supports database installations that have been performed by certified personnel—and if you purchased preinstalled appliances, it is unlikely that you have such people in your project team.

Set Up Support Connections for SAP Support

One of the trademark capabilities of SAP systems when it comes to supportability is the enablement of SAP Support personnel to log on to customer systems via secure, dedicated support connections. If your security policies allow you to open your systems for SAP Support, you should implement the following support connections on your SAP HANA systems (for a full list of support connections that can be meaningful in the context of SAP HANA systems, see the central SAP Note 1635304 for SAP HANA support connections):

▶ **SAP HANA Studio connection**
  Similar to the well-known R/3 support connection, the SAP HANA Studio connection allows SAP Support staff to access your SAP HANA database system from their locally installed SAP HANA Studio through the SAProuter systems. All steps to set up these support connections are described in SAP Note 1592925.

  For any given support incident, you will also have to define an appropriate support user. If you experience problems in an early stage of the setup procedure, you may only have the SYSTEM user available. In Section 14.3.7, we include some considerations for setting up support users.

▶ **Operating system connection**
  If (and only if) the SAP HANA Studio support connection is not sufficient for the support case or is not available, then you may have to open a connection to

the operating system of your SAP HANA database server. The recommended connection type is the so-called TREX/BWA/HANA support connection, as described in SAP Note 1058533.

Alternatively, SAP has standard support connections for SSH or VNC access to backend servers, as described in SAP Note 1275351 and SAP Note 1327257.

▶ **WTS connection**
In the case that you cannot set up the SAP HANA Studio connection or one of the mentioned OS connections, you may still be able to open a connection to a WTS server in your network from which support staff can connect to the SAP HANA server using SAP HANA Studio or SSH. WTS connections are also often needed for supporting SAP BusinessObjects BI tools or SAP Data Services. The connection is described in SAP Note 605795.

Note that SAP Support staff can only use connections as long as they are open. In addition, when opening a connection the credentials for an appropriate user must be given.

You should generally only keep your system connections open as long as they are needed. It is, however, a good idea to set up the connections so that they can quickly be opened before the first support incident.

14.3.2 Preparing the System for Role and User Management

Before we do anything else, we want to get you ready for working with dedicated administration users so that you do not get used to comfortably working along with the overprivileged SYSTEM user.

To this end, there are three major steps to be taken. You may have to prepare for secure user logon by making provisions for SSO login mechanisms and encrypted client connections; you can then set up the environment, roles, and users for role development; and finally, you can define roles and create users for user administration.

Prepare SSO Mechanisms and Client Connection Encryption

If you intend to make use of SSO mechanisms, such as Kerberos authentication (see Chapter 12), why not introduce this technique right from the start? You can implement all setup steps for Kerberos authentication without logging on to the SAP HANA database system. Only when it comes to testing will you need to set up the first user account in SAP HANA. Guidance on setting up Kerberos authentication for SAP HANA is given in the attachment to SAP Note 1837331 and similarly for SAML authentication in SAP Note 1900023.

You may also want to encrypt client connections into the database. See our discussion in Chapter 12, and find the necessary setup steps for encrypting SQL connections to SAP HANA in the *SAP HANA Security Guide* or for encrypting HTTP connections to SAP HANA XS in the *SAP HANA Administration Guide*. Both guides are available at *https://help.sap.com/hana_platform/*.

Set Up Role Development

Role development is a complex matter, as discussed in Chapter 13. In our eyes, there are two reasonable ways of managing roles in SAP HANA: You either have an identity-management (IDM) solution that supports SAP HANA—in this case, you have to set up role development in a way that is compatible with the IDM tool—or you natively develop roles in SAP HANA, in which case the concept of repository roles or design-time roles is most appropriate. In the following discussion, we assume that you will need to design and manage roles with the tools provided by the database system itself. Following our own recommendation, we will only consider repository roles.

> **Note**
>
> SAP does *not* include standard roles for tasks related to administration of the SAP HANA database. While working on the manuscript for this book, we defined a template collection for such standard roles. The documentation of these roles would not have fit into the scope of the book, but we published it in "How to Define Standard Roles for SAP HANA Systems" at *https://scn.sap.com/docs/DOC-53974*. In this chapter, we will frequently refer to this guide, especially when it comes to role definitions.

You may decide to use the roles that are provided alongside the how-to guide. In this case, you may implement the prerequisites mentioned in the guide and import the roles with the SYSTEM user. This procedure will define fully usable roles for role development, user administration, and typical system administration, including security aspects, such as auditing, disk encryption, and so on

In the following discussion, however, we will assume that you create roles step-by-step, mainly for the purpose of showing the relationship between setup steps and privileges or roles.

To fulfill a typical requirement for segregation of duties, role developers must not be able to modify roles granted to them. Combined with the privileges needed for building roles in the repository, it follows that we need to take care when designing the repository structure for role development. The database users who develop roles need certain privileges to do so. These privileges should be collected in a repository role, which naturally is located in some repository package <p1>. All other user roles (roles for administrators, developers, application users, etc.) will be created and maintained by these role developers. They will need a repository package <p2> as working space, and in this package they will have all privileges to create, edit, activate, and delete roles. If <p1> and <p2> refer to the same package, or if <p1> is a subpackage of <p2>, then our role developers will be able to modify and activate their own roles—thus changing their own privileges and violating one of the most basic security rules.

In order to avoid such a violation of security principles, we propose a repository structure for role development as depicted in Figure 14.6. For this proposal, we assume that all roles to be granted to named database users will be maintained in one dedicated part of the repository. In our example, this is the space <base_package>/security—where <base_package> can be an arbitrary location in the repository provided that no regular database user or developer has full privileges on <base_package> (remember that if you have a privilege on a package, you have that same privilege on all subpackages). A typical and recommended choice would be for customers to use their company name as <base_package>.

Within the security package, we have to separate the roles for role developers from the roles created by role developers. In our example, there is a protected package, shown in ❶, that contains the roles for role developers and a common package, shown in ❷, that is the working space of the role developers.

You may have other security-related objects to place into the same repository structure; therefore, we also suggest a roles subpackage in both the protected and common package. Especially in the common/roles package, you may want to create a substructure that reflects the functional areas of the roles.

Now, we can easily describe the actions to be performed with the SYSTEM user in order to set up role development:

1. Create the necessary repository packages up to <base_backage>/security/protected/ (do not create the roles package yet) and <base_package>/security/common/roles (here we do create the roles package).

2. Role development in SAP HANA Studio requires a development project. Set up a project for development with the SYSTEM user, using the package `<base_package>/security/protected` as the development package.

3. Within the development project, create a new package named `roles`.

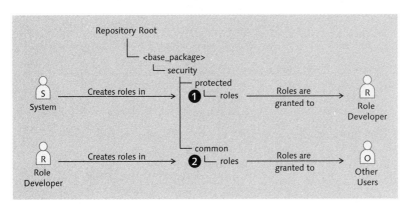

Figure 14.6 Proposed Repository Structure for Role Development

4. Within this new package, create a role that allows role developers to create and activate roles in the package `<base_package>/security/common/roles`. The privileges needed are listed in Table 14.4. In the how-to guide, the corresponding role is named `role_builder_native`.

5. Now, you can create the database users for role development and grant the role to these users. From here onwards, all role development will be done by these database users.

6. Finally, in the how-to guide we suggest the creation of a set of stored procedures related to security management, for example, for granting of repository roles in a way that is restricted to the role development package or for granting and revoking the special catalog role `SAP_INTERNAL_HANA_SUPPORT`. If you want to make use of such procedures, you should now create them within your "protected" development project.

Privilege	What does it do?
EXECUTE on REPOSITORY_REST	General access to the repository
REPO.READ on package <base_package/ security/common/roles	Read content of roles or other objects in the given package

Table 14.4 Privileges for Role Editors

Privilege	What does it do?
REPO.EDIT_NATIVE_OBJECTS on package <base_package/security/common/roles	Create and modify objects in the given package
REPO.ACTIVATE_NATIVE_OBJECTS on package <base_package/security/common/roles	Activate roles and other objects in the package
REPO.MAINTAIN_NATIVE_PACKAGES on package <base_package/security/common/roles	Create, edit, or delete subpackages of the given package

Table 14.4 Privileges for Role Editors (Cont.)

Set Up User Management

Now that we have functioning role editors in place, we can easily set up user administrators:

1. The role developers must create a development project using the package <base_package>/security/common/roles.

2. The first role that the role developers should create is a role for user management. This role may be built along the example of the role user_admin or user_admin_unrestricted from the how-to guide.

3. As SYSTEM user, create the database user for at least one user administrator and grant the user administration role to this user.

Now, you have created all the infrastructure needed to build new roles, create new users, and grant the roles to the users. At this point, we can actually disable the SYSTEM user, because we can now create dedicated roles and users for all upcoming steps.

Deactivate the SYSTEM User

The SYSTEM user can be deactivated by any user administrator. It can be done either in the User Editor of SAP HANA Studio or by using the SQL command:

```
ALTER USER SYSTEM DEACTIVATE USER NOW
```

There may be exceptional situations in which you may have to reactivate the SYSTEM user, for example, if for whatever reason your one and only user administrator gets deactivated. If all user administrators including SYSTEM are locked, then there is an emergency procedure to enable the SYSTEM user and subsequently your user admins, described in "Reactivating the SYSTEM User When No

User with USER ADMIN is Available" at *https://scn.sap.com/community/hana-in-memory/blog/2014/04/28/reactivating-the-system-user-when-no-user-with-user-admin-is-available.*

14.3.3 Creating Database Administrators and Performing Initial Administration

Having deactivated the SYSTEM user, we must now create new users who can administer the database. The goal of the next few steps is to perform vital initial administration steps, such as installing a license key and setting up the backup system so that it works properly and so that the database can be recovered if needed.

Create Database Administrators

We will now define a general-purpose administrator who can fulfill typical tasks such as basic monitoring, changing the database configuration, managing database processes, and, if needed, managing database backups.

The role for this user can be built along the proposed `system_admin_generic` role of the how-to guide. Typically, you may also want to grant predefined roles that come installed with the SAP HANA database software and that are included in the proposed role `system_admin_predefined`.

Create database users for system administration and grant the administration role or roles.

Define the Global Allocation Limit

In case your production license does not cover the entire installed RAM of the SAP HANA database server or you are operating multiple databases on the same physical server, you should define the parameter [memorymanager] • `global_allocation_limit` in configuration file global.ini now to avoid out-of-memory situations or license violations. The unit of measurement for this parameter is megabytes.

> **Privilege Information**
>
> In order to change this parameter (or any other parameter in the configuration files), you need system privilege `INIFILE ADMIN`, which is contained in our proposed role `system_admin_generic`.

Even if you have defined the parameter in the course of system installation, now is a good time to revisit the parameter values.

Install the License Key

Any SAP HANA database system comes with a temporary license that is valid for 90 days. Within this period, you can use the database system without any restrictions. You should, however, install a permanent license as soon as possible.

There is a dialog in SAP HANA Studio that displays license information and also allows you to install or to delete license keys. You can open this dialog by right-clicking on the system entry in the SYSTEMS view and choosing PROPERTIES from the context menu (Figure 14.7, left-hand side, shown in ❶). Within the PROPERTIES dialog, shown in ❷, choose the LICENSE entry.

Privilege Information

To view license information or install new license keys, you need the system privilege LICENSE ADMIN, which is contained in our proposed role system_admin_generic.

If you have purchased an SAP HANA license, you can download the license keys for your production and nonproduction systems from SAP Service Marketplace. When requesting the key, you will need to enter the HARDWARE KEY, which is displayed as part of the license information.

Once a license key is successfully installed, it becomes active immediately, without the need for a system restart or any further configuration.

Process Configuration

Prior to SAP HANA SPS 7, adding or removing data-persistent processes would break the backup history, meaning that a new database backup needs to be done immediately after applying the configuration change. In order to avoid any such problems, we place this type of configuration change in front of the initialization of the backup system.

If you already know that you will configure a different set of running database processes than in a default SAP HANA installation, you should apply this change as early as possible. Such changes may include:

- Starting the script server (see SAP Note 1650957)
- Migrating the statistics service from a dedicated process into a name and index server (SAP Note 1917938)
- Scaling SAP HANA XS (see the *SAP HANA Database Administration Guide*)

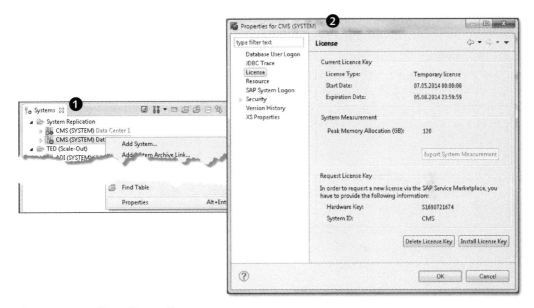

Figure 14.7 Installing a License Key

Initializing the Backup System

Data and log backups are written to the locations specified in file global.ini, in parameters [persistence]•basepath_databackup and [persistence]•basepath_logbackup, respectively. You should make sure that the locations defined in these parameters are the right ones; see our discussion in Chapter 5.

> **Note**
>
> If you are using a third-party backup tool implementing the BackInt interface, this is the right time to configure the tool and the database appropriately. The backup tool will probably need a database user with certain privileges as defined in the tool's documentation. You may therefore have to create a dedicated backup user with an accompanying role.

If the backup locations are correctly defined, then you can perform an initial database backup. The backup will even contain the license key you have installed, so you will not need to reinstall the license key in case a recovery becomes necessary.

The proposed role system_admin_generic contains the privileges required for running data backups so that any of the database administrators you have created in the previous step may execute the backup. Alternatively, we also propose a backup_admin role in the how-to guide, which you may create along with a corresponding database user.

Note

As soon as the data backup is finished, the automatic log backup will be enabled automatically. It is therefore important to verify that the location for log backups also is configured correctly.

Once the data backup is finished, you should verify that the system configuration is set up correctly for automatic log backups (parameter [persistence] • log_mode must be set to normal and [persistence] • enable_auto_log_backup to yes). If you do not intend to use log backups, you have to set log_mode to overwrite and enable_auto_log_backup to no.

14.3.4 Setting Up Initial Security

We have now performed the first necessary steps for ensuring stable system operation, and it is time to think about security aspects before we start bringing in the first nonadministration users. In this section, we will define database roles and users for security-related administration tasks and will configure security settings such as audit logging and disk encryption.

These tasks are technically not required. Whether or not you need to implement the steps in this section depends on the security requirement in your project.

Create Security Administrators

In our role concept, a security administrator is a person who can configure security-related database properties, such as password policies and so on, and can also troubleshoot (trace) security-related issues. The corresponding role in the how-to guide is named security_admin.

In this role, we do not include permissions to manage the audit system of the database. Instead, we foresee a dedicated role for that purpose, named `security_admin_audit`, so that you may have different personnel responsible for basic security configuration on the one hand and audit management on the other hand. A third role related to security administration is the `audit_operator` role, which allows for managing the database table that may serve as an audit target so that you can separate managing the audit configuration from managing the audit data.

Configure Password Policy and Password Blacklist

If name/password authorization is being used, then you should revise the password policy to make sure that it complies with your company requirements. You may also want to or need to maintain a password blacklist in SAP HANA. Both actions are enabled by our proposed role `security_admin`, and the corresponding database configuration is available from within the Security Editor of SAP HANA Studio. See also Chapter 12 for details.

Set Up Audit Logging

For many SAP system administrators, audit logging in the database never played a big role in the past. After all, there was only minimal interaction of natural persons with the database required, because classical SAP systems used the database for data persistence and nothing else. In an SAP HANA system, there is a higher probability by far of having named database users for developers and end users in the database system. In consequence, audit logging in the database will play a more pronounced role in SAP HANA than in other SAP systems.

If audit logging will play a role in your setup, now is a good time to enable it. See Chapter 12 for details.

Enable Disk Encryption

SAP HANA offers a functionality to encrypt data at rest, that is, the contents of the data files. Encryption of the memory contents is not currently foreseen, nor is encryption of the log segments or backup files. If backup encryption is required, the most realistic approach is to handle this encryption in a backup management tool—and this view is shared by SAP.

Data file encryption can be enabled, disabled, and monitored in the Security Editor of SAP HANA Studio, as shown in Figure 14.8. Alternatively, data files can be encrypted via SQL syntax, as given in Listing 14.1.

Privilege Information

System privilege RESOURCE ADMIN is required for managing disk encryption. In the how-to guide on standard roles for SAP HANA, this privilege is contained in the proposed roles user_admin_disk_encryption and system_admin_generic.

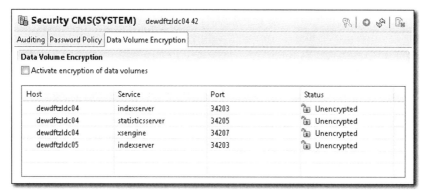

Figure 14.8 Managing Data Volume Encryption in SAP HANA Studio

Data volume encryption will not happen immediately. The system will start encrypting with the next savepoint operation. The actual encryption will take several minutes, obviously depending on the payload of the data volumes. The overall progress can be monitored in the Security Editor or in monitoring view M_PERSISTENCE_ENCRYPTION_STATUS.

```
-- Enable data volume encryption:
alter system persistence encryption on;
-- Moinitor data volume encryption:
select * from M_PERSISTENCE_ENCRYPTION_STATUS;
-- Force an immediate savepoint to decrease the wait time:
alter system savepoint;
-- Switch off data volume encryption:
alter system persistence encryption off;
```

Listing 14.1 SQL Syntax for Managing Disk Encryption

> **Note**
>
> Data volume encryption will only encrypt the current active payload of the data files. If the system has already been used for some time, there will usually be some amount of previously used but now free data pages in the data files. These pages may be overwritten in the future as the data content of the database grows. Initially, however, they will not be encrypted and thus will still contain unencrypted information.
>
> It is therefore recommended to enable disk encryption before starting to load business data into the system. If this is not possible, then you should consider enabling disk encryption, creating a data backup, and then recovering the database from the backup. This procedure will create a new, encrypted data volume without unencrypted pages.

14.3.5 Configuring the System

At this point, our system is prepared for stable and secure operation and we can begin preparing it for day-to-day administration and usage. We will start with the database configuration, such as preparing alerting and monitoring tasks, setting up backup scheduling, and more.

Set Up Alerting

Self-monitoring and proactive alerting are among the most important features for the database administrator, because they drastically decrease the effort of monitoring large system landscapes, allowing the administrators to focus on more demanding tasks. As explained in Chapter 4, the SAP HANA system offers the statistics service for self-monitoring and alerting. The only push mechanism supported by the statistics service is email-based alerting, which can be configured from the ALERTS tab of the Administration Editor in SAP HANA Studio.

If email alerting is not appropriate in your data center, the second SAP-supported way of receiving push notifications from SAP HANA systems is SAP Solution Manager. This tool can connect to SAP HANA systems and receive alerts, and it supports several industry standards, such as SNMP. If SAP Solution Manager also is not an option, you may be fortunate enough to find monitoring tools that either already support SAP HANA or that are easily extendable with some sort of customizing. All current alert information can be retrieved from system view `STATISTICS_CURRENT_ALERTS` in schema `_SYS_STATISTICS`.

Set Up Expensive Statement Trace

SAP HANA can trace information on expensive statements, that is, statements whose run time exceeds a configurable threshold. This tracing is disabled in the initial system configuration. See Chapter 15 for more details.

Set the Default Table Type to Columnar Tables

Because the SAP HANA database supports two fundamentally different table types—columnar and row store tables—it is not clear without ambiguity what kind of table will be created when you run a command like CREATE TABLE <table name> .... The ambiguity is lifted by the database parameter [sql] • default_table_type in configuration file global.ini. The default table type in the initial system configuration is row—so the aforementioned statement would create a row store table.

Because columnar tables are by far more appropriate for most use cases in SAP HANA, we recommend changing the default table type to column so that you will not accidentally create row store tables.

It is, however, good practice to explicitly define the table type in the CREATE TABLE statement. For full details of specifying table types in the create table statement, see the *SAP HANA SQL and System View Reference*, which is available at *https://help.sap.com/hana_platform/*.

Set Up Backup Scheduling

Before you start putting your system to regular use, you should set up backup scheduling with an appropriate frequency; see the discussion in Chapter 5. If you are using a dedicated backup tool that integrates with SAP HANA, the scheduling will be simple.

Because SAP HANA itself does not offer a scheduling service, you need to find other means of backup scheduling. One such way is using a program or script on the Linux operating system that triggers database backups using the hdbsql tool or the ODBC/JDBC database client. This program or script can, for example, be scheduled using the cron daemon of the Linux OS. A working example of such a solution is contained and documented in SAP Note 1651055. The script in this SAP Note also contains some rudimentary functionality for defining backup retention times, so that backups may be overwritten after a configurable number of days, and it provides functions for housekeeping on log backup files.

Start System Replication (If Applicable)

In case you are building a disaster-tolerant system using the system replication technology (see Chapter 5), you may wonder about the optimal point in time to enable continuous replication.

In principle, you can enable system replication right from the beginning. If, however, you are planning significant initial data loads into the SAP HANA system, then we recommend enabling system replication only after these initial data loads are finished. The reason is that with enabled replication you will ship all data twice or even three times to the secondary site: first the log entries, then the delta snapshot. If a given data set is shipped with a delta snapshot before the delta merge on the table has happened, the merged table will be shipped again with a later snapshot. The massive delta snapshot shipments can have an influence on the commit performance (in synchronous replication), thus slowing down the load process.

Because an initial data load can usually be repeated in the worst case, you will have to choose between performance optimization of the initial load and minimizing the impact on the source system of the data load. You do, however, also have data and log backups so that in most circumstances you can avoid having to reload data from the source system. As final justification for our recommendation, the main purpose of system replication—increasing the availability of the SAP HANA system—will normally not play a role at the time of the initial load.

Disable Password Lifetime for Technical Users

For *technical users*, such as the database user for the database connection of an SAP NetWeaver system or the SLT user in SAP HANA, you should disable the password lifetime. Otherwise, the passwords of these technical users will expire and need to be reset in regular interfaces. If you do not notice imminent password expirations of such technical users, you will face system downtimes that—depending on the application—can be accompanied with erratic behavior that may delay problem analysis.

You can disable the password lifetime of a database user either in the User Editor of SAP HANA Studio or by using the SQL syntax:

```
ALTER USER <name> DISABLE PASSWORD LIFETIME;
```

We encourage you to remember this task whenever you add technical users to the database system.

14.3.6 Setting Up the Development Platform

Up to this point, the steps covered in our bootstrapping sequence are not just recommended but in fact essential on any system, regardless of the system use case. If you intend to do any development in the repository of your SAP HANA system, the following additional steps will help you to set up the repository and other aspects of the development platform in a controlled way.

> **Note**
>
> Even if you do not plan any data modeling, XS application development, or other obvious database-side development, you may make use of the development platform in SAP HANA. The most probable case is role management with repository roles.

Set the Vendor Name in the System Configuration

The first step for setting up the development system may be surprising: You need to define the vendor property of our development system. This property will only be needed if you create delivery units later on—either for manual export or for content transports.

The vendor will most probably be your company name or something similar. You can set it in system parameter [repository] • content_vendor of the file indexserver.ini.

Set Up Database Users for Managing the Development Platform

As a next step, we must set up database users that can manage the development aspects of our SAP HANA systems. We suggest a number of administration roles around the development platform in the roles how-to guide. These roles are intended as starting points, and we expect that most customer teams will need to modify them to serve their particular requirements.

You may consider the following database users:

- **Repository manager**
  A user who can define the package structure of the repository and create delivery units. In the proposed role `repo_manager`, we also give read and activation rights to this user but no privilege to edit individual objects.

- **Repository export manager**
  A user who can manually export repository contents. Please see the security considerations in the how-to guide for the role `repo_exporter`.

- **Repository import manager**
  A user who can manually import repository contents. Again, please pay attention to the security considerations for the role `repo_importer`. We strongly suggest that you do not implement this role or grant the privileges within this role to users of security-critical systems.

- **HALM transport manager**
  If you choose to make use of SAP HANA's built-in content transport application named HALM, then you will need a database user who can set up the transport system. The proposed role `content_transport_manager` from the how-to guide describes a user who can perform this transport system configuration. Database users with this role will be needed on all systems that are the target of such transports (or, more precisely, in all SAP HANA systems on which transports are managed; in the default configuration, a transport between two systems is always managed from the target system).

- **HALM transport executor**
  Once the transport system is technically set up, you will need a database user with the privileges from the role `content_transport_executor` on the target system of the transport (and also on the system from which the transport is being managed, in case these two are not the same).

- **HALM transport source user**
  On the source system of a transport, there must be a database user who can provide the content export for the transport. The role for this user is named `content_transport_source` in the how-to guide.

In addition to these administration users, you will also need developers, testers, and other related users. The privileges to be granted to these users will strongly depend on the area of development and also on the database contents, schema layout, and more. Some information on typical development roles is given in the how-to guide.

Define and Create the Fundamental Package Structure

The package structure in the SAP HANA repository is more than just a tool for organizing development artifacts. It also defines the URLs (and thus names) of XS applications, the names of roles in the SAP HANA repository, and more.

It is also difficult (data modeling) or even almost impossible (most other development aspects) to modify the package structure underlying an existing development project without breaking all internal dependencies between objects in this development project.

We therefore encourage you to take some time to set up a package structure and define rules for application developers before creating the developer users. Based on the generic discussion in Chapter 11, we suggest that you create the following packages:

▶ **Public playground for all developers**
In order for developers to be able to test without having to first request a dedicated testing space, we suggest creating a structural subpackage named `public` within the system-delivered package `system-local`.

▶ **Package for developments that shall be promoted to production**
Any development that is supposed to be eventually transported to the production system tier should happen within a dedicated repository package. It is SAP's recommendation that each customer or vendor create their own package directly underneath the root of the SAP HANA repository. We will refer to this package as `<vendor>`.

SAP does not give further guidance regarding the repository structure. Based on security concerns, however, we make at least one recommendation: We assume that you will create security-relevant objects such as roles, privileges, or stored procedures related to security administration within the `<vendor>` package. If this is the case, you must make sure that security-related developments and other developments do not happen within the same branch of the repository tree. You might, for example, create a structure as follows:

  ▶ `<vendor>.security`: Any security-related development

  ▶ `<vendor>.applications`: Contains all XS applications to be developed

- `<vendor>.foundation`: General-purpose development artifacts that may be used across applications

- `<vendor>.vdm`: Contains virtual data models (that are not specific to just one application)

- **Private test packages for projects and individuals—on request**
  Whenever a project team or an individual requires a testing area with access restricted to only select database users, they should be able to request that such a package is created within the system-delivered package `system-local.private`.

An otherwise empty repository for a company named SAP-PRESS with our proposed repository layout is shown in Figure 14.9.

Enable SAP HANA Change Recording/Change Management

As we outlined in Chapter 11, it is now possible to set up content transports in such a way that not all objects modified since the last transport will be transported. This development mode is named SAP HANA CHANGE RECORDING (SPS 8) or SAP HANA CHANGE MANAGEMENT (SPS 7). If change recording is enabled, developers can assign objects to a change—and the change (containing one or multiple objects) can be released for transport after all contributions within the change have been explicitly approved by their respective responsible developers.

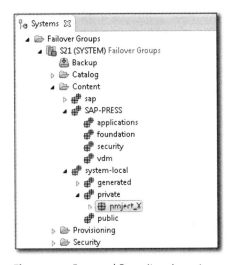

Figure 14.9 Proposed Repository Layout

Change recording affects all developments in a given SAP HANA system (with the exception of developments in the `system-local` package). It is not possible to have some projects use change recording and others not.

The choice for or against SAP HANA Change Recording therefore affects all users that work within the SAP HANA repository, including role developers. In our eyes, the feature clearly improves the manageability of the SAP HANA system, and we therefore recommend enabling it. To ensure that you have a consistent transport mechanism throughout the entire development project, it is best to decide for or against change recording before any serious development happens in your system.

You can enable change recording from within the SAP HANA Application Lifecycle Management (HALM) application, which can be accessed via the URL *http://<hostname>:<port>/hana/xs/lm/xs/* (where <hostname> is the name of a host running the XS server, and <port> is the XS engine's HTTP port, typically defined as 80<instance>, <instance> being the instance number of the SAP HANA system). You need to log on to the application with a database user that has the predelivered role `sap.hana.xs.lm.roles::administrator`. This role is contained in the `repo_manager` role proposed in the roles how-to guide.

Within the HALM application (Figure 14.10), the SETTINGS tab gives you the option to enable change recording/management.

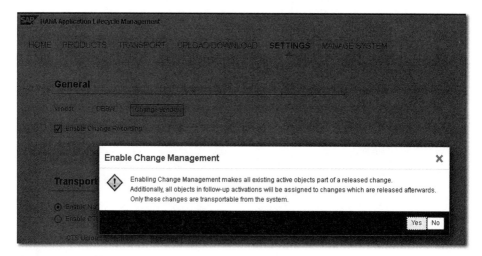

Figure 14.10 Enabling Change Recording

Set Up SAP HANA Content Transports

Finally, it is time to set up content transports for your SAP HANA system. We described the different transport options in Section 14.2.4 (and also in Section 11.5 of Chapter 11). Based on your scenario and existing infrastructure, you can choose the most appropriate transport mechanism and set it up.

14.3.7 Preparing for Support Cases

There will come a time when you need support from SAP for your SAP HANA system. You should already have set up your support connections. Now, it is time to prepare the creation of support users in the database. It is a best practice to create a new support user for each support incident and only grant the necessary privileges to each user.

Define Roles for Support Users

The exact layout of roles for support users depends on the SAP HANA use case to which an incident is related. In the roles how-to guide, we suggest several support users for general database support as well as for application support (related to SAP HANA-side development, such as data modeling).

Prepare for Granting of Special SAP Support Role

SAP HANA systems also come with a predefined role named `SAP_INTERNAL_HANA_SUPPORT`. This role combines multiple privileges that cannot be granted in any other way. The role is intended only for employees of SAP HANA development support and should only be granted if absolutely required. Because it contains rather powerful privileges, it can only be granted to a limited number of users at a time (up to SAP HANA SPS 7, only to one user; starting with SPS 8, the number of users is configurable in system parameter `[authorization]` • `internal_support_user_limit` of the file global.ini).

It is a catalog role; if you followed our recommendations, you will have no user in the system that can grant the role (granting the role would require the `ROLE ADMIN` privilege, which we recommend not to use; hence, the only user that might grant the role is the SYSTEM user, and it should be locked). In the roles how-to guide, we described stored procedures that you can create to grant and revoke the role. You should consider implementing such stored procedures to prepare for the granting and revoking of this special support role.

14.3.8 Final Steps

It is time to say "Congratulations!" You have now set up a manageable SAP HANA system. The last thing to do is to execute a database backup that will freeze the system state directly after this initial set up. Do not forget to also make backup copies of the configuration files for system-wide (*/hana/shared/<SID>/global/hdb/custom/config*) and host-specific configurations (*/hana/shared/<SID>/HDB<instance>/<hostname>*). Then, have a nice cup of coffee.

14.3.9 Propagating Roles from Development to Other Landscape Tiers

Didn't we say you were done? We are not taking this back. This final section simply contains advice on initially transporting your developed roles into the other landscape tiers. After all, many of the setup steps will require appropriate user privileges, so it will help to have all roles in all tiers of your system landscape.

There are two recommended ways to perform this initial transport. The first one is to set up the transport mechanism at this early step. You may create the necessary system users manually with the SYSTEM user. When using the SAP HANA Lifecycle Management (HALM) application, you will need to have a source user with the `sap.hana.xs.lm.roles::Transport` role in each system that is a source of a transport and an administration user with the `sap.hana.xs.lm.roles::Administrator` role in every system from which you manage transports (usually in all target systems). If you do not always manage transports locally in the target systems, you will also need a transport target user with the `sap.hana.xs.lm.roles::Transport` role in each target system. All of these roles come predelivered with your SAP HANA system.

Alternatively, you can manually assign the packages containing your developed roles to a delivery unit, and transport this delivery unit by means of export/import. See the roles `repo_exporter` and `repo_importer` of the roles how-to guide for the required privileges.

14.4 Summary

If your system landscape has been poorly planned, you will probably have a lot of trouble managing it. This is as true for SAP HANA setups as it is for any other type of IT system. We have therefore walked you through the process of getting started with SAP HANA from a technical point of view, beginning with system planning and finishing with the initial system setup.

Query performance is one of the most important aspects of most SAP HANA projects. To achieve the best possible performance, it's useful to know the tools that are at your disposal and how to employ them effectively.

15 Tools for Performance Analysis

A major question that any DBA needs to answer is "Is the system running okay?" Obviously, this question is very general and leaves a lot of room for interpretation. Nevertheless, SAP HANA provides a number of options that will help you answer this question. In this chapter, we look at some of the most important tools for analyzing system and query performance in SAP HANA.

Performance-related tasks for the DBA most often boil down to two activities:

▸ General monitoring of the system performance

▸ Analyzing and probably improving single-query performance

We'll discuss both of these, but, given the high degree of tool support for the monitoring part, we feel there is higher demand for better understanding single-query performance analysis. Therefore, we will put a strong emphasis on single-query performance in this chapter.

The chapter starts with discussions of the load diagram, the ALERTS tab, and the expensive statements trace—all useful tools for understanding the overall well-being of the system. We then dive into two functionalities for analyzing single-statement performance: the EXPLAIN PLAN and, most importantly, the PlanViz tool. We close the chapter with a brief collection of pointers to other important resources on SAP HANA performance.

15.1 Load Diagram

The load diagram (Figure 15.1) visible in SAP HANA STUDIO • ADMINISTRATION CONSOLE • PERFORMANCE • LOAD provides a graphical representation of some performance- and operation-related figures, such as CPU utilization, number of SQL statements/sec, number of blocked statements, and so on. The graph is based on the nameserver.trc file written by every local `nameserver` process. The file itself is written to in a circular manner, always overwriting the oldest records with the newest ones.

The amount of time covered by this trace file depends on the sampling rate, which can be changed if required (as shown in ❶) directly in the UI. The default sampling rate of one sample every 10 seconds should be sufficient for general monitoring. Higher sampling rates will lead to more data and thereby to a quicker overwriting of the old data. Therefore, we recommend cranking up the sampling rate only for specific, short-period monitoring actions.

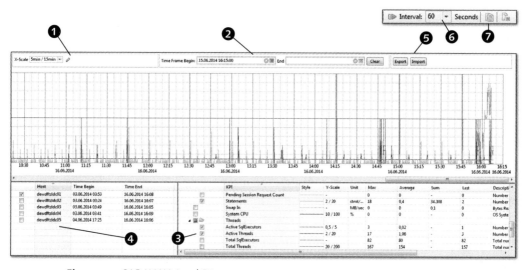

Figure 15.1 SAP HANA Load Diagram

As with all monitoring tools, setting the right scope of data to be looked at can make the difference between getting insight, drowning in data, and starving for information. The most effective option to reduce the amount of data displayed is to set the TIME FRAME borders (as shown in ❷). If the graph stays empty even though KPIs (shown in ❸) and hosts (shown in ❹) have been selected to be displayed, simply click on the X icons in the date-selector boxes to delete the selection. Concerning the actual selection of KPIs, it is important to be clear about what should be monitored. Otherwise, the graph easily becomes completely filled with incomprehensible lines. INDEXSERVER • CPU & MEMORY USED, INDEXSERVER •

THREADS • ACTIVE SQLEXECUTORS, and WAITING SQLEXECUTORS are good general starting selections.

Unfortunately, it is not possible to change the plot style or color for specific KPIs, so either look up the color encoding in the selection box or try to hover over a plotted data line. After a moment, a tool tip with the KPI name should appear.

Two often overlooked but very practical features for the load diagram are the autorefresh (shown in ❻) and the copy to clipboard (shown in ❼) functions. Autorefresh can turn the load diagram into a very simple permanent monitoring dashboard. The copy to clipboard function actually places a screenshot of the current graph into the clipboard. This is particularly useful when documenting certain system states, for example, the normal workload or a problematic situation.

> **Note**
>
> The load diagram typically is used to get an overview impression of the instance and not for detailed root-cause analysis.

A similar overview with a more modern graphic display is provided by the RESOURCE UTILIZATION view (Figure 15.2). Although it provides less functionality than the load diagram, the RESOURCE UTILIZATION display may be useful for a quick interactive analysis. The graphics response times are much better than the in the load diagram. This makes an exploratory way to work with it feasible.

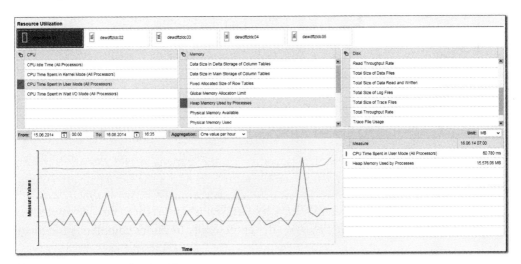

Figure 15.2 Resource Utilization View

15.2 Alerts Tab

One of the simplest tools to you as a DBA is the ALERTS tab, visible in SAP HANA Studio's Administration Console and ALERTS tab (Figure 15.3).

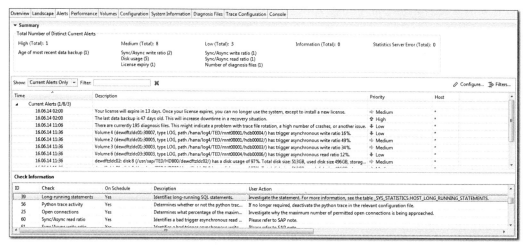

Figure 15.3 SAP HANA Studio Alerts Tab

Although alerts generally are not specifically targeted towards performance problems, alert types such as HOST CPU USAGE, LONG-RUNNING STATEMENTS, or LONG-RUNNING BLOCKING SITUATIONS can provide early pointers to issues that can slow the system down. The list of past and present alerts combined with the option to filter on alerts allows for a quick and easy check if certain alerts occurred only recently or have a standing history in the system. This certainly can be a good starting point for further investigations.

15.3 Expensive Statements Trace

The setup and the technical specifics of the expensive statements trace are described in Chapter 16. Here, we focus on how to use the trace data effectively.

A major use case for the expensive statements trace list is the identification of the top x expensive statements. The idea here is that those statements that take the most time to execute not only use most of the resources but also provide the most potential for improvement.

In order to yield such a top x list, it is necessary to set up the output list (Figure 15.4). First, the displayed columns should be reduced (shown in ❶) in order to speed up the display. The columns shown on the AVAILABLE COLUMNS side of the configuration dialog (shown in ❹) usually can be safely ignored. Next, the list should be filtered (shown in ❷) to *not* include SAP HANA system users, such as SYSTEM or the _SYS_* users. Finally, the resulting list should be sorted (as shown in ❸) by the DURATION_MICROSEC column from large to small values.

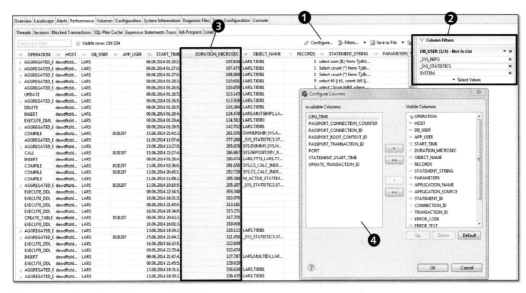

Figure 15.4 Expensive Statements List Setup

Once expensive statements have been identified, the single statement analysis can be started via the context menu navigation to the PlanViz for the selected SQL statement. (PlanViz is discussed in Section 15.5.)

> **Note**
>
> Again, for more information about the expensive statements trace, see Chapter 16.

15.4 EXPLAIN PLAN

The EXPLAIN PLAN was a particularly popular feature in legacy RDBMS systems, because it usually shows how the database will execute an SQL statement. The EXPLAIN PLAN is similar in SAP HANA, with some important differences.

First, unlike in other databases, the costs presented in the EXPLAIN PLAN do not represent an abstract time unit. Instead, it is an internal representation of expected computational effort.

The other important aspect is that SAP HANA only partly predetermines the execution path of a query during the parse and optimize phase. When using column views, like analytic views or calculation views, SAP HANA does an ad hoc optimization based on the actual query that accesses the column views. This includes a new cost evaluation based on the query restriction from the WHERE clause as well as removing unrequested columns from the whole execution chain (column pruning).

Because the EXPLAIN PLAN only has access to the result of the SQL parsing and optimization phase, any access to column views are more or less a dead end for analysis with the EXPLAIN PLAN.

In Figure 15.5, we see a formatted EXPLAIN PLAN for a query accessing a column view. Unfortunately, the original formatting of the EXPLAIN PLAN is not easy to read. The only effective way that we know to read it is to copy and paste the result for the EXPLAIN PLAN command to the clipboard via Ctrl + C, COPY ROWS. From there, it can be easily entered into a spreadsheet application, such as MS Excel. Make sure to format the columns to wrap text and to display the text at the top of the cells.

	A	B	C	D	E	F	G	H	
	OPERATOR_NAME	OPERATOR_DETAILS	EXECUTION_ENGINE	SCHEMA_NAME	TABLE_NAME	TABLE_TYPE	TABLE_SIZE	OUTPUT_SIZE	
11	COLUMN SEARCH	demo/SALES_COMP.SHOP_ID, SUM(demo/SALES_COMP.MARGIN2001), SUM(demo/SALES_COMP.MARGIN2002), SUM(demo/SALES_COMP.AMOUNT_SOLD2001), SUM(demo/SALES_COMP.AMOUNT_SOLD2002), SUM(demo/SALES_COMP.QUANTITY_SOLD2001), SUM(demo/SALES_COMP.QUANTITY_SOLD2002) (LATE MATERIALIZATION)	COLUMN	NULL	NULL	NULL	NULL	50.0	
13	ORDER BY	demo/SALES_COMP.SHOP_ID ASC	COLUMN	NULL	NULL	NULL	NULL	50.0	
	AGGREGATION	GROUPING: demo/SALES_COMP.SHOP_ID, AGGREGATION: SUM(demo/SALES_COMP.MARGIN2001), SUM(demo/SALES_COMP.MARGIN2002), SUM(demo/SALES_COMP.AMOUNT_SOLD2001), SUM(demo/SALES_COMP.AMOUNT_SOLD2002), SUM(demo/SALES_COMP.QUANTITY_SOLD2001), SUM(demo/SALES_COMP.QUANTITY_SOLD2002)	COLUMN	NULL	NULL	NULL	NULL	50.0	
15	COLUMN VIEW		COLUMN	_SYS_BIC	demo/SALES_COMP	CALCULATION VIEW	10000.0	10000.0	

Sheet1 / Sheet2 / Sheet3

Figure 15.5 EXPLAIN PLAN Displayed in MS Excel

Access to the column view _SYS_BIC.demo/SALES_COMP is the lowest level of information available in the EXPLAIN PLAN. Usually helpful figures like TABLE_SIZE/ OUTPUT_SIZE are set to some fixed fantasy value (10,000 rows) that does not have anything to do with what will be returned from the column view.

The takeaway for the EXPLAIN PLAN is that it does not provide crucial information about query processing once column views are involved. Because column views are a major tool for creating SAP HANA applications, this limitation is pretty severe.

Another downside of the EXPLAIN PLAN is that it always only shows the planned execution, not the actual execution. Therefore, it is not possible to find deviations of, for example, the expected from the actual record count numbers that have to be processed by every step of a query.

A useful feature of the EXPLAIN PLAN, however, is the EXECUTION_ENGINE column that indicates for each processing step, for statements that do not involve column views, in which engine it will be processed. As switching engines is particularly expensive, finding and avoiding those switches can be a performance-tuning opportunity.

15.5   PlanViz

The Plan Visualizer, or PlanViz, tool in SAP HANA is the primary tool to understand query runtime performance. The tool is based on two components:

▶ A server-side internal procedure that will execute the statement to be analyzed and that collects runtime information. The internal procedure produces an XML file containing all of the collected runtime information.

▶ A graphical UI that processes the XML data and creates different graphical representations of it.

This split design makes it possible, for example, to create PlanViz files in SAP NetWeaver and save them to disk, even if it is not possible to display the files in SAP NetWeaver directly. Most often, PlanViz is used from within SAP HANA Studio. Also, as the internal procedure is part of the database catalog, it is always updated to the latest capabilities of the SAP HANA engine it is running on. The UI part, on the other hand, is downward compatible and can display any file generated by the older revisions of SAP HANA.

The technical handling of the PlanViz tool is simple compared to the far more difficult capability of correctly interpreting the details it provides or applying this understanding to improvements of the information model or query design. For this reason, we decided *not* to walk you through the tool elements one by one but to design a real-life use case instead. We will show the use of the PlanViz tool and interpretations of the information it provides in the context of this example. We will then dedicate the second part of this section to coverage of the different join implementations in SAP HANA and how you can analyze them with the PlanViz tool.

15.5.1 PlanViz Example

To show you the functionality and recommended usage patterns for the PlanViz tool, we will walk you through a complete example analysis of query runtime.

We will first set the scene by introducing the data model on which our example is based, as well as the example query we will analyze. We will then show how you can use the different features of the PlanViz tool to retrieve and interpret detailed information on the actual query execution. Finally, we will derive potential improvements for the data model and implement and verify them. In the course of this discussion, we will touch on all elements and functionalities of the PlanViz tool that you will need for typical single-query analyses.

> **Note**
>
> Our example is based on a query against an SAP HANA information model; this has been the most common scenario for the use of PlanViz so far. The tool is, however, equally useful for the analysis of any SQL query against regular database tables or views.

The Calculation View

The example we are going to examine is based on the calculation view SALES_COMP shown in Figure 15.6. The view is rather simple; it is supposed to show the sales-related key figures AMOUNT_SOLD, QUANTITY_SOLD, and MARGIN from two years next to each other. That way, a year-to-year comparison will take place—a common pattern in reporting (and thus data modeling) projects.

The calculation view is based on an analytic view, SALES, that is queried twice: once for each year, 2001 and 2002 in our example. The results from these analytic view requests are then joined together so that records from one year always match records from the other year. By filtering on the YR attribute, you ensure that the correct years are selected for the comparison.

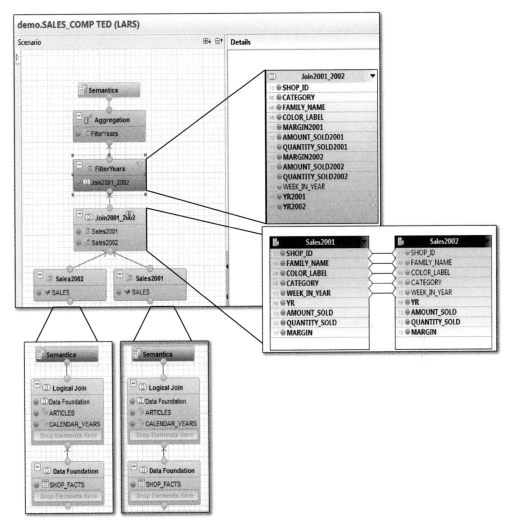

Figure 15.6 Demo Information Model Overview SALES_COMP

The Query Result

The actual SQL query that uses the calculation view (Figure 15.7) simply performs the comparison on the SHOP_ID level, leaving out the other modeled attributes, such as CATEGORY or COLOR. The base SALES_FACT table contains roughly 90,000 records, and the query returns 13 records in about 350 ms with about 120 ms of server processing time.

Although this is well below one second and therefore acceptable for most interactive analytic use cases, the question is, "Is this as quick as possible?"

```
📊 SQL  📄 Result
⊟ SELECT
    "SHOP_ID",
    sum("MARGIN2001") AS "MARGIN2001",
    sum("MARGIN2002") AS "MARGIN2002",
    sum("AMOUNT_SOLD2001") AS "AMOUNT_SOLD2001",
    sum("AMOUNT_SOLD2002") AS "AMOUNT_SOLD2002",
    sum("QUANTITY_SOLD2001") AS "QUANTITY_SOLD2001",
    sum("QUANTITY_SOLD2002") AS "QUANTITY_SOLD2002"
  FROM "_SYS_BIC"."demo/SALES_COMP"
  GROUP BY "SHOP_ID"
  ORDER BY "SHOP_ID"
```

	SHOP_ID	MARGIN2001	MARGIN2002	AMOUNT_SOLD2001	AMOUNT_SOLD2002	QUANTITY_SOLD2001	QUANTITY_SOLD2002
1	3	1696830.4000000008	3066074.1000000006	3848174.5999999917	8233091.500000002	27782	53970
2	64	1858823.6000000015	3413016.799999994	3959645.4000000027	8596670.3	26920	53335
3	110	1917275.6000000015	3480836.1999999974	4042046.9000000027	8585635.900000008	27503	52564
4	137	2384668.1000000024	4121969.8000000054	5206253.1	10657185	36581	67672
5	149	1586372.6000000034	2873304.0000000033	3523313.8000000026	7423951.200000002	25996	49298
6	185	1008759.7000000004	1858314.999999999	2266400.899999998	4968514.599999988	15918	31757
7	197	2779279.5	4905662.399999993	5842416.599999998	12213133.60000...	39932	76418
8	203	1131879.3999999985	2082874.599999999	2505257.0999999996	5535714.099999998	17324	35144
9	261	1364157.900000001	2362288.6999999974	2836717.6000000085	5832704.099999998	18774	35563
10	268	1834100.4999999981	3476781.6999999983	3851488.0000000014	8708860.100000001	26071	54323
11	277	1041428.7000000018	1886589.8000000012	2153542.1000000006	4639491.9	14106	27682
12	351	1761680.5999999992	3190876.5999999987	3822530.999999999	8141219.799999995	26089	50559
13	352	161839.69999999995	312708.79999999993	334876.80000000016	787088.0999999999	2158	4712

Figure 15.7 SALES_COMP Result Set

Calling PlanViz

To understand what SAP HANA does in order to process the query, we choose VISUALIZE PLAN from the context menu in the SQL Editor. A dialog box about switching the perspective to the PLANVIZ perspective may be displayed, and confirming it ensures that all relevant UI displays are visible during the analysis.

The first output PlanViz generates is just a graphical version of the EXPLAIN PLAN (shown in Figure 15.8; compare with Figure 15.5), and we do not see any actual runtime figures. This output also ends at the column view access. To actually start the PlanViz run, EXECUTE has to be selected. Now, the internal procedure is called and executes the statement, including fetching the whole result set.

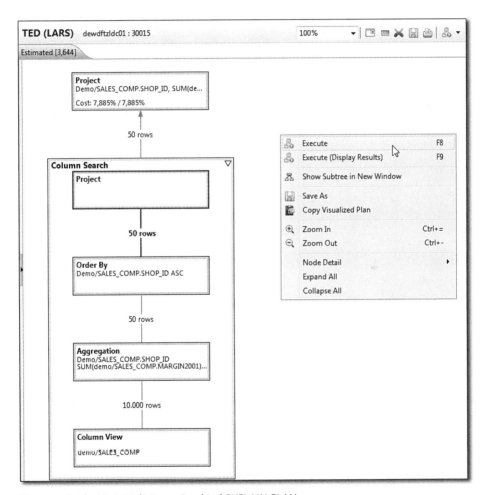

Figure 15.8 PlanViz Initial View—Graphical EXPLAIN PLAN

PlanViz User Interface

Once the statement has been completely executed, the main diagram is displayed (Figure 15.9). Although using PlanViz is pretty straightforward, we briefly look into some aspects that turned out to be useful when working with the tool.

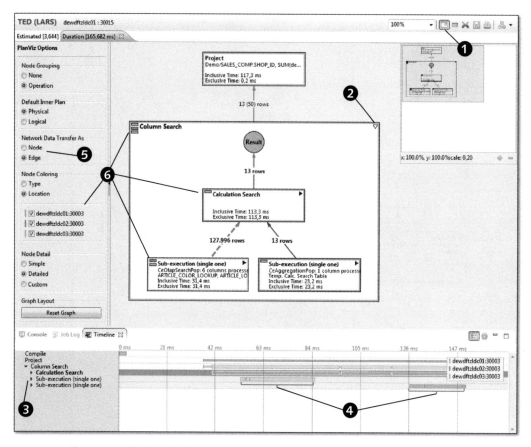

Figure 15.9 PlanViz after Statement Execution

The first element to point out is the overview map tool (shown in ❶) that can be brought up by clicking on the icon in the title bar. For small query graphs, this might seem superfluous, but this tool becomes a lifesaver as soon as the plans get more complicated. Another very useful feature is the save option available via the disk icon in the icon bar. Figure 15.10 shows the SAVE PLAN dialog with the option to save the PlanViz either as a screenshot in various graphic file formats or as a PLV file.

PlanViz files are in fact pseudo-XML files that contain all information of the Plan-Viz execution and can be loaded back via FILE • OPEN FILE... in SAP HANA Studio. This provides the ability to save an interactive PlanViz file and, if you choose, share it with others. The files can be opened and analyzed without any access to the system on which they were created.

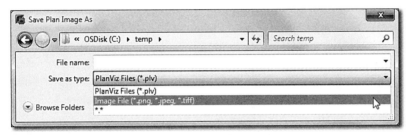

Figure 15.10 Save PlanViz Dialog with File Type Selection

Tip
It is highly recommended that you save the PlanViz PLV files as soon as the query execution is finished. This is especially true for very long-running statements.
In the case that this does not happen and PlanViz accidentally closes or SAP HANA Studio crashes or something else destroys the current PlanViz, it can pay to check the SAP HANA Studio workspace folder, that is, *c:\Users\<username>\hdbstudio*. In there, all PlanViz plans are stored as temporary files named temp_xxx.plv.

The next item of note are the triangles within the boxes (shown in ❷). Each of the boxes represents a unit of work that is performed during query processing. When we want to look inside this unit of work, we need to click on the black triangle. The box then will be enlarged and show what processing happens inside.

On the bottom of the window, there is a timeline display (shown in ❸) that presents a horizontal bar for each processing box visible in the upper area. Both the timeline and the main area are synchronized, so clicking and selecting an activity in one of them will automatically select the corresponding item in the other.

Mapping the Information Model to PlanViz

To get to an understanding of what is happening in PlanViz, it is usually a good start to map the single operations of the information model to the PlanViz output.

> **Note**
>
> Note that detailed and simple display styles are available for the plan operators in Plan-Viz. When zooming out, PlanViz will automatically switch to the simple display mode in order to keep the plan operator labels readable.

Every box in the PlanViz output represents a so-called plan operator (POP). The names of the plan operators provide a hint as to which execution engine processes them. POP names starting with CE are executed in the calculation engine, those starting with BW are executed in the OLAP engine, and those starting with JE are executed in the join engine.

> **Note**
>
> The individual plan operators are not documented (SPS 8). In many cases, however, the names are sufficiently descriptive to make an educated guess.

In the PlanViz display, data flows from bottom to top. That is, our query result is at the top of the view, and the actual data retrieval from database tables is at the bottom. The plan operators in between represent the transformations needed in order to get from the data in the tables to the desired output of the data model. In the modeler interface for calculation views, the data flow direction is also from bottom up. The nodes of the calculation view can be matched to the plan operations almost 1:1.

As our example is rather simple, the mapping is not too difficult. In the calculation view, we have the result node (implicitly containing a projection), an aggregation, and a filter on top of a join of data retrieved from two analytic views.

In PlanViz, we find a node representing a calculation search; expanding this node, we find multiple POPs (Figure 15.11). As you would expect from a calculation search, they are all ce-POPs; there is a `CeProjectionPop`, a `CeAggregationPop`, a `CeJoinPop`, and two `CeOlapSearchPop` nodes. It does not seem bold to assume that these can be mapped to the intrinsic projection of the result node, the aggregation node, the join node, and the analytic view inputs of our calculation view. Once you have figured out the mapping, take a closer look at the provided information.

Notable here is that the input to this POP is not just the result of the underlying `CeJoinPop`; there is also an input of 13 records from an analytical search—queries against analytic views—fed into the aggregation. Checking back with the result set, you will find that this matches the number of groups created by the aggregation. This segregation of different computation steps—here creating the grouping buckets and aggregating data into those buckets—is one of the techniques often employed by SAP HANA to increase the level of parallel computation within a query.

The second input feed to the aggregation is the actual data; resulting from the `CeJoinPop`, we see that 41,888 rows are fed into the aggregation. Such row numbers are information to be looked out for when trying to find potential bottlenecks in a query execution. A rule of thumb here is that the more records are moved between POPs, the more time will be needed.

Another way to look at this is to compare the number of rows that feed into a POP with the number of resulting rows. If this number is not decreased, then the POP effectively performed a row-wise operation, which typically takes a relatively long time.

Farther down in the PlanViz, we find that the `CeJoinPop` is fed from two `CeOlapSearchPop` instances. These are calculation engine wrapper POPs that are used to call the OLAP engine and to access the analytic views. The `CeOlapSearch-Pop` instances are the `Sales2002` and `Sales2001` boxes in the calculation view, and both map to the same analytic view, `SALES`. This information can be found in the yellow details pop-up window.

Taking a look at the record numbers that result from the analytical search POPs, we find that both of them return more than 62,000 records. Given that we are interested in a highly aggregated view of the data (the query result is just 13 records), this could be a first indication of a potential performance issue.

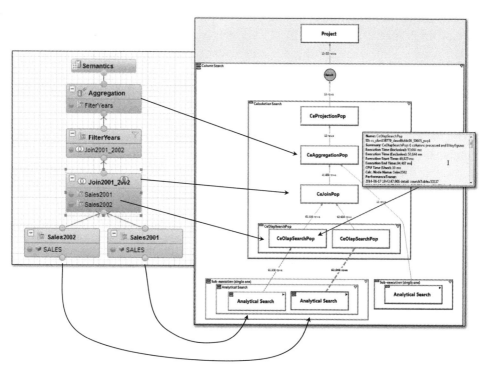

Figure 15.11 Mapping the Calculation View to PlanViz

By hovering over any of the boxes, a DETAILS pop-up window appears that contains information on the specific box. Let's look into one of them in more detail in Table 15.1.

Detail Pop-Up Line	Explanation
Name: CeOlapSearchPop	Type of the plan operation.
ID: cs_plan158779_dewdftz1dc01_30003_pop1	Internal ID within this execution plan.
Summary: CeOlapSearchPop: 6 columns processed and 3 keyfigures	A brief summary of what this POP is doing.
Execution Time (Inclusive): 53,644 ms	The time spent in this POP, including all referenced POPs.

Table 15.1 Interpretation of the Details for a Typical Plan Operator

Detail Pop-Up Line	Explanation
Execution Time (Exclusive): 53,644 ms	The time spent in this POP without the referenced POPs.
Execution Start Time: 40,823 ms	Start time of this POP within this execution of the statement.
Execution End Time: 94,467 ms	End time of this POP within this execution of the statement.
CPU Time (User): 10 ms	CPU time used. This number is currently not to be trusted because CPU time accounting is not yet fully implemented.
Calc. Node Name: Sales2002	The CALCULATION node name. This maps directly to the calculation view, which makes it very helpful in mapping the PlanViz to the model.
PerformanceTracer: 2014-06-17 19:43:47.966 detail: :searchTable=53337 2014-06-17 19:43:47.966 table: _SYS_ BIC:demo/SALES, detail: >>> ceDetails >>> :prepareSO=0:search(65308)=53:pp_ rename=0:pp_removeAttrs=0:setRe- sult(65308)=0: --> overall time=53 <<< ceDetails <<<	Internal details. We have not yet found a useful application for this.
Column Processed: QUANTITY_SOLDsum	The column(s) processed in this request.
PythonTrace: .setNodeName('Sales2002') .setUseInternalTable() pi = fuzzypy.CePlanInput() pi.setName('SALES') .addPopInput(pi) .addViewAttribute('SHOP_ID', datatype=73, sqlType=3, sqlLength=5) .addViewAttribute('YR', datatype=83, sqlType=36, sqlLength=5) .addViewAttribute('CATEGORY', datatype=83, sqlType=36, sqlLength=30) .addViewAttribute('FAMILY_NAME', datatype=83, sqlType=36, sqlLength=30) .addViewAttribute('COLOR_LABEL', datatype=83, sqlType=36, sqlLength=255)	The Python trace section is by far the most cryptic one. It directly relates to the internal structure of the plan operator and the parameters vary between different plan operators. Although this is not documented and might change in the future, as it is not an open API, there still is useful information to be found. .setUseInternalTable() indicates that the result will be stored in an internal table.

Table 15.1 Interpretation of the Details for a Typical Plan Operator (Cont.)

Detail Pop-Up Line	Explanation

`.addViewAttribute('WEEK_IN_YEAR',`
`datatype=73, sqlType=3, sqlLength=5)`
`.setLocale('BINARY')`
`.setUserSchema('LARS')`
`.setPlanOperationFlags(4096)`
`qo = fuzzypy.QueryEntry()`
`qo.setLocation('YR')`
`qo.setValue('2002', '', 'EQ')`
`qo.setValueType('single_quoted')`
`qo.setRowType('ATTRIBUTE')`
`qo.setContentType(fuzzypy.CT_CONTENT)`
`qo.setFuzzySimilarity(-1)`
`qo.setLanguage('NONE')`
`qo.addTermAction(fuzzypy.TA_EXACT)`
`qo.setSearchTermFlags(1)`
`.addPreQueryEntry(qo)`
`.addKeyfigure('MARGIN', 1, 100,`
`sqlType=7, sqlLength=8)`
`.addKeyfigure('AMOUNT_SOLD', 1, 100,`
`sqlType=7, sqlLength=8)`
`.addKeyfigure('QUANTITY_SOLD', 1, 73,`
`sqlType=3, sqlLength=5)`
`.addPlaceholder('$$language$$', 'E')`
`.setSource('_SYS_BIC:demo/SALES')`
	`qo = fuzzypy.QueryEntry()`
	`qo.setLocation('YR')`
	`qo.setValue('2002', '', 'EQ')`
	
	The qo (query optimizer) section shows that the filter conditions are handed down to this POP.
	
	`.setSource('_SYS_BIC:demo/SALES')` shows where the data is coming from. This can be a table or another information model, as is the case in this example.

Table 15.1 Interpretation of the Details for a Typical Plan Operator (Cont.)

At this point in the analysis, we have a rough idea what is happening here: The analytic view SALES is queried twice, each time with the appropriate filter for the year. Still, a lot of records are transferred between the POPs in this PlanViz.

The Timeline Display

In order to confirm if this really is a problem, we need to find out about the time used for each of the POPs. The tool to use here is the TIMELINE at the bottom of the PlanViz window (Figure 15.12).

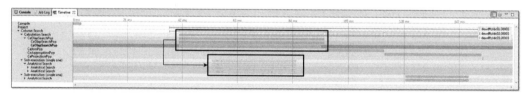

Figure 15.12 Timeline Display for the PlanViz Example

In the TIMELINE display, we find that in fact accessing the analytic views takes a major part of the processing time, even though both of the analytic views are processed in parallel. From the 165,682 ms the total execution took, including compiling and fetching the result set, this step alone consumed 55,005 ms, close to one-third of the total time. Note that in these 55 ms, the time for the data transfer to the next POP, eventually to a different node, is also included.

Remodeling the Calculation View

If we could cut down the number of records resulting from the OLAPSearchPop, this in turn would also decrease the time required for the aggregation POP, because less data would have to be processed. This is in fact what we achieve if we go back and change the model so that we can combine the aggregated data instead of the line-item-level data.

Instead of a join, we are now using a UNION operation to combine the two data sets from the analytic views (Figure 15.13). As UNION will just append one result set after the other, SAP HANA can do this without actually moving the data. Instead, at the end of one result set a memory pointer simply can point to the next result set.

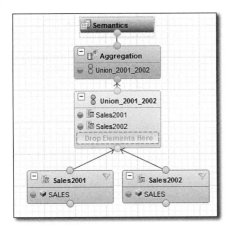

Figure 15.13 Remodeled Example Calculation View

UNION Column Mapping

The only difficulty with using the UNION operation in this example is how to bring the results from both results next to each other. For that, a common trick is used:

The Sales2001 analytic view will deliver 0 values for all 2002 measures, and the Sales2002 analytic view will do the same with the 2001 measures. Because the data will be aggregated via SUM in the next step, the duplicate lines will be merged into single lines carrying the measures for both years. To achieve this in a calculation view, the UNION operator has to be set up with column mappings, as Figure 15.14 shows.

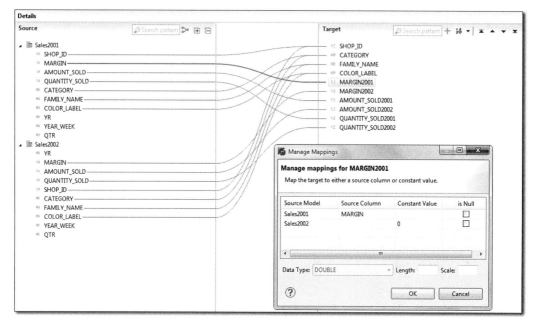

Figure 15.14 Column Mappings for the UNION Operator

Executing the query with this remodeled view already shows that it runs quicker and returns the same data in around 260 ms with around 35 ms of server processing time. Compared to the 350 ms with around 120 ms of server processing time of the original version, the actual processing time was cut down to a third of the original time.

Still, the total execution time is still at roughly two thirds. This is due to the fact that in this case the total execution time is dominated by the time required to transport the data to the client. Because you get the same number of rows back with the remodeled view, this time will stay the same.

Improved Execution PlanViz

Looking at the PlanViz for this model confirms our assumption on the execution steps. In Figure 15.15, you can see that the overall layout of the execution remains unchanged.

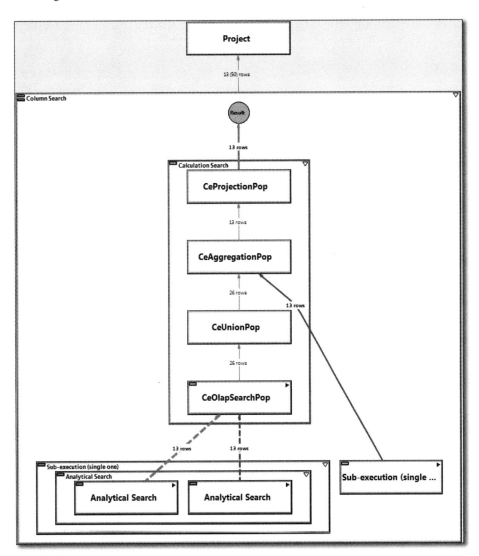

Figure 15.15 PlanViz of Remodeled View

The `CeAggregationPop` still retrieves the 13 records for the aggregation groups from a separate call to the analytic views and the actual to-be-aggregated rows are still delivered from the POP below it. But now, you can see that only 13 rows are fed into the aggregation POP. In fact, even the `CeUnionPop` only has to cope with 26 rows, because the whole aggregation operation was pushed down to the analytic view POPs. Checking the timeline for this execution results in Figure 15.16.

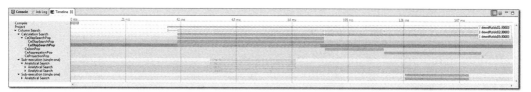

Figure 15.16 Timeline of Remodeled View

Now, all the access to the analytic views is much quicker and takes only a very small share of the total runtime.

Conclusion

You should now know how to use and read PlanViz. A general best practice here is to not get lost in overly detailed observations. Instead, focusing on large data transfers and operations that contribute a large share to the total runtime are effective strategies in finding opportunities to improve performance.

15.5.2 Analyzing Joins with PlanViz

Joins are often among the most expensive contributors to query execution. We will now explain the two most important join implementations in SAP HANA and how to analyze join operations with the PlanViz tool.

There are two major difficulties many users experience when analyzing join queries with PlanViz. The first one is understanding which execution engine does what. The second one is understanding the way in which the database processes join. We will start with a look at the execution engines. The names of the execution engines can be pretty misleading, so let's look at this in a little more detail:

- ▶ **Join engine**

  Performs joins between column tables and can perform filtering, simple aggregation/distinct functions, and sorting and projecting the result set. The main purpose is to provide general join functionality to column store tables.

- ▶ **OLAP engine**

  This engine was originally coupled to analytic views but can also be dynamically invoked by SQL executed statements and calculation views. The main purpose is to support a star schema, such as aggregation queries. Aggregation groups and joins are typically executed at the same time, and special features such as text join or temporal join are supported. The use case for this engine is aggregation and short table chains that should be joined. When calculations are included in analytic views, this will typically lead to a calculation view that gets created as a wrapper around the analytic view. In the activated column views, the analytic view can then be identified by the /olap suffix. The OLAP engine is also the first engine to support and exploit partitioned and distributed tables and replicas.

- ▶ **Calculation engine**

  The calculation engine is the native execution engine for calculation views. These are all about being reusable and stackable elements in larger calculation constructs. A large number of native POPs is supported, including joins, projections, calling analytic views, passing queries to an R server, and so on. The high flexibility and extensibility of the calculation engine make it the execution engine for all cases that cannot be handled in the other two engines. The calculation engine also comes with its own join implementation.

We see that the feature set of the different execution engines does overlap quite a bit. Every engine can perform operations such as filtering and projecting columns or joining tables. Which engine is best used when is always dependent on the problem at hand.

After understanding what the execution engines are, the second hurdle for developers and DBAs used to other databases is to understand the processing of joins. We'll go into that in a little more detail next.

Joins in PlanViz—Join Engine Join

To see how joins are processed in SAP HANA, we will again look at an example. The SQL statement we are going to analyze is shown in Listing 15.1.

```
select f.shop_id, a.family_name, sum (MARGIN) as "MARGIN"
from efashion.shop_facts f
    inner join  efashion.article_lookup a
    on f.article_id = a.article_id
group by f.shop_id, a.family_name
```

Listing 15.1 Join Processing and Aggregation Example Statement

The statement is nothing more than a straightforward inner join with a simple aggregation. Executing it as-is leads to join engine usage and produces a surprisingly complex PlanViz. The reason for this apparent complexity is—again—that decomposing the different tasks that need to be performed for this query can yield much higher parallel degrees of processing.

As the processing of joins in any of the mentioned engines tends to appear rather complex at first sight, we will take you through the simplest case—a join in the join engine—in three steps.

Join Engine Join: Part 1 of 3

The very first step of the join processing (Figure 15.17) is already concerned with optimizing performance. Instead of simply reading all records from the SHOP_FACT table and joining them to the ARTICLE_LOOKUP table, SAP HANA does the sensible thing and preaggregates the large table first. If we supplied filter conditions, they would have been applied in the Search on Table/Delta POPs. The job of the JEEvalPrecond POP here is to turn the row pointers found in the table into an internal intermediate data structure, JEPlanData. This data structure represents the rows without actually materializing them. By doing that, a lot of intermediate memory is saved, and the processing can continue to leverage the SIMD instruction set processor commands.

Next, JEDistinctAttribute prepares the groups for aggregation, and JECreate-NTuple delivers the values for the aggregated column MARGIN. Don't get fooled by the Sorted Merge Join text here. This relates to the join between the groups and the aggregated column, not to the join of two tables.

After the aggregation, the number of records to be joined from the fact table now is only 4,220 rows and is stored in an intermediate temporary table by the Result Assembly and the Create Temp Index POPs.

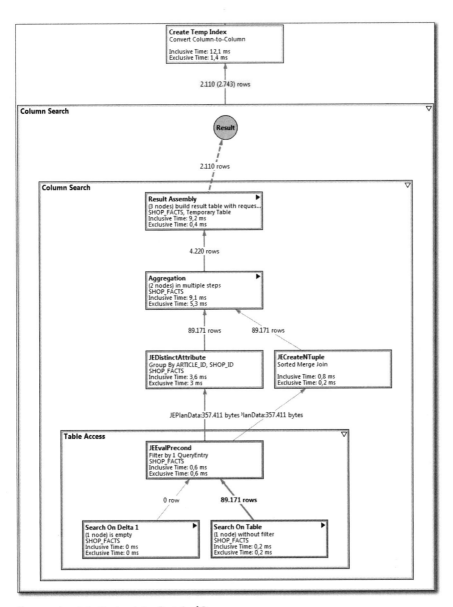

Figure 15.17 Join Engine Join: Part 1 of 3

Join Engine Join: Part 2 of 3

Based on the temporary intermediate result set containing the reduced join data from the fact table, the actual join processing between the two tables can now start. The `Reduction Phase` POP (Figure 15.18) deals with using the join condition to reduce the number of resulting rows. The POPs `JEStep1` to `JEStep4` prepare data structures for the following processing steps. That is the reason for the multiple data streams that leave these POPs and feed into different subsequent steps. Which `JEStep` POPs are employed in a query depends on the query and the possible optimizations.

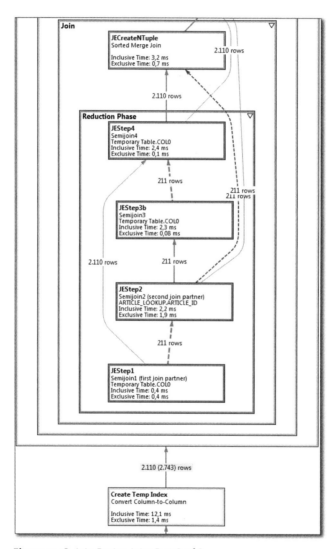

Figure 15.18 Join Engine Join: Part 2 of 3

The actual join is then performed in the JECreateNTuple POP that now only needs to process 2,110 and 211 records.

Join Engine Join: Part 3 of 3

The POPs that are executed after the join is performed combine the joined result set with the grouping and aggregation operations that we requested in the SQL query. This is now done in the Grouping, Aggregation, and Result Assembly POPs (Figure 15.19).

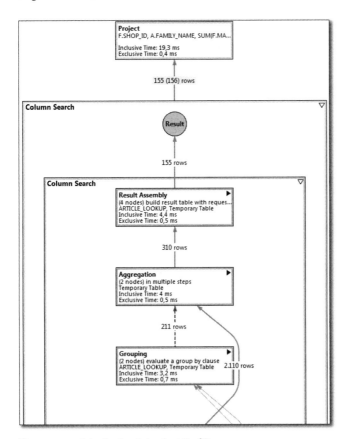

Figure 15.19 Join Engine Join: Part 3 of 3

Joins in PlanViz—OLAP Engine Join

With the insight into join processing in the join engine, we now compare this to the join processing of the OLAP engine. To do this, we usually would have to build an analytic view that resembles the logic in our SQL statement. Fortunately, by using the WITH HINT (OLAP_PARALLEL_AGGREGATION) syntax, SAP HANA can do this on the fly. To understand the OLAP engine join, we break the processing down into two major steps.

OLAP Engine Join: Part 1 of 2

In Figure 15.20, we see that BwPopJoin13 (a combined BwPopJoin1 and BwPopJoin3 that could be used in other scenarios) creates intermediate data structures of type BwDimFn based on the two columns SHOP_ID and ARTICLE_ID that will be used as the group by attributes in our query. BwPopAggregateParallel creates a Parallel-HashMap data structure as the result of a highly parallelized aggregation process. With this and with the actual row information from the BwPopJoin13 POPs, BwPopBuildResultParallel creates an intermediate result set table.

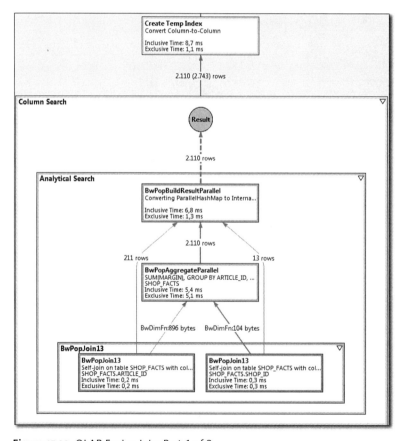

Figure 15.20 OLAP Engine Join: Part 1 of 2

OLAP Engine Join: Part 2 of 2

At this point, the OLAP engine already is at half of the overall processing. Figure 15.21 shows the remaining steps. The intermediate table now is joined to the ARTICLE_LOOKUP table, just as is done in the join engine.

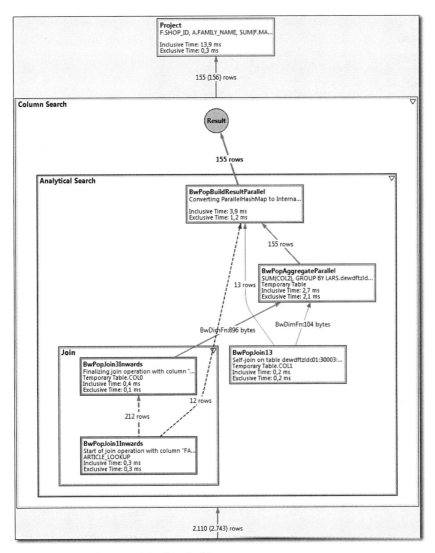

Figure 15.21 OLAP Engine Join: Part 2 of 2

The POPs used for this are BwPopJoin1Inwards and BwPopJoin3Inwards. Again, these POPs create BWDimFn data structures that feed into the BwPopAggregateParallel and `BwPopBuildResultParallel` POPs. The latter also takes the `Parallel-HashMap` generated by the `BWPopAggregateParallel` POP and produces the final result set in the form of an internal temporary table.

Here, we see that in order to perform parallel aggregation, the data from the column store tables needs to be prepared and converted first into special data structures `BWDimFn` and `ParallelHashMap`. This data type conversion usually only pays off for larger amounts of data, so the OLAP engine is not the best choice for all joins.

> **Note**
>
> The actual implementation of joins in any execution engine of SAP HANA will evolve over time and is not officially documented. None of the processing steps are guaranteed to be executed or maintained in future revisions.
>
> However, we believe that the preceding walkthrough provides a good starting point for understanding more about query processing in SAP HANA.

15.6 Further Resources

Performance analysis is a broad topic and could easily fill a book on its own. Although this chapter covers the most important features in detail, the following resources should not go unmentioned; they provide helpful insights and tools for a lot of other performance-related topics.

- The *Performance Analysis Guide* available at *help.sap.com/hana_appliance*.
- SAP Note 1969700 contains a growing number of SQL statements for various use cases. Some of them, for example, `HANA_Resources_CPUAndMemory_History` or `HANA_Workload`, provide easy-to-use overviews of the system usage over time.
- SAP Note 1858357 covers steps to analyze situations in which sessions seem to be stuck due to concurrent access of shared resources.
- SAP Note 1890444 addresses configuration issues that could affect performance negatively.
- Because the options and techniques for performance-related analysis constantly evolve, a book like this can never be at the latest state. To keep updated on these topics, SAP FAQ Note 2000002 should be subscribed to in the SAP Service Marketplace.

15.7 Summary

In this chapter, we provided an overview of different tools and techniques to understand and improve query performance in SAP HANA. If there is one main takeaway, then it might be that it is key not to get lost in details too early. Instead, filter out relevant information—for example, the longest running contributors to the TIMELINE view in PlanViz.

The second item to remember is that PlanViz is the tool of choice for single-statement analysis. SAP HANA also provides a great deal of performance-related information in monitoring views, statistics service views, the load diagram, and other places—and this wealth of information can easily be confusing. Knowing the question that should be answered is the most important step to finding the answer in of all this information.

Your end users complain because "the system is slow." Last night's batches didn't finish. The update process fails. Your developers can no longer activate any data models. These and many more events leave you with two choices: contact SAP Support or find out what's going wrong.

16 Monitoring and Root-Cause Analysis

Troubleshooting or analyzing problems, errors, and unwanted system behavior and finding options to fix or work around them can be looked at as a science, an art, a craft, or a mix of all of them. Typically, good troubleshooters do have a good understanding of the concepts of the system, follow an analytical approach, and usually have a gut feeling about what might be causing the issue at hand. Equally important is the capability to find critical information in order to better understand a given problem.

One prerequisite for developing an intuitive feeling for the system's overall well-being is to understand and adequately use its monitoring capabilities. Although we have discussed some monitoring topics in their relevant chapters throughout the book, we will touch upon general monitoring topics at the beginning of this chapter. We'll then progress to functionalities and techniques relevant for handling individual incidents. To this end, we will start with log and error messages displayed to developers and administrators using SAP HANA Studio and then move on to information collected in diagnostic files and traces of the database server and clients.

16.1 Monitoring

Monitoring describes a regular or continuous observation of system characteristics. The system may collect information on its own (self-monitoring), or administrators may check certain parameters of a system in a manual procedure. Although the latter is, of course, technically possible, manual monitoring is inefficient and will not play a role in our discussion. We will instead focus on the self-monitoring capabilities of SAP HANA—starting with an introduction of the monitoring views of the database and its statistics service. We will not ignore the related topics of accessing the information collected by the system and implementing proactive alerting mechanisms. Finally, we will briefly discuss external tools for monitoring SAP HANA systems, including SAP Solution Manager.

16.1.1 Monitoring Views

The SAP HANA system comes with a large number of tables and views that offer information on the system state. Some of these views describe the comparatively static structural content of the database system, that is, the definitions of database objects. These views make up the database catalog and were the topic of Chapter 7. The monitoring views that we will cover here are very volatile and dynamically reflect the system state. The content of these views is not stored in the database but computed on the fly based on what is currently in memory. This means that the contents of these views will be gone after an instance restart. As an example, monitoring view M_DELTA_MERGE_STATISTICS—which provides information on delta merge executions—only shows the data since the last system restart. For a historic view on some of these monitoring views, the statistics server takes regular snapshots and stores the information in the _SYS_STATISTICS schema.

Sometimes the data content of monitoring views changes so quickly and is so sensitive to different workloads that looking at the absolute total numbers would not provide the desired insight. Instead, it would be interesting to see the change of figures since a specific point in time (e.g., the amount of log data since the start of the data-loading process). For such requirements, SAP HANA comes with a special kind of monitoring view, the resettable views, identifiable by the _RESET suffix. As an example, we use the M_LOG_SEGMENTS view and the resettable twin view M_LOG_SEGMENTS_RESET.

In Figure 16.1, we see the output of M_LOG_SEGMENTS, shown in ❶, which is a list of all processed log segments for the whole SAP HANA instance for every log segment that was created since the instance was restarted. Depending on the workload of the instance, this could mean lots of entries that might be difficult to read. Also, there is no information about the creation time of the log segments, which makes it hard to figure out how many log segments have been created in a certain period of time. By using the command alter system reset monitoring view

M_LOG_SEGMENTS_RESET, a reset timestamp for every entry is created, and the data is now visible in M_LOG_SEGMENTS_RESET, as shown in ❷.

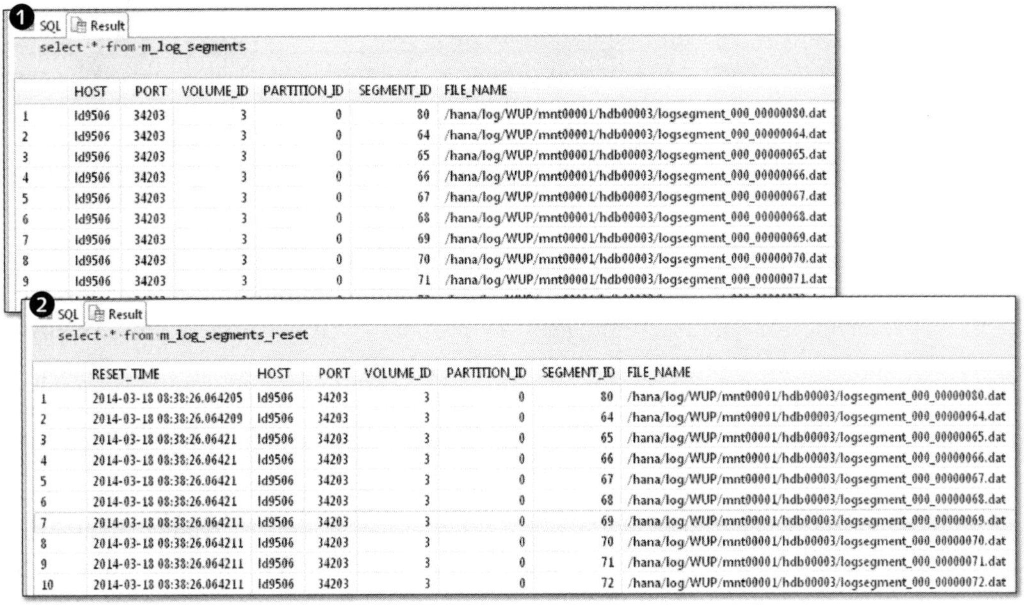

❶ SQL | Result

select * from m_log_segments

	HOST	PORT	VOLUME_ID	PARTITION_ID	SEGMENT_ID	FILE_NAME
1	ld9506	34203	3	0	80	/hana/log/WUP/mnt00001/hdb00003/logsegment_000_00000080.dat
2	ld9506	34203	3	0	64	/hana/log/WUP/mnt00001/hdb00003/logsegment_000_00000064.dat
3	ld9506	34203	3	0	65	/hana/log/WUP/mnt00001/hdb00003/logsegment_000_00000065.dat
4	ld9506	34203	3	0	66	/hana/log/WUP/mnt00001/hdb00003/logsegment_000_00000066.dat
5	ld9506	34203	3	0	67	/hana/log/WUP/mnt00001/hdb00003/logsegment_000_00000067.dat
6	ld9506	34203	3	0	68	/hana/log/WUP/mnt00001/hdb00003/logsegment_000_00000068.dat
7	ld9506	34203	3	0	69	/hana/log/WUP/mnt00001/hdb00003/logsegment_000_00000069.dat
8	ld9506	34203	3	0	70	/hana/log/WUP/mnt00001/hdb00003/logsegment_000_00000070.dat
9	ld9506	34203	3	0	71	/hana/log/WUP/mnt00001/hdb00003/logsegment_000_00000071.dat

❷ SQL | Result

select * from m_log_segments_reset

	RESET_TIME	HOST	PORT	VOLUME_ID	PARTITION_ID	SEGMENT_ID	FILE_NAME
1	2014-03-18 08:38:26.064205	ld9506	34203	3	0	80	/hana/log/WUP/mnt00001/hdb00003/logsegment_000_00000080.dat
2	2014-03-18 08:38:26.064209	ld9506	34203	3	0	64	/hana/log/WUP/mnt00001/hdb00003/logsegment_000_00000064.dat
3	2014-03-18 08:38:26.06421	ld9506	34203	3	0	65	/hana/log/WUP/mnt00001/hdb00003/logsegment_000_00000065.dat
4	2014-03-18 08:38:26.06421	ld9506	34203	3	0	66	/hana/log/WUP/mnt00001/hdb00003/logsegment_000_00000066.dat
5	2014-03-18 08:38:26.06421	ld9506	34203	3	0	67	/hana/log/WUP/mnt00001/hdb00003/logsegment_000_00000067.dat
6	2014-03-18 08:38:26.06421	ld9506	34203	3	0	68	/hana/log/WUP/mnt00001/hdb00003/logsegment_000_00000068.dat
7	2014-03-18 08:38:26.064211	ld9506	34203	3	0	69	/hana/log/WUP/mnt00001/hdb00003/logsegment_000_00000069.dat
8	2014-03-18 08:38:26.064211	ld9506	34203	3	0	70	/hana/log/WUP/mnt00001/hdb00003/logsegment_000_00000070.dat
9	2014-03-18 08:38:26.064211	ld9506	34203	3	0	71	/hana/log/WUP/mnt00001/hdb00003/logsegment_000_00000071.dat
10	2014-03-18 08:38:26.064211	ld9506	34203	3	0	72	/hana/log/WUP/mnt00001/hdb00003/logsegment_000_00000072.dat

Figure 16.1 Output from M_LOG_SEGMENTS and Its RESET Variant

An important detail here is that the reset of the monitoring view does not remove entries from the views. Instead, the _RESET views either carry a reset timestamp or certain counters or key figures in the view are initialized while the records are kept in place. This might be confusing at first, but it makes comparisons between two reset actions easier; after the reset no records will be missing, but the measured values will be set to zero.

SAP HANA Studio as well as the DBA Cockpit for SAP HANA offer dedicated user interfaces for working with the most important monitoring views. In many cases, these user interfaces offer a mixture of administration functionality and monitoring capabilities; we described these aspects in Chapter 4.

Information on all available system views is given in the *SAP HANA SQL and System Views Reference* at *https://help.sap.com/hana_platform/*.

16.1.2 Alerting

The statistics service of SAP HANA performs checks of vital system characteristics and raises alerts when needed. Whenever an alert is raised or the criticality of an alert changes, an entry is written to table STATISTICS__ALERTS in schema _SYS_STATISTICS. For most practical purposes, the subset of alerts exposed by view STATISTICS_CURRENT_ALERTS in the same schema is most relevant.

The built-in method of pushing or distributing alerts is email-based alerting. We described the configuration of the statistics service, including setting up email alerting, in Chapter 4.

If this is not sufficient within your data center setup, there are other means of receiving alert information. The SAP-proposed way is to integrate SAP HANA with your SAP Solution Manager system and make use of SAP Solution Manager's alerting infrastructure. SAP Solution Manager supports several industry standards, such as SNMP, and many third-party tools for monitoring SAP systems come with connectors for SAP Solution Manager.

If SAP Solution Manager is not an option either, you can also pull alert information from the SAP HANA system directly by querying the tables and views of the statistics service. For the purpose of receiving all current alerts from the database, it is sufficient to query the view STATISTICS_CURRENT_ALERTS in schema _SYS_STATISTICS in appropriate intervals.

16.1.3 External Monitoring Tools

Operators of large and diverse data centers must implement a common monitoring infrastructure that encompasses all systems. In most cases, it is therefore not a priority that the system to be monitored provides a feature-complete monitoring environment ready for the end user, but it must provide interfaces or APIs that monitoring solutions can connect to. In the case of SAP HANA, all monitoring and alerting information collected by the database system is exposed to external applications through database views. Thus, monitoring solutions can easily access this information via the database's SQL interface.

Although we cannot cover such external tools in the scope of this book, we will briefly point you to information related to the integration of SAP's standard offering, SAP Solution Manager, and of third-party tools with SAP HANA.

Integration with SAP Solution Manager

SAP's standard solution for managing complex IT landscapes is SAP Solution Manager. By now, SAP HANA is integrated into SAP Solution Manager to the same level as other SAP platforms, so anyone familiar with the tool can easily use it to monitor, administrate, and troubleshoot SAP HANA systems. The integration includes, for example the functionality of alerting, workload and change analysis, and end-to-end tracing.

You can find the documentation for integrating SAP Solution Manager with SAP HANA at *https://service.sap.com/solman-hana*.

Third-Party Tools

The SAP Integration and Certification Center (*https://scn.sap.com/community/icc*) offers certification processes for specialized tools, for example, for monitoring tools, backup tools, ETL tools, and BI tools, and several third-party tools have been certified already. You can see a list of all tools certified for SAP HANA in the SAP Partner Information Center at *www.sap.com/partners/directories/SearchSolution.epx*. For CERTIFICATION CATEGORY, choose SAP CERTIFIED—INTEGRATION WITH SAP HANA.

If your monitoring solution does not yet support SAP HANA but can connect to SAP Solution Manager, then you can set up Solution Manager integration for SAP HANA and use the Solution Manager system as a propagation layer. Alternatively, your solution might offer a generic database connector that you can customize for SAP HANA using either the JDBC or ODBC database client.

16.2   Error Messages

Error messages are your first hint that there is a problem in the system—and also your first step in solving it. In many cases, these error messages already provide the crucial bit of information you need: the date and time when the error occurred, on which node it occurred, with which user account, which database objects and which processes were involved, and so on.

In this section, we'll introduce you to the two most basic tasks in working with error messages: finding out where they are and understanding what they're telling you.

16.2.1 Locating Error Messages

Depending on the application that uses the database, error messages are presented at various different locations. SAP NetWeaver-based systems use their own log and trace file infrastructure, for example, Transactions ST22 (Short Dumps) and ST11 (Developer Traces), to make error messages accessible to the administrator. Other applications will use different facilities to store error information; for the SAP HANA DBA, it is important to find out about these. Otherwise, it is very difficult to know what kind of problem is present.

To help you in this task, we'll walk you through finding error messages for the two most common types of errors: errors displayed in SAP HANA Studio and errors that occur during model activation.

Errors Displayed in SAP HANA Studio

SAP HANA Studio presents error messages typically either in the lower section of the screen, where the tabs Job Log (Figure 16.2) and Error Log (Figure 16.3) are displayed, or in the section below an SQL Editor window.

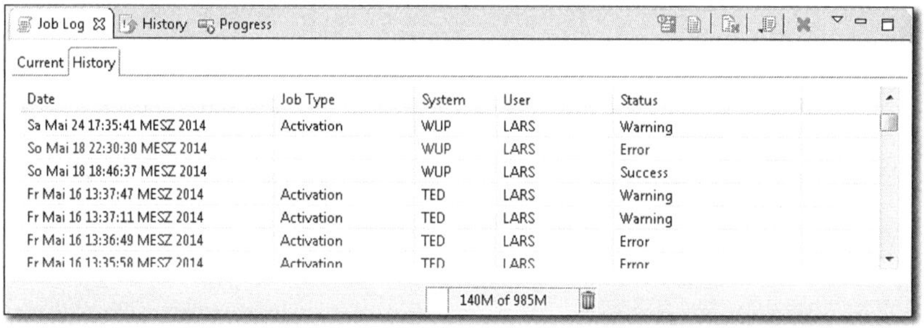

Figure 16.2 SAP HANA Studio Job Log View

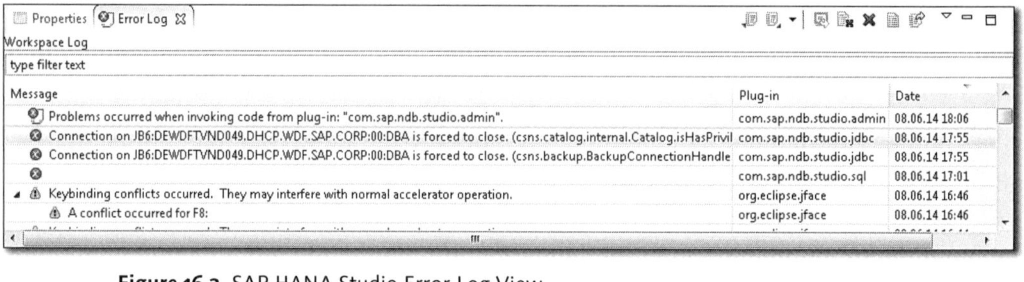

Figure 16.3 SAP HANA Studio Error Log View

Depending on the current perspective and tool used, error messages are sometimes also displayed in the top area of a dialog window. Figure 16.4 shows an example for such editor-specific error output in the Table Editor.

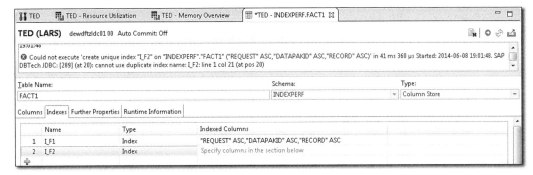

Figure 16.4 Editor-Specific Error Output

Model Activation Errors

When activating or deploying information models, errors are reported by a failed activation job, as shown in Figure 16.5.

Job Type	System	User	Submitted At	Status	
Activation	TED	LARS	Fri Jun 13 14:54:3	Open Job Details	th errors
Activation	TED	LARS	Fri Jun 13 14:53:1	Open Job Log Fi	th errors
Activation	TED	LARS	Fri Jun 13 14:51:5		th errors
				Clear Log Viewer	
				Export Log File	
				Delete Job	

Figure 16.5 Failed Model Activation in SAP HANA Studio

Double-clicking on the failed job entry will bring up an error message summary.

If the error message is not a simple one, the job details (as shown in Figure 16.6) are barely helpful in finding the cause for them. However, selecting OPEN JOB LOG FILE from the context menu provides access to a much better readable representation of the activation log data (Figure 16.7).

The activation logs are automatically saved in the local user's SAP HANA Studio work folder, typically in the folder *%USERPROFILE%\hdbstudio\com.sap.ndb.studio.bi.logs*. This way, the log files can be inspected again or sent to SAP Support even if the error message window was closed in SAP HANA Studio.

> **Note**
>
> Activation log files are not automatically deleted, so, depending on the amount of activations a user routinely performs, cleaning up this folder regularly might be the right thing to do.

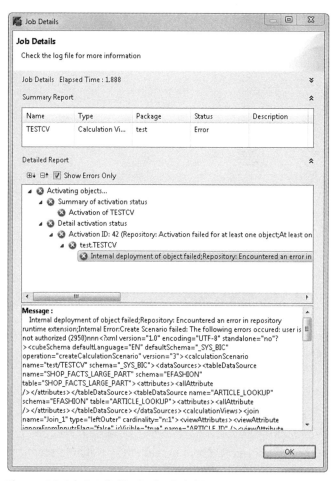

Figure 16.6 Job Details Display for Failed Activation

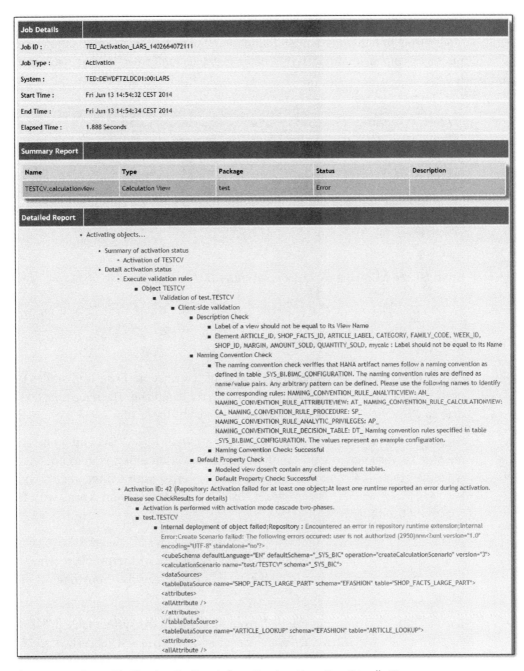

Figure 16.7 Job Log File Showing the Error Information in a More User-Friendly Way

16.2.2 Interpreting Error Messages

Once the error message has been found, we need to make sense of it. Often, error messages contain multiple layers of error-related information that need to be looked at.

> **Note**
>
> Unfortunately, error messages are often badly formatted or not formatted at all. Therefore, it is usually a good idea to copy and paste the full error text into a text editor and reformat the message there. Insert line breaks whenever there is a new error code, a colon (:), or a semi-colon (;). Sometimes, SQLScript code especially can generate n and t characters in trace files and error messages. These n's and t's represent newline and tabulator characters, and replacing them with actual newline and tab characters in a text editor makes the error output far more readable.

Consider the following example error output:

```
Could not execute 'alter table customers add primary key (ID, NAME)'
in 576 ms 810 µs .
SAP DBTech JDBC: [2048]: column store error: set int type and
constraint error:  [56] constraint NOT NULL violation
```

This example error output has three pieces of information. First, it identifies the problem: SAP HANA Studio `could not execute` the command. The remaining text is delivered by the SAP HANA JDBC driver, indicated by the header `SAP DBTech JDBC:`.

Second, the actual error message details are printed. `[2048]` is a common error message for the column store. Without additional information, it does not tell us what the problem was, but there is also auxiliary error information: `set int type and constraint error:`. This makes it clear that something went wrong with the constraint handling.

Finally, the third piece of information in this message is `[56] constraint NOT NULL violation`. This information gives you the root cause of the problem: The `NOT NULL` constraint, implicitly enabled when adding a primary key constraint, is violated.

The meaning of error codes can be looked up either in the system table M_ERROR_ CODES or in the *SAP HANA SQL and System Views Reference* • SQL REFERENCE • SQL ERROR CODES, which is available both on *https://help.sap.com/hana_appliance* and in the built in documentation in SAP HANA Studio. Unfortunately, not every error code is documented this way. In case an undocumented error code requires further clarification, a support call with SAP should be opened.

Alternatively, a new service for finding error documentation and troubleshooting help is *https://answers.saphana.com*. This website is a meta-search engine covering not only the complete set of documentation but also SCN content, training documents, and the like. A direct integration of the website into SAP HANA Studio is available via an Eclipse plug-in that has to be installed separately.

16.3   Diagnostic Files

Diagnostic files are text files in which the database logs events that may help to analyze issues that have occurred in the database, similar to the kernel logs of SAP NetWeaver systems. All of these files are collected on the file system of the SAP HANA database server and are exposed in SAP HANA STUDIO • ADMINISTRATION EDITOR • DIAGNOSIS FILES.

There are two generally different types of such diagnostic files. Dump files are written in exceptional circumstances, such as out-of-memory situations or system crashes, and contain information that will be useful for understanding the root cause of the issue. Trace files contain the output of the database kernel's logging mechanism.

In this section, we will first tell you about the most important aspects of these files and then introduce two tasks that are useful for working with them: collecting diagnostic information on your database system (for example, in order to provide it as auxiliary material to SAP Support), and analyzing trace file contents on your own (via a handy interface in SAP HANA Studio that provides a combined view of all diagnosis files of all services in the database system).

16.3.1   Dump Files

Whenever SAP HANA cannot gracefully handle an error situation, the system needs to abort and crashes or ends a current thread. Instead of writing out a memory dump that might be gigantic and take hours to write to disk, SAP HANA creates a text file that contains nearly everything that could be helpful for understanding the system state that led to the crash/abort. This text file is called a crash dump file and can be found in the DIAGNOSIS FILES tab. All crash dump files have the characters *.crashdump*. as part of the file name. That way, it is easy to find these files in the list of diagnosis files. Apart from the actual crash dump files, SAP HANA can produce dump files with a similar internal structure, such as runtime dump files (*.rtedump.*), emergency dump files (*.emergencydump.*), and out-of-memory dump files (*.oom.*).

The structure of the dump files follows a common layout; refer to Figure 16.8 for an example. A header section that indicates when and where the dump file was created is followed by a table of contents. After that, the content is printed in sections, each starting with the section name in brackets and ending with [OK].

Figure 16.8 Crash Dump File

When displayed in SAP HANA Studio, the dump files can be easily navigated by pressing the ⌜Ctrl⌟ key and clicking on the then-visible hyperlinks in the table of contents.

Note

A common pitfall here is that by default SAP HANA Studio will read only the first 1,000 rows of the dump file. Due to this, many sections will not be loaded into the Diagnosis Files Editor. The table of contents entries referring to these sections will then remain unlinked. To overcome this, simply choose SHOW ENTIRE FILE in the selector at the upper edge of the editor window.

16.3.2 Trace Files

Trace files (sometimes named log files) are another type of diagnostic file that represents the output layer of the database kernel's logging mechanism (named "database trace"). As opposed to dump files, they are continuously written to by the individual database processes. The criticality and consequently the amount of information written to these files depends on the configuration of the database trace (see Section 16.4.1). Each service/process on every host writes into its own set of trace files, the name of which is constructed from the service name, host name, port name, and a running sequence number. The file system location of the trace files written by the services of a given host is */hana/shared/<SID>/<hostname>/trace*. In addition, the trace file folder on each host contains all crash dump and runtime dump files. For most of the trace files, SAP HANA employs an automatic retention mechanism that keeps up to ten files of a maximum of 10 MB size for each process before the oldest file is deleted and a new file is created. The parameters of this file rotation can be configured (Table 16.1).

Besides the standard trace files, simply named by *<servicename>_<hostname>.<portno>.<sequence>.trc*, there is one single alert file for each service into which only trace messages of the highest priorities are written. Especially if the current trace settings lead to a high volume of entries in the regular trace files, it can be easier to find information relevant to a specific error situation in the alert traces. Instead of a file rotation for these alert files, they have a configurable maximum size. Once that size is reached, the oldest file contents will be overwritten. Alert files are simply named *<service>_alert_<host>.trc*.

As Figure 16.9 shows, the trace files for a distributed SAP HANA instance are well spread across different servers and file system folders. The goal behind this rather complex trace/log file handling is twofold:

▶ To prevent loss of potentially important operational information by deleting data too early

▶ To keep the files in manageable sizes and numbers

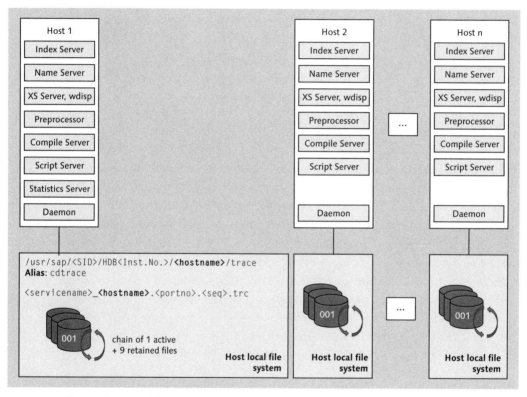

Figure 16.9 Trace Files in SAP HANA

The default settings for trace/log file handling are suitable for a wide range of scenarios. In fact, we never saw a requirement to actually change them in any customer system. However, the `global.ini` • `[trace]` parameters shown in Table 16.1 can be changed to customize the behavior.

Parameter Name (Default Value)	Description
compressioninterval (10)	Interval in seconds to check for large trace files to be compressed
flushinterval (5)	Interval in seconds for trace data to be flushed out into trace files
maxalertfilesize (50000000)	Maximum size in bytes for alert files
maxfiles (10)	Maximum number of sequence files to be kept
Maxfilesize (10000000)	Maximum size in bytes for other trace files, including crash dump files

Table 16.1 Trace File Handling Parameter Settings

The trace files written out by the SAP HANA processes follow a common format. Any message written to the trace files starts with the same set of data. Let's look at the following example to understand this data better (see also Table 16.2):

```
[4869]{301828}[67/1325299]  2014-06-09  21:18:46.357168  i  TraceContext
TraceContext.cpp(00699)  :  UserName=LARS,  ApplicationUserName=I028297,
ApplicationName=HDBStudio
```

Traceline component	Meaning
[4859]	O/S thread ID of the thread that issued the trace line
{301828}	Connection ID of the session
[67/1325299]	Transaction ID/update transaction ID, if applicable; otherwise -1
2014-06-09 21:18:46.357168	Timestamp
i	Trace level indicator (i = info, d = debug, w = warning...)
TraceContext	Name of the trace component
TraceContext.cpp(00699)	Source code module and location
UserName=LARS, ApplicationUserName=I028297, ApplicationName=HDBStudio	Trace line message

Table 16.2 Trace Line Components

Understanding this information can be very useful, such as when following the trace output of a single session through a trace file while other threads write out their trace output in between.

16.3.3 Collecting Diagnostic Files for a Support Incident

The DIAGNOSTICS FILES tab allows for downloading single and multiple files to the local computer on which SAP HANA Studio runs. However, collecting all the diagnosis files typically required for a support incident (dump files, alert files, trace files, etc.) can be cumbersome. To make this easier, SAP HANA Studio provides the COLLECT option in the DIAGNOSIS FILES tab (Figure 16.10).

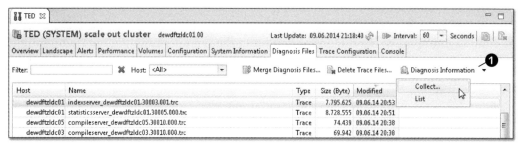

Figure 16.10 Collect Diagnosis Information in SAP HANA Studio

Clicking the DIAGNOSIS INFORMATION button provides a dropdown list for either triggering a new collection of diagnosis information or accessing and managing the already existing information. Clicking COLLECT... brings up a selection window (Figure 16.11) in which you can choose between two options:

- Create a collection of the already available trace and dump files, eventually including current selections from monitoring views from the live system. For this option, you can also provide a filter for the maximum age of files to be included.

- Create so-called runtime dumps. These are files containing current runtime information for all threads and excerpts from monitoring views.

As of SPS 8, the time selection in this dialog is redesigned to be more flexible, and runtime dumps now can be set up to be taken in a series. This can be helpful for analyzing ongoing problem situations.

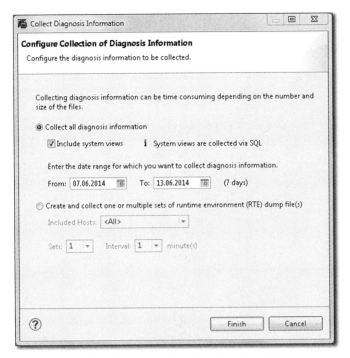

Figure 16.11 Collect Diagnosis Information Selection Dialog

16.3.4 Using the Merged Diagnosis Files Editor

As you have seen, it can be difficult to locate trace file messages for a specific issue in all the different trace files. In order to find the detailed error output for an issue in a scale-out environment, the DBA would need to review the indexserver traces that cover the time when the error occurred on every single host.

To allow for a more efficient approach, SAP HANA provides the MERGED DIAGNOSIS FILES EDITOR (also available in Transaction DBACOCKPIT in SAP NetWeaver systems). This function is available in SAP HANA STUDIO • ADMINISTRATION CONSOLE • DIAGNOSIS FILES • MERGE DIAGNOSIS FILES....

Clicking the button opens a preselection dialog from which the DBA can limit the amount of data that should be processed (Figure 16.12). The longer the time range chosen, the more data will need to be processed, and the longer it will take to gather all information.

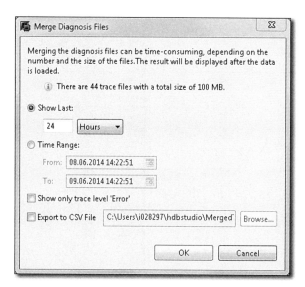

Figure 16.12 Merge Diagnosis Files Selection Dialog

Note

Try to limit the data as much as possible; this will make working with the combined trace file output much quicker and smoother. Finding the right scope of log/trace file information is key to a quick and efficient error analysis.

After clicking the OK button, SAP HANA Studio runs a query against system view M_MERGED_TRACES with the selection criteria provided. Selecting from this system view will trigger a scan of all trace files of all services (indexserver, statisticsserver, xsengine, etc.) based on the provided selection criteria. Although the view can of course be accessed via SQL, it is highly discouraged, because the result set is not buffered. To compensate for this, SAP HANA Studio selects the result of this first query into a local temporary table. All further selections will be performed against this temporary table.

Once the data is read into the temporary table, the MERGED DIAGNOSIS FILES EDITOR (Figure 16.13) is opened; it contains the trace data that is available for the specified time frame.

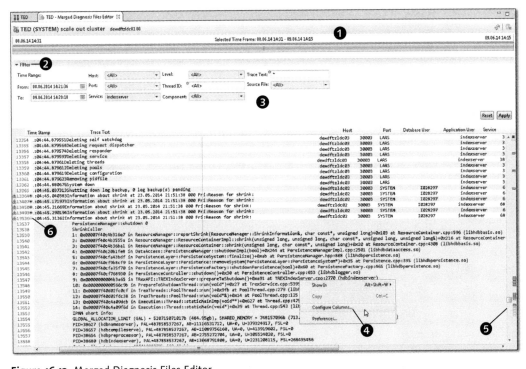

Figure 16.13 Merged Diagnosis Files Editor

Once opened, the time frame cannot be changed; instead, the editor needs to be closed and reopened to select a different time frame.

At the top of the window, a time slider (shown in ❶) can be used to change the displayed time frame within the boundaries of the selection that was made earlier.

Much more important than using the time slider is to open the filter settings (shown in ❷). Because you are now looking at the combined trace output from all services and all hosts, chances are that most of the data displayed will not be of importance (read: noise) to you.

Depending on the type of analysis that should be performed, the filtering strategy (shown in ❸) can be either to exclude what definitively is not relevant (e.g., uncheck all services except INDEXSERVER) or to include only certain types of messages (e.g., only trace level ERROR and WARNING).

It's important for the work with the merged trace files to configure what columns will be actually displayed in the main part of the window. This is done via the context menu option CONFIGURE COLUMNS... (shown in ❹).

We recommend including the columns DATABASE USER, APPLICATION USER, TRACE FILE, and CONNECTION ID and to exclude SOURCE and THREAD ID. (The last two typically do not help in understanding a specific error, whereas the first four help to navigate to the source trace file and to map the error message to other parts of the technology stack.) This is shown in Figure 16.14.

Figure 16.14 Configure Columns for Merged Diagnosis Files Editor

Once all filtering is done and the data is actually displayed, errors and warnings are indicated in the right navigation gutter (shown in ❺) with yellow and red boxes. Clicking on those boxes navigates to the corresponding message in the list.

On the left-hand side of the text grid (shown in ❻), plus icons appear when the displayed trace text spans multiple lines. Initially, each message will be shown on a single line; by clicking on the plus icon, the message can be unfolded to a full display.

Sometimes, the error message text can be too long to fit completely into the display window, though (Figure 16.15).

Time Stamp	Trace Text	
13567	3: Pool/RowEngine	890063560b (848.83mb)
13568	4: Pool/RowEngine/LockTable	536881408b (512mb)
13569	5: AllocateOnlyAllocator-unlimited	285970408b (272.72mb)
13570	6: StackAllocator	245329920b (233.96mb)
13571	7: Pool/malloc	237488344b (226.48mb)
13572	8: Pool/RowEngine/Internal	205573632b (196.04mb)
13573	9: Pool/TTMgr	134242624b (128.02mb)
13574	10: Pool/RowEngine/Transaction	104713688b (99.86mb)
13575	11: Pool/malloc/libhdbbasement.so	91010480b (86.79mb)
13576	12: Pool/malloc/libhdbexpression.so	90487696b (86.29mb)
13577	13: AllocateOnlyAllocator-unlimited/FLA-UL<3145728,1>/MemoryMapLev	
13578	# Text is truncated # (Hold CTRL and click to show more...)	
13579	:04:45.357658Disabling signal handler	
13580	:04:45.357682Stopping self watchdog	

Figure 16.15 Long Trace Message in Merged Diagnosis Files Editor

In this case, the message text is truncated, and the line # Text is truncated # (Hold CTRL and click to show more...) is displayed. Holding down the ⌨Ctrl⌨ key will turn the text into a link, and clicking it opens a dialog window that displays the full text of the message (Figure 16.16).

Figure 16.16 Trace Text Dialog Window

Once an error message is identified, it can be copied and pasted; a specific save-to-file option is not available.

16.4 Server Side Traces

Some problems with SAP HANA will not create error messages. Instead, to understand the cause of the issue, additional information about internal data processing is required. SAP HANA can create additional output of runtime information by means of traces. The traces can be configured, activated, and deactivated in SAP HANA STUDIO • ADMINISTRATION CONSOLE • TRACE CONFIGURATION (Figure 16.17).

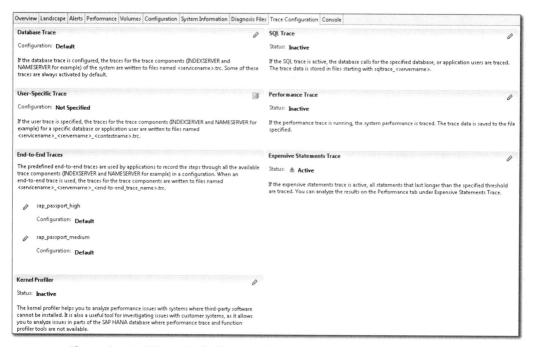

Figure 16.17 SAP HANA Studio Trace Configuration

Most of the server-side traces are aimed at core developers of SAP HANA, SAP HANA development support, or people that otherwise intimately know the internal functions, data structures, and algorithms. In short, this means that only some of the trace options are actually useful for the typical DBA. The two traces that are the most relevant for us are the database trace (with its variants, user-specific trace and end-to-end trace) and the expensive statements trace, and these are covered in detail. Of all the other traces offered by the database system, you may in rare circumstances also encounter the SQL trace, performance trace, and kernel profiler, and we mention them briefly. Table 16.3 provides an overview of the different server-side trace types in an SAP HANA system, including an indication of the most typical usage or target group. For your convenience, we also include other information collectors that can be useful for system or incident analyses, such as the SQL plan cache or PlanViz.

> **Note**
>
> Be aware that activating trace output can (not must) decrease performance of the database system and will likely increase trace file filling speed.

Trace Type	Useful For
Database trace (with the variants user-specific and end-to-end trace)	Single incident analysis; on full detail level, only relevant for SAP HANA development
Expensive statements trace	System overview single statement analysis
SQL trace (Python trace)	SAP HANA development
Performance trace and function profiler	SAP HANA development
Kernel profiler	SAP HANA development
Load diagram	System overview—the big picture
Statistics server	System overview—the big picture
SQL plan cache	System overview/single statement analysis
Explain plan	Single statement analysis
Plan Visualizer (PlanViz)	Single statement analysis

Table 16.3 Overview of Server-Side Traces in SAP HANA

16.4.1 Database Trace and User-Specific Trace

The database trace is the logging mechanism of the SAP HANA kernel. It is the collection of text messages created by the database processes to provide error messages or other output that can help an administrator or an SAP HANA developer understand what happened in the database system. Although each database process maintains its own trace, the tracing follows the same principles throughout the system. We will explain these principles here.

The difference between database trace and user-specific trace is clear by the names. In the database trace, the DBA can set up traces for the whole SAP HANA instance, regardless of the user that runs the session. This can be useful when user-independent activities, e.g., the Mergedog thread, should be traced. The user-specific trace can access the same trace information but also apply a filter for a specific user or application user (the content of the session context variable APPLICATION_USER).

To distinguish the current user-specific trace settings from the default trace, a CONTEXT NAME has to be provided for each user-specific trace. This context name will be added to the trace file name of a user-specific trace so that it is easy to find the corresponding files. The overall system's database trace is always written to the diagnosis files covered in Section 16.3.2. The DATABASE USER field (Figure 16.18) allows filtering on one specific user. It is not possible to activate the trace for multiple users. To trace multiple users at the same time, the database trace must be used.

Alternatively or in addition to the database user, APPLICATION USER can be used to filter the trace output, for example, to a specific end user in an SAP NetWeaver system for which all connections to SAP HANA are performed with the same technical user.

The different traces that can be set up are organized in so-called trace components. These are groups of internal functions that have a shared duty. For example, trace component sqloptstep will write information on SQL query transformation and optimization into the trace file.

Every trace can be set either for all SAP HANA service types or separately just for one service type. Note that it is not possible to activate a trace for any service only on specific nodes. Any trace setting will be applied to all services of the same service type across the SAP HANA instance landscape.

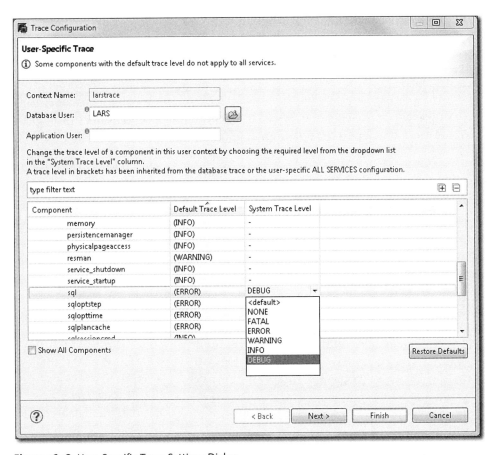

Figure 16.18 User-Specific Trace Settings Dialog

For every trace topic, a trace level can be chosen to select the amount of trace information produced. The available trace levels are designed to start with NONE and range to DEBUG, and every next level includes the output of the levels before:

▶ <DEFAULT>: Output level when no trace level is specified.

▶ NONE: No trace output will be written out.

▶ FATAL: Only very critical errors will be written out (seldom used so far).

▶ ERROR: Trace output will be written out only for errors.

▶ WARNING: Warnings will be written out.

- ► INFO: General runtime information is written out.
- ► DEBUG: Very detailed runtime and debugging information is written out.

Typically, either trace level INFO or DEBUG are used to write additional information into the trace files.

In order to deselect a previously selected trace setting, simply select <DEFAULT>. To deselect all selected trace settings at once, click the RESTORE DEFAULTS button.

16.4.2 End-to-End Trace

The end-to-end trace of SAP Solution Manager collects information on all system components involved in an end-user interaction. In a BI query started in SAP BusinessObjects Web Intelligence against an SAP BW system on SAP HANA, this trace would collect information on the BI server, the SAP BW system, and the SAP HANA database server. On the SAP HANA system, the end-to-end trace will generate trace files, just like a user-specific trace. The string *end-to-end-trace* is used as context in the trace file name.

The end-to-end trace settings do not activate or deactivate a specific trace. Instead, you can specify the levels for the SAP HANA-side tracing for the two different trace levels SAP_PASSPORT_HIGH and SAP_PASSPORT_MEDIUM of the end-to-end trace.

16.4.3 Expensive Statements Trace

You'll recall our discussion of the expensive statements trace in Chapter 15, due to its important role in performance analysis. Because it is also a monitoring tool, we'll briefly discuss it here as well.

One of the most important global monitoring options is the expensive statements trace of SAP HANA (Figure 16.19). Any statement execution running longer than the THRESHOLD DURATION (µs; in microseconds = 1/1.000.000 seconds) will be recorded in the expensive statements trace. Together with the statement text, runtime-related information such as the parameters used for parameterized statements, time spent waiting for locks, and so on is stored. So technically the expensive statements trace should instead be called the *long-running statements trace*, because lock wait times don't make a statement more or less expensive (requiring high effort to compute).

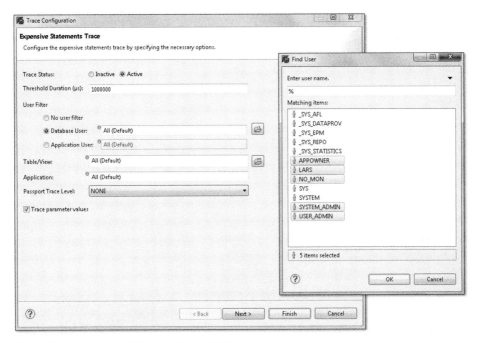

Figure 16.19 Expensive Statements Trace Settings

Even on SAP HANA systems, there are usually still many commands that will take longer than the default threshold of 1 second.

To make working with the expensive statements trace effective, it is a good idea to limit the recorded statements to the interesting ones. This can be done by specifying user or application user filters to include only actual application-related users. _SYS_... users might show long statement runtimes (e.g., _SYS_STATISTICS regularly runs data collection statements that may take some time), but they do not impact end-user performance and cannot be tuned by the DBA.

Another obvious filter is the actual threshold. To find out what would be a good value for the threshold, we can use the system view M_SQL_PLAN_CACHE after the system has running for some time and is in normal condition. The SQL statement shown in Figure 16.20 retrieves an upper-bound threshold and shows which share of the statements would be below this upper-bound threshold.

```
SQL  Result
select n_tile*5 || '% of all statements' as statment_group,
       max(avg_execution_time) as upper_runtime_boundary
from ( select
         avg_execution_time,
         ntile (20) over (order by  avg_execution_time) n_tile
         from "PUBLIC"."M_SQL_PLAN_CACHE")
group by n_tile
order by n_tile
```

	STATMENT_GROUP	UPPER_RUNTIME_BOUNDARY
1	5% of all statements	0
2	10% of all statements	0
3	15% of all statements	0
4	20% of all statements	0
5	25% of all statements	0
6	30% of all statements	0
7	35% of all statements	0
8	40% of all statements	44
9	45% of all statements	103
10	50% of all statements	243
11	55% of all statements	696
12	60% of all statements	1232
13	65% of all statements	2938
14	70% of all statements	3511
15	75% of all statements	4107
16	80% of all statements	6403
17	85% of all statements	8453
18	90% of all statements	16921
19	95% of all statements	42348
20	100% of all statements	271197714

Figure 16.20 Expensive Statements Trace—Choosing a Threshold Value

It is easy to see that in this specific system most statements stay well below the 1,000,000 μs default value. In fact, only the top 5% of all statements run longer than that. The maximum runtime is a couple of hundred seconds in this case, so setting the expensive statements trace threshold to something conservative like 5,000,000 μs should keep the amount of collected data small but focused on possible performance culprits.

Once the trace is activated, the collected data can be reviewed in SAP HANA STU-DIO • ADMINISTRATION CONSOLE • PERFORMANCE • EXPENSIVE STATEMENTS TRACE (Figure 16.21). Key to working successfully with the usually long list is, again, to use sorting (e.g., by DURATION_MICROSEC) and to use the filter conditions. Via the context menu, it is possible to navigate to the PlanViz of the selected statement. (Refer back to Chapter 15 for more about PlanViz.)

With SPS 8, SAP HANA Studio also provides navigation between the expensive statements trace and the SQL plan cache list in the PERFORMANCE tab.

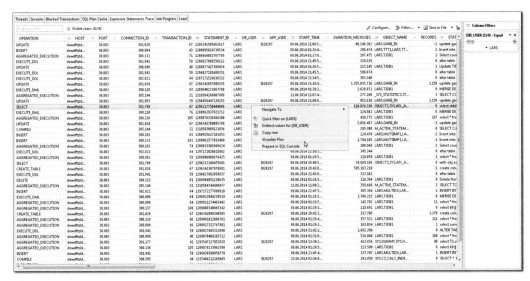

Figure 16.21 Expensive Statements Trace List

A major advantage of the expensive statements trace against the SQL plan cache is that the expensive statements trace focuses on actual execution and keeps track of every single statement execution. This includes the parameters (if used for the statement). With this, the expensive statements trace is the only option to access the call parameters of statements that had been executed in the past.

16.4.4 SQL Trace

The SQL trace captures commands that are sent to SAP HANA and can, depending on the settings, provide information on the total runtime and the error code of the command execution and print out the actual result set of queries into the trace files. It can (and should) be configured to record only the commands executed by a single user or a comma-separated list of users, as shown in Figure 16.22. A useful feature is the ability to filter not on the actual database user but by the application user. In an SAP NetWeaver system on SAP HANA, this application user is the named user in the SAP NetWeaver system. The functionality also works with any other application that uses a single-connection user in the SAP HANA database and sets the application user session parameter in its interactions with SAP HANA.

It is also possible to restrict the tracing to certain types of commands (e.g., only DDL commands) and even to single database objects.

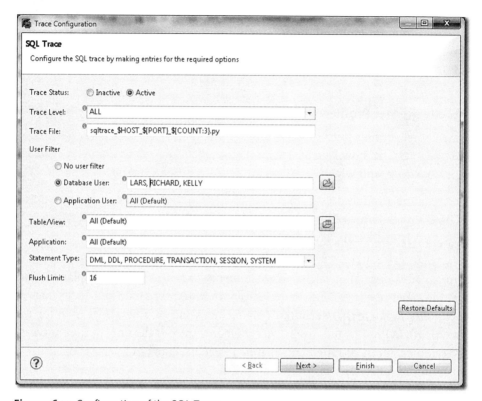

Figure 16.22 Configuration of the SQL Trace

As the SQL trace does not provide information on the actual SAP HANA internal processing of a command, but only on the input or output, this trace lends itself to rather general investigations and data collection. A typical use case is finding the actual SQL statement generated by an application.

16.4.5 Performance Trace

The performance trace allows you to collect a range of different information on request processing in SAP HANA. This includes SQL execution plans, column store plans, execution times, function profile information for internal functions that deliver this kind of data, and the like.

The data produced by this trace is only readable by the HDBAdmin tool, which is neither documented nor supported and typically only used by SAP HANA core developers.

Because most of the information that is gathered by this performance trace is now available via PlanViz and the expensive statements trace, the performance trace is of no practical relevance to the SAP HANA DBA.

16.4.6 Kernel Profiler Trace

The kernel profiler trace samples the SAP HANA internal function calls and collects statistics on how long specific functions have been active, how much time is spent waiting, and which internal function called which other function.

Information produced by this kernel trace really only make sense to someone with intimate knowledge of the SAP HANA source code and the functions used. This makes this kernel trace irrelevant for the practical purposes of a DBA.

Use this trace only when asked by SAP HANA Support.

16.5   Client-Side Traces

Sometimes, it can be important to understand what functions of the database client API are called by a program. Also, it might be relevant to see the exact communication between the client program and the SAP HANA database. For that, there are a number of client traces available. Depending on which client library is used (ODBC, JDBC, SQLDBC, ODBO, etc.), a different trace has to be used.

Content-wise, the traces contain very similar information, although the trace format is quite different with every trace. Because the full interpretation of the traces typically requires a very deep understanding of the SAP HANA communication protocol, we will restrict the discussion to the most important aspects.

16.5.1 JDBC Trace

The JDBC trace can be activated either by the application using the JDBC driver or externally if the application does not provide the option to activate the trace. To set up the JDBC trace externally, the JDBC driver JAR file has to be used, as shown in Figure 16.23.

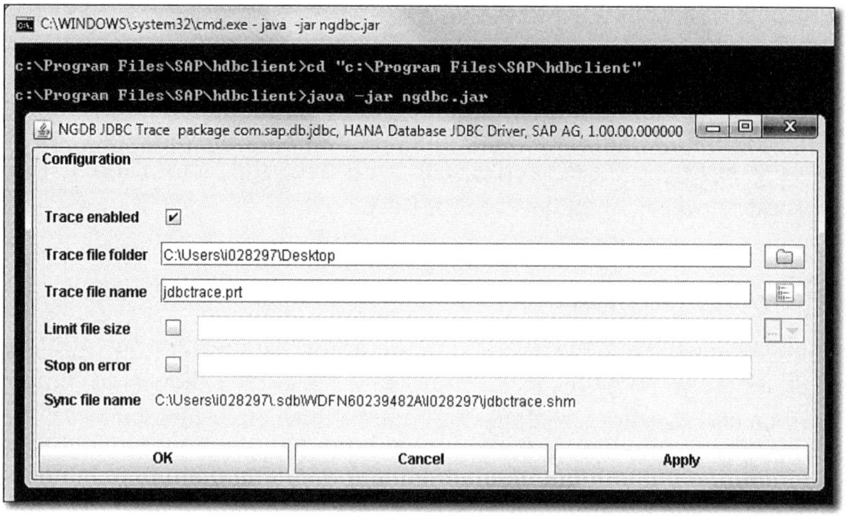

Figure 16.23 Setting Up an External JDBC Trace

When you run the command `java -jar ngdbc.jar` (this is the actual JDBC driver file), a dialog box opens that allows you to specify trace settings. Typically important here is the location of the trace file to be created (TRACE FILE FOLDER) and the file size limitation.

> **Note**
>
> The file size limitation can be especially important for long-term tracing tasks, such as those on an application server, for which the occurrence of the event that should be captured cannot be controlled. In such a situation, it is better to accept the loss of trace data than to risk a file-system-full situation on the application server.

Note that the JDBC trace settings are only valid for the user environment for which they have been set up—not for the whole system. If the process that should be traced runs in another user context, the JDBC trace settings need to be applied within this user context to be effective.

The resulting trace file for the JDBC trace is an XML-like text file that contains the applications' calls of the JDBC API methods and the communication packets exchanged with the SAP HANA database server. Figure 16.24 shows an example of a JDBC trace file.

```
153   com.sap.db.jdbc.ConnectionSapDBFinalize@652db3c1[ID 405569].setClientInfo (APPLICATIONSOURCE, csns.navigator.operations.SAPSystem
154   com.sap.db.jdbc.ConnectionSapDBFinalize@652db3c1[ID 405569].setClientInfo (APPLICATIONVERSION, 1.0.7300)
155   com.sap.db.jdbc.ConnectionSapDBFinalize@652db3c1[ID 405569].prepareStatement (select * from SYS.DUMMY)
156   <Packet SessionID=1741906689247588 PacketCount=3 VarpartLength=728 VarpartSize=129968 NumberOfSegments=1 PacketOptions=0>
157     <Segment Request Length=728 Offset=0 NoOfParts=3 Index=1 SegmentKind=1 MessType=Parse(3) CommitImmediateley=0 CommandOptions=8>
158       <Part PartKind=StatementContext_C Attributes=0 [] ArgCount=1 SegmOffs=0 BufLen=20 BufSize=129944>
164       <Part PartKind=Command_C Attributes=0 [] ArgCount=1 SegmOffs=0 BufLen=23 BufSize=129904>
165         <PartBuffer>
166           [73 65 6c 65 63 74 20 2a 20 66 72 6f 6d 20 53 59 53 2e 44 55 4d 4d 59 ]
167           select * from SYS.DUMMY
168         </PartBuffer>
169       </Part>
170       <Part PartKind=ClientInfo_C Attributes=0 [] ArgCount=4 SegmOffs=0 BufLen=606 BufSize=129864>
176     </Segment>
177   </Packet>
178   <Packet SessionID=1741906689247588 PacketCount=3 VarpartLength=192 VarpartSize=29968 NumberOfSegments=1 PacketOptions=0>
179     <Segment Reply Length=192 Offset=0 NoOfParts=5 Index=1 SegmentKind=2 FunctionCode=Select(5)>
180       <Part PartKind=TableLocation_C Attributes=0 [] ArgCount=1 SegmOffs=0 BufLen=4 BufSize=29928>
186       <Part PartKind=StatementContext_C Attributes=0 [] ArgCount=2 SegmOffs=0 BufLen=30 BufSize=29904>
192       <Part PartKind=StatementID Attributes=0 [] ArgCount=1 SegmOffs=0 BufLen=8 BufSize=29856>
193         <PartBuffer>
197       </Part>
198       <Part PartKind=ResultSetMetaData_C Attributes=0 [] ArgCount=1 SegmOffs=0 BufLen=36 BufSize=29832>
199         <PartBuffer>
200           [02 08 00 00 01 00 00 00 00 00 00 00 ff ff ff ff 06 00 00 00 06 00 00 00 05 44 55 4d 4d 59 05 44 55 4d 4d 59 ]
201           1. Type=CHAR(8) Len=1,0 TableName (OffSet=0) DUMMY SchemaName (OffSet=-1)  Columnname (OffSet=6) DUMMY ColumnDisplayName
```

Figure 16.24 JDBC Trace Example

A special convenience case for setting up the JDBC trace is present in SAP HANA Studio. The trace can be activated in the PROPERTIES dialog for every system/logon maintained in the SYSTEMS navigator tree.

Once activated, the state is indicated by the systems icon in the navigator tree and with a hover-over text box, as shown in Figure 16.25. This feature can be quite useful to find out about commands sent by SAP HANA Studio.

Important to remember here is that the JDBC trace is a local client trace, and activating it in SAP HANA Studio does not imply that JDBC connections from other applications will be traced, too.

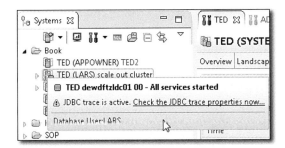

Figure 16.25 JDBC Trace Indication in SAP HANA Studio

16.5.2 The ODBC Trace

Just like the JDBC trace, the ODBC trace is a database client API trace. Therefore, it traces calls to the ODBC API and parts of the communication between the client and the SAP HANA database on the client host on which it is started. It can be activated by running the tool `hdbcodbc_cons` (.exe), located in the client software installation folder; see Figure 16.26.

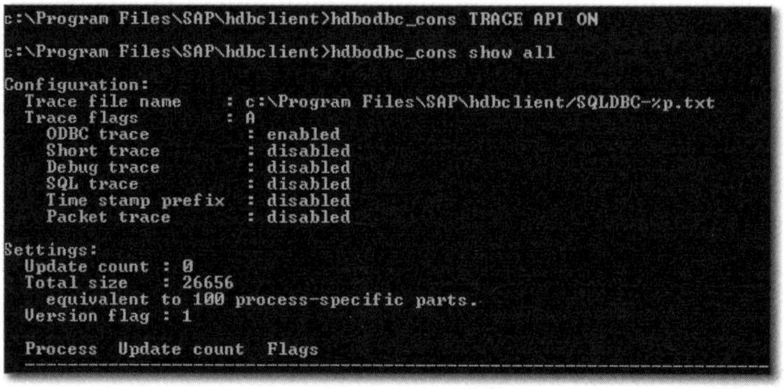

```
c:\Program Files\SAP\hdbclient>hdbodbc_cons TRACE API ON

c:\Program Files\SAP\hdbclient>hdbodbc_cons show all

Configuration:
  Trace file name     : c:\Program Files\SAP\hdbclient/SQLDBC-%p.txt
  Trace flags       : A
    ODBC trace      : enabled
    Short trace     : disabled
    Debug trace     : disabled
    SQL trace       : disabled
    Time stamp prefix : disabled
    Packet trace    : disabled

Settings:
  Update count : 0
  Total size   : 26656
    equivalent to 100 process-specific parts.
  Version flag : 1

  Process  Update count  Flags
```

Figure 16.26 ODBC Client Trace Activation

To activate the ODBC client trace for all processes executed in the current user's session, it is sufficient to specify the `TRACE API ON` switch:

`hdbodbc_cons TRACE API ON`.

The default location for the trace file is the current directory from which `hdbodbc_cons` is being executed.

To get a full list of possible commands for the ODBC trace, it is sufficient to execute the program without any switches or together with the `-h` (help) switch.

There are two common pitfalls that often lead to trace files that just don't seem to get written. The first pitfall is that the ODBC trace has been set up for the wrong bit version of the ODBC driver. On MS Windows client platforms, popular programs such as MS Excel are typically 32-bit programs that need to use the 32-bit ODBC client library. The 32-bit version of the client software is located in *c:\Program Files(x86)\SAP\hdbclient* (default), and only the `hdbodbc_cons` program there can activate the trace for 32-bit clients. Likewise, 64-bit applications make use of the 64-bit ODBC driver, and their interactions with the database can only be traced with the 64-bit `hdbodbc_cons` program.

Note

It is only the bit version of the client program that matters here. The bit version of the client host's operating system is irrelevant.

The second pitfall is the aforementioned default location of the ODBC trace. Typically, the DBA would navigate to the client software folder to start the ODBC trace there. By default, this means that the trace file will be written to the client software installation folder, for example, *c:\Program Files(x86)\SAP\hdbclient*, as shown in Figure 16.26. Note that the %p in the file name is the process ID of the traced process.

Because the program files folders are MS Windows system folders, these cannot be changed with standard user privileges. In turn, the trace file will not be written at all (and no error message will be shown). To change this, the trace file location needs to be changed to a folder that can be written to (Figure 16.27).

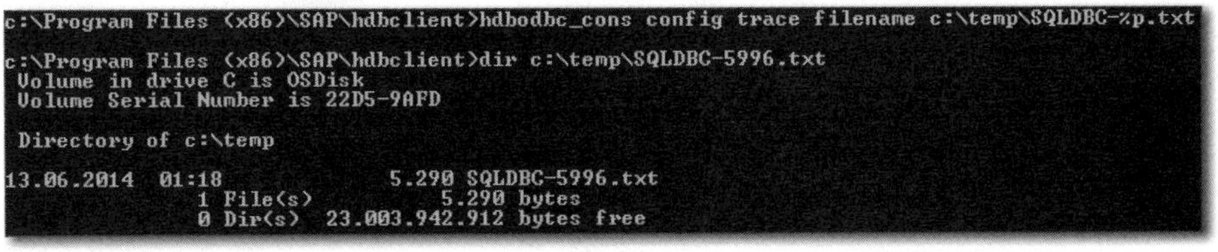

```
c:\Program Files (x86)\SAP\hdbclient>hdbodbc_cons config trace filename c:\temp\SQLDBC-%p.txt

c:\Program Files (x86)\SAP\hdbclient>dir c:\temp\SQLDBC-5996.txt
 Volume in drive C is OSDisk
 Volume Serial Number is 22D5-9AFD

 Directory of c:\temp

13.06.2014  01:18              5.290 SQLDBC-5996.txt
               1 File(s)          5.290 bytes
               0 Dir(s)  23.003.942.912 bytes free
```

Figure 16.27 ODBC Trace Changed Location

For more information, SAP Note 1993254 provides an overview of ODBC trace functions.

16.5.3 SQLDBC Trace

The SQLDBC API is an SAP-owned propriety database client interface that is mainly used by the SAP NetWeaver database interface layer. In most cases, the trace can be conveniently activated via Transaction DBACOCKPIT.

In case the trace needs to be activated and the DBA Cockpit application is not available (e.g., during a system copy/load with `R3Load`), the client software installation folder contains the program `hdbsqldbc_cons`. This trace settings program works similarly to the ODBC trace tool. In fact, most of the switches are precisely the same.

SAP Note 1993251 covers this trace tool.

16.5.4 The ODBO/MDX Trace

When using MDX-based clients, such as the MS Excel integration for SAP HANA, database access is performed via the ODBO (not ODBC) connection. The MDX trace can be set up only when defining the connection settings in the ADVANCED tab of the DATA LINK PROPERTIES dialog (Figure 16.28).

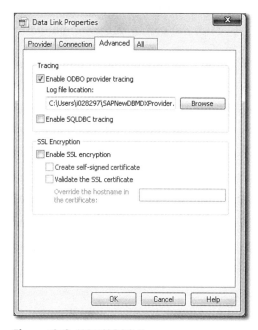

Figure 16.28 MDX/ODBO Trace

Just like the ODBC driver, the ODBO driver uses the SQLDBC driver for server-side communication, and, just as with the ODBC driver, it is possible to activate the SQLDBC trace in one go here. Typically, though, the SQLDBC trace is only usable for SAP HANA development.

16.6 Summary

In this chapter, we have walked you through the tools and functionalities offered by SAP HANA for root-cause analysis. A generic prerequisite for troubleshooting incidents is proper system monitoring so that workload statistics and other information is at hand. You should now be able to identify and work with the monitoring views offered by the database system, including the handy resettable views.

The larger part of the chapter was dedicated to root-cause analysis for individual incidents. This topic is highly complex, and the appropriate tools and techniques depend on the circumstances:

▸ To a database developer or administrator using SAP HANA, the entry point to troubleshooting is the error messages displayed in SAP HANA Studio. We explained the different types of error messages and best practices for understanding them.

▸ For any kind of root-cause analysis, the server-side traces and information written to other diagnostic files can become relevant. After reading the chapter, you should now know the location and purpose of these important files, and you also should know which of the server-side traces are relevant for DBAs and which ones are not. If you need to manually analyze the database traces, the Merged Diagnosis Files Editor will be a helpful tool. If you need to provide system diagnosis information to SAP Support, SAP HANA Studio offers a wizard to easily collect this information.

▸ In many cases, the incident to be analyzed will bridge the boundary between the SAP HANA database system and the client system, so trace information may be needed from both sides. We explained how to activate SAP HANA tracing on both server and client sides.

As a final remark, successful root-cause analysis requires not only experience with the system to be analyzed but also a fair amount of perseverance.

The Authors

Dr. Richard Bremer has worked on SAP's in-memory technologies since 2008, starting as a support consultant for SAP BW Accelerator, and moving to the SAP HANA topic in 2010, working in the RIG / Customer Solution Adoption (CSA) team. He led the global SAP HANA CSA program before moving on to SAP HANA product management. Richard has supported dozens of SAP HANA implementation projects with expertise on data modeling, security, database administration, and system landscape design. He enjoys sharing knowledge and teaching front-line technologies to SAP consultants, customers, and partners. He is a frequent contributor to SAP TechEd events and SAP User Group meetings.

Lars Breddemann has been working with database management systems since 1998 as a developer, DBA, supporter, and systems architect. Having worked in SAP AGS product support since 2003, he has experience with multiple database technologies (Oracle, SAP MaxDB/liveCache), SAP Business Warehouse, and, since 2010, SAP HANA. In 2011, he moved to the Customer Solution Adoption (CSA) team, where he assumed the role of SAP HANA expert. Specializing in core database technology, development, supportability, and performance analysis, Lars educated hundreds of users, partners, and colleagues and has been called into projects around the globe as the go-to authority. Lars is an acclaimed SAP TechEd speaker, a leading SCN contributor and moderator, and was appointed as one of the first SAP HANA Distinguished Engineers in 2012.

Index

M

N

S

T

- ▶ Learn how to perform the tasks of an SAP Basis administrator
- ▶ Dive deep into your system with step-by-step instructions and screenshots
- ▶ Update your skills for SAP HANA administration

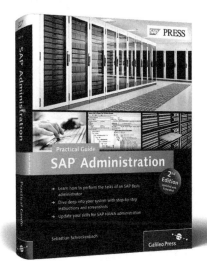

Sebastian Schreckenbach

SAP Administration—Practical Guide

Attention, administrators! Whether you're pursuing a background in SAP Basis or looking to brush up on your skills, this is the book for you! From database management to backup and disaster recovery, learn how to handle everything from the routine to the occasional hiccup. With helpful instructions and screenshots you'll master the tasks and challenges of SAP system administration in no time.

approx. 940 pp., 2nd edition, 2015, $79.95/€79.95
ISBN 978-1-4932-1024-4
www.sap-press.com/3639

▶ Get to know the SAPUI5 IDE, control libraries, model types, and more

▶ Learn how to design and extend modern user interfaces

▶ Apply programming models, controls, and UI elements to real-life scenarios

Miroslav Antolovic

Getting Started with SAPUI5

Develop next-generation UIs for responsive, versatile SAP applications. To understand the pioneering programming language SAPUI5, first walk through basic programming concepts. Then explore the development and runtime environments, tools, and plugins that you'll use throughout the design process. Learn to develop your own apps using step-by-step instructions, sample code listings, and a full-scale model application.

462 pages, 2014, $69.95/€69.95
ISBN 978-1-59229-969-0
www.sap-press.com/3565

www.sap-press.com

▶ Make your SAP system run quickly and efficiently

▶ Master core concepts like sizing, memory management, and database monitoring

▶ Explore new topics such as SAP HANA, SAP Sybase ASE, and innovations in SAP NetWeaver AS Java

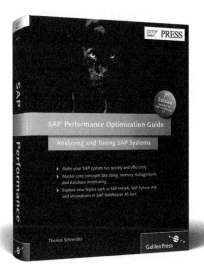

Thomas Schneider

SAP Performance Optimization Guide

Analyzing and Tuning SAP Systems

Is your SAP system as agile as it can be? Optimize system performance with the seventh edition of Thomas Schneider's best-selling resource. Head off any bottlenecks, update your skills for SAP NetWeaver 7.3, and integrate new technologies like SAP HANA and Sybase ASE. Make your SAP system faster, sleeker, and stronger with this updated and revised optimization guide.

837 pages, 7th edition, 2013, $79.95/€79.95
ISBN 978-1-59229-874-7
www.sap-press.com/3360

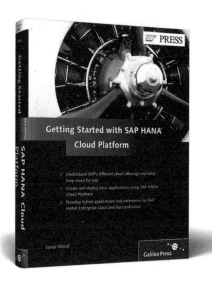

▶ Understand SAP's different cloud offerings and what they mean for you

▶ Create and deploy basic applications using SAP HANA Cloud Platform

▶ Develop hybrid applications and extensions for SAP HANA Enterprise Cloud and Success-Factors

James Wood

Getting Started with SAP HANA Cloud Platform

The cloud is all the rage, but the details are fuzzy. With this book, get the basics of SAP HANA Cloud Platform, and then take the next steps. You'll learn how to use HCP to create, deploy, and secure applications, and how it can be used to extend SuccessFactors and other SAP solutions. There's more to cloud than fluff—find out what it is.

approx. 575 pp., 2015, $69.95/€69.95
ISBN 978-1-4932-1033-6
www.sap-press.com/3638

- ▶ Understand the impact of SAP HANA on ABAP application development

- ▶ Learn how to develop applications for SAP HANA with SAP NetWeaver AS ABAP 7.4

- ▶ Work with advanced functions such as fuzzy search and predictive analysis

Schneider, Westenberger, Gahm

ABAP Development for SAP HANA

They say there's nothing new under the sun—but every once in a while, something novel comes along. With SAP HANA, even the most seasoned ABAP developers have some learning to do. Newbie or not, this book can help: install the Eclipse IDE, brush up your database programming skills, perform runtime and error analysis, transport old ABAP applications to HANA—and more. Expand your horizons!

609 pages, 2014, $69.95/€69.95
ISBN 978-1-59229-859-4
www.sap-press.com/3343

Interested in reading more?

Please visit our website for all new
book and e-book releases from SAP PRESS.

www.sap-press.com